CW00602988

ELVIS
FOR CD FANS ONLY

SECOND EDITION

The Elvis Presley U.S. Compact Disc
Reference and Price Guide

by

DALE HAMPTON

Introduction by Gordon Minto

Copyright © 1998 by Dale Hampton

Elvis: For CD Fans Only   -   Second Edition

Elvis Presley Compact Disc Reference and Price Guide

All Rights Reserved

Manufactured in the United States of America

No part of this book may be reproduced or transmitted in
any form or by any means mechanical or electronic, including
photocopying, recording, or by any information storage and
retrieval system without the express written permission of the
author and publisher, except for reviews where permitted by
law.

Published by: Dale Hampton & WWE Publishing
Distributed by WWE Publishing
            Sarasota, Florida 34276

Cover design and artwork by Jimmy Carpenter

Section III photograph courtesy of Taylor Scott

Library of Congress Catalog Card Number 98-75160

Not responsible for any loss due to transactions based on any
data contained herein.

FOR CD FANS ONLY VOL. 2

DALE HAMPTON

I guess it is an honour to be asked to write the introduction to anyone's book, but it's even more so if the author is a friend of yours. And I'm happy to say that Dale Hampton has been a very good friend of mine since we met several years ago. But that is not the sole reason I agreed to write this, and I would like to explain why.

First of all let me tell you something about the author before looking at this, his latest work. I know he'll squirm with embarrassment when he reads this but I want you to know -- if you didn't already -- that he is a tremendously nice guy, private and very unassuming, who is equally generous in word and deed. I feel privileged to know him and this is a view held by everyone else who I have spoken to about him. Rare among human beings -- never mind other fans! -- he is genuine, thoughtful and caring, going to extraordinary lengths for others, as I know only too well. And that means a lot to me, for there are very few people who you really feel you can trust and who will not let you down. But, as you look at this book, I realise that it's not his fine character you're buying, though I would suggest that it reflects greatly on the quality of his work, as I will now explain.

His devotion to Elvis is well known among his friends and family, but his single-minded determination to making a real contribution to the field of Elvis literature has not been so widely known. Of course it is not a unique aspiration. Many fans have tried and, sadly, most have failed for one reason or another. Not so Dale, though. Some of you will remember that a few years ago he produced a privately published book -- his first -- entitled **'For CD Fans Only'** (circa 300 pages) which dealt with all US CDs to date and enjoyed modest success -- and by that I am referring to sales, not quality. Well if you enjoyed that volume and found its contents of interest and value to you, then you will especially impressed by this his latest piece of research, a greatly extended work which not only supercedes the previous volume, outstrips it in all others ways too. And let me add -- in case you are thinking you've got all this stuff -- this is not just a hastily reworked version of his first book to garner sales -- a popular ploy amongst those with less rigorous scruples. Oh no, it is a major book in its own right. If you are interested in US CDs (which this book deals with almost exclusively) -- indeed Elvis CDs at all -- and especially rarities and promos, wish to know about the variations available and, moreover, want to have some idea what these items are worth, this thorough piece of work is right up your Elvis Presley Boulevard! Indeed, as a CD collector, it will represent an essential adjunct to your collection, all 500 plus pages oozing information and detail, much of it which will surprise and impress you.

Clearly laid out and comprising three main sections: 1) BMG releases, Promos and Special Products; 2) Various Artists; and 3) a Cross Reference section, all neatly captioned in an intelligible and user-friendly way (a must for any serious piece of research), and amply illustrated, the book represents a considerable achievement.. The amount of painstaking research and expense devoted to this product can only be guessed at -- but let me tell you that it is very high on both counts. All too often as I read and review Elvis related books for various magazines, I am saddened by the sloppiness and lack of care evident, frequently by those who ought to know better, but whose main motivation is obviously to reap financial reward. Nothing wrong with making a profit, I hasten to add, but not at the expense of accuracy and integrity. So, believe me, whatever you pay for this book, it will not recompense the author in any significant way (few works like this ever do -- as I know only too well from my own experience!) but it will make him a very happy man if you, the fans, buy the book and enjoy it as much as I have.

Let me conclude with an anecdote that seems very apt in the circumstances. On our visits to the States, and particularly to the wonderful state of Tennessee, Dale has usually accompanied my wife and I when out shopping. We, of course, were totally bemused by the extensive choice and relatively cheap prices in the USA for a whole host of items. Yet as we shopped and considered various items and pondered whether or not to buy them -- a natural British reticence, you might say! -- Dale would stand alongside us and offer words of encouragement (in that great Tennessee drawl of his) long the lines of *'Go on, git it'* -- always adding, *'You need it'* -- at which point we would burst out laughing and I would reach for my credit card -- again! Well, as you consider buying **'For CD Fans Only Revised Edition',** let me tell you -- because he certainly won't -- *'Go on, git it. You need it!'* That's a fact, and you know it well.

Gordon Minto, November 1998

(Gordon Minto is a feature writer for the premier Elvis magazine 'Elvis The Man and His Music', published quarterly , and monthly Rock 'n Roll magazine 'Now Dig This', both UK publications. Gordon has also co-authored Elvis books himself, including 'Elvis UK A Complete guide to Elvis Presley's British Releases 1956-86'; 'Inside Jailhouse Rock' and '60,000,00 Elvis Fans Can't Be Wrong', a book about Elvis's famed appearances on the Ed Sullivan Shows, and is currently working on a sequel to 'Elvis UK' with co-author John Townson.)

ACKNOWLEDGMENTS

I would like to thank a number of very knowledgeable Elvis fans from all over the world who have provided me with a wealth of information for this new edition. I would like to acknowledge their time and effort, which was considerable on both counts. And although some have contributed more than others, every piece of information was of extreme value.

Special thanks, however, need to go to the following people:

Taylor Scott, who did a substantial amount of research on release dates and deletions;

Patsy Anderson, Fan Relations Manager, Marketing Department, Graceland, Division of Elvis Presley Enterprises Inc., who provided key information;

Jimmy Carpenter, for the Cover Artwork and Design; and,

Gordon Minto, for research and editorial assistance.

****

Very special thanks must go to Paul Dowling and WWE Publishing, the publisher and distributor of this Second Edition.

****

The following people (listed in alphabetical order) are also acknowledged for their contributions to this edition.
Peter Baumann
Richard G. Benoit
Eddie Hammer
Dawn Hampton
Dean Hampton
Linda Jones
Bernadette Moore
Jerry Osborne
Walter Piotrowski
Mike Rafferty
Mark Shaffer
Todd Slaughter
Joseph Tunzi
Richard J. Verdi
David Wiese

FORWARD

This reference and price guide is designed to inform you of all known Elvis Presley CD releases in the United States since 1984, and to assist you in determining their value. I have tried to offer as much information as possible on each CD and each pressing. However, I have listed the tracks only on the first pressing of each CD. And for those of you who would like to note which pressing(s) you have in your collection, a check off box is provided to the left of each listing.

In this guide I have tried to make the prices as accurate and realistic as possible. The prices quoted are ones you would expect to pay today, not the price paid for the article originally. Further, you will note that several of the CD's listed here have a considerable number of pressings - some over fifteen! However, remember, this does not necessarily mean that the fifth or sixth pressing is more valuable than the fifteenth. The price demanded reflects a whole host of different factors, not just order of release.

Promotional CD's and those deleted from RCA/BMG's catalog are priced higher than a standard catalog release with multiple pressings - for obvious reasons: there were fewer of them and they are usually much harder to obtain. Also, prices of the same items may vary considerably from place to place in the country. As a result of this, I have listed two prices for each CD: a high and a low one.

The release dates shown for each CD, giving the month and year, are as accurate as possible, and have, in the main, been obtained from RCA/BMG's release sheets and archive files. However, in a small number of cases only the year is shown, particularly where the precise release dates were not available, especially for repressings.

Please note that several of the CD's mentioned in the book were pressed in other countries, but are included here because they were available in the USA. For example, in December 1983, *"Elvis The Legend"* a 3 CD box set was pressed in Germany for worldwide distribution. It was, incidentally the first Elvis CD release in the world, and copies are now very hard to find and so invite a high price tag.

In 1984, RCA released the first US Elvis titles on compact disc:
Elvis Presley - PCD1-1254
Elvis - PCD1-1382
Elvis' Golden Records - PCD1-1707
50,000,000 Elvis Fans Can't Be Wrong - Elvis' Gold Records, Vol 2 - PCD1-2075

Unfortunately, these discs were manufactured in "Electronically Reprocessed Stereo" in error! Nonetheless, if your are fortunate enough to have a copies of these four, then you may be interested to know that they are among the most valuable of all the US releases. At the time, there were no CD pressing plants in the US, so the discs had to be pressed in Japan for distribution in the US. These can be easily identified by the "Made In Japan" inscription on the discs themselves.

However, by the fall of 1984, RCA corrected their mistake and digitally remastered the four titles back into their original mono mode. As these pressings were the first done in the US, they were assigned new catalog numbers, and all four had DIDX on the disc and insert sleeve. Most of following pressings listed DIDX on the sleeve, but not on the disc.

Also in the fall of 1984, RCA released the CD *"Merry Christmas"*, *PCD1-5301*, a CD only release which was deleted from RCA's catalog very shortly after it's release, thus making this the rarest commercial release of any Elvis CD in theUS.

However probably *the* rarest Elvis CD in the world is the 1985 Picture Disc *50,000,000 Elvis Fans Can't Be Wrong - Elvis' Gold Records, Vol. 2*. It is a full color picture disc of Elvis wearing his famous gold lame' suit with the word "Sample" at the bottom of the disc. No-one really knows for sure if this was a special in-house promo or a bootleg. It is my view that it is an in-house pressing, because the matrix number on the disc matches the 1985 fifth pressing, even though RCA claims they have no knowledge of this particular item. But irrespective of whether or not it is a bootleg or promo, it is still extremely collectable and valuable.

There are, of course, several other rarities and promos listed throughout this guide. The ones listed here, are among the most collectable.

LABEL VARIATIONS

Since RCA/BMG started producing their own compact discs in the USA there have been four main label variations. They areas follows:
Silver Discs with Block RCA Logo in White and Print in Blue;
Silver Discs with Block RCA Logo and Print in Black;
Silver and Black Discs with Old RCA Logo (lightning bolt); and,
Elvis In The '90's Black Disc with Old RCA Logo and Print in Silver.

As regards the latter design, there are several variations. Some discs have silver print, others have the silver disc showing thru, though it is not actually silver print. Another variation has print in white.

CATALOG & MATRIX NUMBERS

Wherever possible all catalog and matrix numbers are listed for each pressing.

PROMOTIONAL COPIES

A promotional copy is a compact disc with a special label or insert sleeve with **"Not For Sale"** or **"Promo Only"** printed on the disc and/or the insert sleeve. Not surprisingly, these are among the most collectable - and expensive - of all US compact discs.
Another type of promotional copy is the **"Designated Promo"**. What this means is that essentially the disc is the same as the standard catalog release except for the fact that the discs have a sticker with **"Not For Sale"** on outside of the jewel case, or the front or back insert sleeves. In some cases the discs also have a hole drilled thru the bar code. Consequently the prices for these items are not as high as proper promos, but are normally priced higher than the standard release.

CLUB EDITIONS

Included in this reference and price guide is a list of CD's that were pressed exclusively for BMG and Columbia House Music Mail Order Clubs. The pressings made for these clubs have a special catalog number and, in most cases, have a different matrix number. The price listed on these club editions are slightly higher than the standard releases. In order to obtain these releases a club membership was required and price is determined by a quantity requirement.

BOOTLEGS

This reference and price guide lists standard, promo and club editions only. There are no known bootlegs listed.

LONG BOXES

Long boxes were in existence from 1984 until the end of 1993. Some of the long boxes featured the original artwork which was on the CD sleeve. Some, however, had generic boxes which showed the **"Elvis in the '90's"** Andy Warhol type artwork. The same box was, therefore, used with different CD titles. Others were housed in a generic long box with no artwork, or were offered in a plastic blister pack. Long boxes with each pressing have not been listed. If your copies are still sealed with the original artwork, add $5. If they are in the **"Elvis in the '90's"** boxes, add $1 - $2. Generic long boxes and plastic blister packs add nothing to the value. The packaging on the Box Sets have been included in the value listed in the guide.

VARIOUS ARTISTS

Under the title **"Various Artists"** (*see Section II*), you will find listed a number of CD's known to feature at least one Elvis track. However, this list is not complete, as there are other CD's available - especially of radio shows. Nonetheless, this listing is designed to give you an idea of what is available. Incidentally, some CD's contain anywhere from one to twenty or more Elvis tracks, though inevitably there are tracks by other artists too - which tend to make them less collectable than Elvis only CD's to some fans

As regards the detail included for these releases, you will find the title, catalog number, the Elvis track(s) to be found and the value of the item.

CROSS REFERENCE

A new addition to this volume is the **"Cross Reference"** section (*see Section III*) which contains the cross reference from song title to disc. Within this section you can locate all the CD's that contain a particular song. The alternate takes and home recordings have been shown in bold italics.

THE LOST CD's

Please note: the original title of the May 1991 release *Elvis Presley & Jim Reeves Christmas Favorites* was *Elvis and Jim - Home For Christmas*.

In October 1988 RCA were about to release the third in the **"Rocker"** titled *Rocker III: The Rocker Comes Back, Catalog# 6425-2-R*. It was pressed and ready for release when the decision was made to cancel it.

RCA Special Products pressed the following three titles:

Elvis Presley - The King Of Rock And Roll, Catalog# DMC1-0902 in August 1989, for the Franklin Mint, and a two CD set ***Elvis- His Songs Of Faith And Inspiration, Catalog# DVC2-0728*** in May 1990, for release thru Heartland Music. The first CD featured 20 tracks and the latter 36.

Then in March 1992, RCA Special Products pressed the following title to be sold thru AVON: ***An Elvis Concert Just for You, Catalog# DMC1-1045.*** The disc was never released due to the impending release of RCA's own *Elvis In Concert,* a standard CD issue of the 1977 vinyl album, in May 1992.

Later in August 1993, A&E Cable TV Network advertised the following Limited Edition Set entitled ***Elvis The Beginning,*** which contained a video, an album (pressed on pink vinyl), and compact disc. It contained previously issued material from the Louisiana Hayride, although orders were not filled for the vinyl or compact disc. In 1996, Graceland released a cassette, video and pink vinyl album comprising the same material (using the same title), though a CD was **not** released.

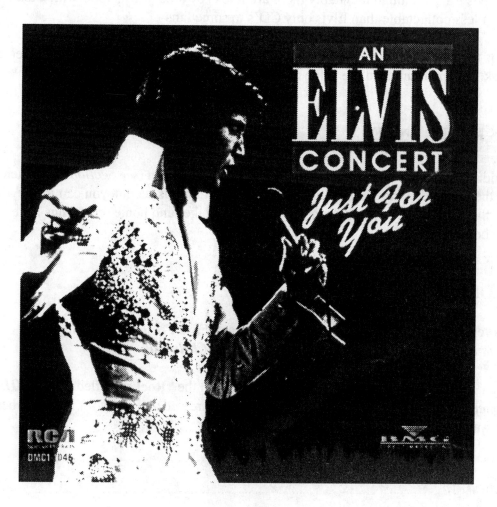

CONTENTS

SECTION I

<u>SECTION II</u> - <u>VARIOUS ARTISTS</u>

SECTION III - CROSS REFERENCE

Section 1

Catalog Releases
Promos
Special Products

A DATE WITH ELVIS

WE'RE GONNA MOVE · BLUE MOON OF KENTUCKY · I WANT TO BE FREE · GOOD ROCKIN' TONIGHT · IS IT SO STRANGE
I FORGOT TO REMEMBER TO FORGET · YOUNG AND BEAUTIFUL · BABY LET'S PLAY HOUSE · BABY I DON'T CARE · MILKCOW BLUES BOOGIE

[ ] **A DATE WITH ELVIS**
Catalog# 2011-2-R   Value $ 10-15
Matrix# W.O. 10973-1 20112R
(Jan. 1989 First Pressing. Midline CD. Silver & Black Disc with old RCA Logo.)
Disc contains the following selections:

Blue Moon of Kentucky   Good Rockin' Tonight
Young and Beautiful   Is It So Strange
Baby I Don't Care   We're Gonna Move
Milkcow Blues Boogie   I Want To Be Free
Baby Let's Play House   I Forgot To Remember To Forget

[ ] **A DATE WITH ELVIS**
Catalog# 2011-2-R   Value $ 10-15
Matrix# W.O. 10973-2 20112R
(1991 Second Pressing. Midline CD. Silver & Black Disc with old RCA Logo.)

[ ] **A DATE WITH ELVIS**
Catalog# 2011-2-R   Value $ 10-12
Matrix# 20112R ++ 64828-01
*(1996 Third Pressing. Midline CD. Silver & Black Disc with old RCA Logo.
"Wise Buy" sticker on shrink wrap.)*

ELVIS
A GOLDEN CELEBRATION
Previously
Unreleased as
4-CD SET
———— Features: ————
Historic TV & Concert Performances
Private Recordings
Rare Photographs
07863-67456-2

A GOLDEN CELEBRATION *(4 CD Set)*

[ ]

Catalog# 07863-67456-2   Value $ 60-70

(Feb. 1998 Release. Packaged in a special 5-1/2" x 10" book type holder.
4 CD Set. Gold Discs with Black and Silver Print. 2 CD's housed in push-in
holder in front cover. 2 CD's housed in push-in holder in back cover. Set contains
32 page booklet with photographs. Digitally Remastered from the original RCA
Record Label Master Tapes. Black and White collectors sticker on shrink wrap.)

Disc #1

Matrix# L801 4494 07863674562-1 H71218-07 A

Disc contains the following selections:

The Sun Sessions-Outtakes-
Memphis, Tennessee, 1954 and 1955
Harbor Lights
That's All Right *(Alt. Takes 1,2,3)*
Blue Moon Of Kentucky *(Alt. Take 1)*
I Don't Care If The Sun Don't Shine *(Alt. Takes)*
I'm Left, You're Right, She's Gone *(Slow Version)*
I'll Never Let You Go *(Alt. Take)*
When It Rains, It Really Pours *(Alt. Takes)*
The Dorsey Bros. Stage Show-
New York, New York - Jan. 28, 1956
Shake, Rattle And Roll/Flip, Flop And Fly
I Got a Woman
The Dorsey Bros. Stage Show -
New York, New York - Feb. 4, 1956
Baby, Lets Play House
Tutti Frutti

The Dorsey Bros. Stage Show -
New York, New York Feb. 11, 1956
Blue Suede Shoes
Heartbreak Hotel
The Dorsey Bros. Stage Show -
New York, New York Feb. 18, 1956
Tutti Frutti
I Was The One
The Dorsey Bros. Stage Show -
New York, New York March 17, 1956
Blue Suede Shoes
Heartbreak Hotel
The Dorsey Bros. Stage Show -
New York, New York March 24, 1956
Money Honey
Heartbreak Hotel

Disc #2

Matrix# L804 4494 07863674562-2 K71219-03 A

Disc contains the following selections:

The Milton Berle Show -
San Diego, California April 3, 1956
Introduction
Heartbreak Hotel
Blue Suede Shoes
Dialogue
Blue Suede Shoes
The Milton Berle Show -
Hollywood, California June 5, 1956
Hound Dog
Dialogue With Milton Berle
I Want You, I Need You, I Love You
The Steve Allen Show -
New York, New York July 1, 1956
Dialogue With Steve Allen
I Want You, I Need You, I Love You
Dialogue With Steve Allen
Hound Dog

The Mississippi -Alabama
Fair And Dairy Show - Tupelo, Miss.
Sept. 26, 1956 - Afternoon Performance
Heartbreak Hotel
Long Tall Sally
Introductions And Presentation
I Was The One
I Want You, I Need You, I Love You
Elvis Talks
I Got A Woman
Don't Be Cruel
Ready Teddy
Love Me Tender
Hound Dog
Vernon & Gladys Presley
Nick Adams
A Fan
Elvis

ELVIS
A GOLDEN CELEBRATION
Previously
Unreleased as
4-CD SET
Features:
Historic TV & Concert Performances
Private Recordings
Rare Photographs
07863-67456-2

Disc #3
Matrix# L804 4494 07863674562-3 K71219-02 A
Disc contains the following selections:

The Mississippi - Alabama
Fair And Dairy Show - Tupelo, Miss.
Sept. 26, 1956 - Evening Performance
Love Me Tender
I Was The One
I Got A Woman
Announcement
Don't Be Cruel
Blue Suede Shoes
Announcement
Baby, Lets Play House
Hound Dog
Announcement
The Ed Sullivan Show -
California and New York, Sept 9, 1956
Don't Be Cruel
Elvis Talks
Love Me Tender
Ready Teddy
Hound Dog

The Ed Sullivan Show -
New York, Oct. 28, 1956
Don't Be Cruel
Ed Sullivan
Love Me Tender
Ed Sullivan Introduces Elvis
Love Me
Hound Dog
Elvis' Closing Remarks
The Ed Sullivan Show -
New York, Jan. 6, 1957
Introduction
Hound Dog
Love Me Tender
Heartbreak Hotel
Don't Be Cruel
Too Much
Elvis Talks
When My Blue Moon Turns To Gold Again
Ed Sullivan Speaks
(There'll Be) Peace In The Valley (For Me)
Ed Sullivan Speaks

Disc #4
Matrix# L801 4494 07863674562-4 H71220-09 A
Disc contains the following selections:

Elvis At Home - Germany 1958-60
Danny Boy
Soldier Boy
The Fool
Earth Angel
I Asked The Lord (He's Only A Prayer Away)
Collectors Treasures -
Discovered At Graceland - Date Unknown
Excerpt From An Interview For TV Guide
My Heart Cries For You
Dark Moon
Write To Me From Naples
Suppose

Elvis - Burbank, California June 27, 1968
Blue Suede Shoes
Tiger Man
That's All Right
Lawdy Miss Clawdy
Baby What You Want Me To Do *(Alt. Take)*
Love Me
Are You Lonesome Tonight?
Baby What You Want Me To Do *(Alt. Take)*
Blue Christmas
One Night
Trying To Get To You

[ ]   # A GOLDEN CELEBRATION *(4 CD Promo Set)*
Catalog# 07863-67456-2   Value $ **70-80**
Disc #1 Matrix# L801 4494 07863674562-1 H71218-07 A
Disc #2 Matrix# L804 4494 07863674562-2 K71219-03 A
Disc #3 Matrix# L804 4494 07863674562-3 K71219-02 A
Disc #4 Matrix# L801 4494 07863674562-4 H71220-09 A
(Feb. 1998 Designated 4 CD Promo Set. Same as regular catalog release with
Black and White sticker "For Promotion Only - Not For Sale P-4/2" under
shrink wrap.)

"A Private Moment with The King"

A never heard ...vate ...home of ...ny Velvet, ...end to Elvis for ...conversation, sing-along jam ...ion,

Join a Private Party with Elvis & Friends

[ ]

A PRIVATE MOMENT WITH THE KING
JOIN A PRIVATE PARTY WITH ELVIS & FRIENDS
Catalog# None   Value $ 20-25
Matrix# 5134-ELVISPM-2 151J 1991
(June 1998 Release from Outwest Entertainment. Black and White Picture Disc.
*4 page insert booklet. Insert booklet dates this as a **1974 home recording**,*
however it may be Dec. 1973. Mail Order Only.)
Disc contains the following Elvis selections:

Spanish Eyes
Baby, What You Want Me To Do
I'm So Lonesome I Could Cry
C.C. Rider

That's All Right
You're Life Has Just Begun
(with Linda Thompson)
Tear Drops *(with Linda Thompson)*

[ ] **A TOUCH OF PLATINUM** *(2 CD's)*
A LIFE IN MUSIC
Catalog# 07863-67592-2   Value $ 25-35
(Feb. 1998 First Pressing. 2 CD's housed in multi disc jewel box. Black and White Picture Discs with 28 page booklet. Contains 44 of the 50 tracks from the first two discs of "Platinum - A Life In Muscic" box set. Silver collectors sticker with black print on front of shrink wrap.)
Disc #1
Matrix# 07863675922D1 ++ 83237-01
Disc contains the following selections:

I'll Never Stand In Your Way *(1954 Acetate)*
That's All Right *(Alternate Takes 1,2,3)*
Blue Moon *(Alternate Take)*
Good Rockin' Tonight *(Master)*
Mystery Train *(Master)*
I Got A Woman *(Alternate Take)*
Heartbreak Hotel *(Alternate Take 6)*
I'm Counting On You *(Alternate Take 13)*
Lawdy, Miss Clawdy *(Alternate Take 1)*
I Want You, I Need You, I Love You *(Alt. Take 4)*
Hound Dog *(From The Milton Berle Show)*

Don't Be Cruel *(Master)*
Rip It Up *(Alternate Take 15)*
Love Me Tender *(From Ed SullivanShow)*
When The Saints Go Marching In *(Home)*
All Shook Up *(Master)*
Peace In The Valley *(Alternate Take 3)*
Blueberry Hill *(Acetate)*
(Let Me Be Your) Teddy Bear *(Master)*
Jailhouse Rock *(Master)*
I Need Your Love Tonight *(Alt. Take 7)*
A Big Hunk O' Love *(Alt. Take 4)*

Disc #2
Matrix# 07863675922D2 ++ 83258-01
Disc contains the following selections:

Stuck On You *(From The Frank Sinatra Show)*
Fame And Fortune *(From The Frank Sinatra Show)*
It's Now Or Never *(Master)*
A Mess Of Blues *(Alternate Take 1)*
Are You Lonesome Tonight? *(Master)*
Reconsider Baby *(Master)*
His Hand In Mine *(Alternate Take 2)*
Milky White Way *(Alternate Take 3)*
I'm Comin' Home *(Alternate Take 3)*
I Feel So Bad *(Alternate Take 1)*
Can't Help Falling In Love *(Master)*

Something Blue *(Alternate Take 1)*
Return To Sender *(Master)*
Bossa Nova Baby *(Alternate Take 2)*
How Great Thou Art *(Alternate Take 4)*
Guitar Man *(Alternate Take 4)*
You'll Never Walk Alone *(Alternate Take 2)*
PRIVATE GRACELAND &
PALM SPRINGS SEGMENT
Oh How I Love Jesus
Tennessee Waltz
Blowin' In The Wind
I'm Beginning To Forget You
After Loving You

[ ] **A TOUCH OF PLATINUM** *(2 CD Promo)*
A LIFE IN MUSIC
Catalog# 07863-67592-2   Value $ 30-40
Disc #1 Matrix# 07863675922D1 ++ 83237-01
Disc #2 Matrix# 07863675922D2 ++ 83258-01
(Feb. 1998 Designated Promo. Same as regular catalog release with Black and White sticker "Not For Sale NFS-1" on front cover of insert booklet. Large drill hole thru back of jewel box.)

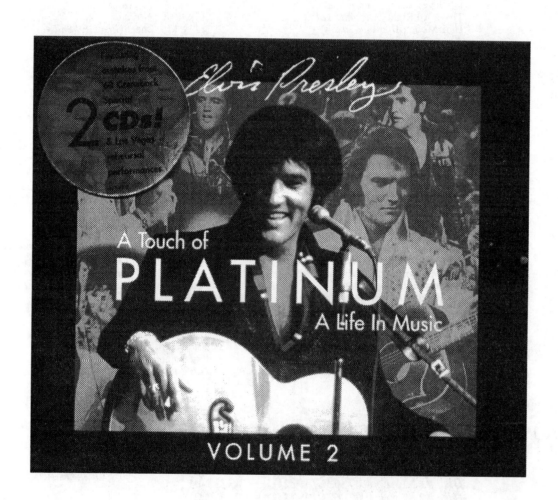

2 CDs!

Elvis Presley

A Touch of
PLATINUM
A Life In Music

VOLUME 2

[ ]   **A TOUCH OF PLATINUM Volume 2**   *(2 CD's)*
A LIFE IN MUSIC
Catalog# 07863-67593-2   **Value $ 25-35**
(July 1998 First Pressing. 2 CD's housed in multi disc jewel box. Black and White Picture Disc with 28 page booklet. Contains 44 of the 50 tracks from the last two discs of "Platinum - A Life In Music" box set. Purple collectors sticker with black print on front of shrink wrap.)
Disc #1
Matrix# 07863675932D1 ++ 85744-01
Disc contains the following selections:

Tiger Man *(Rehearsal)*
When My Blue Moon Turns To Gold Again
(Alternate Take)
Trying To Get To You *(Alternate Take)*
If I Can Dream *(Alternate Take 1)*
In The Ghetto *(Alternate Take 3)*
Suspicious Minds *(Alternate Take 7)*
Baby What You Want Me To Do *(Las Vegas 1969)*
Words *(Las Vegas 1969)*
Johnny B Goode *(Las Vegas 1969)*
Release Me *(Las Vegas 1970)*
See See Rider *(Las Vegas 1970)*

The Wonder Of You *(Las Vegas 1970)*
You Don't Have To Say You Love Me*(Mst)*
Funny How Time Slips Away *(Master)*
LAS VEGAS REHEARSALS:
  I Washed My Hands In Muddy Water
  I Was The One
  Cattle Call
  Baby, Let's Play House
  Don't
  Money Honey
  What'd I Say
Bridge Over Troubled Water*(Las Vegas '70)*

Disc #2
Matrix# 07863675932D2 ++ 85738-01
Disc contains the following selections:

Miracle Of The Rosary *(Alternate Take 1)*
Bosom Of Abraham *(Alternate Take 3)*
I'll Be Home On Christmas Day *(Alternate Take 4)*
Burning Love *(Alternate Take 1)*
Separate Ways *(Alternate Take 25)*
Always On My Mind *(Alternate Take 2)*
An American Trilogy *(Alternate Aloha)*
Take Good Care Of Her *(Alternate Take 4)*
I've Got A Thing About You Baby *(Master)*
Are You Sincere *(Alternate Take 2)*
Promised Land *(Alternate Take 5)*

Steamroller Blues *(Unrel Live Performance)*
And I Love You So *(Alternate Take 2)*
T-R-O-U-B-L-E *(Master)*
Danny Boy *(Alternate Take 9)*
Moody Blue *(Master)*
Hurt *(Alternate Take 2)*
For The Heart *(Alternate Take 1)*
Pledging My Love *(Alternate Take 3)*
Way Down *(Alternate Take 2)*
My Way *(Unreleased Live Performance)*
(Excerpt From) The Jaycees Speech

[ ]   **A TOUCH OF PLATINUM Volume 2**   *(2 CD Promo)*
A LIFE IN MUSIC
Catalog# 07863-67593-2   **Value $ 30-40**
Disc #1 Matrix# 07863675932D1 ++ 85744-01
Disc #2 Matrix# 07863675932D2 ++ 85738-01
(July 1998 Designated Promo. Same as regular catalog release with Black and White sticker "Not For Sale NFS-1" on front cover of insert booklet. Large drill hole thru back of jewel box.)

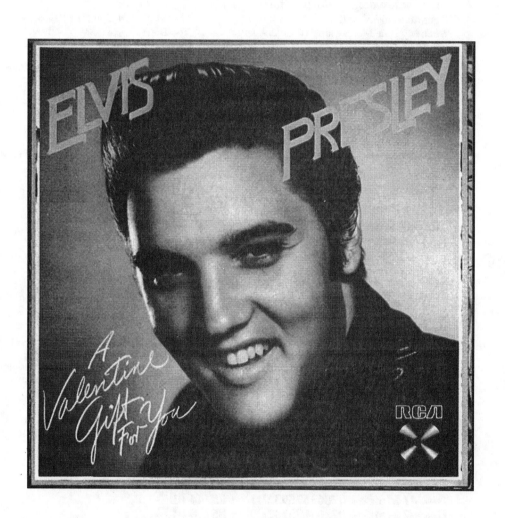

[ ]   **A VALENTINE GIFT FOR YOU**
         Catalog# PCD1-5353   **Value $ 20-25**
         Matrix# PCD-15353 2A1 5Z
         (Aug. 1985 First Pressing. Silver & Blue Disc with block RCA Logo in white.
         Pressed in Japan for U.S. Release.)
         Disc contains the following selections:

Are You Lonesome Tonight?	It Feels So Right
I Need Somebody To Lean On	I Was The One
Young And Beautiful	Fever
Playing For Keeps	Tomorrow Is A Long Time
Tell Me Why	Love Letters
Give Me The Right	Fame And Fortune
	Can't Help Falling In Love

[ ]   **A VALENTINE GIFT FOR YOU**
         Catalog# PCD1-5353   **Value $ 12-15**
         Matrix# PCD-15353 1/88 3A52
         (Jan. 1988 Second Pressing. Silver & Blue Disc with block RCA Logo in white.
         Pressed in U.S.)

[ ]   **A VALENTINE GIFT FOR YOU**
         Catalog# PCD1-5353   **Value $ 12-15**
         Matrix# PCD-15353 2/88 3A55
         (Feb. 1988 Third Pressing. Silver & Blue Disc with block RCA Logo in white.
         Pressed in U.S.)

[ ]   **A VALENTINE GIFT FOR YOU**
         Catalog# PCD1-5353   **Value $ 10-15**
         Matrix# PCD15353 8/90 1DA1X
         (Aug. 1990 Fourth Pressing. Silver & Blue Disc with block RCA Logo in white.
         Pressed in U.S.)

[ ]   **A VALENTINE GIFT FOR YOU**
         Catalog# PCD1-5353   **Value $ 10-15**
         Matrix# PCD15353 10/92 1DA4
         (Oct. 1992 Fifth Pressing. Silver & Blue Disc with block RCA Logo in white.
         Pressed in U.S.)

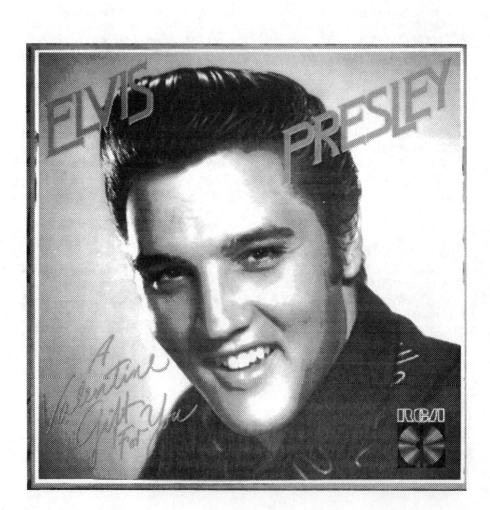

[ ]   **A VALENTINE GIFT FOR YOU**
      Catalog# PCD1-5353   **Value $ 10-15**
      Matrix# PCD15353 5/94 1DA6
      (May 1994 Sixth Pressing. Silver & Blue Disc with block RCA Logo in white.
      Pressed in U.S.)

[ ]   **A VALENTINE GIFT FOR YOU**
      Catalog# PCD1-5353   **Value $ 20-30**
      BMG Music Service Catalog# D 154385
      Matrix# 154385D 6/94 1DA8
      (June 1994 Seventh Pressing. Mfg. for BMG Direct Marketing, Inc. BMG Music
      Service catalog number on disc and back insert cover. Silver & Blue Disc with
      block RCA Logo in white. Pressed in U.S. Only available from BMG Music
      CD Club. Mail Order Only.)

[ ]   **A VALENTINE GIFT FOR YOU**
      Catalog# PCD1-5353   **Value $ 10-15**
      Matrix# PCD15353 3/95 1DB3
      (March 1995 Eighth Pressing. Silver & Blue Disc with block RCA Logo in white.
      "Wise Buy" sticker on shrink wrap. Pressed in U.S.)

[ ]   **A VALENTINE GIFT FOR YOU**
      Catalog# PCD1-5353   **Value $ 20-30**
      BMG Music Service Catalog# D 154385
      Matrix# PCD15353 2/97 1DB5
      (Feb. 1997 Ninth Pressing. Mfg. for BMG Direst Marketing, Inc. BMG Music
      Service catalog number on disc and back insert cover. Silver & Blue Disc with
      block RCA Logo in white. Pressed in U.S. Only available from BMG Music
      CD Club. Mail Order Only.)

[ ]   **A VALENTINE GIFT FOR YOU**
      Catalog# BG2-5353   **Value $ 20-30**
      Matrix# DIDX-037518 01
      (1997 Tenth Pressing. Mfg. by BMG Music for Columbia House Music Club, a
      non-BMG Music CD Club. Columbia House Music Club catalog number on disc,
      spine, front and back insert cover. Silver and Blue Disc with block RCA Logo in
      white. Only available from Columbia House Music CD Club. Mail Order Only.)

[ ]   **ALL SHOOK UP/ ARE YOU LONESOME TONIGHT?**
             Catalog# DRC11810   **Value $ 2-5**
             Matrix# L385 1100 DRC11810 C70722-09
             (Aug. 1997 20th Anniversary CD Single from BMG Special Products for
             Trans World Entertainment Inc. Sold only at TWE outlets- Coconuts, Tape World
             and Record Town. 20th Anniversary Picture Disc. Silver Disc with picture
             of Elvis and Print in Black. Disc housed in a die-cut paper sleeve. This is one of
             five 20th Anniversary CD Singles pressed for TWE.)
             Disc contains the following selections:
             (I'm) All Shook Up   Are You Lonesome Tonight?

[ ]   **ALMOST IN LOVE**
             Catalog# CAD1-2440   **Value $ 20-25**
             Matrix# CAD2440 ++ 73125-01
             (Dec. 1996 BMG Special Products Release for AVON. Silver Disc
             with Black Print. Mail Order Only. This title now deleted.)
             Disc contains the following selections:
             Almost In Love   Rubberneckin'
             Long Legged Girl (With The Short Dress On)   Clean Up Your Own Back Yard
             Edge Of Reality   U.S. Male
             My Little Friend   Charro
             A Little Less Conversation   Stay Away

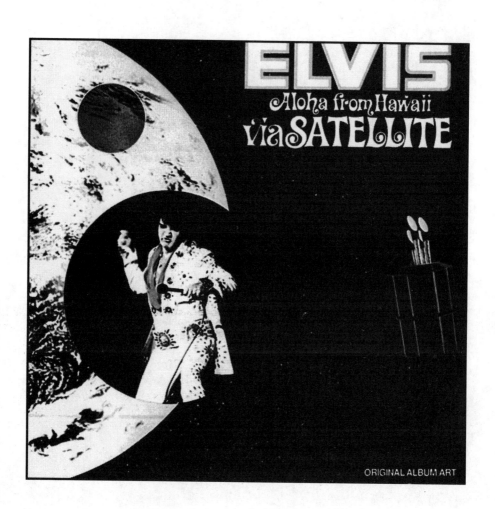

ELVIS
Aloha from Hawaii
via SATELLITE

ORIGINAL ALBUM ART

ALOHA FROM HAWAII VIA SATELLITE

Catalog# 07863-52642-2　　　　　　　　　**Value $ 15-18**

Matrix# 07863-52642-2 Y1D 22

(April 1992 First Pressing. Elvis in the '90's Black Disc with old RCA Logo and Print in Silver. 8 page insert booklet. Digitally Remastered from the original RCA Label Master Tapes.)

Disc contains the following selections:

Introduction: Also Sprach Zarathustra
(Theme from 2001: Space Odyssey)
See See Rider
Burning Love
Something
You Gave Me A Mountain
Steamroller Blues
My Way
Love Me
Johnny B. Goode
It's Over
Blue Suede Shoes
I'm So Lonesome I Could Cry

I Can't Stop Loving You
Hound Dog
What Now My Love
Fever
Welcome To My World
Suspicious Minds
Introductions By Elvis
I'll Remember You
Medley: Long Tall Sally/
Whole Lotta Shakin' Goin' On
American Trilogy
A Big Hunk O' Love
Can't Help Falling In Love

ALOHA FROM HAWAII VIA SATELLITE

Catalog# 07863-52642-2　　　　　　　　　**Value $ 15-18**

Matrix# 07863526422 Y3J11

(1994 Second Pressing. Elvis in the '90's Black Disc with old RCA Logo and Print in Silver. 8 page insert booklet. Elvis in the '90's black and white sticker on shrink wrap. Digitally Remastered from the original RCA Label Master Tapes.)

ALOHA FROM HAWAII VIA SATELLITE

Catalog# 07863-52642-2　　　　　　　　　**Value $ 20-30**

BMG Music Service Catalog# D 118727

Matrix# 07863-52642-2 Y1D 1 7

(July 1997 Third Pressing. Mfg. for BMG Direct Marketing, Inc. BMG Music Service catalog number on disc and insert back cover. Elvis in the '90's Black Disc with old RCA Logo and Print in Silver. 8 page insert booklet. Digitally Remastered from the original RCA Label Master Tapes. Only available from BMG Music CD Club. Mail Order Only.)

ALOHA FROM HAWAII VIA SATELLITE

Catalog# BG2-52642　　　　　　　　　**Value $ 20-30**

Matrix# DIDX-038816 G2 1A 04

(1997 Fourth Pressing. Mfg. by BMG Music for Columbia House Music Club, a non-BMG Music CD Club. Columbia House Music Club catalog number on disc, spine, front and back insert cover. CRC Logo printed above bar code on back insert cover. Elvis in the '90's Black Disc with old RCA Logo and Print in Silver. 8 page insert booklet. Digitally Remastered from the original RCA Label Master Tapes. Only available from Columbia House Music CD Club. Mail Order Only.)

ELVIS PRESLEY
ALOHA
FROM HAWAII
VIA SATELLITE

Special
25th Anniversary
Edition

Includes 5 Bonus Songs:
Blue Hawaii
No More
Ku-U-I-Po
Hawaiian Wedding Song
Early Morning Rain

Digitally Remastered
Includes New Liner Notes and Photos!

In Stores Now

 The RCA Records Label is a unit of BMG Entertainment Tmk(s) Registered • Marca(s)
Registrada(s) ® ®General Electric., USA • BMG logo is a trademark of BMG Music

[ ] **ALOHA FROM HAWAII VIA SATELLITE**
Catalog# 07863-52642-2   Value $ 20-30
BMG Music Service Catalog # D 118727
Matrix# IFPI 07863526422 Y5J 12
*(Jan. 1998 Fifth Pressing. Mfg. for BMG Direct Marketing, Inc. BMG Music
Service catalog number on disc and insert back cover. Elvis in the '90's Black
Disc with old RCA Logo and Print in Silver. 8 page insert booklet. Digitally
Remastered from the original RCA Label Master Tapes. Only available from
BMG Music CD Club. Mail Order Only.)*

[ ] **ALOHA FROM HAWAII VIA SATELLITE**
25th ANNIVERSARY EDITION
Catalog# 07863-67609-2   Value $ 13-18
Matrix# L804 4494 07863676092 K80323-01 A
*(April 1998 Reissue with new catalog number, artwork and 5 additional tracks.
Purple Disc with Red and Gold Print. Contains 12 page insert booklet.
Purple and White 25th Anniversary Edition collectors sticker on front of shrink
wrap. Digitally Remastered from the original RCA Label Master Tapes with
improved sound.)*
Disc contains the following selections:

Introduction: Also Sprach Zarathustra	Fever
See See Rider	Welcome To My World
Burning Love	Suspicious Minds
Something	Introductions By Elvis
You Gave Me A Mountain	I'll Remember You
Steamroller Blues	Long Tall Sally/
My Way	Whole Lotta Shakin' Goin' On
Love Me	An American Trilogy
Johnny B. Goode	A Big Hunk O' Love
It's Over	Can't Help Falling In Love
Blue Suede Shoes	Blue Hawaii
I'm So Lonesome I Could Cry	Ku-U-I-Po
I Can't Stop Loving You	No More
Hound Dog	Hawaiian Wedding Song
What Now My Love	Early Morning Rain

[ ] **ALOHA FROM HAWAII VIA SATELLITE**
25th ANNIVERSARY EDITION
Catalog# 07863-67609-2   Value $20-30
BMG Music Service Catalog# D 122908
Matrix# L385 1099 07863676092 C80720-04 A
*(Aug. 1998 Second Pressing. Mfg. for BMG Direct Marketing, Inc. BMG Music
Service catalog number on disc and insert back cover. Purple Disc with Red and
Gold Print. Contains 12 page insert booklet. Digitally Remastered from the
original RCA Label Master Tapes. Only available from BMG Music CD Club.
Mail Order Only.)*

[ ] **ALOHA VIA SATELLITE**
Catalog# DPC 12214   **Value $ 60-65**
Matrix# L385 1100 DPC12214 C80921-15 A
(Oct. 1998 Limited Edition from BMG Special Products for JAT Publishing.
Package includes book, CD and 8"x10" bonus photo. Price above includes entire
package. Mail order Only.)
Disc contains the following selections:

Welcome To My World   It's Over
What Now My Love   Dialogue/I'll Remember You
Steamroller Blues

[ ] The **ALTERNATE ALOHA**
Catalog# 6985-2-R   **Value $ 15-18**
Matrix# 69852R 5/88 2DC1
(May 1988 First Pressing. First commercial U.S. Elvis Picture Disc with
8 page insert booklet.)
Disc contains the following selections:

Also Sprach Zarathustra   What Now My Love
See See Rider   Fever
Burning Love   Welcome To My World
Something   Suspicious Minds
You Gave Me A Mountain   Introductions By Elvis
Steamroller Blues ·   I'll Remember You
My Way   American Trilogy
Love Me   A Big Hunk O' Love
It's Over   Can't Help Falling In Love
Blue Suede Shoes   Blue Hawaii
I'm So Lonesome I Could Cry   Hawaiian Wedding Song
Hound Dog   KU-U-I-PO

[ ] The **ALTERNATE ALOHA**
Catalog# 6985-2-R   **Value $ 15-18**
Matrix# 69852R 5/88 2DD3
(May 1988 Second Pressing. Picture Disc. Contains 8 page insert booklet.)

[ ] The **ALTERNATE ALOHA**
Catalog# 6985-2-R   **Value $ 12-15**
Matrix# 69852R 1/91 5DA2X
(Jan. 1991 Third Pressing. Picture Disc. Contains 8 page insert booklet.)

[ ] The **ALTERNATE ALOHA**
Catalog# 6985-2-R   Value $ 12-15
Matrix# 69852R 3/91 5DB2X
(March 1991 Fourth Pressing. Picture Disc. Contains 8 page insert booklet.)

[ ] The **ALTERNATE ALOHA**
Catalog# 6985-2-R   Value $ 12-15
Matrix# 69852R 10/92 5DB9
(Oct. 1992 Fifth Pressing. Picture Disc. Contains 8 page insert booklet.)

[ ] The **ALTERNATE ALOHA**
Catalog# 6985-2-R   Value $ 12-15
Matrix# 69852R 7/93 6DA2
(July 1993 Sixth Pressing. Picture Disc. Contains 8 page insert booklet.)

[ ] The **ALTERNATE ALOHA**
Catalog# 6985-2-R   Value $ 12-15
Matrix# 69852R 1/95 6DA7
(January 1995 Seventh Pressing. Picture Disc. Contains 8 page insert booklet.)

[ ] The **ALTERNATE ALOHA**
Catalog# 6985-2-R   Value $ 12-15
Matrix# 69852R 10/95 6DB1
(Oct. 1995 Eighth Pressing. Picture Disc. Contains 8 page insert booklet.)

[ ] The **ALTERNATE ALOHA**
Catalog# 6985-2-R   Value $ 12-15
Matrix# 69852R 6/96 6DB2
(June 1996 Ninth Pressing. Picture Disc. Contains 8 page insert booklet.)

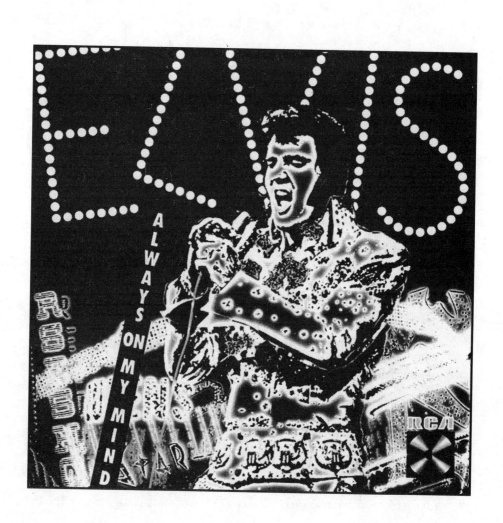

[ ] **ALWAYS ON MY MIND**
Catalog# PCD1-5430   Value $ 20-25
Matrix# PCD-15430 1A2 63
(July 1985 First Pressing. Silver & Blue Disc with block RCA Logo in white.
Pressed in Japan for U.S. Release.)
Disc contains the following selections:

Separate Ways	Pieces Of My Life
Don't Cry Daddy	I Miss You
My Boy	It's Midnight
Solitaire	I've Lost You
Bitter They Are, Harder They Fall	You Gave Me A Mountain
Hurt	Unchained Melody
	Always On My Mind

[ ] **ALWAYS ON MY MIND**
Catalog# PCD1-5430   Value $ 15-18
Matrix# PCD-15430 1A11 6X
(1985 Second Pressing. Silver & Blue Disc with block RCA Logo in white.
Pressed in Japan for U.S. Release.)

[ ] **ALWAYS ON MY MIND**
Catalog# PCD1-5430   Value $ 15-18
Matrix# PCD-15430 1A14 72
(1985 Third Pressing. Silver & Blue Disc with block RCA Logo in white.
Pressed in Japan for U.S. Release.)

[ ] **ALWAYS ON MY MIND**
Catalog# PCD1-5430   Value $ 12-15
Matrix# PCD-15430 1/88 2A6
(January 1988 Fourth Pressing. Silver & Blue Disc with block RCA Logo in
white. Pressed in U.S.)

[ ] **ALWAYS ON MY MIND**
Catalog# PCD1-5430   Value $ 12-15
Matrix# PCD-15430 8/88 2A56
(August 1988 Fifth Pressing. Silver & Blue Disc with block RCA Logo in white.
Pressed in U.S.)

[ ] **ALWAYS ON MY MIND**
Catalog# PCD1-5430   Value $ 12-15
Matrix# PCD-15430 10/88 2A58
(Oct. 1988 Sixth Pressing. Silver & Blue Disc with block RCA Logo in white.
Pressed in U.S.)

[ ]   **ALWAYS ON MY MIND**
    Catalog# PCD1-5430   Value $ 12-15
    Matrix# PCD-15430 8/89 1DA2
    (August 1989 Seventh Pressing. Silver & Blue Disc with block RCA Logo in
    white. Pressed in U.S.)

[ ]   **ALWAYS ON MY MIND**
    Catalog# PCD1-5430   Value $ 12-15
    Matrix# PCD1-5430 32T 13
    (1990 Eighth Pressing. Silver & Black Disc with old RCA Logo with
    *"**Wise Buy**" sticker on shrink wrap. Pressed in U.S.)*

[ ]   **ALWAYS ON MY MIND**
    Catalog # PCD1-5430   Value $ 12-15
    Matrix# PCD1-5430 42T 14
    (1991 Ninth Pressing. Silver & Black Disc with old RCA Logo with
    *"**Wise Buy**" sticker on shrink wrap. Pressed in U.S.)*

[ ]   **ALWAYS ON MY MIND**
    Catalog# PCD1-5430   Value $ 10-12
    Matrix# PCD1-5430 42T 16
    (1991 Tenth Pressing. Silver & Black Disc with old RCA Logo with
    *"**Wise Buy**" sticker on shrink wrap. Pressed in U.S.)*

[ ]   **ALWAYS ON MY MIND**
    Catalog# PCD1-5430   Value $ 10-12
    Matrix# PCD1-5430 42T 25
    (1991 Eleventh Pressing. Silver & Black Disc with old RCA Logo with
    *"**Wise Buy**" sticker on shrink wrap. Pressed in U.S.)*

[ ]   **ALWAYS ON MY MIND**
    Catalog# PCD1-5430   Value $ 10-12
    Matrix# PCD1-5430 42T 27
    (1992 Twelfth Pressing. Silver & Black Disc with old RCA Logo.
    Pressed in U.S.)

ELVIS PRESLEY
Amazing Grace

His Greatest
Sacred Performances

2 Compact Discs

55 Classic Songs of Faith and Inspiration on
2 compact discs or cassettes

Including Amazing Grace • Crying In The Chapel
His Hand In Mine • How Great Thou Art

Plus 5 previously unreleased "jam session" tracks
Booklet includes rare photos and extensive liner notes
07863 66421-2/4

[ ]   **AMAZING GRACE** *(2 CD Set)*
        HIS GREATEST SACRED PERFORMANCES
        Catalog# 07863-66421-2   **Value $ 25-30**
        (Oct. 1994 First Pressing. Lavender Discs with old RCA Logo and print in black.
        Contains 32 page insert booklet. Discs housed in multi disc jewel box. Full
        color photo of Elvis under each disc in jewel box. Jewel box packaged with outer
        bellyband with same artwork as jewel box. Lavender sticker on bellyband shrink
        wrap. Set contains five previously unreleased performances.)
        Disc #1
        Matrix# 07863664212P1 ++ 50719-01
        Disc contains the following selections:

I Believe   Working On The Building
(There'll Be) Peace In The Valley (For Me)   Crying In The Chapel
Take My Hand Precious Lord   Run On
It Is No Secret (What God Can Do)   How Great Thou Art
Milky White Way   Stand By Me
His Hand In Mine   Where No One Stands Alone
I Believe In The Man In The Sky   So High
He Knows Just What I Need   Farther Along
Mansion Over The Hilltop   By And By
In My Father's House   In The Garden
Joshua Fit The Battle   Somebody Bigger Than You And I
Swing Down Sweet Chariot   Without Him
I'm Gonna Walk Dem Golden Stairs   If The Lord Wasn't Walking By My Side
If We Never Meet Again   Where Could I Go But To The Lord
Known Only To Him

Disc #2
Matrix# 07863664212P2 ++ 50169-01
Disc contains the following selections:

We Call On Him ·   He Is My Everything
You'll Never Walk Alone   There Is No God But God
Only Believe   I, John
Amazing Grace   Bosom Of Abraham
Miracle Of The Rosary   Help Me
Lead Me, Guide Me   If That Isn't Love
He Touched Me   Why Me Lord *(Live Version)*
I've Got Confidence   How Great Thou Art *(Live Version)*
An Evening Prayer   I, John *(Previously Unreleased)*
Seeing Is Believing   Bosom Of Abraham*(Previously Unreleased)*
A Thing Called Love   You Better Run *(Previously Unreleased)*
Put Your Hand In The Hand   Lead Me, Guide Me*(Previously Unreleased)*
Reach Out To Jesus   Turn Your Eyes Upon Jesus/Nearer My God
                                                    To Thee *(Previously Unreleased)*

[ ]   **AMAZING GRACE** *(2 CD Promo Set)*
        HIS GREATEST SACRED PERFORMANCES
        Catalog# 07863-66421-2   **Value $ 30-35**
        Disc #1 Matrix# 07863664212P1 ++ 50719-01
        Disc #2 Matrix# 07863664212P2 ++ 50169-01
        (Oct. 1994 Designated Promo. Same as regular catalog release with Black and
        *White sticker "**Not For Sale NFS-1** " on front cover of bellyband. Bar code has*
        been scratched off the bellyband.)

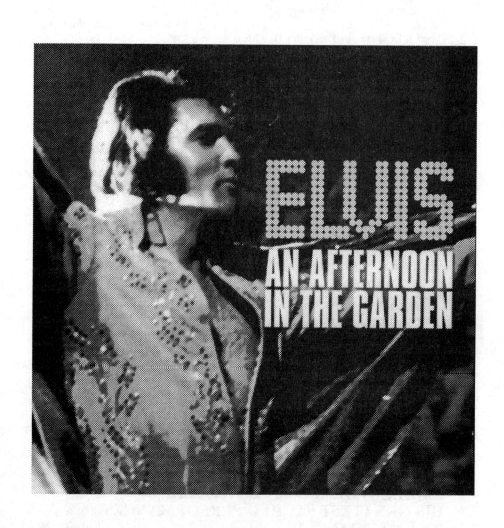

[ ]   **AMAZING GRACE** *(2 CD Set)*
HIS GREATEST SACRED PERFORMANCES
Catalog# 07863-66421-2   Value $ 30-40
BMG Music Service Catalog# D 2059977
Disc #1 Matrix# 07863664212P1 ++ 50719-01
Disc #2 Matrix# 07863664212P2 ++ 50890-03
*(1995 Second Pressing. Mfg. for BMG Direct Marketing, Inc. BMG Music
Service catalog number on discs, insert covers and booklet. Second disc is darker
lavender color and bolder print. Disc housed in multi disc jewel box without
bellyband. Only available from BMG Music CD Club. Mail Order Only.)*

[ ]   **AN AFTERNOON IN THE GARDEN**
Catalog# 07863-67457-2   Value $ 15-18
Matrix# 07863674572 ++ 74401-02
*(March 1997 First Pressing. Blue Picture Disc of crowd attending the concert.
Elvis in Yellow and all other print in Silver. Contains 12 page insert booklet.
Yellow collectors sticker with black print on front of shrink wrap. Digitally
Remastered from the original RCA Label Master Tapes.)*
Disc contains the following selections:

Also Sprach Zarathustra	Love Me Tender
That's All Right	Blue Suede Shoes
Proud Mary	Reconsider Baby
Never Been To Spain	Hound Dog
You Don't Have To Say You Love Me	I'll Remember You
Until It's Time For You To Go	Suspicious Minds
You've Lost That Lovin' Feelin'	Introductions By Elvis
Polk Salad Annie	For The Good Times
Love Me	An American Trilogy
All Shook Up	Funny How Time Slips Away
Heartbreak Hotel	I Can't Stop Loving You
(Let Me Be Your) Teddy Bear/Don't Be Cruel	Can't Help Falling In Love

[ ]   **AN AFTERNOON IN THE GARDEN** *(Promo)*
Catalog# 07863-67457-2   Value $ 20-25
Matrix# 07863674572 ++ 74401-02
*(March 1997 Designated Promo. Same as regular catalog release with black and
white sticker "Not For Sale NFS-1" on front cover of insert sleeve. Drill hole
thru back of jewel box.)*

[ ]   **AN AFTERNOON IN THE GARDEN**
Catalog# 07863-67457-2   Value $ 20-30
BMG Music Service Catalog# D 118206
Matrix# 07863674572 ++ 74401-02
*(May 1997 Second Pressing. Mfg. for BMG Direct Marketing, Inc. BMG Music
Service catalog number on disc and back insert cover. Blue crowd picture disc.
Contains 12 page insert booklet. Only available from BMG Music CD Club.
Mail Order Only.)*

GOLD STANDARD SINGLE

ARE YOU LONESOME TONIGHT?

ELVIS PRESLEY
with The Jordinaires

I GOTTA KNOW

8994-2-RH

COMMEMORATIVE JUKE BOX SERIES

  Tmk(s) ® Registered • Marca(s) Registrada(s) RCA Corporation. BMG logo ® BMG Music
© 1989 BMG Music • Manufactured and Distributed by BMG Music, New York, N.Y. • Printed in U.S.A.

[ ]

AN ELVIS DOUBLE FEATURE: SPEEDWAY, CLAMBAKE

Catalog# PDC2-1250 CXD-3017   Value $ 20-25
Matrix# W.O. 12927-1 PDC2-1250

*(Sept. 1989 RCA Special Products Release on the Pair Label. Silver & Black Disc with RCA and Pair Logos in Blue. **This title is now deleted from catalog.**)*
Disc contains the following selections:

Speedway
There Ain't Nothing Like A Song*(with Nancy Sinatra)*
Who Are You? (Who Am I?)
Let Yourself Go
Your Groovy Self*
Western Union
Goin' Home
Suppose
Nancy Sinatra track

Guitar Man
Clambake
A House That Has Everything
Hey, Hey, Hey
The Girl I Never Loved
How Can You Lose What...
You Never Had
Big Boss Man
Just Call Me Lonesome

[ ]

ARE YOU LONESOME TONIGHT/I GOTTA KNOW

Catalog# 8994-2-RH   Value $10-20
Matrix# W.O. 75056-1 89942RH

(May 1989 Commemorative Juke Box Gold Standard Series CD Single. Silver & Black Disc with old RCA Logo. Gold Standard insert sleeve. One of five Elvis CD singles pressed for Jukebox only.)
Disc contains the following selections:

Are You Lonesome Tonight?   I Gotta Know

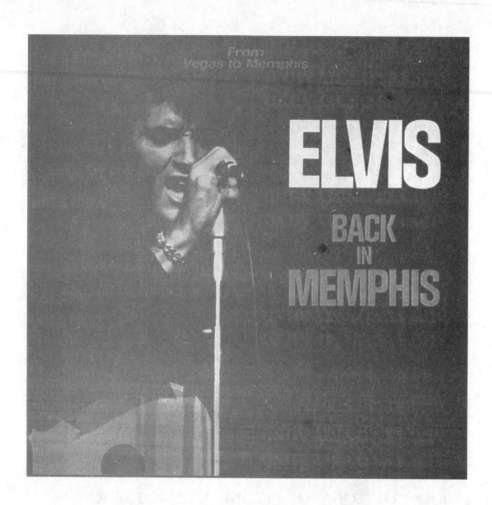

[ ]   **BACK IN MEMPHIS**
     Catalog# 07863-61081-2   Value $ 12-15
     Matrix# W.O. 27623-1 07863610812
     *(Oct. 1992 First Pressing. Elvis in the '90's Black Disc with old RCA
     Logo and Print in Silver. 6 page insert booklet. Digitally Remastered
     from the original RCA Label Master Tapes.)*
     Disc contains the following selections:

     Inherit The Wind   Do You Konw Who I Am?
     This Is The Story   From A Jack To A King
     Stranger In My Own Home Town   The Fair's Moving On
     A Little Bit Of Green   You'll Think Of Me
     And The Grass Won't Pay No Mind   Without Love (There Is Nothing)

[ ]   **BACK IN MEMPHIS**
     Catalog# BG2-61081   Value $ 20-30
     Matrix# E1 1ABG261081 03
     *(1997 Second Pressing. Mfg. by BMG Music for Columbia House Music Club,
     a non-BMG Music Club. Columbia House Music Club catalog number on disc,
     spine, booklet and back insert cover. CRC Logo printed above bar code on back
     insert cover. Elvis in the '90's Black Disc with old RCA Logo and Print in Silver.
     6 page insert booklet. Digitally Remastered from the original RCA Label Master
     Tapes. Only available from Columbia House Music CD Club. Mail Order Only.)*

[ ]   **BLUE CHRISTMAS**
     Catalog# 07863-59800-2   Value $ 10-15
     Matrix# 07863-59800-2 1D 21
     *(July 1992 First Pressing. Country Budget CD. Elvis in the '90's Black Disc
     with old RCA Logo and Print in Silver. RCA Sound Saver Release. Contains only
     8 Tracks. Digitally Mixed and Mastered in Nashville using the latest
     restoration equipment.)*
     Disc contains the following selections:

     O Come, All Ye Faithful   Blue Christmas
     The First Noel   Silent Night
     Winter Wonderland   White Christmas
     Silver Bells   I'll Be Home For Christmas

[ ]   **BLUE CHRISTMAS**
     Catalog# 07863-59800-2   Value $ 10-15
     Matrix# 07863-59800-2 1D 22
     *(Oct. 1995 Second Pressing. Elvis in the '90's Black Disc with old RCA Logo
     and Print in Silver. RCA Sound Saver Release. "Wise Buy" sticker on shrink
     wrap.)*

[ ] **BLUE HAWAII**
Catalog# 3683-2-R   Value $ 12-15
Matrix# W.O. 10144-1 36832R
(April 1988 First Pressing. Midline CD. Silver & Black Disc with old RCA Logo.
Back cover printed "Digitally Remastered ADD".)
Disc contains the following selections:

Blue Hawaii	Ku-U-I-Po
Almost Always True	Ito Eats
Aloha Oe	Slicin' Sand
No More	Hawaiian Sunset
Can't Help Falling In Love	Beach Boy Blues
Rock-A-Hula Baby	Island Of Love
Moonlight Swim	Hawaiian Wedding Song

[ ] **BLUE HAWAII**
Catalog# 3683-2-R   Value $ 10-12
Matrix# W.O. 10144-1 36832R
(1991 Second Pressing. Midline CD. Silver & Black Disc with old RCA Logo.
Back cover printed "Digitally Remastered" without ADD.)

[ ] **BLUE HAWAII**
Catalog# 3683-2-R   Value $ 10-12
Matrix# W.O. 10144-2 36832R
(1992 Third Pressing. Midline CD. Silver & Black Disc with old RCA Logo.)

[ ] **BLUE HAWAII**
Catalog# 3683-2-R   Value 20-30
BMG Music Service Catalog# D 163932
Matrix# W.O. 10144-2M 36832R
(1993 Fourth Pressing. Mfg. for BMG Direct Marketing, Inc. BMG Music
Service catalog number on disc and back insert cover. Midline CD. Silver &
Black Disc with old RCA Logo. Only available from BMG Music CD Club.
Mail Order Only.)

[ ] **BLUE HAWAII**
Catalog# 3683-2-R   Value $ 10-12
Matrix# W.O. 10144-3 36832R
(1995 Fifth Pressing. Midline CD. Silver & Black Disc with old RCA Logo.
"Wise Buy" sticker on shrink wrap.)

[ ] **BLUE HAWAII**
Catalog# 3683-2-R   Value $ 20-30
BMG Music Service Catalog# D 163932
Matrix# W.O. 10144-3 36832R
(1995 Sixth Pressing. Mfg. for BMG Direct Marketing, Inc. BMG Music
Service catalog number on disc and back insert cover. Midline CD. Silver &
Black Disc with old RCA Logo. Only available from BMG Music CD Club.
Mail Order Only.)

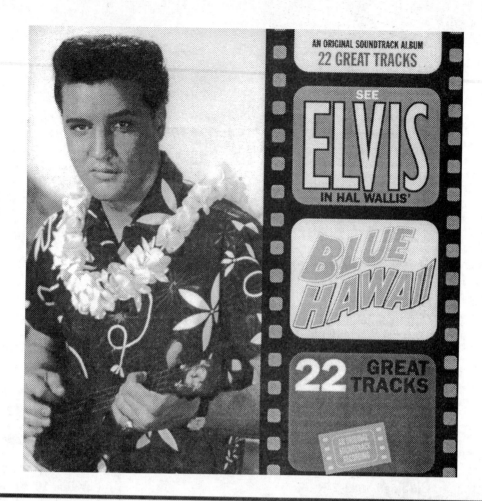

[ ] **BLUE HAWAII**
Catalog# 07863-66959-2   Value $ 15-18
Matrix# 07863669592 ++ 75353-01
*(April 1997 Reissue with new catalog number plus 8 additional alternate masters
and outtakes. Blue Picture Disc. Contains 8 page insert booklet. Black collectors
sticker with yellow and white print on front of shrink wrap. Digitally remastered
from the original RCA Label Master Tapes.)*
Disc contains the following selections:

Blue Hawaii	Beach Boy Blues
Almost Always True	Island Of Love
Alohe Oe	Hawaiian Wedding Song
No More	Steppin' Out Of Line
Can't Help Falling In Love	Can't Help Falling In Love *(Take 23)*
Rock-A-Hula Baby	Slicin' Sand *(Alt. Take 4)*
Moonlight Swim	No More *(Alt. Take 7)*
Ku-U-I-Po	Rock-A- Hula Baby *(Alt. Take 1)*
Ito Eats	Beach Boy Blues *(Movie Version, Take 3)*
Slicin' Sand	Steppin' Out Of Line *(Movie Vers. Take 19)*
Hawaiian Sunset	Blue Hawaii *(Alt. Take 3)*

[ ] **BLUE HAWAII** *(Promo)*
Catalog# 07863-66959-2   Value $ 18-20
Matrix# 07863669592 ++ 75353-01
*(April 1997 Designated Promo. Same as regular catalog release with black and
white sticker "Not For Sale NFS-1" on front cover of jewel box. Drill hole thru
back of jewel box.)*

[ ] **BLUE HAWAII** *(Collectors Edition)*
Catalog# 07863-67459-2   Value $ 20-25
Matrix# 07863674592 ++ 75302-01
*(April 1997 Reissue Special Collectors Edition. Rust Picture Disc with Blue
lettering. Contains 28 page booklet housed in deluxe edition hard cover book.
CD contained in back of booklet in attached picture sleeve. Black collectors
sticker with yellow and white print "Special Deluxe Collectors Edition" on
shrink wrap.)*
Disc contains the following selections:

Blue Hawaii	Beach Boy Blues
Almost Always True	Island Of Love
Aloha Oe	Hawaiian Wedding Song
No More	Steppin' Out Of Line
Can't Help Falling In Love	Can't Help Falling In Love *(Take 23)*
Rock-A-Hula Baby	Slicin' Sand *(Alt. Take 4)*
Moonlight Swim	No More *(Alt. Take 7)*
Ku-U-I-Po	Rock-A-Hula Baby *(Alt. Take 1)*
Ito Eats	Beach Boy Blues *(Movie Version, Take 3)*
Slicin' Sand	Steppin' Out Of Line *(Movie Ver.Take 19)*
Hawaiian Sunset	Blue Hawaii *(Alt. Take 3)*

THE BLUE SUEDE BOX

ELVIS

HIS GREATEST SOUNDTRACKS

[ ]   The **BLUE SUEDE BOX** *(5 CD Box Set)*
ELVIS: HIS GREATEST SOUNDTRACKS
BMG Music Service Catalog# D 207350   Value $ 75-100
(Aug. 1997 Limited Edition 5 CD Box Set. A BMG Music CD Club exclusive.
Contains three regular catalog releases - "Jailhouse Rock", "Loving You", and
"King Creole" plus the two collectors editions "G.I. Blues" and " Blue Hawaii".
Discs housed in a 5-3/4" x 5-1/2" Blue Suede Slipcase. Only available from
BMG Music CD Club. Mail Order Only.)

Disc #1 **LOVING YOU**
Matrix# 07863674522 ++ 74993-01
Disc contains the following selections:

Mean Woman Blues	Have I Told You Lately That I Love You
(Let Me Be Your) Teddy Bear	I Need You So
Loving You	Tell Me Why
Got A Lot O' Livin' To Do!	Is It So Strange
Lonesome Cowboy	One Night Of Sin
Hot Dog	When It Rains, It Really Pours
Party	I Beg Of You *(Alternate Master, Take 12)*
Blueberry Hill	Party *(Alternate Master, Take 7)*
True Love	Loving You *(Uptempo Version, Take 13)*
Don't Leave Me Now	Got A Lot O' Livin' To Do! *(Finale)*

Disc #2 **JAILHOUSE ROCK and LOVE ME TENDER**
Matrix# 07863674532 ++ 75317-01
Disc contains the following selections:

Jailhouse Rock	Don't Leave Me Now *(Alternate Master)*
Treat Me Nice	Love Me Tender
I Want To Be Free	Poor Boy
Don't Leave Me Now	Let Me
Young And Beautiful	We're Gonna Move
(You're So Square) Baby, I Don't Care	Love Me Tender *(End Title Version)*
Jailhouse Rock *(Movie Version)*	Let Me *(Solo)*
Treat Me Nice *(Movie Version)*	We're Gonna Move *(Stereo Take 9)*
I Want To Be Free *(Movie Version)*	Poor Boy *(Stereo)*
Young And Beautiful *(Movie Version)*	Love Me Tender *(Stereo)*

Disc #3 **KING CREOLE**
Matrix# 07863674542 ++ 75315-03
Disc contains the following selections:

King Creole	Steadfast, Loyal And True
As Long As I Have You	New Orleans
Hard Headed Woman	King Creole *(Alt. Take 18)*
Trouble	As Long As I Have You *(Movie Ver Take 4)*
Dixieland Rock	Danny
Don't Ask Me Why	Lover Doll *(Undubbed)*
Lover Doll	Steadfast, Loyal And True *(Alt. Master)*
Crawfish	As Long As I Have You *(Movie Ver Take 8)*
Young Dreams	King Creole *(Alt. Take 3)*

THE BLUE SUEDE BOX

ELVIS

HIS GREATEST SOUNDTRACKS

Disc #4 **BLUE HAWAII** *(Collectors Edition)*
Matrix# 07863674592 ++ 75302-01
Disc contains the following selections:

Blue Hawaii
Almost Always True
Ahoha Oe
No More
Can't Help Falling In Love
Rock-A-Hula Baby
Moonlight Swim
Ku-U-I-Po
Ito Eats
Slicin' Sand
Hawaiian Sunset

Beach Boy Blues
Island Of Love
Hawaiian Wedding Song
Steppin' Out Of Line
Can't Help Falling In Love *(Take 23)*
Slicin' Sand *(Alt. Take 4)*
No More *(Alt. Take 7)*
Rock-A-Hula Baby *(Alt. Take 1)*
Beach Boy Blues *(Movie Version, Take 3)*
Steppin' Out Of Line *(Movie Ver. Take 19)*
Blue Hawaii *(Alt. Take 3)*

Disc #5 **G. I. BLUES** *(Collectors Edition)*
Matrix# 07863674602 ++ 75335-01
Disc contains the following selections:

Tonight Is So Right For Love
What's She Really Like
Frankfort Special
Wooden Heart
G.I. Blues
Pocketful Of Rainbows
Shoppin' Around
Big Boots
Didja' Ever
Blue Suede Shoes

Doin' The Best I Can
Tonight's All Right For Love
Big Boots *(Fast Version)*
Shoppin' Around *(Alt. Take 11)*
Frankfort Special *(Fast Version Take 2)*
Pocketful Of Rainbows *(Alt. Take 2)*
Didja' Ever *(Alt. Take 1)*
Big Boots *(Acoustic Version, Take 2)*
What's She Really Like *(Alt. Take 7)*
Doin' The Best I Can *(Alt. Take 9)*

GOLD
STANDARD SINGLE

BLUE SUEDE SHOES

ELVIS PRESLEY

TUTTI FRUTTI

8993-2-RH

COMMEMORATIVE JUKE BOX SERIES

  Tmk(s) ® Registered • Marca(s) Registrada(s) RCA Corporation. BMG logo ® BMG Music
© 1989 BMG Music • Manufactured and Distributed by BMG Music, New York, N.Y. • Printed in U.S.A.

[ ] **BLUE SUEDE SHOES**   *(Original Soundtrack 2 CD Set)*
Catalog# 07863-67458-2   **Value $ 25-35**
(April 1997 Release. An original soundtrack recording from the touring rock
ballet "Blue Suede Shoes". Contains 16 page booklet. Silver Discs with Blue Print
and original artwork in Blue.. 2 CD's in multi disc jewel box. Red and White
collectors sticker on shrink wrap. This set contains overdubs and sweetening.
All tracks have been enhanced and remixed.
Contains alternate take of "I Want You, I Need You, I Love You".
"One Night Of Sin" incorrectly listed as "One Night" on back cover and booklet.)
Disc #1
Matrix# 07863674582D1 ++ 75329-01
Disc contains the following selections:

Guitar Man *(Uneditted Version)*   A Big Hunk O' Love
Blue Suede Shoes   Hard Headed Woman
Wear My Ring Around Your Neck   Steadfast, Loyal And True
I Want You, I Need You, I Love You *(Alt. Take)*   Soldier Boy
Stuck On You   Frankfort Special
Don't Be Cruel   Wooden Heart *(Music Box Intro.)*
(Let Me Be Your) Teddy Bear   Young And Beautiful *(Music Box Intro.)*
Hot Dog   Are You Lonesome Tonight?
Tutti Frutti   Love Me Tender
(You're The) Devil In Disguise

Disc #2
Matrix# 07863674582D2 ++ 75304-01
Disc contains the following selections:

(It's A) Long, Lonely Highway   Bossa Nova Baby
Heartbreak Hotel   Big Boss Man
Stranger In My Own Home Town   Trouble *(Drum Intro.)*
Mama Liked The Roses *(Chimes Intro.)*   One Night Of Sin *(Sax Overdub)*
In The Ghetto   Jailhouse Rock *(Sax Overdub)*
Starting Today   Hound Dog *(Instrumental)*
Got A Lot O' Livin' To Do!   Shake, Rattle And Roll *(Instrumental)*
Rip It Up   Blue Suede Shoes *(Instrumental)*
Long Tall Sally

[ ] **BLUE SUEDE SHOES/TUTTI FRUTTI**
Catalog# 8993-2-RH   **Value $ 10-20**
Matrix# W.O. 75067-1 89932RH
(May 1989 Commemorative Juke Box Gold Standard Series CD Single.
Silver & Black Disc with old RCA Logo. Gold Standard insert sleeve.
One of five Elvis CD singles pressed for Jukebox only.)
Disc contains the following selections:
Blue Suede Shoes   Tutti Frutti

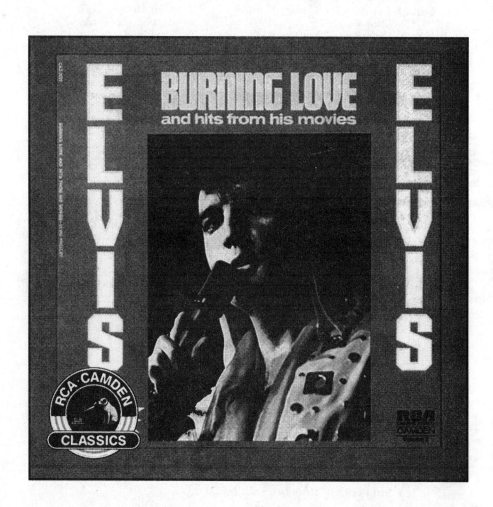

[ ]
BURNING LOVE AND HITS FROM HIS MOVIES Vol. 2
Catalog# CAD1-2595   Value $ 7-10
Matrix# Y2E CAD1-2595
(Aug. 1987 RCA Special Products - RCA Camden Classics Release. Distributed by The Special Music Co. Disc pressed in Canada for release in Canada & U.S. Silver & Black Disc with old RCA Logo, Nipper, Camden & Special Music Co. Logos in Blue. Insert cover printed in U.S.)
Disc contains the following selections:

Burning Love	It's A Matter Of Time
Tender Feelings	No More
Am I Ready	Santa Lucia
Tonight Is So Right For Love	We'll Be Together
Guadalajara	I Love Only One Girl

[ ]
BURNING LOVE AND HITS FROM HIS MOVIES Vol. 2
Catalog# CAD1-2595   Value $ 7-10
Matrix# 8SR/CAD1-2595
(1991 Second Pressing. RCA Special Products. Distributed by The Special Music Co. Disc pressed in Canada for release in U.S. Silver & Black Disc with block RCA Logo, Nipper and Special Produts in Blue. Insert cover printed in Canada.)

[ ]
BURNING LOVE AND HITS FROM HIS MOVIES Vol. 2
Catalog# CAD1-2595   Value $ 10-12
Matrix# CAD1-2595 15054A 02!
(June 1996 Third Pressing. RCA Special Products Release for AVON. Silver & Black Disc with block RCA Logo, Nipper and Special Products in Red. Disc and Insert cover printed in U.S.)

CAN'T HELP FALLING IN LOVE

ELVIS PRESLEY
with The Jordinaires

ROCK-A-HULA BABY ("Twist" Special)

8991-2-RH

COMMEMORATIVE JUKE BOX SERIES

   Tmk(s) ® Registered • Marca(s) Registrada(s) RCA Corporation. BMG logo ® BMG Music © 1989 BMG Music • Manufactured and Distributed by BMG Music, New York, N.Y. • Printed in U.S.A.

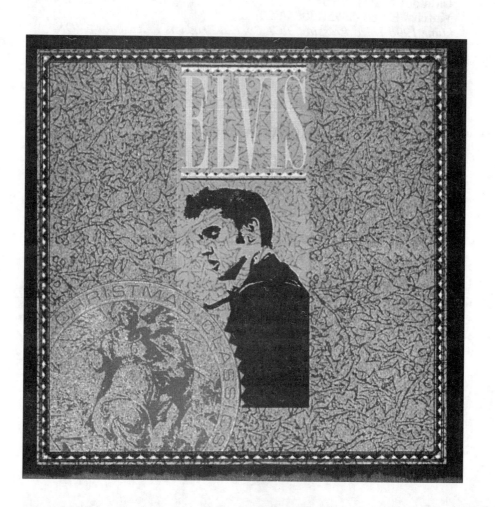

[ ]

CAN'T HELP FALLING IN LOVE/ROCK-A-HULA BABY
Catalog# 8991-2-RH   **Value $ 10-20**
Matrix# W.O. 75055-1 89912RH
(May 1989 Commemorative Juke Box Gold Standard Series CD Single.
Silver & Black Disc with old RCA Logo. Gold Standard insert sleeve.
One of five Elvis CD singles pressed for Jukebox only.)
Disc contains the following selections:
Can't Help Falling In Love   Rock -A-Hula Baby ("Twist" Special)

[ ]

CHRISTMAS CLASSICS
Catalog# 9801-2-R   **Value $ 10-15**
Matrix# W.O. 12449-1 98012R
(July 1989 First Pressing. C & W Midline CD. Silver & Black Disc with old
RCA Logo. RCA Sound Value Release. Contains only 9 tracks. Original artwork
on back cover.)
Disc contains the following selections:

Blue Christmas	O Come, All Ye Faithful
Silent Night	The First Noel
White Christmas	Winter Wonderland
I'll Be Home For Christmas	Silver Bells
Oh Little Town Of Bethlehem	

[ ]

CHRISTMAS CLASSICS
Catalog# 9801-2-RRE   **Value $ 8-12**
Matrix# W.O. 12449-1 90812R
(Oct 1992 Second Pressing. Silver & Black Disc with old RCA Logo.
RCA Sound Saver Release. New improved sound. Digitally Mixed
and Mastered in Nashville using the latest restoration equipment.
Back cover white with black print.)

[ ]

CHRISTMAS CLASSICS
Catalog# 9801-2-RRE   **Value $ 8-12**
Matrix# W.O. 12449-2P 90812R
(Oct. 1995 Third Pressing. Silver & Black Disc with old RCA Logo.
RCA Sound Saver Release. "Wise Buy" sticker on shrink wrap.
Back cover white with black print.)

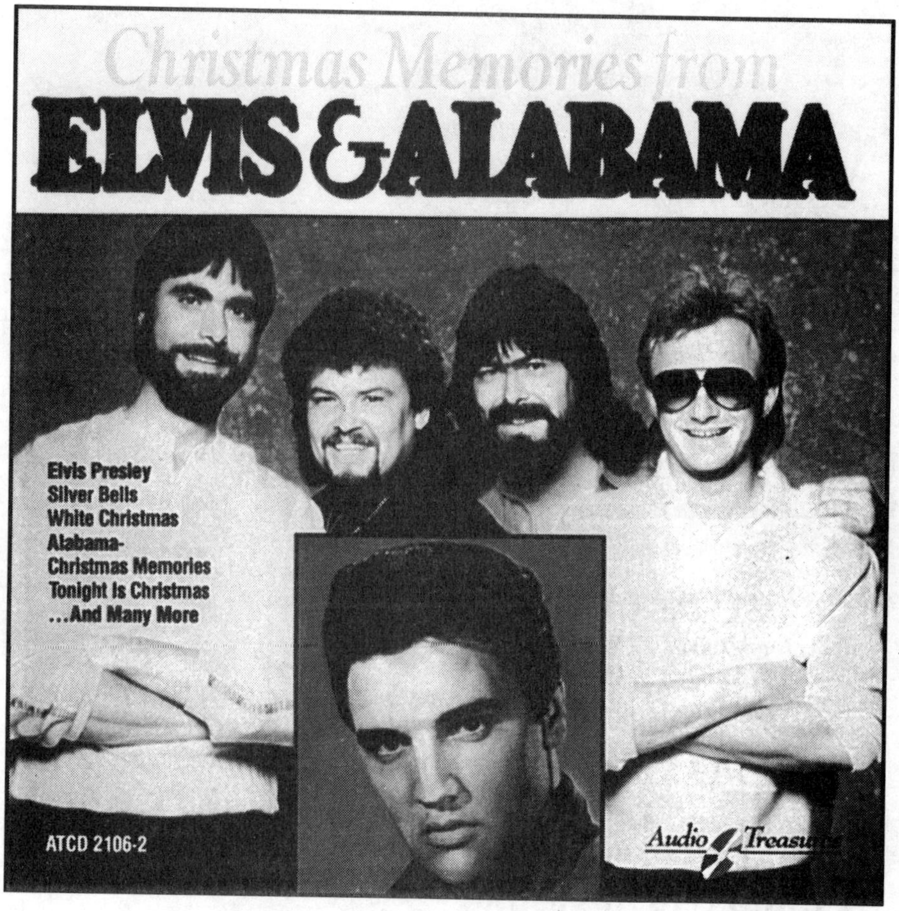
Christmas Memories from
ELVIS & ALABAMA
Elvis Presley
Silver Bells
White Christmas
Alabama-
Christmas Memories
Tonight Is Christmas
...And Many More
ATCD 2106-2
Audio Treasures

[ ]

CHRISTMAS MEMORIES FROM ELVIS & ALABAMA
Catalog# ATCD 2106-2   **Value $ 15-20**
Matrix# W.O. 17532-1 ATCD2106-2
(May 1991 RCA Special Products Release. Sold only in budget Department Stores during Christmas season. Distributed by Audio Treasures Inc., Troy, Michigan. Silver Disc. Block RCA & Nipper Logos in Red. Print in Black. Back insert cover White with Black Print. This is one of four CD's using Elvis with one other artist. This release has now been deleted.)
Disc contains the following selections:

Silver Bells - *Elvis*
Christmas Memories - *Alabama*
O Come All Ye Faithful - *Elvis*
Christmas In Dixie - *Alabama*
Tonight Is Christmas - *Alabama*

Silent Night - *Elvis*
Tennessee Christmas - *Alabama*
White Christmas - *Elvis*
Winter Wonderland - *Elvis*
Thistlehair The Christmas Bear - *Alabama*

[ ]

CHRISTMAS MEMORIES FROM ELVIS & ALABAMA
Catalog# ATCD 2106-2   **Value $ 10-15**
Matrix# DDX2517-3 01# ++ 30804
(Oct. 1996 Reissue from RCA Special Products. Sold only in budget Department Stores during Christmas season. This is the same disc used on the Deco Disc Pop-Out CD and Ornament. Now housed in jewel case with insert cover as above but with red border around photo on front insert cover. Back insert cover is Red with Print in White and Black. Contains same six tracks as on Deco Disc.)
Disc contains the following selections:

Elvis Presley Sings...
White Christmas
Silver Bells
O Come, All Ye Faithful
Santa Claus Is Back In Town
Winter Wonderland
Silent Night

Alabama Sings...
Christmas In Dixie
Homecoming Christmas
Christmas Memories
Thistlehair The Christmas Bear
Tonight Is Christmas
Tennessee Christmas

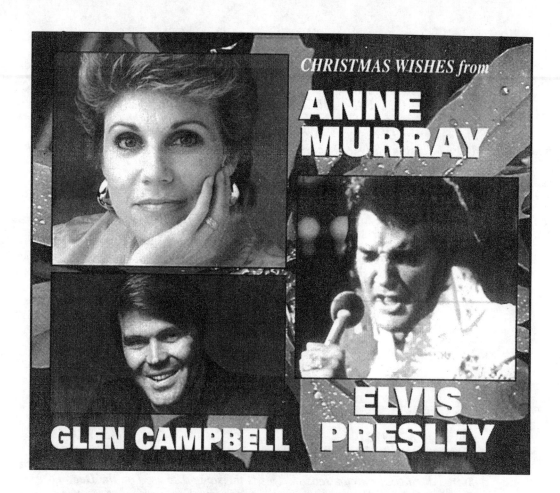

CHRISTMAS WISHES *from*
ANNE MURRAY

GLEN CAMPBELL

ELVIS PRESLEY

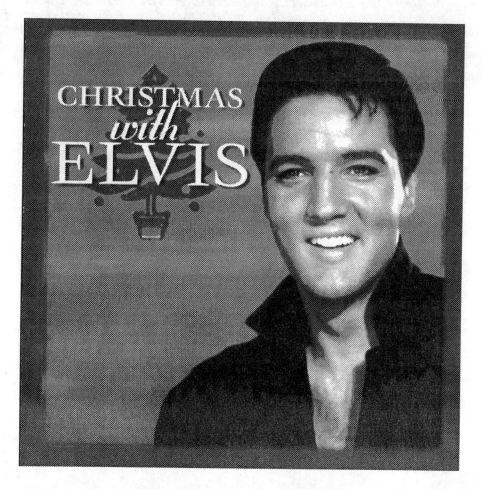

CHRISTMAS *with* ELVIS

[ ]   **CHRISTMAS WISHES** *(3 CD Set)*
From ANNE MURRAY,GLEN CAMPBELL& ELVIS PRESLEY
Catalog# 15035   Value $ 40-50
Matrix# E6Z1<005>CAD12428
*(Oct. 1992 RCA Special Products Release for GSC Music. Distributed by
Entertainment Distributing Inc., Eugene, Oregon. Packaged in multi-disc
jewel box. Each artist featured on individual disc. Elvis disc originally released
as "Elvis' Christmas Album" on Camden label from Special Music Co.
Silver Disc with block RCA Logo and Special Products in Blue. Print in Black.
Disc pressed in Canada for U.S. release in this set. Mail Order Only.
This set is now deleted.)*
Disc contains the following selections:

Blue Christmas
Silent Night
White Christmas
Santa Claus Is Back In Town
I'll Be Home For Christmas

If Every Day Was Like Christmas
Here Comes Santa Claus
Oh Little Town Of Bethlehem
Santa Bring My Baby Back To Me
Mama Liked The Roses

[ ]   **CHRISTMAS WITH ELVIS**
Catalog# DIR 9003-2   Value $ 20-25
Matrix# L384 1100 DRC11715 B70724-12
*(Aug. 1997 Release from BMG Special Products for Razor & Tie Direct LLC.
Red and White Picture Disc. Contains 4 page insert cover. Mail Order Only.)*
Disc contains the following selections:

Santa Claus Is Back In Town
Blue Christmas
Santa Bring My Baby Back (To Me)
If Every Day Was Like Christmas
Here Comes Santa Claus
White Christmas
Silver Bells
Merry Christmas Baby
Winter Wonderland
If I Get Home On Christmas Day

Holly Leaves And Christmas Trees
O Little Town Of Bethlehem
I'll Be Home On Christmas Day
It Won't Seem Like Christmas
The Wonderful World Of Christmas
The First Noel
On A Snowy Christmas Night
I'll Be Home For Christmas
O Come All Ye Faithful
Christmas Message From Elvis/
Silent Night

[ ]

COLLECTORS GOLD *(3 CD Box Set)*
Catalog# 3114-2-R   Value $ 30-40
*(Aug. 1991 First Pressing. Packaged in a Special Long Box. Three colored discs
in multi disc jewel box. Includes 20 page insert booklet. Contains 48 unreleased
performances. Digitally Remastered from the original RCA Label Master Tapes.
Pink & Black Collectors sticker on shrink wrap.)*
Disc #1 HOLLYWOOD (Green Disc)
Matrix# W.O. 16955-2 31142R-1
Disc contains the following selections:

G. I. Blues *(Take1)*
Pocket Full Of Rainbows *(Takes 22 & 17)*
Big Boots *(Take 10)*
Black Star *(Take Unknown)*
Summer Kisses, Winter Tears *(Takes 1 & 14)*
I Slipped, I Stumbled, I Fell *(Take 18)*
Lonely Man *(Take 4)*
What A Wonderful Life *(Takes 2 & 1)*
A Whistling Tune *(Take 4)*

Beyond The Bend *(Takes 1 & 2)*
One Broken Heart For Sale *(Take 1)*
You're The Boss *(Take Unknown)*
Roustabout *(Take 6)*
Girl Happy *(Take 4)*
So Close, Yet So Far *(Take 4)*
Stop, Look And Listen *(Take 3)*
Am I Ready *(Take 1)*
How Can You Lose What You Never Had
(Takes 1 & 3)

Disc #2 NASHVILLE (Orange Disc)
Matrix# W.O. 16956-1 31142R-2
Disc contains the following selections:

Like A Baby *(Takes 1 & 2)*
There's Always Me *(Take 4)*
I Want You With Me *(Take 1)*
Gently *(Take 3)*
Give Me The Right *(Take 1)*
I Met Her Today *(Take 1)*
Night Rider *(Takes 1 & 2)*

Just Tell Her Jim Said Hello *(Take 1)*
Ask Me *(Take 2)*
Memphis, Tennessee *(Take 2)*
Love Me Tonight *(Take 1)*
Witchcraft *(Take 1)*
Come What May (You Are Mine) *(Take 6)*
Love Letters *(Takes 4 & 7)*
Going Home *(Takes 24 & 21)*

Disc #3 LIVE IN LAS VEGAS (Pink Disc)
Matrix# W.O. 16957-1 31142R-3
Disc contains the following selections:

Blue Suede Shoes
I Got A Woman
Heartbreak Hotel
Love Me Tender
Baby, What You Want Me To Do
Runaway
Surrender/Are You Lonesome Tonight
Rubber Neckin'

Memories
Introductions by Elvis Presley
Jailhouse Rock/Don't Be Cruel
Inherit The Wind
This Is The Story
Mystery Train/Tiger Man
Funny How Time Slips Away
Loving You/Reconsider Baby
What'd I Say

[ ]

COLLECTORS GOLD *(3 CD Box Set)*
LIMITED EDITION WOODEN BOX SET
Catalog# 3114-2-R   Value $ 250-350
Disc #1 Matrix# W.O. 16955-2 31142R-1
Disc #2 Matrix# W.O. 16956-1 31142R-2
Disc #3 Matrix# W.O. 16957-1 31142R-3
*(Sept. 1991 Special Collectors Edition in 12"x12" Blue/Grey Wooden Box with
photo from "King Creole" on Box cover. Box made by Per Post in Germany
for U.S. release. Limited edition of 300 copies. Contains 20 page booklet
and Certificate of Authenticity. The colored discs and booklet are manufactured
in the U.S. and are the standard U.S. catalog release. Mail Order Only.)*

[ ]

COMMAND PERFORMANCES *(2 CD Set)*
THE ESSENTIAL 60's MASTERS II
Catalog# 07863-66601-2   **Value 30-35**

(July 1995 First Pressing. Disc housed in multi-disc jewel box. Photo of Elvis under each disc in jewel box. Jewel box packaged with outer bellyband with same artwork as jewel box. Blue and White sticker on bellyband shrink wrap. Contains 24 page full color booklet complete with liner notes and movie poster memorabilia. Digitally Remastered from the original RCA Label Master Tapes.)

Disc #1 (Copper Matte Finish Picture Disc)
Matrix# 07863666012P1 ++ 54618-02
Disc contains the following selections:

G.I. Blues	Girls!Girls!Girls!
Wooden Heart	Because Of Love
Shoppin' Around	Return To Sender
Doin' The Best I Can	One Broken Heart For Sale
Flaming Star	I'm Falling In Love Tonight
Wild In The Country	They Remind Me Too Much Of You
Lonely Man	Fun In Acapulco
Blue Hawaii	Bossa Nova Baby
Rock-A-Hula Baby	Marguerita
Can't Help Falling In Love	Mexico
Beach Boy Blues	Kissin' Cousins
Hawaiian Wedding Song	One Boy, Two Little Girls
Follow That Dream *(Alt. Take 2)*	Once Is Enough
Angel	Viva Las Vegas
King Of The Whole Wide World	What'd I Say
I Got Lucky	

Disc #2 (Green Matte Finish Picture Disc)
Matrix# 07863666012P2 ++ 54871-01
Disc contains the following selections:

Roustabout	Easy Come, Easy Go
Poison Ivy League	Double Trouble
Little Egypt	Long Legged GirlWith The Short Dress On
There's A Brand New Day On The Horizon	Clambake
Girl Happy	You Don't Know Me
Puppet On A String	Stay Away, Joe
Do The Clam	Speedway
Harem Holiday	Your Time Hasn't Come Yet Baby
So Close, Yet So Far	Let Yourself Go
Frankie And Johnny	Almost In Love
Please Don't Stop Loving Me	A Little Less Conversation
Paradise, Hawaiian Style	Edge Of Reality
This Is My Heaven	Charro!
Spinout	Clean Up Your Own Back Yard
All That I Am	Change Of Habit
I'll Be Back	

[ ]

COMMAND PERFORMANCES *(2 CD Promo Set)*
THE ESSENTIAL 60's MASTERS II
Catalog# 07863-66601-2   **Value $ 35-40**
Disc #1 **Matrix# 07863666012P1 ++ 54618-02**
Disc #2 **Matrix# 07863666012P2 ++ 54871-01**
(July 1995 Designated Promo. Same as regular catalog release with Black and White sticker "Not For Sale NFS-1 " on front cover of bellyband. Bar code has been scratched off the bellyband.)

GOLD
STANDARD SINGLE

HOUND DOG

ELVIS PRESLEY

DON'T BE CRUEL

8990-2-RH
COMMEMORATIVE JUKE BOX SERIES

Tmk(s) ® Registered • Marca(s) Registrada(s) RCA Corporation. BMG logo ® BMG Music © 1989 BMG Music • Manufactured and Distributed by BMG Music, New York, N.Y. • Printed in U.S.A.

GOLD
STANDARD SINGLE

CAN'T HELP FALLING IN LOVE

ELVIS PRESLEY
with The Jordinaires

ROCK-A-HULA BABY ("Twist" Special)

8991-2-RH
COMMEMORATIVE JUKE BOX SERIES

Tmk(s) ® Registered • Marca(s) Registrada(s) RCA Corporation. BMG logo ® BMG Music © 1989 BMG Music • Manufactured and Distributed by BMG Music, New York, N.Y. • Printed in U.S.A.

GOLD
STANDARD SINGLE

JAILHOUSE ROCK

ELVIS PRESLEY

TREAT ME NICE

8992-2-RH
COMMEMORATIVE JUKE BOX SERIES

Tmk(s) ® Registered • Marca(s) Registrada(s) RCA Corporation. BMG logo ® BMG Music © 1989 BMG Music • Manufactured and Distributed by BMG Music, New York, N.Y. • Printed in U.S.A.

GOLD
STANDARD SINGLE

BLUE SUEDE SHOES

ELVIS PRESLEY

TUTTI FRUTTI

8993-2-RH
COMMEMORATIVE JUKE BOX SERIES

Tmk(s) ® Registered • Marca(s) Registrada(s) RCA Corporation. BMG logo ® BMG Music © 1989 BMG Music • Manufactured and Distributed by BMG Music, New York, N.Y. • Printed in U.S.A.

GOLD
STANDARD SINGLE

ARE YOU LONESOME TONIGHT?

ELVIS PRESLEY
with The Jordinaires

I GOTTA KNOW

8994-2-RH
COMMEMORATIVE JUKE BOX SERIES

Tmk(s) ® Registered • Marca(s) Registrada(s) RCA Corporation. BMG logo ® BMG Music © 1989 BMG Music • Manufactured and Distributed by BMG Music, New York, N.Y. • Printed in U.S.A.

[ ]   # COMMEMORATIVE JUKEBOX SERIES *(5 CD Set)*
                                    Value $ 100-125

*(May 1989 Commemorative Juke Box Gold Standard Series Release.
Silver & Black Discs with old RCA Logos. Gold Standard Insert Sleeves.
The discs are listed alphabetically in this price guide but were also sold
as a 5 disc set with Jukebox Title Strips. The value listed is for the set.
Also available as "Promo Copy" with insert cover stamped "Demonstration-
Not For Sale". RCA does not acknowledge a promo of this set.)*

Disc #1
Catalog# 8990-2-RH
Matrix# W.O. 75061-1 89902RH
Disc contains the following selections:
Hound Dog   Don't Be Cruel

Disc #2
Catalog# 8991-2-RH
Matrix# W.O. 75055-1 89912RH
Disc contains the following selections:
Can't Help Falling In Love   Rock-A-Hula Baby ("Twist" Special)

Disc #3
Catalog# 8992-2-RH
Matrix# W.O. 75068-1 89922RH
Disc contains the following selections:
Jailhouse Rock   Treat Me Nice

Disc #4
Catalog# 8993-2-RH
Matrix# W.O. 75067-1 89932RH
Disc contains the following selections:
Blue Suede Shoes   Tutti Frutti

Disc #5
Catalog# 8994-2-RH
Matrix# W.O. 75056-1 89942RH
Disc contains the following selections:
Are You Lonesome Tonight?   I Gotta Know

[ ] **COUNTRY CHRISTMAS**
ELVIS PRESLEY'S COUNTRY CHRISTMAS
JIM REEVES' HOLIDAY HITS

Catalog# DDX2508-3 01#   **Value $ 25-30**
Matrix# DDX 2508-3 01# 30805

(Oct. 1993 Pressing. RCA Special Products Release. Sold only in budget Department Stores for two weeks during 1993 Christmas season. Deco Disc Pop Out CD & Ornament. Made to be hung as a Christmas ornament with a Pop-Out CD that is playable. A collectable with digital sound.)

Disc contains the following selections:

Elvis Presley's Country Christmas

Blue Christmas
Here Comes Santa Claus
It Is No Secret (What God Can Do)
Take My Hand Precious Lord
(There'll Be) Peace In The Valley (For Me)
I'll Be Home For Christmas

Jim Reeves' Holiday Hits

Jingle Bells
Silent Night
Silver Bells
O Come, All Ye Faithful
O Little Town Of Bethlehem
An Old Christmas Card

[ ] **COUNTRY CHRISTMAS**
ELVIS PRESLEY'S COUNTRY STYLE CHRISTMAS
ALABAMA'S DOWN HOME CHRISTMAS

Catalog# DDX 2517-3 01#   **Value $ 25-30**
Matrix# DDX 2517-3 01# 30804

(Oct. 1993 Pressing. RCA Special Products Release. Sold only in budget Department Stores for two weeks during 1993 Christmas season. Deco Disc Pop-Out CD & Ornament. Made to be hung as a Christmas ornament with a Pop Out CD that is playable. A collectable with digital sound.)

Disc contains the following selections:

Elvis Presley's Country Style Christmas

White Christmas
Silver Bells
O Come, All Ye Faithful
Santa Claus Is Back In Town
Winter Wonderland
Silent Night

Alabama's Down Home Christmas

Christmas In Dixie
Homecoming Christmas
Christmas Memories
Thistlehair The Christmas Bear
Tonight Is Christmas
Tennessee Christmas

[ ] **DOUBLE DYNAMITE**
Catalog# PDC2-1010   **Value $ 15-20**
Matrix# PDC2-1010 2A2 76
*(1987 RCA Special Products Release on the Pair Label. Silver Disc with Block
RCA & Pair Logos in Blue - other printing in Black. Pair Logo at bottom of disc.
Special Products in large print. Disc pressed in Japan by RCA/Ariola
International for U.S. release.)*
Disc contains the following selections:

Burning Love	Rubberneckin'
I'll Be There	U.S. Male
Fools Fall In Love	Frankie And Johnny
Follow That Dream	Easy Come, Easy Go
Flaming Star	Separate Ways
Yellow Rose Of Texas	Peace In The Valley
Old Shep	Big Boss Man
Mama	It's A Matter Of Time

[ ] **DOUBLE DYNAMITE**
Catalog# PDC2-1010   **Value $ 10-12**
Matrix# PDC2-1010 4S 21
*(1992 Second Pressing from RCA Special Products on the Pair Label.
Silver Disc with Block RCA, Pair Logos & Nipper in Blue - other printing in
Black. Disc pressed in U.S. by RCA/Ariola International. On this Pressing
"Ariola" is misspelled "Arila". Pair Logo is located on right side of disc. Special
Products in small print. Front insert cover has dark brown border surrounding
Elvis picture on first pressing. This pressing has lighter brown border.)*

[ ] **DOUBLE DYNAMITE**
Catalog# PDC2-1010   **Value $ 10-12**
Matrix# PDC2-1010 15075A 01!
*(1993 Third Pressing from RCA Special Products on the Pair Label.
Silver Disc with Block RCA, Pair Logos & Nipper in Red - other printing in
Black. Disc pressed in U.S. by RCA/Ariola International. On this pressing
"Ariola" is spelled correctly. Pair Logo is locatd on right side of disc. Special
Products in small print. This pressing again has darker brown border on insert
cover.)*

[ ] **DOUBLE DYNAMITE**
Catalog# PDC2-1010   **Value $ 10-12**
Matrix# PDC21010 W.O.#8487-1
*(1995 Fourth Pressing from RCA Special Products on the Pair Label.
Silver Disc with Old RCA, Pair Logos & Nipper in Blue - other printing in Black.
Disc pressed in U.S. by RCA/Ariola International. Pair Logo is located on
bottom of disc. Special Products in small print and underlined. Insert cover same
as third pressing.)*

[ ]   **DON'T BE CRUEL**
        Catalog# 07863-62404-2   **Value $ 15-20**
        Matrix# W.O. 28047-1M07863624042
        (Oct. 1992, 5 Track Mustard Colored Picture Disc pressed for Jukebox only,
        with two Jukebox Title Strips. To promote "The King Of Rock 'N' Roll-
        Complete 50's Masters" Box Set. Disc is available without title strips in $8-12
        price range. The value listed above is with title strips.)
        Disc contains the following selections:
        Don't Be Cruel
        Ain't That Loving You Baby (*Fast Version Alternate Take 11*)
        Blue Christmas
        Love Me Tender
        Heartbreak Hotel

[ ]   **DON'T BE CRUEL/ CAN'T HELP FALLING IN LOVE**
        Catalog# DRC11809   **Value $ 2-5**
        Matrix# L385 1100 DRC11809 C70718-30
        (Aug. 1997 20th Anniversary CD Single from BMG Special Products for
        Trans World Entertainment Inc. Sold only at TWE outlets- Coconuts, Tape World
        and Record Town. 20th Anniversary Picture Disc. Silver Disc with picture of
        Elvis and Print in Black. Disc housed in a die-cut paper sleeve. This is one of
        five 20th Anniversary CD Singles pressed for TWE.)
        Disc contains the following selections:
        Don't Be Cruel   Can't Help Falling In Love

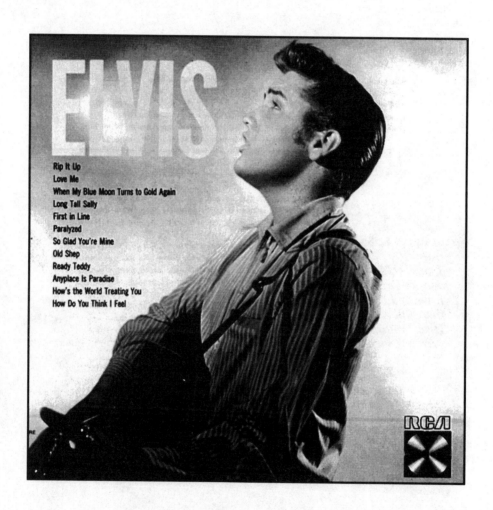

[ ]   **ELVIS**
           Catalog# PCD1-1382   **Value $250-300**
           Matrix# PCD-11382 1A1-48
           (Sept. 1984 First Pressing in Electronic Stereo. Silver & Blue Disc with block
           RCA Logo in white. Pressed in Japan for U.S. Release.)
           Disc contains the following selections:
           Rip It Up   So Glad You're Mine
           Love Me   Old Shep
           When My Blue Moon Turns To Gold Again   Ready Teddy
           Long Tall Sally   Anyplace Is Paradise
           First In Line   How's The World Treating You
           Paralyzed   How Do You Think I Feel

[ ]   **ELVIS**
           Catalog# PCD1-5199   **Value $ 30-40**
           Matrix# DIDX 183 31A3
           (Nov. 1984 Reissue. Digitally Remastered to Original Mono. DIDX on disc and
           insert sleeve. Silver & Blue Disc with block RCA Logo in white. This title has
           been given a new catalog number. Pressed in U.S.)

[ ]   **ELVIS**
           Catalog# PCD1-5199   **Value $ 12-15**
           Matrix# PCD-15199 1A6 6Z 78
           (1985 Second Pressing. Silver & Blue Disc with block RCA Logo in white.
           Pressed in U.S.)

[ ]   **ELVIS**
           Catalog# PCD1-5199   **Value $ 12-15**
           Matrix# PCD-15199 1A7 D71
           (1985 Third Pressing. Silver & Blue Disc with block RCA Logo in white.
           Pressed in U.S.)

[ ]   **ELVIS**
           Catalog# PCD1-5199   **Value $ 12-15**
           Matrix# PCD-15199 1B2 D74
           (1986 Fourth Pressing. Silver & Blue Disc with block RCA Logo in white.
           Pressed in U.S.)

[ ]   **ELVIS**
           Catalog# PCD1-5199   **Value $ 12-15**
           Matrix# PCD-15199 8/87 1A52
           (Aug. 1987 Fifth Pressing. Silver & Blue Disc with block RCA Logo in white.
           Pressed in U.S.)

[ ]   **ELVIS**
          Catalog# PCD1-5199   **Value $ 12-15**
          Matrix# PCD15199 8/88 1C51
          (Aug. 1988 Sixth Pressing. Silver & Blue Disc with block RCA Logo in white.
          Pressed in U.S.)

[ ]   **ELVIS**
          Catalog# PCD1-5199   **Value $ 12-15**
          Matrix# PCD15199 2/89 2DA7
          (Feb. 1989 Seventh Pressing. Silver & Blue Disc with block RCA Logo in white.
          Pressed in U.S.)

[ ]   **ELVIS**
          Catalog# PCD1-5199   **Value $ 10-12**
          Matrix# PCD1-5199-1T 13
          (1991 Eighth Pressing. Silver & Black Disc with old RCA Logo.
          Pressed in U.S.)

[ ]   **ELVIS**
          Catalog# PCD1-5199   **Value $ 10-12**
          Matrix# PCD1-5199 2T 11
          (1992 Ninth Pressing. Silver & Black Disc with old RCA Logo.
          Pressed in U.S.)

[ ]   **ELVIS**
          Catalog# PCD1-5199   **Value $ 10-12**
          Matrix# PCD1-5199 2T 13
          (1993 Tenth Pressing. Silver & Black Disc with old RCA Logo.
          Pressed in U.S.)

[ ]   **ELVIS**
          Catalog# PCD1-5199   **Value $ 10-12**
          Matrix# PCD1-5199 2T 14
          (1994 Eleventh Pressing. Silver & Black Disc with old RCA Logo.
          *Pressed in U.S. **RCA deleted this title from their catalog in Dec. 1997.**)*

[ ]   **ELVIS**
          Catalog# PCD1-5199   **Value $ 20-30**
          Matrix# 5 PCD 05199-2 SRC##01 M1S1
          (1997 Twelfth Pressing. Mfg. by BMG Music for Columbia House Music Club, a
          non-BMG Music CD Club. Silver & Black Disc with old RCA Logo. Only
          available from Columbia House Music CD Club. Mail Order Only.)

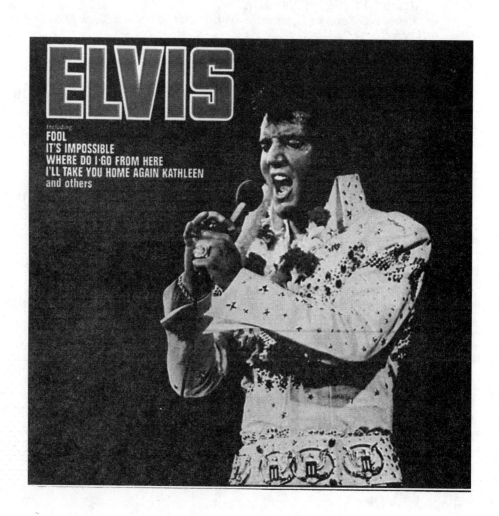

[ ]   **ELVIS** (aka "The Fool Album")
        Catalog# 07863-50283-2   **Value $ 15-20**
        Matrix# 07863502832 01# 4004
        *(March 1994 First Pressing. Elvis in the '90's Black Disc with The RCA
        Records Label and Nipper above new silver line. Print in silver. Contains 8
        page insert booklet including original cover art for "Fool" 45.
        Digitally Remastered from the original RCA Label Master Tapes. **RCA deleted
        this title from their catalog in July, 1998.**)*
        Disc contains the following selections:

Fool	(That's What You Get) For Lovin' Me
Where Do I Go From Here	Padre
Love Me, Love The Life I Lead	I'll Take You Home Again Kathleen
It's Still Here	I Will Be True
It's Impossible	Don't Think Twice, It's All Right

[ ]   **ELVIS** (aka "The Fool Album") *(Promo)*
        Catalog# 07863-50283-2 NFS-1   **Value $ 20-25**
        Matrix# 07863502832 01# 4004
        *(March 1994 Designated Promo. Same as regular catalog release with black and
        white sticker "**Not For Sale NFS-1**" on front cover of jewel box. Drill hole thru
        back of jewel box.)*

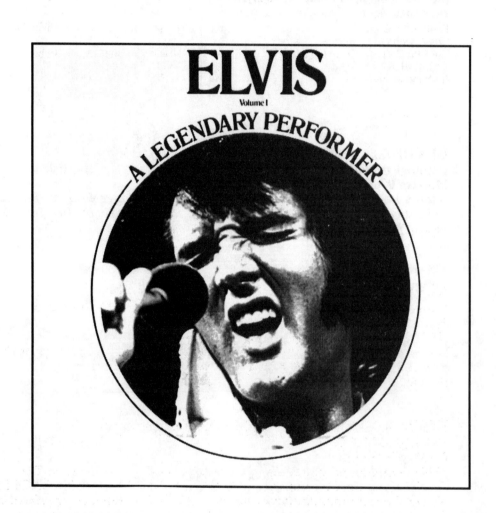

[ ] **ELVIS A LEGENDARY PERFORMER** Volume 1
Catalog# CAD1-2705   Value $ 7-10
Matrix# CAD1-2705 SRC-01
(Aug. 1989 First Pressing. RCA Special Products Release. Distributed by The Special Music Co. Disc pressed in Canada for release in Canada & U.S. Silver & Black Disc with RCA Special Products Logo in Blue. Insert cover printed in Canada.)
Disc contains the following selections:

That's All Right   Peace In The Valley
Heartbreak Hotel   Elvis*(excerpt from interview Sept. 22, 1958)*
Elvis*(excerpt from interview Sept. 22,1958)*   Tonight's All Right For Love
Don't Be Cruel   Can't Help Falling In Love
Trying To Get To You
Love Me Tender

[ ] **ELVIS A LEGENDARY PERFORMER** Volume 1
Catalog# CAD1-2705   Value $ 7-10
Matrix# CAD1-2705 1B 22
(1991 Second Pressing. RCA Special Products Release. Distributed by The Special Music Co. Disc pressed in U.S. Silver & Black Disc with RCA Special Products, Nipper & Special Music Co. Logos in Blue. Insert cover printed in U.S.)

[ ] **ELVIS A LEGENDARY PERFORMER** Volume 1
Catalog# CAD1-2705   Value $ 7-10
Matrix# CAD1-2705 1B 23
(1992 Third Pressing. RCA Special Products Release. Distributed by The Special Music Co. Disc pressed in U.S. Silver & Black Disc with RCA Special Products, Nipper & Special Music Co. Logos in Blue. Insert cover printed in U.S.)

[ ] **ELVIS A LEGENDARY PERFORMER** Volume 1
Catalog# CAD1-2705   Value $ 7-10
No Matrix Number
(1995 Fourth Pressing. RCA Special Products Release. Distributed by The Special Music Co. Disc pressed in U.S. Silver & Black Disc with block RCA Logo, Nipper, Special Products and Special Music Co. in Red. Insert cover printed in U.S. One of several Special Music Co. releases that were pressed without a matrix number.)

[ ] **ELVIS A LEGENDARY PERFORMER** Volume 1
Catalog# CAD1-2705   Value $ 7-10
Matrix# CAD1-2705 15062A 01!
(1996 Fifth Pressing. RCA Special Products Release. Distributed by The Special Music Co. Disc pressed in U.S. Silver & Black Disc with block RCA Logo, Nippper, Special Products and Special Music Co. in Red. Insert cover printed in U.S.)

[ ] **ELVIS A LEGENDARY PERFORMER** Volume 2

Catalog# CAD1-2706   Value $ 7-10

Matrix# 4DE/CAD1-2706

(Jan. 1990 First Pressing. RCA Special Products Release. Distributed by The Special Music Co. Disc pressed in Canada for release in Canada & U.S. Silver & Black Disc with RCA Special Products Logo in Blue. Insert cover printed in Canada.)

Disc contains the following selections:

Harbor Lights	Blue Suede Shoes
I Want You, I Need You, I Love You	Such A Night
Blue Hawaii	Baby What You Want Me To Do
Jailhouse Rock	How Great Thou Art
It's Now Or Never	If I Can Dream

[ ] **ELVIS A LEGENDARY PERFORMER** Volume 2

Catalog# CAD1-2706   Value $ 7-10

Matrix# CAD1-2706 4D 22

(1991 Second Pressing. RCA Special Products Release. Distributed by The Special Music Co. Disc pressed in U.S. Silver & Black Disc with RCA Special Products, Nipper & Special Music Co. Logos in Blue. Insert cover printed in U.S.)

[ ] **ELVIS A LEGENDARY PERFORMER** Volume 2

Catalog# CAD1-2706   Value $ 7-10

Matrix# CAD1-2706 4D 23

(1992 Third Pressing. RCA Special Products Release. Distributed by The Special Music Co. Disc pressed in U.S. Silver & Black Disc with RCA Special Products & Nipper in Blue. Disc without Special Music Co. Logo. Insert cover printed in U.S.)

[ ] **ELVIS A LEGENDARY PERFORMER** Volume 2

Catalog# CAD1-2706   Value $ 7-10

No Matrix Number

(1995 Fourth Pressing. RCA Special Products Release. Disstributed by The Special Music Co. Disc pressed in Canada. Silver & Black Disc with block RCA Logo, Nipper, Special Products and Special Music Co. in Red. Insert cover printed in U.S. One of several Special Music Co. releases that were pressed without a matrix number.)

[ ] **ELVIS A LEGENDARY PERFORMER** Volume 2

Catalog# CAD1-2706   Value $ 7-10

Matrix# CAD1-2706 15063A 01!

(1996 Fifth Pressing. RCA Special Products Release. Distributed by The Special Music Co. Disc pressed in U.S. Silver & Black Disc with block RCA Logo, Nipper, Special Products and Special Music Co. in Red. Insert cover printed in U.S.)

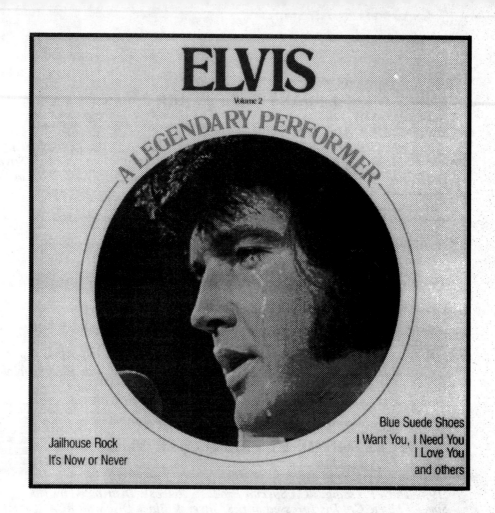

ELVIS
Volume 2

A LEGENDARY PERFORMER

Jailhouse Rock
It's Now or Never

Blue Suede Shoes
I Want You, I Need You
I Love You
and others

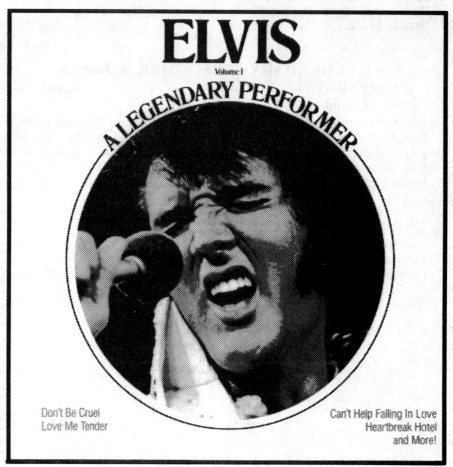

ELVIS
Volume 1

A LEGENDARY PERFORMER

Don't Be Cruel
Love Me Tender

Can't Help Falling In Love
Heartbreak Hotel
and More!

[ ] **ELVIS A LEGENDARY PERFORMER** *(Limited Edition)*
Elvis T-Shirt & Audio Gift Pak   Value $ 25-35
(Oct. 1992 RCA Special Products Limited Edition. 12"x15" Box contains Elvis
Official U.S. Postal Commemorative Stamp T-Shirt and two Legendary Performer
CD's. Distributed by UAV, Charlotte, N.C. This package is no longer available.)

Disc #1 **ELVIS A LEGENDARY PERFORMER** Volume 1
Catalog# CAD1-2705
Matrix# CAD1-2705 1B 23
Disc contains the following selections:

That's All Right
Heartbreak Hotel
Elvis *(excerpt from interview Sept. 22, 1958)*
Don't Be Cruel
Trying To Get to You
Love Me Tender

Peace In The Valley
Elvis *(excerpt from interview Sept. 22, 1958)*
Tonight's All Right For Love
Can't Help Falling In Love

Disc #2 **ELVIS A LEGENDARY PERFORMER** Volume 2
Catalog# CAD1-2706
Matrix# 4DE/CAD1-2706
Disc contains the following selections:

Harbor Lights
I Want You, I Need You, I Love You
Blue Hawaii
Jailhouse Rock
It's Now Or Never

Blue Suede Shoes
Such A Night
Baby What You Want Me To Do
How Great Thou Art
If I Can Dream

ELVIS ARON
PRESLEY
PREVIOUSLY
UNRELEASED ON CD!
Digitally Remastered
4-CD Set Features Rare
Historic Performances:
Las Vegas 1956 • Hawaiian Benefit
Concert 1961 • On Tour 1975
Plus
ELVIS AT THE PIANO &
the Lost Singles
07863 67455-2

[ ]

ELVIS ARON PRESLEY *(4 CD Set)*
Catalog# 07863-67455-2
Value $ 60-70

*(April 1998 Release. Packaged in a special 5-1/2" x 10" book type holder.
4 CD Set. Each disc is a different color with Black and Silver Print. 2 CD's
housed in push-in holder in front cover. 2 CD's housed in push-in holder in back
cover. Set contains 36 page booklet with photographs. Digitally Remastered from
the original RCA Record Label Master Tapes. Blue and White collectors sticker
on shrink wrap.)*

Matrix# L804 4494 07863674552-1 K80224-07 A

Disc #1 Raspberry
Disc contains the following selections:

An Early Live Performance - Las Vegas 1956
Heartbreak Hotel
Long Tall Sally
Blue Suede Shoes
Money Honey
An Elvis Monolog
Monolog

**An Early Benefit Performance
Honolulu, Hawaii 1961**
Introduction
Heartbreak Hotel
All Shook Up
A Fool Such As I
I Got A Woman
Love Me
Introductions
Such A Night
Reconsider Baby
I Need Your Love Tonight
That's All Right
Don't Be Cruel
One Night
Are You Lonesome Tonight?
It's Now Or Never
Swing Down Sweet Chariot
Hound Dog

Matrix# L804 4494 0786367455-2 K80223-15 A

Disc #2 Yellow
Disc contains the following selections:

Collectors' Gold From The Movie Years
They Remind Me Too Much Of You *(Alt. Take 1)*
Tonight's All Right For Love *(Alt. Takes 3,4,7, 8)*
Follow That Dream *(Alt. Take 2)*
Wild In The Country *(Alt. Take 16)*
Datin' *(Alt. Takes 6-8, 11-12)*
Shoppin' Around *(Alt. Takes 3, 5)*
Can't Help Falling In Love *(Alt. Take 24)*
A Dog's Life *(Alt. Takes 4-6)*
I'm Falling In Love Tonight *(Alt. Takes 1-4)*
Thanks To The Rolling Sea *(Alt. Take 10)*

The TV Specials
Jailhouse Rock
Suspicious Minds
Lawdy Miss Clawdy/
Baby What You Want Me To Do
Blue Christmas
You Gave Me A Mountain
Welcome To My World
Trying To Get To You
I'll Remember You
My Way

ELVIS ARON
P R E S L E Y
PREVIOUSLY
UNRELEASED ON CD!
Digitally Remastered
4-CD Set Features Rare
Historic Performances:
Las Vegas 1956 • Hawaiian Benefit
Concert 1961 • On Tour 1975
Plus
ELVIS AT THE PIANO &
the Lost Singles
07863 67455-2

Matrix# L804 4494 07863674552-3 K80224-08 A
Disc #3 Orange
Disc contains the following selections:

The Las Vegas Years
Polk Salad Annie
You've Lost That Lovin' Feelin'
Sweet Caroline
Kentucky Rain
Are You Lonesome Tonight? *(Laughing)*
My Babe
In The Ghetto
An American Trilogy
Little Sister/Get Back
Yesterday

Lost Singles
I'm Leavin'
The First Time Ever I Saw Your Face
Hi-Heel Sneakers *(Single Version)*
Softly, As I Leave You
Unchained Melody
Fool
Rags To Riches
It's Only Love
America The Beautiful
Elvis At The Piano
It's Still Here
I'll Take You Home Again Kathleen
Beyond The Reef
I Will Be True

Matrix# L804 4494 07863674552-4 K80224-06 A
Disc #4 Lavender
Disc contains the following selections:

The Concert Years - Part 1
Elvis In Concert 1975
Also Sprach Zarathustra
(Theme from 2001:A Space Odyssey)
See See Rider
Medley: I Got A Woman/Amen
Love Me
If You Love Me (Let Me Know)
Love Me Tender
All Shook Up
Medley: (Let Me Be Your) Teddy Bear/
Don't Be Cruel

The Concert Years - Concluded
Elvis In Concert 1975
Hound Dog
The Wonder Of You
Burning Love
Introductions
Johnny B. Goode
Introductions/Long Live Rock And Roll
T-R-O-U-B-L-E
Why Me Lord?
How Great Thou Art
Let Me Be There
An American Trilogy
Funny How Time Slips Away
Little Darlin'
Medley: Mystery Train/Tiger Man
Can't Help Falling In Love
Closing Vamp

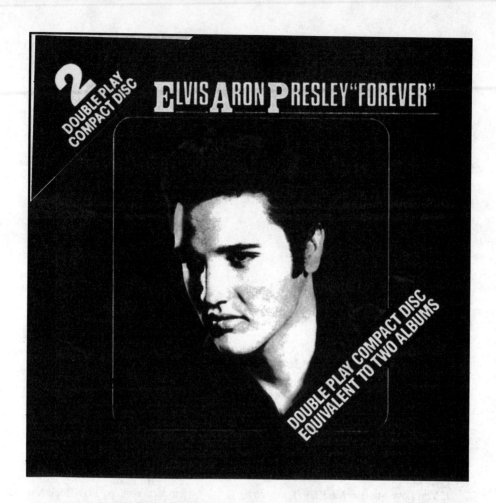

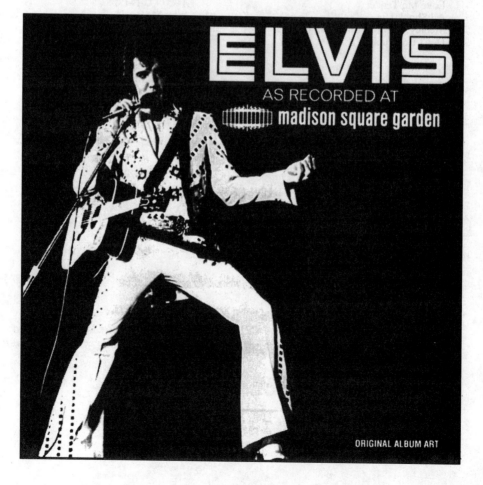

[ ] **ELVIS ARON PRESLEY - FOREVER**
Catalog# PDC2-1185   Value $ 15-25
Matrix# W.O. 10008-4 PDC2-1185
*(Dec. 1987 RCA Special Products Release on the Pair Label. Silver Disc with RCA & Pair Logos in Blue - other printing in Black. **This title now deleted from catalog.**)*
Disc contains the following selections:

Blue Hawaii	Mean Woman Blues
Hawaiian Wedding Song	Loving You
No More	Got A Lot O' Livin' To Do!
Early Mornin' Rain	Blueberry Hill
Pieces Of My Life	T-R-O-U-B-L-E
I Can Help	And I Love You So
Bringin' It Back	Woman Without Love
Green, Green Grass Of Home	Shake A Hand

[ ] **ELVIS AS RECORDED AT MADISON SQUARE GARDEN**
Catalog# 07863 54776-2   Value $ 12-15
Matrix# 07863-54776-2 1D 11
(April 1992 First Pressing. Elvis in the '90's Black Disc with old RCA Logo and Print in Silver. 8 page insert booklet. Digitally Remastered from the original RCA Label Master Tapes.)
Disc contains the following selections:

Introduction: Also Sprach Zarathustra	Medley: Teddy Bear/Don't Be Cruel
(Theme from 2001: A Space Odyssey)	Love Me Tender
That's All Right	The Impossible Dream
Proud Mary	Introductions by Elvis
Never Been To Spain	Hound Dog
You Don't Have To Say You Love Me	Suspicious Minds
You've Lost That Lovin' Feelin'	For The Good Times
Polk Salad Annie	American Trilogy
Love Me	Funny How Time Slips Away
I'm All Shook Up	I Can't Stop Loving You
Heartbreak Hotel	Can't Help Falling In Love
	End Theme

[ ] **ELVIS AS RECORDED AT MADISON SQUARE GARDEN**
Catalog# 07863 54776-2   Value $ 12-15
Matrix# 07863-54776-2 2D 28
(1994 Second Pressing. Elvis in the '90's Black Disc with old RCA Logo and Print in Silver. 8 page insert booklet. Digitally Remastered from the original RCA Label Master Tapes.)

[ ] **ELVIS AS RECORDED AT MADISON SQUARE GARDEN**
Catalog# 07863 54776-2   Value $ 12-15
Matrix# 07863-54776-2 3C 10
(1995 Third Pressing. Elvis in the '90's Black Disc with old RCA Logo and Print in Silver. 8 page insert booklet. Digitally Remastered from the original RCA Label Master Tapes.)

ELVIS AT HIS ROMANTIC BEST

RCA
Special Products
DPC1-0984

BMG
DIRECT MARKETING

ELVIS
BIRTHDAY TRIBUTE

[ ] **ELVIS AT HIS ROMANTIC BEST**

Catalog# DPC1-0984   Value $ 20-30

Matrix# W.O. 18225-2 DPC1-0984

(July 1991 First Pressing. RCA Special Products Release for AVON.
Silver Disc with block RCA and Nipper in Red. Printing in Black. Mail Order
Only.)

Disc contains the following selections:

One Night   Love Me
Fever   Help Me Make It Through The Night
Love Letters   Unchained Melody
You Don't Know Me   Let It Be Me
The Wonder Of You   I Really Don't Want To Know
And I Love You So   Until It's Time For You To Go
Always On My Mind   Anyway You Want Me

[ ] **ELVIS AT HIS ROMANTIC BEST**

Catalog# DPC1-0984   Value $ 20-30

Matrix# W.O 18225-3 DPC1-0984

(Feb. 1992 Second Pressing. RCA Special Products Release for AVON.
Silver Disc with block RCA and Nipper in Red. Printing in Black. Mail Order
Only. This title is now deleted.)

[ ] **ELVIS BIRTHDAY TRIBUTE RADIO PROGRAM**

Catalog# Creative Radio   Value $ 30-40

Matrix# H8NR0100D

(Dec. 1992 Limited Edition Release from the Creative Radio Network
for broadcast on Elvis' birthday 1/8/93. Pink Disc. Not sold in stores.
Contains 4 page insert booklet with cue sheets.)

Disc contains the following selections:

Elvis Medley   Love Me Tender
That's All Right Mama   Jailhouse Rock
Heartbreak Hotel   Suspicious Minds
All Shook Up   Hound Dog
Teddy Bear   My Way
Blue Suede Shoes   Don't Be Cruel
                                    I'll Remember You (*Music Fades*)

[ ] **ELVIS' CHRISTMAS ALBUM**
Catalog# PCD1-5486   Value $ 15-25
Matrix# PCD-15486 1A1 58
(Aug. 1985 First Pressing. Silver & Blue Disc with block RCA Logo in white.
Pressed in Japan for U.S. Release. Contains 16 page insert booklet.)
Disc contains the following selections:

Santa Claus Is Back In Town	Oh Little Town Of Bethlehem
White Christmas	Silent Night
Here Comes Santa Claus	Peace In The Valley
I'll Be Home For Christmas	I Believe
Blue Christmas	Take My Hand, Precious Lord
Santa Bring My Baby Back (To Me)	It Is No Secret

[ ] **ELVIS' CHRISTMAS ALBUM**
Catalog# PCD1-5486   Value $ 14-18
Matrix# PCD-15486 1A5 5X 6X
(Nov. 1985 Second Pressing. Silver & Blue Disc with block RCA Logo in white.
Pressed in Japan for U.S. Release. Contains 16 page insert booklet.)

[ ] **ELVIS' CHRISTMAS ALBUM**
Catalog# PCD1-5486   Value $ 10-15
Matrix# PCD-15486 1A7 D79
(Aug. 1986 Third Pressing. Silver & Blue Disc with block RCA Logo in white.
Pressed in U.S. Contains 16 page insert booklet.)

[ ] **ELVIS' CHRISTMAS ALBUM**
Catalog# PCD1-5486   Value $ 10-15
Matrix# PCD-15486 9/87 1A54
(Sept. 1987 Fourth Pressing. Silver & Blue Disc with block RCA Logo in white.
Pressed in U.S. Contains 16 page insert booklet.)

[ ] **ELVIS' CHRISTMAS ALBUM**
Catalog# PCD1-5486   Value $ 10-15
Matrix# PCD15486 2/90 1DA1
(Feb. 1990 Fifth Pressing. Silver & Blue Disc with block RCA Logo in white.
Pressed in U.S. Contains 16 page insert booklet.)

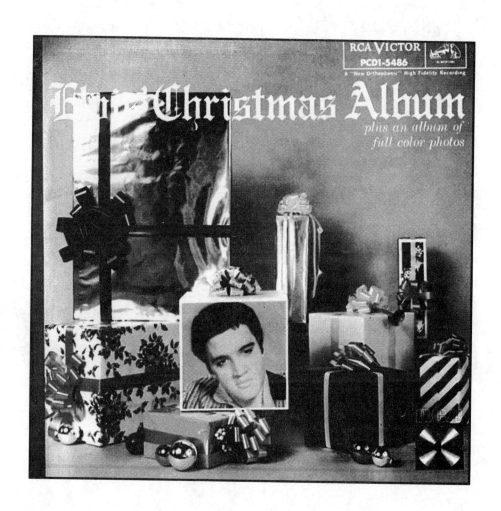

[ ] **ELVIS' CHRISTMAS ALBUM**
Catalog# PCD1-5486   Value $ 10-15
Matrix# PCD15486 8/91 2DA7X
(Aug. 1991 Sixth Pressing. Silver & Blue Disc with block RCA Logo in white. Pressed in U.S. Contains 16 page insert booklet.)

[ ] **ELVIS' CHRISTMAS ALBUM**
Catalog# PCD1-5486   Value $ 10-15
Matrix# PCD15486 10/91 2DA10
(Oct. 1991 Seventh Pressing. Silver & Blue Disc with block RCA Logo in white. Pressed in U.S. Contains 16 page insert booklet.)

[ ] **ELVIS' CHRISTMAS ALBUM**
Catalog# PCD1-5486   Value $ 10-15
Matrix# PCD15486 11/92 3DA5
(Nov. 1992 Eighth Pressing. Silver & Blue Disc with block RCA Logo in white. Pressed in U.S. Contains 16 page insert booklet.)

[ ] **ELVIS' CHRISTMAS ALBUM**
Catalog# PCD1-5486   Value $ 15-20
Matrix# PCD15486 01 # ++ 30596
*(Aug. 1994 Ninth Pressing. Silver & Black Disc without RCA Logo. **It appears block RCA Logo omitted in error.** Pressed in U.S. Contains 16 page insert booklet. This also available with "Wise Buy" sticker on shrink wrap.)*

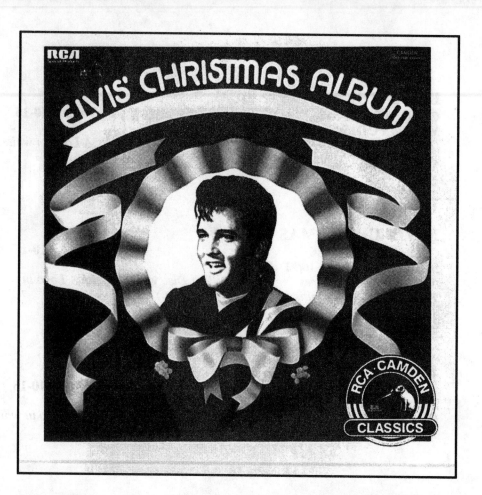

[ ]
ELVIS' CHRISTMAS ALBUM
Catalog# CAD1-2428   Value $ 7-10
Matrix# CAD1-12428 SA8368
*(Aug. 1987 First Pressing. RCA Special Products - RCA Camden Classics
Release. Distributed by The Special Music Co. Disc pressed in Canada for
release in Canada & U.S. Silver & Black Disc with old RCA Logo, Camden &
Special Music Co. Logos in Blue. Disc made by Diaque Americ Inc. Canada.
Insert cover printed in Canada.)*
Disc contains the following selections:

Blue Christmas	If Every Day Was Like Christmas
Silent Night	Here Comes Santa Claus
White Christmas	Oh Little Town Of Bethlehem
Santa Claus Is Back In Town	Santa Bring My Baby Back (to Me)
I'll Be Home For Christmas	Mama Liked The Roses

[ ]
ELVIS' CHRISTMAS ALBUM
Catalog# CAD1-2428   Value $ 7-10
Matrix# 7V7/CAD1-2428
*(1991 Second Pressing. RCA Special Products. Distributed by The Special Music
Co. Disc pressed in Canada for release in U.S. Silver & Black Disc with block
RCA Logo, Nipper and Special Products in Blue. Disc made by Fabrique' par
Disque Americ, Canada. Insert cover printed in U.S.)*

[ ]
ELVIS' CHRISTMAS ALBUM
Catalog# CAD1-2428   Value $ 7-10
Matrix# CAD1-2428 15052A 01!
*(1993 Third Pressing. RCA Special Products. Distributed by The Special Music
Co. Disc pressed in U.S. Silver & Black Disc with block RCA Logo, Nipper,
Special Products and Special Music Co. in Red. Front and back insert covers
read "Printed in U.S.A. Made in Canada".)*

[ ]
ELVIS' CHRISTMAS ALBUM
Catalog# CAD1-2428   Value $ 7-10
Matrix# CAD 12428 15052A 03@
*(1994 Fourth Pressing. RCA Special Products. Distributed by The Special Music
Co. Disc pressed in U.S. Silver & Black Disc with block RCA Logo, Nipper
Special Products and Special Music Co. in Red. Front and back insert covers
read "Printed in U.S.A. Made in Canada".)*

[ ]
ELVIS' CHRISTMAS ALBUM
Catalog# CAD1-2428   Value $ 7-10
Matrix# CAD 12428 15052A 03@
*(Sept. 1995 Reissue. RCA Special Products. Distributed by The Special
Music Co., a Division of Essex Entertainment, Inc. Green Disc with Silver and
Black Lettering. Different cover than above pressings. Both cover and disc
show title as "Elvis' Christmas", Correct title is on spine. Pressed in U.S. for
U.S. Release. Contains same Matrix number as Fourth Pressing.)*

[ ] **ELVIS COUNTRY**
"I'M 10,000 YEARS OLD"
Catalog# 07863-66279-2   Value $ 12-15
Matrix# 07863662792 01# ++
*(June 1993 First Pressing. Elvis in the '90's Black Matte Disc with old RCA
Logo and Print in Silver. 4 page insert booklet. Segments of the song
"I Was Born About Ten Thousand Years Ago" are heard at the end of each
track. Digitally Remastered from the original RCA Label Master Tapes.)*
Disc contains the following selections:

Snowbird   There Goes My Everything
Tomorrow Never Comes   It's Your Baby, You Rock It
Little Cabin On The Hill   The Fool
Whole Lot-ta Shakin' Goin' On   Faded Love
Funny How Time Slips Away   I Wash My Hands In Muddy Water
I Really Don't Want To Know   Make The World Go Away

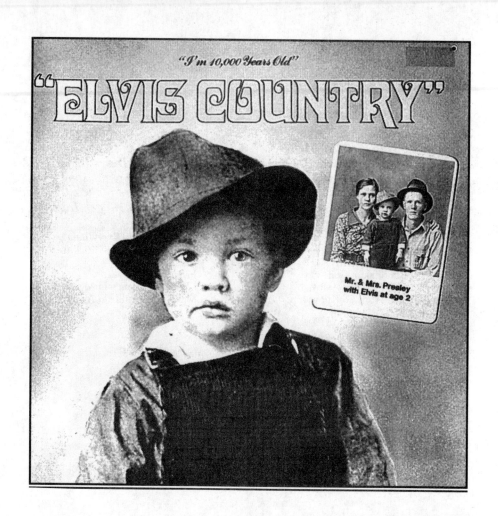

[ ]   **ELVIS COUNTRY**

Catalog# 6330-2-R   **Value $ 20 -30**

Matrix# W.O. #9010-1 63302R

(Oct. 1988 First Pressing. Silver & Black Disc with old RCA Logo.
RCA Sound Value Release. Contains only 8 Tracks.
"Elvis Country" LP cover released in error.)
Disc contains the following selections:

Whole Lot-ta-Shakin' Goin' On	Lovin' Arms *(1980 Remix Version)*
Funny How Time Slips Away	You Asked Me To *(1980 Remix Version)*
Baby Lets Play House *(1983 Overdub Version)*	She Thinks I Still Care *(1980 Remix Ver.)*
Rip It Up *(1983 Overdub Version)*	Paralyzed *(1983 Overdub Version)*

[ ]   **ELVIS COUNTRY**

Catalog# 6330-2-R   **Value $ 10-15**

Matrix# W.O. #9010-1 63302R

(Nov. 1988 Reissue. Silver & Black Disc with old RCA Logo.
RCA Sound Value Release. Contains only 8 tracks.
"Elvis Country" LP cover replaced with Sound Value "I Was The One" LP
Artwork cover. Black Background with White Print on back cover.)

[ ]   **ELVIS COUNTRY**

Catalog# 6330-2-R   **Value $ 10-15**

Matrix# W.O. 9010-2 66302R

(1990 Second Pressing. Silver & Black Disc with old RCA Logo.
RCA Sound Value Release. Contains only 8 tracks.
Black Background with White Print on back cover.)

[ ]   **ELVIS COUNTRY**

Catalog# 6330-2-RRE   **Value $ 10-15**

Matrix# W.O. 9010-2 63302R

(1992 Third Pressing. Silver & Black Disc with old RCA Logo.
RCA Sound Value Release. Contains only 8 tracks.
White Background with Black Print on back cover.)

[ ]   **ELVIS COUNTRY**

Catalog# 07863-66405-2   **Value $ 10-15**

Matrix# 07863664052 5F 13

(June 1994 Reissue. Red & Black Disc with Nipper and Print in Silver.
RCA Sound Value Release. Contains only 8 tracks. This title has been given
a new catalog number by RCA Nashville.
The front insert cover of the 1988 & 1992 pressings used a copy of the cassette
cover and therefore had Program 1 and Program 2 listed. This release is
different in that the insert cover does not list Program 1 and Program 2.
The "Sound Value" Logo has moved from upper left corner of cassette cover
to the lower right hand corner of the CD cover. The titles on the back cover
have been reprinted to give songwriting credits. Black Background with White
Print on back cover. RCA deleted this title from their catalog in 1996.)

ELVIS DOUBLE FEATURES *(4 CD Canister Set)*

Catalog# 07863-61835-2   Value $ 100-150

*(Jan. 1993 Limited Edition of 15,000 Picture Disc Sets from TV QVC Home
Shopping Network. Comes in 12" Metal Film Canister. Package includes
20 page booklet, four 8" x 10" photos, Elvis pin and Certificate of Authenticity.)*

Disc #1 KID GALAHAD and GIRLS! GIRLS! GIRLS!

Matrix# W.O. 28350-1M 07863618352-A

Disc contains the following selections:

King Of The Whole Wide World	Earth Boy
This Is Living	Return To Sender
Riding The Rainbow	Because Of Love
Home Is Where The Heart Is	Thanks To The Rolling Sea
I Got Lucky	Song Of The Shrimp
A Whistling Tune	The Walls Have Ears
Girls! Girls! Girls!	We're Coming In Loaded
I Don't Wanna Be Tied	Mama
Where Do You Come From	Plantation Rock
I Don't Want To	Dainty Little Moonbeams
We'll Be Together	Girls! Girls! Girls! *(End Title Version)*
A Boy Like Me, A Girl Like You	

Disc #2 IT HAPPENED AT THE WORLD'S FAIR and FUN IN ACAPULCO

Matrix# W.O. 28351-1M 07863618352-B

Disc contains the following selections:

Beyond The Bend	Fun In Acapulco
Relax	Vino, Dinero Y Amor
Take Me To The Fair	Mexico
They Remind Me Too Much Of You	El Toro
One Broken Heart For Sale *(Film Version)*	Marguerita
I'm Falling In Love Tonight	The Bullfighter Was A Lady
Cotton Candy Land	No Room To Rhumba In A Sports Car
A World Of Our Own	I Think I'm Gonna Like It Here
How Would You Like To Be	Bossa Nova Baby
Happy Ending	You Can't Say No In Acapulco
One Broken Heart For Sale *(Single Version)*	Guadalajara

Disc #3 VIVA LAS VEGAS and ROUSTABOUT
Matrix# W.O. 28352-2M 07863618352-C
Disc contains the following selections:

Viva Las Vegas
If You Think I Don't Need You
I Need Somebody To Lean On
You're The Boss *(with Ann-Margret)*
What'd I Say
Do The Vega
C'mon Everybody
The Lady Loves Me *(with Ann-Margret)*
Night Life
Today, Tomorrow And Forever
The Yellow Rose Of Texas/The Eyes
Of Tesas *(Medley)*
Santa Lucia *(Traditional)*

Roustabout
Little Egypt
Poison Ivy League
Hard Knocks
It's A Wonderful World
Big Love Big Heartache
One Track Heart
It's Carnival Time
Carny Town
There's A Brand New Day On The Horizon
Wheels On My Heels

Disc #4 HARUM SCARUM and GIRL HAPPY
Matrix# W.O. 28353-1 07863618352-D
Disc contains the following selections:

Harem Holiday
My Desert Serenade
Go East - Young Man
Mirage
Kismet
Shake That Tambourine
Hey Little Girl
Golden Coins
So Close, Yet So Far (From Paradise)
Animal Instinct
Wisdom Of The Ages

Girl Happy
Spring Fever
Fort Lauderdale Chamber Of Commerce
Startin' Tonight
Wolf Call
Do Not Disturb
Cross My Heart And Hope To Die
The Meanest Girl In Town
Do The Clam
Puppet On A String
I've Got To Find My Baby

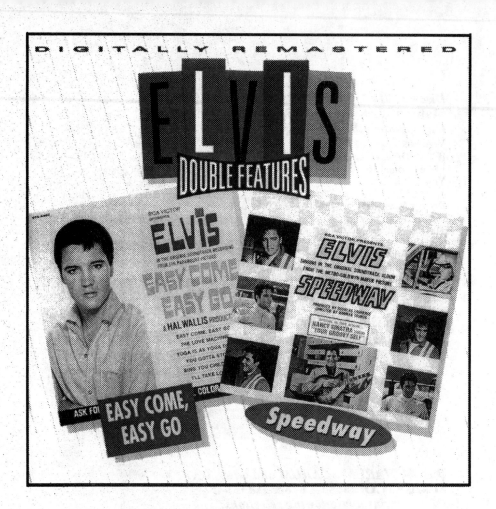

[ ]   **ELVIS DOUBLE FEATURES**
EASY COME, EASY GO and SPEEDWAY
Catalog# 07863-66558-2   Value $ 13-18
Matrix# 07863665582 ++ 53404-01
*(March 1995 First Pressing. Elvis in the '90's Black Disc with old RCA Logo
and Print in Silver. Contains 12 page insert booklet with Sessionography and
Historical Movie Data. Two complete soundtracks on one CD. Digitally
Remastered from the original RCA Label Master Tapes.* **RCA deleted this title
from their catalog in Dec. 1997.)**
Disc contains the following selections:

Easy Come, Easy Go	Suppose *(Alt. Master)*
The Love Machine	Speedway
Yoga Is As Yoga Does	There Ain't Nothing Like A Song
You Gotta Stop	Your Time Hasn't Come Yet, Baby
Sing You Children	Who Are You (Who Am I?)
I'll Take Love	He's Your Uncle Not Your Dad
She's A Machine	Let Yourself Go
The Love Machine *(Alt. Take 11)*	Five Sleepy Heads
Sing You Children *(Alt. Take 1)*	Suppose
She's A Machine *(Alt. Take 13)*	Your Groovy Self *(Nancy Sinatra)*

[ ]   **ELVIS DOUBLE FEATURES**   *(Promo)*
EASY COME, EASY GO and SPEEDWAY
Catalog# 07863-66558-2   Value $ 15-20
Matrix# 07863665582 ++ 53404-01
*(March 1995 Designated Promo. Same as regular catalog release with Black and
White sticker* **"Not For Sale NFS-1"** *on front cover of jewel box. Drill hole thru
back of jewel box.)*

[ ]   **ELVIS DOUBLE FEATURES**   *(Promo)*
EASY COME, EASY GO and SPEEDWAY
Catalog# RJC 66558-2   Value $ 75-100
Matrix# 07863665582 ++ 53404-01
*(March 1995 Promo Only. Elvis in the '90's Black Disc with old RCA Logo and
Print in Silver. Catalog#* **RJC 66558-2** *and* **"Not For Sale"** *printed on disc.
Black and White sticker* **"Not For Sale NFS-1"** *on front insert booklet. Hole
punched thru the bar code on back insert cover. One of three of the Double
Features to have a promo. Rare.)*

[ ]   **ELVIS DOUBLE FEATURES**
EASY COME, EASY GO and SPEEDWAY
Catalog# BG2-66558   Value $ 20-30
Matrix# E3 1ABG266558 01
*(1996 Second Pressing. Mfg. by BMG Music for Columbia House Music
Club, a non-BMG Music CD Club. Columbia Hous Music Club catalog number
on disc, spine, booklet and back insert cover. CRC Logo printed above bar code
on back insert cover. Elvis in the '90' Black Disc with old RCA Logo and Print in
Silver. Contains 12 page insert booklet. Digitally Remastered from the original
RCA Label Master Tapes. Only available from Columbia House Music CD Club.
Mail Order Only.)*

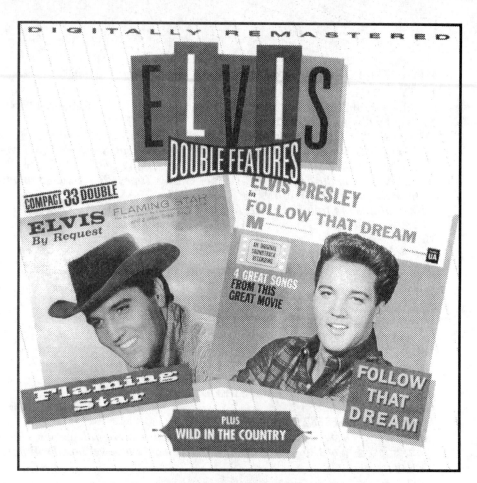

[ ]   **ELVIS DOUBLE FEATURES**
FLAMING STAR, WILD IN THE COUNTRY & FOLLOW THAT DREAM
Catalog# 07863-66557-2   Value $ 13-18
Matrix# 07863665572 ++ 53450-01
*(March 1995 First Pressing. Elvis in the '90's Black Disc with old RCA Logo
and Print in Silver. Contains 12 page insert booklet with Sessionography and
Historical Movie Data. Three complete soundtracks on one CD. Digitally
Remastered from the original RCA Label Master Tapes. RCA deleted this title
from their catalog in July, 1998.)*
Disc contains the following selections:

Flaming Star	In My Way
Summer Kisses Winter Tears	Forget Me Never
Britches	Lonely Man *(Solo)*
A Cane And A High Starch Collar	I Slipped. I Stumbled, I Fell *(Alt.Master)*
Black Star	Follow That Dream
Summer Kisses Winter Tears *(Movie Version)*	Angel
Flaming Star *(End Title Version)*	What A Wonderful Life
Wild In The Country	I'm Not The Marrying Kind
I Slipped, I Stumbled, I Fell	A Whistling Tune
Lonely Man	Sound Advice

[ ]   **ELVIS DOUBLE FEATURES**   *(Promo)*
FLAMING STAR, WILD IN THE COUNTRY & FOLLOW THAT DREAM
Catalog# 07863-66557-2   Value $ 15-20
Matrix# 07863665572 ++ 53450-01
*(March 1995 Designated Promo. Same as regular catalog release with Black and
White sticker "Not For Sale NFS-1" on front cover of jewel box. Drill hole thru
back of jewel box.)*

[ ]   **ELVIS DOUBLE FEATURES**   *(Promo)*
FLAMING STAR, WILD IN THE COUNTRY & FOLLOW THAT DREAM
Catalog# RJC 66557-2   Value $ 75-100
Matrix# 07863665572 ++ 53450-01
*(March 1995 Promo Only. Elvis in the '90's Black Disc with old RCA Logo and
Print in Silver. Catalog# RJC 66557-2 and "Not For Sale" printed on disc.
Black and White sticker "Not For Sale NFS-1" on front insert booklet. Hole
punched thru the bar code on back insert cover. One of three of the Double
Features to have a promo. Rare.)*

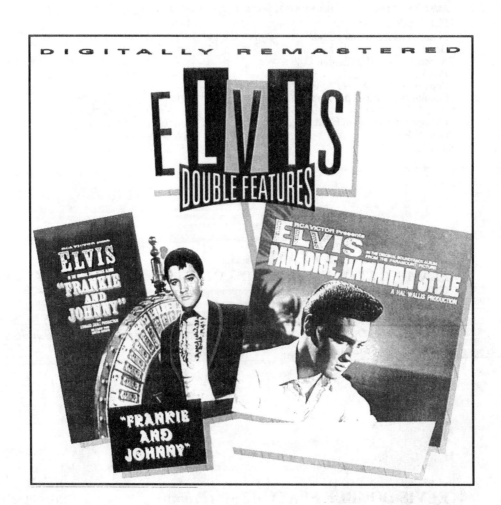

[ ]

ELVIS DOUBLE FEATURES
FRANKIE AND JOHNNY and PARADISE, HAWAIIAN STYLE
Catalog# 07863-66360-2   Value $ 13-18
Matrix# 07863663602 42327 #
*(June 1994 First Pressing. Elvis in the '90's Black Disc with The RCA
Records Label and Nipper above new silver line. Print in Silver. Contains 12
page insert booklet. Black & White sticker on shrink wrap reads - "2 Complete
Soundtracks on 1 CD" Digitally Remastered from the original RCA Records
Label - 2 And/Or 3 Track Masters. Includes Sessionography & Historical Movie
Data #SND-2. RCA deleted this title from their catalog in July, 1998.)*
Disc contains the following selections:

Frankie And Johnny	Paradise, Hawaiian Style
Come Along	Queenie Wahine's Papaya
Petunia, The Gardener's Daughter	Scratch My Back
Chesay	Drums Of The Island
What Every Woman Lives For	Datin'
Look Out, Broadway	A Dog's Life
Beginner's Luck	House Of Sand
Down By The Riverside And	Stop Where You Are
When The Saints Go Marching In	This Is My Heaven
Shout It Out	Sand Castles
Hard Luck	
Please Don't Stop Loving Me	
Everybody Come Aboard	

[ ]

ELVIS DOUBLE FEATURES *(Promo)*
FRANKIE AND JOHNNY and PARADISE, HAWAIIAN STYLE
Catalog# 07863-66360-2   Value $ 15-20
Matrix# 07863663602 42327 #
*(June 1994 Designated Promo. Same as regular catalog release with Black and
White sticker "Not For Sale NFS-1" on front cover of jewel box. Drill hole thru
back of jewel box.)*

[ ]

ELVIS DOUBLE FEATURES
FRANKIE AND JOHNNY and PARADISE, HAWAIIAN STYLE
Catalog# BG2-66360   Value $ 20-30
Matrix# E3 1ABG266360 01
*(1996 Second Pressing. Mfg. by BMG Music for Columbia House Music Club,
a non-BMG Music CD Club. Columbia House Music Club catalog number on
disc, spine, booklet and back insert cover. CRC Logo printed above bar code on
back insert cover. Elvis in the '90's Black Disc with old RCA Logo and Print in
Silver. Contains 12 page insert booklet. Digitally Remastered from the original
RCA Label Master Tapes. Only available from Columbia House Music CD Club.
Mail Order Only.)*

[ ]
ELVIS DOUBLE FEATURES
HARUM SCARUM and GIRL HAPPY
Catalog# 07863-66128-2   **Value $ 13-18**
Matrix# W.O. 28510-1M 07863661282
(Feb. 1993 First Pressing. Elvis in the '90's Black Disc with old RCA Logo and Print in Silver. Contains 16 page insert booklet with Sessionography and Historical Movie Data. Two complete soundtracks on one CD. Digitally Remastered from the original RCA Label Master Tapes.)
Disc contains the following selections:

Harem Holiday	Girl Happy
My Desert Serenade	Spring Fever
Go East - Young Man	Fort Lauderdale Chamber Of Commerce
Mirage	Startin' Tonight
Kismet	Wolf Call
Shake That Tambourine	Do Not Disturb
Hey Little Girl	Cross My Heart And Hope To Die
Golden Coins	The Meanest Girl In Town
So Close, Yet So Far (From Paradise)	Do The Clam
Animal Instinct	Puppet On A String
Wisdom Of The Ages	I've Got To Find My Baby

[ ]
ELVIS DOUBLE FEATURES
HARUM SCARUM and GIRL HAPPY
Catalog# 07863-66128-2   **Value $ 13-18**
Matrix# 07863661282 ++ 65111-01
*(Oct 1996 Second Pressing. Elvis in the '90's Black Disc with old RCA Logo and Print in Silver. Contains 16 page insert booklet with Sessionagraphy and Historical Movie Data. Two complete soundtracks on one CD. Digitally Remastered from the original RCA Label Master Tapes. **RCA deleted this title from their catalog in Dec. 1997.**)*

[ ]
ELVIS DOUBLE FEATURES
HARUM SCARUM and GIRL HAPPY
Catalog# BG2-66128   **Value $ 20-30**
Matrix# E2 1ABG266128 01
(1996 Third Pressing. Mfg. by BMG Music for Columbia House Music Club, a non-BMG Music Club. Columbia House Music Club catalog number on disc, spine, booklet and back insert cover. CRC Logo printed above bar code on back insert cover. Elvis in the '90's Black Disc with old RCA Logo and Print in Silver. Contains 16 page insert booklet. Digitally Remastered from the original RCA Master Tapes. Only available from Columbia House Music CD Club. Mail Order Only.)

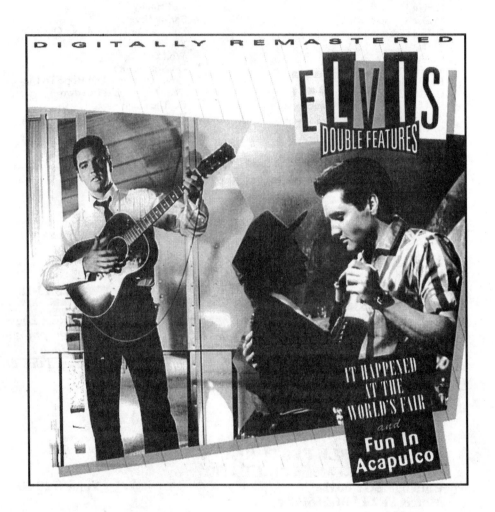

[ ] **ELVIS DOUBLE FEATURES**
IT HAPPENED AT THE WORLD'S FAIR and FUN IN ACAPULCO
Catalog# 07863-66131-2   Value $ 13-18
Matrix# W.O. 28513-1M 07863661312
(Feb. 1993 First Pressing. Elvis in the '90's Black Disc with old RCA
Logo and Print in Silver. Contains 16 page insert booklet with Sessionography
and Historical Movie Data. Two complete soundtracks on one CD. Digitally
Remastered from the original RCA Label Master Tapes.)
Disc contains the following selections:

Beyond The Bend	Fun In Acapulco
Relax	Vino, Dinero Y Amor
Take Me To The Fair	Mexico
They Remind Me Too Much Of You	El Toro
One Broken Heart For Sale *(Film Version)*	Marguerita
I'm Falling In Love Tonight	The Bullfighter Was A Lady
Cotton Candy Land	No Room To Rhumba In A Sports Car
A World Of Our Own	I Think I'm Gonna Like It Here
How Would You Like To Be	Bossa Nova Baby
Happy Ending	You Can't Say No In Acapulco
One Broken Heart For Sale *(Single Version)*	Guadalajara

[ ] **ELVIS DOUBLE FEATURES**
IT HAPPENED AT THE WORLD'S FAIR and FUN IN ACAPULCO
Catalog# 07863-66131-2   Value $ 13-18
Matrix# 07863661312 ++ 64823-01
(Oct. 1996 Second Pressing. Elvis In the '90's Black Disc with old RCA Logo
and Print in Silver. Contains 16 page insert booklet with Sessionography and
Historical Movie Data. Two complete soundtracks on one CD. Digitally
*Remastered from the original RCA Label Master Tapes. **RCA deleted this title***
from their catalog in July, 1998)

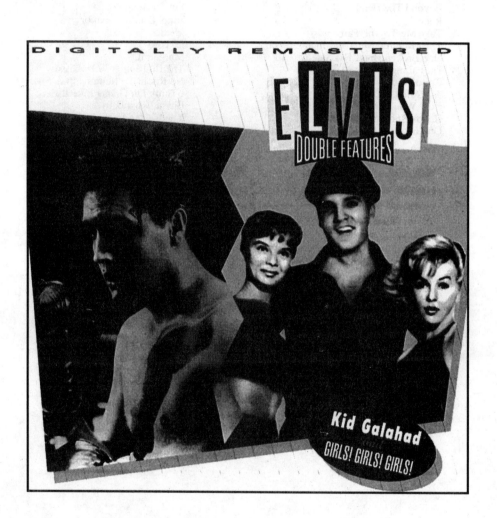

[ ]

ELVIS DOUBLE FEATURES
KID GALAHAD and GIRLS! GIRLS! GIRLS!
Catalog# 07863-66130-2   Value $ 13-18
Matrix# W.O. 28512-1 07863661302

*(Feb. 1993 First Pressing. Elvis in the '90's Black Disc with old RCA Logo and Print in Silver. Contains 16 page insert booklet with Sessionography and Historical Movie Data. Two complete soundtracks on one CD. Digitally Remastered from the original RCA Label Master Tapes. **RCA deleted this title from their catalog in July, 1998.**)*

Disc contains the following selections:

King Of The Whole Wide World	Earth Boy
This Is Living	Return To Sender
Riding The Rainbow	Because Of Love
Home Is Where The Heart Is	Thanks To The Rolling Sea
I Got Lucky	Song Of The Shrimp
A Whistling Tune	The Walls Have Ears
Girls! Girls! Girls!	We're Coming In Loaded
I Don't Wanna Be Tied	Mama
Where Do You Come From	Plantation Rock
I Don't Want To	Dainty Little Moonbeams
We'll Be Together	Girls! Girls! Girls! *(End Title Version)*
A Boy Like Me, A Girl Like You	

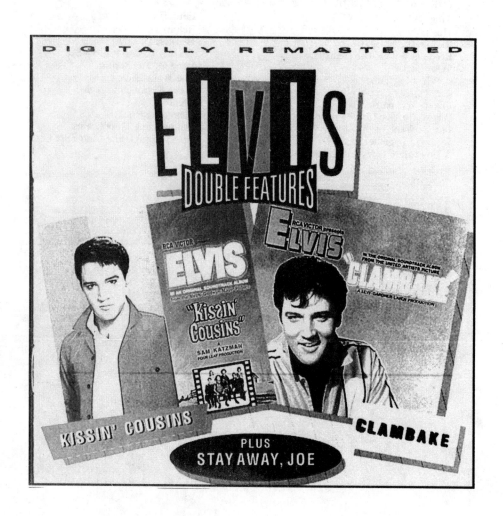

[ ] **ELVIS DOUBLE FEATURES**
KISSIN' COUSINS, CLAMBAKE and STAY AWAY, JOE
Catalog# 07863-66362-2   Value $ 13-18
Matrix# 07863663622 02# 42001
*(June 1994 First Pressing. Elvis in the '90's Black Disc with The RCA
Records Label and Nipper above new silver line. Print in Silver. Contains 12
page insert booklet. Black and White sticker on shrink wrap reads "3 Complete
Soundtracks on 1 CS/CD". Digitally Remastered from the original RCA Records
Label 2 And/Or 3 Track Masters. Includes Sessionography & Historical Movie
Data #EPSND-4/2. RCA deleted this title from their catalog in Dec. 1997.)*
Disc contains the following selections:

Kissin' Cousins *(Number 2)*	A House That Has Everything
Smokey Mountain Boy	Confidence
There's Gold In The Mountains	Hey, Hey, Hey
One Boy, Two Little Girls	You Don't Know Me *(Orig.Film Version)*
Catchin' On Fast	The Girl I Never Loved
Tender Feelings	How Can You Lose What You Never Had
Anyone (Could Fall In Love With You)	Clambake *(Reprise)*
Barefoot Ballad	Stay Away, Joe
Once Is Enough	Dominic
Kissin' Cousins	All I Needed Was The Rain
Clambake	Goin' Home
Who Needs Money?	Stay Away

[ ] **ELVIS DOUBLE FEATURES** *(Promo)*
KISSIN' COUSINS, CLAMBAKE and STAY AWAY, JOE
Catalog# 07863-66362-2   Value $ 15-20
Matrix# 07863663622 02# 42001
*(June 1994 Designated Promo. Same as regular catalog release with Black and
White sticker "**Not For Sale NFS-1**" on front cover of jewel box. Drill hole thru
back cover of jewel box.)*

[ ] **ELVIS DOUBLE FEATURES**
KISSIN' COUSINS, CLAMBAKE and STAY AWAY, JOE
Catalog# BG2-66362   Value $ 20-30
Matrix# E3 ABG266362 01
*(1996 Second Pressing. Mfg. by BMG Music for Columbia House Music Club,
a non-BMG Music CD Club. Columbia House Music Club catalog number on
disc, spine, booklet and back insert cover. CRC Logo printed above bar code on
back insert cover. Elvis in the '90's Black Disc with old RCA Logo and Print in
Silver. Contains 12 page insert booklet. Digitally Remastered from the original
RCA Label master Tapes. Only available from Columbia House Music CD Club.
Mail Order Only.)*

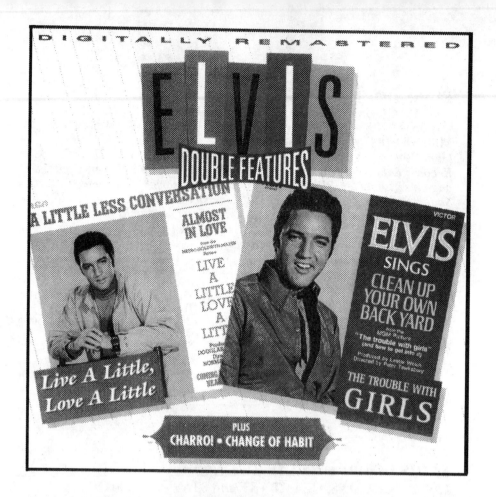

[ ] **ELVIS DOUBLE FEATURES**
LIVE A LITTLE, LOVE A LITTLE, CHARRO!
THE TROUBLE WITH GIRLS and CHANGE OF HABIT
Catalog# 07863-66559-2   Value $ 13-18
Matrix# 07863665592 ++ 53393-01
*(March 1995 First Pressing. Elvis in the '90's Black Disc with old RCA Logo
and Print in Silver. Contains 12 page insert booklet with Sessionography and
Historical Movie Data. Four complete soundtracks on one CD. Digitally
Remastered from the original RCA Label Master Tapes. RCA deleted this title
from their catalog in Dec. 1997.)*
Disc contains the following selections:

Almost In Love	Almost
A Little Less Conversation	The Whiffenpoof Song
Wonderful World	Violet
Edge Of Reality	Clean Up Your Own Backyard *(Undub Ver)*
A Little Less Conversation *(Album Version)*	Almost *(Undubbed Version)*
Charro!	Have A Happy
Let's Forget About The Stars	Let's Be Friends
Clean Up Your Own Back Yard	Change Of Habit
Swing Down, Sweet Chariot	Let Us Pray
Signs Of The Zodiac	Rubberneckin'

[ ] **ELVIS DOUBLE FEATURES**   *(Promo)*
LIVE A LITTLE, LOVE A LITTLE, CHARRO!
THE TROUBLE WITH GIRLS and CHANGE OF HABIT
Catalog# 07863-66559-2   Value $ 15-20
Matrix# 07863665592 ++ 53393-01
*(March 1995 Designated Promo. Same as regular catalog release with Black and
White sticker "Not For Sale NFS-1"on front cover of jewel box. Drill hole thru
back of jewel box.)*

[ ] **ELVIS DOUBLE FEATURES**   *(Promo)*
LIVE A LITTLE, LOVE A LITTLE, CHARRO!
THE TROUBLE WITH GIRLS and CHANGE OF HABIT
Catalog# RJC 66559-2   Value $ 75-100
Matrix# 07863665592 ++ 53393-01
*(March 1995 Promo Only. Elvis in the '90's Black Disc with old RCA Logo and
Print in Silver. Catalog# RJC 66559-2 and "Not For Sale" printed on disc.
Black and White sticker "Not For Sale NFS-1" on front insert booklet. Hole
punched thru the bar code on back insert cover. One of three of the Double
Features to have a promo. Rare.)*

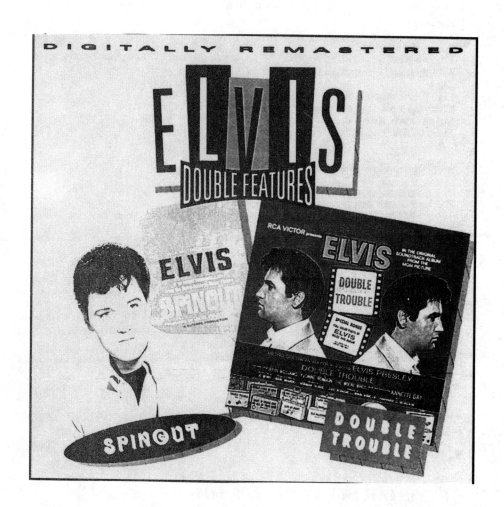

[ ] **ELVIS DOUBLE FEATURES**
SPINOUT and DOUBLE TROUBLE
Catalog# 07863-66361-2   Value $ 13-18
Matrix# 07863663612 01# 41590
(June 1994 First Pressing. Elvis in the '90's Black Disc with The RCA
Records Label and Nipper above new silver line. This pressing has wide silver
line around edge of disc. Print in Silver. Contains 12 page insert booklet.
Black & White sticker on shrink wrap reads "2 Complete Soundtracks on 1 CD".
Digitally Remastered from the original RCA Records Label 2 And/Or 3 Track
Masters. Includes Sessionography & Historical Movie Data #SND-2.
RCA deleted this title from their catalog in July, 1998.)
Disc contains the following selections:

Stop, Look And Listen	Double Trouble
Adam And Evil	Baby, If You'll Give Me All Of Your Love
All That I Am	Could I Fall In Love
Never Say Yes	Long Legged Girl (WithThe ShortDressOn)
Am I Ready	City By Night
Beach Shack	Old MacDonald
Spinout	I Love Only One Girl
Smorgasbord	There Is So Much World To See
I'll Be Back	It Won't Be Long

[ ] **ELVIS DOUBLE FEATURES** *(Promo)*
SPINOUT and DOUBLE TROUBLE
Catalog# 07863-66361-2   Value $ 15-20
Matrix# 07863663612 01# 41590
(June 1994 Designated Promo. Same as regular catalog release with Black and
White sticker "Not For Sale NFS-1" on fron cover of jewel box. Drill hole thru
back cover of jewel box.)

[ ] **ELVIS DOUBLE FEATURES**
SPINOUT and DOUBLE TROUBLE
Catalog# BG2-66361   Value $ 20-30
Matrix# E2 1ABG266361 01
(1996 Second Pressing. Mfg. by BMG Music for Columbia House Music Club,
a non-BMG Music CD Club. Columbia House Music Club catalog number on
disc, spine, booklet and back insert cover. CRC Logo printed above bar code on
back insert cover. Elvis in the '90's Black Disc with old RCA Logo and Print in
Silver. Contains 12 page insert booklet. Digitally Remastered from the original
RCA Label Master Tapes. Only available from Columbia House Music CD Club.
Mail Order Only.)

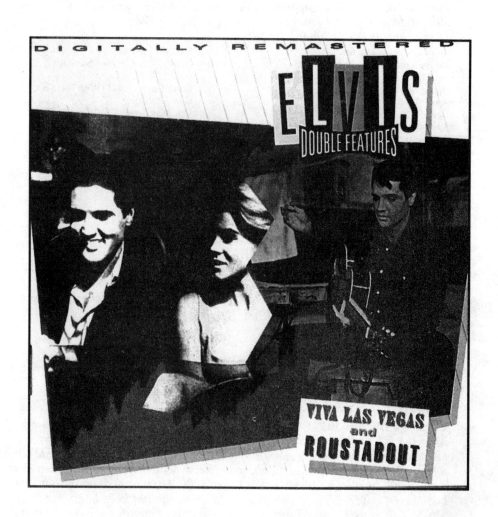

[ ] **ELVIS DOUBLE FEATURES**
VIVA LAS VEGAS and ROUSTABOUT
Catalog# 07863-66129-2   **Value $ 13-18**
Matrix# W.O. 28511-1M 07863661292
*(Feb. 1993 First Pressing. Elvis in the '90's Black Disc with old RCA
Logo and Print in Silver. Contains 16 page insert booklet with Sessionography
and Historical Movie Data. Two complete soundtracks on one CD. Digitally
Remastered from the original RCA Label MasterTapes.)*
Disc contains the following selections:

Viva Las Vegas	Roustabout
If You Think I Don't Need You	Little Egypt
I Need Somebody To Lean On	Poison Ivy League
You're The Boss *(with Ann-Margret)*	Hard Knocks
What'd I Say	It's A Wonderful World
Do The Vega	Big Love Big Heartache
C'mon Everybody	One Track Heart
The Lady Loves Me *(with Ann-Margret)*	It's Carnival Time
Night Life	Carny Town
Today, Tomorrow And Forever	There's A Brand New Day On The Horizon
The Yellow Rose Of Texas/	Wheels On My Heels
The Eyes Of Texas *(Medley)*	
Santa Lucia *(Traditional)*	

[ ] **ELVIS DOUBLE FEATURES**
VIVA LAS VEGAS and ROUSTABOUT
Catalog# 07863-66129-2   **Value $ 13-18**
Matrix# W.O. 28511-2 07863661292
*(1995 Second Pressing. Elvis in the '90's Black Disc with old RCA
Logo and Print in Silver. Contains 16 page insert booklet. Black & White
sticker on shrink wrap reads "2 Complete Soundtracks on 1 CD". Digitally
Remastered from the original RCA Records Label 2 And/Or 3 Track Masters.
Includes Sessionography & Historical Movie Data #SND-2.)*

[ ] **ELVIS DOUBLE FEATURES**
VIVA LAS VEGAS and ROUSTABOUT
Catalog# 07863-66129-2   **Value $ 20-30**
BMG Music Service Catalog# D 101154
Matrix# W.O. 28511-2 07863661292
*(1995 Third Pressing. Mfg. for BMG Direct Marketing, Inc. BMG Music
Service catalog number on disc and back insert cover. Elvis in the '90's Black
Disc with old RCA Logo and Print in Silver. Contains 16 page insert booklet.
Only available from BMG Music CD Club. Mail Order Only.)*

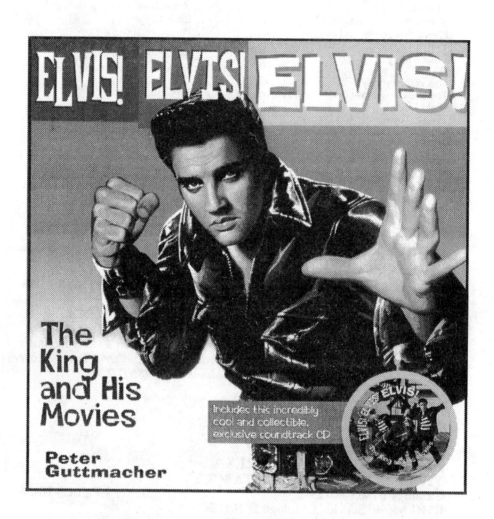

[ ]
ELVIS DOUBLE FEATURES
VIVA LAS VEGAS and ROUSTABOUT
Catalog# 07863-66129-2   **Value $ 20-30**
BMG Music Service Catalog# D 101154
Matrix# 07863661292 ++ 64832-01
(Oct. 1996 Fourth Pressing. Mfg. for BMG Direst Marketing, Inc. BMG Music Service catalog number on disc and back insert cover. Elvis in the '90's Black Disc with old RCA Logo and Print in Silver. Contains 16 page insert booklet. Only available from BMG Music CD Club. Mail Order Only.)

[ ]
ELVIS DOUBLE FEATURES
VIVA LAS VEGAS and ROUSTABOUT
Catalog# BG2-66129   **Value $ 20-30**
Matrix# E2 1ABG266129 01
(1996 Fifth Pressing. Mfg. by BMG Music for Columbia House Music Club, a non-BMG Music Club. Columbia House Music Club catalog number on disc, spine, booklet and back insert cover. CRC Logo printed above bar code on back insert cover. Elvis in the '90's Black Disc with old RCA Logo and Print in Silver. Contains 16 page insert booklet. Digitally Remastered from the original RCA Label Master Tapes. Only available from Columbia House Music CD Club. Mail Order Only.)

[ ]
ELVIS! ELVIS! ELVIS!
THE KING AND HIS MOVIES
Catalog# DPC11624   **Value $ 25-30**
Matrix# L385 1100 DPC11624 C70705-13
(Aug. 1997 Release from BMG Special Products. Silver Disc with Black Print. The CD was included in the book Elvis! Elvis! Elvis! by Peter Guttmacher. This hardback book is oversized at 11-1/4" x 11-1/4" with 128 pages. Distributed by Friedman/Fairfax Publishers, New York , New York.)
Disc contains the following selections:

Love Me Tender	Relax
Jailhouse Rock	(You're So Square) Baby I Don't Care
Mean Woman Blues	Viva Las Vegas
Crawfish	There Ain't Nothing Like A Song
King Creole	*(with Nancy Sinatra)*
Trouble	King Of The Whole Wide World
Double Trouble	Can't Help Falling In Love
Spinout	Lonesome Cowboy

53450-2

[ ] **ELVIS FOR EVERYONE!**
Catalog# 3450-2-R   Value $ 25-30
Matrix# W.O. 15627-1 34502R
*(Oct. 1990 First Pressing. Midline CD. Silver & Black Disc with old RCA Logo.
Contains alternate take of "In My Way" with 4 page insert booklet.*
RCA deleted this title from their catalog in April 1992.)
Disc contains the following selections:

Your Cheatin' Heart	For The Millionth And The Last Time
Summer Kisses, Winter Tears	Forget Me Never
Finders Keepers, Losers Weepers	Sound Advice
In My Way *(Alternate Take)*	Santa Lucia
Tomorrow Night	I Met Her Today
Memphis, Tennessee	When It Rains, It Really Pours

[ ] **ELVIS FOR EVERYONE!**
Catalog# 07863-53450-2   Value $ 15-20
Matrix# 07863534502 ++ 53449-01
*(April 1995 Reissue with new catalog number. Midline CD. Elvis in the '90's
Black Disc with old RCA Logo and Print in Silver. This reissue contains same
tracks as above with the exception of the alternate take of "In My Way".
Contains 8 page four fold insert booklet with rare UK LP cover photo.
Digitally Remastered from the original RCA Label Master Tapes.*
RCA deleted this title from their catalog in 1997.)

[ ] **ELVIS FOR EVERYONE!**   *(Promo)*
Catalog# 07863-53450-2   Value $ 20-25
Matrix# 07863534502 ++ 53449-01
*(April 1995 Designated Promo. Same as regular catalog release with Black and
White sticker "**Not For Sale NFS-1**" on front cover of jewel box. Drill hole thru
back of jewel box.)*

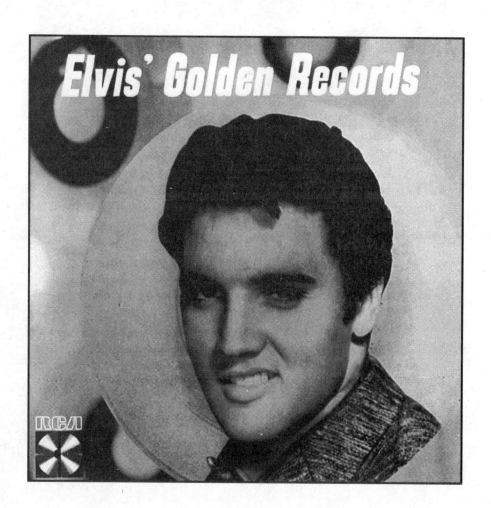

[ ] ELVIS' GOLDEN RECORDS
Catalog# PCD1-1707   Value $ 250-300
Matrix# PCD-11707 1A5-47
(Jan. 1984 First Pressing in Electronic Stereo. Silver & Blue Disc with block RCA Logo in white. Contains 8 page insert booklet. Pressed in Japan for U.S. Release.)
Disc contains the following selections:

Hound Dog	Don't Be Cruel
Loving You	That's When Your Heartaches Begin
All Shook Up	(Let Me Be Your) Teddy Bear
Heartbreak Hotel	Love Me Tender
Jailhouse Rock	Treat Me Nice
Love Me	Anyway You Want Me
Too Much	I Want You, I Need You, I Love You

[ ] ELVIS' GOLDEN RECORDS
Catalog# PCD1-5196   Value $ 30-40
Matrix# DIDX 185 21B6
(Nov. 1984 Reissue. Digitally Remastered to Original Mono. DIDX on disc and insert sleeve. Silver & Blue Disc with block RCA Logo in white. This title has been given a new catalog number. Contains 8 page insert booklet. Pressed in U.S.)

[ ] ELVIS' GOLDEN RECORDS
Catalog# PCD1-5196   Value $ 15-18
Matrix# PCD-15196 1B5 71
(1985 Second Pressing. Silver & Blue Disc with block RCA Logo in white. Contains 8 page insert booklet. Pressed in Japan for U.S. Release.)

[ ] ELVIS' GOLDEN RECORDS
Catalog# PCD1-5196   Value $ 15-18
Matrix# PCD-15196 1B9 72
(1986 Third Pressing. Silver & Blue Disc with block RCA Logo in white. Contains 8 page insert booklet. Pressed in Japan for U.S. Release.)

[ ] ELVIS' GOLDEN RECORDS
Catalog# PCD1-5196   Value $ 12-15
Matrix# PCD-15196 9/87 2C1
(Sept. 1987 Fourth Pressing. Silver & Blue Disc with block RCA Logo in white. Contains 8 page insert booklet. Pressed in U.S.)

[ ] ELVIS' GOLDEN RECORDS
Catalog# PCD1-5196   Value $ 12-15
Matrix# PCD15196 7/88 2DA2
(July 1988 Fifth Pressing. Silver & Blue Disc with block RCA Logo in white. Contains 8 page insert booklet. Pressed in U.S.)

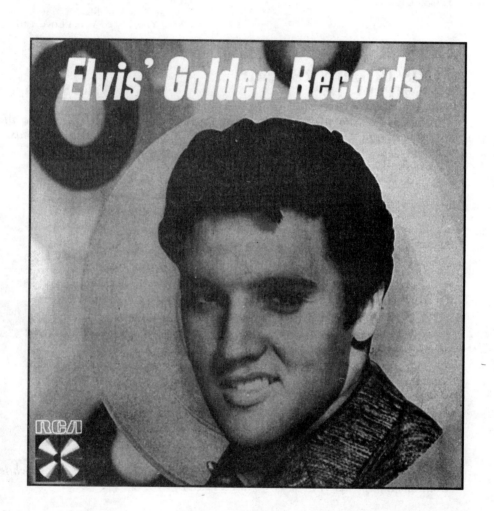

[ ]   **ELVIS' GOLDEN RECORDS**
        Catalog# PCD1-5196   Value $ 12-15
        Matrix# PCD15196 8/88 2DA5
        (Aug. 1988 Sixth Pressing. Silver & Blue Disc with block RCA Logo in white.
        Contains 8 page insert booklet. Pressed in U.S.)

[ ]   **ELVIS' GOLDEN RECORDS**
        Catalog# PCD1-5196   Value $ 10-12
        Matrix# PCD1-5196 1T12
        (1989 Seventh Pressing. Sliver & Black Disc with block RCA Logo.
        Contains 8 page insert booklet. Pressed in U.S.)

[ ]   **ELVIS' GOLDEN RECORDS**
        Catalog# PCD1-5196   Value $ 10-12
        Matrix# PCD1-5196 1T 21
        (1990 Eighth Pressing. Silver & Black Disc with block RCA Logo.
        Contains 8 page insert booklet. Pressed in U.S.)

[ ]   **ELVIS' GOLDEN RECORDS**
        Catalog# PCD1-5196   Value $ 10-12
        Matrix# PCD1-5196 4T 23
        (1990 Ninth Pressing. Silver & Black Disc with block RCA Logo.
        Contains 8 page insert booklet. Pressed in U.S.)

[ ]   **ELVIS' GOLDEN RECORDS**
        Catalog# PCD1-5196   Value $10-12
        Matrix# PCD1-5196 4T 27
        (1991 Tenth Pressing. Silver & Black Disc with block RCA Logo.
        Contains 8 page insert booklet. Pressed in U.S.)

[ ]   **ELVIS' GOLDEN RECORDS**
        Catalog# PCD1-5196   Value $ 10-12
        Matrix# PCD1-5196 3S 23
        (1991 Eleventh Pressing. Silver & Black Disc with block RCA Logo.
        Contains 8 page insert booklet. Pressed in U.S.)

[ ]   **ELVIS' GOLDEN RECORDS**
        Catalog #PCD1-5196   Value $ 20-30
        BMG Music Service Catalog# D133855
        Matrix# PCD1-5196 4T 01
        (1994 Twelfth Pressing. Mfg. for BMG Direct Marketing, Inc. BMG Music
        Service catalog number on disc and back insert cover. Silver & Black Disc with
        block RCA Logo. Contains 8 page insert booklet. Pressed in U.S.
        Mail Order Only.)

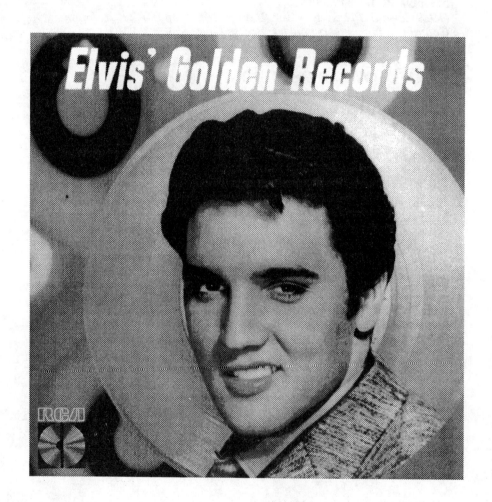

[ ] **ELVIS' GOLDEN RECORDS**
Catalog# PCD1-5196   Value $ 20-30
BMG Music Service Catalog# D133855
Matrix# PCD1-5196 4T 03
*(1994 Thirteenth Pressing. Mfg. for BMG Direct Marketing, Inc. BMG Music
Service catalog number on disc and back insert cover. Silver & Black Disc with
block RCA Logo. Contains 8 page insert booklet. Pressed in U.S.
Mail Order Only.)*

[ ] **ELVIS' GOLDEN RECORDS**
Catalog# PCD1-5196   Value $ 10-12
Matrix# PCD15196 02# ++ 40388
*(1994 Fourteenth Pressing. Special Elvis in the '90's Silver Disc with The RCA
Records Label and Nipper above black line. Print in Black. Same disc as used
in the "Elvis His Life And Music" Ltd. Edition box set. Contains 8 page insert
booklet. "Wise Buy" sticker on shrink wrap. Pressed in U.S.)*

[ ] **ELVIS' GOLDEN RECORDS**
Catalog# PCD1-5196   Value $ 20-30
BMG Music Service Catalog# D 133855
Matrix# PCD1-5196 4T 61
*(1995 Fifteenth Pressing. Mfg. for BMG Direct Marketing, Inc. BMG Music
Service catalog number on disc and back insert cover. Silver & Black Disc with
block RCA Logo. Contains 8 page insert booklet. Pressed in U.S.
Mail Order Only.)*

[ ] **ELVIS' GOLDEN RECORDS**
Catalog# PCD1-5196   Value $ 20-30
BMG Music Service Catalog# D133855
Matrix# PCD1-5196 4T 66
*(1995 Sixteenth Pressing. Mfg. for BMG Direct Marketing, Inc. BMG Music
Service catalog number on disc and back insert cover. Silver & Black Disc with
block RCA Logo. Contains 8 page insert booklet. Pressed in U.S.
Mail Order Only.)*

[ ] **ELVIS' GOLDEN RECORDS**
Catalog# PCD1-5196   Value $ 20-30
Matrix# 5 PCD 05196-2 SRC##01 M1S3
*(1997 Seventeenth Pressing. Mfg. by BMG Music for Columbia House Music
Club, a non-BMG Music CD Club. CRC Logo printed above bar code on back
insert cover. Silver & Black Disc with block RCA Logo. Contains 8 page insert
booklet. Only available from Columbia House Music CD Club. Mail Order Only.)*

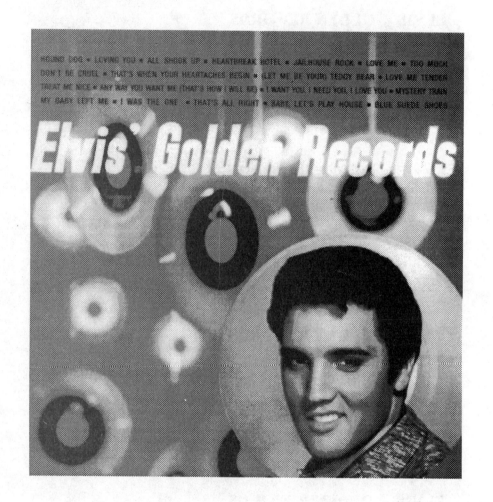

[ ]
ELVIS' GOLDEN RECORDS
Catalog# 07863-67462-2   **Value $ 13-18**
Matrix# 07863674622 ++ 76423-01

(July 1997 Reissue. Disc is made to simulate a gold '45 record with Dark Blue Label and White Print with simulated Gold spindle adapter. Contains 8 page insert booklet. Back cover has new artwork, which is a color "Jailhouse Rock" publicity photo of Elvis. Also contains 6 bonus tracks not included on all previous issues. Gold collectors sticker with black print on front of shrink wrap. Wording on sticker was printed for European market and does not apply to the U.S. The 6 bonus tracks were not on the original U.S. LP. Digitally Remastered from the original RCA Label Master Tapes.)
Disc contains the following selections:

Hound Dog	Love Me Tender
Loving You	Treat Me Nice
All Shook Up	Any Way You Want Me
Heartbreak Hotel	I Want You, I Need You, I Love You
Jailhouse Rock	My Baby Left Me
Love Me	I Was The One
Too Much	That's All Right
Don't Be Cruel	Baby, Let's Play House
That's When Your Heartaches Begin	Mystery Train
(Let Me Be Your) Teddy Bear	Blue Suede Shoes

[ ]
ELVIS' GOLDEN RECORDS *(Promo)*
Catalog# 07863-67462-2   **Value $ 15-20**
Matrix# 07863674622 ++ 76423-01

(July 1997 Designated Promo. Same as regular catalog release with black and white sticker "Not For Sale NFS-1" on front of insert booklet. Drill hole thru back of jewel box.)

[ ] **ELVIS' GOLD RECORDS**
Volume 2 - 50,000,000 ELVIS FANS CAN'T BE WRONG
Catalog# PCD1-2075   Value $ 250-300
Matrix# PCD-12075 1A1-48
(Sept. 1984 First Pressing in Electronic Stereo. Silver & Blue Disc with block
RCA Logo in white. Contains 4 page insert booklet. Pressed in Japan for U.S.
Release.)
Disc contains the following selections:

I Need Your Love Tonight	One Night
Don't	A Big Hunk O' Love
Wear My Ring Around Your Neck	I Beg Of You
My Wish Came True	A Fool Such As I
I Got Stung	Doncha' Think It's Time

[ ] **ELVIS' GOLD RECORDS**
Volume 2 - 50,000,000 ELVIS FANS CAN'T BE WRONG
Catalog# PCD1-5197   Value $ 30-40
Matrix# DIDX 184 11A1
(Nov. 1984 Reissue. Digitally Remastered to Original Mono. DIDX on disc and
insert sleeve. Silver & Blue Disc with block RCA Logo in white. This title has
been given a new catalog number. Contains 4 page insert booklet. Pressed in
U.S.)

[ ] **ELVIS' GOLD RECORDS**
Volume 2 - 50,000,000 ELVIS FANS CAN'T BE WRONG
Catalog# PCD1-5197   Value $ 30-40
Matrix# DIDX 184 21A3
(Feb. 1985 Second Pressing. Digitally Remastered to Original Mono. DIDX on
disc and insert sleeve. Silver & Blue Disc with block RCA Logo in white. Contains
4 page insert booklet. Pressed in U.S.)

[ ] **ELVIS' GOLD RECORDS**
Volume 2 - 50,000,000 ELVIS FANS CAN'T BE WRONG
Catalog# PCD1-5197   Value $ 15-18
Matrix# PCD-15197 1A6 65 Z
(1985 Third Pressing. Silver & Blue Disc with block RCA Logo in white.
Contains 4 page insert booklet. Pressed in Japan for U.S. Release.)

[ ] **ELVIS' GOLD RECORDS**
Volume 2 - 50,000,000 ELVIS FANS CAN'T BE WRONG
Catalog# PCD1-5197   Value $ 15-18
Matrix# PCD-15197 1A8 67 Z
(1985 Fourth Pressing. Silver & Blue Disc with block RCA Logo in white.
Contains 4 page insert booklet. Pressed in Japan for U.S. Release.)

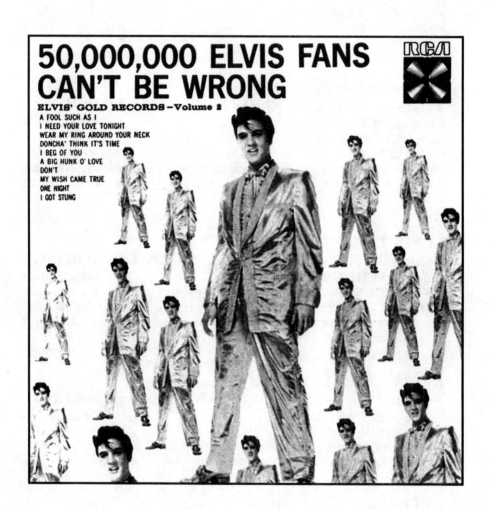

[ ] **ELVIS' GOLD RECORDS**
Volume 2 - 50,000,000 ELVIS FANS CAN'T BE WRONG
Catalog# PCD1-5197   Value $ 12-15
Matrix# PCD-15197 2A1 D74
(1985 Fifth Pressing. Silver & Blue Disc with block RCA Logo in white.
Contains 4 page insert booklet. Pressed in U.S.)

[ ] **ELVIS' GOLD RECORDS**
Volume 2 - 50,000,000 ELVIS FANS CAN'T BE WRONG
Catalog# PCD1-5197   Value $ 12-15
Matrix# PCD-15197 6/87 2C2
(June 1987 Sixth Pressing. Silver & Blue Disc with block RCA Logo in white.
Contains 4 page insert booklet. Pressed in U.S.)

[ ] **ELVIS' GOLD RECORDS**
Volume 2 - 50,000,000 ELVIS FANS CAN'T BE WRONG
Catalog# PCD1-5197   Value $ 12-15
Matrix# PCD15197 4/89 4A51
(April 1989 Seventh Pressing. Silver & Blue Disc with block RCA Logo in white.
Contains 4 page insert booklet. Pressed in U.S.)

[ ] **ELVIS' GOLD RECORDS**
Volume 2 - 50,000,000 ELVIS FANS CAN'T BE WRONG
Catalog# PCD1-5197-RE   Value $ 12-15
Matrix# PCD115197 10/89 2D52
(Oct. 1989 Eighth Pressing. Silver & Blue Disc with block RCA Logo in white.
Original artwork back cover with RE. Contains 4 page insert booklet.
Pressed in U.S.)

[ ] **ELVIS' GOLD RECORDS**
Volume 2 - 50,000,000 ELVIS FANS CAN'T BE WRONG
Catalog# PCD1-5197-RE   Value $ 10-12
Matrix# PCD15197 1/90 1DA2
(Jan. 1990 Ninth Pressing. Silver & Blue Disc with block RCA Logo in white.
Plain white back cover with RE. Contains 4 page insert booklet. Pressed in U.S.)

[ ] **ELVIS' GOLD RECORDS**
Volume 2 - 50,000,000 ELVIS FANS CAN'T BE WRONG
Catalog# PCD1-5197-RE   Value $ 10-12
Matrix# PCD15197 10/91 1DA3
(Oct. 1991 Tenth Pressing. Silver & Blue Disc with RCA Logo in white.
Plain white back cover with RE. Contains 4 page insert booklet. Pressed in U.S.)

SAMPLE

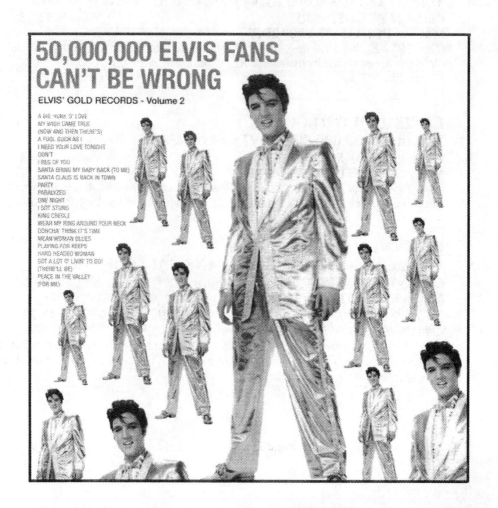

50,000,000 ELVIS FANS CAN'T BE WRONG

ELVIS' GOLD RECORDS ~ Volume 2

[ ]   **ELVIS' GOLD RECORDS**
Volume 2 - 50,000,000 ELVIS FANS CAN'T BE WRONG
Catalog# PCD1-5197-RE   Value $ 10-12
Matrix# PCD15197 02# ++ 40361
*(1994 Eleventh Pressing. Special Elvis in the '90's Silver Disc with The RCA
Records Label and Nipper above black line. Print in Black. Same disc as used
in the "Elvis His Life And Music" Ltd. Edition Box Set. Plain White back cover
with RE. Contains 4 page insert booklet. "**Wise Buy**" sticker on shrink wrap.
Pressed in U.S.)*

[ ]   **ELVIS' GOLD RECORDS**   *(Promo)*
Volume 2 - 50,000,000 ELVIS FANS CAN'T BE WRONG
Catalog# PCD1-5197   Value $ 700-1000
Matrix# PCD-15197 2A1 D74
*(1985 Super Rare "In House" Promo Picture Disc. With "Sample" on Disc.
This was the first Elvis picture disc. Very few copies were pressed.
Same tracks as the standard release. Contains 4 page insert booklet.
Pressed in U.S.?)*

[ ]   **ELVIS' GOLD RECORDS**
Volume 2 - 50,000,000 ELVIS FANS CAN'T BE WRONG
Catalog# 07863-67463-2   Value $ 13-18
Matrix# 07863674632 ++ 76352-01
*(July 1997 Reissue. Disc is made to simulate a gold '45 record with Red Label
and White Print with simulated Gold spindle adapter. Contains 8 page insert
booklet. Back cover has new artwork, which is a 1958 color publicity photo of
Elvis. Also contains 10 bonus tracks not included in all previous issues. Gold
collectors sticker with black print on front of shrink wrap. Wording on sticker was
printed for European market and does not apply to U.S. The 10 bonus tracks were
not on the original U.S. LP. Digitally remastered from the original RCA Label
MasterTapes.)*
Disc contains the following selections:

A Big Hunk O' Love	One Night
My Wish Came True	I Got Stung
(Now And Then There's) A Fool Such As I	King Creole
I Need Your Love Tonight	Wear My Ring Around Your Neck
Don't	Dontcha' Think It's Time
I Beg Of You	Mean Woman Blues
Santa Bring My Baby Back (To Me)	Playing For Keeps
Santa Claus Is Back In Town	Hard Headed Woman
Party	Got A Lot O' Livin' To Do!
Paralyzed	(There'll Be) Peace In TheValley (For Me)

[ ]   **ELVIS' GOLD RECORDS** *(Promo)*
Volume 2 - 50,000,000 ELVIS FANS CAN'T BE WRONG
Catalog# 07863-67463-2   Value $ 15-20
Matrix# 07863674632 ++ 76352-01
*(July 1997 Designated Promo. Same as regular catalog release with black and
white sticker "**Not For Sale NFS-1**" on front of insert booklet. Drill hole thru
back of jewel box.)*

[ ] **ELVIS' GOLDEN RECORDS Volume 3**
Catalog# 2765-2-R   Value $ 12-15
Matrix# W.O. 13706-1 27652R
(April 1990 First Pressing. Midline CD. Silver & Black Disc with old RCA Logo.)
Disc contains the following selections:

It's Now Or Never	Are You Lonesome Tonight?
Stuck On You	(Marie's The Name) His Latest Flame
Fame And Fortune	Little Sister
I Gotta Know	Good Luck Charm
Surrender	Anything That's Part Of You
I Feel So Bad	She's Not You

[ ] **ELVIS' GOLDEN RECORDS Volume 3**
Catalog# 2765-2-R   Value $ 12-15
Matrix# W.O. 13706-2M 27652R
(1992 Second Pressing. Midline CD. Silver & Black Disc with old RCA Logo.)

[ ] **ELVIS' GOLDEN RECORDS Volume 3**
Catalog# 2765-2-R   Value $ 12-15
Matrix# 27652R 02# ++ 40357
(1994 Third Pressing. Midline CD. Silver & Black Disc with old RCA Logo.)

[ ] **ELVIS' GOLDEN RECORDS Volume 3**
Catalog# 2765-2-R   Value $ 12-15
Matrix# 27652R 02# ++ 40357
*(1994 Fourth Pressing. Midline CD. Special Elvis in the '90's Silver Disc with
The RCA Records Label and Nipper above black line. Print in Black. Same disc
as used in the "Elvis His Life And Music" Ltd. Edition box set. "Wise Buy" sticker
on shrink wrap.)*

[ ] **ELVIS' GOLDEN RECORDS** Volume 3
     Catalog# 07863-67464-2   Value $ 13-18
     Matrix# 07863674642 ++ 76296-03
     *(July 1997 Reissue. Disc is made to simulate a gold '45 record with Light Blue
     Label and White Print with simulated Gold spindle adapter. Contains 8 page
     insert booklet. Back cover has new artwork, which is a color "It Happened At The
     Worlds Fair" publicity photo of Elvis. Also contains 6 bonus tracks not included
     in all previous issues. Gold collectors sticker with black print on front of shrink
     wrap. Wording on sticker was printed for European market and does not apply to
     U.S. The 6 bonus tracks were not on the original LP. Digitally Remastered from
     the original RCA Label Master Tapes.)*
     Disc contains the following selections:

It's Now Or Never	Good Luck Charm
Stuck On You	Anything That's Part Of You
Fame And Fortune	She's Not You
I Gotta Know	Wild In The Country
Surrender	Wooden Heart
I Feel So Bad	The Girl Of My Best Friend
Are You Lonesome Tonight?	Follow That Dream
His Latest Flame	King Of The Whole Wide World
Little Sister	Can't Help Falling In Love

[ ] **ELVIS' GOLDEN RECORDS** Volume 3 *(Promo)*
     Catalog# 07863-67464-2   Value $ 15-20
     Matrix# 07863674642 ++ 76296-03
     *(July 1997 Designated Promo. Same as regular catalog release with black and
     white sticker "**Not For Sale NFS-1**" on front of insert booklet. Drill hole thru
     back of jewel box.)*

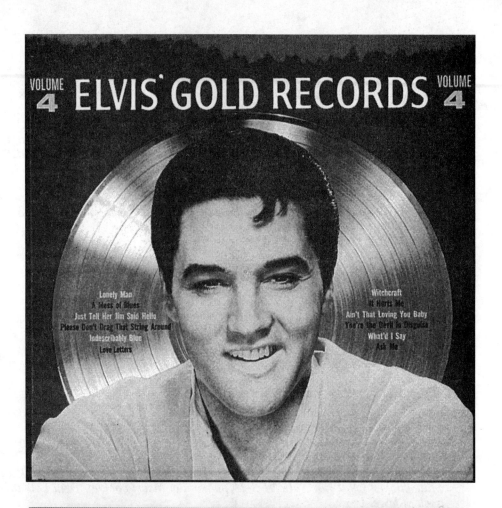

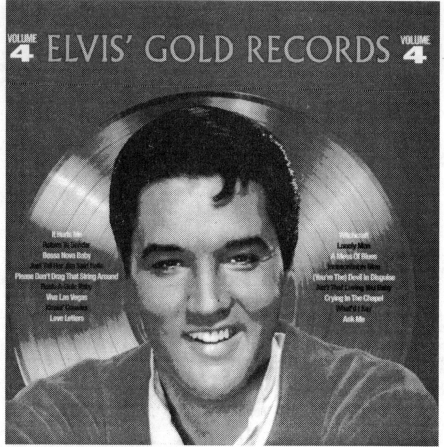

[ ] **ELVIS' GOLD RECORDS Volume 4**
Catalog# 1297-2-R   Value $ 12-15
Matrix# W.O. 14543-1 12972R
(July 1990 First Pressing. Midline CD. Silver & Black Disc with old RCA Logo.
Contains 4 page insert booklet.)
Disc contains the following selections:

Love Letters	You're The Devil In Disguise
Witchcraft	Lonely Man
It Hurts Me	A Mess Of Blues
What'd I Say	Ask Me
Please Don't Drag That String Around	Ain't That Loving You Baby
Indescribably Blue	Just Tell Her Jim Said Hello

[ ] **ELVIS' GOLD RECORDS Volume 4**
Catalog# 1297-2-R   Value $ 12-15
Matrix# 12972R 01# ++ 40845
(1994 Second Pressing. Midline CD. Silver & Black Disc with old RCA Logo.
Contains 4 page insert booklet.)

[ ] **ELVIS' GOLD RECORDS Volume 4**
Catalog# 1297-2-R   Value $ 12-15
Matrix# 12972R 01# ++ 40845
(1994 Third Pressing. Midline CD. Special Elvis in the '90's Silver Disc with
The RCA Records Label and Nipper above black line. Print in Black. Same disc
as used in the "Elvis His Life And Music" Ltd. Edition box set. "Wise Buy"
sticker on shrink wrap.)

[ ] **ELVIS' GOLD RECORDS Volume 4**
Catalog# 07863-67465-2   Value $ 13-18
Matrix# 07863674652 ++ 76353-01
(July 1997 Reissue. Disc is made to simulate a gold '45 record with Green Label
and White Print with simulated Gold spindle adapter. Contains 8 page insert
booklet. Back cover has new artwork, which is a color "Double Trouble"
publicity photo of Elvis. Aso contains 6 bonus tracks not included on all previous
issues. Gold collectors sticker with black print on front of shrink wrap. Wording
on sticker was printed for European market and does not apply to the U.S.
The 6 bonus tracks were not on the original U.S. LP. Digitally Remastered from
the original RCA Label Master Tapes.)
Disc contains the following selections:

Return To Sender	Please Don't Drag That String Around
Rock-A-Hula Baby	Indescribably Blue
Love Letters	(You're The) Devil In Disguise
Bossa Nova Baby	Lonely Man
Witchcraft	A Mess Of Blues
Kissin' Cousins	Ask Me
It Hurts Me	Ain't That Loving You Baby
Viva Las Vegas	Just Tell Her Jim Said Hello
What'd I Say	Crying In The Chapel

[ ] **ELVIS' GOLD RECORDS Volume 4 *(Promo)***
Catalog# 07863-67465-2   Value $ 15-20
Matrix# 07863674652 ++ 76353-01
(July 1997 Designated Promo. Same as regular catalog release with black and
white sticxker "Not For Sale NFS-1" on front of insert booklet. Drill hole thru
back of jewel box.)

[ ] **ELVIS' GOLD RECORDS** Volume 5
Catalog# PCD1-4941   Value $ 20-25
Matrix# PCD-14941 1A3-49
(May 1984 First Pressing. Silver & Blue Disc with block RCA Logo in white.
Contains 4 page insert booklet. Pressed in Japan for U.S. Release.)
Disc contains the following selections:

Suspicious Minds	Burning Love
Kentucky Rain	If You Talk In Your Sleep
In The Ghetto	For The Heart
Clean Up Your Own Back Yard	Moody Blue
If I Can Dream	Way Down

[ ] **ELVIS' GOLD RECORDS** Volume 5
Catalog# PCD1-4941   Value $ 15-20
Matrix# PCD-14941 1A9 5X
(1984 Second Pressing. Silver & Blue Disc with block RCA Logo in white.
Contains 4 page insert booklet. Pressed in Japan for U.S. Release.)

[ ] **ELVIS' GOLD RECORDS** Volume 5
Catalog# PCD1-4941   Value $ 12-15
Matrix# PCD-14941 2A2 D72
(1985 Third Pressing. Silver & Blue Disc with block RCA Logo in white.
Contains 4 page insert booklet. Pressed in U.S.)

[ ] **ELVIS' GOLD RECORDS** Volume 5
Catalog# PCD1-4941   Value $ 12-15
Matrix# PCD14941 3/88 2A54
(March 1988 Fourth Pressing. Silver & Blue Disc with block RCA Logo in white.
Contains 4 page insert booklet. Pressed in U.S.)

[ ] **ELVIS' GOLD RECORDS** Volume 5
Catalog# PCD1-4941   Value $ 12-15
Matrix# PCD14941 11/88 1DA2
(Nov. 1988 Fifth Pressing. Silver & Blue Disc with block RCA Logo in white.
Contains 4 page insert booklet. Pressed in U.S.)

[ ] **ELVIS GOLD RECORDS** Volume 5
Catalog# PCD1-4941   Value $ 12-15
Matrix# PCD14941 2/89 1DA3
(Feb. 1989 Sixth Pressing. Silver & Blue Disc with block RCA Logo in white.
Contains 4 page insert booklet. Pressed in U.S.)

[ ] **ELVIS' GOLD RECORDS** Volume 5
Catalog# PCD1-4941   Value $ 10-12
Matrix# PCD14941 4S 13
(1990 Seventh Pressing. Silver & Black Disc with old RCA Logo. Contains 4
*page insert booklet. **"Best Buy"** sticker on shrink wrap. Pressed in U.S.)*

[ ] **ELVIS' GOLD RECORDS** Volume 5
Catalog# PCD1-4941   Value $ 10-12
Matrix# PCD1-4941 32T 21
(1991 Eighth Pressing. Silver & Black Disc with old RCA Logo.
Contains 4 page insert booklet. "Best Buy" sticker on shrink wrap
Pressed in U.S.)

[ ] **ELVIS' GOLD RECORDS** Volume 5
Catalog# PCD1-4941   Value $ 20-30
BMG Music Service Catalog# D 143781
Matrix# PCD1-4941 4S 22
(1994 Ninth Pressing. Mfg. for BMG Direct Marketing, Inc. BMG Music
Service catalog number on disc and back insert cover. Silver & Black Disc
with old RCA Logo. Contains 4 page insert booklet. Pressed in U.S.
Only available from BMG Music CD Club. Mail Order Only.)

[ ] **ELVIS' GOLD RECORDS** Volume 5
Catalog# PCD1-4941   Value $ 10-12
Matrix# PCD14941 5F 11
(1995 Tenth Pressing. Silver & Black Disc with old RCA Logo. "Wise Buy"
sticker on shrink wrap. Contains 4 page insert booklet. Pressed in U.S.)

[ ] **ELVIS' GOLD RECORDS** Volume 5
Catalog# 07863-67466-2   Value $ 13-18
Matrix# 07863674662 ++ 76354-01
(July 1997 Reissue. Disc is made to simulate a gold '45 record with Medium Blue
Label and White Print with simulated Gold spindle adapter. Contains 8 page
insert booklet. Back cover has new artwork, which is a 1968 color publicity photo
of Elvis. Also contains 6 bonus tracks not included on all previous issues. Gold
collectors sticker with black print on front of shrink wrap. Wording os sticker was
printed for European market and does not apply to the U.S. The 6 bonus tracks
were not on the original U.S. LP. Digitally Remastered from the original RCA
Label Master Tapes.)
Disc contains the following selections:

Suspicious Minds	Way Down
Kentucky Rain	Big Boss Man
In The Ghetto	Guitar Man
Clean Up Your Own Back Yard	U.S. Male
Burning Love	You Don't Have To Say You Love Me
If You Talk In Your Sleep	Edge Of Reality
For The Heart	Memories
Moody Blue	If I Can Dream

[ ] **ELVIS' GOLD RECORDS** Volume 5 *(Promo)*
Catalog# 07863-67466-2   Value $ 15-20
Matrix# 07863674662 ++ 76354-01
(July 1997 Designated Promo. Same as regular catalog release with black and
white sticker "Not For Sale NFS-1" on front of insert booklet. Drill hole thru
back of jewel box.)

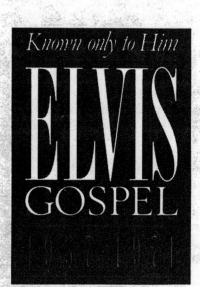

Known only to Him

ELVIS
GOSPEL

[ ]   **ELVIS GOSPEL 1957-1971: KNOWN ONLY TO HIM**
       Catalog# 9586-2-R   Value $ 14-18
       Matrix# W.O. 11713-1 95862R
       (April 1989 First Pressing. Silver & Black Disc with old RCA Logo. Four fold
       insert information booklet.)
       Disc contains the following selections:
       Peace In The Valley   Run On
       Take My Hand, Precious Lord   Where Could I Go But To The Lord
       I'm Gonna Walk Dem Golden Stairs   So High
       I Believe In The Man In The Sky   We Call On Him
       Joshua Fit The Battle   Who Am I
       Swing Down Sweet Chariot   Lead Me, Guide Me
       Stand By Me   Known Only To Him

[ ]   **ELVIS GOSPEL 1957-1971: KNOWN ONLY TO HIM**
       Catalog# 9856-2-R   Value $ 14-18
       Matrix# W.O. 11713-3M 95862R
       (1995 Second Pressing. Silver & Black Disc with old RCA Logo. Four fold insert
       information booklet.)

[ ] **ELVIS' GREATEST JUKEBOX HITS**
Catalog# 07863-67565-2   **Value $ 14-18**
Matrix# 07863675652 ++ 80449-01
*(Sept. 1997 First Pressing. Disc is made to simulate a '45 Black record with
Yellow Label and Black Print with simulated spindle adapter. Contained in a
wood grained tri-fold cardboard digi-pack with die-cut front cover. Grey, Yellow
and White collectors sticker "23 Smash Hits" on front cover of shrink wrap.
Digitally Remastered from the original RCA Label Master Tapes.)*
Disc contains the following selections:

Good Rockin' Tonight	Stuck On You
Baby, Let's Play House	It's Now Or Never
Heartbreak Hotel	Little Sister
Don't Be Cruel	Good Luck Charm
Hound Dog	She's Not You
Too Much	Return To Sender
All Shook Up	(You're The) Devil In Disguise
(Let Me Be Your) Teddy Bear	Viva Las Vegas
Jailhouse Rock	Suspicious Minds
Hard Headed Woman	Burning Love
I Got Stung	Way Down
A Big Hunk O' Love	

[ ] **ELVIS' GREATEST JUKEBOX HITS**   *(Promo)*
Catalog# 07863-67565-2   **Value $15-20**
Matrix# 07863675652 ++ 80449-01
*(Sept. 1997 Designated Promo. Same as regular catalog release with Black and
White sticker "Not For Sale NFS-1" on back of digi-pack over bar code.)*

[ ] **ELVIS' GREATEST JUKEBOX HITS**
Catalog# 07863-67565-2   **Value $ 20-30**
BMG Music Service Catalog# D 120986
Matrix# 07863675652 ++ 80449-01
*(Oct. 1997 Second Pressing. Mfg. for BMG Direct Marketing, Inc. BMG Music
Service catalog number on back of digi-pack over bar code. Only available from
BMG Music CD Club. Mail Order Only.)*

[ ] **ELVIS GREATEST JUKEBOX HITS**
Catalog# BG2-67565   **Value $ 20-30**
Matrix# DIDX-059604 1 A02
*(July 1998 Third Pressing. Mfg. by BMG Music for Columbia House Music Club,
a non-BMG Music CD Club. Columbia House Music Club catalog number on
disc, spine and back cover of digi-pack. CRC Logo printed above bar code on
back cover. Only available from Columbia House Music CD Club.
Mail Order Only.)*

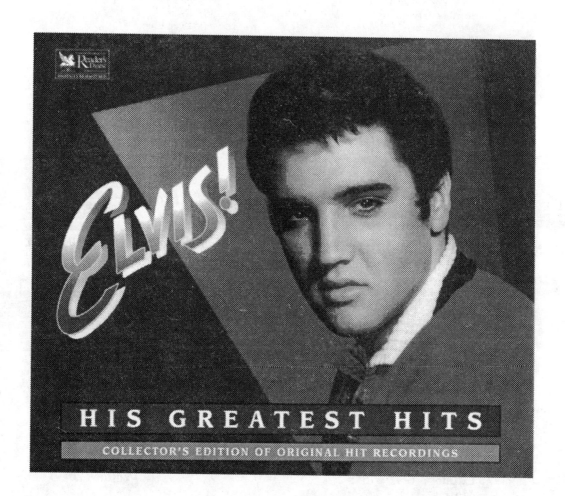

ELVIS! HIS GREATEST HITS *(4 CD Set)*

Catalog# RDU 010   **Value $ 55-60**

(Oct. 1996 Special Collectors Edition from Readers Digest Music. Turquoise and Grey Picture Discs with Turquoise and White Print. 4 CD's in multi-disc Jewel Box. Contains 48 page insert booklet. Mail Order Only.)

Disc #1 Elvis's Greatest Hits 1956-1958
Matrix# RD7A-010-1 ++ 68122-01
Disc contains the following selections:

Heartbreak Hotel
Don't Be Cruel (to a Heart That's True)
I Want You, I Need You, I Love You
Any Way You Want Me
Hound Dog
Love Me Tender
Too Much
That's When Your Heartaches Begin
Love Me
I Was The One
(Let Me Be Your) Teddy Bear

Playing For Keeps
Blue Suede Shoes
Loving You
All Shook Up
Treat Me Nice
Blue Christmas
Jailhouse Rock
I Beg Of You
Don't
Wear My Ring Around Your Neck

Disc #2 Elvis's Greatest Hits 1958-1961
Matrix# RD7A-010-2 ++ 68123-01
Disc contains the following selections:

One Night
King Creole
Hard Headed Woman
I Got Stung
A Fool Such As I
I Need Your Love Tonight
My Wish Came True
Doncha' Think It's Time
A Big Hunk O' Love
Are You Lonesome Tonight?
A Mess O' Blues

Stuck On You
I Gotta Know
Fame And Fortune
It's Now Or Never
Can't Help Falling In Love
Surrender
Little Sister
Flaming Star
I Feel So Bad
His Latest Flame

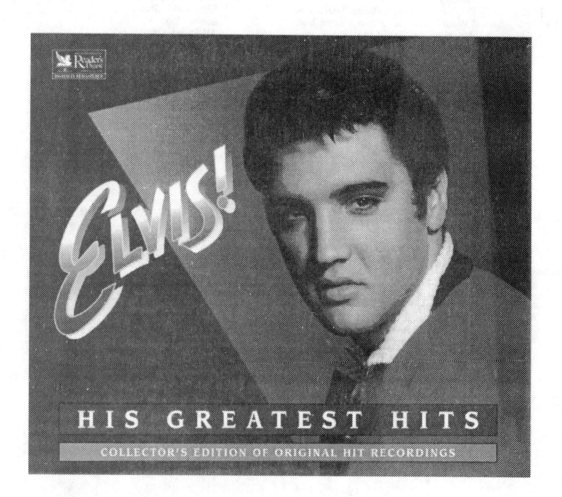

Disc #3 Elvis's Greatest Hits 1962-1969
Matrix# RD7A-010-3 ++ 68124-01
Disc contains the following selections:

Return To Sender
Good Luck Charm
Follow That Dream
Wooden Heart
She's Not You
Rock-A-Hula Baby
Blue Hawaii
One Broken Heart For Sale
Bossa Nova Baby
King Of The Whole Wide World
Ask Me

Such A Night
What'd I Say
Kiisin' Cousins
Ain't That Loving You Baby
You're The Devil In Disguise
Viva Las Vegas
(Such An) Easy Question
Puppet On A String
Kiss Me Quick
Don't Cry Daddy
If I Can Dream

Disc #4 Elvis's Greatest Hits 1969-1977
Matrix# RD7A-010-4 ++ 68311-01
Disc contains the following selections:

Suspicious Minds
In The Ghetto
You Don't Have To Say You Love Me
Burning Love

The Wonder Of You
Kentucky Rain
Steamroller Blues
My Way

Early Elvis 1954-1955

That's All Right
I'm Left, You're Right, She's Gone
Mystery Train

I Forgot To Remember To Forget
Baby, Let's Play House
You're A Heartbreaker

Country Classics

Your Cheatin' Heart
I Really Don't Want To Know
When My Blue Moon Turns To Gold Again

There Goes My Everything
Have I Told You Lately That I Love You
I Can't Stop Loving You

Numbered Limited Edition

Long Live the King!

Elvis Presley is the best-selling recording and pop-memorabilia star of all time. And now, you can follow his meteoric career with the ultimate Elvis celebration, Elvis: His Life and Music.

48 GOLDEN HITS, INCLUDING:

- TEDDY BEAR
- LOVE ME TENDER
- DON'T BE CRUEL
- ALL SHOOK UP
- WHAT'D I SAY
- (YOU'RE THE) DEVIL IN DISGUISE
- HEARTBREAK HOTEL
- HOUND DOG
- IT'S NOW OR NEVER
- WITCHCRAFT

Elvis: His Life and Music by *Timothy Frew*
- 176-page photobiography, oversized at 11¼" x 11¼"
- Over 200 color and black-and-white photographs and illustrations
- Illuminating text spans the King's life, from Tupelo to Graceland
- Comprehensive discography and filmography

Golden Hits of the 50s and 60s
- 4 digitally remastered CDs
- 48 essential tracks
- Each one a million-selling single

Session Journal by *Andrew G. Hager*
- 16 pages of session notes
- Invaluable information for the audiophile, including recording dates, personnel, and alternate takes
- Lavishly illustrated with rare and candid studio photographs

This numbered Collector's Edition of Elvis: His Life and Music *is a must for fans and friends alike. An invaluable collectible and the perfect gift for anyone who loves the King, this package is the final word on the legendary Elvis Presley.*

SUGGESTED RETAIL PRICE: $89.95

ISBN 1-56799-111-4 NB2I

FRIEDMAN/FAIRFAX PUBLISHERS
15 WEST 26 STREET NEW YORK, NY 10010

[ ]   **ELVIS - HIS LIFE AND MUSIC** *(Limited Edition Box Set)*

Value $ 90-100

(Aug. 1994 Release. 4 Digitally Remastered CD's containing Elvis' Gold Records, Volume 1-4. Special Elvis in the '90's Silver discs with The RCA Records Label and Nipper above black line. Print in Black. Contains 16 page Sessions Journal by Andrew G. Hager. Sessions notes and discs in 11-1/2" x 11-1/2" black gatefold cover. Information includes recording dates, personnel and alternate takes. Illustrated with rare studio photographs. Also included is a 176 page photobiography hardback book "Elvis: His Life and Music" by Timothy Frew. The book is oversized at 11-1/4" x 11-1/4" which contains over 200 color and black and white photos and illustrations. Text spans Tupelo to Graceland. Contains discography and filmography. Total package is housed in a black hard slipcase 11-3/4" x 11-3/4" x 1-1/2" and is a numbered Collector's Edition. Gold limited edition sticker on front of slipcase.
First sold through QVC Home Shopping Television Network.
Distributed by Friedman / Fairfax Publishers, New York, N.Y.)

Disc #1 ELVIS' GOLDEN RECORDS, Vol. 1
Catalog# PCD1-5196 Matrix# PCD15196 02# ++ 40388
Disc contains the following selections:

Hound Dog	Don't Be Cruel
Loving You	That's When Your Heartaches Begin
All Shook Up	(Let Me Be Your) Teddy Bear
Heartbreak Hotel	Love Me Tender
Jailhouse Rock	Treat Me Nice
Love Me	Anyway You Want Me
Too Much	I Want You, I Need You, I Love You

Disc #2 ELVIS' GOLD RECORDS, Vol. 2
Catalog# PCD1-5197 Matrix# PCD15197 02# ++ 40361
Disc contains the following selections:

I Need Your Love Tonight	One Night
Don't	A Big Hunk O' Love
Wear My Ring Around Your Neck	I Beg Of You
My Wish Came True	A Fool Such As I
I Got Stung	Doncha' Think Its Time

Disc #3 ELVIS' GOLDEN RECORDS, Vol. 3
Catalog# 2765-2-R Matrix# 27652R 02# ++ 40357
Disc contains the following selections:

It's Now Or Never	Are You Lonesome Tonight?
Stuck On You	(Marie's The Name) His Latest Flame
Fame And Fortune	Little Sister
I Gotta Know	Good Luck Charm
Surrender	Anything That's Part Of You
I Feel So Bad	She's Not You

Disc #4 ELVIS' GOLD RECORDS, Vol. 4
Catalog# 1297-2-R Matrix# 12972R 01# ++ 40845
Disc contains the following selections:

Love Letters	You're The Devil In Disguise
Witchcraft	Lonely Man
It Hurts Me	A Mess Of Blues
What'd I Say	Ask Me
Please Don't Drag That String Around	Ain't That Loving You Baby
Indescribably Blue	Just Tell Her Jim Said Hello

ELVIS IN CONCERT

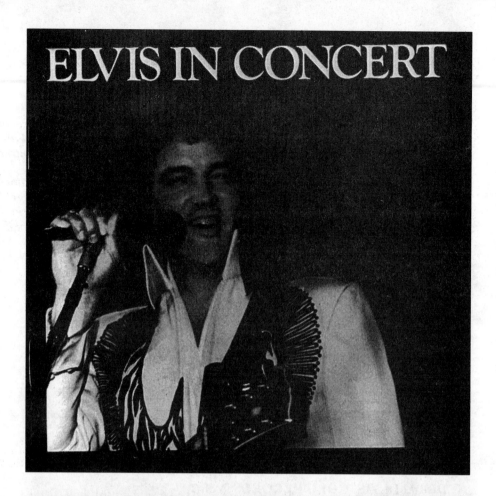

ELVIS IN HOLLYWOOD [50's THE]

CANDID
INTERVIEWS
featuring
EXCLUSIVE EXCERPTS from INTERVIEWS
with the following FRIENDS & ASSOCIATES

1 SCOTTY MOORE

2 JUNE JUANICO

3 JERRY LEIBER & MIKE STOLLER

4 BOB RELYEA

5 HAL KANTER

6 TRUDE FORSHER

7 GEORGE KLEIN

8 JAN SHEPARD

74321 15811 2
Running Time: 21.57

GOLDMAN-TAYLOR
ENTERTAINMENT CO

COMPACT
disc
DIGITAL AUDIO

©1993 Goldman-Taylor Entertainment Co., Inc. and Elvis Presley Enterprises, Inc.
under exclusive license to BMG Video International, a division of BMG Music.
Distributed by BMG, a Bertelsmann Music Group Company. All trademarks and logos are protected. Manufactured in the UK.

[ ] **ELVIS IN CONCERT**
Catalog# 07863 52587-2   **Value $ 15-20**
Matrix# 07863-52587-2-1 Y1D 11
*(May 1992 First Pressing. Elvis in the '90's Black Disc with old RCA
Logo and Print in Silver. 8 page insert booklet. Digitally Remastered
from the original RCA Label Master Tapes.)*
Disc contains the following selections:

Elvis Fans' Comments/Opening Riff	My Way
Also Sprach Zarathustra	Can't Help Falling In Love
See See Rider	Closing Riff/Message From Elvis' Father
That's All Right	I Got A Woman/Amen
Are You Lonesome Tonight?	Elvis Talks
Teddy Bear/Don't Be Cruel	Love Me
Elvis Fans' Comments II	If You Love Me (Let Me Know)
You Gave Me A Mountain	O Sole Mio/It's Now Or Never
Jailhouse Rock	Trying To Get To You
Elvis Fans' Comments III	Hawaiian Wedding Song
How Great Thou Art	Fairytale
Elvis Fans' Comments IV	Little Sister
I Really Don't Want To Know	Early Morning Rain
Elvis Introduces His Father	What'd I Say
Hurt	Johhny B. Goode
Hound Dog	And I Love You So

[ ] **ELVIS IN CONCERT**
Catalog# BG2-52587   **Value $ 20-30**
Matrix# E2 1ABG252587 01
*(1997 Second Pressing. Mfg. by BMG Music for Columbia House Music Club,
a non-BMG Music CD Club. Columbia House Music Club catalog number on
disc, spine, front and back insert cover. CRC Logo printed above bar code on
back insert cover. Elvis in the '90's Black Disc with old RCA Logo and Print in
Silver. 8 page insert booklet. Digitally Remastered from the original RCA Label
Master Tapes. Only available from Columbia House Music CD Club. Mail
Order Only.)*

[ ] **ELVIS IN HOLLYWOOD**
Catalog# 74321-15811-2   **Value $ 45-55**
Matrix# 74321158112
*(Dec. 1993 Limited Edition. Set sold through TV QVC Home Shopping Network.
5000 pressed, only 250 sold, balance returned to RCA warehouse. Comes in
12" x 9" Collectors Box. Package includes 65 min. Video, 16 page
full color booklet, 4 limited prints and bonus CD featuring rare and exclusive
interviews. Interviews with Elvis' friends and co-workers. No Elvis interviews
on disc. CD comes enclosed in cardboard Elvis picture sleeve. Disc pressed in
France for U.S. release.)*
Disc contains the following interviews:

Scotty Moore	Hal Kanter
June Juanico	Trude Forsher
Jerry Leiber & Mike Stoller	George Klein
Bob Relyea	Jan Shepard

ELVIS IN NASH VILLE

1956 — 1971

Between 1956 and 1971, Elvis Presley recorded some 250 songs at 26 sessions in Nashville. This album represents the first retrospective to focus on this enormous body of work.

(CONTINUED)

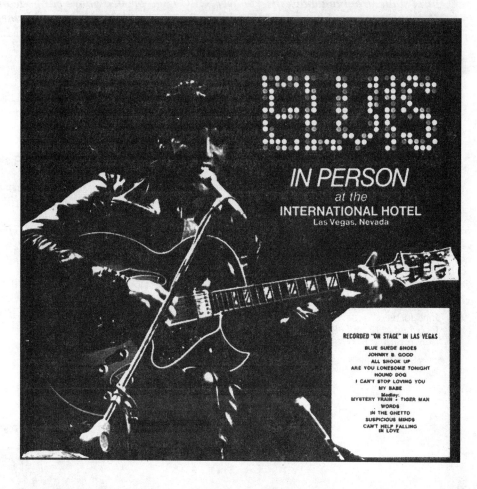

ELVIS

IN PERSON
at the
INTERNATIONAL HOTEL
Las Vegas, Nevada

RECORDED "ON STAGE" IN LAS VEGAS

BLUE SUEDE SHOES
JOHNNY B. GOOD
ALL SHOOK UP
ARE YOU LONESOME TONIGHT
HOUND DOG
I CAN'T STOP LOVING YOU
MY BABE
Medley:
MYSTERY TRAIN - TIGER MAN
WORDS
IN THE GHETTO
SUSPICIOUS MINDS
CAN'T HELP FALLING
IN LOVE

[ ]   **ELVIS IN NASHVILLE 1956-1971**

Catalog# 8468-2-R   **Value $ 20-25**

Matrix# C-4357/8468-2-R C

(Oct. 1988 First Pressing. Silver and Black Disc with old RCA Logo.
8 page insert booklet. Pressed in Germany for U.S. Release.
Contains alternate take of "Anything That's Part Of You".)
Disc contains the following selections:

I Got A Woman	Just Call Me Lonesome
A Big Hunk O' Love	Guitar Man
Working On The Building	Little Cabin On The Hill
Judy	It's Your Baby, You Rock It
Anything That's Part Of You *(Alternate Take1)*	Early Morning Rain
Night Rider	It's Still Here
Where No One Stands Alone	I, John

[ ]   **ELVIS IN NASHVILLE 1956-1971**

Catalog# 8468-2-R   **Value $ 30-40**

Matrix# 8468-2-R-3T 22

(1990 Second Pressing. Silver & Black Disc with old RCA Logo.
8 page insert booklet. This rare pressing made in U.S. Sold through
BMG Music Service CD Club. **RCA deleted this title from their catalog**
in April 1992.*)*

[ ]   **ELVIS IN PERSON AT THE INTERNATIONAL HOTEL**

Catalog# 07863-53892-2   **Value $ 12-15**

Matrix# W.O. 27769-1 07863538922

(Oct. 1992 First Pressing. Elvis in the '90's Black Disc with old RCA Logo
and Print in Siilver. 8 page insert booklet. Digitally Remastered from the
original RCA Label Master Tapes.)
Disc contains the following selections:

Blue Suede Shoes	Medley: Mystery Train/Tiger Man
Johnny B. Goode	Words
All Shook Up	In The Ghetto
Are You Lonesome Tonight?	Suspicious Minds
Hound Dog	Can't Help Falling In Love
I Can't Stop Loving You	
My Babe	

[ ]   **ELVIS IN PERSON AT THE INTERNATIONAL HOTEL**

Catalog# 07863-53892-2   **Value $ 20-30**

BMG Music Service Catalog# D 118726

Matrix# IFPI L239 07863538922 1J 13

(1996 Second Pressing. Mfg. for BMG Direct Marketing, Inc. BMG Music Serivce
catalog number on disc and insert covers. Elvis in the '90's Black Disc with old
RCA Logo and Print in Silver. 8 page insert booklet. Digitally Remastered from
the original RCA Label Master Tapes. Only available from BMG Music CD Club.
Mail Order Only.)

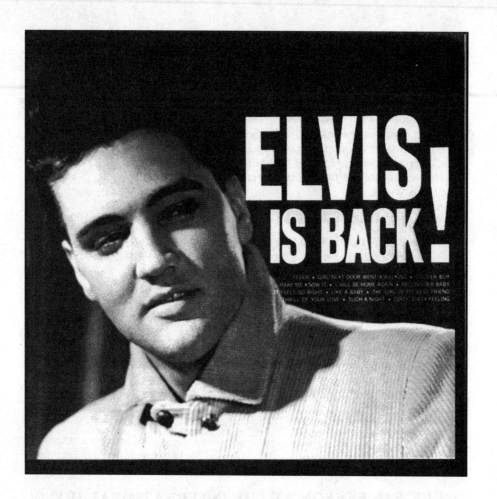

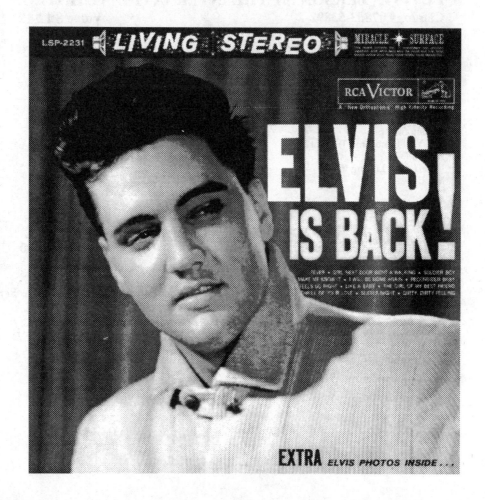

[ ] **ELVIS IS BACK!**
Catalog# 2231-2-R   Value $ 12-15
Matrix# W.O. 10683-1 22312R
(Nov. 1988 First Pressing. Midline CD. Silver & Black Disc with old RCA Logo.)
Disc contains the following selections:

Make Me Know It	Soldier Boy
Fever	Such A Night
The Girl Of My Best Friend	It Feels So Right
I Will Be Home Again	Girl Next Door Went A' Walking
Dirty, Dirty Feeling	Like A Baby
Thrill Of Your Love	Reconsider Baby

[ ] **ELVIS IS BACK!**
Catalog# 2231-2-R   Value $ 10-12
Matrix# W.O. 10683-2 22312R
(1991 Second Pressing. Midline CD. Silver & Black Disc with old RCA Logo.)

[ ] **ELVIS IS BACK!**
Catalog# 2231-2-R   Value $ 10-12
Matrix# W.O. 10683-3M 22312R
(1993 Third Pressing. Midline CD. Silver & Black Disc with old RCA Logo.)

[ ] **ELVIS IS BACK!**
Catalog# 2231-2-R   Value $ 10-12
Matrix# 22312R ++ 64596-01
(1996 Fourth Pressing. Midline CD. Silver & Black Disc with old RCA Logo.)

[ ] **ELVIS IS BACK!**
24 KARAT GOLD DISC
Catalog# GZS-1111   Value $ 25-35
Matrix# GZS1111-2
(June 1997 DCC Compact Classics 24 Kt. Gold Disc. Gold Disc with Black Print. Produced under license from BMG Direct Marketing Inc. CD and jewel case housed in slipcase. Gold disc is visable thru front of slipcase. Contains 8 page insert booklet which includes complete original artwork including "Living Stereo" logo. CD in Pop-Up Jewel Box. Limited Edition numbered sticker on back of slip case. Digitally Remastered from the original Master Tapes.)
Disc contains the following selections:

Make Me Know It	Soldier Boy
Fever	Such A Night *(With False Starts)*
The Girl Of My Best Friend	It FeelsSo Right
I Will Be Home Again	Girl Next Door Went A'Walking
Dirty, Dirty Feeling	Like A Baby
Thrill Of Your Love	Reconsider Baby

[ ] **ELVIS IS BACK!** *(Promo)*
24 KARAT GOLD DISC
Catalog# GZS-1111   Value $ 75-100
Matrix# GZS1111-2
(May 1997 Advance Promo for DCC Compact Classics 24 kt. Gold Disc. Gold Disc with Black Print. "Not For Sale" on center spindle of disc. CD housed in clear jewel box without art work. Contains same tracks as regular release.)

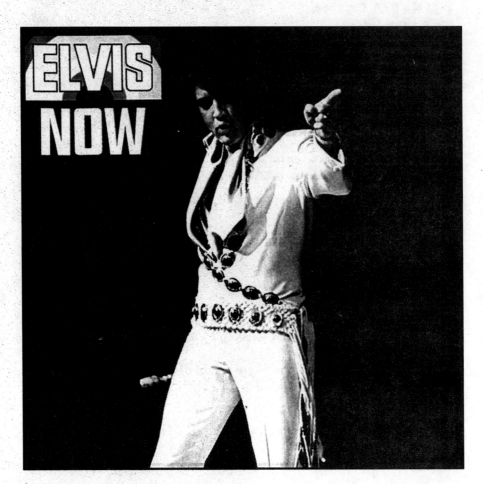

[ ] **ELVIS / NBC-TV SPECIAL**
Catalog# 07863-61021-2   **Value $ 12-15**
Matrix# W.O. 17779-2 07863610212
(Aug. 1991 First Pressing. Midline CD. Silver & Black Disc with old RCA Logo.
Newly restored disc including 8 Digitally Remastered Bonus Tracks not on the
original LP. Contains 8 page insert booklet. Back cover has photo of Elvis in
white suit "If I Can Dream"". This photo not used on original LP.)
Disc contains the following selections:
Trouble/Guitar Man
Lawdy,Miss Clawdy/Baby, What You Want Me To Do
Dialog/Medley:Heartbreak Hotel/Hound Dog/All Shook Up/Can't Help Falling In Love/
Jailhouse Rock/Don't Be Cruel/Blue Suede Shoes/Love Me Tender
Dialog/Where Could I Go But To The Lord/Up Above My Head/Saved
Baby, What You Want Me To Do/That's All Right /Blue Christmas/One Night/Tiger Man/
Trying To Get to You
Memories
Medley: Nothingville/Big Boss Man/Let Yourself Go/It Hurts Me/Guitar Man/Little Egypt/
Trouble/Guitar Man
If I Can Dream

[ ] **ELVIS/ NBC-TV SPECIAL**
Catalog# 07863-61021-2   **Value $ 12-15**
Matrix# W.O. 17779-3 07863610212
(1994 Second Pressing. Midline CD. Silver & Black Disc with old RCA Logo.
Contains 8 page insert booklet.)

[ ] **ELVIS/ NBC-TV SPECIAL**
Catalog# 07863-61021-2   **Value $ 12-15**
Matrix# 07863610212 ++ 64020-01
(1996 Third Pressing. Midline CD. Silver & Black Disc with old RCA Logo.
Contains 8 page insert booklet.)

[ ] **ELVIS/ NBC-TV SPECIAL**
Catalog# BG2-61021   **Value $ 20-30**
Matrix# E1 1ABG261021 01
(1997 Fourth Pressing. Mfg. by BMG Music for Columbia House Music Club,
a non-BMG Music CD Club. Columia House Music Club catalog number on
disc, spine, front and back insert cover. CRC Logo printed above bar code on
back insert cover. Silver & Black Disc with old RCA Logo. Contains 8 page
insert booklet. Only available from Columbia House Music CD Club. Mail
Order Only.)

[ ] **ELVIS NOW**
Catalog# 07863-54671-2   **Value $ 12-15**
Matrix# 078635-4671-2 01#
(June 1993 First Pressing. Elvis in the '90's Black Matte Disc with old RCA
Logo and Print in Silver. 4 page insert booklet. Digitally Remastered
from the original RCA Label Master Tapes.)
Disc contains the following selections:

Help Me Make It Through The Night	We Can Make The Morning
Miracle of the Rosary	Early Mornin' Rain
Hey Jude	Sylvia
Put Your Hand In The Hand	Fools Rush In
Until It's Time For You To Go	I Was Born About Ten Thousand Years Ago

[ ] **ELVIS PRESLEY**
Catalog# PCD1-1254   Value $ 250-300
Matrix# PCD-11254 1A1-48
(Sept. 1984 First Pressing in Electronic Stereo. Silver & Blue Disc with block
RCA Logo in white. Pressed in Japan for U.S. Release.)
Disc contains the following selections:

Blue Suede Shoes	Tutti Frutti
I'm Counting On You	Tryin' To Get to You
I Got A Woman	I'm Gonna Sit Right Down And Cry
One-Sided Love Affair	I'll Never Let You Go (Little Darlin')
I Love You Because	Blue Moon
Just Because	Money Honey

ELVIS PRESLEY
Catalog# PCD1-5198   Value $ 30-40
Matrix# DIDX 182 51A1
(Nov. 1984 Reissue. Digitally Remastered to Original Mono. DIDX on disc and
insert sleeve. Silver & Blue Disc with block RCA Logo in white. This title has
been given a new catalog number. Pressed in U.S.)

[ ] **ELVIS PRESLEY**
Catalog# PCD1-5198   Value $ 15-18
Matrix# PCD-15198 1A2 66 7
(1985 Second Pressing. Silver & Blue Disc with block RCA Logo
in white. Pressed in Japan for U.S. Release.)

[ ] **ELVIS PRESLEY**
Catalog# PCD1-5198   Value $ 12-15
Matrix# PCD-15198 1A3 62
(1985 Third Pressing. Silver & Blue Disc with block RCA Logo
in white. Pressed in U.S.)

[ ] **ELVIS PRESLEY**
Catalog# PCD1-5198   Value $ 12-15
Matrix# PCD-15198 2A1 D74
1986 Fourth Pressing. Silver & Blue Disc with block RCA Logo
in white. Pressed In U.S.)

[ ] **ELVIS PRESLEY**
Catalog# PCD1-5198   Value $ 12-15
Matrix# PCD-15198 11-87 2A52
(Nov. 1987 Fifth Pressing. Silver & Blue Disc with block RCA Logo
in white. Pressed in U.S.)

[ ] **ELVIS PRESLEY**
Catalog# PCD1-5198   Value $ 10-12
Matrix# PCD-15198 2C1 D75
(1990 Sixth Pressing. Silver & Blue Disc with block RCA Logo in white.
Pressed in U.S.)

[ ]   **ELVIS PRESLEY**
       Catalog# PCD1-5198   **Value $ 10-12**
       Matrix# PCD-15198 3/91 2C2X
       (March 1991 Seventh Pressing. Silver & Black Disc with old RCA Logo
       Pressed in U.S.)

[ ]   **ELVIS PRESLEY**
       Catalog# PCD1-5198   **Value $ 10-12**
       Matrix# PCD15198 7/92 1DA1
       (July 1992 Eighth Pressing. Silver & Blue Disc with block RCA Logo
       in white. Pressed in U.S.)

[ ]   **ELVIS PRESLEY**
       Catalog# PCD1-5198   **Value $ 10-12**
       Matrix# PCD15198 9/93 1DA4
       (Sept. 1993 Ninth Pressing. Silver & Blue Disc with block RCA Logo
       in white. Pressed in U.S.)

[ ]   **ELVIS PRESLEY**
       Catalog# PCD1-5198   **Value $ 10-12**
       Matrix# PCD15198 10/93 2DA1
       (Oct 1993 Tenth Pressing. Silver & Blue Disc with block RCA Logo
       in white. Pressed in U.S.)

[ ]   **ELVIS PRESLEY**
       Catalog# PCD1-5198   **Value $ 10-12**
       Matrix# PCD15198 1/95 2DB7
       (Jan. 1995 Elevemnth Pressing. Silver & Blue Disc with block RCA Logo
       in white. Pressed in U.S.)

[ ]   **ELVIS PRESLEY**
       Catalog# PCD1-5198   **Value $ 10-12**
       Matrix# PCD15198 2/95 2DB9
       (Feb. 1995 Twelfth Pressing. Silver & Blue Disc with block RCA Logo
       in white. Pressed in U.S.)

[ ]   **ELVIS PRESLEY**
       Catalog# PCD1-5198   **Value $ 10-12**
       Matrix# PCD15198 5/95 2DB10
       (May 1995 Thirteenth Pressing. Silver & Blue Disc with block RCA Logo
       in white. Pressed in U.S.)

[ ]   **ELVIS PRESLEY**
       Catalog# PCD1-5198   **Value $ 10-12**
       Matrix# PCD15198 4/96 2DB13
       (April 1996 Fourteenth Pressing. Silver & Blue Disc with block RCA Logo
       in white. Pressed in U.S.)

[ ]   **ELVIS PRESLEY**
            Catalog# PCD1-5198   **Value $ 10-12**
            Matrix# PCD15198 5/96 2DB17
            (May 1996 Fifteenth Pressing. Silver & Blue Disc with block RCA Logo
            in white. Pressed in U.S.)

[ ]   **ELVIS PRESLEY**
            Catalog# PCD1-5198   **Value $ 10-12**
            Matrix# PCD15198 6/96 2DB19
            (June 1996 Sixteenth Pressing. Silver & Blue Disc with block RCA Logo
            in white. Pressed in U.S.)

[ ]   **ELVIS PRESLEY**
            Catalog# PCD1-5198   **Value $ 10-12**
            Matrix# PCD15198 9/96 2DC2
            (Sept. 1996 Seventeenth Pressing. Silver & Blue Disc with block RCA Logo
            in white. Pressed in U.S.)

[ ]   **ELVIS PRESLEY**
            Catalog# PCD1-5198   **Value $ 10-12**
            Matrix# PCD15198 10/96 2DC4
            (Oct. 1996 Eighteenth Pressing. Silver & Blue Disc with block RCA Logo
            in white. Pressed in U.S.)

[ ]   **ELVIS PRESLEY**
            Catalog# PCD1-5198   **Value $ 20-30**
            Matrix# 5 PCD 05198-2 SRC@@01 M1S2
            (1997 Ninteenth Pressing. Mfg. by BMG Music for Columbia House Music Club,
            a non-BMG Music CD Club. Silver & Black Disc with block RCA Logo in white.
            Only available from Columbia House Music CD Club. Mail Order Only.
            Pressed in U.S.)

[ ]   **ELVIS PRESLEY**
            Catalog# PCD1-5198   **Value $ 10-12**
            Matrix# *4D* PCD15198 1FP1L431 B 5A
            (May 1998 Twentieth Pressing. Silver & Blue Disc with block RCA Logo
            in white. Pressed in U.S.)

COLLECTOR'S EDITION • 24 KARAT GOLD DISC

ELVIS PRESLEY

24 KARAT GOLD DISC
A Classic CD For The Serious Collector

Ultimate Audio Quality & Clarity
State-of-the-art audio restoration
Remastered from original first generation
session & multi-track tapes

Deluxe Packaging
original artwork, liner notes, lyrics & credits

Let *YOUR EARS* Decide
GOLD • 2

INTERVIEW PICTURE DISC AND FULLY ILLUSTRATED BOOK

ELVIS PRESLEY

COLLECTORS EDITION

[ ] **ELVIS PRESLEY** *(Collector's Edition)*
Catalog# 07863-66659-2   Value $ 30-35
Matrix# 07863666592 1H 12
(July 1995 First Pressing. RCA Collectors's Edition - 24 kt. Gold Disc.
CD and jewel case housed in slipcase. The gold disc is visable thru a window
in the back of the slipcase. Large block Elvis Presley in Black on Gold Disk.
Collectors black and white sticker on shrink wrap "A Classic CD For The Serious
Collector - Ultimate Audio Quality & Clarity - State Of The Art Audio
Restoration - Remastered From Original First Generation Session & Multi-track
Tapes. Deluxe Packaging - Original Artwork, Liner Notes, Lyrics & Credits -
Let YOUR EARS Decide - Gold -2". Contains 4 page insert booklet. Booklet
does not contain lyrics as noted on sticker. **RCA deleted this title from their**
catalog in July, 1998.)
Disc contains the following selections:

Blue Suede Shoes	Tutti Frutti
I'm Counting On You	Tryin' To Get To You
I Got A Woman	I'm Gonna Set Right Down And Cry
One Sided Love Affair	I'll Never Let You Go (Little Darlin')
I Love You Because	Blue Moon
Just Because	Money Honey

[ ] **ELVIS PRESLEY** *(Collector's Edition Promo)*
Catalog# 07863-66659-2   Value $ 35-40
Matrix# 07863666592 1H 12
(July 1995 Designated Promo. Same as regular catalog release with black and
white sticker "For Promotion Only Not For Sale P-4/2" on back cover of
the slipcase.)

[ ] **ELVIS PRESLEY**
INTERVIEW PICTURE DISC AND FULLY ILLUSTRATED BOOK
Catalog# 8046   Value $ 7-10
Matrix# MT8046 (97118207)
(Dec. 1996 MasterTone MultiMedia Ltd. Release. Picture Disc with an exclusive
Elvis interview. Package contains collectors edition interview picture disc with
fully illustrated 118 page book and a chronological discography. Housed in
cardboard slipcase. Back of slipcase lists compact disc made in U.S.A. Book
printed in U.K. Printing on disc "Made In Holland". Sold thru "Best Buy" stores.)
Disc contains following Elvis Interviews:

Texarkana Interview	Biloxi, Mississippi Interview
St. Petersburg, Florida Interview	Houston Press Conference 3/27/70
Wichita Falls Interview	New York 1972 Press Conference
New Orleans Interview	

THE ELVIS PRESLEY BIRTHDAY TRIBUTE
UNISTAR
RADIO PROGRAMMING
FROM Ed Salamon, President/Programming
TO: "THE ELVIS PRESLEY BIRTHDAY TRIB
THE ELVIS PRESLEY BIRTHDAY TRIBUTE
UNISTAR
RADIO PROGRAMMING
Elvis Presley Birthday

[ ]   The **ELVIS PRESLEY BIRTHDAY TRIBUTE** *(4 CD Radio Show)*
Catalog# Unistar 01/03 - 01/08   **Value $ 100-125**
*(Jan. 1992 Limited Edition 4 CD Radio Show from the Unistar Radio Network
Silver Elvis Picture Disc with Blue Print. Contains Cue Sheets for 4 hour Elvis
Radio Show broadcast 1/3 - 1/8. Disc and Cue Sheets enclosed in "the Original
CD Shortbox". Drawing of Elvis on Shortbox.)*

Disc #1
Matrix# A7X20100C Hour 1
Disc contains the following selections:

All Shook Up   Can't Help Falling In Love
Are You Lonesome Tonight?   Crying In The Chapel
Baby, Let's Play House   Don't
Big Hunk O' Love   Don't Be Cruel
Blue Suede Shoes   Don't Cry Daddy
Bossa Nova Baby   Elvis Medley
Burning Love   Good Luck Charm

Disc #2
Matrix# A7X30100A Hour 2
Disc contains the following selections:

Guitar Man   I Gotta Know
Hard Headed Woman   I Need Your Love Tonight
Heartbreak Hotel   I Want You, I Need You, I Love You
Hound Dog   If I Can Dream
I Beg Of You   I'm Yours
I Feel So Bad   In The Ghetto
I Got Stung   It's Now Or Never
                                      Jailhouse Rock

Disc #3
Matrix# A7X40100C Hour 3
Disc contains the following selections:

Kentucky Rain   Moody Blue
(Let Me Be Your) Teddy Bear   My Way
Little Sister   Mystery Train
Love Me   (Now And Then There's) A Fool Such As I
Love Me Tender   One Broken Heart For Sale
Loving You   One Night
(Marie's The Name) His Latest Flame   Promised Land

Disc #4
Matrix# A7X50100C Hour 4
Disc contains the following selections:

Return To Sender   That's All Right Mama
Separate Ways   Too Much
She's Not You   Treat Me Nice
Steamroller Blues   Viva Las Vegas
Stuck On You   Way Down
Surrender   Wear My Ring Around Your Neck
Suspicious Minds   The Wonder Of You
                                      (You're The) Devil In Disguise

Page 179

The **ELVIS PRESLEY COLLECTION** *(2 CD's)*
COUNTRY
Catalog# R806-04 07863-69403-2   **Value $ 20-25**

*(Jan. 1998 First Pressing. BMG Release for Time/Life Music. 2 CD's housed in Double Slimline jewel case. Lavender and Black Picture Discs with Silver and Black Print. BMG, RCA and Time/Life Logos on discs and insert sleeves. 16 page insert booklet. Blue, white and black sticker **"Includes An Unreleased Bonus Cut"** on shrink wrap. This is the fourth of a series of Elvis Time/Life CD's, each having a different theme and containing a previously unreleased song. This CD contains the previously unreleased undubbed master of "Snowbird" from Sept. 1970 Nashville recording session. Mail Order Only.)*

Disc #1
Matrix# 07863694032D1 ++ 82865-02
Disc contains the following selections:

Blue Moon Of Kentucky
When My Blue Moon Turns To Gold Again
A Fool Such As I
You Don't Know Me
Gentle On My Mind
It Keeps Right On A-Hurtin'
From A Jack To A King
Make The World Go Away

Kentucky Rain
Good Time Charlie's Got The Blues
Are You Sincere
She Thinks I Still Care
I've Got A Thing About You Baby
He'll Have To Go
I'm So Lonesome I Could Cry

Disc #2
Matrix# 07863694032D2 ++ 82861-01
Disc contains the following selections:

I Forgot To Remember To Forget
Have I Told You Lately That I Love You
Old Shep
Your Cheatin' Heart
Just Call Me Lonesome
Early Morning Rain
Green, Green Grass Of Home
There Goes My Everything

Moody Blue
I Really Don't Want To Know
I'm Movin' On
Blue Eyes Crying In The Rain
Take Good Care Of Her
Funny How Time Slips Away
Welcome To My World
Snowbird *(Undubbed Master)*

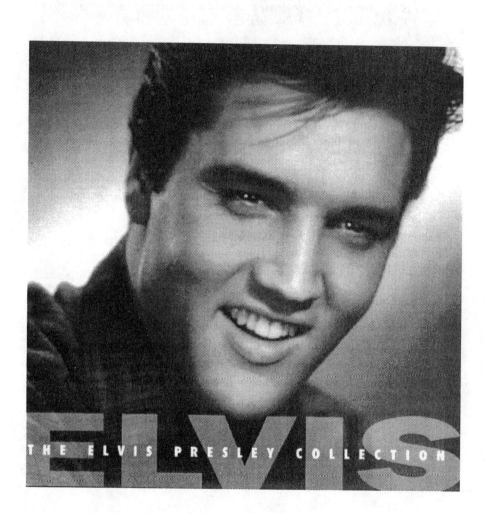

THE ELVIS PRESLEY COLLECTION

[ ] The **ELVIS PRESLEY COLLECTION** *(2 CD's)*
FROM THE HEART
Catalog# R806-03 07863-69402-2   Value $ 20-25
(Feb. 1998 First Pressing. BMG Release for Time/Life Music. 2 CD's housed in Double Slimline jewel case. Green and Black Pixcture Discs with Silver and Black Print. BMG, RCA and Time/Life Logos on discs and insert sleeves. 16 page insert booklet. Blue, white and black sticker "Includes An Unreleased Bonus Cut" on shrink wrap. This is Volume 3, but was released as the fifth in the series of Elvis Time/Life CD', each having a different theme and containing a previously unreleased song. This CD contains the previously unreleased song "Separate Ways" an alternate take from March 27, 1972. Mail Order Only.)
Disc #1
Matrix# 07863694022D1 ++ 83933-02
Disc contains the following selections:

You Don't Have To Say You Love Me
Without Love (There Is Nothing)
In The Ghetto
Memories
Mama Liked The Roses
Spanish Eyes
I'm Leavin'
Let It Be Me

Mary In The Morning
It's Only Love
Fool
I've Lost You
Danny Boy
Hurt
My Way *(Studio Master)*

Disc #2
Matrix# 07863694022D2 ++ 83909-01
Disccontains the following selections:

Only The Strong Survive
Any Day Now
Don't Cry Daddy
If I Can Drream
Fools Rush In (Where Angels Fear To Tread)
Bridge Over Troubled Water
It's Impossible
An American Trilogy

Rags To Riches
For Ol' Times Sake
My Boy
Pieces Of My Life
The Last Farewell
I'll Never Fall In Love Again
Pledging My Love
Separate Ways *(Alternate Take)*

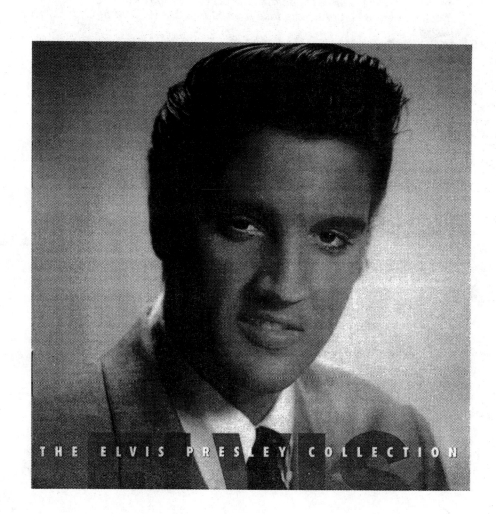

THE ELVIS PRESLEY COLLECTION

[ ]

The **ELVIS PRESLEY COLLECTION** *(2 CD's)*
GOSPEL
Catalog# R806-09 07863-69408-2   Value $ 20-25

*(Sept. 1998 First Pressing. BMG Release for Time/Life Music. 2 CD's housed in Double Slimline jewel case. Light Blue and Black Picture Discs with Silver and Black Print. BMG, RCA and Time/Life Logos on discs and insert sleeves. 16 page insert booklet. Blue, white and black sticker "**Includes An Unreleased Bonus Cut**" on shrink wrap. This is the ninth of a series of Elvis Time/Life CD's, each having a different theme and containing a previously unreleased song. This CD contains the previously unreleased alternate tale of "We Call On Him" from the September 1967 RCA Nashville sessions. Mail Order Only.)*

Disc #1
Matrix# 07863694082D1 ++ 90246-01
Disc contains the following selections:

Joshua Fit The Battle
I Believe In The Man In The Sky
(There'll Be) Peace In The Valley
I Believe
Mansion Over The Hilltop
Working On The Building
His Hand In Mine
Crying In The Chapel

By And By
How Great Thou Art
You'll Never Walk Alone
Bosom Of Abraham
Stand By Me
He Touched Me
He Is My Everything
Amazing Grace

Disc #2
Matrix# 07863694082D2 ++ 90267-01
Disc contains the following selections:

Swing Down Sweet Chariot
Milky White Way
It Is No Secret (What God Can Do)
He Knows Just What I Need
Take My Hand, Precious Lord
I'm Gonna Walk Them Golden Stairs
If We Never Meet Again
In The Garden

Run On
Known Only To Him
Farther Along
Where Could I Go But To The Lord
Where No One Stands Alone
Reach Out To Jesus
We Call On Him *(Alternate Take)*

[ ]   The **ELVIS PRESLEY COLLECTION** *(2 CD's)*
LOVE SONGS
Catalog# R806-01 07863-69400-2   Value $ 20-25

*(Sept. 1997 First Pressing. BMG Release for Time/Life Music. 2 CD's housed in Double Slimline jewel case. Red and Black Picture Discs with Silver and Black Print. BMG, RCA and Time/Life Logos on discs and insert sleeves. 16 page insert booklet. Blue, white and black sticker **"Includes An Unreleased Bonus Cut"** on shrink wrap. This is the first of a series of Elvis Time/Life CD's, each having a different theme and containing a previously unreleased song. This CD contains the previously unreleased song "If I Loved You" from a 1966 home recording. The first 50 orders of this CD received the 12"x11" hardback book "Elvis" 20th Anniversary Edition. Mail Order Only.)*

Disc #1
Matrix# 07863694002D1 ++ 80757-01
Disc contains the following selections:

Love Me
Don't
Loving You
It's Now Or Never
Are You Lonesome Tonight?
Young And Beautiful
Starting Today
That's Someone You Never Forget

Surrender
Anything That's Part Of You
I'm Yours
Suspicious Minds
Until It's Time For You To Go
Always On My Mind
The Wonder Of You

Disc #2
Matrix# 07863694002D2 ++ 80778-01
Disc contains the following selections:

I Want You, I Need You, I Love You
Love Me Tender
I Was The One
Anyway You Want Me
Puppet On A String
Can't Help Falling In Love
Love Letters
Blue Hawaii

Suspicion
As Long As I Have You
She's Not You
Lovin' Arms
Help Me Make It Through The Night
For The Good Times
I Just Can't Help Believin'
If I Loved You *(Home Recording)*

THE ELVIS PRESLEY COLLECTION

[ ]   The **ELVIS PRESLEY COLLECTION** *(2 CD's)*
MOVIE MAGIC
Catalog# R806-05 07863-69404-2   **Value $20-25**
*(Dec. 1997 First Pressing. BMG Release for Time/Life Music. 2 CD's housed in
Double Slimline jewel case. Mustard and Black Picture Discs with Silver and
Black Print. BMG, RCA and Time/Life Logos on discs and insert sleeve.
16 page insert booklet. Blue, white and black sticker "**Includes An Unreleased
Bonus Cut**" on shrink wrap. This is Volume 5 but was released as third in the
series of Elvis Time/Life CD's, each having a different theme and containing
a previously unreleased song. This CD contains the previously unreleased song
"Little Egypt" an alternate take from "Roustabout". Mail Order Only.)*
Disc #1
Matrix# 07863694042D1 ++ 82477-01
Disc contains the following selections:

Party
Got A Lot O' Livin' To Do!
Lonesome Cowboy
Treat Me Nice
(You're So Square) Baby I Don't Care
Danny
Crawfish
Wooden Heart

King Of The Whole Wide World
Home Is Where The Heart Is
Girls! Girls! Girls!
They Remind Me Too Much Of You
Viva Las Vegas
C'Mon Everybody
Let Yourself Go

Disc #2
Matrix# 07863694042D2 ++ 82753-01
Disc contains the following selections:

Mean Woman Blues
Loving You *(Fast Version)*
I Want To Be Free
Jailhouse Rock *(Movie Version)*
Trouble
King Creole
Shoppin' Around
Pocketful Of Rainbows

Follow That Dream
Flaming Star
Can't Help Falling In Love *(Alt. Take 23)*
One Broken Heart For Sale
Bossa Nova Baby
The Lady Loves Me *(with Ann-Margret)*
I'll Be Back
Little Egypt *(Alternate Take 21)*

THE ELVIS PRESLEY COLLECTION

[ ]

The ELVIS PRESLEY COLLECTION *(2 CD's)*
RHYTHM & BLUES
Catalog# R806-08 07863-69407-2   Value $ 20-25

*(July 1998 First Pressing. BMG Release for Time/Life Music. 2 CD's housed in Double Slimline jewel case. Orange and Black Picture Discs with Silver and Black Print. BMG, RCA and Time/Life Logos on disc and insert sleeve. 16 page insert booklet. Blue, white and black sticker "**Includes Unreleased Bonus Cut**" on shrink wrap. This is the eighth of a series of Elvis Time/Life CD's, each having a different theme and containing a previously unreleased song. This CD contains the previously unreleased alternate take of "Wearin' That Loved On Look" from the 1969 Memphis American Studios sessions. Mail Order Only.)*

Disc #1
Matrix# 07863694072D1 ++ 85531-01
Disc contains the following selections:

Milk Cow Blues Boogie
My Baby Left Me
One Night Of Sin
Ain't That Loving You Baby *(Fast Ver. Alt Take 11)*
Any Place Is Paradise
Such a Night
It Feels So Right
I Feel So Bad

Like A Baby
Memphis Tennessee
Big Boss Man
Trying To Get to You *(NBC TV Special)*
After Loving You
Medley: Got My Mojo Working/
Keep Your Hands Off Of It
Steamroller Blues
Shake A Hand

Disc #2
Matrix# 07863694072D2 ++ 85979-01
Disc contains the following selections:

Baby Let's Play House
So Glad You're Mine
When It Rains, It Really Pours
I Need You So
A Mess Of Blues
Tell Me Why
Fever
Reconsider Baby

What'd I Say
Down In The Alley
Medley: Lawdy, Miss Clawdy/
Baby, What You Want Me To Do*(NBC TV)*
Tiger Man *(NBC TV Special)*
My Babe
Just A Little Bit
Wearin' That Loved On Look *(Alt. Take)*

[ ]

The ELVIS PRESLEY COLLECTION *(2 CD's)*
ROCK 'N' ROLL
Catalog# R806-02 07863-69401-2   **Value $ 20-25**

*(Nov. 1997 First Pressing. BMG Release for Time/Life Music. 2 CD's housed in
Double Slimline jewel case. Blue and Black Picture Discs with Silver and Black
Print. BMG, RCA and Time/Life Logos on discs and insert sleeve. 16 page insert
booklet. Blue, white and black sticker "Includes An Unreleased Bonus Cut"
on shrink wrap. This is the second of a series of Elvis Time/Life CD's, each
having a different theme and containing a previously unreleased song. This CD
contains the previously unreleased song "Baby What You Want Me To Do" from
a 1968 dressing room jam session. Mail Order Only.)*

Disc #1
Matrix# 07863694012D1 ++ 81696-01
Disc contains the following selections:

Good Rockin' Tonight	Hard Headed Woman
Hound Dog	(Let Me Be Your) Teddy Bear
Jailhouse Rock	Return to Sender
Tryin' To Get to You	(Marie's The Name) His Latest Flame
Wear My Ring Around Your Neck	(You're The) Devil In Disguise
One Night	Guitar Man
I Need Your Love Tonight	U.S. Male
Too Much	Burning Love

Disc #2
Matrix# 07863694012D2 ++ 81695-01
Disc contains the following selections:

That's All Right	Stuck On You
Heartbreak Hotel	Little Sister
Blue Suede Shoes	Good Luck Charm
Don't Be Cruel	Hi-Heel Sneakers
Ready Teddy	The Promised Land
All Shook Up	T-R-O-U-B-L-E
Lawdy, Miss Clawdy	Baby What You Want Me To Do
A Big Hunk O' Love	*(Dressing Room Jam)*

[ ]

The ELVIS PRESLEY COLLECTION   *(2 CD's)*
THE ROCKER
Catalog# R806-06 07863-69405-2   **Value $ 20-25**

*(April 1998 First Pressing. BMG Release for Time/Life Music. 2 CD's housed in Double Slimline jewel case. Green and Black Picture Discs with Silver and Black Print. BMG, RCA and Time/Life Logos on discs and insert sleeve. 16 page insert booklet. Blue, white and black sticker "**Includes An Unreleased Bonus Cut**" on shrink wrap. This is the sixth of a series of Elvis Time/Life CD's, each having a different theme and containing a previously unreleased song. This CD contains the previously unreleased alternate take of "Burning Love" from the March 1972 RCA Hollywood sessions. Mail Order Only.)*

Disc #1
Matrix# 07863694052D1 ++ 84233-01
Disc contains the following selections:

Mystery Train	Girl Of My Best Friend
Long Tall Sally	Rock-A-Hula Baby
Paralyzed	Kissin' Cousins
I Got Stung	Dirty, Dirty Feeling
Tutti Frutti	The Fool
I Beg Of You	I Washed My Hands In Muddy Water
Doncha Think It's Time	See See Rider
Make Me Know It	Way Down

Disc #2
Matrix# 07863694052D2 ++ 84234-01
Disc contains the following selections:

Money Honey	Put The Blame On Me
Rip It Up	I'm Comin' Home
Shake, Rattle And Roll	Witchcraft
One-Sided Love Affair	Too Much Monkey Business
Ain't That Loving You Baby	Patch It Up
Hot Dog	Polk Salad Annie
Dixieland Rock	Burning Love *(Alternate Take)*
I Gotta Know	

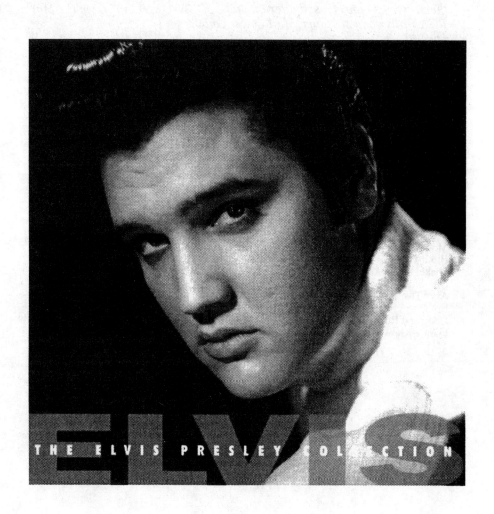

[ ]

The ELVIS PRESLEY COLLECTION *(2 CD's)*
THE ROMANTIC
Catalog# R806-07 07863-69406-2   **Value $ 20-25**

(June 1998 First Pressing. BMG Release for Time/Life Music. 2 CD's housed in Double Slimline jewel case. Pink and Black Picture Disc with Silver and Black Print. BMG, RCA and Time/Life Logos on disc and insert sleeve. 16 page insert booklet. Blue, white and black sticker "Includes An Unreleased Bonus Cut" on shrink wrap. This is the seventh of a series of Elvis Time/Life CD's, each having a different theme and containing a previously unreleased song. This CD contains the previously unreleased alternate take of "For The Good Times" from the March 1972 RCA Hollywood sessions. Mail Order Only.)

Disc #1
Matrix# 07863694062D1 ++ 84865-01
Disc contains the following selections:

That's When Your Heartaches Begin
True Love
Fame And Fortune
My Wish Came True
I Will Be Home Again
It Hurts Me
Starting Today
Something Blue

Tonight Is So Right For Love
(Such An) Easy Question
Angel
Please Don't Stop Loving Me
If I'm A Fool (For Loving You)
I'll Hold You In My Heart (Till I Can Hold You In My Arms)
Just Pretend

Disc #2
Matrix# 07863690462D2 ++ 84868-01
Disc contains the following selections:

Blue Moon
Playing For Keeps
Soldier Boy
Doin' The Best I Can
Give Me The Right
Hawaiian Wedding Song
For The Millionth And The Last Time
I Need Somebody To Lean On

Kiss Me Quick
Wild In The Country
There's Always Me
Ask Me
Indescribably Blue
It's Midnight
And I Love You So
For The Good Times *(Alternate Take)*

Page 197

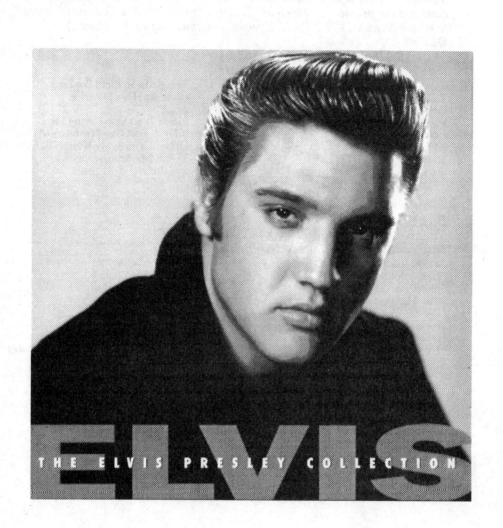

[ ] The **ELVIS PRESLEY COLLECTION** *(2 CD's)*
TREASURES '53 TO '58
Catalog# R806-10 07863-69409-2   Value $ 20-25
(Oct. 1998 First Pressing. BMG Release for Time/Life Music. 2 CD's housed in Double Slimline jewel case. Light Blue and Black Picture Discs with Silver and Black Print. BMG, RCA and Time/Life Logos on discs and insert sleeves. 16 page insert booklet. Blue, white and black sticker **"Includes An Unreleased Bonus Cut"** *on shrink wrap. This is the tenth of a series of Elvis Time/Life CD's, each having a different theme and containing a previously unreleased song. This CD contains the previously unreleased alternate take of "I Was The One" from the January 1956 RCA Nashville sessions. Mail Order Only.)*
Disc #1
Matrix# 07863694092D1 ++ 91826-01
Disc contains the following selections:
That's When Your Heartaches Begin *(1953 Acetate)*   Money Honey *(1956 Dorsey Bros. Show)*
I Don't Care If The Sun Don't Shine   How Do You Think I Feel
Tomorrow Night   Is It So Strange
I'm Left, You're Right, She's Gone   Don't Leave Me Now
I Love You Because   New Orleans
I'm Gonna Sit Right Down And Cry (Over You)   Lover Doll
We're Gonna Move   Don't Ask Me Why
How's The World Treating You   TV Guide Interview

Disc #2
Matrix# 07863694092D2 ++ 91828-01
Disc contains the following selections:
Blue Moon Of Kentucky *(Alternate Take 1)*   Too Much *(1957 Ed Sullivan Show)*
Harbor Lights   Blueberry Hill
Just Because   First In Line
You're A Heartbreaker   Loving You *(Uptempo Ver. Alt. Take 13)*
I'll Never Let You Go (Little Darlin')   Young Dreams
Poor Boy   Steadfast, Loyal And True
Let Me   I Was The One *(Alternate Take 3)*
I'm Counting On You

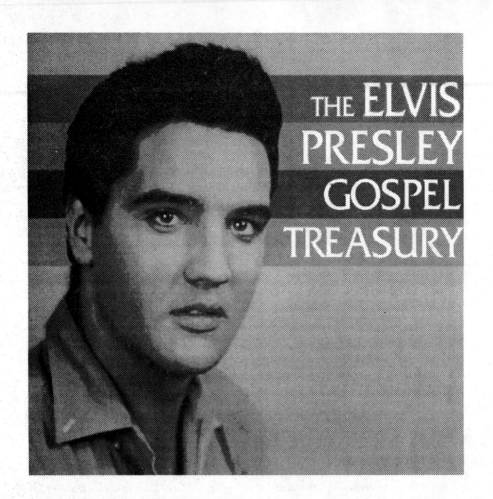

THE ELVIS
PRESLEY
GOSPEL
TREASURY

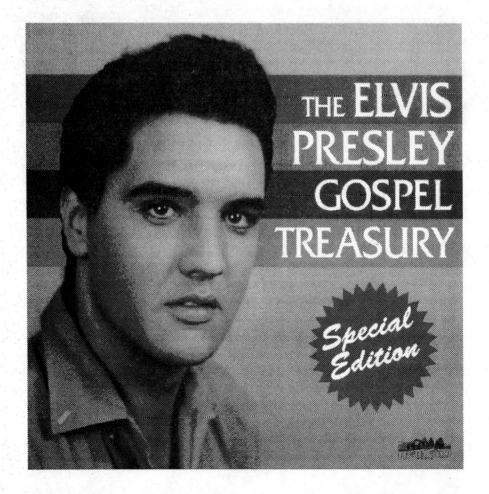

THE ELVIS
PRESLEY
GOSPEL
TREASURY

Special Edition

[ ]   The **ELVIS PRESLEY GOSPEL TREASURY** *(2 CD's)*
        Catalog# 3571-2 DMC2-1427   **Value $ 20-25**
        (Dec. 1996 First Pressing. BMG Special Products Release for Heartland Music.
        2 CD's housed in Double Slimline jewel case. Silver Discs with Black Print.
        BMG Special Products and Heartland Music Logos on discs and insert sleeves.
        4 page insert booklet. Black, white and grey sticker **"Contains Two CD's"** *on*
        shrink wrap. Selection #12 on Disc 1 "Where No One Stands Alone" incorrectly
        listed as "Where No Man Stands Alone" on both disc and insert sleeves. Available
        from TV ad or direct from Heartland Music.)
        Disc #1
        Matrix# L385 1100 DMC214271 C61209-16
        Disc contains the following selections:

Amazing Grace	Bosom Of Abraham
In The Garden	I Believe
Joshua Fit The Battle	Crying In The Chapel
How Great Thou Art	I'm Gonna Walk Dem Golden Stairs
Farther Along	Where No Man Stands Alone
Milky White Way	It Is No Secret
Peace In The Valley	

Disc #2
Matrix# L385 1100 DMC214272 C61209-05
Disc contains the following selections:

Swing Down Sweet Chariot	Working On The Building
Where Could I Go But To The Lord	Mansion Over The Hilltop
You'll Never Walk Alone	Stand By Me
Reach Out To Jesus	He Knows Just What I Need
Take My Hand Precious Lord	If We Never Meet Again
By And By	His Hand In Mine
He Touched Me	

[ ]   The **ELVIS PRESLEY GOSPEL TREASURY** *(Special Edition)*
        Catalog# H004-29 TCD-804   **Value $ 15-25**
        Matrix# L385 1108 TCD804 C71123-05 A
        (Nov.1997 BMG Special Products Release for Heartland Music. Available only
        from Publishers Clearing House in September and October of 1998. Silver Disc
        with Black Print. BMG Special Products and Heartland Music Logos on discs
        and insert sleeves. "Special Edition " on front and back covers. Mail Order
        Only.)
        Disc contains the following selections:

Amazing Grace	Working On The Building
Joshua Fit The Battle	Take My Hand, Precious Lord
How Great Thou Art	Where Could I Go But To The Lord
Farther Along	He Touched Me
Milky White Way	(There'll Be) Peace In The Valley
In The Garden	Crying In The Chapel

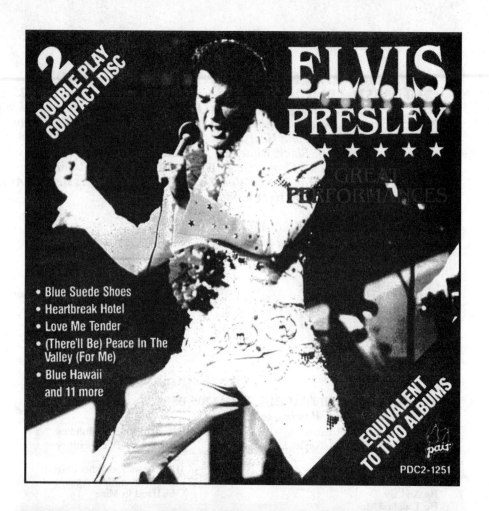

ELVIS PRESLEY: GREAT PERFORMANCES

[ ]

Catalog# PDC2-1251 CXD-3018   Value $ 10-12
Matrix# W.O. 13478-1 PDC1-1251

*(Jan. 1990 First Pressing. RCA Special Products Release on the Pair Label.
Silver & Black Disc with RCA & Nipper Logos in Blue. Disc pressed in Canada
for release in U.S. Back cover Black with Red and White Print. 4 page insert
booklet contains the Pair Records CD catalog selections.)*

Disc contains the following selections:

That's All Right	I Want You, I Need You, I Love You
Heartbreak Hotel	Blue Hawaii
Don't Be Cruel	Jailhouse Rock
Trying To Get To You	It's Now Or Never
Love Me Tender	Blue Suede Shoes
Peace In The Valley	Such A Night
Tonight's All Right For Love	Baby What You Want Me To Do
Can't Help Falling In Love	If I Can Dream

ELVIS PRESLEY: GREAT PERFORMANCES

[ ]

Catalog# PCD-2-1251 CXD-3018   Value $ 10-12
No Matrix Number

*(1993 Second Pressing. RCA Special Products on the Pair Label. Silver & Black
Disc with Pair, RCA & Nipper Logos in Red. Disc pressed in U.S. All else same
as first pressing. Matrix number trailed off and unreadable.)*

ELVIS PRESLEY: GREAT PERFORMANCES

[ ]

Catalog# PDC-2-1251 CXD-3018   Value $ 10-12
Matrix# PDC2-1251 15117 A011

*(1994 Third Pressing. RCA Special Products on the Pair Label. Silver & Blue
Disc with Pair Records Rocks Label in Black & White. Disc pressed in U.S.
Insert front cover different from other pressings. ESX Entertainment Label on
back cover. Back cover Tan with Black Print. 4 page insert booklet contains ESX
Label and 2 page history of Elvis.)*

THE

LASERLIGHT AUDIO BOOK ON CD

PRESLEY INTERVIEWS

3 CD - SET

TALKING WITH THE KING

WRITTEN & NARRATED
BY GEOFFREY GIULIANO

LASERLIGHT
DIGITAL
55 581

[ ]   The **ELVIS PRESLEY INTERVIEWS**   *(3 CD Set)*
TALKING WITH THE KING
Catalog# 55 581   **Value $ 15-20**
(Sept. 1996 Release from Laserlight Digital. This is a Laserlight Audio Book
Set on CD. Contains 3 CD's in a slipcase. The 3 CD's are also sold individually.
All Discs are Silver and Yellow with Black Print. Written and Narrated by
Geoffrey Giuliano. These are interview only CD's.)
Disc #1 IN THE BEGINNING
Matrix# 12787 Y6718G IFPI L532
Disc contains the following interviews:
Introduction
Presley Interview 1962 Part 1
Presley Interview 1962 Part 2
Presley Interview A
Presley Interview B
Presley Interview Little Rock, Arkansas

Disc #2 EYE OF THE HURRICANE
Matrix# 12788 Y6718B IFPI L532
Disc contains the following interviews:
Introduction
Presley Interview Lakeland, Florida Aug. 6, 1956
Presley Interview Ottawa, Canada
Presley Interview New York, New York
Presley Interview C
Presley Interview D
Presley Press Conference

Disc #3 ON THE ROAD INTERVIEWS
Matrix# 12789 Y6723C IFPI L532
Disc contains the following interviews:
Introduction
Presley Press Conference, 1961 Part 1
Presley Press Conference, 1961 Part 2
Presly in La Crosse Interview
Presley Interview E
Presley Interview F
Presley Interview G

[ ]   **ELVIS PRESLEY & JIM REEVES CHRISTMAS FAVORITES**
           Catalog# ATCD-2107-2   Value $ 15-20
           Matrix# W.O. 17534-1 ATCD2107-2
           (May 1991 RCA Special Products Release. Sold only in budget Department
           Stores during the Christmas season. Distributed by Audio Treasures Inc.
           Troy, Michigan. Silver Disc with block RCA & Nipper in Red. Print in Black.
           Back insert cover White with Black Print. This is one of four CD's using Elvis
           *with one other artist. **This release is now deleted.**)*
           Disc contains the following selections:

Here Comes Santa Claus - *Elvis*	I'll Be Home For Christmas - *Elvis*
Silent Night - *Jim Reeves*	Jingle Bells - *Jim Reeves*
Blue Christmas - *Elvis*	Take My Hand Precious Lord - *Elvis*
O Little Town Of Bethlehem - *Jim Reeves*	Silver Bells - *Jim Reeves*
O Come All Ye Faithful - *Jim Reeves*	Peace In the Valley - *Elvis*

[ ]   **ELVIS PRESLEY & JIM REEVES CHRISTMAS FAVORITES**
           Catalog# ATCD-2107-2   Value $10-15
           Matrix# DDX2508-3 01# ++ 30805
           (Oct. 1996 Reissue from RCA Special Products. Sold only in budget Department
           Stores during Christmas season. This is the same disc used on the Deco Disc
           Pop-Out CD and Ornament. Now housed in jewel case with insert cover as above
           but with dark green border around photo on front insert cover. Back insert cover
           is Green with Print in White and Black. Contains same six tracks as on
           Deco Disc.)
           Disc contains the following selections:

Elvis Presley Sings...	**Jim Reeves Sings...**
Blue Christmas	Jingle Bells
Here Comes Santa Claus	Silent Night
It Is No Secret (What God Can Do)	Silver Bells
Take My Hand, Precious Lord	O Come, All Ye Faithful
(There'll Be) Peace In The Valley (For Me)	O Little Town Of Bethlehem
I'll Be Home For Christmas	An Old Christmas Card

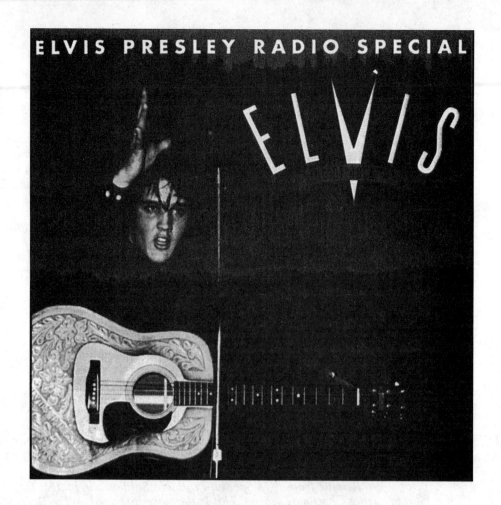

ELVIS PRESLEY RADIO SPECIAL

ELVIS

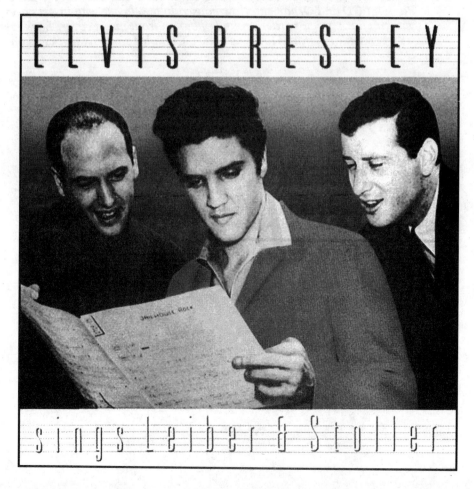

ELVIS PRESLEY

sings Leiber & Stoller

[ ] **ELVIS PRESLEY RADIO SPECIAL** *(Promo)*
Catalog# RDJ-66121-2   Value $ 50-75
Matrix# W.O. 76797-2 RDJ661212
*(Nov. 1992 Promo Only CD issued to promote the Complete 50's Masters Box
Set. Contains 17 Tracks plus Interviews. Also comes with Radio Survey Postcard.
Silver Disc - RCA and Elvis in the '90's Logos and Print in Black.*
"Promo Only - Not For Sale" *on CD and insert sleeve.)*
Disc contains the following selections:

That's All Right	Love Me
Mystery Train	Let Me Be Your Teddy Bear
Heartbreak Hotel	One Night Of Sin
Hound Dog	Don't
Don't Be Cruel	Blue Christmas
Blue Suede Shoes	Jailhouse Rock
Love Me Tender	Treat Me Nice
All Shook Up	A Big Hunk O' Love
That's When Your Heartaches Begin	Theme Music: Nine String Blues

[ ] **ELVIS PRESLEY SINGS LEIBER & STOLLER**
Catalog# 3026-2-R   Value $ 15-20
Matrix# W.O. 16429-1 30262R
*(April 1991 First Pressing. Midline CD. Silver & Black Disc with old RCA Logo.
Contains 6 page trifold insert booklet. First CD to contain the unreleased
Elvis - Ann-Margret duet "You're The Boss".)*
Disc contains the following selections:

Hound Dog	King Creole
Love Me	Steadfast, Loyal And True
Loving You	Dirty, Dirty Feeling
Hot Dog	Just Tell Her Jim Said Hello
I Want To Be Free	Girls! Girls! Girls!
Jailhouse Rock	Bossa Nova Baby
Treat Me Nice	You're The Boss *(with Ann-Margret)*
Baby I Don't Care	Little Egypt
Santa Claus Is Back In Town	Fools Fall In love
Don't	Saved
Trouble	

[ ] **ELVIS PRESLEY SINGS LEIBER & STOLLER**
Catalog# 3026-2-R   Value $ 15-20
Matrix# W.O. 16429-2M 30262R
*(1994 Second Pressing. Midline CD. Silver & Black Disc with old RCA Logo.
Contains 6 page trifold insert booklet.)*

[ ] **ELVIS PRESLEY SINGS LEIBER & STOLLER**
Catalog# 3026-2-R   Value $ 15-20
Matrix# 64845-01 30262R
*(1995 Third Pressing. Midline CD. Silver & Black Disc with old RCA Logo.
Contains 6 page trifold insert booklet.* ***RCA deleted this title from their catalog
in 1996.****)*

DELUXE 4 CD SET

ELVIS

The King Of
Rock & Roll
At His Best...

Greatest Hits

Movie Hits

Gospel Hits

Interviews

[ ]

ELVIS PRESLEY- *(4 CD Box Set)*
THE KING OF ROCK & ROLL AT HIS BEST
Catalog# S4D-4965 SC   Value $ 100-150

*(Sept. 1991 RCA Special Products Release for The Special Music Co.
Distributed by Entertainment Distributing Inc. Eugene, Oregon. Packaged
in a Special Longbox. Discs were pressed in Canada for release in U.S. Silver
Discs with Logos in Blue. Printing in Black. All 4 discs were originally released
as single CD's in 1980's. Longbox has color photo of Elvis In Concert on front
cover. Back cover has color photos of the 4 CD's. The 4 CD's are housed in a
Library Slipcase inside the Longbox. **This set has now been deleted.**)*

Disc #1 YOU'LL NEVER WALK ALONE
Matrix# Y28 CAD1-2472
Disc contains the following selections:

You'll Never Walk Alone
Who Am I?
Let Us Pray
Peace In The Valley
We Call On Him

I Believe
It Is No Secret (What God Can Do)
Sing You Children
Take My Hand, Precious Lord

Disc #2 BURNING LOVE AND HITS FROM HIS MOVIES Vol. 2
Matrix# Y2E CAD1-2595
Disc contains the following selections:

Burning Love
Tender Feelings
Am I Ready
Tonight Is So Right For Love
Guadalajara

It's A Matter Of Time
No More
Santa Lucia
We'll Be Together
I Love Only One Girl

Disc #3 A LEGENDARY PERFORMER, Volume 1
Matrix# CVC1 <005> CAD1-2705
Disc contains the following selections:

That's All Right
Heartbreak Hotel
Elvis *(excerpt from interview Sept.22,1958)*
Don't Be Cruel
Trying To Get To You
Love Me Tender

Peace In The Valley
Elvis *(excerpt from interview Sept.22,1958)*
Tonight's All Right For Love
Can't Help Falling In Love

Disc #4 A LEGENDARY PERFORMER, Volume 2
Matrix# B43 <005> CAD1-2706
Disc contains the following selections:

Harbor Lights
I Want You, I Need You, I Love You
Blue Hawaii
Jailhouse Rock
It's Now Or Never

Blue Suede Shoes
Such A Night
Baby What You Want Me To Do
How Great Thou Art
If I Can Dream

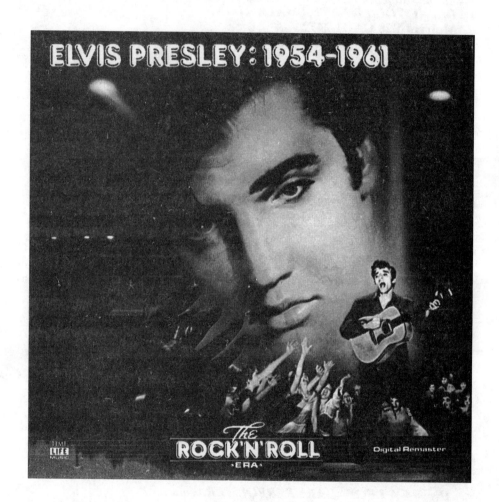

[ ]

ELVIS PRESLEY: 1954-1961

Catalog# 2RNR-06 TCD-106

Value $ 15-20

Matrix# W.O. 10015-2 TCD-106

(March 1988 Time/Life Music Release. Silver Disc with Black Print.
Contains 8 page insert booklet with Discography. Mail Order Only.
Digitally Remastered. This CD is part of the Time/Life Rock 'N' Roll Era series.)
Disc contains the following selections:

That's All Right	Hard Headed Woman
Heartbreak Hotel	One Night
Hound Dog	Wear My Ring Around Your Neck
Love Me Tender	A Fool Such As I
Don't Be Cruel	Don't
All Shook Up	A Big Hunk O' Love
I Want You, I Need You, I Love You	It's Now Or Never
Jailhouse Rock	Stuck On You
Love Me	Are You Lonesome Tonight?
Teddy Bear	Little Sister
Too Much	Can't Help Falling In Love

[ ]

ELVIS PRESLEY: 1954-1961

Catalog# 2RNR-06 TCD-106

Value $ 15-20

Matrix# L384 1100 TCD106 B60604-02

(1997 Second Pressing from Time/Life Music. Silver Disc with Black Print.
Contains 8 page insert booklet with Discography. Mail Order Only.
Digitally Remastered. This CD is part of the Time/Life Rock 'N' Roll Era series.
Red & White sticker "Double Length Equivement to 2 LP's" on shrink wrap.)

ELVIS
HEARTBREAK HOTEL
DON'T BE CRUEL
HOUND DOG
LOVE ME TENDER
SUSPICIOUS MINDS
IN THE GHETTO
RETURN TO SENDER
TEDDY BEAR
IT'S NOW OR NEVER
KENTUCKY RAIN
CAN'T HELP FALLIN' IN LOVE WITH YOU
AND MANY MORE!
COMPACT disc DIGITAL AUDIO

[ ]   **ELVIS PRESLEY - 50 GREATEST HITS** *(2 CD Box Set)*
        Catalog# 15018-2   **Value $ 150-200**
        (Oct. 1991 RCA Special Products Release. Packaged in a Special Longbox.
        Distributed by Entertainment Distributing Inc. Eugene, Oregon. Longbox
        printed in Canada. Both Discs were originally released as a 2 CD Set
        "Elvis - 50 Years - 50 Hits" without the longbox. Box has color "Aloha" photo of
        Elvis on front cover. Back cover has song titles. Two CD's in multi disc jewel box.
        Silver Disc with block RCA Logo and Nipper in Red. Print in Black. Mail Order
        Only. This set has now been deleted.)
        Disc #1 Volume 1
        Matrix# SVC2-0710-1 1S
        Disc contains the following selections:

Heartbreak Hotel   All Shook Up
Don't Be Cruel   Love Me Tender
I Want You, I Need You, I Love You   What'd I Say
(You're The) Devil In Disguise   Don't
I Need Your Love Tonight   One Broken Heart For Sale
Too Much   Danny Boy
Viva Las Vegas   Teddy Bear
Hound Dog   Good Luck Charm
Old Shep   Suspicious Minds
The Wonder Of You   Treat Me Nice
Loving You   Return To Sender
Kissin' Cousins   If I Can Dream
Suspicion

Disc #2 Volume II
Matrix# SVC2-0710-2 1S
Disc contains the following selections:

A Big Hunk O' Love   Stuck On You
One Night   (Such An) Easy Question
Such A Night   Hard Headed Woman
Love Me   I Beg Of You
Don't Cry Daddy   You Don't Have To Say You Love Me
Wear My Ring Around Your Neck   Crying In The Chapel
It's Now Or Never   She's Not You
My Wish Came True   Puppet On A String
I Got Stung   Moody Blue
(Now And Then There's) A Fool Such As I Surrender
Blue Hawaii   In The Ghetto
Kentucky Rain   Memories
Can't Help Falling In Love

[ ] **ELVIS RECORDED LIVE ON STAGE IN MEMPHIS**
Catalog# 07863-50606-2   Value $ 12-15
Matrix# 0786350606-2 01#
*(March 1994 First Pressing. Elvis in the '90's Black Disc with The RCA
Records Label and Nipper above new silver line. Print in Silver. Contains 8
page insert booklet. Digitally Remastered from the original RCA Label
Master Tapes.)*
Disc contains the following selections:

See See Rider   Medley:*Blueberry Hill/*
I Got A Woman   *I Can't Stop Loving You*
Love Me   Help Me
Trying To Get To You   An American Trilogy
Medley: *Long Tall Sally/*   Let Me Be There
Whole Lotta Shakin' Goin' On/   My Baby Left Me
Mama Don't Dance/Flip,Flop & Fly/   Lawdy, Miss Clawdy
Jailhouse Rock/Hound Dog   Can't Help Falling In Love
Why Me Lord   Closing-Vamp
How Great Thou Art

[ ] **ELVIS RECORDED LIVE ON STAGE IN MEMPHIS** *(Promo)*
Catalog# 07863-50606-2 NFS-1   Value # 15-20
Matrix# 0786350606-2 01#
*(March 1994 Designated Promo. Same as regular catalog release with Black and
White sticker "Not For Sale NFS-1" on front cover of jewel box. Drill hole thru
back of jewel box.)*

[ ] **ELVIS SINGS FOR CHILDREN AND GROWNUPS TOO!**
Catalog# CAD1-2704   Value $ 7-10
Matrix# CAD1-2704 SRC-01
*(Aug. 1989 RCA Special Products Release. Distributed by The Special Music Co.
Disc pressed in Canada for Release in Canada & U.S. Silver & Black Disc
with RCA Logo in Blue.)*
Disc contains the following selections:

Teddy Bear   Old MacDonald
Wooden Heart   How Would You Like To Be
Five Sleepyheads   Cotton Candy Land
Puppet On A String   Old Shep
Angel   Have A Happy

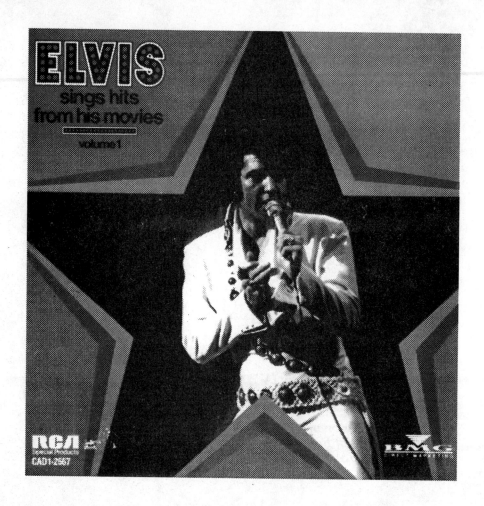

ELVIS SINGS HITS FROM HIS MOVIES Volume 1
Catalog# CAD1-2567   Value $ 20-25
Matrix# IFPI L238 CAD12567 2H 12
*(June 1996 First Pressing. RCA Special Products Release for AVON.
Silver & Black Disc with block RCA Logo, Nipper and Special Products in Blue.
Mail Order Only. This title now deleted.)*
Disc contains the following selections:

Down By The Riverside/
When The Saints Go Marching In
They Remind Me Too Much Of You
Confidence
Frankie And Johnny
Guitar Man

Long Legged Girl(With The Short DressOn)
You Don't Know Me
How Would You Like To Be
Big Boss Man
Old MacDonald

[ ]

ELVIS SINGS THE WONDERFUL WORLD OF CHRISTMAS
Catalog# 4579-2-R   Value $ 12-15
Matrix# W.O. 10525-1 45792R
*(Aug. 1988 First Pressing. Midline CD. Silver & Black Disc with old RCA Logo.
Contains one Bonus Track not on the original Album. Black Background with
White Print on back cover.)*
Disc contains the following selections:

O Come, All Ye Faithful
The First Noel
On A Snowy Christmas Night
Winter Wonderland
The Wonderful World Of Christmas
It Won't Seem Like Christmas (Without You)

I'll Be Home On Christmas Day
If I Get Home On Christmas Day
Holly Leaves And Christmas Trees
Merry Christmas Baby *(Extended Version)*
Silver Bells
Blue Christmas *(Bonus Track)*

[ ]

ELVIS SINGS THE WONDERFUL WORLD OF CHRISTMAS
Catalog# 4579-2-RRE   Value $ 10-12
Matrix# W.O. 10525-1 45792R
*(Oct. 1993 Second Pressing. Midline CD. Silver & Black Disc with old RCA
Logo. White Background with Black Print on back cover.)*

[ ]

ELVIS SINGS THE WONDERFUL WORLD OF CHRISTMAS
Catalog# 4579-2-RRE   Value $ 10-12
Matrix# W.O. 10525-2M 45792R
*(Sept. 1994 Third Pressing. Midline CD. Silver & Black Disc with old RCA
Logo. White Background with Black Print on back cover.)*

[ ]

ELVIS SINGS THE WONDERFUL WORLD OF CHRISTMAS
Catalog# 4579-2-RRE   Value $ 10-12
Matrix# W.O. 10425-3 45792R
*(Oct. 1995 Fourth Pressing. Midline CD. Silver & Black Disc with old RCA
Logo. White Background with Black Print on back cover. "Wise Buy" sticker
on shrink wrap.)*

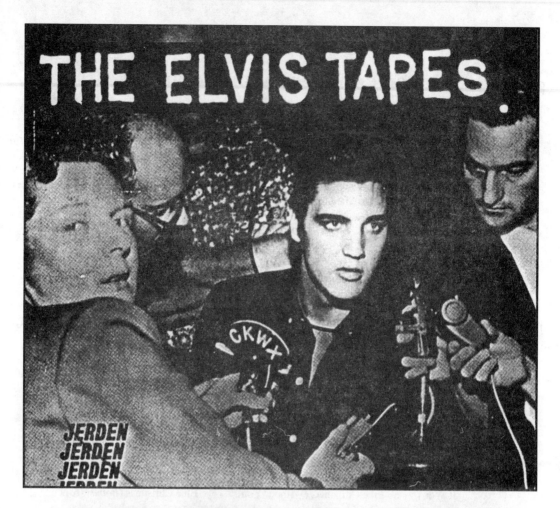

THE ELVIS TAPES

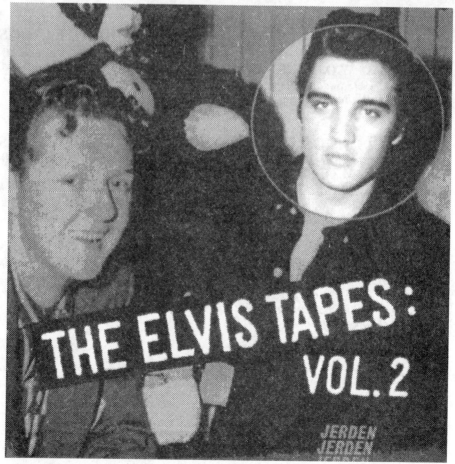

THE ELVIS TAPES: VOL. 2

[ ] **The ELVIS TAPES**
Catalog# JRCD 7005   Value $ 10-15
Matrix# TS 92056
(1992 Interview Only CD. Released on the Jerden Label. Produced by
Redwood Music Inc., Vancouver, B.C., Canada. Issued by the Great
Northwest Music Co. in the U.S. Silver Disc with Black Print & Green Logo.
Comes in oversized cardboard gatefold sleeve. Part of the ReUnion Series.)
Disc contains the following interviews:
Elvis Interview Vancouver, Canada 1957   Elvis In Memphis 1961

[ ] **The ELVIS TAPES**
Catalog# JRCD 7005   Value $ 10-15
Matrix# 5 JRCD 7005-2 SRC*02 **** M3S1 ****
(1994 Second Pressing. Released on the Jerden Label. Produced by
Redwood Music Inc., Vancouver, B.C., Canada. Issued by the Great Northwest
Music Co. in the U.S. Silver Disc with Black Print & Green Logo. Comes in
oversized cardboard gatefold sleeve. Part of the ReUnion Series.)

[ ] **The ELVIS TAPES VOL. 2**
Catalog# JRCD 7017   Value $ 15-18
Matrix# C2 123483-02 JRCD 7017
(Sept. 1997 First Pressing. Released on the Jerden Records Label. Silver Disc
with Black Print and Green Logo. Contained in a regular jewel box.)
Disc contains the following interviews:
Elvis On CKOY, Ottawa, Canada 1957   Elvis Armed Forces Radio Germany 1960
Elvis With Peter Noone, Hawaii 1965

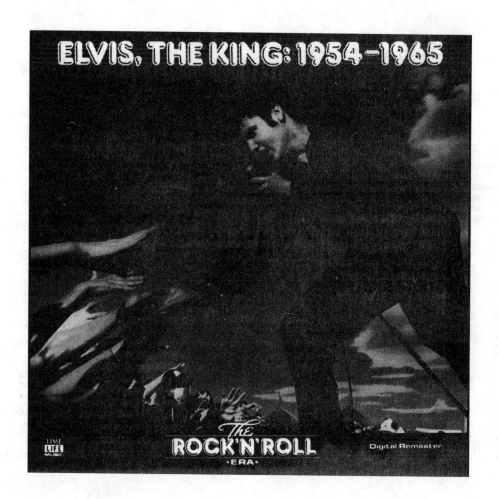

[ ] **ELVIS, THE KING: 1954-1965**
Catalog# 2RNR-26 TCD-126   Value $ 15-20
Matrix# W.O. 13755-2 TCD-126
(1990 First Pressing from Time/Life Music. Silver Disc with Black Print.
Contains 8 page insert booklet with Discography. Mail Order Only.
Digitally Remastered. This CD is part of the Time/Life Rock 'N' Roll Era series.
Red & White sticker "Double Length Equivalent to 2 LP's " on shrink wrap.)
Disc contains the following selections:

Good Rockin' Tonight	Party
My Baby Left Me	I Feel So Bad
Any Way You Want Me	Return To Sender
Blue Suede Shoes	(You're The) Devil In Disguise
Lawdy, Miss Clawdy	I Got Stung
That's When Your Heartaches Begin	I Need Your Love Tonight
Mystery Train	(Marie's The Name) His Latest Flame
Treat Me Nice	Such A Night
Money Honey	Good Luck Charm
(You're So Square) Baby I Don't Care	A Mess Of Blues
Loving You	Crying In The Chapel

[ ] **ELVIS, THE KING: 1954-1965**
Catalog# 2RNR-26 TCD-126   Value $ 15-20
Matrix# W.O. 13755-3M TCD-126
(1993 Second Pressing from Time/Life Music. Silver Disc with Black Print.
Contains 8 page insert booklet with Discography. Mail Order Only.
Digitally Remastered. This CD is part of the Time/Life Rock 'N' Roll Era series.
Red & White sticker "Double Length Equivalent to 2 LP's " on shrink wrap.)

[ ] **ELVIS, THE KING: 1954-1965**
Catalog# 2RNR-26 TCD-126   Value $ 15-20
Matrix# L384 1108 TCD126 B70117-08
(1997 Third Pressing from Time/Life Music. Silver Disc with Black Print.
Contains 8 page insert booklet with Discography. Mail Order Only.
Digitally Remastered. This CD is part of the Time/Life Rock 'N' Roll Era series.
Red & White sticker "Double Length Equivelent to 2 LP's " on shrink wrap.)

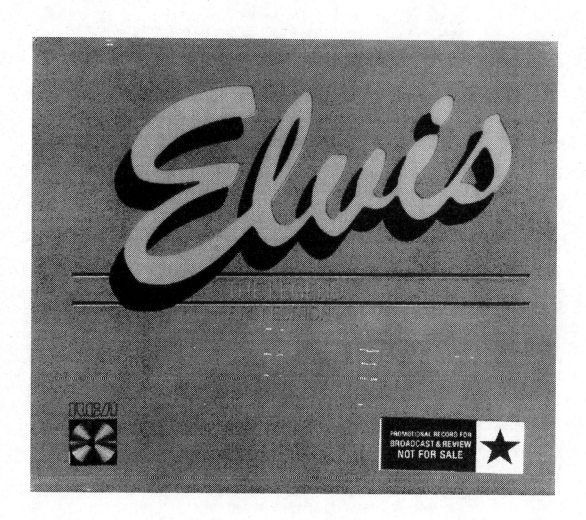

[ ]   **ELVIS THE LEGEND**   *(3 CD Box Set)*
           Catalog# PD 89061/PD89062/PD89063   **Value $ 400-500**
           (Dec. 1983 First Edition from RCA, West Germany. Contains 3 Gold Discs with
           Red Print in individual jewel cases. Each has an 8 page insert booklet with a
           different photo of Elvis on the sleeve. These are contained in a gold slipcase with
           a limited edition numbered certificate. RCA commissioned the manufacture of
           these three special Compact Discs featuring a total of 60 Elvis Presley songs. The
           first 5000 of each of these discs - the first Compact Discs of Elvis Presley music
           ever pressed - are packaged in special limited edition numbered box sets. The CD
           is listed here because of the importance of this release. Although this is a West
           German pressing it was exported to a number of countries as the first Elvis CD.
           The set was sold in the U.S in the spring of 1984.)

Disc #1 - **Volume One**
Matrix# PD 89061 2893 254 01
Disc contains the following selections:

That's All Right	All Shook Up
Heartbreak Hotel	That's When Your Heartaches Begin
I Was The One	(There'll Be) Peace In The Valley (For Me)
Blue Suede Shoes	One Night
My Baby Left Me	Loving You
I Want You, I Need You, I Love You	Teddy Bear
Hound Dog	Party
Don't Be Cruel	Jailhouse Rock
Love Me Tender	Don't
Love Me	King Creole

Disc #2 - **Volume Two**
Matrix# PD 89062 2893 255 01
Disc contains the following selections:

Wear My Ring Around Your Neck	Wooden Heart
A Big Hunk O' Love	Surrender
A Fool Such As I	Wild In The Country
My Wish Came True	Can't Help Falling In Love
I Got Stung	Rock A Hula Baby
It's Now Or Never	His Latest Flame
Stuck On You	Follow That Dream
The Girl Of My Best Friend	Good Luck Charm
A Mess Of Blues	She's Not You
Are You Lonesome Tonight	Return To Sender

Disc #3 - **Volume Three**
Matrix# PD 89063 2893 256 02
Disc contains the following selections:

Devil In Disguise	Don't Cry Daddy
Bossa Nova Baby	The Wonder Of You
Such A Night	You Don't Have To Say You Love Me
Crying In The Chapel	There Goes My Everything
Love Letters	Rags To Riches
Guitar Man	I Just Can't Help Believing
U.S. Male	An American Trilogy
If I Can Dream	Burning Love
In The Ghetto	Always On My Mind
Suspicious Minds	It's Only Love

[ ]   **ELVIS THE LEGEND**   *(3 CD Promo Box Set)*
           Catalog# PD 89061/PD 89062/ PD 89063   **Value $ 600-700**
           Matrix# PD89061 2893 254 01, PD89062 28093 255 01, PD89063 2893 256 02
           (Dec. 1983 Designated Promo. Same as regular catalog release with Purple and
           White sticker "Promotional Record For Broadcast & Review Not For Sale"
           on front of slipcase. Only a few copies in the U.S. were designated as Promos.)

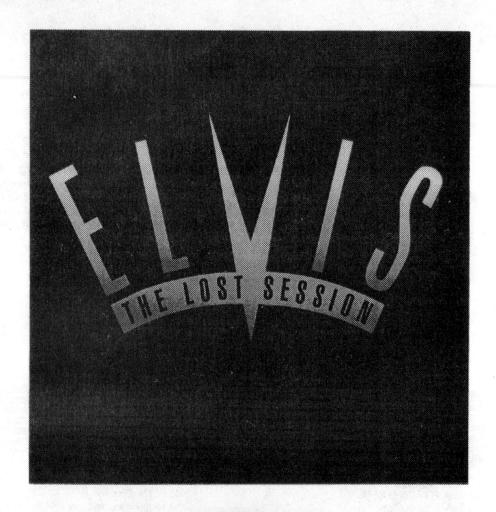

RCA

RCA RECORDS LABEL

RDJ64860-2

ELVIS PRESLEY

PROMOTION ONLY.
NOT FOR SALE

1: THE LOST SESSION
:24/3:58/:06/FADE

[ ]   **ELVIS THE LOST SESSION** *(Promo)*
Catalog# RDJ64880-2   Value $ 25-30
Matrix# IFPI L238

(May 1997 Promo Only from RCA Nashville. Red and Black Disc with Print in Silver. This CD contains no Elvis track although Elvis listed on insert covers and CD. This was a promotional ploy by RCA Nashville to get air play for their new artist Sarah Evans. This was sent to selected country stations throughout the U.S. "Promotional Only - Not For Sale" on back insert cover and CD.)
Song title listed:
1. The Lost Session :24/3:58/:06 Fade *(this is not Elvis)*

ELVIS

THE OTHER SIDES

WORLDWIDE GOLD AWARD HITS · VOLUME 2

2 Compact Disc Set

25TH ANNIVERSARY EDITION

[ ]   **ELVIS THE OTHER SIDES** *(2 CD Box Set)*
WORLDWIDE GOLD AWARD HITS - VOLUME 2
Catalog# 07863-66921-2   **Value $ 25-30**
*(Aug. 1996 First Pressing. Packaged in Special Longbox. A numbered collectable
2 CD Box Set. Each CD has it's own jewel box with it's individual insert sleeve.
Each CD is a picture disc. Original Album Cover Artwork is on back cover of
insert sleeves. Red, White and Blue collectors sticker on shrink wrap.
"25th Anniversary Limited Edition Individually Numbered 2 CD Set - Special
Bonus Original First Day of Issue Elvis Stamp on Limited Edition RCA Envelope
12 page Souvenir Booklet - First Time On CD". Digitally Remastered from the
original RCA Record Label Master Tapes.)*
Disc# 1 Gold and Black Picture Disc
Matrix# 07863669212D1 ++ 67968-01
Disc contain the following selections:

My Baby Left Me	One Night
We're Gonna Move	Young And Beautiful
Poor Boy	I Want To Be Free
Let Me	(You're So Square) Baby I Don't Care
Love Me	My Wish Came True
Paralyzed	Dixieland Rock
When My Blue Moon Turns To Gold Again	Lover Doll
Rip It Up	New Orleans
Tell Me Why	Don't Ask Me Why
Got A Lot O' Livin' To Do!	Crawfish
Mean Woman Blues	King Creole
Hot Dog	As Long As I Have You
Lonesome Cowboy	

Disc# 2 Gold and Black Picture Disc
Matrix# 07863669212D2 ++ 67969-01
Disc contains the following selections:

Trouble	Ask Me
Young Dreams	It Hurts Me
Doncha' Think It's Time	Puppet On A String
I Need Your Love Tonight	Any Day Now
Fame And Fortune	You'll Think Of Me
I Believe In The Man In The Sky	The Wonder Of You
Lonely Man	I've Lost You
Wild In The Country	The Next Step Is Love
His Latest Flame	You Don't Have To Say You Love Me
Just Tell Her Jim Said Hello	Patch It Up
They Remind Me Too Much Of You	There Goes My Everything
Please Don't Drag That String Around	I Really Don't Want To Know
Witchcraft	

[ ]   **ELVIS THE OTHER SIDES**   *(Promo Box Set)*
WORLDWIDE GOLD AWARD HITS - VOLUME 2
Catalog# 07863-66921-2   **Value $ 30-40**
Disc #1 Matrix# 07863669212D1 ++ 67968-01
Disc #2 Matrix# 07863669212D2 ++ 67969-01
*(Aug. 1996 Designated Promo Box Set. Same as regular catalog release with
Black and White sticker "For Promotion Only - Not For Sale P-4/2" under
shrink wrap.)*

ORIGINAL ALBUM ART

[ ]   **ELVIS THE TRIBUTE**   *(3 CD Radio Show)*
       A BIOGRAPHY
       Catalog# Entertainment Radio Network   **Value $ 100-125**
       (Sept. 1994 Limited Edition 3 CD Radio Show. Contains Cue Sheets for
       3 hour Elvis Radio Show broadcast 9/30 - 10/8 to promote Graceland's
       "Elvis - The Tribute" show on Pay-Per-View. Digitally Remastered by AMI.)
       Disc #1 Red, Black & Silver Picture Disc
       Matrix# ECD-041-0015 G1 940928 Elvis Hour 1
       Disc contains the following selections:

Good Rockin' Tonight	Tutti Frutti
Don't Be Cruel	Too Much
A Big Hunk O' Love	Mystery Train
All Shook Up	I Got Stung
Teddy Bear	I Need Your Love Tonight
Blue Moon Of Kentucky	Little Sister
Devil In Disguise	Such A Night
Blue Suede Shoes *(Live Version)*	Jailhouse Rock

Disc #2 Blue, Black & Silver Picture Disc
Matrix# ECD-041-0016 G1 940928 Elvis Hour 2
Disc contains the following selections:

Viva Las Vegas	That's All Right
Are You Lonesome Tonight?	Kentucky Rain
Loving You	It's Now Or Never
Love Me Tender	Treat Me Nice
The Wonder Of You	One Night
Crying In The Chapel	A Fool Such As I
Heartbreak Hotel	Return To Sender

Disc #3 Purple, Black & Silver Picture Disc
Matrix# ECD-041-0017 G1 940928 Elvis Hour 3
Disc contains the following selections:

Bossa Nova Baby	Can't Help Falling In Love
Money Honey	Good Luck Charm
Don't Cry Daddy	Kissin' Cousins
Shake, Rattle & Roll	Wear My Ring Aroung Your Neck
Baby Let's Play House	Burning Love
In The Ghetto	If I Can Dream
Hound Dog	Memories
Stuck On You	Suspicious Minds
King Creole *(Alternate Take)*	

[ ]   **ELVIS TODAY**
       Catalog# 51039-2   **Value $ 12-15**
       Matrix# 07863-51039-2 1C 24
       (April 1992 First Pressing. Elvis in the '90's Black Disc with old RCA
       Logo and Print in Silver. 8 page insert booklet. Digitally Remastered
       from the original RCA Label Master Tapes.)
       Disc contains the following selections:

T-R-O-U-B-L-E	Pieces Of My Life
And I Love You So	Fairytale
Susan When She Tried	I Can Help
Woman Without Love	Bringin' It Back
Shake A Hand	Green, Green Grass Of Home

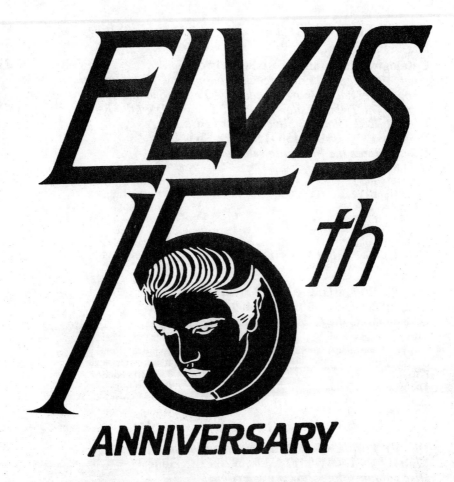

SIX HOUR RADIO TRIBUTE

**THE CREATIVE
RADIO NETWORK**

[ ]   **ELVIS 15th ANNIVERSARY RADIO SHOW** *(6 CD Box Set)*
Catalog# Creative Radio   **Value $ 125-135**
(Aug. 1992 Limited Edition 15th Anniversary Set from Creative Radio. Only 500
pressed. Black Discs with "Elvis 15th Anniversary" Logo and Print in Gold.
Contains folder with information and Cue Sheets for six hour Elvis Radio Show.
85% Music and 15% Talk. Packaged in 8-1/2" x 11" x 2" box with Radio Show
Logos.)
Disc #1
Matrix# ABMPO100C
Disc contains the following selections:

2001: *(Opening)*   Johnny B. Goode
Old Shep   Good Rockin' Tonight
Music Montage   Hard Headed Woman
That's When Your Heartaches Begin   Don't Be Cruel
My Happiness   Shake, Rattle And Roll
That's All Right Mama   Trouble
Baby Let's Play House   Long Tall Sally

Disc #2
Matrix# ABMRO100A
Disc contains the following selections:

Montage #2   The Wonder Of You
Treat Me Nice   Love Me
Heartbreak Hotel   Love Me Tender
Devil In Disguise   Too Much
Return To Sender   Viva Las Vegas
Moody Blue   My Babe
Any Way You Want Me   Money Honey
Don't

Disc #3
Matrix# ABMTO200B
Disc contains the following selections:

I Got A Woman   Tutti Frutti
You're A Heartbreaker   I Need Your Love Tonight
Down By The Riverside   G. I. Blues
Polk Salad Annie   Didj' Ever
A Big Hunk O' Love   Rags To Riches
One Night Of Sin   Hurt
Double Trouble   There'll Be Peace In The Valley
Loving You   I Believe

ELVIS 15th ANNIVERSARY

SIX HOUR RADIO TRIBUTE

**THE CREATIVE
RADIO NETWORK**

Disc #4
Matrix# ABMUO100B
Disc contains the following selections:

Teddy Bear
The Last Farewell
Frankfort Special
Have I Told You Lately That I Love You
Young And Beautiful
Wooden Heart
All Shook Up
Stuck On You

It's Now Or Never
Are You Lonesome Tonight?
Long Tall Sally
Rock-A-Hula Baby
When My Blue Moon Turns To Gold Again
Loving You
Gotta Lotta Livin To Do

Disc #5
Matrix# ABMWO100A
Disc contains the following selections:

Music Montage
One Sided Love Affair
Wear My Ring Around Your Neck
Welcome To My World
If I Can Dream
Blue Suede Shoes
Lawdy, Miss Clawdy
My Baby Left Me

Follow That Dream
Burning Love
Something
Good Luck Charm
Don't Cry Daddy
She's Not You
Can't Help Falling In Love

Disc #6
Matrix# ABMXO200C
Disc contains the following selections:

Guitar Man
Memories
What Now My Love
Fever
See See Rider
Suspicious Minds

You Gave Me A Mochill
Way Down
Crying In The Chapel
How Great Thou Art
Unchained Melody
Mystery Train (*Music Fades*)

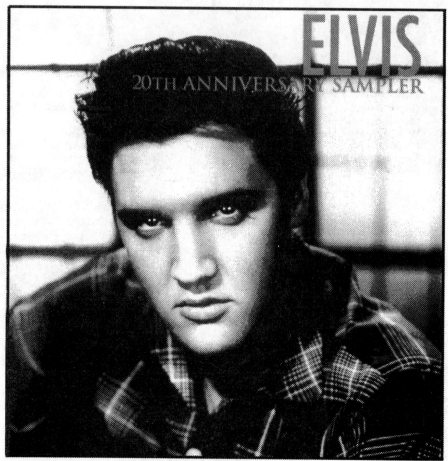

[ ]   **ELVIS 20th ANNIVERSARY RADIO SHOW** *(3 CD Box Set)*
Catalog# Creative Radio 818 991 3892   **Value $ 60-75**
(Aug. 1997 Limited Edition 20th Anniversary Set from Creative Radio.
Gold Discs with "Elvis 20th Anniversary" Logo and Print in Silver. Comes with
information and Cue Sheets for three hour Elvis Radio Show. Packaged in a
5-1/4" square cardboard flip-top box. CD's in white paper die-cut protective
sleeve.)
Disc #1
Matrix# A3610 AF EP797-2.1 70 *M1 S2
Disc contains the following selections:

Elvis Medley	American Trilogy
I Want You, I Need You, I Love You	It's Now Or Never
Love Me Tender	Twelfth Of Never
Blue Suede Shoes	What'd I Say
Harbor Lights	Heartbreak Hotel
That's All Right Mama	Wear My Ring Around Your Neck
I Can't Stop Loving You	

Disc #2
Matrix# B3138 AF EP797-2.2 70 *M1 S2
Disc contains the following selections:

Wonder Of You	Can't Help Falling In Love
All Shook Up	Hound Dog
Lawdy Miss Clawdy	Steamroller Blues
Kentucky Rain	Don't Cry Daddy
Too Much	Return To Sender
I'll Remember You	In The Ghetto
Rock Medley	If I Can Dream
Treat Me Nice	

Disc #3
Matrix# B3139 AF EP797-2.3 70 *M1 S1
Disc contains the following selections:

Love Me	Follow That Dream
Elvis Medley	I Got A Woman
A Fool Such As I	The Impossible Dream
Good Luck Charm	His Latest Flame
There Goes My Everything	You Gave Me A Mountain
Devil In Disguise	Don't Be Cruel
A Big Hunk O' Love	As Long As I Have You
Suspicious Minds	Memories

[ ]   **ELVIS 20TH ANNIVERSARY SAMPLER**
Catalog# 07863-67537-2   **Value $ 10-20**
Matrix# 07863675372 ++ 76007-01
(June 1997 Limited Edition 6 track sampler made exclusively for Blockbuster
Music stores. Black and White Picture Disc with "Blockbuster Exclusive" in
Blue and Gold on disc and back cover. Tracks 1, 2 and 4 from "Platinum -
A Life In Music". Track 3 from "Blue Hawaii" standard and collectors edition.
Track 5 from "Elvis Aron Presley" (Silver Box). Track 6 from "A Golden
Celebration" (Gold Box). Track 4,5 and 6 never before released on CD.
Contains 4 page insert booklet.)
Disc contains the following selections:

Jailhouse Rock	Burning Love *(Alternate Take1)*
All Shook Up	America The Beautiful
Can't Help Falling In Love *(Movie Ver., Alt.Take 23)*	The Fool *(1959 Home Recording)*

SONG TITLES:
1. Heartbreak Hotel / Love Me Tender   4:46
2. Hound Dog / It's Now or Never   5:29
3. Don't Be Cruel / Can't Help Falling In Love   5:01
4. All Shook Up / Are You Lonesome Tonight   5:05
5. In The Ghetto / Stuck on You   5:01

[ ]   **ELVIS 20th ANNIVERSARY SINGLES SET** *(5 CD Box Set)*
Catalog# 159ECDBOL-4A   **Value $ 12-25**
*(Aug. 1997 20th Anniversary 5 CD Singles Box Set from BMG Special Products
for Trans World Entertainment Inc. Sold only at TWE outlets- Coconuts,
Tape World and Record Town. 20th Anniversary Picture Discs. Discs with picture
of Elvis and Print in Black. Discs contained in individual die-cut paper sleeves
and housed in 5"x6-1/4" Black Collectors Box with full color 1970's picture of
Elvis on stage on the front cover. Back cover lists short history of Elvis. These
discs are also individually listed alphabetically in this price guide as CD Singles.
Most of the discs were sold as individual CD Singles. Very few box sets were
available. Green and black sticker "5 CD Singles" on front of shrink wrap.
Back of shrink wrap has black and white sticker listing song titles of the 5 CD
Singles.)*

Disc #1
Matrix# L385 1100 DRC11807 C70717-10
Disc contains the following selections:
Heartbreak Hotel   Love Me Tender

Disc #2
Matrix# L385 1100 DRC11808 C70717-11
Disc contains the following selections:
Hound Dog   It's Now Or Never

Disc #3
Matrix# L385 1100 DRC11809 C70718-30
Disc contains the following selections:
Don't Be Cruel   Can't Help Falling In Love

Disc #4
Matrix# L385 1100 DRC11810 C70722-09
Disc contains the following selections:
(I'm) All Shook Up   Are You Lonesome Tonight?

Disc #5
Matrix# L384 1100 DRC11811 B70718-01
Disc contains the following selections:
In The Ghetto   Stuck On You

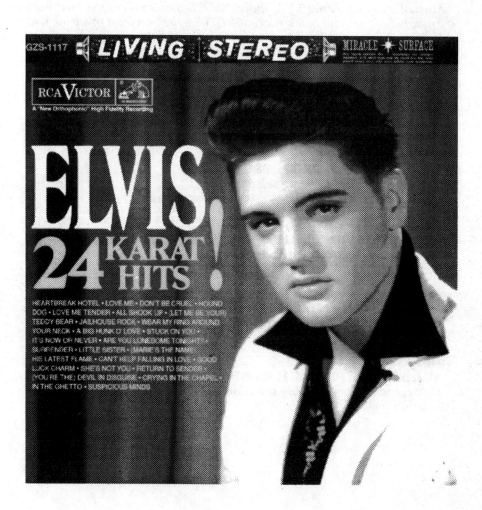

[ ]   # ELVIS 24 KARAT HITS!
        Catalog# GZS-1117   **Value $ 30-40**
        Matrix# $GZS-1117 Y7810C
        *(Sept. 1997 DCC Compact Classics 24 kt. Gold Disc. Gold Disc with Black Print.
        Produced under license from BMG Direct Marketing Inc. CD and jewel case
        housed in slipcase. Gold disc is visable thru front of slip case. Contains 12 page
        insert booklet. CD in Pop-Up Jewel Box. Limited Edition numbered sticker on
        back of slipcase. Black and Gold collectors sticker on front of slipcase "Limited
        Numbered Edition - The Ultimate Sounding Elvis Hits Collection!". Digitally
        Remastered from the original Master Tapes.)*
        Disc contains the following selections:

Heartbreak Hotel	Are You Lonesome Tonight?
Love Me	Surrender
Don't Be Cruel	(Marie's The Name) His Latest Flame
Hound Dog	Little Sister
Love Me Tender *(stereo)*	Can't Help Falling In Love
All Shook Up	Good Luck Charm
(Let Me Be Your) Teddy Bear	She's Not You
Jailhouse Rock	Return to Sender
Wear My Ring Around Your Neck	(You're The) Devil In Disguise
A Big Hunk O' Love	Crying In The Chapel
Stuck On You	In The Ghetto
It's Now Or Never	Suspicious Minds

[ ]   # ELVIS 24 KARAT HITS! *(Promo)*
        Catalog# GZS-1117   **Value $ 75-100**
        Matrix# $GZS-1117 Y7810C
        *(August 1997 Advance Promo for DCC Compact Classics 24 kt. Gold Disc.
        Gold Disc with Black Print. "Promotional Use Only - Not For Sale" on center
        spindle of disc. CD housed in jewel box with without art work. Contains same
        tracks as regular release.)*

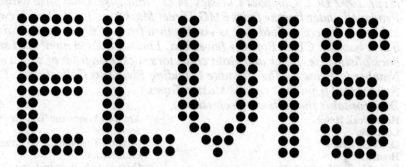

ELVIS

50 WORLDWIDE GOLD HITS
VOLUME 1
PART 1

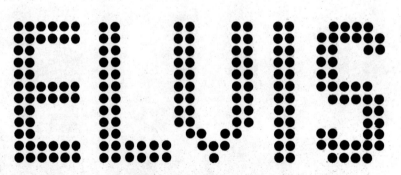

ELVIS

50 WORLDWIDE GOLD HITS
VOLUME 1
PART 2

ELVIS 50 WORLDWIDE GOLD HITS Vol. 1 *(2 CD's)*

[ ]

Catalog# 6401-2-R   **Value $ 40-50**

(Aug. 1988 First Pressing, Midline CD. Light Gold Title Side, Gold Playing Surface. Each disc is housed in it's own jewel box with four page insert booklet. The first pressing discs were housed in white plastic disc trays. Contains alternate take of "Anything That's Part Of You".)

Disc #1 Volume 1 - Part 1 Mono
Matrix# W.O. 10441-1 64012R-2
Disc contains the following selections:

Heartbreak Hotel	Teddy Bear
I Was The One	Jailhouse Rock
I Want You, I Need You, I Love You	Treat Me Nice
Hound Dog	Don't
Don't Be Cruel	Hard Headed Woman
Anyway You Want Me	Wear My Ring Around Your Neck
Love Me Tender	A Big Hunk O' Love
Playin' For Keeps	Ain't That Loving You Baby
Too Much	A Fool Such As I
All Shook Up	I Got Stung
That's When Your Heartaches Begin	Interviews *(from "Elvis Sails")*
I Beg Of You	Crying In The Chapel
Loving You	Viva Las Vegas

Disc #2 Volume 1 - Part 2 Stereo
Matrix# W.O. 10440T-1 64012R-2
Disc contains the following selections:

Stuck On You	She's Not You
A Mess Of Blues	Where Do You Come From
It's Now Or Never	Return To Sender
I Gotta Know	One Broken Heart For Sale
Are You Lonesome Tonight?	Bossa Nova Baby
Wooden Heart	(You're The) Devil In Disguise
Surrender	Kissin' Cousins
I Feel So Bad	If I Can Dream
Little Sister	Don't Cry Daddy
Can't Help Falling In Love	In The Ghetto
Rock - A - Hula Baby	Kentucky Rain
Good Luck Charm	Suspicious Minds
Anything That's Part Of You *(Alternate Take)*	

ELVIS 50 WORLDWIDE GOLD HITS Vol. 1 *(2 CD's)*

[ ]

Catalog# 6401-2-R   **Value $ 20-30**
Disc #1 Matrix# W.O. 10441-1 64012R-2
Disc #2 Matrix# W.O. 10440T-2 64012R-2
(Aug. 1989 Second Pressing. Dark Gold Title Side. Silver Playing Surface. Each disc is housed in it's own jewel box with four page insert booklet. The second pressing discs were housed in black plastic disc trays.)

ELVIS 50 WORLDWIDE GOLD HITS Vol. 1 *(2 CD's)*

[ ]

Catalog# 6401-2-R   **Value $ 20-30**
Disc #1 Matrix# W.O. 10441-1 64012R-2
Disc #2 Matrix# W.O. 10440T-3 64012R-2
(1992 Third Pressing. Dark Gold Title Side. Silver Playing Surface. Each disc housed in it's own jewel box with four page insert booklet. The Third pressing also housed in black plastic disc trays.)

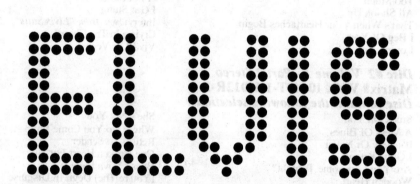

ELVIS

50 WORLDWIDE GOLD HITS
VOLUME 1
PART 1 AND PART 2

2 COMPACT DISCS

[ ] **ELVIS 50 WORLDWIDE GOLD HITS Vol. 1** *(2 CD's)*
Catalog# 6401-2-R   Value $ 20-30
Disc #1 Matrix# W.O. 10441-4M 64012R-2
Disc #2 Matrix# W.O. 10440T-5M 64012R-2
(1993 Fourth Pressing. Dark Gold Title side. Silver Playing Surface.
Each disc housed in its own jewel box with four page insert booklet.
The Fourth pressing also housed in black plastic disc trays.)

[ ] **ELVIS 50 WORLDWIDE GOLD HITS Vol.1** *(2 CD's)*
Catalog# 6401-2-R   Value $ 30-40
BMG Music Service Catalog# D 220600
Disc #1 Matrix# W.O. 10441-5M 64012R-1
Disc #2 Matrix# W.O. 10440T-5M 64012R-2
(1994 Fifth Pressing. Mfg. for BMG Direct Marketing, Inc. BMG Music Service
Catalog number on disc and back insert cover. Dark Gold Title Side, Silver
Playing Surface. Each disc housed in it's own jewel box with four page insert
booklet. Housed in black plastic disc trays. Only available from BMG Music
CD Club. Mail Order Only.)

[ ] **ELVIS 50 WORLDWIDE GOLD HITS Vol. 1** *(2 CD's)*
Catalog# 6401-2-R   Value $ 30-40
BMG Music Service Catalog# D 220600
Disc #1 Matrix# 64012R-1 ++ 65180-01
Disc #2 Matrix# 64012R-2 ++ 65181-01
(1995 Sixth Pressing. Mfg for BMG Direct Marketing, Inc. BMG Music Service.
Catalog number on disc and front and back insert covers. Dark Gold Title Side,
Silver Playing Surface. Discs housed in multi disc jewel box. Previous releases
were in 2 individual jewel boxes. Front and back insert covers have track
listings. Artwork is now on inside of jewel box. Only available from BMG Music
CD Club. Mail Order Only.)

[ ] **ELVIS 50 WORLDWIDE GOLD HITS Vol. 1** *(2 CD Set)*
Catalog# 07863-56401-2   Value $ 20-30
Disc #1 Matrix# 64012R-1 ++ 65180-01
Disc #2 Matrix# 64012R-2 ++ 65181-01
(April 1996 Reissue with new catalog number. Dark Gold Title Side with Silver
outer band, Silver Playing Surface. This title has been given a new catalog
number. Contains 4 page insert booklet with RE on back page. Discs housed in
multi disc jewel box. Jewel box packaged with outer bellyband with same artwork
as jewel box.)

[ ] **ELVIS 50 WORLDWIDE GOLD HITS VOL. 1** *(2 CD Set)*
Catalog# 07863-56401-2   Value $ 30 -40
BMG Music Service Catalog# D220600
Disc #1 Matrix# 64012R-1 ++ 65180-01
Disc #2 Matrix# 64012R-2 ++ 65181-01
(May 1996 Second Pressing. Mfg. for BMG Direct Marketing, Inc. BMG Music
Service Catalog number on discs, spine, back of insert booklet and back insert
cover. Dark Gold Title Side, Silver Playing Surface. Contains 4 page insert
booklet with RE on back page. Discs housed in multi-disc jewel box. Only
available from BMG Music CD Club. Mail Order Only.)

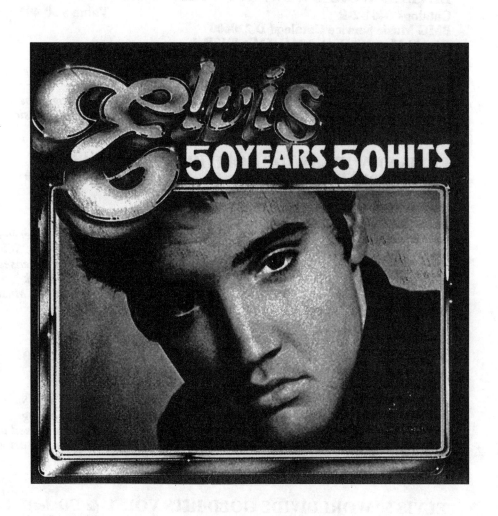

[ ]   **ELVIS - 50 YEARS - 50 HITS**   *(2 CD's)*

Catalog# SVC2-0710-1 & 2   **Value $ 25-30**

(Sept 1990 RCA Special Products Release. First Pressing. Silver Disc with block RCA Logo and Nipper in Red. Printing in Black. Two CD's in multi disc jewel box. Mail Order Only.)

Disc #1 Volume 1

Matrix# W.O. 15560-1 SVC2-0710-1

Disc contains the following selections:

Heartbreak Hotel	All Shook Up
Don't Be Cruel	Love Me Tender
I Want You, I Need You, I Love You	What'd I Say
(You're The) Devil In Disguise	Don't
I Need Your Love Tonight	One Broken Heart For Sale
Too Much	Danny Boy
Viva Las Vegas	Teddy Bear
Hound Dog	Good Luck Charm
Old Shep	Suspicious Minds
The Wonder Of You	Treat Me Nice
Loving You	Return To Sender
Kissin' Cousins	If I Can Dream
Suspicion	

Disc #2 Volume II

Matrix# W.O. 15561-3 SVC2-0710-2

Disc contains the following selections:

A Big Hunk O' Love	Stuck On You
One Night	(Such An) Easy Question
Such A Night	Hard Headed Woman
Love Me	I Beg Of You
Don't Cry Daddy	You Don't Have To Say You Love Me
Wear My Ring Around Your Neck	Crying In The Chapel
It's Now Or Never	She's Not You
My Wish Came True	Puppet On A String
I Got Stung	Moody Blue
(Now And Then There's) A Fool Such As I	Surrender
Blue Hawaii	In The Ghetto
Kentucky Rain	Memories
Can't Help Fallin' In Love	

[ ]   **ELVIS - 50 YEARS - 50 HITS**   *(2 CD's)*

Catalog# SVC2-0710-1 & 2   **Value $ 20-25**

Disc #1 Matrix# SVC2-0710-1 1S

Disc #2 Matrix# SVC2-0710-2 1S

(Aug. 1991 RCA Special Products Release. Second Pressing. Silver Disc with block RCA Logo and Nipper in Red. Printing in Black. Two CD's in multi disc jewel box. Mail Order Only.)

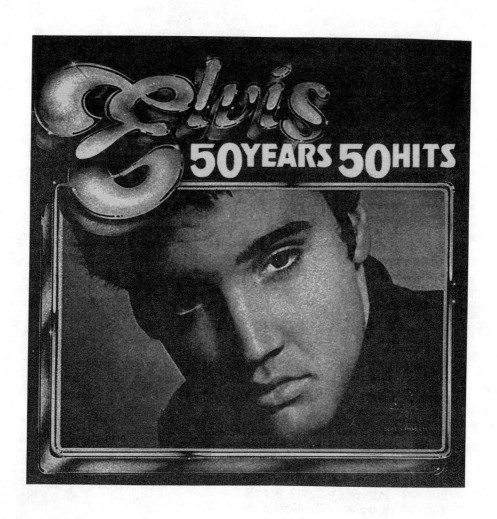

[ ] **ELVIS - 50 YEARS - 50 HITS** *(2 CD's)*
Catalog# SVC2-0710-1 & 2   Value $ 20-25
Disc #1 **Matrix# SVC2-0710-1 1S11**
Disc #2 **Matrix# SVC2-0710-2 1S12**
(1993 RCA Special Products Release. Third Pressing. Silver Disc with block RCA Logo and Nipper in Red. Printing in Black. Two CD's in multi disc jewel box. Mail Order Only.)

[ ] **ELVIS - 50 YEARS - 50 HITS** *(2 CD's)*
Catalog# SVC2-0710-1 & 2   Value $ 20-25
Disc #1 **Matrix# SVC2-0710-1 Y2C 12**
Disc #2 **Matrix# SVC2-0710-2 Y2C 11**
(1995 RCA Special Products Release. Fourth Pressing. Silver Disc with block RCA Logo and Nipper in Red. Printing in Black. First three pressings had dark blue background on front insert cover. This pressing has purple background on front insert cover. Two CD's in Double Slimline jewel case. First three pressings were in multi disc jewel box. Mail Order Only.)

[ ] **ELVIS - 50 YEARS - 50 HITS** *(2 CD's)*
Catalog# SVC2-0710-1& 2   Value $ 20-25
Disc #1 **Matrix# SVC20710D1 ++ 83761-01**
Disc #2 **Matrix# SVC20710D2 ++ 83771-01**
(Feb. 1998 Fifth Pressing. RCA Special Products Release for AVON. Silver Disc with block RCA Logo and Nipper in Red. Printing in Black. Same front insert cover as Fourth Pressing. Two CD's in Double Slimline jewel case. Mail Order Only.)

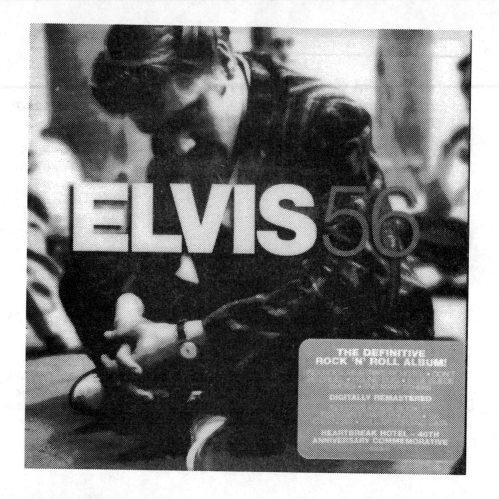

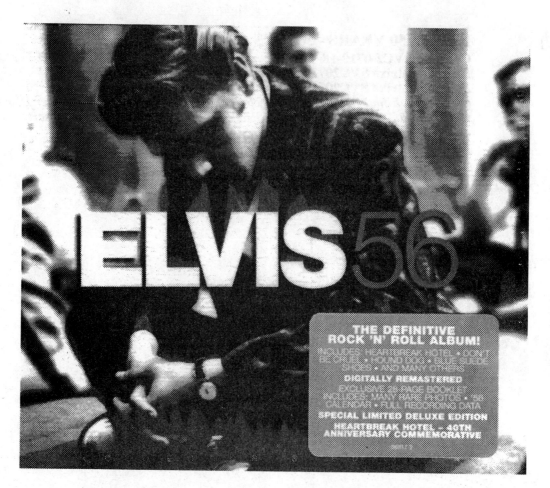

[ ]   **ELVIS 56**
        Catalog# 07863 66856-2   **Value $ 13-18**
        Matrix# 07863668562 ++ 64679-02
        (April 1996 First Pressing. A light black and white matte finish Picture Disc with
        old RCA Logo and print in white. Contains 8 page insert booklet. Black and white
        photo of Elvis under disc in jewel box. Red and White collectors sticker "The
        Definitive Rock 'N' Roll Album!" on shrink wrap.)
        Disc contains the following selections:

Heartbreak Hotel	Hound Dog
My Baby Left Me	Any Way You Want Me
Blue Suede Shoes	Don't Be Cruel
So Glad You're Mine	Lawdy, Miss Clawdy
Tutti Frutti	Shake, Rattle And Roll *(Alternate Take 8)*
One - Sided Love Affair	I Want You, I Need You, I Love You
Love Me	Rip It Up
Anyplace Is Paradise	Heartbreak Hotel *(Alt. Take 5 Prev. Unrlsd.)*
Paralyzed	I Got A Woman
Ready Teddy	I Was The One
Too Much	Money Honey

[ ]   **ELVIS 56**   *(Promo)*
        Catalog# 07863 66856-2   **Value $ 20-25**
        Matrix# 07863668562 ++ 64679-02
        (April 1996 Designated Promo. Same as regular catalog release with Black &
        White sticker "Not For Sale NFS-1" on fron cover of jewel box. Drill hole thru
        back of jewel box.)

[ ]   **ELVIS 56**   *(Collectors Edition)*
        Catalog# 07863 66817-2   **Value $ 20-25**
        Matrix# 07863668172 ++ 64626 -01
        (April 1996 Special Collectors Edition. A dark black and white matte finish
        Picture Disc with old RCA Logo and print in white. Contains 28 page booklet
        which contain many rare photos, '56 calendar and full recording data housed in a
        deluxe edition hardcover book. CD contained in back of booklet in attached
        picture sleeve. Red and White collectors sticker "The Definitive Rock 'N' Roll
        Album - Special Limited Deluxe Edition" on shrink wrap.)
        Disc contains the following selections:

Heartbreak Hotel	Hound Dog
My Baby Left Me	Any Way You Want Me
Blue Suede Shoes	Don't Be Cruel
So Glad You're Mine	Lawdy, Miss Clawdy
Tutti Frutti	Shake Rattle And Roll *(Alternate Take 8)*
One - Sided Love Affair	I Want You, I Need You, I Love You
Love Me	Rip It Up
Anyplace Is Paradise	Heartbreak Hotel *(Alt. Take 5 Prev. Unrlsd.)*
Paralyzed	I Got A Woman
Ready Teddy	I Was The One
Too Much	Money Honey

[ ]   **ELVIS 56**   *(Collectors Edition Promo)*
        Catalog# 07863 66817-2   **Value $ 30-35**
        Matrix# 07863668172 ++ 64626-01
        (April 1996 Designated Promo. Same as regular catalog release with Black &
        White sticker "For Promotion Only Not For Sale P-4/2" over bar code on back
        cover of jewel box.)

ELVIS '56
ADVANCE MUSIC

1 HEARTBREAK HOTEL 2:08 2 MY BABY LEFT ME 2:11
3 BLUE SUEDE SHOES 1:58 4 SO GLAD YOU'RE MINE 2:20
5 TUTTI FRUTTI 1:58 6 ONE-SIDED LOVE AFFAIR 2:09
7 LOVE ME 2:43 8 ANYPLACE IS PARADISE 2:26
9 PARALYZED 2:23 10 READY TEDDY 1:56
11 TOO MUCH 2:31 12 HOUND DOG 2:16
13 ANY WAY YOU WANT ME (THAT'S HOW I WILL BE) 2:13
14 DON'T BE CRUEL 2:02 15 LAWDY, MISS CLAWDY 2:08
16 SHAKE, RATTLE AND ROLL (ALTERNATE TAKE 8) 2:37
17 I WANT YOU, I NEED YOU, I LOVE YOU 2:40 18 RIP IT UP 1:53
19 HEARTBREAK HOTEL (ALTERNATE TAKE 5-INTRO-PREVIOUSLY UNRELEASED) 2:13
20 I GOT A WOMAN 2:23
21 I WAS THE ONE 2:33 22 MONEY HONEY 2:34

TRACKS 7-14, 16 WITH THE JORDANAIRES • COMPILATION PRODUCED BY ERNST MIKAEL JORGENSEN AND ROGER SEMON
• EXECUTIVE PRODUCER: PAUL WILLIAMS

NOT FOR SALE OR RADIO AIRPLAY

P 1996 BMG Entertainment

Manufactured and distributed by BMG Distribution, a unit of BMG
Entertainment, 1540 Broadway, New York, New York 10036-4098

THE RCA RECORDS LABEL.
TMK(S) ® REGISTERED
MARCA(S) REGISTRADA(S)
GENERAL ELECTRIC, USA.
BMG LOGO ® BMG MUSIC
© 1996 BMG ENTERTAINMENT

[ ] **ELVIS '56 ADVANCE MUSIC** *(Promo)*
Catalog# RADV-66856-2   **Value $ 75-100**
Matrix# 07863668562 ++ 64679-02
(February 1996 Promo Only. Silver Disc with old RCA Logo and Print in Black.
"Elvis '56 Advance Music - Not For Sale Or Radio Airplay" printed on disc.
Black and White sticker "Not For Radio Airplay - ACD-2" on front of jewel
case. No front cover insert. Back insert cover white with song titles and
"Not For Sale Or Radio Airplay" in black print.)
Disc contains the following selections:

Heartbreak Hotel	Hound Dog
My Baby Left Me	Any Way You Want Me
Blue Suede Shoes	Don't Be Cruel
So Glad You're Mine	Lawdy, Miss Clawdy
Tutti Frutti	Shake, Rattle And Roll *(Alternate Take 8)*
One - Sided Love Affair	I Want You, I Need You, I Love You
Love Me	Rip It Up
Any Place Is Paradise	Heartbreak Hotel
Paralyzed	*(Alt. Take 5 - Intro - Previoulsy Unreleased)*
Ready Teddy	I Got A Woman
Too Much	I Was The One
	Money Honey

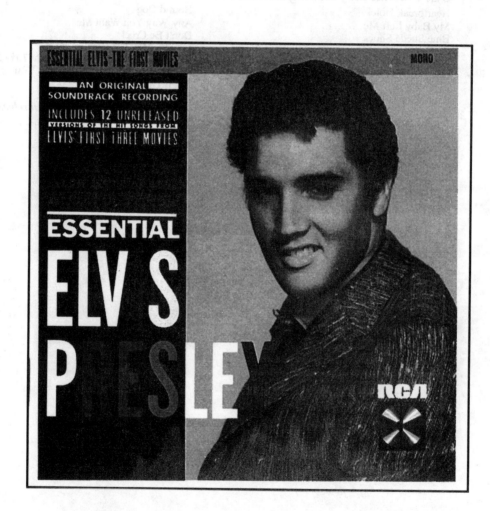

[ ] **ESSENTIAL ELVIS - THE FIRST MOVIES**
Catalog# 6738-2-R   Value $ 14-18
Matrix# W.O. 8754-1 67382R
(Jan. 1988 First Pressing. Silver & Black Disc with old RCA Logo.
Contains 8 page insert booklet. An original soundtrack recording.
Includes 12 unreleased versions of the hit songs from Elvis' first three
movies. "Love Me Tender", "Loving You" & "Jailhouse Rock".)
Disc contains the following selections:

Love Me Tender	Jailhouse Rock *(Vocal Overdub Take 6)*
Let Me	Treat Me Nice*(Unreleased Version Take 10)*
Poor Boy	Young And Beautiful *(Unrel. Ver. Take 12)*
We're Gonna Move	Don't Leave Me Now *(Orig. Ver. Take 12)*
Loving You *(Slow Version Take 10)*	I Want To Be Free *(Orig. Version Take 11)*
Party *(Unreleased Version Alternate Master Take 7)*	Baby I Don't Care *(Take 16 and Take 6)*
Hot Dog	Jailhouse Rock *(Unrel. Ver. Take 5)*
Teddy Bear	Got A Lot O' Livin' To Do
Loving You *(Fast Version Takes 20-21)*	Loving You *(Slow Version Take 1)*
Mean Woman Blues *(Alt. Film Version)*	Mean Woman Blues
Got A Lot O' Livin' To Do *(Unreleased Version)*	Loving You *(Fast Version Take 8)*
Loving You *(Fast Version Take 1)*	Treat Me Nice
Party	Love Me Tender *(Unreleased Version)*
Lonesome Cowboy	

[ ] **ESSENTIAL ELVIS - THE FIRST MOVIES**
Catalog# 6738-2-R   Value $ 12-15
Matrix# W.O. 8754-2 67382R
(1990 Second Pressing. Silver & Black Disc with old RCA Logo.
Contains 8 page insert booklet. An original soundtrack recording.)

[ ] **ESSENTIAL ELVIS - THE FIRST MOVIES**
Catalog# 6738-2-R   Value $ 12-15
Matrix# W.O. 8754-3 67382R
(1992 Third Pressing. Silver & Black Disc with old RCA Logo.
Contains 8 page insert booklet. An original soundtrack recording.)

[ ] **ESSENTIAL ELVIS - THE FIRST MOVIES**
Catalog# 6738-2-R   Value $ 12-15
Matrix# W.O. 8754-4V 67382R
(1994 Fourth Pressing. Silver & Black Disc with old RCA Logo.
Contains 8 page insert booklet. An original soundtrack recording.)

[ ] **ESSENTIAL ELVIS - THE FIRST MOVIES**
Catalog# 6738-2-R   Value $ 12-15
Matrix# 67382R ++ 64561-01
(1996 Fifth Pressing. Silver & Black Disc with old RCA Logo.
Contains 8 page insert booklet. An original soundtrack recording.)

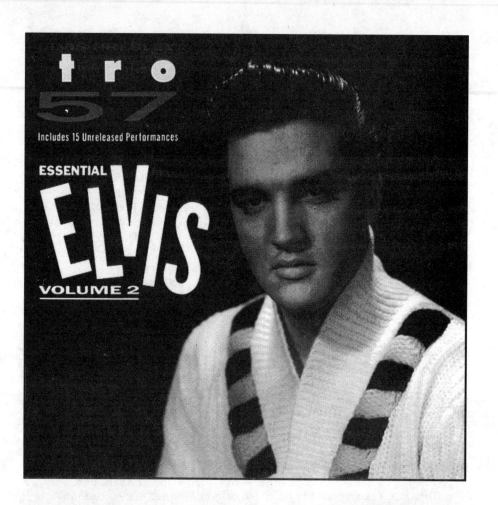

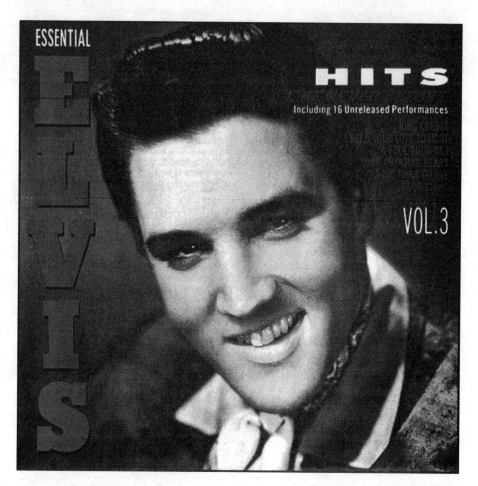

[ ] **ESSENTIAL ELVIS Vol. 2 - STEREO '57**
Catalog# 9589-2-R   **Value $ 14-18**
Matrix# W.O. 11106-4 95892R
(Feb. 1989 First Pressing. Silver & Black Disc with old RCA Logo. Contains
10 page insert booklet. Includes 15 unreleased performances.)
Disc contains the following selections:

I Beg Of You *(Take 1)*   Is It So Strange *(Takes 7,11)*
Is It So Strange *(Take 1)*   I Beg Of You *(Takes 6,8)*
Have I Told You Lately That I Love You *(Take 2)*   Peace In The Valley *(Take 7)*
It Is No Secret *(Takes 1,2,3)*   Have I Told You Lately That I Love You-
Blueberry Hill *(Take 2)*   *(Takes 12,13)*
Mean Woman Blues *(Take 14)*   I Beg Of You *(Take 12)*
Peace In The Valley *(Takes 2,3)*   I Believe *(Take 4)*
Have I Told You Lately That I Love You *(Take 6)*   Tell Me Why *(Take 5)*
Blueberry Hill *(Take 7)*   Got A Lot O' Livin' To Do! *(Take 9)*
That's When Your Heartaches Begin *(Takes 4,5,6)*   All Shook Up *(Take 10)*
                                                           Take My Hand, Precious Lord *(Take 14)*

[ ] **ESSENTIAL ELVIS Vol. 2 - STEREO '57**
Catalog# 9589-2-R   **Value $ 12-15**
Matrix# W.O. 11106-6M 95892R
(1994 Second Pressing. Silver & Black Disc with old RCA Logo. Contains
10 page insert booklet.)

[ ] **ESSENTIAL ELVIS Vol. 3 / HITS LIKE NEVER BEFORE**
Catalog# 2229-2-R   **Value $ 14-18**
Matrix# W.O. 14692-1 22292R
(Jan. 1991 First Pressing. Silver & Black Disc with old RCA Logo.
Contains 8 page insert booklet. Includes 16 unreleased performances.)
Disc contains the following selections:

King Creole *Track E, Take 18*   Crawfish *Track F Take 7*
(Unreleased Master Recording)   *(Unreleased Full Length Version)*
I Got Stung *Take 1*   A Big Hunk O' Love *Take 1*
(Unreleased Version)   *(Unreleased Version)*
A Fool Such As I *Take 3*   Ain't That Loving You Baby *Takes 5,11*
(Unreleased Version)   *(Unreleased Fast Version)*
Wear My Ring Around Your Neck *Take 22*   I Got Stung *Takes 13.14*
(Original Undubbed Version)   *(Unreleased Version with False Start)*
Your Cheating Heart *Take 9*   Your Cheating Heart *Take 10*
Ain't That Loving You Baby *Take 1*   Wear My Ring Around Your Neck *Take 22*
(Unreleased Mid Tempo Version)   *(Original Single Version)*
Doncha' Think It's Time *Take 40*   Steadfast, Loyal And True *Track M Take 6*
I Need Your Love Tonight *Takes 2,10*   *(Unreleased Version)*
(Unreleased False Start & Complete Take)   I Need Your Love Tonight *Take 5*
Lover Doll *Track H Take 7*   *(Unreleased Version)*
(Original Undubbed Version)   Doncha' Think It's Time *Spliced*
As Long As I Have You *Track N Take 8*   *(Original Single Version)*
(Unreleased Version)   I Got Stung *Take 12*
Danny *Take Unknown*   *(Unreleased Version)*
King Creole *Track E Take 3*   King Creole *Track R Take 8*
(Unreleased Version)   *(Main Title Instrumental Version)*
                                                          As Long As I Have You *Track N Take 4*
                                                          (Unreleased Version)

[ ] **ESSENTIAL ELVIS Vol. 3 / HITS LIKE NEVER BEFORE**
Catalog# 2229-2-R   **Value $ 12-15**
Matrix# W.O. 14692-5M 22292R
(1993 Second Pressing. Silver & Black Disc with old RCA Logo. 8 page booklet.)

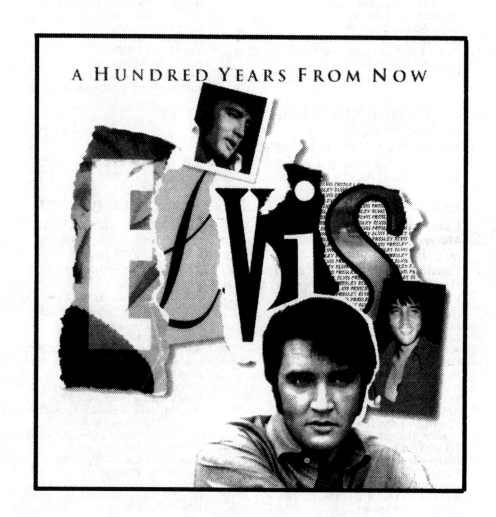

A HUNDRED YEARS FROM NOW

[ ] **ESSENTIAL ELVIS Vol. 4 - A HUNDRED YEARS FROM NOW**
Catalog# 07863-66866-2   Value $ 14-18
Matrix# 07863668662 ++ 67967-01
(July 1996 First Pressing. Grey Disc with Black Print. Block RCA Logos. Two Logos in Red and One Small Logo in Black. Disc artwork is reproduction of RCA tape reel. Contains 8 page insert booklet. Black and White picture of RCA tape box and recording session sheets under disc in jewel box. Black and White collectors sticker "22 Great Tracks Featuring 18 Previously Unreleased Performances!" on shrink wrap.)
Disc contains the following selections:

I Didn't Make It On Playing Guitar *(Informal Jam)*
I Washed My Hands In Muddy Water *(Undubbed/Unedited)*
Little Cabin On The Hill *(Alternate Take 1)*
A Hundred Years From Now *(Alternate Take 2)*
I've Lost You *(Alternate Take 6)*
Got My Mojo Working *(Undubbed/Unedited Master)*
You Don't Have To Say You Love Me *(Alternate Take 2)*
It Ain't No Big Thing *(Alternate Take 2)*
Cindy, Cindy *(Alternate Take 1)*
Faded Love *(Country Version)*
The Fool *(Alternate Take 1)*
Rags To Riches *(Alternate Take 3)*
Just Pretend *(Alternate Take 2)*

If I Were You *(Alternate Take 5)*
Faded Love *(Alternate Take 3)*
Where Did They Go Lord?
(Alternate Take 1)
It's Only Love *(Alternate Take 9)*
Until It's Time For You To Go
(Alternate Master, Take 10)
Patch It Up *(Alternate Take 9)*
Whole Lotta Shakin' Goin' On
(Undubbed/Unedited Master)
Bridge Over Troubled Water
(Alternate Take 5)
The Lord's Prayer
(Informal Performance)

[ ] **ESSENTIAL ELVIS Vol. 4 - *(Promo)***
A HUNDRED YEARS FROM NOW
Catalog# RJC 66866-2   Value $ 40-50
Matrix# 07863668662 ++ 67967-01
(July 1996 Promo Only. Gray Disc with Black Print. Block RCA Logo. Two Logos in Red and One Small Logo in Black. Catalog# RJC 66866-2 and "Not For Sale" printed on disc. Black and White sticker "Not For Sale NFS-1" on front onsert booklet. Hole punched thru the bar code on back insert cover.)

[ ] **ESSENTIAL ELVIS Vol. 4**
A HUNDRED YEARS FROM NOW
Catalog# BG2-66866   Value $ 20-30
Matrix# DIDX-039672 1
(Sept. 1998 Second Pressing. Mfg. by BMG Music for Columbia House Music Club, a non-BMG Music CD Club. Columbia House Music Club catalog number on disc and spine. CRC Logo printed above bar code on back insert cover. Gray Disc with Black Print. Block RCA Logo. Two Logos in Red and One Small Logo in Black. Contains 8 page insert booklet. Only available from Columbia House Music CD Club. Mail Order Only.)

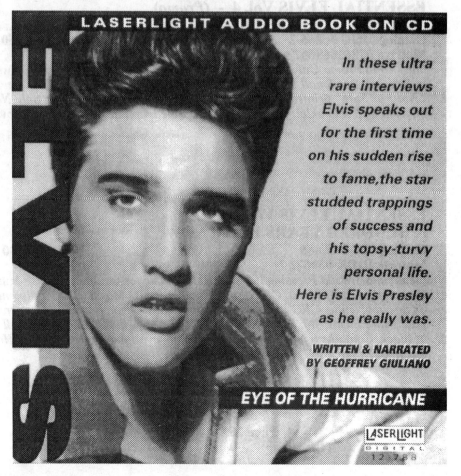

[ ]   **ESSENTIAL ELVIS Vol. 5 - RHYTHM AND COUNTRY**
Catalog# 07863-67672-2   Value $ 14-18
Matrix# 07863676722 ++ 86623-01
(Aug.1998 First Pressing. Cream & Light Orange Disc with Brown Print.
Contains 12 page insert booklet. Light blue collectors sticker with brown print
on front of shrink wrap. Digitally Remastered from the original RCA Label
Master Tapes.)
Disc contains the following selections:

I Got A Feeling In My Body *(Alt. Take 1)*
Loving Arms *(Alt. Take 2)*
I've Got A Thing About You Baby *(Alt. Take 14)*
She Wears My Ring *(Alt. Take 8)*
You Asked Me To *(Alt. Take 2)*
There's A Honky Tonk Angel *(Alt. Take 1)*
Good Time Charlie's Got The Blues *(Alt. Take 8)*
Find Out What's Happening *(Alt. Take 6)*
For Ol' Times Sake *(Alt. Take 3)*

If You Don't Come Back *(Alt. Take 3)*
Promised Land *(Alt. Take 4)*
Thinking About You *(Alt. Take 4)*
Three Corn Patches *(Alt. Take 14)*
Girl Of Mine *(Alt. Take 9)*
Your Love's Been A Long Time Coming
   (Alt. Take 4)
Spanish Eyes *(Alt. Take 2)*
Talk About The Good Times *(Alt. Take 3)*
If That Isn't Love *(Alt. Take 1)*

[ ]   **EYE OF THE HURRICANE**
Catalog# 12 788   Value $ 6-8
Matrix# 12788 Y6718B IFPI L532
(Sept. 1996 Release from Laserlight Digital. This is a Laserlight Audio Book on
CD. Contains 4 page insert booklet. Silver and Yellow Disc with Black Print.
Written and Narrated by Geoffrey Giuliano. This is an interview only CD.)
Disc contains the following interviews:

Introduction
Presley Interview, Lakeland Florida Aug. 6, 1956
Presley Interview, Ottawa, Canada
Presley Interview, New York, New York
Presley Interview C
Presley Interview D
Presley Press Conference

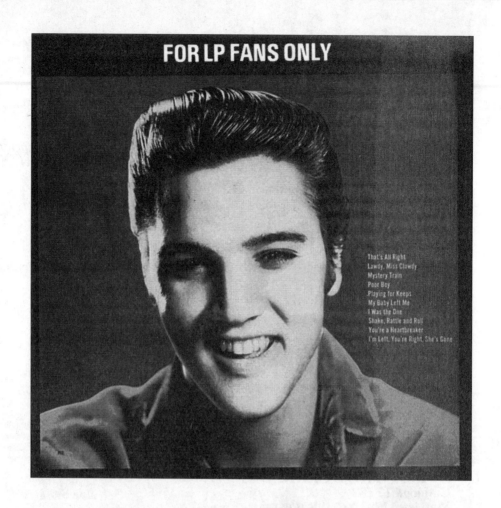

[ ] **FOR LP FANS ONLY**
Catalog# 1990-2-R   Value $ 10-15
Matrix# W.O. 11698-2 19902R
(April 1989 First Pressing. Midline CD. Silver & Black Disc with old RCA Logo.
Bold printing on disc.)
Disc contains the following selections:

That's All Right	My Baby Left Me
Lawdy, Miss Clawdy	I Was The One
Mystery Train	Shake, Rattle And Roll
Playing For Keeps	I'm Left, You're Right, She's Gone
Poor Boy	You're A Heartbreaker

[ ] **FOR LP FANS ONLY**
Catalog# 1990-2-R   Value $ 10-15
Matrix# W.O. 11698-2 19902R
(1991 Second Pressing. Midline CD. Silver & Black Disc with old RCA Logo.
Lighter printing on disc.)

[ ] **FOR LP FANS ONLY**
Catalog# 1990-2-R   Value $ 10-12
Matrix# 19902R ++ 64113-01
(1996 Third Pressing. Midline CD. Silver & Black Disc with old RCA Logo.
"Wise Buy" sticker on shrink wrap.)

[ ] **FROM ELVIS IN MEMPHIS**
Catalog# 07863-51456-2   Value $ 12-15
Matrix# W.O. 17780-1 07863514562
(Aug. 1991 First Pressing. Midline CD. Silver & Black Disc with old RCA Logo.
Contains 8 page insert booklet.)
Disc contains the following selections:

Wearin' That Loved On Look	Power Of My Love
Only The Strong Survive	Gentle On My Mind
I'll Hold You In My Heart	After Loving You
Long Black Limousine	True Love Travels On A Gravel Road
It Keeps Right On A-Hurtin'	Any Day Now
I'm Movin' On	In The Ghetto

[ ] **FROM ELVIS IN MEMPHIS**
Catalog# 07863-51456-2   Value $ 10-12
Matrix# ISPI L238 07863514562 1H 21
(1997 Second Pressing. Midline CD. Silver & Black Disc with old RCA Logo.
Contains 8 page insert booklet. "Wise Buy" sticker on shrink wrap.)

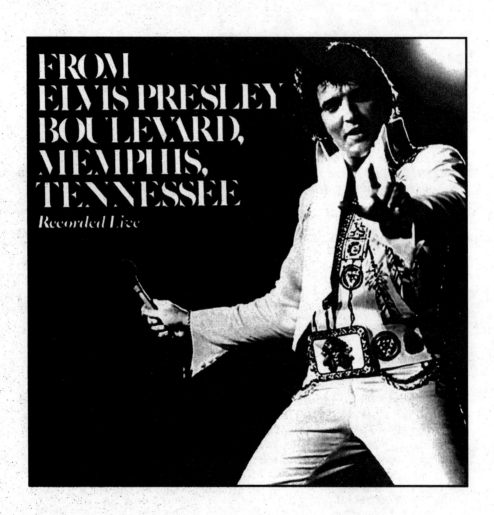

[ ]   **FROM ELVIS PRESLEY BOULEVARD**
MEMPHIS, TENNESSEE Recorded Live
Catalog# 1506-2-R   Value $ 12-15
Matrix# W.O. 10168-2 15062R
(April 1988 First Pressing. Midline CD. Silver & Black Disc with old RCA Logo.
Back cover printed "Digitally Remastered ADD".)
Disc contains the following selections:

Hurt	For The Heart
Never Again	Bitter They Are, Harder They Fall
Blue Eyes Crying In The Rain	Solitaire
Danny Boy	Love Coming Down
The Last Farewell	I'll Never Fall In Love Again

[ ]   **FROM ELVIS PRESLEY BOULEVARD**
MEMPHIS, TENNESSEE Recorded Live
Catalog# 1506-2-R   Value $ 10-12
Matrix# W.O. 10168-2 15062R
(1991 Second Pressing. Midline CD. Silver & Black Disc with old RCA Logo.
Back cover printed "Digitally Remastered" without ADD.)

[ ] **FROM NASHVILLE TO MEMPHIS** *(5 CD Box Set)*
THE ESSENTIAL 60's MASTERS I
Catalog# 07863-66160-2   Value $ 70-80
*(Sept. 1993 First Pressing. Packaged in Special Longbox. A Numbered
collectable 5 CD Box Set - 130 Tracks. Includes Nineteen previously
unreleased/alternate performances. Each CD has its own jewel box with it's
individual insert sleeve. Each CD is a picture disc. Box contains a 94 page
booklet with recording session data and complete 60's Discography plus
a sheet of 36 full-color promotional stamps depicting Elvis' RCA 60's Record
Covers. Digitally Remastered from the original RCA Label Master Tapes.
Yellow & Red Collectors sticker on shrink wrap.)*
Disc #1 Lavender and Black Picture Disc
Matrix# 07863661602P1 01# ++
Disc contains the following selections:

Make Me Know It
Soldier Boy
Stuck On You
Fame And Fortune
A Mess Of Blues
It Feels So Right
Fever
Like A Baby
It's Now Or Never
The Girl Of My Best Friend
Dirty, Dirty Feeling
Thrill Of Your Love
I Gotta Know
Such A Night

Are You Lonesome Tonight?
Girl Next Door Went A' Walking
I Will Be Home Again
Reconsider Baby
Surrender
I'm Coming Home
Gently
In Your Arms
Give Me The Right
I Feel So Bad
It's A Sin
I Want You With Me
There's Always Me

Disc #2 Pink and Black Picture Disc
Matrix# 07863661602P2 03# ++
Disc contains the following selections:

Starting Today
Sentimental Me
Judy
Put The Blame On Me
Kiss Me Quick
That's Someone You Never Forget
I'm Yours
His Latest Flame
Little Sister
For The Millionth And The Last Time
Good Luck Charm
Anything That's Part Of You
I Met Her Today
Night Rider
Something Blue
Gonna Get Back Home Somehow

(Such An) Easy Question
Fountain Of Love
Just For Old Time Sake
You'll Be Gone
I Feel That I've Known You Forever
Just Tell Her Jim Said Hello
Suspicion
She's Not You
Echoes Of Love
Please Don't Drag That String Around
(You're The) Devil In Disguise
Never Ending
What Now, What Next, Where To
Witchcraft
Finders Keepers, Losers Weepers
Love Me Tonight

Disc #3 Red and Black Picture Disc
Matrix# 07863661602P3 01# ++
Disc contains the following selections:

(It's A) Long Lonely Highway
Western Union
Slowly But Surely
Blue River
Memphis, Tennessee
Ask Me
It Hurts Me
Down In The Alley
Tomorrow Is A Long Time
Love Letters
Beyond The Reef (*Original Undubbed Master*)
Come What May (*Alternate Take 7*)
Fools Fall In Love
Indescribably Blue

I'll Remember You (*Orig. Unedit. Master*)
If Every Day Was Like Christmas
Suppose (*Master*)
Guitar Man/What'd I Say...
(*Original Unedited Master*)
Big Boss Man
Mine
Just Call Me Lonesome
Hi-Heel Sneakers (*Orig. Unedit. Master*)
You Don't Know Me
Singing Tree
Too Much Monkey Business
U.S. Male

Disc #4 Mustard and Black Picture Disc
Matrix# 07863661602P4 01# ++ 30634
Disc contains the following selections:

Long Black Limousine
This Is The Story
Wearin' That Loved On Look
You'll Think Of Me
A Little Bit Of Green
Gentle On My Mind
I'm Movin' On
Don't Cry Daddy
Inherit The Wind
Mama Liked The Roses
My Little Friend
In The Ghetto

Rubberneckin'
From A Jack To A King
Hey Jude
Without Love (There Is Nothing)
I'll Hold You In My Heart
I'll Be There
Suspicious Minds
True Love Travels On A Gravel Road
Stranger In My Own Home Town
And The Grass Won't Pay No Mind
Power Of My Love

Disc #5 Blue and Black Picture Disc
Matrix# 07863661602P5 03# ++ 30675
Disc contains the following selections:

After Loving You
Do You Know Who I Am
Kentucky Rain
Only The Strong Survive
It Keeps Right On A-Hurtin'
Any Day Now
If I'm A Fool (For Loving You)
The Fair Is Moving On
Who Am I?
This Time/I Can't Stop Loving You
(*Informal Recording*)
In The Ghetto (*Alternate Take 4*)

Suspicious Minds (*Alternate Take 6*)
Kentucky Rain (*Alternate Take 9*)
Big Boss Man (*Alternate Take 2*)
Down In The Alley (*Alternate Take 1*)
Memphis, Tennessee
(*Alt. Take 1 from the "1963 Session"*)
I'm Yours (*Alt. Take 1 Undubbed Version*)
His Latest Flame (*Alternate Take 4*)
That's Someone You Never Forget
(*Alternate Take 1*)
Surrender (*Alternate Take 1*)
It's Now Or Never
(*Original Undubbed Master*)
Love Me Tender/Witchcraft
(*From "The Frank Sinatra Timex Special
recorded March 26, 1960 at
Hotel Fontainebleau, Miami*)

[ ]   **FROM NASHVILLE TO MEMPHIS** *(Promo Box Set)*
        THE ESSENTIAL 60's MASTERS I
        Catalog# 07863-66160-2 NFS-1 or PRES-4/2   **Value $ 90-100**
        Disc #1 **Matrix# 07863661602P1 01#**
        Disc #2 **Matrix# 07863661602P2 03#**
        Disc #3 **Matrix# 07863661602P3 01#**
        Disc #4 **Matrix# 07863661602P4 02#**
        Disc #5 **Matrix# 07863661602P5 03#**
        (Sept. 1993 Designated Promo Box Set. Same as regular catalog release with
        Black and White sticker "Not For Sale NFS-1" under shrink wrap.
        This was also issued on a promo with the Black and White sticker
        "For Promotion Only Not For Sale PRES-4/2")

3735-2-R

1. TONIGHT IS SO RIGHT FOR LOVE (Sid Wayne - Silver Joe Lilly) 2:15
2. SHE'S ALL MINE 2:17
3. FRANKFORT SPECIAL (Sid Wayne - Sherman Edwards) 2:55
4. WOODEN HEART (Fred Wise - Ben Weisman - Kay Twoney) 2:02
5. G.I. BLUES (Tepper - Bennett) 3:37
6. POCKET FULL OF RAINBOWS (Fred Wise - Ben Weisman) 2:29
7. SHOPPIN' AROUND (Tepper - Bennett - Schroeder) 2:24
8. BIG BOOTS (Wayne - Edwards) 1:29
9. DIDJA' EVER (Sid Wayne - Sherman Edwards) 2:36
10. BLUE SUEDE SHOES (Carl Perkins) Hill and Range Songs, Inc., BMI 2:05
11. DOIN' THE BEST I CAN (Doc Pomus - Mort Shuman) 3:10
12. TONIGHT IS SO RIGHT FOR LOVE (Alternate Version) 1:21
    (Sid Wayne - Silver Joe Lilly)

All Selections From The Hal Wallis Production "G.I. Blues," A Paramount Picture

Digital Series Executive Producer - Don Wardell
Digital Series Remastering Engineer/Producer: Rick Rowe

BMG   RCA

Tmk(s) ® Registered • Marca(s) Registrada(s) RCA Corporation, except BMG logo TM BMG Music
1960 BMG Music • Manufactured and Distributed by BMG Music, New York, N.Y. • Printed in U.S.A.

3735-2-R

1. TONIGHT IS SO RIGHT FOR LOVE (Sid Wayne - Silver Joe Lilly) 2:15
2. SHE'S ALL MINE 2:17
3. FRANKFORT SPECIAL (Sid Wayne - Sherman Edwards) 2:55
4. WOODEN HEART (Fred Wise - Ben Weisman - Kay Twoney) 2:02
5. G.I. BLUES (Tepper - Bennett) 3:37
6. POCKET FULL OF RAINBOWS (Fred Wise - Ben Weisman) 2:29
7. SHOPPIN' AROUND (Tepper - Bennett - Schroeder) 2:24
8. BIG BOOTS (Wayne - Edwards) 1:29
9. DIDJA' EVER (Sid Wayne - Sherman Edwards) 2:36
10. BLUE SUEDE SHOES (Carl Perkins) Hill and Range Songs, Inc., BMI 2:05
11. DOIN' THE BEST I CAN (Doc Pomus - Mort Shuman) 3:10
12. TONIGHT IS SO RIGHT FOR LOVE (Alternate Version) 1:21
    (Sid Wayne - Silver Joe Lilly)

All Selections From The Hal Wallis Production "G.I. Blues," A Paramount Picture

Digital Series Executive Producer - Don Wardell
Digital Series Remastering Engineer/Producer: Rick Rowe

BMG   RCA

Tmk(s) ® Registered • Marca(s) Registrada(s) RCA Corporation, except BMG logo TM BMG Music
1960 BMG Music • Manufactured and Distributed by BMG Music, New York, N.Y. • Printed in U.S.A.

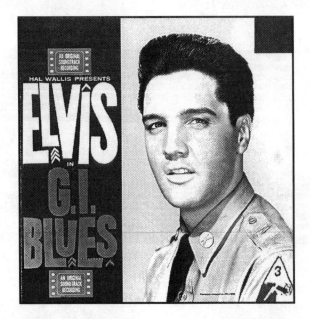

AN ORIGINAL SOUNDTRACK RECORDING
HAL WALLIS PRESENTS
ELVIS in G.I. BLUES
AN ORIGINAL SOUND TRACK RECORDING

3735-2-R

1. TONIGHT IS SO RIGHT FOR LOVE (Sid Wayne - Silver Joe Lilly) 2:15
2. WHAT'S SHE REALLY LIKE 2:17
3. FRANKFORT SPECIAL (Sid Wayne - Sherman Edwards) 2:55
4. WOODEN HEART (Fred Wise - Ben Weisman - Kay Twoney) 2:02
5. G.I. BLUES (Tepper - Bennett) 3:37
6. POCKET FULL OF RAINBOWS (Fred Wise - Ben Weisman) 2:29
7. SHOPPIN' AROUND (Tepper - Bennett - Schroeder) 2:24
8. BIG BOOTS (Wayne - Edwards) 1:29
9. DIDJA' EVER (Sid Wayne - Sherman Edwards) 2:36
10. BLUE SUEDE SHOES (Carl Perkins) Hill and Range Songs, Inc., BMI 2:05
11. DOIN' THE BEST I CAN (Doc Pomus - Mort Shuman) 3:10
12. TONIGHT IS SO RIGHT FOR LOVE (Alternate Version) 1:21
    (Sid Wayne - Silver Joe Lilly)

All Selections From The Hal Wallis Production "G.I. Blues," A Paramount Picture

Digital Series Executive Producer - Don Wardell
Digital Series Remastering Engineer/Producer: Rick Rowe

BMG   RCA

Tmk(s) ® Registered • Marca(s) Registrada(s) RCA Corporation, except BMG logo TM BMG Music
1960 BMG Music • Manufactured and Distributed by BMG Music, New York, N.Y. • Printed in U.S.A.   RE

3735-2-R

1. TONIGHT IS SO RIGHT FOR LOVE (Sid Wayne - Silver Joe Lilly) 2:15
2. WHAT'S SHE REALLY LIKE (Sid Wayne-Silver Joe Lilly) 2:17
3. FRANKFORT SPECIAL (Sid Wayne - Sherman Edwards) 2:55
4. WOODEN HEART (Fred Wise - Ben Weisman - Kay Twoney) 2:02
5. G.I. BLUES (Tepper - Bennett) 3:37
6. POCKET FULL OF RAINBOWS (Fred Wise - Ben Weisman) 2:29
7. SHOPPIN' AROUND (Tepper - Bennett - Schroeder) 2:24
8. BIG BOOTS (Wayne - Edwards) 1:29
9. DIDJA' EVER (Sid Wayne - Sherman Edwards) 2:36
10. BLUE SUEDE SHOES (Carl Perkins) Hill and Range Songs, Inc., BMI 2:05
11. DOIN' THE BEST I CAN (Doc Pomus - Mort Shuman) 3:10
12. TONIGHT IS SO RIGHT FOR LOVE (Alternate Version) 1:21
    (Sid Wayne - Silver Joe Lilly)

All Selections From The Hal Wallis Production "G.I. Blues," A Paramount Picture

Digital Series Executive Producer - Don Wardell
Digital Series Remastering Engineer/Producer: Rick Rowe

BMG   RCA

Tmk(s) ® Registered • Marca(s) Registrada(s) RCA Corporation, except BMG logo TM BMG Music
1960 BMG Music • Manufactured and Distributed by BMG Music, New York, N.Y. • Printed in U.S.A.   RE-1

[ ]   **G. I. BLUES**
Catalog# 3735-2-R   Value $ 12-15
Matrix# W.O. 10143-4 37352R
(April 1988 First Pressing. Midline CD. Silver & Black Disc with old RCA Logo.
Back cover printed "Digitally Remastered ADD".)
Disc contains the following selections:

Tonight Is So Right For Love	Shoppin' Around
She's All Mine	Big Boots
Frankfort Special	Didja' Ever
Wooden Heart	Blue Suede Shoes
G.I.Blues	Doin' The Best I Can
Pocket Full Of Rainbows	Tonight Is So Right For Love *(Alt. Version)*

[ ]   **G. I. BLUES**
Catalog# 3735-2-R   Value $ 10-12
Matrix# W.O. 10143-4 37352R
(1991 Second Pressing. Midline CD. Silver & Black Disc with old RCA Logo.
Back cover printed "Digitally Remastered" without ADD.)

[ ]   **G. I. BLUES**
Catalog# 3735-2-RRE   Value $ 10-12
Matrix# W.O. 10143-4 37352R
(1993 Third Pressing. Midline CD. Silver & Black Disc with old RCA Logo.
First and Second Pressings incorrectly listed "What's She Really Like" as
"She's All Mine". This pressing lists the correct title on insert sleeve.
Printing is lighter and smaller on disc. Insert and back cover with RE.)

[ ]   **G. I. BLUES**
Catalog# 3735-2-RRE-1   Value $ 10-12
Matrix# W. O. 10143-4 37352R
(1994 Fourth Pressing. Midline CD. Silver & Black Disc with old RCA Logo.
Insert sleeve and back cover give song writing credit on "What's She Really Like"
for first time Printing on disc lighter than third pressing. Insert and back
cover with RE-1.)

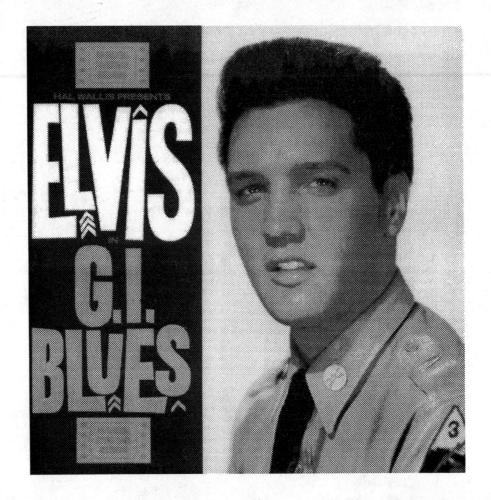

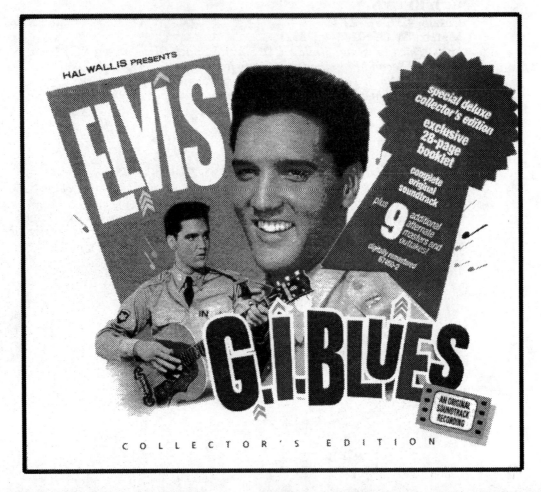

[ ] **G. I. BLUES**
Catalog# 07863-66960-2   **Value $ 15-18**
Matrix# 07863669602 ++ 75356-01
(April 1997 Reissue with new catalog number plus 9 additional alternate masters
and outtakes. Black and White Picture Disc. Contains 8 page insert booklet.
Red collectors sticker with yellow and white print on front of shrink wrap.
Digitally remastered from the original RCA Label Master Tapes.)
Disc contains the following selections:

Tonight Is So Right For Love	Doin' The Best I Can
What's She Really Like	Tonight's Alright For Love
Frankfort Special	Big Boots *(Fast Version Take 7)*
Wooden Heart	Shoppin' Around *(Alt. Take 11)*
G.I. Blues	Frankfort Special *(Fast Version Take 2)*
Pocketful Of Rainbows	Pocketful Of Rainbows *(Alt. Take 2)*
Shoppin' Around	Didja' Ever *(Alt. Take 1)*
Big Boots	Big Boots *(Acoustic Version Take 2)*
Didja' Ever	What's She Really Like *(Alt Take 7)*
Blue Suede Shoes	Doin' The Best I Can *(Alt. Take 9)*

[ ] **G. I. BLUES** *(Promo)*
Catalog# 07863-66960-2   **Value $ 18-20**
Matrix# 07863669602 ++ 75356-01
(April 1997 Designated Promo. Same as regular catalog release with black and
white sticker "Not For Sale NFS-1" on front cover of jewel box. Drill hole thru
back of jewel box.)

[ ] **G. I. BLUES** *(Collectors Edition)*
Catalog# 07863-67460-2   **Value $ 20-25**
Matrix# 07863674602 ++ 75335-01
(April 1997 Reissue Special Collectors Edition. Dark Red Picture Disc with Blue
lettering. Contains 28 page booklet housed in deluxe edition hard cover book.
CD contained in back of book in attached picture sleeve. Red collectors sticker
with yellow and white print "Special Deluxe Collectors Edition" on shrink wrap.)
Disc contains the following selections:

Tonight Is So Right For Love	Doin' The Best I Can
What's She Really Like	Tonight's All Right For Love
Frankfort Special	Big Boots *(Fast Version Take 7)*
Wooden Heart	Shoppin' Around *(Alt. Take 11)*
G.I. Blues	Frankfort Special *(Fast Version Take 2)*
Pocketful Of Rainbows	Pocketful Of Rainbows *(Alt. Take 2)*
Shoppin' Around	Didja' Ever *(Alt. Take 1)*
Big Boots	Big Boots *(Acoustic Version Take 2)*
Didja' Ever	What's She Really Like *(Alt. Take 7)*
Blue Suede Shoes	Doin' The Best I Can *(Alt. Take 9)*

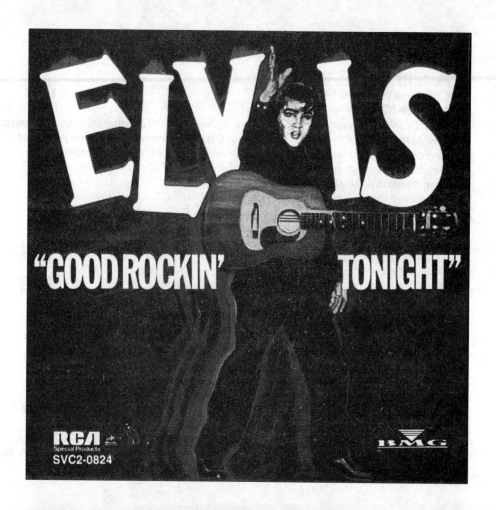

[ ] **GOOD ROCKIN' TONIGHT** *(2 CD Set)*
Catalog# SVC2-0824   **Value $ 75-100**
*(Jan. 1988 RCA Special Products Release. Silver Disc with block RCA Logo and Nipper in Red. Printing in Black. Two CD's in multi disc jewel box. Contains 4 page insert booklet. Mail Order Only. **This set is now deleted.**)*
Disc #1
Matrix# W.O. 10137-1 SVC2-0824-1
Disc contains the following selections:

Good Rockin' Tonight	Hound Dog
Jailhouse Rock	Tutti Frutti
Blue Suede Shoes	Hard Headed Woman
Little Sister	I Got A Woman
Tryin' To Get To You	Baby Let's Play House
Lawdy, Miss Clawdy	I Feel So Bad
Heartbreak Hotel	Mean Woman Blues
That's All Right	I Got Stung

Disc #2
Matrix# W.O. 10138-1 SVC2-0824-2
Disc contains the following selections:

One Night	Mystery Train
It Feels So Right	Ready Teddy
Fever	A Big Hunk O' Love
I Want You With Me	(Marie's The Name) His Latest Flame
Too Much	So Glad You're Mine
Money Honey	Like A Baby
Rip It Up	I Was The One
Down In The Alley	Soldier Boy

[ ] **GOOD TIMES**
Catalog# 07863-50475-2   **Value $ 12-15**
Matrix# 07863504752 01#
(March 1994 First Pressing. Elvis in the '90's Black Disc with The RCA Records Label and Nipper above new silver line. Print in Silver. Contains 8 page insert booklet including original single cover art for "Take Good Care Of Her" 45. Digitally Remastered from the original RCA Label Master Tapes.)
Disc contains the following selections:

Take Good Care Of Her	I've Got A Thing About You Baby
Loving Arms	My Boy
I Got A Feelin' In My Body	Spanish Eyes
If That Isn't Love	Talk About The Good Times
She Wears My Ring	Good Time Charlie's Got The Blues

[ ] **GOOD TIMES** *(Promo)*
Catalog# 07863-50475-2 NFS-1   **Value $ 15-20**
Matrix# 07863504752-01#
(March 1994 Designated Promo. Same as regular catalog release with black and white sticker "Not For Sale NFS-1" on front cover of jewel box. Drill hole) thru back of jewel box.)

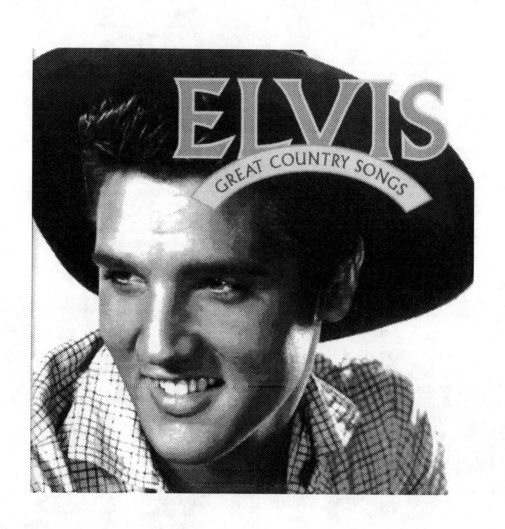

[ ] **GREAT COUNTRY SONGS**
Catalog# 07863 66880-2   Value $ 14-18
Matrix# 07863668802 ++ 70843-01
(Oct. 1996 First Pressing. Red Disc with Silver & Gold Print. Contains 12 page tri-fold insert booklet. Black Collectors sticker with red bar and white print on front cover of shrink wrap. "24 Great Tracks - Featuring 5 Previously Unreleased Performances". Digitally Remastered from the original RCA Label Master Tapes.)
Disc contains the following selections:

I Forgot To Remember To Forget	It Keeps Right On A-Hurtin'
Blue Moon Of Kentucky	Green, Green Grass Of Home *(Alt. Take 1)*
When My Blue Moon Turns To Gold Again	Fairytale *(Alternate Take 2)*
Old Shep	Gentle On My Mind
Your Cheatin' Heart *(Alternate Take 9)*	Make The World Go Away
(Now And Then There's) A Fool Such As I	You Asked Me To
Just Call Me Lonesome *(Alternate Take 6)*	Funny How Time Slips Away
There Goes My Everything *(Alternate Take 1)*	Help Me Make It Thru The Night *(Alt #3)*
Kentucky Rain	Susan When She Tried
From A Jack To A King	He'll Have To Go
I'll Hold You In My Heart	Always On My Mind
I Really Don't Want To Know	Guitar Man *(Remake)*

[ ] **GREAT COUNTRY SONGS** *(Promo)*
Catalog# 07863 66880-2   Value $ 15-20
Matrix# 07863668802 ++ 70843-01
(Oct. 1996 Designated Promo. Same as regular catalog release with Black and White sticker "Not For Sale NFS-1" on front cover of jewel box. Drill hole thru back of jewel box.)

[ ] **GREAT COUNTRY SONGS** *(Promo)*
Catalog# RJC 66880-2   Value $ 40-50
Matrix# 07863668802 ++ 70843-01
(Oct. 1996 Promo Only. Red Disc with Silver & Gold Print. Catalog #RJC 66880-2 and "Not For Sale" printed on disc. Black and White sticker "Not For Sale NFS-1" on front insert booklet. Hole punched thru the bar code on back insert cover.)

[ ] **GREAT COUNTRY SONGS**
Catalog# BG2-66880   Value $ 20-30
Matrix# DIDX-045601 G3 1A 07
(1998 Second Pressing. Mfg. by BMG Music for Columbia House Music Club. a non-BMG Music CD Club. Columbia House Music Club catalog number on disc and spine. CRC Logo printed below bar code on back insert cover. Red Disc with Silver & Gold Print. Contains 12 page tri-fold insert booklet. Digitally Remastered from the original RCA Label Master Tapes. Only available from Columbia House Music CD Club. Mail Order Only.)

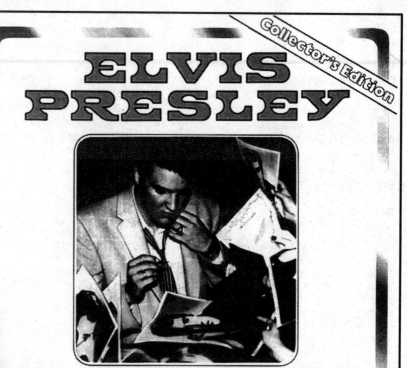

ELVIS PRESLEY

Collector's Edition

Great Hits of 1956-57

Reader's Digest

DIGITALLY REMASTERED

THE GREAT PERFORMANCES

ELVIS

[ ] **GREAT HITS OF 1956-57**
Catalog# RBD-072/CD1   Value $ 50-75
Matrix# W.O. 15436-1 XCD1-5721
*(July 1990 Special Collectors Edition from Reader's Digest Music.
Silver Disc with Black Print. Offered as a Bonus CD with the purchase
of the 4 CD Set "The Heart 'n' Soul of Rock 'n' Roll" which does not
contain any Elvis songs. Mail Order Only.)*
Disc contains the following selections:

Hound Dog	Blue Suede Shoes
Don't Be Cruel	I Was The One
Love Me Tender	Love Me
I Want You, I Need You, I Love You	Teddy Bear
Heartbreak Hotel	Any Way You Want Me
Playing For Keeps	Too Much

[ ] The **GREAT PERFORMANCES**
Catalog# 2227-2-R   Value $ 15-18
Matrix# W.O. 14882-2 22272R
*(Aug. 1990 First Pressing. Silver & Black Disc with old RCA Logo.
Contains 6 page trifold insert booklet. First CD to contain "My Happiness"
and stereo version of "Treat Me Nice".)*
Disc contains the following selections:

My Happiness *(1953 Acetate)*	Treat Me Nice *(Stereo)*
That's All Right	King Creole
Shake, Rattle & Roll/Flip Flop & Fly	Trouble
Heartbreak Hotel	Fame And Fortune
Blue Suede Shoes	Return To Sender
Ready Teddy	Always On My Mind
Don't Be Cruel	American Trilogy
Teddy Bear	If I Can Dream
Got A Lot Of Livin' To Do	Unchained Melody
Jailhouse Rock	Memories

[ ] The **GREAT PERFORMANCES**
Catalog# 2227-2-R   Value $ 12-15
Matrix# W.O. 14882-5M 22272R
*(1993 Second Pressing. Silver & Black Disc with old RCA Logo. Contains
6 page trifold insert booklet.)*

[ ] The **GREAT PERFORMANCES**
Catalog# 2227-2-R   Value $ 12-15
Matrix# W.O. 14882-6 22272R
*(1994 Third Pressing. Silver & Black Disc with old RCA Logo. Contains
6 page trifold insert booklet.)*

[ ] The **GREAT PERFORMANCES**
Catalog# 2227-2-R   Value $ 12-15
Matrix# 64564-01 22272R
*(1996 Fourth Pressing. Silver & Black Disc with old RCA Logo. Contains
6 page trifold insert booklet.)*

ORIGINAL ALBUM ART

"H"

[ ]   **HE TOUCHED ME**

Catalog# 07863-51923-2   **Value $ 12-15**

Matrix# 07863-51923-2 1C 11

(April 1992 First Pressing. Elvis in the '90's Black Disc with old RCA Logo and Print in Silver. 8 page insert booklet. Digitally Remastered from the original RCA Label Master Tapes.)

Disc contains the following selections:

He Touched Me
I've Got Confidence
Amazing Grace
Seeing Is Believing
He Is My Everything
Bosom Of Abraham

An Evening Prayer
Lead Me, Guide Me
There Is No God But God
A Thing Called Love
I, John
Reach Out To Jesus

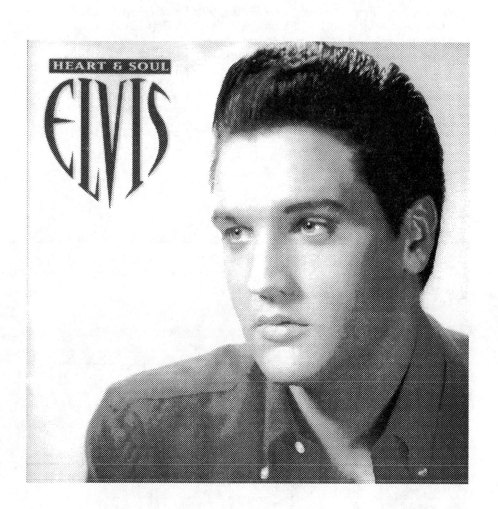

[ ]   **HEART AND SOUL**
Catalog# 07863 66532-2   **Value $ 14-18**
Matrix# 07863665322++52445-01
(Jan. 1995 First Pressing. Elvis in the '90's Black Disc with old RCA Logo
above new silver line. BMG has eliminated Nipper on this label. Print in Silver.
Contains 4 page trifold insert booklet. Maroon collectors sticker on front cover
of shrink wrap. First release of "Love Me Tender" and "I've Lost You" in stereo.
Also first time release of "Bridge Over Troubled Water" without dubbed
applause. Digitally Remastered from the original RCA Label Master Tapes.)
Disc contains the following selections:

Love Me Tender *(Unreleased Stereo)*	She's Not You
Young And Beautiful	Anything That's Part Of You
Love Me	Love Letters
I Want You, I Need You, I Love You	It's Now Or Never
Don't	It Hurts Me
As Long As I Have You	I Just Can't Help Believin'
Loving You	Always On My Mind
Fame And Fortune	Suspicious Minds
The Girl Of My Best Friend	I've Lost You *(Unreleased Stereo)*
Are You Lonesome Tonight?	You Don't Have To Say You Love Me
Can't Help Falling In Love	Bridge Over Troubled Water
	(Unreleased Undubbed Version)

[ ]   **HEART AND SOUL**   *(Promo)*
Catalog# 07863 66532-2   **Value $ 15-20**
Matrix# 07863665322++52445-01
(Jan. 1995 Designated Promo. Same as regular catalog release with black and
*white sticker "**Not For Sale NFS-1**" on front cover of jewel box. Drill hole thru*
back of jewel box.)

[ ]   **HEART AND SOUL**
Catalog# 07863 66532-2   **Value $ 20-30**
BMG Music Service Catalog# D 106881
Matrix# 07863665322++52445-01
(Feb. 1995 Second Pressing. Mfg. for BMG Direct Marketing, Inc. BMG Music
Service catalog number on disc and insert back cover. Elvis in the 90's Black Disc
with old RCA Logo above new silver line. Digitally Remastered from the original
RCA Label Master Tapes. Only available from BMG Music CD Club.
Mail Order Only.)

[ ]   **HEART AND SOUL**
Catalog# 07863 66532-2   **Value $ 20-30**
BMG Music Service Catalog# D 106881
Matrix# 07863665322 ++ 74228-03
(Jan. 1997 Third Pressing. Mfg for BMG Direct Marketing, Inc. BMG Music
Service catalog number on disc and insert back cover. Elvis in the 90's Black
Disc with old RCA Logo above new silver line. Digitally Remastered from the
original RCA Label Master Tapes. Only available from BMG Music CD Club.
Mail Order Only.)

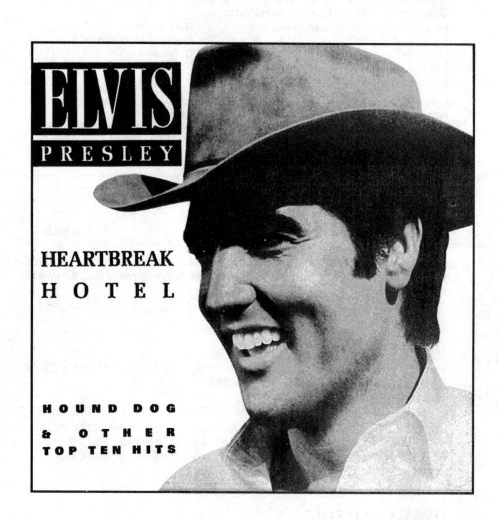

[ ]   **HEARTBREAK HOTEL, HOUND DOG & TOP TEN HITS**
Catalog# 2079-2-R   Value $ 8-12
Matrix# W.O. 15235-1 20792R
(Sept. 1990 First Pressing. Silver & Black Disc with old RCA Logo.
4 page insert booklet. RCA Sound Value Release. Contains 8 tracks.)
Disc contains the following selections:

Heartbreak Hotel	Jailhouse Rock
Hound Dog	Anyway You Want Me
Don't Be Cruel	That's When Your Heartaches Begin
Love Me Tender	Teddy Bear

[ ]   **HEARTBREAK HOTEL, HOUND DOG & TOP TEN HITS**
Catalog# 2079-2-R   Value $ 8-12
Matrix# W.O. 15235-2 20792R
(1994 Second Pressing. Silver & Black Disc with old RCA Logo.
4 page insert booklet. RCA Sound Value Release. "Wise Buy" sticker on
shrink wrap.)

[ ]   **HEARTBREAK HOTEL, HOUND DOG & TOP TEN HITS**
Catalog# 2079-2-R   Value $ 8-12
Matrix# 64743-01 20792R
(1996 Third Pressing. Silver & Black Disc with old RCA Logo.
4 page insert booklet. RCA Sound Value Release.)

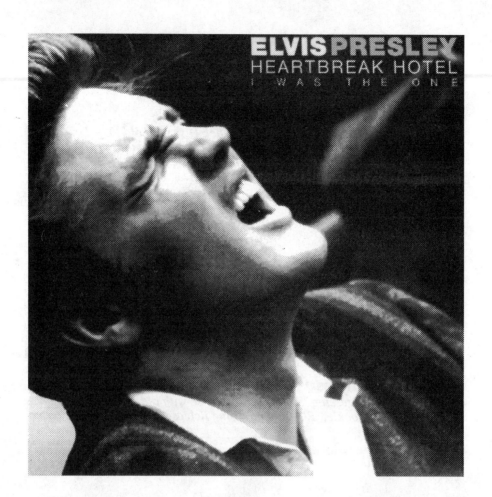

ELVIS PRESLEY
HEARTBREAK HOTEL
I WAS THE ONE

[ ]   **HEARTBREAK HOTEL**
         I WAS THE ONE
         Catalog# 07863 64475-2   Value $ 8-12
         Matrix# 07863644752 ++ 64583-01
         (April 1996 4 Track Matte finish Picture Disc. To promote "Elvis 56" CD.
         This is the only release that contains Alternate Take 2 of "I Was The One".)
         Disc contains the following selections:

         Heartbreak Hotel   Heartbreak Hotel *(Alternate Take 5)*
         I Was The One   I Was The One *(Alternate Take 2)*

[ ]   **HEARTBREAK HOTEL/ LOVE ME TENDER**
         Catalog# DRC11807   Value $ 2-5
         Matrix# L385 1100 DRC11807 C70717-10
         (Aug. 1997 20th Anniversary CD Single from BMG Special Products for
         Trans World Entertainment Inc. Sold only at TWE outlets- Coconuts, Tape World
         and Record Town. 20th Anniversary Picture Disc. Silver Disc with picture of
         Elvis and Print in Black. Disc housed in a die-cut paper sleeve. This is one of
         five 20th Anniversary CD Singles pressed for TWE.)
         Disc contains the following selections:
         Heartbreak Hotel   Love Me Tender

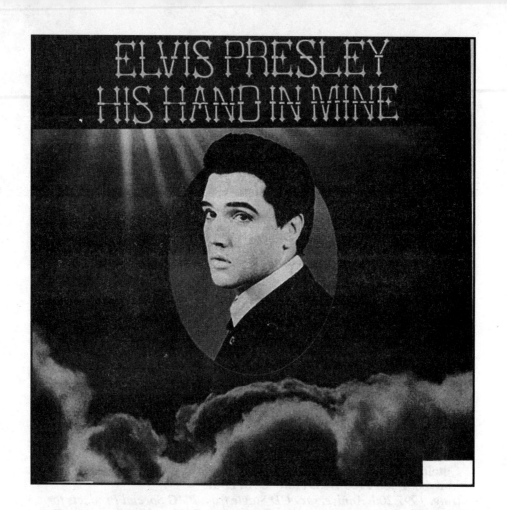

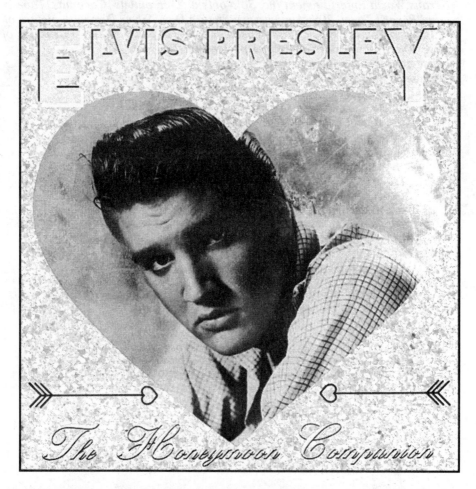

[ ]   **HIS HAND IN MINE**
           Catalog# 1319-2-R   **Value $ 12-15**
           Matrix# W.O. 10497-1 13192R
           (Aug. 1988 First Pressing. Midline CD. Silver & Black Disc with old RCA Logo.
           Contains three bonus tracks not included on the original Album.)
           Disc contains the following selections:

His Hand In Mine	Swing Down Sweet Chariot
(I'm) Gonna Walk Dem Golden Stairs	Mansion Over The Hilltop
In My Fathers House	If We Never Meet Again
Milky White Way	Working On The Building
Known Only To Him	It Is No Secret *(Bonus Track)*
I Believe In The Man In The Sky	You'll Never Walk Alone *(Bonus Track)*
Joshua Fit The Battle	Who Am I *(Bonus Track)*
He Knows Just What I Need	

[ ]   **HIS HAND IN MINE**
           Catalog# 1319-2-R   **Value $ 12-15**
           Matrix# W.O. 10497-2 13192R
           (1993 Second Pressing. Midline CD. Silver & Black Disc with old RCA Logo.)

[ ]   **HIS HAND IN MINE**
           Catalog# 1319-2-R   **Value $ 12-15**
           Matrix# 13192R ++ 64133-01
           (1996 Third Pressing. Midline CD. Silver & Black Disc with old RCA Logo
           with "Wise Buy" sticker on shrink wrap.)

[ ]   **HIS HAND IN MINE**
           Catalog# BG2-01319   **Value $ 20-30**
           Matrix# DIDX-036304 1
           (1998 Fourth Pressing. Mfg. by BMG Music for Columbia House Music Club,
           a non-BMG Music CD Club. Columbia House Music Club catalog number on
           disc, spine, front and back insert cover. Silver & Black Disc with old RCA Logo.
           Only available from Columbia House Music CD Club. Mail Order Only.)

[ ]   The **HONEYMOON COMPANION** *(Promo)*
           Catalog# RDJ 66124-2   **Value $ 75-100**
           Matrix# W.O. 76808-1 RDJ661242
           (Nov. 1992 RCA Promo Only Hologram Picture Disc sent to Radio Stations and
           CD Retail Stores to promote Elvis' original versions of the 13 songs used in the
           movie "Honeymoon In Vegas" and the "King of Rock 'N' Roll" Box Set.
           "Promo Only" and "Not For Sale" printed on CD and jewel box sleeve.
           Picture Disc is Silver with Pink printing.)
           Disc contains the following selections:

All Shook Up	(You're The) Devil In Disguise
Wear My Ring Around Your Neck	Hound Dog
Love Me Tender	That's All Right
Burning Love	Jailhouse Rock
Heartbreak Hotel	Blue Hawaii
Are You Lonesome Tonight?	Can't Help Falling In Love
Suspicious Minds	

GOLD
RCA
STANDARD SINGLE

HOUND DOG

ELVIS PRESLEY

DON'T BE CRUEL

8990-2-RH

COMMEMORATIVE JUKE BOX SERIES

BMG · RCA · Tmk(s) ® Registered · Marca(s) Registrada(s) RCA Corporation. BMG logo ® BMG Music © 1989 BMG Music · Manufactured and Distributed by BMG Music, New York, N.Y. · Printed in U.S.A.

[ ] **HOUND DOG / DON'T BE CRUEL**
Catalog# 8990-2-RH   Value $ 10-20
Matrix# W. O. 75061-1 89902RH
(May 1989 Commemorative Juke Box Gold Standard Series CD Single.
Silver & Black Disc with old RCA Logo. Gold Standard insert sleeve.
One of five Elvis CD singles pressed for Jukebox only.)
Disc contains the following selections:
Hound Dog   Don't Be Cruel

[ ] **HOUND DOG/ IT'S NOW OR NEVER**
Catalog# DRC11808   Value $ 2-5
Matrix# L385 1100 DRC11808 C70717-11
(Aug. 1997 20th Anniversary CD Single from BMG Special Products for
Trans World Entertainment Inc. Sold only at TWE outlets- Coconuts, Tape World
and Record Town. 20th Anniversary Picture Disc. Silver Disc with picture of
Elvis and Print in Black. Disc housed in a die-cut paper sleeve. This is one of
five 20th Anniversary CD Singles pressed for TWE.)
Disc contains the following selections:
Hound Dog   It's Now Or Never

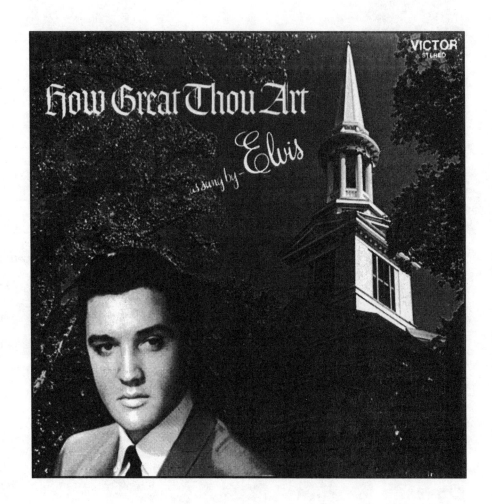

[ ]   **HOW GREAT THOU ART**
        Catalog# 3758-2-R   **Value $ 12-15**
        Matrix# W.O. 10562-2 37582R
        (Aug. 1988 First Pressing. Midline CD. Silver & Black Disc with old RCA Logo.
        Contains one bonus track not included on the original Album.)
        Disc contains the following selections:

How Great Thou Art   Where Could I Go But To The Lord
In The Garden   By And By
Somebody Bigger Than You And I   If The Lord Wasn't Walking By My Side
Farther Along   Run On
Stand By Me   Where No One Stands Alone
Without Him   Crying In The Chapel
So High   Peace In The Valley *(Bonus Track)*

[ ]   **HOW GREAT THOU ART**
        Catalog# 3758-2-R   **Value $ 10-12**
        Matrix# W.O. 10562-3 37582R
        (1991 Second Pressing. Midline CD. Silver & Black Disc with old RCA Logo.)

[ ]   **HOW GREAT THOU ART**
        Catalog# 3758-2-R   **Value $ 10-12**
        Matrix# W.O. 10562-7V 37582R
        (1993 Third Pressing. Midline CD. Silver & Black Disc with old RCA Logo.)

[ ]   **HOW GREAT THOU ART**
        Catalog# 3758-2-R   **Value $ 10-12**
        Matrix# 37582R ++ 64600-01
        (1997 Fourth Pressing. Midline CD. Silver & Black Disc with old RCA Logo.)

[ ]   **HOW GREAT THOU ART**
        Catalog# 3758-2-R   **Value $ 20-30**
        BMG Music Service Catalog# D140770
        Matrix# 37582R ++ 64600-01
        (1997 Fifth Pressing. Mfg. for BMG Direct Marketing, Inc. BMG Music Service
        catalog number over bar code on back insert cover. Silver & Black Disc with old
        RCA Logo. Only available from BMG Music CD Club. Mail Order Only.)

[ ]   **HOW GREAT THOU ART**
        Catalog# BG2-3758   **Value $ 20-30**
        Matrix# DIDX-036310 1
        (1997 Sixth Pressing. Mfg. by BMG Music for Columbia House Music Club,
        a non-BMG Music CD Club. Columbia House Music Club catalog number on
        disc, spine, front and back insert cover. Silver & Black Disc with old RCA Logo.
        Only available from Columbia House Music CD Club. Mail Order Only.)

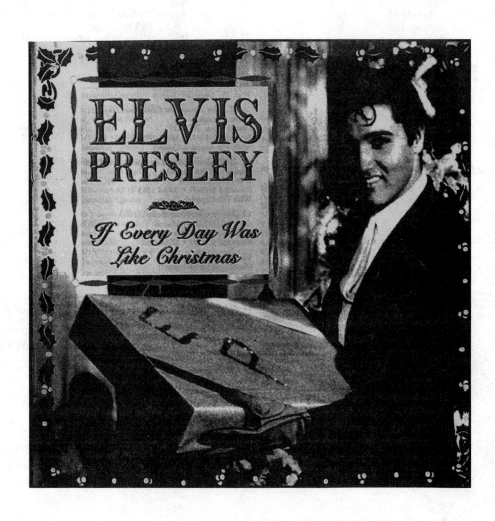

[ ]   **IF EVERY DAY WAS LIKE CHRISTMAS**
Catalog# 07863 66482-2   **Value $ 15-18**
Matrix# 50340-01 ++ 07863664822
*(Oct. 1994 First Pressing. Red Disc with old RCA Logo and Print in Gold.
Contains 16 page insert booklet. Dark Blue collectors sticker on jewel box shrink
wrap. Disc contains two previously unreleased alternate takes.)*
Disc contains the following selections:

If Every Day Was Like Christmas	Silver Bells
Blue Christmas	I'll Be Home On Christmas Day *(Alt.Vers.)*
Here Comes Santa Claus	On A Snowy Christmas Night
White Christmas	Winter Wonderland
Santa Bring My Baby Back (To Me)	The Wonderful World Of Christmas
I'll Be Home For Christmas	O Come All Ye Faithful
O Little Town Of Bethlehem	The First Noel
Santa Claus IsBack In Town	It Won't Seem Like Christmas(WithoutYou)
It Won't Seem Like Christmas (Without You)	*(Unreleased Alternate Take 6)*
If I Get Home On Christmas Day	Silver Bells *(Alternate Take 1)*
Holly Leaves And Christmas Trees	Holly Leaves And Christmas Trees
Merry Christmas Baby	*(Unreleased Alternate Take 8)*
	I'll Be Home On Christmas Day
	Christmas Message From Elvis/
	Silent Night

[ ]   **IF EVERYDAY WAS LIKE CHRISTMAS** *(Promo)*
Catalog# 07863 66482-2   **Value $ 18-20**
Matrix# 50340-01 ++ 07863664822
*(Oct. 1994 Designated Promo. Same as regular catalog release with Black &
White sticker "**Not For Sale NFS-1**" on front cover of jewel box. Drill hole
thru back of jewel box.)*

[ ]   **IF EVERYDAY WAS LIKE CHRISTMAS**
Catalog# 07863 66482-2   **Value $ 20-30**
BMG Music Service Catalog# D 108799
Matrix# 50340-01 ++ 07863664822
*(Nov. 1994 Second Pressing. Mfg. for BMG Direct Marketing, Inc. BMG Music
Service catalog number on disc and back insert cover. Red Disc with old RCA
Logo and Print in Gold. Contains 16 page insert booklet. Only available from
BMG Music CD Club. Mail Order Only.)*

[ ]   **IF EVERYDAY WAS LIKE CHRISTMAS**
Catalog# BG2-66482   **Value $ 20-30**
Matrix# 5 BG2 66482-2 SRC@ @01 xM2 S3
*(1997 Third Pressing. Mfg. by BMG Music for Columbia House Music Club, a
non-BMG Music CD Club. Columbia House Music Club catalog number on disc,
spine, front and back insert covers. CRC Logo printed above bar code on back
insert cover. Red Disc with old RCA Logo and Print in Gold. Contains 16 page
insert booklet. Only available from Columbia House Music CD Club.
Mail Order Only.)*

ELVIS PRESLEY

If Every Day Was Like Christmas

TO:

FROM:

SPECIAL COLLECTOR'S EDITION:
A full-color 12x12 "Winter at
Graceland" 3-dimensional pop-up.
Specially packaged with "If Every Day
Was Like Christmas" (cd only)
24 Classic Christmas Songs on 1 CD
Including 2 Unreleased Alternate Takes "It
Won't Seem Like Christmas (Without You)"
& "Holly Leaves And Christmas Trees"
2 Rare Alternate Takes "I'll Be Home On
Christmas Day" & "Silver Bells"
And A Special Christmas Message
From Elvis Himself!
07863 66406 2

SPECIAL COLLECTOR'S EDITION

[ ]   **IF EVERY DAY WAS LIKE CHRISTMAS**
SPECIAL COLLECTORS EDITION
Catalog# 07863 66506 2   Value $ 20-25
Matrix# W.O. 101819-1 07863665062
(Nov. 1994 Special Collectors Edition. Red Disc with old RCA Logo and Print in Gold. Contains 16 page insert booklet. This package is 6" x12" and opens up to 12" x 12" full color "Winter at Graceland" three dimensional Pop-Up. Disc housed in cardboard slip-case inside the 6" x 12" package.
Dark blue special collectors edition sticker on shrink wrap. "To & From" Christmas package tag also on shrink wrap. Disc contains two previously unreleased alternate takes.)
Disc contains the following selections:

If Every Day Was Like Christmas	Silver Bells
Blue Christmas	I'll Be Home On Christmas Day *(Alt. Vers.)*
Here Comes Santa Claus	On A Snowy Christmas Night
White Christmas	Winter Wonderland
Santa Bring My Baby Back (To Me)	The Wonderful World Of Christmas
I'll Be Home For Christmas	O Come All Ye Faithful
O Little Town Of Bethlehem	The First Noel
Santa Claus Is Back In Town	It Won't Seem Like Christmas(WithoutYou)
It Won't Seem Like Christmas (Without You)	*(Unreleased Alternate Take 6)*
If I Get Home On Christmas Day	Silver Bells *(Alternate Take 1)*
Holly Leaves And Christmas Trees	Holly Leaves And Christmas Trees
Merry Christmas Baby	*(Unreleased Alternate Take 8)*
	I'll Be Home On Christmas Day
	Christmas Mesage From Elvis/
	Silent Night

[ ]   **IF EVERY DAY WAS LIKE CHRISTMAS** *(Promo)*
SPECIAL COLLECTORS EDITION
Catalog# 07863 66506 2   Value $ 25-30
Matrix# W.O. 101819-1 07863665062
(Nov. 1994 Special Collectors Edition Designated Promo. Same as regular catalog release with Black & White sticker "Not For Sale - NFS-1" over bar code.)

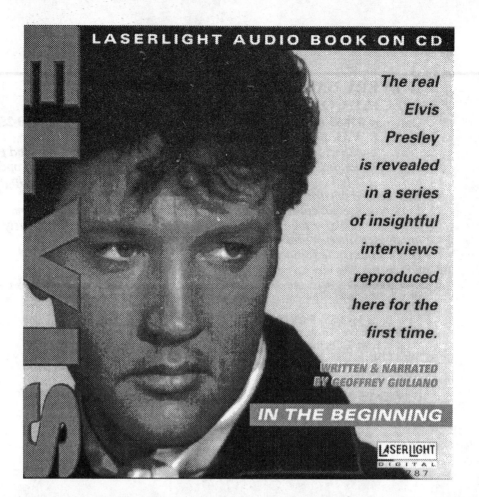

LASERLIGHT AUDIO BOOK ON CD

The real Elvis Presley is revealed in a series of insightful interviews reproduced here for the first time.

WRITTEN & NARRATED BY GEOFFREY GIULIANO

IN THE BEGINNING

LaserLight DIGITAL

[ ]   **IN THE BEGINNING**
            Catalog# 12 787   **Value $ 6-8**
            Matrix# 12787 Y6718G IFPI L532

(Sept 1996 Release from Laserlight Digital. This is a Laserlight Audio Book on CD. Contains 4 page insert booklet. Silver and Yellow Disc with Black Print. Written and Narrated by Geoffrey Giuliano. This is an interview only CD.)
Disc contains the following interviews:

Introduction
Presley Interview 1962 Part 1
Presley Interview 1962 Part 2
Presley Interview A
Presley Interview B
Presley Interview Little Rock, Arkansas

[ ]   **IN THE GHETTO/ STUCK ON YOU**
            Catalog# DRC11811   **Value $ 2-5**
            Matrix# L384 1100 DRC11811 B70718-01

(Aug. 1997 20th Anniversary CD Single from BMG Special Products for Trans World Entertainment Inc. Sold only at TWE outlets- Coconuts, Tape World and Record Town. 20th Anniversary Picture Disc. Silver Disc with picture of Elvis and Print in Black. Disc housed in a die-cut paper sleeve. This is one of five 20th Anniversary CD Singles pressed for TWE.)
Disc contains the following selections:

In The Ghetto   Stuck On You

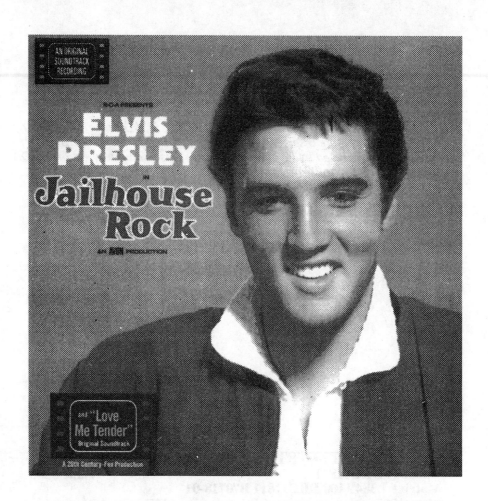

JAILHOUSE ROCK

ELVIS PRESLEY

TREAT ME NICE

8992-2-RH

COMMEMORATIVE JUKE BOX SERIES

  Tmk(s) ® Registered • Marca(s) Registrada(s) RCA Corporation. BMG logo ® BMG Music © 1989 BMG Music • Manufactured and Distributed by BMG Music, New York, N.Y. • Printed in U.S.A.

"J"

[ ] **JAILHOUSE ROCK**
and LOVE ME TENDER
Catalog# 07863-67453-2   **Value $ 15-18**
Matrix# 07863674532 ++ 75317-01
(April 1997 First Pressing. Red and Black Picture Disc. Contains 12 page insert booklet. Black collectors sticker with yellow and white print on front of shrink wrap. Digitally Remastered from the original RCA Label Master Tapes.)
Disc contains the following selections:

Jailhouse Rock	Don't Leave Me Now *(Alternate Master)*
Treat Me Nice	Love Me Tender
I Want To Be Free	Poor Boy
Don't Leave Me Now	Let Me
Young And Beautiful	We're Gonna Move
(You're So Square) Baby, I Don't Care	Love Me Tender *(End Title Version)*
Jailhouse Rock *(Movie Version)*	Let Me *(Solo)*
Treat Me Nice *(Movie Version)*	We're Gonna Move *(Stereo Take 9)*
I Want To Be Free *(Movie Version)*	Poor Boy *(Stereo)*
Young And Beautiful *(Movie Version)*	Love Me Tender *(Stereo)*

[ ] **JAILHOUSE ROCK** *(Promo)*
and LOVE ME TENDER
Catalog# 07863-67453-2   **Value $ 18-20**
Matrix# 07863674532 ++ 75317-01
(April 1997 Designated Promo. Same as regular catalog release with black and white sticker "Not For Sale NFS-1" on front cover of jewel box. Drill hole thru back of jewel box.)

[ ] **JAILHOUSE ROCK / TREAT ME NICE**
Catalog# 8992-2-RH   **Value $ 10-20**
Matrix# W.O. 75068-1 89922RH
(May 1989 Commemorative Juke Box Gold Standard Series CD Single. Silver & Black Disc with old RCA Logo. Gold Standard insert sleeve. One of five Elvis CD singles. Pressed for Jukebox Only.)
Disc contains the following selections:

Jailhouse Rock	Treat Me Nice

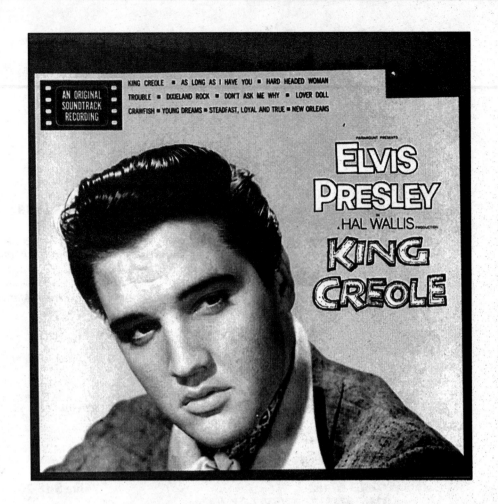

KING CREOLE ■ AS LONG AS I HAVE YOU ■ HARD HEADED WOMAN
TROUBLE ■ DIXIELAND ROCK ■ DON'T ASK ME WHY ■ LOVER DOLL
CRAWFISH ■ YOUNG DREAMS ■ STEADFAST, LOYAL AND TRUE ■ NEW ORLEANS

AN ORIGINAL SOUNDTRACK RECORDING

PARAMOUNT PRESENTS
ELVIS PRESLEY
A HAL WALLIS PRODUCTION
KING CREOLE

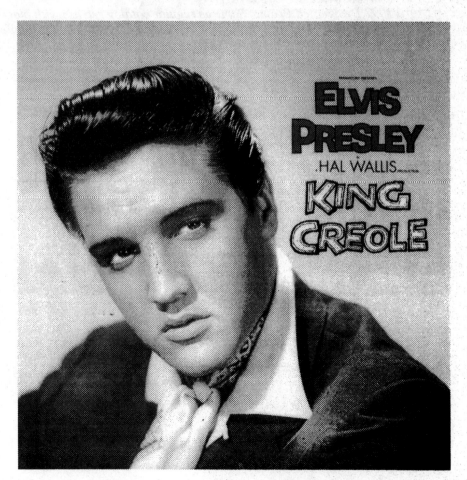

PARAMOUNT PRESENTS
ELVIS PRESLEY
A HAL WALLIS PRODUCTION
KING CREOLE

[ ]

KING CREOLE
Catalog# 3733-2-R   Value $ 12-15
Matrix# W.O. 10169-2 37332R
*(April 1988 First Pressing. Midline CD. Silver & Black Disc with old RCA Logo.
Back cover printed "Digitally Remastered ADD".)*
Disc contains the following selections:

King Creole	Lover Doll
As Long As I Have You	Crawfish
Hard Headed Woman	Young Dreams
Trouble	Steadfast, Loyal And True
Dixieland Rock	New Orleans
Don't Ask Me Why	

[ ]

KING CREOLE
Catalog# 3733-2-R   Value $ 10-12
Matrix# W.O. 10169-2 37332R
*(1991 Second Pressing. Midline CD. Silver & Black Disc with old RCA Logo.
Back cover printed "Digitally Remastered" without ADD.)*

[ ]

KING CREOLE
Catalog# 07863-67454-2   Value $ 15-18
Matrix# 07863674542 ++ 75315-03
*(April 1997 Reissue with new catalog number plus 7 additional alternate masters.
Brown and White Picture Disc. Contains 8 page insert booklet. Black collectors
sticker with yellow and white print on front of shrink wrap. Digitally remastered
from the original RCA Label Master Tapes.)*
Disc contains the following selections:

King Creole	Steadfast, Loyal And True
As Long As I Have You	New Orleans
Hard Headed Woman	King Creole *(Alt. Take 18)*
Trouble	As Long As I Have You*(Movie Ver. Take 4)*
Dixieland Rock	Danny
Don't Ask Me Why	Lover Doll *(Undubbed)*
Lover Doll	Steadfast, Loyal And True *(Alt. Master)*
Crawfish	As Long As I Have You*(Movie Ver Take 8)*
Young Dreams	King Creole *(Alt. Take 3)*

[ ]

KING CREOLE *(Promo)*
Catalog# 07863-67454-2   Value $ 18-20
Matrix# 07863674542 ++ 75315-03
*(April 1997 Designated Promo. Same as regular catalog release with black and
white sticker "Not For Sale NFS-1" on front cover of jewel box. Drill hole thru
back of jewel box.)*

[ ]

The KING OF ROCK 'N' ROLL *(5 CD Box Set)*
THE COMPLETE 50's MASTERS
Catalog# 07863-66050-2   **Value $ 70-80**

(June 1992 First Pressing. Packaged in Special Longbox. A numbered collectable 5 CD Box Set - 140 Tracks. Includes Fourteen previously unreleased performances. Each CD has it's own jewel box with it's individual insert sleeve. Each CD is a picture disc. Box contains a 92 page four-color booklet with complete 50's Sessionography and Discography plus a sheet of RCA Records Label stamps with photos of all the Elvis 45's, EP's and LP's from the 50's. Digitally Remastered from the original RCA Record Label and Sun Master Recordings. Pink & Black Collectors sticker on shrink wrap.)

Disc #1 Black and Pale Yellow Picture Disc
Matrix# W.O. 26259-1 07863660502

Disc contains the following selections:

My Happiness *(1953 Acetate)*
That's All Right
I Love You Because
Harbor Lights
Blue Moon Of Kentucky
Blue Moon
Tomorrow Night
I'll Never Let You Go (Little Darlin')
I Don't Care If The Sun Don't Shine
Just Because
Good Rockin' Tonight
Milkcow Blues Boogie
You're A Heartbreaker
Baby Let's Play House
I'm Left, You're Right, She's Gone

Mystery Train
I Forgot To Remember To Forget
Trying To Get to You
When It Rains, It Really Pours
I Got A Woman
Heartbreak Hotel
Money Honey
I'm Counting On You
I Was The One
Blue Suede Shoes
My Baby Left Me
One - Sided Love Affair
So Glad You're Mine
I'm Gonna Sit Right Down And Cry
Tutti Frutti

Disc #2 Black and Pink Picture Disc
Matrix# W.O. 26261-3 07863660502-2

Disc contains the following selections:

Lawdy, Miss Clawdy
Shake, Rattle And Roll
I Want You, I Need You, I Love You
Hound Dog
Don't Be Cruel
Any Way You Want Me
We're Gonna Move
Love Me Tender
Poor Boy
Let Me
Playing For Keeps
Love Me
Paralyzed
How Do You Think I Feel

How's The World Treating You
When My Blue Moon Turns To Gold Again
Long Tall Sally
Old Shep
Too Much
Any Place Is Paradise
Ready Teddy
First In Line
Rip It Up
I Believe
Tell Me Why
Got A Lot O' Livin' To Do!
All Shook Up
Mean Woman Blues
Peace In The Valley

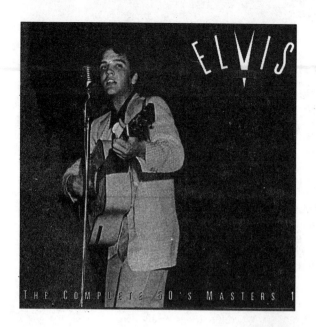

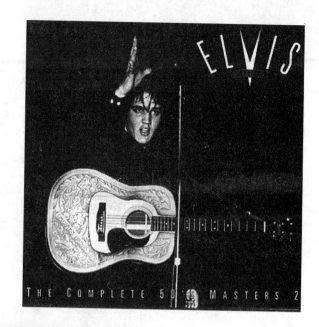

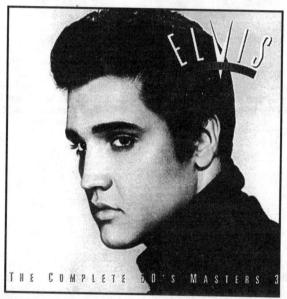

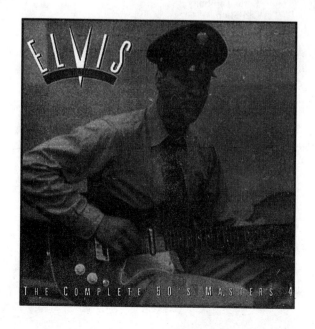

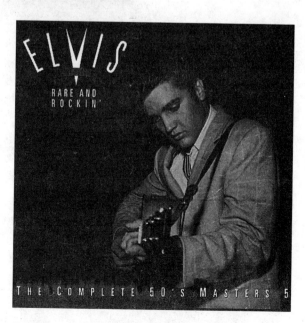

Disc #3 Black and Turquoise Picture Disc
Matrix# W.O. 26262-1 07863660502-3
Disc contains the following selections:

That's When Your Heartaches Begin
Take My Hand, Precious Lord
It Is No Secret (What God Can Do)
Blueberry Hill
Have I Told You Lately That I Love You
Is It So Strange
Party
Lonesome Cowboy
Hot Dog
One Night Of Sin
Teddy Bear
Don't Leave Me Now
I Beg Of You
One Night
True Love

I Need You So
Loving You
When It Rains, It Really Pours
Jailhouse Rock
Young And Beautiful
I Want To Be Free
(You're So Square) Baby I Don't Care
Don't Leave Me Now
Blue Christmas
White Christmas
Here Comes Santa Claus
Silent Night
O Little Town Of Bethlehem
Santa Bring My Baby Back (To Me)
Santa Claus Is Back In Town
I'll Be Home For Christmas

Disc #4 Black and Pale Blue Picture Disc
Matrix# W.O. 26263-4 07863660502-4
Disc contains the following selections:

Treat Me Nice
My Wish Came True
Don't
Danny
Hard Headed Woman
Trouble
New Orleans
Crawfish
Dixieland Rock
Lover Doll
Don't Ask Me Why
As Long As I Have You

King Creole
Young Dreams
Steadfast, Loyal And True
Doncha' Think It's Time
Your Cheatin' Heart
Wear My Ring Around Your Neck
I Need Your Love Tonight
A Big Hunk O' Love
Ain't That Loving You Baby
(Now And Then There's) A Fool Such As I
I Got Stung
Interview With Elvis

Disc #5 RARE AND ROCKIN' Black and Lavender Picture Disc
Matrix# W.O 26264-3 07863660502-5
Disc contains the following selections:

That's When Your Heartaches Begin *(1953 Acetate)*
Fool, Fool, Fool *(1955 Acetate)*
Tweedle Dee *(Texas 1954)*
Maybellene *(Louisiana 1955)*
Shake, Rattle And Roll *(1955 Acetate)*
Blue Moon Of Kentucky *(Alternate Take)*
Blue Moon *(Alternate Take 1)*
I'm Left, You're Right, She's Gone *(Alt. Take 11)*
Reconsider Baby *(Million Dollar Quartet)*
Lawdy, Miss Clawdy *(Alternate Take 3)*
Shake, Rattle And Roll *(Alternate Take 8)*
I Want You, I Need You, I Love You *(Alt. Take 16)*
Heartbreak Hotel *(Las Vegas 1956)*

Long Tall Sally *(Las Vegas 1956)*
Blue Suede Shoes *(Las Vegas 1956)*
Money Honey *(Las Vegas 1956)*
We're Gonna Move *(Alternate Take 4)*
Old Shep *(Alternate Take 5)*
I Beg Of You *(Alternate Master Take 12)*
Loving You *(Slow Version Alt. Take 12)*
Loving You *(Uptempo Version Alt. Take 13)*
Young And Beautiful *(Alternate Take 3)*
I Want To Be Free *(Alternate Take 10)*
King Creole *(Alternate Take 3)*
As Long As I Have You *(Alternate Take 8)*
Ain't That Loving You Baby
(Fast Version Take 11)

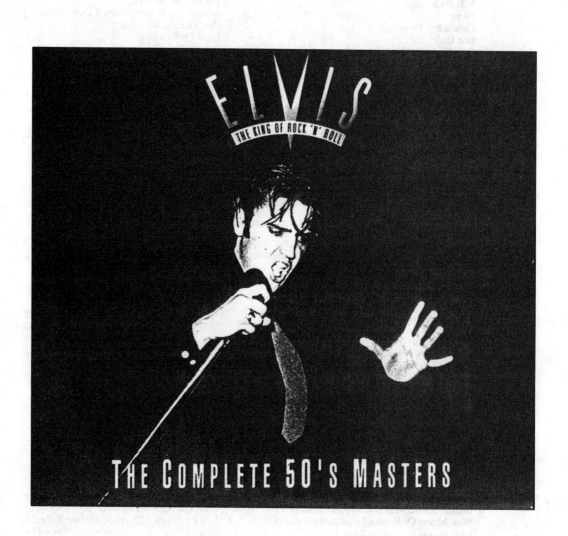

[ ] The **KING OF ROCK 'N' ROLL** *(5 CD Box Set)*
THE COMPLETE 50's MASTERS
Catalog# 07863-66050-2   Value $ 70-80
Disc #1 Matrix# W.O. 26259-3M 07863660502
Disc #2 Matrix# W.O. 26261-5M 07863660502-2
Disc #3 Matrix# W.O. 26262-3V 07863660502-3
Disc #4 Marix# W.O. 26263-6   07863660502
Disc #5 Matrix# W.O. 26264-6   07863660502-5
(1994 Second Pressing. Packaging same as First Pressing.)

[ ] The **KING OF ROCK 'N' ROLL** *(Promo Box Set)*
THE COMPLETE 50's MASTERS
Catalog# 07863-66050-2 PRES-4/2   Value $ 100-150
Disc #1 Matrix# W.O. 26259-1 07863660502
Disc #2 Matrix# W.O. 26261-3 07863660502-2
Disc #3 Matrix# W.O. 26262-1 07863660502-3
Disc #4 Matrix# W.O. 26263-4 07863660502-4
Disc #5 Matrix# W.O. 26264-3 07863660502-5
*(May 1992 Designated Promo Box Set. Same as regular catalog release, but with
the following added items. Folder with the same artwork and Elvis photo as on
front of longbox, 2 black and white 8" x 10" photo of Elvis, sheet of 36
collectable stamps, two pages of press release information on McMullen &
Company letterhead and black and white sticker reading "**For Promotion Only -
Not For Sale PRES-4/2**" under shrink wrap.)*

[ ] The **KING OF ROCK 'N' ROLL** *(Promo)*
THE COMPLETE 50's MASTERS
Catalog# 7432102022   Value $ 100-150
Matrix# S 74321102022 02
*(June 1992 Six Track Promo Release. Silver Disc with Red and Black Print.
Cardboard gatefold sleeve. This Promo CD was said to be pressed
in the U.S. to promote the Box Set in Germany. Listed here for that reason.)*
Disc contains the following selections:

Mystery Train	Trouble
All Shook Up	Shake, Rattle And Roll
(You're So Square) Baby I Don't Care	Don't Leave Me Now

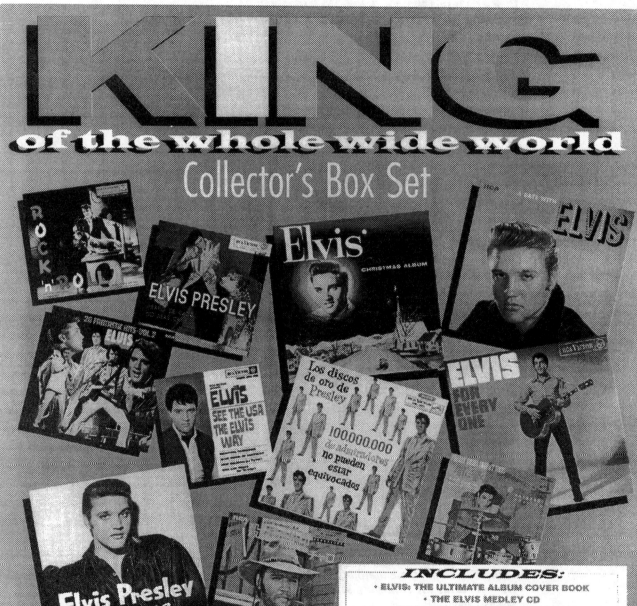

[ ]   **KING OF THE WHOLE WIDE WORLD** *(Collectors Box Set)*
        Catalog# WWE 001   **Value $ 100-125**
        (Oct. 1996 Collectors Box Set from Worldwide Elvis. Includes "Elvis: The
        Ultimate Album Cover Book", "The Elvis Medley CD", "The Gold Suit Elvis
        Phone Card" and "The Ultimate Album Cover Price Guide Booklet" which was
        contained in a 11" x 10-1/2" full color box. Although this CD is a Mexico only
        release, it is listed here because the box set was sold throughout the U.S.
        Mail Order Only.)
        Disc - **The Elvis Medley**
        Catalog# 7 48211 13562 2
        Matrix# IFPIL025 748211135622
        Disc contains the following selections:

The Elvis Medley	Burning Love
Jailhouse Rock	Suspicious Minds
Teddy Bear	Always On My Mind
Hound Dog	Heartbreak Hotel
Don't Be Cruel	Hard Headed Woman

COLLECTOR'S EDITION

THE LEGEND LIVES ON

"L"

[ ] The **LEGEND LIVES ON**   *(4 CD Set)*
Catalog# RBD-191/CD1   Value $ 55-60
(Oct. 1993 Special Collectors Edition from Reader's Digest Music. Silver Disc with Black Print. Title and Logos in Blue. Four CD's in multi disc Jewel Box. Mail Order Only. Contains 48 page insert booklet.)

Disc #1
Matrix# BCD45591 Y1D
Disc contains the following selections:

Medley: Also Sprach Zarathustra/That's All Right
Medley: Mystery Train/Tiger Man
Medley: Teddy Bear/Don't Be Cruel
Medley: LongTallSally/WholeLot-taShakin'Goin'On
Little Darlin'
Johnny B. Goode
See See Rider
Fever
A Big Hunk O' Love
Jailhouse Rock
Love Me
All Shook Up
I Just Can't Help Believin'
You Don't Have To Say You Love Me
Little Sister
You've Lost That Lovin' Feelin'
In The Ghetto
Suspicious Minds
What Now My Love
Are You Lonesome Tonight?
Medley: I Got A Woman/Amen
Medley: O Sole Mio/It's Now Or Never
Unchained Melody
Let It Be Me

Disc #2
Matrix# BCD45592 Y1C
Disc contains the following selections:

Burning Love
Steamroller Blues
It's Impossible
An American Trilogy
Let Me Be There
Bridge Over Troubled Waters
Kentucky Rain
Don't Cry Daddy
Fairytale
You Gave Me A Mountain
My Way
The Impossible Dream
Good Rockin' Tonight
Tryin' to Get to You
Shake, Rattle & Roll/Flip Flop & Fly
Heartbreak Hotel
Hound Dog
Don't Be Cruel (To A Heart That's True)
Rip It Up
Money Honey
Blue Moon
One-Sided Love Affair
Got A Lot O' Livin' To Do
Ready Teddy

COLLECTOR'S EDITION

Elvis

THE LEGEND LIVES ON

Reader's Digest

Disc #3
Matrix# BCD45593 1D
Disc contains the following selections:

Release Me (And Let Me Love Again)
Help Me Make It Through The Night
Always On My Mind
I'm So Lonesome I Could Cry
I Can't Stop Loving You
Green, Green Grass Of Home
Welcome To My World
And I Love You So
Mary In The Morning

Can't Help Falling In Love
Love Letters
Until It's Time For You To Go
Hurt
Separate Ways
Indescribably Blue
Fool
I've Lost You
For The Good Times

Disc #4
Matrix# BCD45594 1D
Disc contains the following selections:

Blue Suede Shoes
Medley:Lawdy, Miss Clawdy/
BabyWhat You Want Me To Do
Medley:Heartbreak Hotel/HoundDog/AllShookUp
Love Me Tender
Blue Christmas
One Night
Promised Land
U.S. Male
I'm Leavin'

Early Mornin' Rain
Moody Blue
Way Down
The Elvis Medley
Loving Arms
Funny How Time Slips Away
Yesterday
Memories
Life

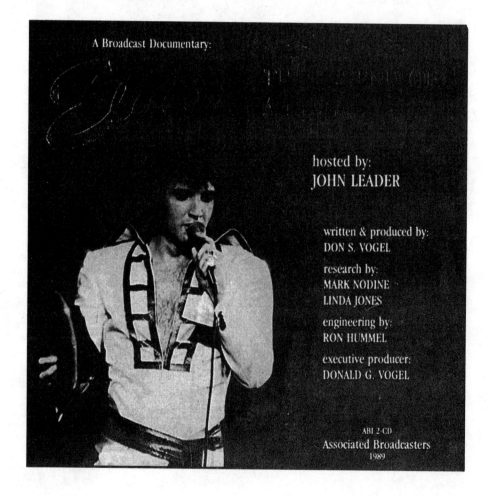

A Broadcast Documentary:

hosted by:
JOHN LEADER

written & produced by:
DON S. VOGEL

research by:
MARK NODINE
LINDA JONES

engineering by:
RON HUMMEL

executive producer:
DONALD G. VOGEL

ABI 2-CD
Associated Broadcasters
1989

[ ]   The **LEGEND OF A KING**   *(2 CD Set)*
Catalog# AB1-2CD   **Value $ 100-125**
(Aug. 1989 Associated Broadcasters Radio Station Only Release. A Broadcast Documentary on two Picture Discs in multi disc jewel box. Contains 10 page insert booklet. Limited Numbered Edition, only 1000 pressed. Twenty five full length songs in True Mono and Full Stereo with interviews.
"For Broadcast Only - Not For Sale" printed on disc and back cover.)

Disc #1
Matrix# 7TU0200B
Disc contains the following selections:

Old Shep   Trouble
That's All Right   All Shook Up
Good Rockin' Tonight   A Fool Such As I
Mystery Train   My Wish Came True
Heartbreak Hotel   It's Now Or Never
Don't Be Cruel   Can't Help Falling In Love
Love Me Tender   Return to Sender
Jailhouse Rock

Disc #2
Matrix# 7TW0400A
Disc contains the following selections:

If I Can Dream   Moody Blue
Suspicious Minds   Way Down
Johnny B. Goode   How Great Thou Art
Love Me, Love The Life I Lead   Memories
Separate Ways   American Trilogy

[ ]   The **LOST ALBUM**
        Catalog# 07863-61024-2   Value $ 14-18
        Matrix# 07863-61024-2 1T 12
        (Nov. 1991 First Pressing. Silver & Black Disc with old RCA Logo.
        Contains 4 page insert booklet.)
        Disc contains the following selections:
        Long Lonely Highway   Devil In Disguise
        Western Union   Finders Keepers, Losers Weepers
        Witchcraft   Echoes Of Love
        Love Me Tonight   Slowly But Surely
        What Now, What Next, Where To   It Hurts Me
        Please Don't Drag That String Around Memphis, Tennessee
        Blue River   Ask Me
        Never Ending

[ ]   The **LOST ALBUM**
        Catalog# 07863-61024-2   Value $ 12-15
        Matrix# 07863-61024-2 1T 25
        (1992 Second Pressing. Silver & Black Disc with old RCA Logo.
        Contains 4 page insert booklet.)

[ ]   The **LOST ALBUM**
        Catalog# 07863-61024-2   Value $ 12-15
        Matrix# 07863-61024-2 2T 11
        (1993 Third Pressing. Silver & Black Disc with old RCA Logo.
        Contains 4 page insert booklet.)

[ ]   The **LOST ALBUM**
        Catalog# 07863-61024-2   Value $ 12-15
        Matrix# 07863-61024-2 3C 11
        (1994 Fourth Pressing. Silver & Black Disc with old RCA Logo.
        Contains 4 page insert booklet.)

[ ]   The **LOST ALBUM**
        Catalog# 07863-61024-2   Value $ 12-15
        Matrix# 07863-61024-2 3C 27
        (1995 Fifth Pressing. Silver & Black Disc with old RCA Logo.
        *Contains 4 page insert booklet. **"Wise Buy"** sticker on shrink wrap.)*

THE LOUISIANA HAYRIDE

ANTHOLOGIES OF LEGENDS

ELVIS PRESLEY

Featuring Some of the Live Performances Which Made Him Famous

featuring a rare cover of
"Hearts Of Stone"

Louisiana Hayride

volume 1

The Louisiana Hayride
ARCHIVES

[ ] ## The LOUISIANA HAYRIDE
ANTHOLOGIES OF LEGENDS - ELVIS PRESLEY
Catalog# None   **Value $ 15-20**
Matrix# 0J544<5032>CDHRS4451R ADFL/NCD
(Dec. 1997 First Pressing from IMC Licensing, SA, Bobby & Ray Williams Partnership. Silver Disc with Black Print. 4 page insert. Re-Mix and Re-Mastered at Strawberry Skys Recording Studio, W. Columbia, S.C. from the original acetates. Song titles different from the original "Tweedle Dee", "Maybellene" and " Baby Let's Play House". Available from Critics Choice Music. Mail Order Only.)
Disc contains the following selections:

Narration	Narration
That's Alright Mama	Play House
Blue Moon	Maybaleen
Narration	That's Alright Mama (Version 2)
Hearts Of Stone	Tweedaly Dee (Version 2)
Money Honey	Narration
I Don't Care If The Sun Don't Shine	I Was The One
Good Rockin' Tonight	Love Me Tender
I Got A Woman	Hound Dog
Narration	"Elvis Has Left The Building"
Tweedaly Dee	Narration

[ ] ## The LOUISIANA HAYRIDE ARCHIVES, Volume 1
Catalog# BGR-02462   **Value $ 15-20**
Matrix# IFPI L791 145747-2W1-6183-A TAPESPECBGR02462****
(July 1996 First Pressing from Branson Gold, Inc. Mfg. & Distributed by Calf Creek Distribution. 1996 Pepper Ridge Productions, LLC. Silver Disc with Black Print. Single sheet insert cover. Group photo, but no mention of Elvis. No booklet included in original release. This release features Elvis' Hayride appearances with narration by Hayride announcer, Frank Page.)
Disc contains the following selections:

That's All Right, Mama 10/16/54	Baby, Let's Play House 8/20/55
Blue Moon Of Kentucky 10/16/54	Maybellene 8/20/55
Hearts Of Stone 1/15/55	That's All Right, Mama 11/19/55
Money Honey 1/22/55	Tweedle Dee 12/17/55
I Don't Care If The Sun Don't Shine 1/22/55	I Was The One 12/15/56
Good Rockin' Tonight 6/25/55	Love Me Tender 12/15/56
I Got A Woman 4/9/55	Hound Dog 12/15/56
Tweedle Dee 4/30/55	"Elvis Has Left The Building" 12/15/56

[ ] ## The LOUISIANA HAYRIDE ARCHIVES, Volume 1
Catalog# BGR-02462   **Value $ 15-20**
Matrix# IFPI L791 145747-2W1-6183-A TAPRSPECBGR02462****
(Sept. 1996 Reissue from Branson Gold, Inc. Mfg. & Distributed by Calf Creek Distribution. 1996 Pepper Ridge Productions, LLC. Silver Disc with Black Print. 12 page insert booklet with 10 photos from Elvis' Hayride performances. Same background artwork as first pressing but now has Elvis photo superinposed on front cover and different wording including "ELVIS PRESLEY" in black. All else same as first pressing.)

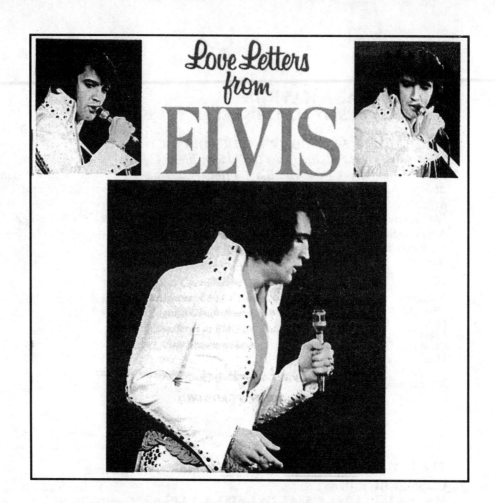

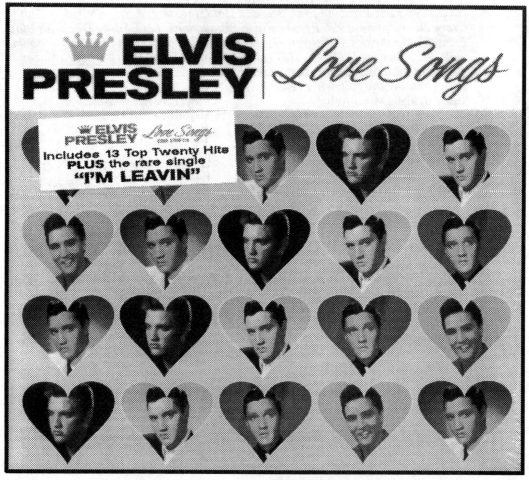

[ ] **LOVE LETTERS FROM ELVIS**
Catalog# 07863-54350-2   Value $ 12-15
Matrix# W.O. 27736-2M 07863543502
*(Oct. 1992 First Pressing. Elvis in the '90's Black Disc with old RCA
Logo and Print in Silver. 8 page insert booklet. Digitally Remastered
from the original RCA Label Master Tapes.)*
Disc contains the following selections:

Love Letters   This Is Our Dance
When I'm Over You   Cindy, Cindy
If I Were You   I'll Never Know
Got My Mojo Working   It Ain't No Big Thing (But It's Growing)
Heart Of Rome   Life
Only Believe

[ ] **LOVE SONGS**
Catalog# 07863-67595-2   Value $ 14-18
Matrix# 07863675952 ++ 82950-01
*(Jan. 1998 First Pressing. Disc is Silver with Yellow Hearts and Silver Crown in
center of Heart. Print in Black. Contained in a tri-fold cardboard digi-pack.
Blue, Black and White collectors sticker "Includes 13 Top Twenty Hits Plus the
rare single I'm Leavin" on front cover of shrink wrap. Single sheet promoting
Graceland Mail Order catalog included in the trifold. Digitally Remastered
from the original RCA Label Master Tapes.)*
Disc contains the following selections:

Unchained Melody   I'm Leavin'
Surrender   Love Me Tender *(Stereo)*
Are You Lonesome Tonight?   She's Not You
It's Now Or Never   That's Someone You Never Forget
Can't Help Falling In Love   Puppet On A String
Such A Night   Spanish Eyes
Good Luck Charm   Separate Ways
Suspicious Minds   You Gave Me A Mountain
Kentucky Rain   The Wonder Of You

[ ] **LOVE SONGS**   *(Promo)*
Catalog# 07863-67595-2   Value $ 15-20
Matrix# 07863675952 ++ 82950-01
*(Jan. 1998 Designated Promo. Same as regular catalog release with Black and
White sticker "**For Promotion Only Not For Sale P-4/2**" on back of digi-pack
over bar code.)*

[ ] **LOVE SONGS**
Catalog# 07863-67595-2   Value $ 20-30
BMG Music Service Catalog# D121742
Matrix# 07863675952 ++ 82950-01
*(Jan. 1998 Second Pressing. Mfg. for BMG Direct Marketing, Inc. BMG Music
Service catalog number printed on disc and back cover of digi-pack under bar
code. Only available from BMG Music CD Club. Mail Order Only.)*

[ ]   **LOVE ME TENDER** *(Shaped Disc)*
         Catalog# 07863-64885-2   **Value $ 10-15**
         Matrix# *RCA/Elvis RE1* 2706-1-1
         (July 1997 Release. Black & White Picture Disc. This is the first U.S. Elvis
         Shaped Picture Disc. Mfg. by Shape CD, Inc., Orlando, Florida for BMG.
         Available exclusively at Target Stores for a limited time.. Housed in a clear
         see-thru jewel case. This CD Single contains only one track.)
         Disc contains the following selection:
         Love Me Tender *(Stereo)*

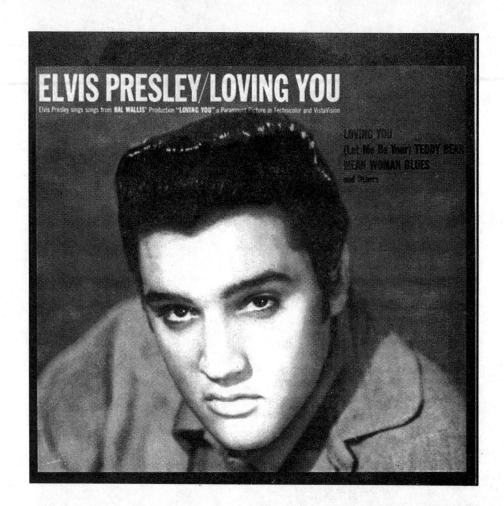

[ ]   **LOVING YOU**
    Catalog# 1515-2-R   **Value $ 12-15**
    Matrix# W.O. 10142-1 151522R
    (April 1988 First Pressing. Midline CD. Silver & Black Disc with old RCA Logo.
    Back cover printed "Digitally Remastered ADD".)
    Disc contains the following selections:

Mean Woman Blues	Party
Teddy Bear	Blueberry Hill
Loving You	True Love
Got A Lot O' Livin' To Do	Don't Leave Me Now
Lonesome Cowboy	Have I Told You Lately That I Love You
Hot Dog	I Need You So

[ ]   **LOVING YOU**
    Catalog# 1515-2-R   **Value $ 10-12**
    Matrix# W.O. 10142-1 151522R
    (1991 Second Pressing. Midline CD. Silver & Black Disc with old RCA Logo.
    Back cover printed "Digitally Remastered" without ADD.)

[ ]   **LOVING YOU**
    Catalog# BG2-1515   **Value $ 20-30**
    Matrix# 5 BG2 01515-2 SRC##01 M1S1
    (1997 Third Pressing. Mfg. by BMG Music for Columbia House Music Club, a
    non-BMG Music Club. Columbia House Music Club catalog number on disc,
    spine, booklet and back insert cover. CRC Logo printed below bar code on back
    insert cover. Silver & Black Disc with old RCA Logo. Only available from
    Columbia House Music CD Club. mail Order Only.)

[ ]   **LOVING YOU**
    Catalog# 07863-67452-2   **Value $ 15-18**
    Matrix# 07863674522 ++ 74993-01
    (April 1997 Reissue with new catalog number plus 8 additional alternate masters
    and outtakes. Brown and Red Picture Disc. Contains 8 page insert booklet.
    Red heart shaped collectors sticker with blue and white print on front of shrink
    wrap. Digitally remastered from the original RCA Label Master Tapes.)
    Disc contains the following selections:

Mean Woman Blues	Have I Told You Lately That I Love You
(Let Me Be Your) Teddy Bear	I Need You So
Loving You	Tell Me Why
Got A Lot O' Livin' To Do!	Is It So Strange
Lonesome Cowboy	One Night Of Sin
Hot Dog	When It Rains, It Really Pours
Party	I Beg Of You *(Alternate Master Take 12)*
Blueberry Hill	Party *(Alternate Master Take 7)*
True Love	Loving You *(Uptempo Ver. Alt. Take 13))*
Don't Leave Me Now	Got A Lot O' Livin' To Do! *(Finale)*

[ ]   **LOVING YOU** *(Promo)*
    Catalog# 07863-67452-2   **Value $ 18-20**
    Matrix# 07863674522 ++ 74993-01
    (April 1997 Designated Promo. Same as regular catalog release with black and
    *white sticker "**Not For Sale NFS-1**" on front cover of jewel box. Drill hole thru*
    back of jewel box.)

MAHALO from ELVIS

Ku-U-I-PO
Blue Hawaii
Early Mornin' Rain
Hawaiian Wedding Song
One Broken Heart For Sale

Relax
No More
Happy Ending
So Close, Yet So Far
Baby, If You'll Give Me
All Of Your Love

RCA · CAMDEN
CLASSICS

MEMORIESTHE'68COMEBACKSPECIAL

[ ]

MAHALO FROM ELVIS
Catalog# CCD-7064   **Value $ 20-25**
Matrix# #910518DD CCD-7064
(Nov. 1991 First Pressing. Canada Only Release. RCA Camden Classics.
Silver & Black Disc with old RCA and Camden Logos. 4 page insert booklet.
This CD is listed here as it was available for sale in the U.S.)
Disc contains the following selections:

Blue Hawaii	Relax
Early Mornin' Rain	Baby, If You'll Give Me All Of Your Love
Hawaiian Wedding Song	One Broken Heart For Sale
Ku-U-I-Po	So Close, Yet So Far (From Paradise)
No More	Happy Ending

[ ]

MEMORIES   *(2 CD's)*
THE '68 COMEBACK SPECIAL
Catalog# 07863-67612-2   **Value $ 25 - 30**
(Oct. 1998 First Pressing. A 2 CD Picture Disc Set housed in Double Slimline
jewel case. Contains 24 page insert booklet. Red collectors sticker with black
print on front of shrink wrap. 30th Anniversary Edition of '68 Comeback Special.
Digitally Remastered from the original RCA Label Master Tapes.)
Disc #1 Red & Silver Picture Disc
Matrix# 07863676122D1 ++ 91686-01
Disc contains the following selections:

June 29, 1968 Stand Up Show	**Gospel Medley:** Sometimes I Feel Like A
Trouble/Guitar Man	Motherless Child/Where Could I Go But To
Heartbreak Hotel	The Lord/Up Above My Head/Saved
Hound Dog	Memories
All Shook Up	A Little Less Conversation(*PrevUnreleased*)
Can't Help Falling In Love	**Road Medley:**Nothingville/Big Boss Man/
Jailhouse Rock (*Previously Unreleased*)	Let Yourself Go/ It Hurts Me/Guitar Man/
Don't Be Cruel (*Previously Unreleased*)	Little Egypt/ Trouble
Blue Suede Shoes (*Previously Unreleased*)	If I Can Dream
Love Me Tender (*Previously Unreleased*)	
Baby What You Want Me To Do (*Prev. Unreleased*)	
Trouble/Guitar Man (*Previously Unreleased*)	

Disc #2 Black & Silver Picture Disc
Matrix# 07863676122D2 ++ 91687-01
Disc contains the following selections:

Dress Rehearsal	Lawdy, Miss Clawdy (*Prev. Unreleased*)
When It Rains It Really Pours (*Prev. Unreleased*)	Are You Lonesome Tonight (*Prev. Unrelsd*)
Lawdy Miss Clawdy (*Previously Unreleased*)	When My Blue Moon Turns To Gold Again
Baby What You Want Me To Do (*Prev. Unreleased*)	(*Previously Unreleased*)
June 27, 1968 Sit Down Show	Blue Christmas (*Previously Unreleased*)
That's All Right (*Previously Unreleased*)	Trying To Get To You (*Prev. Unreleased*)
Heartbreak Hotel (*Previously Unreleased*)	One Night (*Previously Unreleased*)
Love Me (*Previously Unreleased*)	Baby What You Want Me To Do
Baby What You Want Me To Do (*Prev. Unreleased*)	One Night
Blue Suede Shoes	Memories (*Previously Unreleased*)
Baby What You Want Me To Do	If I Can Dream (*Previously Unreleased*)

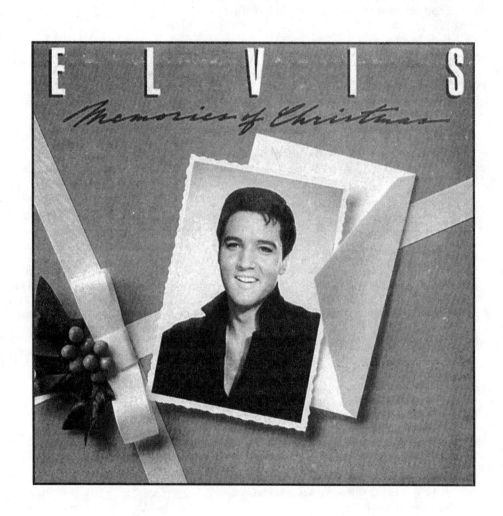

[ ] **MEMORIES OF CHRISTMAS**
Catalog# 4395-2-R   Value $ 12-15
Matrix# 43952R 9/87 1DD1
(Sept 1987 First Pressing. Silver & Black Disc with old RCA Logo.
Red Background with White Print on back cover.)
Disc contains the following selections:

Oh Come, All Ye Faithful	Santa Claus Is Back In Town
(Unreleased Version)	Merry Christmas Baby
Silver Bells	*(Unreleased Complete Studio Performance)*
I'll Be Home On Christmas Day	If Every Day Was Like Christmas
Blue Christmas	*(Unreleased Version)*
	Christmas Message From Elvis/Silent Night

[ ] **MEMORIES OF CHRISTMAS**
Catalog# 4395-2-RRE   Value $ 10-12
Matrix# 43952R 9/89 1DD6
(Sept 1989 Second Pressing. Silver & Black Disc with old RCA Logo.
White Background with Black Print on back cover.)

[ ] **MEMORIES OF CHRISTMAS**
Catalog# 4395-2-RRE   Value $ 10-12
Matrix# 43952R 8/91 3DA3X
(Aug. 1991 Third Pressing. Silver & Black Disc with old RCA Logo.
White Background with Black Print on back cover.)

[ ] **MEMORIES OF CHRISTMAS**
Catalog# 4395-2-RRE   Value $ 10-12
Matrix# 43952R 8/91 3DB1X
(Aug. 1991 Fourth Pressing. Silver & Black Disc with old RCA Logo.
White Background with Black Print on back cover.)

[ ] **MEMORIES OF CHRISTMAS**
Catalog# 4395-2-RRE   Value $ 10-12
Matrix# 43952R 6/94 3D84
(June 1994 Fifth Pressing. Silver & Black Disc with old RCA Logo.
White Background with Black Print on back cover.)

[ ] **MEMORIES OF CHRISTMAS**
Catalog# 4395-2-RRE   Value $ 10-12
Matrix# 43952R 11/94 6DA1
(Nov. 1994 Sixth Pressing. Silver & Black Disc with old RCA Logo with
"Wise Buy" sticker on shrink wrap. White Background with Black Print on
back cover.)

[ ] **MEMORIES OF CHRISTMAS**
Catalog# 4395-2-RRE   Value $ 10-12
Matrix# 43952R 7/95 6DA7
(July 1995 Seventh Pressing. Silver & Black Disc with old RCA Logo with
"Wise Buy" sticker on shrink wrap. White Background with Black Print on
back cover.)

MEMORIES OF ELVIS

RADIO PROGRAMMING

06-08-90

MEMORIES OF ELVIS *(4 CD Radio Show)*
Catalog# Unistar 08/09-08/16   Value $ 100-125
(June 1991 Limited Edition 4 CD Radio Show from the Unistar Radio Network.
Silver Elvis Picture Disc with Blue Print. Contains Cue Sheets for 4 hour Elvis
Radio Show broadcast 8/9 - 8-16. Disc and Cue Sheets enclosed in "the Original
CD Shortbox". Drawing of Elvis on Shortbox.)
Disc #1
Matrix# A4XX0100B Hour 1
Disc contains the following selections:

Hard Headed Woman
One Broken Heart For Sale
I Beg Of You
Steamroller Blues
I Need Your Love Tonight
Loving You
Bossa Nova Baby
G.I. Blues

(Marie's The Name) His Latest Flame
I Got Stung
Don't
You Don't Have To Say You Love Me
Treat Me Nice
Big Hunk O' Love
My Wish Came True
Love Me
When My Blue Moon Turns To Gold Again

Disc #2
Matrix# A4XY0100C Hour 2
Disc contains the following selections:

My Boy
Too Much
Surrender
I Feel So Bad
Mystery Train
Viva Las Vegas
Such A Night
I Was The One

She's Not You
Stuck On You
Crying In The Chapel
Good Luck Charm
Follow That Dream
(You're The) Devil In Disguise
One Night
Promised Land

Disc #3
Matrix# A4Y00100A Hour 3
Disc contains the following selections:

Guitar Man
Don't Cry Daddy
(Now And Then There's) A Fool Such As I
Separate Ways
That's All Right Mama
Baby Let's Play House
It's Now Or Never
Wear My Ring Around Your Neck

Way Down
If I Can Dream
Little Sister
Teddy Bear
Blue Suede Shoes
Burning Love
Return To Sender
In The Ghetto

Disc #4
Matrix# A4Y10100C Hour 4
Disc contains the following selections:

My Way
Are You Lonesome Tonight
Kentucky Rain
The Wonder Of You
All Shook Up
Don't Be Cruel

Hound Dog
I Want You, I Need You, I Love You
Heartbreak Hotel
Love Me Tender
Can't Help Falling In Love
Suspicious Minds
Jailhouse Rock

Memories of ELVIS

UNISTAR
RADIO PROGRAMMING

08-13-93

[ ]   **MEMORIES OF ELVIS** *(3 CD Radio Show)*
             Catalog# Unistar 08/13-08/15   **Value $ 75-100**
             (Aug. 1993 Limited Edition 3 CD Radio Show from the Unistar Radio Network.
             Silver Discs with Black Print. Contans Cue Sheets for 3 hour Elvis Radio Show
             broadcast 8/13 - 8/16. Discs and Cue Sheets enclosed in "the Original CD
             Shortbox".)
             Disc #1
             Matrix# HEW80100A Hour 1
             Disc contains the following selections:

That's All Right Mama   Don't Be Cruel
Baby, Let's Play House   Love Me Tender
Mystery Train   Love Me
Heartbreak Hotel   Too Much
Blue Suede Shoes   All Shook Up
I Want You, I Need You, I Love You   (Let Me Be Your) Teddy Bear
Hound Dog   Loving You
                                               Jailhouse Rock

Disc #2
Matrix# HEW90200A Hour 2
Disc contains the following selections:

Treat Me Nice   I Need Your Love Tonight
Don't   Big Hunk O' Love
I Beg O You   Stuck On You
Wear My Ring Around Your Neck   It's Now Or Never
Hard Headed Woman   Are You Lonesome To-Night?
One Night   Surrender
I Got Stung   Little Sister
(Now And Then There's) A Fool Such As I   (Marie's The Name) His Latest Flame
                                               Can't Help Falling In Love

Disc #3
Matrix# HEWA0200C Hour 3
Disc contains the following selections:

Good Luck Charm   Suspicious Minds
Return To Sender   Don't Cry Daddy
(You're The) Devil In Disguise   The Wonder Of You
Bossa Nova Baby   Burning Love
Crying In The Chapel   Separate Ways
If I Can Dream   Way Down
In The Ghetto   My Way

ELVIS The Memphis Record EXTRA

DIGITALLY REMASTERED   RCA

1969: YEAR IN REVIEW

ACADEMY AWARD WINNERS

☐ **Best Picture**
Midnight Cowboy

☐ **Best Actor**
John Wayne, True Grit

☐ **Best Actress**
Maggie Smith, The Prime Of Miss Jean Brodie

☐ **Best Supporting Actor**
Gig Young, They Shoot Horses, Don't They?

☐ **Best Supporting Actress**
Goldie Hawn, Cactus Flower

GRAMMY WINNERS

☐ **Record Of The Year**
Aquarius/Let The Sunshine In, 5th Dimension

☐ **Album Of The Year**
Blood, Sweat & Tears, Blood, Sweat & Tears

☐ **Song Of The Year**
Games People Play, Joe South

☐ **Best New Artist**
Crosby, Stills And Nash

COMEBACK Elvis Presley as he appeared in December, 1968 NBC television special.

THE YEAR'S NO. 1 HITS

I Heard It Through The Grapevine – Marvin Gaye

Crimson And Clover – Tommy James & The Shondells

Everyday People – Sly & The Family Stone

Dizzy – Tommy Roe

Aquarius/Let The Sunshine In – 5th Dimension

Get Back – Beatles

Love Theme From "Romeo & Juliet" – Henry Mancini

In The Year 2525 – Zager & Evans

Honky Tonk Woman – Rolling Stones

ELVIS PRESLEY COMMEMORATIVE ISSUE

■ **PRESLEY RETURNS HOME FOR FIRST MEMPHIS SESSIONS SINCE MID-1950's**

■ **FIRST MAN WALKS ON MOON**

■ **HALF MILLION IN ATTENDANCE AT WOODSTOCK FESTIVAL**

■ **NEW YORK METS WIN WORLD SERIES**

■ **NIXON SWORN IN AS NATION'S 37TH PRESIDENT**

■ **JETS UPSET COLTS IN SUPER BOWL III**

[ ] The **MEMPHIS RECORD**
Catalog# 6221-2-R   Value $ 15-20
Matrix# 1A1 73 R-6221
(June 1987 First Pressing. Silver & Blue Disc with block RCA Logo in white.
Pressed in Japan for U.S. Release. Contains 12 page insert booklet.)
Disc contains the following selections:

Stranger In My Own Home Town	True Love Travels On A Gravel Road
Power Of My Love	It Keeps Right On A-Hurtin'
Only The Strong Survive	You'll Think Of Me
Any Day Now	Mama Liked The Roses
Suspicious Minds	Don't Cry Daddy
Long Black Limousine	In The Ghetto
Wearin' That Loved On Look	The Fair Is Moving On
I'll Hold You In My Heart	Inherit The Wind
After Lovin' You	Kentucky Rain
Rubberneckin'	Without Love
I'm Movin' On	Who Am I?
Gentle On My Mind	

[ ] The **MEMPHIS RECORD**
Catalog# 6221-2-R   Value $ 12-15
Matrix# 62212R 10/89 1B54
(Oct. 1989 Second Pressing. Silver & Black Disc with block RCA Logo.
Pressed in U.S. Contains 12 page insert booklet.)

[ ] The **MEMPHIS RECORD**
Catalog# 6221-2-R   Value $ 12-15
Matrix# W.O. 14168-9 62212R
(1991 Third Pressing. Silver & Black Disc with old RCA Logo.
Pressed in U.S. Contains 12 page insert booklet. **RCA deleted this title from their**
catalog in July, 1998)

[ ] The **MEMPHIS RECORD**
Catalog# 6221-2-RRE   Value $ 20-30
BMG Music Service Catalog# D 254097
Matrix# W.O. 14168-3 62212R
(1993 Fourth Pressing. Mfg. for BMG Direct Marketing, Inc. BMG Music Service
catalog number on disc and back insert cover. Silver & Black Disc with old RCA
Logo. Pressed in U.S. Contains 12 page insert booklet. Only available from
BMG Music CD Club. Mail Order Only.)

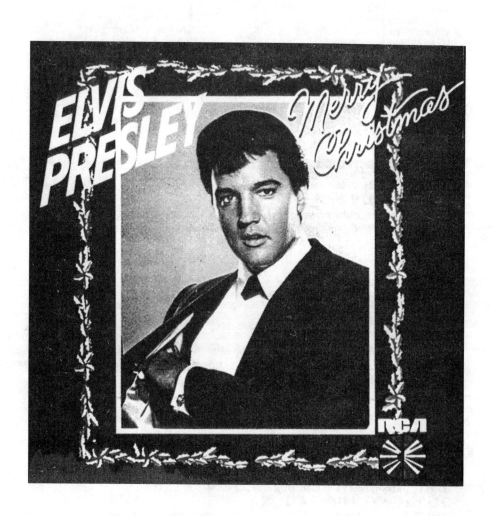

[ ]   The **MEMPHIS RECORD**
          Catalog# 6221-2-RRE   Value $ 20-30
          BMG Music Service Catalog# D 254097
          Matrix# W.O. 14168-11 62212R
          (1995 Fifth Pressing. Mfg. for BMG Direct Marketing, Inc. BMG Music Service
          catalog number on disc and back insert cover. Silver & Black Disc with old RCA
          Logo. Pressed in U.S. Contains 12 page insert booklet. Only available from
          BMG Music CD Club. Mail Order Only.)

[ ]   The **MEMPHIS RECORD**
          Catalog# BG2-6221 RE   Value $ 20-30
          Matrix# BG2-06221 F3 1A 08
          (1996 Sixth Pressing. Mfg. by BMG Music for Columbia House Music Club, a
          non-BMG Music Club. Columbia House Music Club catalog number on disc,
          spine, booklet and back insert cover. CRC Logo printed below bar code on back
          insert cover. Silver & Black Disc with old RCA Logo. Contains 12 page insert
          booklet. Only available from Columbia House Music CD Club. Mail Order Only.)

[ ]   **MERRY CHRISTMAS**
          Catalog# PCD1-5301   Value $ 300-400
          Matrix# PCD-15301 1A1-48
          (Nov. 1984 Release. Silver & Blue Disc with block RCA Logo in white.
          Pressed in Japan for U.S. Release. One of the Rarest U.S. CD's.
          Was available for a short period. RCA has deleted this title from their catalog.)
          Disc contains the following selections:

I'll Be Home For Christmas	O Come, All Ye Faithful
White Christmas	The First Noel
Blue Christmas	Oh Little Town Of Bethlehem
Santa Claus Is Back In Town	Silent Night
Merry Christmas Baby	Peace In The Valley

ELVIS PRESLEY

The Million Dollar Quartet

[ ] The **MILLION DOLLAR QUARTET**
Catalog# 2023-2-R   Value $ 12-15
Matrix# W.O. 13694-1 20232R
(March 1990 First Pressing. Four color matte finish picture disc with RCA and
Sun Logos. Includes 6 page insert booklet. Disc contains songs by
Elvis Presley with Jerry Lee Lewis and Carl Perkins.)
Disc contains the following selections:

You Belong To My Heart	Out Of Sight, Out Of Mind
When God Dips His Love In My Heart	Brown Eyed Handsome Man
Just A Little Talk With Jesus	Don't Be Cruel
Jesus Walk That Lonesome Valley	Don't Be Cruel
I Shall Not Be Moved	Paralyzed
Peace In The Valley	Don't Be Cruel
Down By The Riverside	There's No Place Like Home
I'm With A Crowd But So Alone	When The Saints Go Marchin' In
Farther Along	Softly And Tenderly
Blessed Jesus (Hold My Hand)	Is It So Strange
As We Travel Along On The Jerico Road	That's When Your Heartaches Begin
I Just Can't Make It By Myself	Brown Eyed Handsome Man
Little Cabin Home On The Hill	Rip It Up
Summertime Is Past And Gone	I'm Gonna Bid My Blues Goodbye
I Hear A Sweet Voice Calling	Crazy Arms
Sweetheart You Done Me Wrong	That's My Desire
Keeper Of The Key	End Of The Road
Crazy Arms	Black Bottom Stomp
Don't Forbid Me	You're The Only Star In My Blue Heaven
Too Much Monkey Business	Elvis
Brown Eyed Handsome Man	

[ ] The **MILLION DOLLAR QUARTET**
Catalog# 2023-2-R   Value $ 12-15
Matrix# W.O. 13694-1 20232R
(1991 Second Pressing. Four color matte finish picture disc with RCA and
Sun Logos. Picture disc is darker color than first pressing. Includes 6 page
insert booklet.)

[ ] The **MILLION DOLLAR QUARTET**
Catalog# 2023-2-R   Value $ 12-15
Matrix# W.O. 13694-4P 20232R
(1993 Third Pressing. Four color matte finish picture disc with RCA and
Sun Logos. Includes 6 page insert booklet.)

[ ] The **MILLION DOLLAR QUARTET**
Catalog# 2023-2-R   Value $ 12-15
Matrix# 20232R ++ 64866-01
(1996 Fourth Pressing. Four color matte finish picture disc with RCA and
Sun Logos. Includes 6 page insert booklet.)

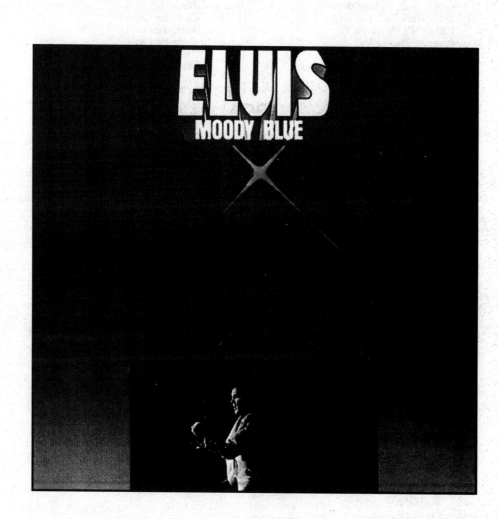

[ ]   **MOODY BLUE**
Catalog# 2428-2-R   **Value $ 15-18**
Matrix# W.O. 10167-1 24282R
(May 1988 First Pressing. Midline CD. Light Blue matte finish Disc with old RCA Logo in Black. Back cover printed "Digitally Remastered ADD".)
Disc contains the following selections:

Unchained Melody	Way Down
If You Love Me (Let Me Know)	Pledging My Love
Little Darlin'	Moody Blue
He'll Have To Go	She Thinks I Still Care
Let Me Be There	It's Easy For You

[ ]   **MOODY BLUE**
Catalog# 2428-2-R   **Value $ 12-15**
Matrix# W.O. 10167-1 24282R
(1991 Second Pressing. Midline CD. Dark Blue shiny finish Disc with old RCA Logo in Black. Back cover printed "Digitally Remastered" without ADD. "Best Buy" sticker on blister pack.)

[ ]   **MOODY BLUE**
Catalog# 2428-2-R   **Value $ 12-15**
Matrix# W.O. 10167-2 24282R
(1994 Third Pressing. Midline CD. Light Blue shiny finish Disc with old RCA Logo in Black. Back cover printed "Digitally Remastered" without ADD.)

[ ]   **MOODY BLUE**
Catalog# 2428-2-R   **Value $ 20-30**
BMG Music Service Catalog# D 153717
Matrix# W.O. 10167-2 24282R
(1994 Fourth Pressing. Mfg. for BMG Direct Marketing, Inc. BMG Music Service catalog number on disc and back insert cover. Midline CD. Light Blue shiny finish Disc with old RCA Logo in Black. Back cover printed "Digitally Remastered" without ADD. Only available from BMG Music CD Club. Mail Order Only.)

[ ]   **MOODY BLUE**
Catalog# BG2-2428   **Value $ 20-30**
Matrix# 5 BG2 02428-2 SRC # 01   M1S2
(1997 Fifth Pressing. Mfg. by BMG Music for Columbia House Music Club, a non-BMG Music CD Club. Columbia House Music Club catalog number on disc, spine, booklet and back insert cover. Light Blue shiny finish Disc with old RCA Logo in Black. Back cover printed "Digitally Remastered" without ADD. Only available from Columbia House Music CD Club. Mail Order Only.)

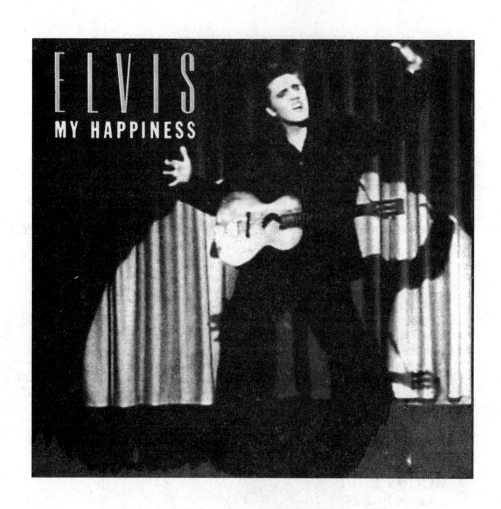

[ ] **MY HAPPINESS** *(Promo)*
Catalog# 2654-2-RDJ   Value $ 40-60
Matrix# W.O. 75376-1 26542RDJ
(Aug. 1990 Promo Only CD issued to promote "The Great Performances" CD.
Silver & Black Disc with old RCA Logo. Contains 4 page insert booklet....
Front cover has original photo of Elvis' screen test for Paramount.
"Promo Only - Not For Sale" printed on front and back covers.)
Disc contains the following selection:
My Happiness *(1953 Acetate)*

[ ] **The NUMBER ONE HITS**
    Catalog# 6382-2-R   **Value $ 20-25**
    Matrix# 1A5 75 R-6382
    (June 1987 First Pressing. Silver & Blue Disc with block RCA Logo in white.
    Pressed in Japan for U.S. Rekease.)
    Disc contains the following selections:

Heartbreak Hotel	Don't
I Want You, I Need You, I Love You	Hard Headed Woman
Hound Dog	A Big Hunk O' Love
Don't Be Cruel	Stuck On You
Love Me Tender	It's Now Or Never
Too Much	Are You Lonesome Tonight
All Shook Up	Surrender
Teddy Bear	Good Luck Charm
Jailhouse Rock	Suspicious Minds

[ ] **The NUMBER ONE HITS**
    Catalog# 6382-2-R   **Value $ 15-18**
    Matrix# 6382-2-R 1T21
    (1989 Second Pressing. Silver & Black Disc with block RCA Logo.
    Pressed in U.S.)

[ ] **The NUMBER ONE HITS**
    Catalog# 6382-2-R   **Value $ 12-15**
    Matrix# 6382-2-R 2A 512
    (1990 Third Pressing. Silver & Black Disc with block RCA Logo.
    RE printed on back cover of insert sleeve. Pressed in U.S.)

[ ] **The NUMBER ONE HITS**
    Catalog# 6382-2-R   **Value $ 12-15**
    Matrix# 6382-2-R 2S 11
    (1990 Fourth Pressing. Silver & Black Disc with block RCA Logo.
    RE printed on back cover of insert sleeve. Pressed in U.S.)

[ ] **The NUMBER ONE HITS**
    Catalog# 6382-2-R   **Value $ 12-15**
    Matrix# 6382-2-R 4C 11
    (1991 Fifth Pressing. Silver & Black Disc with block RCA Logo.
    RE printed on back cover of insert sleeve. Pressed in U.S.)

[ ] **The NUMBER ONE HITS**
    Catalog# 6382-2-R   **Value $ 12-15**
    Matrix# 6382-2-R 4C 13
    (1991 Sixth Pressing. Silver & Black Disc with block RCA Logo.
    RE printed on back cover of insert sleeve. Pressed in U.S.)

[ ]   The **NUMBER ONE HITS**
      Catalog# 6382-2-RRE-1   **Value $ 20-30**
      BMG Music Service Catalog# D 172190
      Matrix# 6382-2-R 4C 36
      (1993 Seventh Pressing. Mfg. for BMG Direct Marketing, Inc. BMG Music
      Service catalog number on disc and insert covers. RE-1 printed on spine.
      Silver & Black Disc with block RCA Logo. Pressed in U.S. Only available from
      BMG Music CD Club. Mail Order Only.)

[ ]   The **NUMBER ONE HITS**
      Catalog# 6382-2-RRE-1   **Value $ 20-30**
      BMG Music Service Catalog# D 172190
      Matrix# 6382-2-R 4C 310
      (1994 Eighth Pressing. Mfg. for BMG Direct Marketing, Inc. BMG Music
      Service catalog number on disc and insert covers. RE-1 printed on spine.
      Silver & Black Disc with block RCA Logo. Pressed in U.S. Only available from
      BMG Music CD Club. Mail Order Only)

[ ]   The **NUMBER ONE HITS**
      Catalog# 6382-2-RRE-1   **Value $ 20-30**
      BMG Music Service Catalog# D 172190
      Matrix# 6382-2-R 5C 12
      (1995 Ninth Pressing. Mfg. for BMG Direct Marketing, Inc. BMG Music
      Service catalog number on disc and insert covers. RE-1 printed on spine.
      Silver & Black Disc with block RCA Logo. Pressed in U.S. Only available from
      BMG Music CD Club. Mail Order Only.)

[ ]   The **NUMBER ONE HITS**
      Catalog# 6382-2-RRE-1   **Value $ 20-30**
      BMG Music Service Catalog# D 172190
      Matrix# IFPI L238 63822R 8H 11
      (Feb. 1996 Tenth Pressing. Mfg. for BMG Direct Marketing, Inc. BMG Music
      Service catalog number on disc and insert covers. RE-1 printed on spine.
      Silver & Black Disc with block RCA Logo. Pressed in U.S. Only available from
      BMG Music CD Club. Mail Order Only.)

[ ]   The **NUMBER ONE HITS**
      Catalog# 6382-2-RRE-1   **Value $ 20-30**
      BMG Music Service Catalog# D 172190
      Matrix# IFPI L238 63822R 8H 15
      (June 1996 Eleventh Pressing. Mfg. for BMG Direct Marketing, Inc. BMG Music
      Service catalog number on disc and insert covers. RE-1 printed on spine.
      Silver & Black Disc with block RCA Logo. Pressed in U.S. Only available from
      BMG Music CD Club. Mail Order Only.)

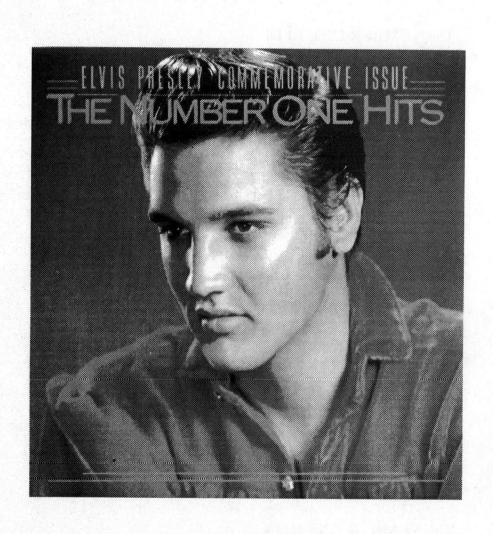

[ ]   The **NUMBER ONE HITS**
Catalog# 6382-2-RRE-1   **Value $ 20-30**
BMG Music Service Catalog# D 172190
Matrix# **IFPI L238 63822R 8H** 19
*(Sept. 1996 Twelfth Pressing. Mfg. for BMG Direct Marketing, Inc. BMG Music
Service catalog number on disc and insert cover. RE-1 printed on spine.
Silver & Black Disc with block RCA Logo. Pressed in U.S. Only available from
BMG Music CD Club. Mail Order Only.)*

[ ]   The **NUMBER ONE HITS**
Catalog# BG2-6382   **Value $ 20-30**
Matrix# **5 BG2 06382-2 SRC ## 01** M1S29
*(1997 Thirteenth Pressing. Mfg. by BMG Music for Columbia House Music Club,
a non-BMG Music CD Club. Columbia House Music Club catalog number on
disc, spine, front and back insert covers. CRC Logo printed above bar code on
back insert cover. RE printed on back of front insert cover. Silver & Black Disc
with block RCA Logo. Only available from Columbia House Music CD Club.
Mail Order Only.)*

February, 1970

ON STAGE

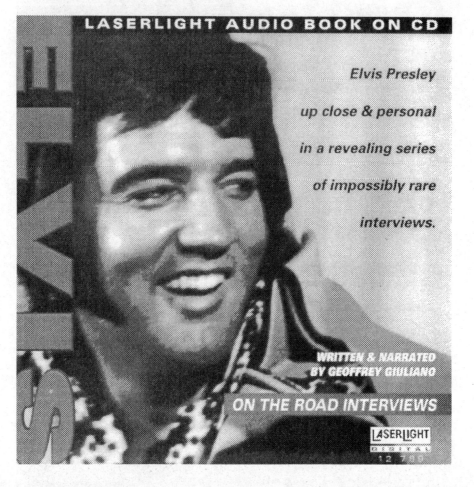

LASERLIGHT AUDIO BOOK ON CD

Elvis Presley

up close & personal

in a revealing series

of impossibly rare

interviews.

WRITTEN & NARRATED
BY GEOFFREY GIULIANO

ON THE ROAD INTERVIEWS

LASERLIGHT
DIGITAL
12

[ ] **ON STAGE February, 1970**
Catalog# 07863-54362-2   Value $ 10-15
Matrix# W.O. 17781-1 07863543622
(Aug. 1991 First Pressing. Midline CD. Silver & Black Disc with old RCA Logo.
Contains 4 page insert booklet.)
Disc contains the following selections:

C. C. Rider	Polk Salad Annie
Release Me	Yesterday
Sweet Caroline	Proud Mary
Runaway	Walk A Mile In My Shoes
The Wonder Of You	Let It Be Me (Je T' Appartiens)

[ ] **ON STAGE February, 1970**
Catalog# 07863-54362-2   Value $ 10-15
Matrix# W.O. 17781-2M 07863543622
(1995 Second Pressing. Midline CD. Silver & Black Disc with old RCA Logo
*with "**Wise Buy**" sticker on shrink wrap. Contains 4 page insert booklet.)*

[ ] **ON THE ROAD INTERVIEWS**
Catalog# 12 789   Value $ 6-8
Matrix# 12789 Y6723C IFPI L532
(Sept. 1996 Release from Laserlight Digital. This is a Laserlight Audio Book on
CD. Contains 4 page insert booklet. Silver and Yellow Disc with Black Print.
Written and Narrated by Geoffrey Giuliano. This is an interview only CD.)
Disc contains the following interviews:

Introduction
Presley Press Conference, 1961 Part 1
Presley Press Conference, 1961 Part 2
Presley in La Crosse Interview
Presley Interview E
Presley Interview F
Presley Interview G

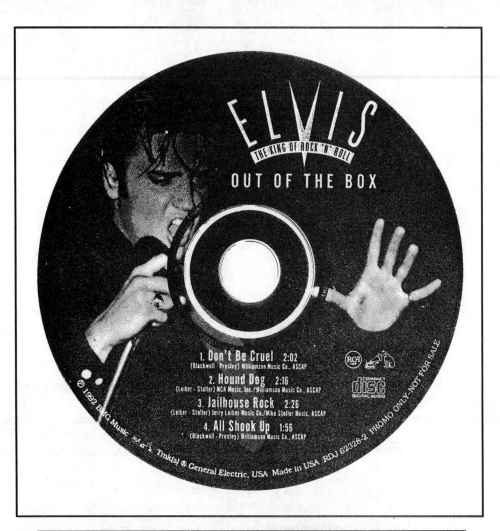

ELVIS
THE KING OF ROCK 'N' ROLL
OUT OF THE BOX

1. Don't Be Cruel 2:02
(Blackwell - Presley) Williamson Music Co., ASCAP

2. Hound Dog 2:16
(Leiber - Stoller) MCA Music, Inc./Williamson Music Co., ASCAP

3. Jailhouse Rock 2:26
(Leiber - Stoller) Jerry Leiber Music Co./Mike Stoller Music, ASCAP

4. All Shook Up 1:56
(Blackwell - Presley) Williamson Music Co., ASCAP

© 1992 BMG Music ™ ⑧ ⑤ ⑥ ⑦. Tmk(s) ® General Electric, USA Made in USA RDJ 62328-2 PROMO ONLY-NOT FOR SALE

RCA

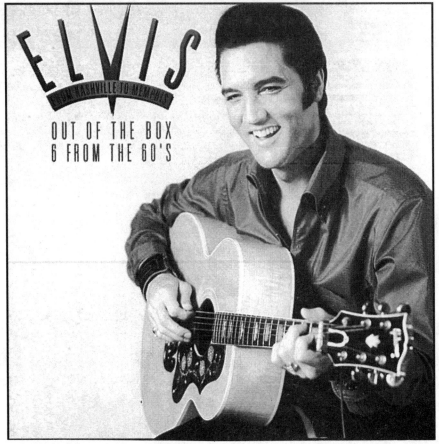

ELVIS
FROM NASHVILLE TO MEMPHIS
OUT OF THE BOX
6 FROM THE 60'S

[ ] **OUT OF THE BOX** *(Promo)*
Catalog# RDJ 62328-2   Value $ 35-50
Matrix# W.O. 76613-1 RDJ623282
(May 1992 Promo Only CD issued to promote the Complete 50's Masters Box Set.
Picture Disc is Black matte finish with Blue Logo and Print. Only 800 Pressed.
Disc doesn't have insert front cover in jewel box. Aqua colored back cover with
"Promo Only - Not For Sale")
Disc contains the following selections:

Don't Be Cruel   Jailhouse Rock
Hound Dog   All Shook Up

[ ] **OUT OF THE BOX - 6 FROM THE 60's** *(Promo)*
Catalog# RDJ 62624-2   Value $ 25-40
Matrix# RDJ626242 01#
(Aug. 1993 Promo Only CD issued to promote The Essential 60's Box Set.
Picture Disc is Yellow matte finish with Blue Logo and Print. Contains
4 page insert booklet. "Promotional Copy - Not For Sale" printed on disc,
insert sleeve and back cover.)
Disc contains the following selections:

Suspicion   Suspicious Minds *(Alternate Take 6)*
The Girl Of My Best Friend   His Latest Flame *(Alternate Take 4)*
Memphis, Tennessee *(Alternate Take 1)*   It's Now Or Never *(Orig. Undubbed Master)*

Elvis Presley

PLATINUM

THE ULTIMATE ELVIS PRESLEY COLLECTION!
100 TRACKS

FEATURING 77 RARE & PREVIOUSLY UNRELEASED PERFORMANCES

Includes: The recently discovered 1954 demo —
I'LL NEVER STAND IN YOUR WAY
plus Classic Masters, Private Recordings,
Rare Rehearsals & Live Performances

4-CD SET
with DELUXE 48 page
full-color booklet

A LIFE IN MUSIC

[ ]   **PLATINUM** *(4 CD Set)*
        A LIFE IN MUSIC
        Catalog# 07863-67469-2   Value $ 60-70
        (July 1997 Release. Packaged in a special 5-1/2" x 10" book type holder.
        4 CD Picture Disc set - 100 tracks. Includes 77 previously unreleaased
        performances. 2 CD's housed in push-in holder in front cover. 2 CD's housed in
        push-in holder in back cover. Set contains 48 page deluxe booklet with rare
        photographs. Digitally Remastered from the original RCA Record Label Master
        Tapes. Blue and White collectors sticker on shrink wrap. Set available only thru
        Dec.'97)
        Disc #1 Black and White Picture Disc
        Matrix# 07863674692D1 ++ 75870-01
        Disc contains the following selections:

I'll Never Stand In Your Way *(1954 Acetate)*   All Shook Up *(Master)*
That's All Right *(Alternate Takes 1,2,3)*   Peace In The Valley *(Alternate Take 3)*
Blue Moon *(Alternate Take)*   Blueberry Hill *(Acetate)*
Good Rockin' Tonight *(Master)*   (Let Me Be Your) Teddy Bear *(Master)*
Mystery Train *(Master)*   Jailhouse Rock *(Master)*
I Got A Woman *(Alternate Take)*   New Orleans *(Master)*
Heartbreak Hotel *(Alternate Take 6)*   I Need Your Love Tonight *(Alt. Take 7)*
I'm Counting On You *(Alternate Take 13)*   A Big Hunk O' Love *(Alternate Take 4)*
Shake Rattle And Roll/Flip Flop And Fly   Bad Nauheim Medley:
(From Dorsey Bros. TV "Stage Show")   I'll Take You Home Again Kathleen
Lawdy Miss Clawdy *(Alternate Take 1)*   I Will Be True
I Want You, I Need You, I Love You *(Alternate Take 4)* It's Been So Long Darling
Hound Dog *(From the Milton Berle Show)*   Apron Strings
Don't Be Cruel *(Master)*   There's No Tomorrow
Rip It Up *(Alternate Take 15)*   *(Private Recordings)*
Love Me Tender *(From the Ed Sullivan Show)*
When The Saints Go Marching In *(Home Recording)*

        Disc #2 Black and White Picture Disc
        Matrix# 07863674692D2 ++ 75871-01
        Disc contains the following selections:

Stuck On You *(From the Frank Sinatra Show)*   Something Blue *(Alternate Take 1)*
Fame And Fortune *(From the Frank Sinatra Show)*   Return To Sender *(Master)*
It's Now Or Never *(Master)*   Bossa Nova Baby *(Alternate Take 2)*
It Feels So Right *(Alternate Take 3)*   How Great Thou Art *(Alternate Take 4)*
A Mess Of Blues *(Alternate Take 1)*   Guitar Man *(Alternate Take 4)*
Are You Lonesome Tonight? *(Master)*   You'll Never Walk Alone *(Alternate Take 2)*
Reconsider Baby *(Master)*   PRIVATE GRACELAND &
Tonight Is So Right For Love *(Alternate Take 3)*   PALM SPRINGS SEGMENT:
His Hand In Mine *(Alternate Take 2)*   Oh How I Love Jesus
Milky White Way *(Alternate Take 3)*   Tennessee Waltz
I'm Comin' Home *(Alternate Take 3)*   Blowin' In The Wind
I Feel So Bad *(Alternate Take 1)*   I Can't Help It
Can't Help Falling In Love *(Master)*   I'm Beginning To Forget You
                                                    After Loving You

Disc #3 Black and White Picture Disc
Matrix# 07863674692D3 ++ 75872-01
Disc contains the following selections:
'68 COMEBACK SPECIAL:
  I Got A Woman *(Rehearsal)*
  Tiger Man *(Rehearsal)*
  When My Blue Moon Turns to Gold Again
  (Alternate Take)
  Trying To Get to You *(Alternate Take)*
If I Can Dream *(Alternate Take 1)*
In The Ghetto *(Alternate Take 3)*
Suspicious Minds *(Alternate Take 7)*
Power Of My Love *(Alternate Take 3)*
Baby What You Want Me To Do *(Las Vegas 1969)*
Words *(Las Vegas 1969)*
Johnny B. Goode *(Las Vegas 1969)*
Release Me *(Las Vegas 1970)*

See See Rider *(Las Vegas 1970)*
The Wonder Of You *(Las Vegas 1970)*
The Sound Of Your Cry *(Alternate Take 3)*
You Don't Have To Say You Love Me *(Mst)*
Funny How Time Slips Away *(Master)*
LAS VEGAS REHEARSALS:
  I Washed My Hands In Muddy Water
  I Was The One
  Cattle Call
  Baby, Let's Play House
  Don't
  Money Honey
  What'd I Say
Bridge Over Troubled Water *(Las Vegas'70)*

Disc #4 Black and White Picture Disc
Matrix# 07863674692D4 ++ 75873-01
Disc contains the following selections:
Miracle Of The Rosary *(Alternate Take 1)*
He Touched Me *(Alternate Take 2)*
Bosom Of Abraham *(Alternate Take 3)*
I'll Be Home On Christmas Day *(Alternate Take 4)*
For The Good Times *(Alternate Take 3)*
Burning Love *(Alternate Take 1)*
Separate Ways *(Alternate Take 25)*
Always On My Mind *(Alternate Take 2)*
An American Trilogy *(Alternate Aloha)*
Take Good Care Of Her *(Alternate Take 4)*
I've Got A Thing About You Baby *(Master)*
Are You Sincere *(Alternate Take 2)*
It's Midnight *(Alternate Take 10)*

Promised Land *(Alternate Take 5)*
Steamroller Blues *(Unrel Live Performance)*
And I Love You So *(Alternate Take 2)*
T-R-O-U-B-L-E *(Master)*
Danny Boy *(Alternate Take 9)*
Moody Blue *(Master)*
Hurt *(Alternate Take 2)*
For The Heart *(Alternate Take 1)*
Pledging My Love *(Alternate Take 3)*
Way Down *(Alternate Take 2)*
My Way *(Unreleased Live Performance)*
(Excerpt From) The Jaycees Speech

[ ] **PLATINUM** *(4 CD Set)*
A LIFE IN MUSIC
Catalog# 07863-67469-2   Value $ 70-80
BMG Music Service Catalog# D 207367
Disc #1 **Matrix# 07863674692D1 ++ 75870-01**
Disc #2 **Matrix# 07863674692D2 ++ 75871-01**
Disc #3 **Matrix# 07863674692D3 ++ 75872-01**
Disc #4 **Matrix# 07863674692D4 ++ 75873-01**
(July 1997. Mfg. for BMG Direct Marketing, Inc. BMG Music Service catalog
number on back cover over bar code. Only available from BMG Music CD Club.
Mail Order Only.)

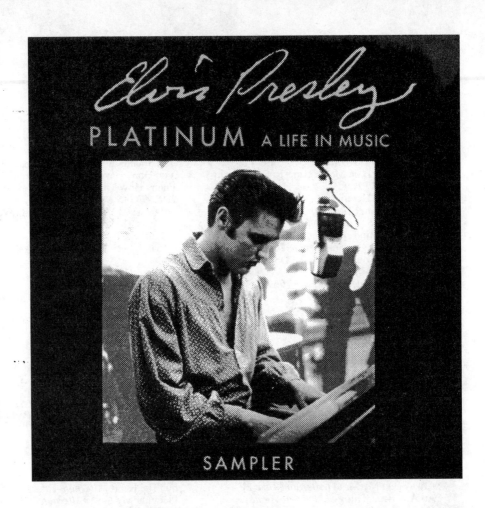

ELVIS PRESLEY
PLATINUM
IN-STORE SAMPLER

1. I'LL NEVER STAND IN YOUR WAY 2:01
2. WHEN THE SAINTS GO MARCHING IN 1:22
3. A BIG HUNK O' LOVE (ALT. TAKE 4) 2:12
4. ARE YOU LONESOME TONIGHT? 3:06
5. BOSSA NOVA BABY (ALT. TAKE 2) 2:14
6. OH HOW I LOVE JESUS 1:37
7. IN THE GHETTO (ALT. TAKE 3) 2:40
8. BABY WHAT YOU WANT ME TO DO 2:18
9. BRIDGE OVER TROUBLED WATER 4:12
10. BURNING LOVE (ALT. TAKE) 3:04
11. ALWAYS ON MY MIND (ALT. TAKE 2) 3:32
12. FOR THE HEART (ALT. TAKE 1) 3:47

PRODUCED BY ERNST MIKAEL JORGENSEN · ENGINEERED BY DENNIS FERRANTE ·
TAKEN FROM ELVIS PRESLEY · PLATINUM - A LIFE IN MUSIC 07863-67469-2/4

NOT FOR SALE

®1997 BMG Entertainment
Manufactured and distributed by BMG Distribution, a unit of BMG
Entertainment, 1540 Broadway, New York, New York 10036-4098

[ ]   **PLATINUM SAMPLER** *(Promo)*
Catalog# RDJ-67529-2   **Value $ 75-125**
Matrix# RDJ675292 ++ 75770-01
(May 1997 Promo Only CD. Issued to promote the Elvis Presley Platinum -
A Life In Music Box Set. In house promo for BMG Marketing convention in
New York. White Disc with old RCA Logo and Print in Black.
Contains 2 page insert. "Not For Sale - Or Radio Air Play" printed on disc
and back insert cover.)
Disc contains the following selections:
I'll Never Stand In Your Way *(1954 Acetate)*   Oh How I Love Jesus *(Home Recording)*
A Big Hunk O' Love *(Alternate Take 4)*   For The Heart *(Alternate Take 1)*

[ ]   **PLATINUM IN-STORE SAMPLER** *(Promo)*
Catalog# RJC -67568-2   **Value $ 50-75**
Matrix# 07863675682 ++ 80455-01
(August 1997 Promo Only CD. Issued to promote the Elvis Presley Platinum-
A Life In Music Box Set. Silver Disc with old RCA Logo and Print in Black.
No front insert cover. "Not For Sale" printed on disc and back insert cover.
Back cover Gray with Blue Print.)
Disc contains the following selections:

I'll Never Stand In Your Way	In The Ghetto *(Alt. Take 3)*
When The Saints Go Marching In	Baby What You Want Me To Do
A Big Hunk O' Love *(Alt. Take 4)*	Bridge Over Troubled Water
Are You Lonesome Tonight?	Burning Love *(Alt. Take 1)*
Bossa Nova Baby *(Alt. Take 2)*	Always On My Mind *(Alt. Take 2)*
Oh How I Loved Jesus	For The Heart *(Alt. Take 1)*

POT LUCK
WITH
ELVIS

KISS ME QUICK • JUST FOR OLD TIME SAKE
GONNA GET BACK HOME SOMEHOW
(SUCH AN) EASY QUESTION • STEPPIN' OUT OF LINE
I'M YOURS • SOMETHING BLUE • SUSPICION
I FEEL THAT I'VE KNOWN YOU FOREVER
NIGHT RIDER • FOUNTAIN OF LOVE
THAT'S SOMEONE YOU NEVER FORGET

THE *PRIVATE PRESLEY* CD

1. ELVIS IN GERMANY 1958-ELVIS GREETS
   THE PRESS (IN PRESS) 0:50
2. TWEEDLE DEE (Winfield/Scott) Intersong
   Recorded December 8, 1954. 2:13
3. ELVIS IN THE ARMY (INTERVIEW) 1:00
4. I GOT A WOMAN (R. Charles/Renal Connelly
   Recorded October 23, 1954 2:31
5. WE WANT ELVIS (Fan chant for Elvis) 0:35
6. ELVIS IN THE ARMY (INTERVIEW) 0:37

Available only with the book
PRIVATE PRESLEY

All rights of the producer and of the owner
of the work reproduced reserved.
Unauthorized copying, hiring, lending,
public performance and broadcasting
of this record prohibited. Made in the USA

MORROW

COMPACT
disc
DIGITAL AUDIO

0-688-04609-6

7. MAYBELLENE (Berry/Fratto/Freed) ARC Music Corp
   Recorded October 23, 1954 2:34
8. THAT'S ALRIGHT (MAMA) (Arthur Crudup) Carlin Music
   Recorded October 23, 1954 2:58
9. BLUE MOON OF KENTUCKY (Bill Monroe) Peer International Corp
   Recorded October 23, 1954 2:04
10. THERE'S GOOD ROCKIN' TONIGHT (Ray Brown) Intersong
    Recorded December 16, 1954 2:05
11. ELVIS RETURNS HOME (INTERVIEW) Recorded at Graceland
    (IN PRESS)
12. BABY LET'S PLAY HOUSE (Arthur Gunter) Carlin Music
    Recorded December 16, 1954 3:09

[ ] **POT LUCK WITH ELVIS**
Catalog# 2523-2-R   Value $ 20-25
Matrix# W.O. 10145-1 25232R
*(April 1988 First Pressing. Midline CD. Silver & Black Disc with old RCA Logo.
Back cover printed "Digitally Remastered ADD".)*
Disc contains the following selections:

Kiss Me Quick	Something Blue
Just For Old Times Sake	Suspicion
Gonna Get Back Home Somehow	I Feel That I've Known You Forever
Easy Question	Night Rider
Steppin' Out Of Line	Fountain Of Love
I'm Yours	That's Someone You Never Forget

[ ] **POT LUCK WITH ELVIS**
Catalog# 2523-2-R   Value $ 25-35
Matrix# W.O. 10145-1 25232R
*(1991 Second Pressing. Midline CD. Silver & Black Disc with old RCA Logo.
Back cover printed "Digitally Remastered" without ADD.)*

[ ] **POT LUCK WITH ELVIS**
Catalog# 2523-2-R   Value $ 15-20
Matrix# W.O. 10145-3 25232R
*(1995 Third Pressing. Midline CD. Silver & Black Disc with old RCA Logo.
Back cover printed same as first pressing "Digitally Remastered ADD".
RCA deleted this title from their catalog in 1997.)*

[ ] The **PRIVATE PRESLEY CD**
Catalog# 0-688-04609-6   Value $ 25-30
Matrix# 0688-4609-06-01#
*(Aug. 1993 Pressing on the Morrow Label from the Merlin Group. CD included
as a bonus with the hard cover book "Private Presley".)*
Disc contains the following selections:

Elvis In Germany 1958 *(Interview)*	Maybellene
Tweedle Dee	That's All Right Mama
Elvis In The Army *(Interview)*	Blue Moon Of Kentucky
I Got A Woman	There's Good Rockin' Tonight
We Want Elvis *(Fans Chant for Elvis)*	Elvis Returns Home *(Graceland Interview)*
Elvis In the Army *(Interview)*	Baby Let's Play House

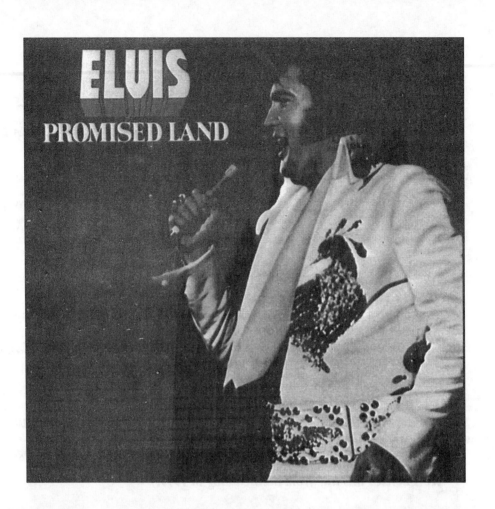

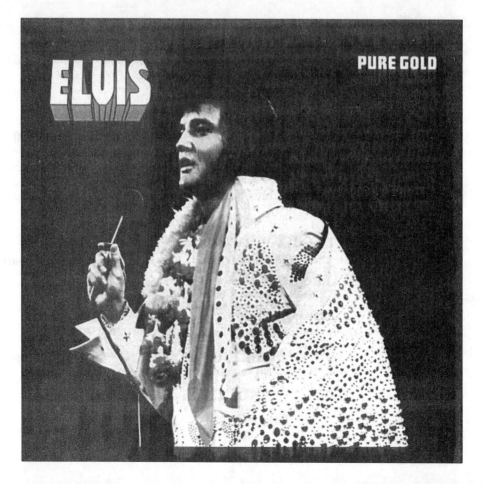

[ ] **PROMISED LAND**
Catalog# 0873-2-R   Value $ 12-15
Matrix# W.O. 11652-1 08732R
(April 1989 First Pressing. Midline CD. Silver & Black Disc with old RCA Logo.)
Disc contains the following selections:

Promised Land   It's Midnight
There's A Honky Tonk Angel   Your Love's Been A Long Time Coming
Help Me   If You Talk In Your Sleep
Mr. Songman   Thinking About You
Love Song Of The Year   You Asked Me To

[ ] **PROMISED LAND**
Catalog# 0873-2-R   Value $ 12-15
Matrix# W.O. 11652-3M 08732R
*(1995 Second Pressing. Midline CD. Silver & Black Disc with old RCA Logo
with "Wise Buy" sticker on shrink wrap.)*

[ ] **PURE GOLD**
Catalog# 07863-53732-2   Value $ 12-15
Matrix# 07863-53732-2 1D 11
*(May 1992 First Pressing. Elvis in the '90's Black Disc with old RCA
Logo and Print in Silver. 6 page insert booklet. Digitally Remastered
from the original RCA Label Master Tapes.)*
Disc contains the following selections:

Kentucky Rain   I Got A Woman
Fever   All Shook Up
It's Impossible   Loving You
Jailhouse Rock   In The Ghetto
Don't Be Cruel   Love Me Tender

[ ] **PURE GOLD**
Catalog# 07863-53732-2   Value $ 12-15
Matrix# 07863-53732-2 1D 5v
*(1994 Second Pressing. Elvis in the '90's Black Disc with old RCA Logo and
Print in Silver. 6 page insert booklet. Elvis in the '90's sticker on shrink wrap.)*

[ ] **PURE GOLD**
Catalog# 07863-53732-2   Value $ 12-15
Matrix# 07863-53732-2 1D 27
*(1996 Third Pressing. Elvis in the '90's Black Disc with old RCA Logo and Print
in Silver. 6 page insert booklet. Elvis in the '90's sticker on shrink wrap.)*

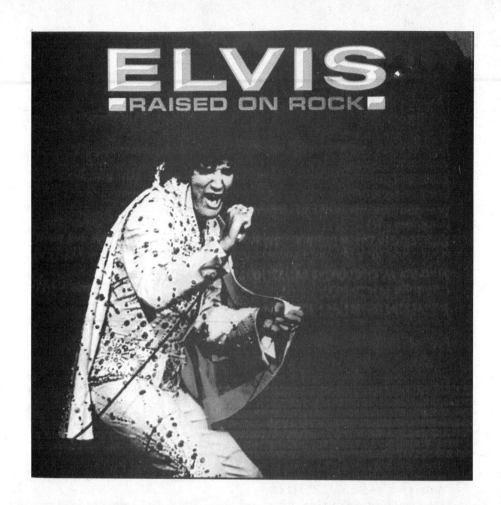

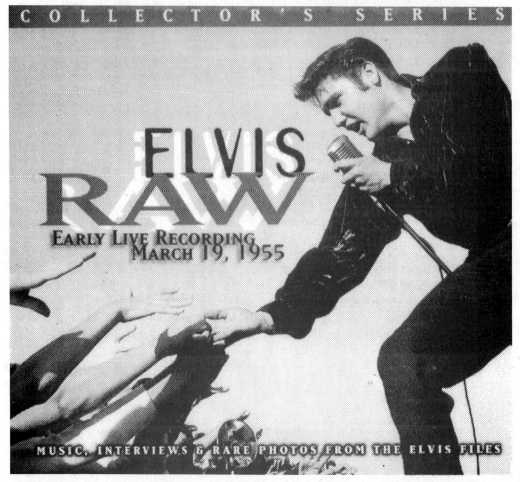

"R"

[ ] **RAISED ON ROCK**
Catalog$ 07863-50388-2   Value $ 12-15
Matrix# 07863 50388-2 01# 40146
(March 1994 First Pressing. Elvis in the '90's Black Disc with The RCA Records
Label and Nipper above new silver line. Print in Silver. Contains 8 page
insert booklet including original single cover art for "Raised On Rock" 45.
Digitally Remastered from the original RCA Label Master Tapes.
RCA deleted this title from their catalog in 1997.)
Disc contains the following selections:

Raised On Rock	For Ol' Times Sake
Are You Sincere	If You Don't Come Back
Find Out What's Happening	Just A Little Bit
I Miss You	Sweet Angeline
Girl Of Mine	Three Corn Patches

[ ] **RAISED ON ROCK**   *(Promo)*
Catalog# 07863-50388-2   Value $ 15-20
Matrix# 07863 50388-2 01# 40146
(March 1994 Designated Promo. Same as regular catalog release with black
*and white sticker "**Not For Sale NFS-1**" on front cover of jewel box.*
Drill hole thru back of jewel box.)

[ ] **RAW ELVIS - COLLECTORS SERIES**
Early Live Recording March 19, 1955
Catalog# 9210-2 DRC 11739   Value $ 14-18
Matrix# L385 1100 DRC11739 C70519-09
(June 1997 BMG Special Products Release for Outwest Records. Distributed
by PPI Entertainment Group, a division of Peter Pan Industries Inc., Newark,
N.J. A Black and White Picture Disc housed in a tri-fold digi-pack. Contains
music, interviews and rare photos from the Elvis files with a 12 page insert
booklet.)
Disc contains the following selections:

Interview With Biff Collie	Good Rockin' Tonight
Baby, Let's Play House	Thats All Right
Blue Moon Of Kentucky	Interview With Scotty Moore
I Got A Woman	

[ ]
RECONSIDER BABY
Catalog # PCD1-5418
Matrix# PCD-15418 1A1 55
(March 1985 First Pressing. Silver & Blue Disc with block RCA Logo in white.
4 page insert booklet. Pressed in Japan for U.S. Release.)
Disc contains the following selections:

Value $ 20-25

Reconsider Baby
Tomorrow Night *(Unreleased Sun Master)*
So Glad You're Mine
One Night *(Alternate Take)*
When It Rains, It Pours
My Baby Left Me

Ain't That Loving You Baby *(Alt. Take)*
I Feel So Bad
Down In The Alley
Hi-Heeled Sneakers
Stranger In My Own Home Town *(Alt.Mix)*
Merry Christmas Baby *(Alternate Edit.)*

[ ]
RECONSIDER BABY
Catalog# PCD1-5418
Matrix# PCD-15418 3A9 6Y
(1985 Second Pressing. Silver & Blue Disc with block RCA Logo in white.
4 page insert booklet. Pressed in Japan for U.S. Release.)

Value $ 15-18

[ ]
RECONSIDER BABY
Catalog# PCD1-5418
Matrix# PCD-15418 10B2 D74
(1986 Third Pressing. Silver & Blue Disc with block RCA Logo in white.
4 page insert booklet. Pressed in Japan for U.S. Release.)

Value $ 15-18

[ ]
RECONSIDER BABY
Catalog# PCD1-5418
Matrix# PCD-15418 10B5 D75
(1986 Fourth Pressing. Silver & Blue Disc with block RCA Logo in white.
4 page insert booklet. Pressed in Japan for U.S. Release.)

Value $ 15-18

[ ]
RECONSIDER BABY
Catalog# PCD1-5418
Matrix# PCD-15418 12T 12
(1990 Fifth Pressing. Silver & Black Disc with old RCA Logo.
4 page insert booklet. Pressed in U.S.)

Value $ 10-12

[ ]
RECONSIDER BABY
Catalog# PCD1-5418
Matrix# PCD1-5418 12T 13
(1991 Sixth Pressing. Silver & Black Disc with old RCA Logo.
4 page insert booklet. Pressed in U.S.)

Value $ 10-12

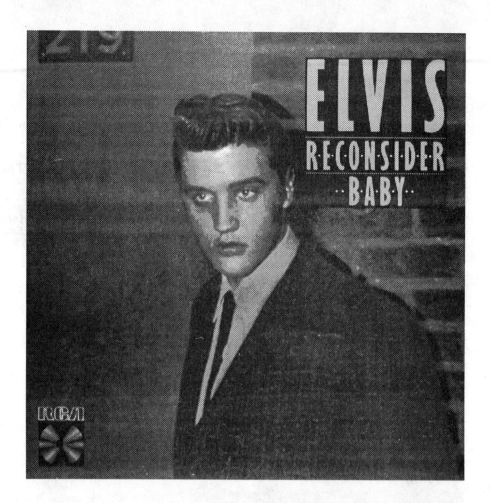

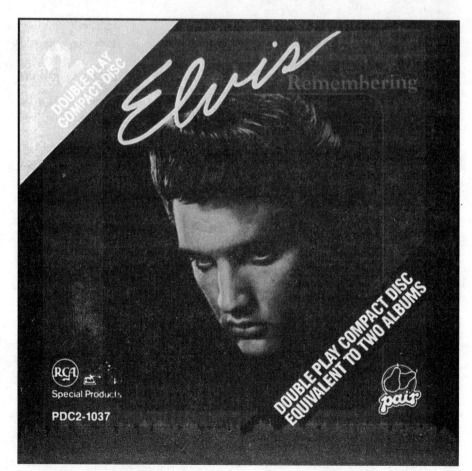

[ ] **RECONSIDER BABY**
Catalog# PCD1-5418   Value $ **10-12**
Matrix# PCD1-5418 12T 14
(1991 Seventh Pressing. Silver & Black Disc with old RCA Logo.
4 Page insert booklet. "Sound Value" sticker on shrink wrap. Pressed in U.S.
RCA deleted this title from their catalog in July, 1998.)

[ ] **RECONSIDER BABY**
Catalog# BG2-5418   Value $ **20-30**
Matrix# BG2-05418 F2 1A 03
(1997 Eighth Pressing. Mfg. by BMG Music for Coumbia House Music Club, a
non-BMG Music Club. Columbia House Music Club catalog number on disc,
spine, booklet and back insert cover. CRC Logo printed below bar code on back
insert cover. Silver & Black Disc with old RCA Logo. 4 page insert booklet.
Only available from Columbia House Music CD Club. Mail Order Only.)

[ ] **REMEMBERING ELVIS**
Catalog# PDC2-1037   Value $ **20 -25**
Matrix# W.O. 10003-1 PCD2-1037
(Feb. 1988 RCA Special Products Release on the Pair Label. Silver Disc with
*RCA & Pair Logos in Blue - other printing in Black. **This title has been deleted***
from catalog.)
Disc contains the following selections:

Blue Moon Of Kentucky	Kiss Me Quick
Young And Beautiful	Just For Old Time Sake
Milkcow Blues Boogie	Gonna Get Back Home Somehow
Baby Let's Play House	(Such An) Easy Question
Good Rockin' Tonight	Suspicion
We're Gonna Move	I Feel That I've Known You Forever
I Want To Be Free	Night Rider
I Forgot To Remember To Forget	Fountain Of Love

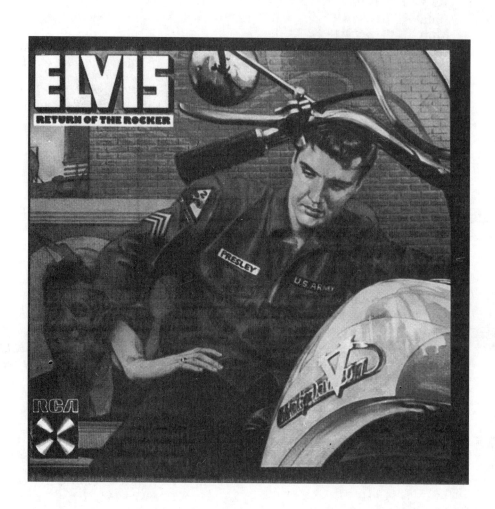

[ ]   **RETURN OF THE ROCKER**
Catalog# 5600-2-R   **Value $ 20-25**
Matrix# R-5600 1A2 6X
(June 1986 First Pressing. Silver & Blue Disc with block RCA Logo in white.
4 page insert booklet. Pressed in Japan for U.S. Release.)
Disc contains the following selections:

King Of The Whole Wide World	Stuck On You
(Marie's The Name) His Latest Flame	Return To Sender
Little Sister	Make Me Know It
A Mess Of Blues	Witchcraft
Like A Baby	I'm Coming Home
I Want You With Me	Follow That Dream

[ ]   **RETURN OF THE ROCKER**
Catalog# 5600-2-R   **Value $ 15-20**
Matrix# R-5600 1D1 D7X
(1987 Second Pressing. Silver & Blue Disc with block RCA Logo in white.
4 page insert booklet. Pressed in U.S.)

[ ]   **RETURN OF THE ROCKER**
Catalog# 5600-2-R   **Value $ 15-20**
Matrix# 56002R 2/89 2A51
(Feb. 1989 Third Pressing. Silver & Black Disc with block RCA Logo.
4 page insert booklet. Pressed in U.S.)

[ ]   **RETURN OF THE ROCKER**
Catalog# 5600-2-R   **Value $ 15-20**
Matrix# 56002R 8/89 2A52
(Aug. 1989 Fourth Pressing. Silver & Black Disc with block RCA Logo.
4 page insert booklet. Pressed in U.S.)

[ ]   **RETURN OF THE ROCKER**
Catalog# 5600-2-R   **Value $ 15-20**
Matrix# 5600-2-R 12T 11
(1990 Fifth Pressing. Silver & Black Disc with old RCA Logo. 4 page insert
*booklet. Pressed in U.S. **RCA deleted this title from their catalog in April 1992.**)*

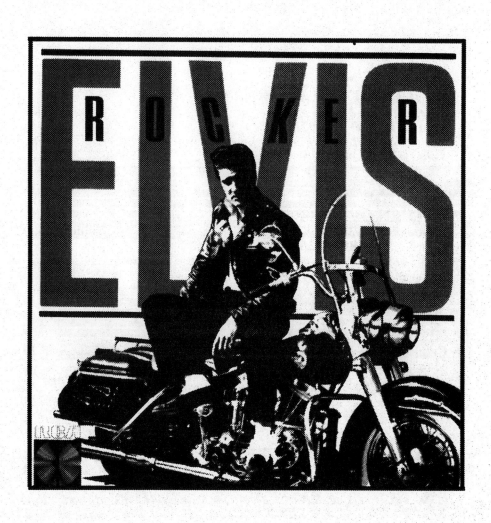

[ ] **ROCKER**
Catalog# PCD1-5182   **Value $ 20-25**
Matrix# **DIDX-181 11A2**
(Nov. 1984 First Pressing. Silver & Blue Disc with block RCA Logo in white.
4 page insert booklet. Pressed in Japan for U.S. Release.)
Disc contains the following selections:

Jailhouse Rock	Ready Teddy
Blue Suede Shoes	Rip It Up
Tutti Frutti	Shake, Rattle & Roll
Lawdy Miss Clawdy	Long Tall Sally
I Got A Woman	(You're So Square) Baby I Don't Care
Money Honey	Hound Dog

[ ] **ROCKER**
Catalog# PCD1-5182   **Value $ 15-18**
Matrix# **PCD-15182 1A6 62**
(1985 Second Pressing. Silver & Blue Disc with block RCA Logo in white.
4 page insert booklet. Pressed in Japan for U.S. Release.)

[ ] **ROCKER**
Catalog# PCD1-5182   **Value $ 15-18**
Matrix# **PCD-15182 1A8 6Y**
(1985 Third Pressing. Silver & Blue Disc with block RCA Logo in white.
4 page insert booklet. Pressed in Japan for U.S. Release.)

[ ] **ROCKER**
Catalog# PCD1-5182   **Value $ 15-18**
Matrix# **PCD-15182 1A15 72**
(1986 Fourth Pressing. Silver & Blue Disc with block RCA Logo in white.
4 page insert booklet. Pressed in Japan for U.S. Release.)

[ ] **ROCKER**
Catalog# PCD1-5182   **Value $ 12-15**
Matrix# **PCD15182 8/88 2B58**
(Aug. 1988 Fifth Pressing. Silver & Blue Disc with block RCA Logo in white.
4 page insert booklet. Pressed in U.S.)

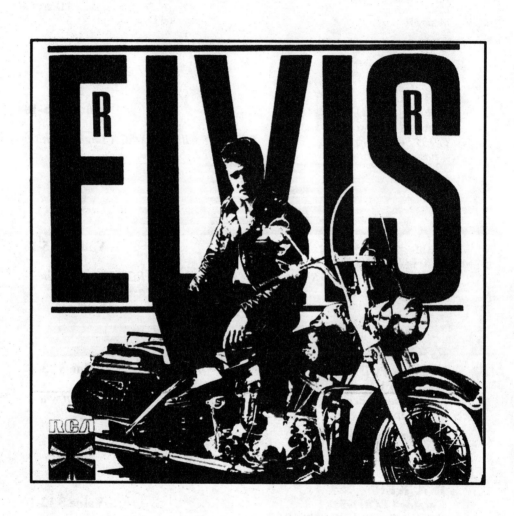

[ ]   **ROCKER**
      Catalog# PCD1-5182   **Value 12-15**
      Matrix# PCD15182 1/89 1DA2
      (Jan. 1989 Sixth Pressing. Silver & Blue Disc with block RCA Logo in white.
      4 page insert booklet. Pressed in U.S.)

[ ]   **ROCKER**
      Catalog# PCD1-5182   **Value $ 10-12**
      Matrix# PCD1-5182 3S 13
      (1991 Seventh Pressing. Silver & Black Disc with old RCA Logo.
      4 page insert booklet. Pressed in U.S.)

[ ]   **ROCKER**
      Catalog# PCD1-5182   **Value $ 10-12**
      Matrix# PCD1-5182 3S 23
      (1993 Eighth Pressing. Silver & Black Disc with old RCA Logo.
      4 page insert booklet. Pressed in U.S.)

[ ]   **ROCKER**
      Catalog# PCD1-5182   **Value $ 10-12**
      Matrix# PCD1-5182 4C 13
      (1995 Ninth Pressing. Silver & Black Disc with old RCA Logo.
      4 page insert booklet with "Wise Buy" sticker on shrink wrap. Pressed in U.S.)

[ ]   **ROCKER**
      Catalog# PCD1-5182   **Value $ 10-12**
      Matrix# PCD1-5182 4C 14
      (1996 Tenth Pressing. Silver & Black Disc with old RCA Logo.
      4 page insert booklet. Pressed in U.S.)

SANTA CLAUS IS BACK IN TOWN

1997 Seasons Greetings from Graceland

SANTA CLAUS IS BACK IN TOWN

© 1957 (Renewed)
Jerry Leiber Music & Mike Stoller Music

Special thanks to RCA Records
for their _____ _____.

Elvis Presley's
Graceland.

1997 Seasons Greetings

© 1997 E.P.E., Inc.

[ ]

SANTA CLAUS IS BACK IN TOWN
1997 SEASONS GREETINGS FROM GRACELAND
Catalog# None   Value $ 100-300
Matrix# POLLYDISC LNIX-GRACE L809 4446 LNIXGRACE S71129-01 A
*(Nov. 1997 Release. Black Disc with Silver Print housed in a 5" x 5" full color
cardboard sleeve. Contains an insert in the sleeve from Priscilla Presley and
Lisa Marie Presley with best wishes for the holiday season. Mailed only to the
Elvis Presley Fan Club Presidents from Graceland as a special way to say
"seasons greetings" instead of mailing a Christmas card. Since this was not
available to the general public, it is a collectors item.)*
Disc contains the following selection:
Santa Claus Is Back In Town

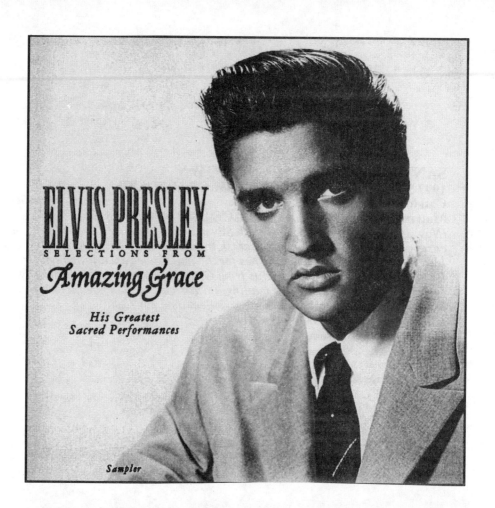

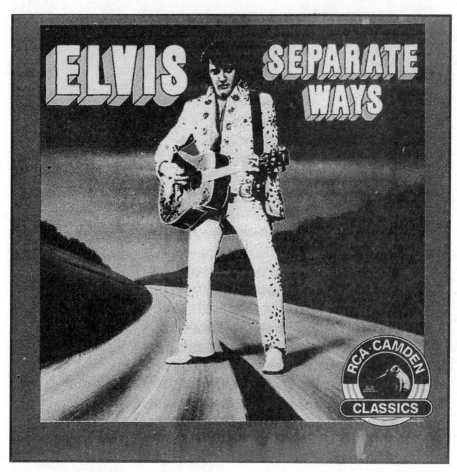

[ ] **SELECTIONS FROM AMAZING GRACE** *(Promo)*
HIS GREATEST SACRED PERFORMANCES
Catalog# RJC 66512-2   Value $ 35-50
Matrix# 50410-01 ++ RJC665122
*(Oct. 1994 Promo Only CD issued to promote Amazing Grace 2 CD Set.
Silver Disc with old RCA Logo and Print in Dark Blue. Contains 4 page insert
booklet. "Sampler" printed on front insert cover. "Not For Sale" printed
on back of front insert cover and back cover.)*
Disc contains the following selections:

Amazing Grace	Bosom Of Abraham
Milky White Way	You Better Run
Run On	Lead Me, Guide Me
I, John	Turn Your Eyes Upon Jesus/
	Nearer My God To Thee

[ ] **SEPARATE WAYS**
Catalog# CCD-2611   Value $ 20-25
Matrix# #910517AA CCD-2611
*(Nov. 1991 First Pressing. Canada Only Release. RCA Camden Classics.
Silver & Black Disc with old RCA and Camden Logos. 4 page insert booklet.
This CD is listed here as it was available for sale in the U.S.)*
Disc contains the following selections:

Separate Ways	Always On My Mind
Sentimental Me	I Slipped, I Stumbled, I Fell
In My Way	Is It So Strange
I Met Her Today	Forget Me Never
What Now, What Next, Where To	Old Shep

from the beginning
we made music
shake,
rattle
+ roll*

*build for future generations

SIXTIES LEGENDS

ELVIS PRESLEY

RADIO PROGRAMMING

[ ] **SHAKE, RATTLE & ROLL** *(Promo)*
Catalog# 6382-2-RDJ   Value $ 75-125
Matrix# 6382-2-R 3S 02
(Jan. 1992 - 18 Track Promo to promote the Elvis in the '90's Series.
Elvis in the '90's Black Disc with old RCA Logo and Print in Silver.
4 page insert booklet. Contains same tracks as 1987 "The Number One Hits".
"Not For Sale" printed on disc. "Promotional Copy - Not For Sale" printed on
back cover. Digitally Remastered from the original RCA Label Master Tapes.)
Disc contains the following selections:

Heartbreak Hotel	Don't
I Want You, I Need You, I Love You	Hard Headed Woman
Hound Dog	A Big Hunk O' Love
Don't Be Cruel	Stuck On You
Love Me Tender	It's Now Or Never
Too Much	Are You Lonesome Tonight?
All Shook Up	Surrender
Teddy Bear	Good Luck Charm
Jailhouse Rock	Suspicious Minds

[ ] **SIXTIES LEGENDS - ELVIS PRESLEY** *(2 CD Radio Show)*
Catalog# Unistar 05/22-05/24   Value $ 50-60
(May 1992 Limited Edition 2 CD Radio Show from the Unistar Radio Network.
Silver Disc with Red Print. Contains Cue Sheets for 2 hour Elvis Radio Show
broadcast 05/22-05/24. Disc and Cue Sheets enclosed in "the Original CD
Shortbox".)
Disc #1
Matrix# H2EU0200C Hour 1
Disc contains the following selections:

Stuck On You	Can't Help Falling In Love
It's Now Or Never	Good Luck Charm
Are You Lonesome Tonight?	Follow That Dream
Surrender	She's Not You
Flaming Star	Return To Sender
I Feel So Bad	(You're The) Devil In Disguise
Little Sister	Bossa Nova Baby
(Marie's The Name) His Latest Flame	Such A Night

Disc #2
Matrix# H2EW0100C Hour 2
Disc contains the following selections:

Ask Me	Suspicious Minds
Crying In The Chapel	Don't Cry Daddy
If I Can Dream	The Wonder Of You
In The Ghetto	

[ ] **SOMETHING FOR EVERYBODY**
Catalog# 2370-2-R   Value $ 20-25
Matrix# W.O. 12161-2 23702R
(Oct. 1989 First Pressing. Midline CD. Silver & Black Disc with old RCA Logo.)
Disc contains the following selections:

There's Always Me   I'm Comin' Hone
Give Me The Right   In Your Arms
It's A Sin   Put The Blame On Me
Sentimental Me   Judy
Starting Today   I Want You With Me
Gently   I Slipped, I Stumbled, I Fell

[ ] **SOMETHING FOR EVERYBODY**
Catalog# 2370-2-R   Value $ 15-20
Matrix# W.O. 12161-3V 23702R
*(1994 Second Pressing. Midline CD. Silver & Black Disc with old RCA Logo with "Wise Buy" sticker on shrink wrap. **RCA deleted this title from their catalog in 1997.**)*

[ ] The **SUN SESSIONS CD**
Catalog# 6414-2-R   **Value $ 15-18**
Matrix# C105857 64142R 10001
*(June 1987 First Pressing. Silver & Blue Disc with block RCA Logo in Blue.
12 page insert booklet.)*
Disc contains the following selections:
THE MASTER TAKES
That's All Right   Mystery Train
Blue Moon Of Kentucky   I Forgot To Remember to Forget
Good Rockin' Tonight   I Love You Because
I Don' Care If The Sun Don't Shine   Blue Moon
Milkcow Blues Boogie   Tomorrow Night
You're A Heartbreaker   I'll Never Let You Go (Little Darlin')
Baby Let's Play House   Just Because
I'm Left, You're Right, She's Gone   Trying To Get To You

THE OUTTAKES
Harbor Lights   I Don't Care If The Sun Don't Shine
I Love You Because - *take 2*   I'm Left, You're Right, She's Gone -
That's All Right   (My Baby's Gone) - *take 9*
Blue Moon Of Kentucky   I'll Never Let You Go (Little Darlin')
                                           When It Rains, It Really Pours

THE ALTERNATE TAKES *(Previously Unreleased)*
I Love You Because - *take 3*   I'm Left, You're Right, She's Gone -
I Love You Because - *take 5*   (My Baby's Gone) - *take 7*
                                           I'm Left, You're Right, She's Gone -
                                               (My Baby's Gone) - *take 12*

[ ] The **SUN SESSIONS CD**
Catalog# 6414-2-R   **Value $ 12-15**
Matrix# W.O. 5857-5M 64142R
*(1991 Second Pressing. Silver & Black Disc with block RCA Logo.
Contains 12 page insert booklet.)*

[ ] The **SUN SESSIONS CD**
Catalog# 6414-2-R   **Value $ 20-30**
BMG Music Service Catalog# D 272289
Matrix# W.O. 5857-5M 64142R
*(1993 Third Pressing. Mfg. for BMG Direct Marketing, Inc. BMG Music
Service catalog number on disc and insert covers. Silver & Black Disc with
block RCA Logo. Pressed in U.S. Contains 12 page insert booklet.
Only available from BMG Music CD Club. Mail Order Only.)*

[ ] The **SUN SESSIONS CD**
Catalog# 6414-2-R   **Value $ 12-15**
Matrix# W.O. 5857-6 64142R
*(1994 Fourth Pressing. Silver & Black Disc with block RCA Logo. Contains 12
page insert booklet.* **RCA deleted this title from their catalog in July, 1998.***)*

[ ] The **SUN SESSIONS CD**
Catalog# 6414-2-R   **Value $ 20-30**
BMG Music Service Catalog# D 272289
Matrix# 64142R ++ 64117-01
*(1996 Fifth Pressing. Mfg. for BMG Direct Marketing, Inc. BMG Music
Service catalog number on disc and insert covers. Silver & Black Disc with
block RCA Logo. Pressed in U.S. Contains 12 page insert booklet.
Only available from BMG Music CD Club. Mail Order Only.)*

[ ] **THAT'S THE WAY IT IS**
ORIGINAL MASTER RECORDING
Catalog# UDCD-560   **Value $ 30-45**
Matrix# SP-ROA UDCD-560
(May 1992 Mobile Fidelity Original Master Recording on 24 kt. Gold plated Ultradisc. Black Disc with Gold Print. Under license agreement from RCA/BMG Records. 12 page insert booklet including fold out mini poster. New Pop Up Jewel Box. Pressed in Japan for U.S. Release.)
Disc contains the following selections:

I Just Can't Help Believin'	You've Lost That Lovin' Feelin'
Twenty Days And Twenty Nights	I've Lost You
How The Web Was Woven	Just Pretend
Patch It Up	Stranger In The Crowd
Mary In The Morning	The Next Step Is Love
You Don't Have To Say You Love Me	Bridge Over Troubled Water

[ ] **THAT'S THE WAY IT IS**
ORIGINAL MASTER RECORDING
Catalog# UDCD-560   **Value $ 30-45**
Matrix# UDCD-560 1D 12
(Jan. 1993 Second Pressing. Mobile Fidelity Original Master Recording on 24 kt. Gold plated Ultradisc II. Black Disc with Gold Print. Under license agreement from RCA/BMG Records. 12 page insert booklet including fold out mini poster. New Pop Up Jewel box. Comes in Limited Edition Collectors Ultradisc II Longbox with jewel box housed in half slipcase. Pressed in U.S.)

[ ] **THAT'S THE WAY IT IS**
Catalog# 07863-54114-2   **Value $ 12-15**
Matrix# 0786354114 A1
(June 1993 First Pressing. Elvis in the '90's Black Matte Disc with old RCA Logo and Print in Silver. 4 page insert booklet. Digitally Remastered from the original RCA Label Master Tapes.)
Disc contains the following selections:

I Just Can't Help Believin'	You've Lost That Lovin' Feelin'
Twenty Days and Twenty Nights	I've Lost You
How the Web Was Woven	Just Pretend
Patch It Up	Stranger In The Crowd
Mary In The Morning	The Next Step Is Love
You Don't Have to Say You Love Me	Bridge Over Troubled Water

[ ] **TIGER MAN**
Catalog# 07863-67611-2   Value $ 14-18
Matrix# 07863676112 ++ 90366-01
(Sept. 1998 First Pressing. Black & Gold Disc with Black Print. Contains 12
page insert booklet. Black and Orange Tiger Stripe collectors stickers with white
print on front of shrink wrap. 30th Anniversary Edition of "68 Comeback Special,
complete uneditied 8 P.M. "Sit Down" show includes 7 unreleased performances.
Digitally Remastered from the original RCA Label Master Tapes.)
Disc contains the following Elvis selections:

Heartbreak Hotel *(Previously Unreleased)*   Love Me
Baby What You Want Me To Do *(Pre. Unreleased)* Trying To Get To You
Introductions   Lawdy Miss Clawdy
That's All Right   Santa Claus Is Back In Town *(Prev.Unrel)*
Are You Lonesome Tonight?   Blue Christmas
Baby What You Want Me to Do (version 2)   Tiger Man
(Previously Unreleased)   When My Blue Moon Turns To Gold Again
Blue Suede Shoes   *(Previously Unreleased)*
One Night *(Previously Unreleased)*   Memories *(Previously Unreleased)*

[ ] **TIGER MAN** *(Promo)*
Catalog# 07863-67611-2   Value $ 15-20
Matrix# 07863676112 ++ 90366-01
(Sept. 1998 Designated Promo. Same as regular release with Black and White
sticker "Not For Sale NFS-1" on front cover of jewel box. Drill hole thru back
of jewel box.)

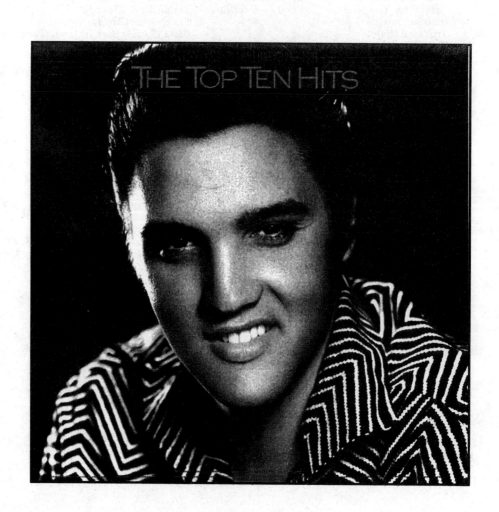

[ ]   The **TOP TEN HITS** *(2 CD's)*

Catalog# 6383-2-R-P1,2   **Value $ 40-50**
(June 1987 First Pressing. Silver & Blue Discs with block RCA Logo in white. Pressed in Japan for U.S. Release.)
Disc #1
Matrix# 1A2 75 R1-6383
Disc contains the following selections:

Heartbreak Hotel	Don't
I Want You, I Need You, I Love You	I Beg Of You
Hound Dog	Wear My Ring Around Your Neck
Don't Be Cruel	Hard Headed Woman
Love Me Tender	One Night
Love Me	I Got Stung
Too Much	A Fool Such As I
All Shook Up	I Need Your Love Tonight
Teddy Bear	A Big Hunk O' Love
Jailhouse Rock	

Disc #2
Matrix# 1B1 75 R2-6383
Disc contains the following selections:

Stuck On You	Return To Sender
It's Now Or Never	Devil In Disguise
Are You Lonesome Tonight?	Bossa Nova Baby
Surrender	Crying In The Chapel
I Feel So Bad	In The Ghetto
Little Sister	Suspicious Minds
His Latest Flame	Don't Cry Daddy
Can't Help Falling In Love	The Wonder Of You
Good Luck Charm	Burning Love
She's Not You	

[ ]   The **TOP TEN HITS** *(2 CD's)*

Catalog # 6383-2-R-P1,2   **Value $ 20-25**
Disc #1 **Matrix# 1/88 2A515 R16383**
Disc #2 **Matrix# 1/88 1C53 R26383**
(Jan. 1988 Second Pressing. Silver & Black Discs with block RCA Logo. Pressed in U.S.)

[ ]   The **TOP TEN HITS** *(2 CD's)*

Catalog# 6383-2-R-P1,2   **Value $ 20-25**
Disc #1 **Matrix# 6/89 2DA6 63832R-1S**
Disc #2 **Matrix# 6/89 3DA10 63832R 2S**
(June 1989 Third Pressing. Silver & Black Discs with block RCA Logo. Pressed in U.S.)

[ ]   The **TOP TEN HITS** *(2 CD's)*

Catalog# 6383-2-R-P1,2   **Value $ 20-25**
Disc #1 **Matrix# W.O. 8801-3 63832R 1S**
Disc #2 **Matrix# W.O. 8802-5 63832R 2S**
(1991 Fourth Pressing. Silver & Black Discs with block RCA Logo. Pressed in U.S.)

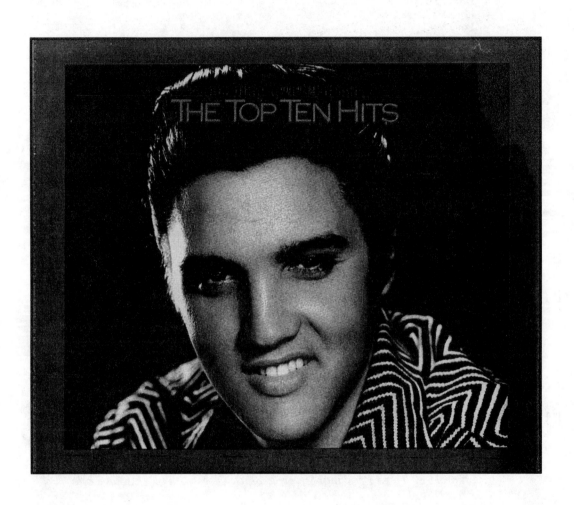

[ ]   The **TOP TEN HITS** *(2 CD's)*

Catalog# 6383-2-R-P1,2 RE   Value $ 20-25
Disc #1 Matrix# W.O. 8801-3 63832R1
Disc #2 Matrix# W.O. 8802-8 63832R2
(1992 Fifth Pressing. Silver & Black Disc with old RCA Logo. RE printed on back of insert sleeve. Pressed in U.S.)

[ ]   The **TOP TEN HITS** *(2 CD's)*

Catalog# 6383-2-R-P1,2 RE-1   Value $ 30-40
BMG Music Service Catalog# D 243910-1-2
Disc #1 Matrix# W.O. 8801-6M 63832R1
Disc #2 Matrix# W.O. 8802-9P 63832R-2
(1993 Sixth Pressing. Mfg. for BMG Direct Marketing, Inc. BMG Music Service catalog number on discs and insert covers. RE-1 printed on back cover. Silver & Black Discs with old RCA Logo. Pressed in U.S. Only available from BMG Music CD Club. Mail Order Only)

[ ]   The **TOP TEN HITS** *(2 CD's)*

Catalog# 6383-2-R-P1,2 RE-1   Value $ 30-40
BMG Music Service Catalog# D 243910-1-2
Disc #1 Matrix# W.O. 8801-7 63832R1
Disc #2 Matrix# W.O. 8802-9P 63832R-2
(1995 Seventh Pressing. Mfg. for BMG Direct Marketing, Inc. BMG Music Service catalog number on discs and insert covers. RE-1 printed on back cover. Silver & Black Discs with old RCA Logo. Pressed in U.S. Only available from BMG Music CD Club. Mail Order Only)

[ ]   The **TOP TEN HITS** *(2 CD Set)*

Catalog# 07863-56383-2   Value $ 20-25
Disc #1 Matrix# W.O. 8801-7 63832R1
Disc #2 Matrix# W.O. 8802-13 S.O. 63832R-2
(May 1996 Reissue with new catalog number. Silver & Black Discs with old RCA Logo. This title has been given a new catalog number. Contains 4 page insert booklet with RE on back page. Discs housed in multi disc jewel box. Jewel box packaged with outer bellyband with same artwork as jewel box. Previous releases were in 2 individual jewel boxes.. Same photo of Elvis as previous releases but with light brown border around the photo on bellyband and insert cover. Pressed in U.S.)

[ ]   The **TOP TEN HITS** *(2 CD Set)*

Catalog# 07863-56383-2   Value $ 20-25
Disc #1 Matrix# 63832RP1 ++ 65399-01
Disc #2 Matrix# 63832RP2 ++ 65378-01
(July 1996 Second Pressing. Silver & Black Discs with old RCA Logo. Contains 4 page insert booklet with RE on back page. Same information as May 1996 issue. This was a free CD from the GLAD Rocks CD Offer (First Brands Corp). Pressed in U.S.)

ELVIS
PRESLEY

• "The TRUTH About Me"
  Interview — *Intimate Thoughts*
• Reproduction of
  The Gold Vinyl record
  from the Magazine
• Personal Conversations
  Including out-takes

℗ ©1996 **RAINBO** RECORDS AND CASSETTES
1738 BERKELEY ST. • SANTA MONICA, CA 90404 • 310-829-3476

[ ]   The **TRUTH ABOUT ME**
Catalog# Rainbo Records   Value $ 30-40
Matrix # RBOEL VISRAINBO RAINBO
(Feb. 1997 Release. CD is part of special Collectors Set which includes
Reprint of the original 34 page "Elvis Answers Back" magazine and gold playable
2 minute record, a 10" gold vinyl 20 minute interview and full length 20 minute
picture CD. All presented in an album sized gatefold clear vinyl sleeve.
This is an exact reproduction of the ultra-rare highly collectable magazine that
was never sold. Includes 18 minutes of previously unheard conversation with
Elvis. Value listed is for the complete set. Mail Order Only.)
Disc contains the following Elvis interview:
Original 20 minute interview, recorded Aug. 1956

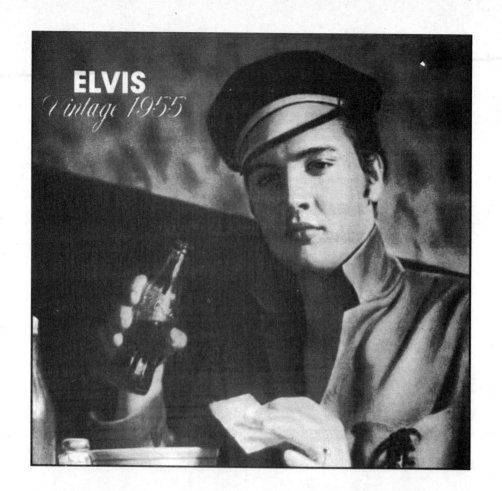

[ ] **VINTAGE '55 ELVIS**
Catalog# OAK-1003 NR 18245   **Value $ 50-75**
Matrix# NR 18245 (V)
(1990 Release on the OAK Records Label. Black & White front insert cover with Vintage 55 and Elvis in Pink. Back insert cover White with Black Print. Silver Disc with Black Print. Single page insert sleeve. Available only for a short time in 1990. Mail Order Only.)
Disc contains the following selections:

Interview: Biff Collie	There's Good Rockin' Tonight
Baby Let's Play House	That's All Right Little Mama
Blue Moon Of Kentucky	Interview: Scotty Moore - Tells The
I've Got A Woman	Beginnings of Elvis

[ ] **VINTAGE 55 ELVIS**
Catalog# OAK-1003 NR 18245   **Value $ 20-25**
Matrix# C2 113869-01 OAK-1003
(June 1998 Reissue on the Oak Records Label. Distributed by Outwest Entertainment. Full color front insert cover with Vintage 55 and Elvis in Blue. Back insert cover Brown background with CD and song titles in Blue. All other print in White. Silver Disc with Black Print. Single page insert sleeve. Mail Order Only.)

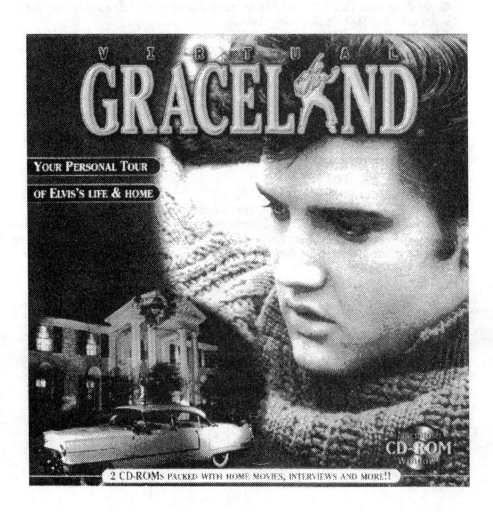

[ ]   **VIRTUAL GRACELAND**   *(2 Disc CD-ROM Set)*
Standard Edition
Catalog# 1246-73702-2   Value $ 45-55
Disc 1 **Matrix# IFPI L238 CD0113A R1H** 11
Disc 2 **Matrix# IFPI L239 CD0113B R1J** 12
(Sept. 1996 Release from Highway One Media Entertainment. A 2 Disc CD-ROM
Set for Macintosh and Windows computers. This is a personal tour of Elvis' life
and home. Contains home movies, interviews, music and more. These are picture
discs. Pale Blue Discs with Black & White different "Jailhouse Rock" publicity
pose on each disc. Disc 1 titled "Graceland" printed in Silver and Disc 2 titled
"Estate" printed in Silver. Has 8 page insert booklet. The two discs are housed
in a 9-1/2" x 7-3/4" glossy hard cover box. This was also available as a
"Platinum Collectors Edition" which contained all of the above plus a 12 page
photo filled booklet, artist's rendering of the estate map - suitable for framing
with hardbound cover. Price on collectors edition $100. This release is included
here because it contains Elvis' performances even though this is technically
not a music CD.)
Discs contain the following selections:

All Shook Up	Lead Me, Oh Lord
Are You Lonesome Tonight	Love Me Tender
Burning Love	Suspicious Minds
Don't Be Cruel (To A Heart That's True)	Teddy Bear
Heartbreak Hotel	That's All Right Mama
Hound Dog	Unchained Melody
Jailhouse Rock	

[ ]   **VIRTUAL GRACELAND**   *(2 Disc CD-ROM Set)*
Catalog# 1246-71702-2   Value $ 30-40
Disc 1 **Matrix# IFRI L238 CD0113A R1H** 11
Disc 2 **Matrix# IFPI L239 CD0113B R1J** 12
(Dec. 1996 Reissue. 2 CD-ROMs now housed in jewel case format. All else the
same except the packaging.)

"W"

[ ]

WALK A MILE IN MY SHOES *(5 CD Box Set)*
THE ESSENTIAL 70's MASTERS
Catalog# 07863 66670-2   **Value $ 70-80**

(Oct. 1995 First Pressing. Packaged in a Special Longbox. A numbered collectable. 5 CD Box Set - 120 Tracks. Includes 7 previously unreleased songs. Each CD has it's own jewel box with it's individual insert sleeve. Each CD is a picture disc. Box contains a 94 page full color booklet. Booklet has full supporting recording data and Discography plus a sheet of RCA Records Label stamps depicting Elvis' 70's Record Covers. Digitally Remastered from the original RCA Record Label Master Tapes. Aqua and White collectors sticker on shrink wrap.)

Disc #1 THE SINGLES Lavender and Black Picture Disc
Matrix# 07863666702P1 ++ 60138-01
Disc contains the following selections:

The Wonder Of You	It's Only Love
I've Lost You	The Sound Of Your Cry
The Next Step Is Love	I Just Can't Help Believin'
You Don't Have To Say You Love Me	How The Web Was Woven
Patch It Up	Until It's Time For You To Go
I Really Don't Want To Know	We Can Make The Morning
There Goes My Everything	An American Trilogy
Rags To Riches	The First Time Ever I Saw Your Face
Where Did They Go, Lord	Burning Love
Life	It's A Matter Of Time
I'm Leavin'	Separate Ways
Heart Of Rome	

Disc # 2 THE SINGLES Aqua and Black Picture Disc
Matrix# 07863666702P2 ++ 60139-01
Disc contains the following selections:

Always On My Mind	T-R-O-U-B-L-E
Fool	Mr. Songman
Steamroller Blues	Bringing It Back
Raised On Rock	Pieces Of My Life
For Ol' Times Sake	Green, Green Grass Of Home
I've Got A Thing About You Baby	Thinking About You
Take Good Care Of Her	Hurt
If You Talk In Your Sleep	For The Heart
Promised Land	Moody Blue
It's Midnight	She Thinks I Still Care
My Boy	Way Down
Loving Arms	Pledging My Love

Disc #3 STUDIO HIGHLIGHTS 1970-1971 *Purple and Black Picture Disc*
Matrix# 07863666702P3 ++ 60143-01
Disc contains the following selections:

Twenty Days And Twenty Nights
I Was Born About Ten Thousand Years Ago
The Fool
A Hundred Years From Now *(Informal Recording)*
Little Cabin On The Hill
Cindy, Cindy
Bridge Over Troubled Water
Got My Mojo Working/Keep Your Hands Off Of It
It's Your Baby, You Rock It
Stranger In The Crowd
Mary In The Morning
It Ain't No Big Thing (But It's Growing)

Just Pretend
Faded Love *(Original Unedited Version)*
Tomorrow Never Comes *(Includes False Sr)*
Make The World Go Away
Funny How Time Slips Away
I Washed My Hands In Muddy Waters -
(Long Version)
Snowbird
Whole Lot-ta Shakin' Goin' On
Amazing Grace *(Alternate Take 2)*
(That's What You Get) For Lovin' Me
Lady Madonna *(Informal Recording)*

Disc #4 STUDIO HIGHLIGHTS 1971-1976 *Orange and Black Picture Disc*
Matrix# 07863666702P4 ++ 60459-01
Disc contains the following selections:

Merry Christmas Baby
I Shall Be Released *(Informal Recording)*
Don't Think Twice, It's All Right *(Jam Edit)*
It's Still Here *(Original Unedited Version)*
I'll Take You Home Again Kathleen -
(Original Undubbed Version)
I Will Be True
My Way *(Studio Master)*
For The Good Times *(Master)*
Just A Little Bit
It's Different Now *(Rehearsal)*
Are You Sincere

I Got A Feelin' In My Body
You Asked Me To
Good Time Charlie's Got The Blues
Talk About The Good Times
Tiger Man *(Jam)*
I Can Help
Susan When She Tried
Shake A Hand
She Thinks I Still Care *(Alternate Take 2B)*
Danny Boy
Love Coming Down
He'll Have To Go

Disc #5 THE ELVIS PRESLEY SHOW *Gold and Black Picture Disc*
Matrix# 07863666702P5 ++ 60057-01
Disc contains the following selections:

See See Rider
Men With Broken Hearts *(Short Poem)*
Walk A Mile In My Shoes
Polk Salad Annie
Let It Be Me (Je T' Appartiens)
Proud Mary
Something *(Master)*
You've Lost That Lovin' Feelin'
Heartbreak Hotel *(Previously Unreleased)*
I Was The One *(Previously Unreleased)*
One Night *(Previously Unreleased)*
Never Been To Spain *(Master)*
You Gave Me A Mountain *(Master)*
It's Impossible

A Big Hunk O' Love *(Master)*
It's Over *(Master)*
The Impossible Dream (The Quest)
Reconsider Baby
I'll Remember You
I'm So Lonesome I Could Cry
Suspicious Minds
Unchained Melody
The Twelfth Of Never *(Rehearsal)*
Softly As I Leave You *(Rehearsal)*
Alla' En El "Rancho Grande" *(Rehearsal)*
Froggy Went A Courtin' *(Rehearsal)*
Stranger In My Own Home Town -
(Informal Rehearsal)

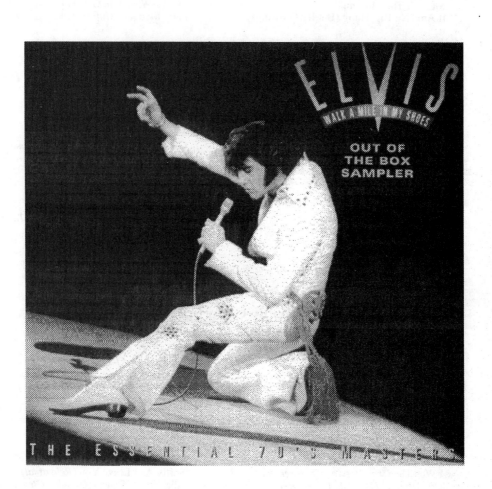

[ ] **WALK A MILE IN MY SHOES**   *(Promo Box Set)*
THE ESSENTIAL 70's MASTERS
Catalog# 07863 66670-2 PRES-4/2   Value $ 90-100
Disc #1 Matrix# 07863666702P1 ++ 60138-01
Disc #2 Matrix# 07863666702P2 ++ 60139-01
Disc #3 Matrix# 07863666702P3 ++ 60143-01
Disc #4 Matrix# 07863666702P4 ++ 60459-01
Disc #5 Matrix# 07863666702P5 ++ 60057-01
(Oct. 1995 Designated Promo Box Set. Same as regular catalog release with
black and white sticker **"For Promotional Only - Not For Sale PRES-4/2"**
under shrink wrap.)

[ ] **WALK A MILE IN MY SHOES**   *(Promo)*
OUT OF THE BOX SAMPLER
Catalog# RJC-66765-2   Value $ 40-50
Matrix# RJC667652 ++ 60996-01
(Aug. 1995 Promo Only CD Picture Disc issued to promote the Essential 70's
Box Set. Picture Disc is matte finish Dark Blue and White. Contains 4 page
insert booklet. **"Not For Sale"** *printed on disc.* **"Promotional Use Only -**
Not For Sale" *printed on back insert cover.)*
Disc contains the following selections:

Men With Broken Hearts *(Short Poem)*	Faded Love *(Original Unedited Version)*
Walk A Mile In My Shoes	A Hundred Years From Now *(Inf. Record)*
I Just Can't Help Believin'	My Way *(Studio Master)*
Burning Love	Good Time Charlie's Got The Blues
Promised Land	You Gave Me A Mountain *(Master)*
T-R-O-U-B-L-E	The Twelfth Of Never *(Rehearsal)*

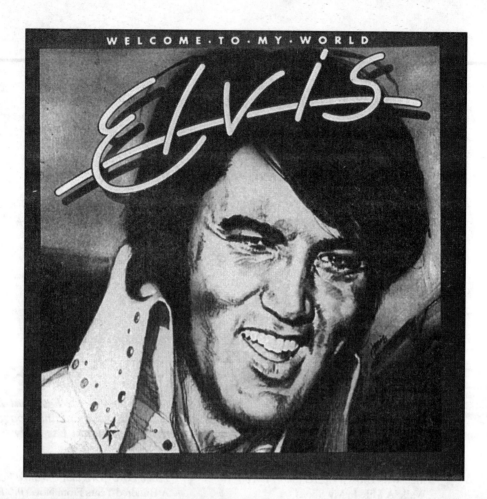

WELCOME·TO·MY·WORLD

ELVIS

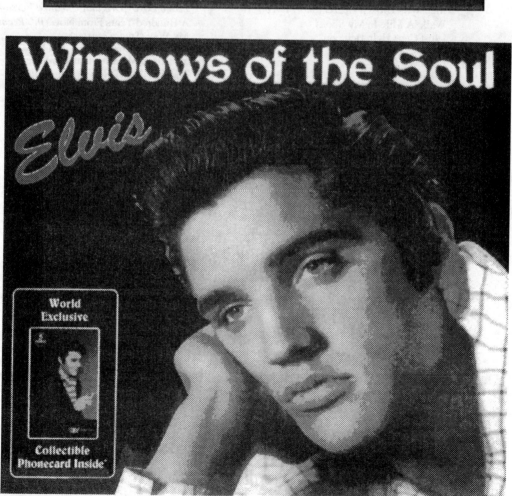

Windows of the Soul

Elvis

World
Exclusive

Collectible
Phonecard Inside

[ ] **WELCOME TO MY WORLD**
Catalog# 07863-52274-2   Value $ 12-15
Matrix# 07863-52274-2 1D 11
*(May 1992 First Pressing. Elvis in the '90's Black Disc with old RCA Logo
and Print in Silver. 8 page insert booklet. Digitally Remastered from the
original RCA Label Master Tapes. Contains alternate take of
"Your Cheatin' Heart".)*
Disc contains the following selections:

Welcome To My World	Make The World Go Away
Help Me Make It Through The Night	Gentle On My Mind
Release Me (And Let Me Love Again)	I'm So Lonesome I Could Cry
I Really Don't Want To Know	Your Cheatin' Heart *(Alternate Take)*
For The Good Times	I Can't Stop Loving You

[ ] **WELCOME TO MY WORLD**
Catalog# 07863-52274-2   Value $ 12-15
Matrix# 07863-52274-2 1D 13
*(1995 Second Pressing. Elvis in the '90's Black Disc with old RCA Logo
and Print in Silver. 8 page insert booklet.)*

[ ] **WELCOME TO MY WORLD**
Catalog# 07863-52274-2   Value $ 12-15
Matrix# 07863-52274-2 2D 17
*(1997 Third Pressing. Elvis in the '90's Black Disc with old RCA Logo
and Print in Silver. 8 page insert booklet.)*

[ ] **WINDOWS OF THE SOUL**
Catalog# GLCD 02041313   Value $ 25-30
Matrix# L383 7090 ELVIS A60719-14
*(Sept. 1996 Release from ERIKA Records, Inc. Interview Disc with Phone Card.
Black Disc with Silver Print and Elvis in Blue. Contains 12 page insert booklet.
Housed in cardboard digi-pack. First U.S. CD released to contain a Phonecard.
Disc contains 1956 Little Rock Interviews by Ray Green.)*

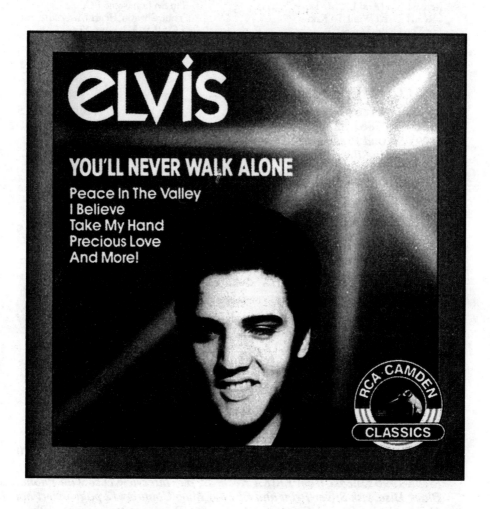

[ ] **YOU'LL NEVER WALK ALONE**
Catalog# CAD1-2472   Value $ 7-10
Matrix# Y28 CAD1-2472
*(Aug. 1987 First Pressing. RCA Special Products - RCA Camden Classics
Release. Distributed by The Special Music Co. Disc pressed in Canada for
release in Canada & U.S. Silver & Black Disc with old RCA Logo, Camden
and Special Music Co. Logos in Blue. Insert cover printed in U.S.)*
Disc contains the following selections:

You'll Never Walk Alone	I Believe
Who Am I?	It Is No Secret (What God Can Do)
Let Us Pray	Sing You Children
Peace In The Valley	Take My Hand, Precious Lord
We Call On Him	

[ ] **YOU'LL NEVER WALK ALONE**
Catalog# CAD1-2472   Value $ 7-10
Matrix# Y28 CAD1-2472
*(1989 Second Pressing. RCA Special Products - RCA Camden Classics Release.
Distributed by The Special Music Co. Disc pressed in Canada for release in
Canada & U.S. Silver & Black Disc with block RCA Logo, Nipper and
Special Products in Blue. Insert cover printed in Canada.)*

[ ] **YOU'LL NEVER WALK ALONE**
Catalog# CAD1-2472   Value $ 7-10
Matrix# CAD1-2472 1C 13
*(1991 Third Pressing. RCA Special Products. Distributed by The Special
Music Co. Disc pressed in U.S. Silver & Black Disc with block RCA Logo,
Nipper and Special Products in Blue. Insert cover printed in U.S.)*

[ ] **YOU'LL NEVER WALK ALONE**
Catalog# CAD1-2472   Value $ 7-10
Matrix# CAD1-2472 1C 14
*(1992 Fourth Pressing. RCA Special Products. Distributed by The Special
Music Co. Disc pressed in U.S. Silver & Black Disc with block RCA Logo,
Nipper and Special Products in Blue. Insert cover printed in U.S.)*

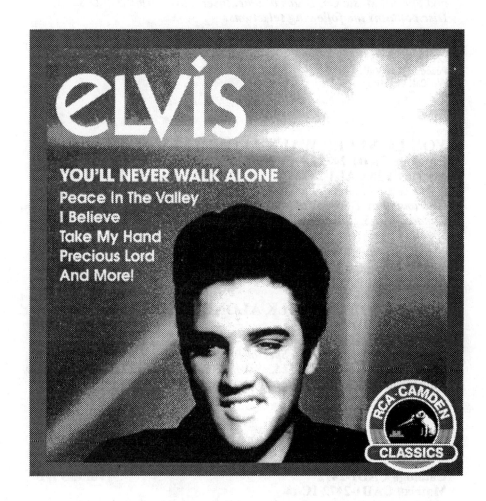

[ ] **YOU'LL NEVER WALK ALONE**
Catalog# CAD1-2472   Value $ 7-10
Matrix# CAD1-2472 1502/A
*(1994 Fifth Pressing. RCA Special Products. Distributed by The Special
Music Co. Disc pressed in U.S. Silver & Black Disc with block RCA Logo,
Nipper, Special Products and Special Music Co. in Red. Insert cover
printed in U.S.)*

[ ] **YOU'LL NEVER WALK ALONE**
Catalog# CAD1-2472   Value $ 7-10
Matrix# CAD1-2472 15027A 01!
*(1995 Sixth Pressing. RCA Special Products. Distributed by The Special
Music Co. Disc pressed in U.S. Silver & Black Disc with block RCA Logo,
Nipper, Special Products and Special Music Co. in Red. Insert cover
printed in U.S.)*

[ ] **YOU'LL NEVER WALK ALONE**
Catalog# CAD1-2472A   Value $ 7-10
Matrix# CAD1-2472 15027A 01!
*(October 1998 Reissue. RCA Special Products Release for AVON.
Disc pressed in U.S. Dark Red Disc with block RCA Logo, Nipper, Special
Products and Camden in Silver. Title in Dark Yellow. Does not have Special
Music Co. on disc or insert cover. Back cover Dark Red with White Print. All
previous pressings had Tan back cover with Black Print. Insert cover printed
in U.S. Contains same Matrix number as Sixth Pressing.)*

Section 11

Various Artists

****VARIOUS ARTISTS RELEASES****

All of the Following Contain at Least One Elvis Track

[ ] **A CELEBRATION OF COUNTRY 'N' POP MUSIC** *(4 CD Set)*
Catalog# RB7-218C-1,2,3,4   Value $ 55-60
(1995 Readers Digest Music Release. A 4 CD Set with 48 page insert booklet. Mail Order Only.)
Discs contain the following Elvis selections:
Gentle On My Mind   You Don't Know Me

[ ] **A CELEBRATION OF FAITH & JOY** *(4 CD Set)*
Catalog# RBD-196/CD1   Value $ 55-60
(1993 Readers Digest Music Release. A 4 CD Set. Mail Order Only.)
Discs contain the following Elvis selections:
Somebody Bigger Than You And I   His Hand In Mine
Joshua Fit The Battle Of Jericho   An Evening Prayer

[ ] **A COUNTRY CHRISTMAS** *(3 CD Set)*
Catalog# RBD-166/CD1   Value $ 45-50
(1992 Readers Digest Music Release. A 3 CD Set. Contains 40 page insert booklet. Mail Order Only.)
Discs contain the following Elvis selections:
White Christmas   Here Comes Santa Claus

[ ] **A COUNTRY CHRISTMAS Volume 2**
Catalog# 4809-2-R   Value $ 12-15
(Aug. 1987 First Pressing. RCA Release.)
Disc contains the following Elvis selection:
Silver Bells

[ ] **A COUNTRY CHRISTMAS Volume 2**
Catalog# 4809-2-R   Value $ 12-15
(Aug. 1991 Second Pressing. RCA Release.)

[ ] **A FIRESIDE CHRISTMAS** *(2 CD Set)*
Catalog# PCD2-1219   Value $ 15-20
(1988 RCA Special Products Release on the Pair Label. A 2 CD Set.)
Discs contains the following Elvis selection:
If Every Day Was Like Christmas

A GIFT OF MUSIC   *(Promo)*
Catalog# RDJ66341-2   Value $ 25-30
(1993 BMG Promo Only Release for J & R Music World. To promote various artists on the BMG label. "Not For Sale" on disc and cardboard sleeve.)
Disc contains the following Elvis selection:
Suspicious Minds *(Alternate Take)*

A HOLIDAY HAPPENING/   *(Promo)*
CHRISTMAS RARITIES ON CD VOLUME 8
Catalog# WESTWOOD ONE   Value $ 50-75
(1991 Westwood One Radio Promo CD with "Not For Sale" on disc.)
Disc contains the following Elvis selection:
Santa Claus Is Back In Town

A LIFE LESS ORDINARY   *(Original Soundtrack)*
Catalog# 314-540-809   Value #15-20
(1997 Soundtrack CD on London. Distributed by PolyGram.)
Disc contains the following Elvis selection:
Always On My Mind

The ALBUM NETWORK CHRISTMAS CD TUNEUP *(Promo)*
Catalog# Christmas 87   Value $ 30-40
(1987 Album Network Release. "For Promotion Only Not for Sale". Contains 6 page tri-fold insert booklet. Promo CD sent to Album Network affiliates.)
Disc contains the following Elvis selection:
Santa Bring My Baby Back (To Me)

AMERICAN BANDSTAND   *(3 CD Radio Show)*
40th ANNIVERSARY SPECIAL
Catalog# 92-05   Value $ 20-25
(1992 Unistar Radio Network Inc. 3 CD Set with Cue sheets.)
Discs contain the following Elvis selection:
Jailhouse Rock

AMERICAN COUNTRY COUNTDOWN   *(4 CD Radio Show)*
With Bob Kingsley
Catalog# 91-1 Show #1   Value $ 25-30
(1991 4 CD Set for ABC Radio Network. Contained in "the Original CD Shortbox" with Cue sheets.)
Discs contain the following Elvis selection:
If I Can Dream

[ ]   **AMERICAN COUNTRY COUNTDOWN** *(4 CD Radio Show)*
      With Bob Kingsley
      Catalog# 94-6 Show #25   **Value $ 25-30**
      (1994 4 CD Set for ABC Radio Network. Contained in "the Original
      CD Shortbox" with Cue sheets.)
      Discs contain the following Elvis selection:
      Moody Blue

[ ]   **AMERICAN COUNTRY COUNTDOWN** *(4 CD Radio Show)*
      With Bob Kingsley
      Catalog# 94-10 Show #43   **Value $ 25-30**
      (1994 4 CD Set for ABC Radio Network. Contained in "the Original
      CD Shortbox" with Cue sheets.)
      Discs contain the following Elvis selection:
      Funny How Time Slips Away

[ ]   **AMERICAN GOLD** *(4 CD Radio Show)*
      With Dick Bartley
      Catalog# 93-12 Show 51   **Value $ 25-30**
      (1993 4 CD Set for ABC Radio Network. Contained in "the Original CD
      Shortbox" with Cue sheets.)
      Discs contain the following Elvis selections:
      Santa Claus Is Back In Town   Blue Christmas

[ ]   **AMERICAN GOLD** *(4 CD Radio Show)*
      With Dick Bartley
      Catalog# 95-2 Show# 6   **Value 25-30**
      (1995 4 CD Set for ABC Radio Network. Contained in "the Original CD
      Shortbox" with Cue sheets.)
      Discs contain the following Elvis selection:
      Can't Help Falling In Love

[ ]   **AMERICAN GOLD** *(4 CD Radio Show)*
      With Dick Bartley
      Catalog# 96-3 Show# 10   **Value $ 25-30**
      (1996 4 CD Set for ABC Radio Network. Contained in "the Original CD
      Shortbox" with Cue sheets.)
      Discs contain the following Elvis selections:
      Jailhouse Rock   Suspicious Minds

[ ]   **AMERICAN GOLD** *(4 CD Radio Show)*
      With Dick Bartley
      Catalog# 97-12 Show# 51   **Value $ 25-30**
      (1997 4 CD Set for ABC Radio Network. Contained in 7" x 9" mailing envelope
      with Cue sheets.)
      Discs contain the following Elvis selections:
      Santa Claus Is Back In Town   Blue Christmas

[ ] **ANGELS AMONG US**
Catalog# 07863-67623-2   Value $ 8-12
(1998 RCA Release.)
Disc contains the following Elvis selection:
Fools Rush In (Where Angels Fear To Tread)

[ ] **BACK TO THE 50's** *(2 CD Set)*
Catalog# DVC 2-1068-1/2   Value $ 25-30
(1993 Heartland Music Release. A 2 CD Set. Mail Order Only.)
Discs contain the following Elvis selections:
(Let Me Be Your) Teddy Bear   All Shook Up

[ ] The **BEST OF CHRISTMAS**
Catalog# 7013-2-R   Value $ 12-15
(1990 RCA Release.)
Disc contains the following Elvis selection:
Silver Bells

[ ] **BILLBOARD CHRISTMAS FOUR-PACK!** *(4 CD Box Set)*
Catalog# R2 72540   Value $ 40-50
*(1996 Rhino Records Release. 4 CD Box Set in Slipcase. Contains
"Billboard Greatest Christmas Hits 1935 - 1954", "Billboard Greatest Christmas
Hits 1955-Present", "Billboard Greatest R & B Christmas Hits" and
"Billboard Rock 'N' Roll Christmas".These discs were also sold individually.)*
Discs contain the following Elvis selection:
Blue Christmas

[ ] **BILLBOARD GREATEST CHRISTMAS HITS
1955 - PRESENT**
Catalog# R2-70636 DPC1-0885   Value $ 10-12
(1989 Rhino Records Release.)
Disc contains the following Elvis selection:
Blue Christmas

[ ] **BILLBOARD TOP ROCK 'N' ROLL HITS - 1956**
Catalog# R2-70599 DPC1-0890   Value $ 10-12
(1989 Rhino Records Release.)
Disc contains the following Elvis selections:
Don't Be Cruel   Hound Dog

[ ] **BILLBOARD TOP ROCK 'N' ROLL HITS - 1957**
Catalog# R2-70618 DPC1-0827   Value $ 10-12
(1988 Rhino Records Release.)
Disc contains the following Elvis selections:
All Shook Up   Jailhouse Rock

[ ]   **BILLBOARD TOP ROCK 'N' ROLL HITS - 1958**
                Catalog# R2-70619 DPC1-0828   **Value $ 10-12**
                (1988 Rhino Records Release.)
                Disc contains the following Elvis Selection:
                Hard Headed Woman

[ ]   **BILLBOARD TOP ROCK 'N' ROLL HITS - 1959**
                Catalog# R2-70620 DPC1-0829   **Value $ 10-12**
                (1988 Rhino Records Release.)
                Disc contains the following Elvis selection:
                A Big Hunk O' Love

[ ]   **BILLBOARD TOP ROCK 'N' ROLL HITS - 1960**
                Catalog# R2-70621 DPC1-0830   **Value $ 15-20**
                (1988 Rhino Records Release. 1993 Re-Issue does not contain Elvis selections.)
                Disc contains the following Elvis selections:
                Stuck On You   It's Now Or Never

[ ]   **BILLBOARD 1957 - 1961:**   *(5 CD Box Set)*
                TOP ROCK 'N' ROLL HITS
                Catalog# R2 72004   **Value $ 50-55**
                (1989 Rhino Records Special Value. 5 CD Box Set. These discs were also sold
                *individually. **This set has been deleted from catalog.**)*
                Discs contain the following Elvis selections:
                All Shook Up   A Big Hunk O' Love
                Jailhouse Rock   Stuck On You
                Hard Headed Woman   It's Now Or Never

[ ]   **BLUES NOTES AND BLACK: BLUES SUR**
                Catalog# 8827   **Value $ 14-18**
                (1993 Phontastic Label Release.)
                Disc contains the following Elvis selection:
                That's All Right

[ ]   The **BOY FROM TUPELO**
                Catalog# PS1 359CD   **Value $ 25-35**
                (1993. Distributed by Paradise Sounds, Inc. Hendersonville, TN. Sold by
                The Elvis Hour, a syndicated radio show from Creative Radio Network. Songs by
                Shaun Nielson, former Elvis backup singer. Contains previously unreleased
                1974 Elvis vocal recorded at home in Palm springs. Full color Elvis insert cover.)
                Disc contains the following Elvis selection:
                Blue Spanish Eyes *(Unreleased Home Recording)*

[ ] **CHRISTMAS CLASSICS, Volume 1**
Catalog# 07863-66301-2   Value $ 12-15
(1993 RCA Release.)
Disc contains the following Elvis selection:
Blue Christmas

[ ] **CHRISTMAS CLASSICS, Volume 2**
Catalog# 07863-66302-2   Value $ 12-15
(1993 RCA Release.)
Disc contains the following Elvis selection:
Santa Claus Is Back In Town

[ ] **CHRISTMAS IN AMERICA** *(3 CD Set)*
Catalog# RBD-177/CD1   Value $ 45-50
(1988 Readers Digest Music Release. 3 CD Set. Mail Order Only.)
Discs contain the following Elvis selection:
A Special Christmas Message From Elvis - Silent Night

[ ] **CLASSIC COUNTRY MUSIC II** *(4 CD Box Set)*
A Smithsonian Collection
Catalog# RD 042-2   Value $ 65-75
*(1990 Smithsonian Recording Collection "Revised Edition". 4 CD Box Set
contained in LP sized box with 92 page booklet. Discs are also sold individually
in $15-20 each range. Elvis selection only on second disc. Produced in
association with and manufactured by RCA Special Products. Mail Order Only.)*
Discs contain the following Elvis selection:
Blue Moon Of Kentucky

[ ] **CLASSIC COUNTRY 1965-1969** *(2 CD Set)*
Catalog# TCD 808 R808-02   Value $ 20-25
*(1998 Time - Life Music Release. 2 CD's housed in Double Slimline jewel case.
Contains 10 page five-fold insert booklet. Mail Order Only.)*
Disc contains the following Elvis selections:
Crying In The Chapel   Suspicious Minds

[ ] **CONTEMPORARY COUNTRY Volume 1**
The Late '70's
Catalog# TCD-140   Value $ 15-20
*(1991 Time - Life Music Release. Contains 8 page insert booklet.
Mail Order Only. This title is now deleted.)*
Disc contains the following Elvis selection:
Moody Blue

[ ]   **CONTEMPORARY COUNTRY Volume 3**
The Late '70's - Hot Hits
Catalog# TCD-142   **Value $ 15-20**
*(1993 Time - Life Music Release. Contains 8 page insert booklet.
Mail Order Only.* **This title is now deleted.***)*
Disc contains the following Elvis selection:
Way Down

[ ]   **CONTEMPORARY COUNTRY Volume 4**
The Early '80's - Hot Hits
Catalog# TCD-143   **Value $ 15-20**
*(1993 Time - Life Music Release. Contains 8 page insert booklet.
Mail Order Only.* **This title is now deleted.***)*
Disc contains the following Elvis selection:
Guitar Man *(Remixed Version)*

[ ]   **COUNTRY CHRISTMAS**   *(2 CD Set)*
Catalog# TCD-109 A/B   **Value $ 20-25**
(1988 Time - Life Music Release. 2 CD Set. Mail Order Only.)
Discs contain the following Elvis selections:
I'll Be Home For Christmas   Blue Christmas
If Every Day Was Like Christmas

[ ]   **COUNTRY MEMORIES**   *(4 CD Set)*
Catalog# RBD-066/CD1   **Value $ 55-60**
*(1989 Reader's Digest Music Release. 4 CD Set with 64 page insert booklet.
Mail Order Only.)*
Discs contain the following Elvis selections:
Don't Be Cruel   Crying In The Chapel
A Fool Such As I   Don't Cry Daddy
Love Me Tender   Kentucky Rain

[ ]   **COUNTRY SOFT 'N' MELLOW**   *(4 CD Set)*
Catalog# RBD-200/CD1   **Value $ 55-60**
*(1989 Reader's Digest Music Release. 4 CD Set with 64 page insert booklet.
Mail Order Only.)*
Discs contain the following Elvis selections:
Bridge Over Troubled Waters   Always On My Mind
Memories

[ ]   **COUNTRY SONGS THAT WILL LAST FOREVER** *(4 CD Set)*
Catalog# RBD-202/CD1   **Value $ 55-60**
*(1993 Reader's Digest Music Release. 4 CD Set with bonus booklet. Mail Order
Only.)*
Discs contain the following Elvis selections:
I Really Don't Want To Know   She Thinks I Still Care

[ ]   **COUNTRY SWEET 'N' SENTIMENTAL** *(4 CD Set)*
        Catalog# RBD-241/CD1   **Value $ 55-60**
        (1993 Readers Digest Music Release. 4 CD Set. Contains 48 page insert booklet.
        Mail Order Only.)
        Discs contain the following Elvis selections:
        It Keeps Right On A-Hurtin'   Put Your Hand In The Hand

[ ]   **COUNTRY USA - 1954**
        Catalog# TCD-117   **Value $ 15-20**
        (1990 Time - Life Release. Mail Order Only. This title is now deleted.)
        Disc contains the following Elvis selection:
        Blue Moon Of Kentucky

[ ]   **COUNTRY USA - 1955**
        Catalog# TCD-118   **Value $ 15-20**
        (1990 Time - Life Music Release. Mail Order Only. This title is now deleted.)
        Disc contains the following Elvis selections:
        I Forgot To Remember To Forget   Mystery Train

[ ]   **COUNTRY USA - 1956**
        Catalog# TCD-119   **Value $ 15-20**
        (1990 Time - Life Music Release. Mail Order Only. Elvis, Scotty & Bill cover.
        This title is now deleted.)
        Disc contains the following Elvis selections:
        Heartbreak Hotel   I Want You, I Need You, I Love You

[ ]   **COUNTRY USA - 1958**
        Catalog# TCD-112   **Value $ 15-20**
        (1989 Time - Life Music Release. Mail Order Only. This title is now deleted.)
        Disc contains the following Elvis selection:
        Don't

[ ]   **COUNTRY USA - 1969**
        Catalog# TCD-113   **Value $ 15-20**
        (1990 Time - Life Music Release. Mail Order Only. This title is now deleted.)
        Disc contains the following Elvis selection:
        Suspicious Minds

[ ]   **CREATIVE RADIO NETWORK** *(Radio Demo Sampler)*
        Catalog# None   **Value $ 25-30**
        (1993 Creative Radio Network 20th Anniversary Radio Demo Sampler.
        Highlighting the Christmas and Special Program Radio Shows.)
        Disc contains the following Elvis selections:
        Cut 5 Christmas With Elvis   Cut 12 Elvis The Country Side
        Cut 10 Elvis Birthday Tribute   Cut 17 The Elvis Hour
        Cut 11 Memories Of Elvis

[ ] **CRUISIN' AMERICA with COUSIN BRUCIE***(3 CD Radio Show)*
Catalog# 92-30   Value $ 10-15
(1992. A 3 CD Set from CBS Radio with Cue sheets.)
Discs contain the following Elvis selection:
Hard Headed Woman

[ ] **CRUISIN' AMERICA with COUSIN BRUCIE***(3 CD Radio Show)*
Catalog# 92-32   Value $ 10-15
(1992. A 3 CD Set from CBS Radio with Cue sheets.)
Discs contain the following Elvis selections:
When My Blue Moon Turns To Gold Again

[ ] **DECEMBER SONGS**   *(Promo)*
Catalog# RJC 66546-2   Value $ 20-30
(1994 BMG Promo Only Release. White Disc with Red Print.
"Promo Only - Not For Sale" on inside circle of disc and "Not for Sale"
on back cover. No insert front cover.)
Disc contains the following Elvis selections:
Merry Christmas Baby   Santa Bring My Baby Back (To Me)

[ ] **DICK CLARK'S ROCK 'N' ROLL CHRISTMAS** *(2 CD's)*
Catalog# TCD-805 R129-02 A/B   Value $ 15-25
(1997 Time - Life Music Release from BMG Special Products. 2 CD Set.
Mail Order Only.)
Discs contain the following Elvis selections:
Blue Christmas   If Every Day Was Like Christmas
Snata Claus Is Back In Town

[ ] **DICK CLARK'S ROCK ROLL & REMEMBER***(4 CD Radio Sh.)*
Catalog# Unistar 1/3-1/5   Value $ 30-40
(1992 Limited Edition 4 CD Set for the Unistar Radio Network. Contained in
"the Original CD Shortbox" with cue sheets.)
Discs contain the following Elvis selections:

Don't Be Cruel	Jailhouse Rock
Ready Teddy	It's Now Or Never
Love Me Tender	Surrender
That's All Right	Are You Lonesome Tonight?
Heartbreak Hotel	Crying In The Chapel
A Big Hunk O' Love	Kentucky Rain
Hound Dog	Burning Love
Teddy Bear	Fame And Fortune
One Night	If I Can Dream

[ ] **DICK CLARK'S ROCK ROLL& REMEMBER***(4 CD Radio Sh.)*
Catalog# Westwood One 08/12-08/14   **Value $ 30-40**
(1994 Limited Edition 4 CD Set for the Unistar/Westwood One Radio Networks.
Contained in "the Original CD Shortbox" with Cue sheets. ***"Not For Sale -***
For Licensed Broadcast Use Only" *on Disc.)*
Disc contains the following Elvis selections:

Jailhouse Rock	(Marie's The Name) His Latest Flame
Don't Be Cruel	I Really Don't Want To Know
Heartbreak Hotel	Can't Help Falling In Love
Hound Dog	It's Now Or Never
(Let Me Be Your) Teddy Bear	Surrender
(You're The) Devil In Disguise	Are You Lonesome Tonight?
She's Not You	Suspicious Minds
Crying In The Chapel	A Fool Such As I
	Burning Love

[ ] **DICK CLARK'S ROCK ROLL& REMEMBER***(4 CD Radio Sh.)*
Catalog# Westwood One 09/02-09/04   **Value $ 30-40**
(1994 Limited Edition. 4 CD Set for the Unistar/Westwood One Radio Networks.
Contained in "the Original CD Shortbox" with Cue sheets. ***"Not For Sale -***
For Licensed Broadcast Use Only" *on Disc.)*
Discs contain the following Elvis selections:

I Want You, I Need You, I Love You	Elvis Interview

[ ] **DINER**   *(Original Soundtrack)*
Catalog# 60107-2   **Value $ 14-18**
(1987 Elektra Records Release.)
Disc contains the following Elvis selection:
Don't Be Cruel

[ ] **DINER**   *(Original Soundtrack)*
Catalog# 60107-2   **Value $ 20-25**
BMG Music Service Catalog# D 116492
(1995 Second Pressing. Mfg. for BMG Direct Marketing Inc. BMG Music Service
catalog number on disc and back insert cover. Mail Order Only.)

[ ] **DO YOU LOVE ME?**
ALL-TIME BEST LOVE SONGS
Catalog# 07863 66812-2   **Value $ 15-18**
(1996 RCA Release. Contains 8 page quad-fold insert cover.)
Disc contains the following Elvis selection:
Always On My Mind

[ ] **DON KIRSHNER'S 35th ANNIVERSARY OF ROCK** *(2 CD's)*
GREAT VOCALISTS
Catalog# DK35 1/2   **Value $ 40-50**
(1990 - 2 CD Radio Show with Cue sheets.)
Discs contain the following Elvis selection:
Good Luck Charm

[ ]   **DRIVER'S FAVORITE SONGS**
Catalog# 3100   Value $ 14-18
(1998 Four O Four Label Release.)
Disc contains the following Elvis selection:
Amazing Grace

[ ]   **EASY LISTENING HITS OF THE 60's & '70's** *(4 CD Set)*
Catalog# RBD-040/CD1   Value $ 55-60
(1989 Reader's Digest Music Release. 4 CD Set with 64 page insert booklet.
Mail Order Only.)
Discs contain the following Elvis selections:

Until It's Time For You To Go	My Way
Can't Help Falling In Love	Memories

[ ]   **ELVIS MANIA** *(2 CD Set)*
Catalog# LG 40004/50005   Value $ 20-25
(1991 Live Gold Productions 2 CD Set. Contains 52 Novelty & Tribute Songs
with insert booklet. Pressed in Czechoslovakia for U.S. Release.)
Contains Elvis Interview

[ ]   **ELVIS MANIA 2**
Catalog# LG 120012   Value $ 15-18
(1992 Live Gold Productions. Contains 27 Novelty & Tribute Songs with
insert booklet. Pressed in Czechoslovakia for U.S. Release.)
Contains Only Portions of Several Elvis Songs

[ ]   The **ELVIS PRESLEY YEARS** *(4 CD Set)*
       Catalog# RBD-236/CD1   **Value $ 60-70**
       (1991 Reader's Digest Music Release. Four CD's in a multi disc jewel box.
       Silver Disc with Reader's Digest Title and Logos in Blue. Print in Black.
       Contains 48 page insert booklet.)
       Disc #1 Catalog# RB7-236-1 XCD4-5921 1954-1959
       Disc contains the following Elvis selections:

That's All Right Mama	All Shook Up
Good Rockin' Tonight	Teddy Bear
Love Me Tender	Wear My Ring Around Your Neck
Heartbreak Hotel	Hard Headed Woman

       Disc #2 Catalog# RB7-236-2 XCD4-5922 1959-(continued from Disc 1)-1965
       Disc contains the following Elvis selections:

A Big Hunk O' Love	Return To Sender
I Need Your Love Tonight	Good Luck Charm
Can't Help Falling In Love	Such A Night
It's Now Or Never	Crying In The Chapel

       Disc #3 Catalog# RB7-236-3 XCD4-5923 1965-1971
       Disc contains the following Elvis selections:

Big Boss Man	If I Can Dream
Love Letters	The Wonder Of You
Don't Cry Daddy	Kentucky Rain

       Disc #4 Catalog# RB7-236-4 XCD4-5924 1970-1977
       Disc contains the following Elvis selections:

Steamroller Blues	Promised Land
Burning Love	Way Down
My Boy	My Way

[ ]   **EMI MUSIC PUBLISHING**   *(2 CD Promo Set)*
       CHRISTMAS SONGS
       Catalog# None   **Value $ 40-50**
       (1996 Promo Only from EMI Music Publishing Co. "For Promotional Use Only"
       on back cover and insert booklet.)
       Discs contain the following Elvis selection:
       On A Snowy Christmas Night

[ ]   The **FAMILY CHRISTMAS COLLECTION** *(4 CD Set)*
       Catalog# TCD-131A/B/C/D   **Value $ 50-60**
       (1990 Time-Life Music Release. 4 CD Set. Mail Order Only.)
       Discs contain the following Elvis selections:

White Christmas	If Every Day Was Like Christmas
I'll Be Home For Christmas	

[ ]   **FEEL 21 AGAIN/ RARITIES VOLUME 4**   *(Promo)*
       Catalog# WESTWOOD ONE   **Value $ 40-60**
       (1991 Westwood One Radio Promo CD. Contains Alternate Take of "Old Shep".)
       Disc contains the following Elvis selection:
       Old Shep *(Alternate Take)*

[ ]   **FIFTY YEARS OF HITS** *(11 CD Promo Box Set)*
            Catalog# DIDX 011839-49   **Value $ 200-250**
            (1992 Promo Only Release from Opryland Music Group - Acuff Rose Music Inc.
            In House promo presented to selected producers, A & R reps, and artists here
            and abroad . Contains 269 recordings of 237 of Acuff Rose's most popular songs.
            "Promotional Only - Not For Sale" *on box, discs and sleeves.)*
            Discs contain the following Elvis selection:
            An American Trilogy

[ ]   **FORREST GUMP** *(Original Soundtrack 2 CD Set)*
            Catalog# E2K 66329-2   **Value $ 20-25**
            (1994 Epic Label Release. 2 CD Set in Multi-Disc Jewel Box. Contains 14 page
            insert foldout.)
            Discs contain the following Elvis selection:
            Hound Dog

[ ]   **GOD BLESS THE U.S.A.** *(4 CD Set)*
            Catalog# RBD-018/CD1   **Value $ 55-60**
            (1992 Reader's Digest Music Release. 4 CD Set. Contains 48 page insert booklet.
            Mail Order Only.)
            Discs contain the following Elvis selections:
            Unchained Melody   America The Beautiful
            My Way

[ ]   **GOLD AND PLATINUM** *(6 CD Set)*
       THE ULTIMATE ROCK COLLECTION
            Catalog# None   **Value $ 120 -130**
            (1997 Time-Life Music Release. 6 CD Set with 80 page Commemorative book.
            Each track is certified by RIAA to be Gold or Platinum. Mail Order Only.)
            Discs contain the following Elvis selection:
            Suspicious Minds

[ ]   **GOLD DISC 1001**   *(Radio Show)*
            Catalog# 1001   **Value $ 15-20**
            (1995 TM Century, Inc. Release. "For Broadcast Only".)
            Disc contains the following Elvis selection:
            In The Ghetto

[ ]   **GOLDEN COUNTRY OLDIES** *(Promo)*
            Catalog# 5962-2-RDJ   **Value $ 150-200**
            (1987 RCA Promo Only Release. Remixed version of "Kentucky Rain"
            released by mistake. ***"Promo Only - Not For Sale"*** *on disc.)*
            Disc contains the following Elvis selections:
            Kentucky Rain *(Unreleased Remixed Version)*   Suspicious Minds

[ ] The **GOLDEN DAYS OF ROCK 'N' ROLL** *(3 CD Set)*
Catalog# RC7-085-1/2/3   Value $ 45-50
(1997 Readers Digest Music Release. 3 CD Set. Contains 48 page booklet.
Mail Order Only.)
Discs contain the following Elvis selections:
Hound Dog   (Let Me Be Your) Teddy Bear

[ ] **GOODTIME OLDIES THEME PARTY**   *(12 CD Radio Show)*
Catalog# 93-36   Value $ 75-100
(1993 Westwood One Radio Show. With Cue sheets.)
Discs contain the following Elvis selections:
Good Luck Charm   Return to Sender
Jailhouse Rock

[ ] The **GREAT AMERICAN VOCALISTS**
Catalog# 9965-2-R   Value $ 15-20
(1990 RCA Release. This title now deleted from catalog.)
Disc contains the following Elvis selection:
One Night

[ ] The **GREAT VICTOR DUETS**
Catalog# 9967-2-R   Value $ 15-20
(1990 RCA Release. This title now deleated from catalog.)
Disc contains the following Elvis selection:
The Lady Loves Me *(with Ann-Margret)*

[ ] **GREATEST HITS OF THE '50's**
Catalog# DPC1-1056   Value $ 8-12
(1992 RCA Special Products Release.)
Disc contains the following Elvis selection:
Hound Dog

[ ] **HAPPY HOLIDAYS**   *(Promo)*
Catalog# 6C WC XMAS93-2   Value $ 40-50
(1993 Warner/Chappell Music Promo Only Release. Housed in a two-fold
Christmas Card. Card states "Warner/Chappell Music Wishes You And Your
Family A Joyous Holiday Season. And In Keeping With The Holiday Spirit,
We Have Made A Donation In Your Name To The Following Charities:
Greenpeace - Los Angeles Mission - Neil Bogart Memorial Laboratories -
Sickle Cell Anemia Research Foundation." "For Promotional Use Only -
Not For Sale" on disc.)
Disc contains the following Elvis selection:
Merry Christmas Baby

[ ]   **HAPPY HOLIDAYS FROM ASCAP**   *(Promo)*
       THE ASCAP HOLIDAY MUSIC SPECIAL
       Catalog# Deco Disc DD1   Value $ 30-40
       (1993 Allied Record Co. Promo Only Release. Pop Out CD housed in a postcard.
       "Not For Sale - Promotion Only" on back of postcard.)
       Disc contains the following Elvis selection:
       Blue Christmas

[ ]   **HAPPY HOLIDAYS VOLUME 25**   *(2 CD Set)*
       Catalog# DPL2-0936   Value $ 20-25
       (1990 RCA Special Products Release for True Value Hardware. For the 25th
       Edition of this series in 1990. For the only time, it issued a 2 - record set: it also
       for the first time issued a compact disc, a 2 CD set. Because of declining sales
       this was the last vinyl release.. Available only from True Value Hardware stores.)
       Discs contain the following Elvis selection:
       If Every Day Was Like Christmas

[ ]   **HAPPY HOLIDAYS VOLUME 28**
       Catalog# DPC 1-1107   Value $ 10-15
       (1993 RCA Special Products Release for True Value Hardware. Available only
       from True Value Hardware stores.)
       Disc contains the following Elvis selection:
       Here Comes Santa Claus

[ ]   **HAPPY HOLIDAYS VOLUME 32**
       Catalog# DPC1-1662   Value $ 10-15
       (1997 BMG Special Products Release for True Value Hardware. Available only
       from True Value Hardware stores.)
       Disc contains the following Elvis selection:
       Santa Bring My Baby Back (To Me)

[ ]   The **HEART 'N' SOUL OF ROCK 'N' ROLL** *(4 CD Set)*
       Catalog# RD7-008-1/2/3/4   Valuer $ 55-60
       (1997 Readers Digest Music Reissue. 4 CD Set. Contains 48 page booklet.
       Originally released in 1990 with no Elvis track but had a bonus CD of all Elvis,
       titled "Great Hits Of 1956-57". Mail Order Only.)
       Discs contain the following Elvis selection:
       I Want You, I Need You, I Love You

[ ]   **HEART OF DIXIE** *(Original Soundtrack)*
       Catalog# A & M CD 3930   Value $ 14-18
       (1989 A & M Records Release.)
       Disc contains the following Elvis selections:
       I Want You, I Need You, I Love You   Blue Suede Shoes

[ ]   **HEART OF DIXIE** *(Original Soundtrack Promo)*
               Catalog# A & M CD 3930   **Value $ 20-25**
               (1989 A & M Records Designated Promo with "Not For Sale" sticker.)
               Disc contains the following Elvis selections:

I Want You, I Need You, I Love You   Blue Suede Shoes

[ ]   **HEARTBREAK HOTEL**   *(Original Soundtrack)*
               Catalog# 8533-2-R   **Value $ 20-25**
               Matrix# W.O. 10707-3 85332R
               (Nov. 1988 Release. Silver & Black Disc with old RCA Logo
               with 4 page insert booklet. The original soundtrack from the
               *Touchstone Film "Heartbreak Hotel". **RCA has deleted this***
               ***title from their catalog.**)*
               Disc contains the following Elvis selections:

Heartbreak Hotel   Ready Teddy
One Night   If I Can Dream
Burning Love

[ ]   **HOLIDAY MUSIC COLLECTION**
               Catalog# DPC1-1004   **Value $ 15-20**
               (1991 RCA Special Products Release.)
               Disc contains the following Elvis selection:

Merry Christmas Baby

[ ]   **HOLIDAY MUSIC 1992 COLLECTION**
               Catalog# DPC1-1037   **Value $ 25-35**
               (1992 RCA Special Products Release. A limited release for Winston Cigarettes.)
               Disc contains the following Elvis selections:

Blue Christmas   If Every Day Was Like Christmas

[ ]   The **HOLLYWOOD MEN**
               Catalog# 9966-2-R   **Value $ 15-20**
               *(1990 RCA Release. **This title now deleted from catalog.**)*
               Disc contains the following Elvis selection:

How Would You Like To Be?

[ ]   **HONKY TONK CHRISTMAS WITH ALAN JACKSON***(3 CD's)*
               Catalog# 93-51   **Value $ 20-25**
               (1993. A 3 CD Set from Westwood One Radio Networks, Inc. with Cue sheets.)
               Discs contain the following Elvis selections:

Here Comes Santa Claus   Blue Christmas

[ ]   **HOORAY FOR HOLLYWOOD** *(2 CD Set)*
               Catalog# 66099-2   **Value $ 20-25**
               (1992 RCA Release. 2 CD Set with 16 page color booklet.)
               Discs contain the following Elvis selection:

How Would You Like To Be?

[ ]   **I BELIEVE** *(4 CD Set)*
BEST - LOVE STARS OF INSPIRATION
Catalog# RB7-163-1,2,3,4   **Value $ 60-70**
(1998 Readers Digest Music Release. 4 CD Set with 48 page booklet.
Contains Alternate Take of "If I Can Dream". Mail Order Only.)
Discs contain the following Elvis selections:

He Is My Everything   If I Can Dream *(Alternate Take)*
Swing Down, Sweet Chariot   O Little Town Of Bethlehem
He Touched Me   Blue Christmas

[ ]   **JERRY MAGUIRE** *(Original Soundtrack)*
Catalog# EK 67910   **Value $ 15-18**
(1996 Epic Soundtrack Release. 4-Fold insert booklet. Contains previously
unreleased performance of "Pocketful Of Rainbows".)
Disc contains the following Elvis selection:
Pocketful Of Rainbows *(False Start, Alternate Take)*

[ ]   **JUKEBOX FAVORITES!** *(2 CD Set)*
MUSICAL MEMORIES FROM THE 50's & 60's
Catalog# DMC2-1136-1/2   **Value $ 40-50**
(1993 First Pressing. RCA Special Products Release for Publishers Clearing
House limited to Presidents Club members. RCA Special Products & BMG Direct
Mkt. on spine only of insert sleeve. Mail Order Only.)
Discs contain the following Elvis selections:
All Shook Up   Return to Sender

[ ]   **JUKEBOX FAVORITES!** *(2 CD Set)*
MUSICAL MEMORIES FROM THE 50's & 60's
Catalog# DMC2-1136-1/2   **Value $ 40-50**
(1995 Second Pressing. RCA Special Products Release for Publishers Clearing
House limited to Presidents Club members. Back insert cover different from first
pressing. Smaller print and RCA Special Products & BMG Direct Mkt. on back of
insert cover only, not on spine. Mail Order Only.)

[ ]   **K-TEL'S CHRISTMAS ROCK GREATS**
Catalog# 4146   **Value $ 10-12**
(1998 K-Tel Label Release.)
Disc contains the following Elvis selection:
Blue Christmas

[ ]   **KEEPIN' THE 70s ALIVE!** *(3 CD Radio Show)*
Catalog# 95-34   **Value $ 25-30**
(1995 On The Radio Broadcasting. For broadcast the weekend of Aug. 18-20,
1995. With Cue sheets.)
Discs contain the following Elvis selection.
Burning Love

[ ]   The **LEGENDS OF ROCK 'N' ROLL**

Catalog# DMC1-1100   **Value $ 30-40**

(1993 Mfg. for Warner Custom Music by RCA Special Products. To commemorate "The Legends Of Rock 'N' Roll Rythum & Blues" U.S. Postal stamp. Comes in collectors box with 24 page book and 20 mint stamps. Mail Order Only.)

Disc contains the following Elvis selections:

Return To Sender   Heartbreak Hotel

Don't Be Cruel

[ ]   The **LEGENDS OF ROCK 'N' ROLL**

Catalog# DMC1-1100   **Value $ 15-20**

(1993 Mfg. for Warner Custom Music by RCA Special Products. Disc in jewel box without extras. Mail Order Only.)

[ ]   The **LEGENDS OF ROCK 'N' ROLL** *(Promo)*

Catalog# DMC1-1100   **Value $ 40-50**

(1993 Promo Release of the above set. This box stamped "Demonstration - Not For Sale". RCA does not acknowledge a promo of this set.)

[ ]   **LEIBER & STOLLER** *(Promo)*
THE FIFTIES

Catalog# LS. CD1   **Value $ 30-40**

(1992 Promo Only Release from Leiber & Stoller Publishing. With 6 page tri-fold insert cover.)

Disc contains the following Elvis selections:

Hound Dog   Treat Me Nice

Jailhouse Rock   Santa Claus Is Back In Town

Love Me   Don't

Loving You   Trouble

[ ]   **LEIBER & STOLLER** *(Promo)*
THE 60's, '70's & '80's

Catalog# LS. CD2   **Value $ 30-40**

(1992 Promo Only Release from Leiber & Stoller Publishing. With 6 page tri-fold insert cover.)

Disc contains the following Elvis selections:

She's Not You   Bossa Nova Baby

[ ] **LEIBER & STOLLER MUSIC PUBLISHING** *(6 CD Promo Set)*
Catalog# LS 206   **Value $ 150-200**
(1994. A 6 CD Set from Leiber & Stoller Publishing. Plastic insert sleeves housed in a Gold deluxe 2 ring binder with Black lettering which is contained in a 6" x 8" Black slipcase with Gold lettering. "For Promotion Only - Owership Reserved by Leiber & Stoller Music Publishing - Sale Is Unlawful".
Disc 6 is all Elvis.)
Discs contain the following Elvis selections:

Good Rockin' Tonight	Steadfast, Loyal And True
Love Me	Dirty, Dirty Feeling
Hot Dog	Fever
Loving You	She's Not You
Jailhouse Rock	Just Tell Her Jim Said Hello
Treat Me Nice	Girls! Girls! Girls!
Baby I Don't Care	Bossa Nova Baby
I Want To Be Free	You're The Boss *(with Ann-Margret)*
Santa Claus Is Back In Town	Little Egypt
Don't	Come What May
King Creole	Fools Fall In Love
Trouble	Saved

[ ] **LET ME ENTERTAIN YOU**
Catalog# 07863-6682-2   **Value $ 15-18**
(1996 RCA Release. This is an all Ann-Margret CD but contains one duet with Elvis and Ann-Margret.)
Disc contains the following Elvis selection:
The Lady Loves Me *(Duet with Elvis & Ann Margret)*

[ ] **LET ME ENTERTAIN YOU**
Catalog# 07863-6682-2   **Value $ 20-25**
BMG Music Service Catalog# D 114940
(1996 Second Pressing. Mfg. for BMG Direct Marketing, Inc. BMG Music Service catalog number on disc and back insert cover. Mail Order Only.)

[ ] **LOVE ME TENDER** *(2 CD Set)*
Catalog# TCD-133 R103-27 A/B   **Value $ 15-25**
(1991 Time - Life Music Release. 2 CD Set. Mail Order Only.)
Discs contain the following Elvis selections:

Love Me Tender	Can't Help Falling In Love
Are You Lonesome Tonight?	

[ ] **LOWERY COUNTRY GOLD Vol. 3** *(Promo)*
Catalog# LGY-008   **Value $ 15-25**
(1991 Lowery Music Release. This CD "For Broadcast Only - Not For Sale" Mail Order Only.)
Disc contains the following Elvis selection:
Walk A Mile In My Shoes

[ ] **MADE IN AMERICA** *(12 CD Radio Show)*
Catalog# 91-27   Value $ 75-100
(1991 Westwood One 12 hour Radio Show with Cue sheets.)
Discs contain the following Elvis selections:
Jailhouse Rock   All Shook Up
Hard Headed Woman

[ ] **MADE IN AMERICA** *(12 CD Radio Show)*
Catalog# 93-27   Value $ 75-100
(1993 Westwood One 12 hour Radio Show with Cue sheets.)
Discs contain the following Elvis selections:
Stuck On You   Suspicious Minds

[ ] **MADE IN AMERICA** *(12 CD Radio Show)*
Catalog# 94-27   Value $ 75-100
(1994 Westwood One 12 hour Radio Show with Cue sheets.)
Discs contain the following Elvis selection:
Suspicious Minds

[ ] The **MANY MOODS OF ROMANCE**
AS TIME GOES BY
Catalog# TCD-303 R974-04   Value $ 15-20
(1994 Time-Life Music Release. Contains 8 page insert booklet. Mail Order Only.)
Disc contains the following Elvis selection:
Can't Help Falling In Love

[ ] The **MANY MOODS OF ROMANCE**
MY HEART REMINDS ME
Catalog# TCD-301 R974-02   Value $15-20
(1994 Time-Life Music Release. Contaions 8 page insert booklet. Mail Order Only.)
Disc contains the following Elvis selection:
Don't

[ ] **MILLION DOLLAR MEMORIES** *(4 CD Set)*
OF THE '50s AND '60s
Catalog# RC7-135-1,2,3&4   Value $ 55-60
(1998 Readers Digest Music Release. A 4 CD Set with 48 page booklet. Mail Order Only.)
Discs contains the following Elvis selection:
Are You Lonesome Tonight?

[ ]   **MIRACLE ON 34th STREET**   *(Original Soundtrack)*
        Catalog# 07822-11022-2   **Value $ 15-20**
        (1994 Fox Records Inc. Release.)
        Disc contains the following Elvis selection:
        Santa Claus Is Back In Town

[ ]   **MISTLETOE AND MEMORIES**
        Catalog# 8732-R   **Value $ 12-15**
        (1988 RCA Release.)
        Disc contains the following Elvis selection:
        O Come, All Ye Faithful

[ ]   **MONSTER ROCK 'N' ROLL SHOW**
        Catalog# DZS-050   **Value $ 15-20**
        (1990 DCC Compact Classics Release.)
        Disc contains the following Elvis selections:
        One Night   I Got Stung

[ ]   The **MUSIC THAT MADE MEMPHIS**
        Catalog# OPCD 1726   **Value $ 40-50**
        (1996 Release. Produced and manufactured for the Memphis Convention &
        Visitors Bureau by Warner Special Products. Three-fold insert booklet.
        The Elvis tracks are from 1953 acetates. Sold only at the Memphis Visitors
        Information Center.)
        Disc contains the following Elvis selections:
        My Happiness   That's When Your Heartaches Begin

[ ]   **MY FELLOW AMERICANS**   *(Original Soundtrack)*
        Catalog# TVT 8090-2   **Value $ 15-20**
        (1996 TVT Records Release.)
        Disc contains the following Elvis selection:
        Treat Me Nice

[ ]   **MYSTERY TRAIN**   *(Original Soundtrack)*
        Catalog# 60367-2-RC   **Value $ 14-18**
        (1989 RCA Release.)
        Disc contains the following Elvis selections:
        Mystery Train   Blue Moon

[ ] The **NASHVILLE EXPLOSION** *(Promo)*
COUNTRY MUSIC'S GREATEST HITS
Catalog# **PIP-CD 001**   **Value $ 50-75**
(1989 PolyGram Promo Only Release. "For Promotional Use Only - Not For Sale" on front insert cover.)
Disc contains the following Elvis selection:
Are You Sincere

[ ] **NEW GOLD ON CD:**   *(Radio Show)*
THE WEEK OF July 13, 1992
Catalog# **92-28**   **Value $ 15-20**
(1992 Westwood One Radio Networks Radio show with Cue sheets.)
Disc contains the following Elvis selection:
Fame And Fortune

[ ] **NIPPER'S GREATEST CHRISTMAS HITS**
Catalog# **9859-2-R**   **Value $ 12-15**
(1991 RCA Release.)
Disc contains the following Elvis selection:
Here Comes Santa Claus

[ ] **NIPPER'S GREATEST HITS - The '50's, Vol.1**
Catalog# **8466-2-R**   **Value $ 12-15**
(1988 RCA Release.)
Disc contains the following Elvis selection:
Heartbreak Hotel

[ ] **NIPPER'S GREATEST HITS - The '50's, Vol. 2**
Catalog# **8467-2-R**   **Value $ 12-15**
(1988 RCA Release.)
Disc contains the following Elvis selection:
Don't Be Cruel

[ ] **NIPPER'S GREATEST HITS - The '60's, Vol. 1**
Catalog# **8474-2-R**   **Value $ 12-15**
(1988 RCA Release.)
Disc contains the following Elvis selection:
It's Now Or Never

[ ] **NIPPER'S GREATEST HITS - The '60's, Vol. 2**
Catalog# **8475-2-R**   **Value $ 12-15**
(1988 RCA Release.)
Disc contains the following Elvis selection:
Suspicious Minds

[ ]   **NIPPER'S GREATEST HITS - The '70's**
        Catalog# 8476-2-R   Value $ 12-15
        (1988 RCA Release.)
        Disc contains the following Elvis selection:
        Burning Love

[ ]   **NIPPER'S GREATEST HITS - The '70's**
        Catalog# 9684-2-R   Value $ 20-25
        (1989 RCA Release. This is a variation of the above release. It has a different
        catalog number and the printing on the disc is a variation of the above.)
        Disc contains the following Elvis selection:
        Burning Love

[ ]   **NIPPER'S GREATEST HITS - The '80's**
        Catalog # 9970-2-R   Value $ 12-15
        (1990 RCA Release.)
        Disc contains the following Elvis selection:
        Guitar Man *(1980 Remix Version)*

[ ]   **NIPPER'S HOLIDAY FAVORITES** *(Promo)*
        Catalog# RDJ62699-2   Value $ 30-40
        (1993 RCA Promo Only Release. "Promotional Use Only - Not For Sale" on
        disc and back cover.)
        Disc contains the following Elvis selection:
        Silver Bells *(Alternate Take)*

[ ]   **NIPPER'S HOLIDAY FAVORITES II** *(Promo)*
        Catalog# RDJ62722-2   Value $ 30-40
        (1993 RCA Promo Only Release. "Promotional Use Only - Not For Sale" on
        disc and back cover.)
        Disc contains the following Elvis selection:
        Silver Bells *(Alternate Take)*

[ ]   **NIPPER'S #1 HITS (1956-1986)**
        Catalog# 9902-2-R   Value $ 12-15
        (1989 RCA Release.)
        Disc contains the following Elvis selections:
        Hard Headed Woman   Suspicious Minds

[ ]   The **OLDIES COUNTDOWN** *(2 CD Radio Show)*
        Catalog# OC-11   Value $ 20-25
        (1991. A 2 CD Set from MJI Broadcasting with Cue sheets. This radio series was
        only broadcast for six months and then was deleted.)
        Discs contain the following Elvis selection:
        Burning Love

[ ] **PRECIOUS MEMORIES** *(2 CD Set)*
Catalog# TCD-127A/B   Value $ 30-35
(1993 Time - Life Music Release. 2 CD Set. Mail Order Only through TV spots.
Same catalog number and tracks as "Songs Of Faith And Inspiration".
This title has now been deleted.)
Discs contains the following Elvis selections:
How Great Thou Art   His Hand In Mine

[ ] **PRACTICAL MAGIC** *(Original Soundtrack)*
Catalog# 47140   Value $ 12-15
(1998 WEA/Warner Brothers Label Release.)
 Disc contains the following Elvis selection:
 Always On My Mind

[ ] **RCA CHRISTMAS 1996** *(Promo)*
Catalog# RDJ64688-2   Value $ 25-30
(1996 RCA Nashville Promo Only Release. Sent to country music radio stations
only.)
Disc contains the following Elvis selection:
Blue Christmas

[ ] **RCA CHRISTMAS 1997** *(Promo)*
Catalog# RDJ65327-2   Value $ 25-30
(1997 RCA Nashville Promo Only Release. Sent to country music radio stations
only.)
Disc contains the following Elvis selection:
Blue Christmas

[ ] **RCA NASHVILLE 60 YEARS 1928-1988** *(3 CD Promo Set)*
Catalog# 6864-2-RDJ   Value $ 150-200
(1988 RCA Country Music Foundation Release. 3 CD Promo Set. 48 page insert
booklet.)
Discs contain the following Elvis selection:
Hound Dog

[ ] The **RCA RECORDS LABEL** *(3 CD Set)*
THE FIRST NOTE IN BLACK MUSIC
Catalog# 61144-2   Value $ 25-30
(1992 RCA Release. 3 CD Set with 32 page insert booklet.)
Discs contain the following Elvis selection:
All Shook Up

[ ]   The **RCA RECORDS LABEL** *(3 CD Promo Set)*
THE FIRST NOTE IN BLACK MUSIC
Catalog# RDJ 61144-2   Value $ 40-50
(1992 RCA Promo Copy. 3 CD Set with 32 page insert booklet. "Promotional
Copy - Not For Sale" on back insert cover. "Not For Sale" on disc.)
Disc contains the following Elvis selection:
All Shook Up

[ ]   **RCA 24 KARAT GOLD SAMPLER** *(Promo)*
Catalog# RJC 66713-2   Value $ 30-40
(July 1995 Promo Only CD issued to promote the RCA 24 kt. Gold
Releases. Gold & Black Disc. No front insert cover. Gold & Black back cover.
"Not For Sale" on disc and back cover.)
Disc contains the following Elvis selections:
Tutti Frutti   I'm Gonna Sit Right Down And Cry

[ ]   **REACH OUT AND TOUCH** *(4 CD Set)*
Catalog# RCD-077/CD1   Value $ 55-60
(1991 Reader's Digest Music Release. 4 CD Set with 48 page insert booklet.
Mail Order Only.)
Discs contain the following Elvis selections:
You'll Never Walk Alone   He Touched Me
How Great Thou Art   An American Trilogy

[ ]   **REELIN' IN THE YEARS** *(2 CD Radio Show)*
Catalog# 08/15-16   Value $ 15-25
(1992 Global Satellite Network. 2 CD Set with Cue sheet. Contains interview with
Elvis historian and former RCA employee Don Wardell.)
Discs contain the following Elvis selection:
That's All Right

[ ]   **ROCK 'N' ROLL CLASSICS 1954-1956**
Catalog# TCD-160   Value $ 15-20
(1992 Time - Life Music Release. A double play CD with 24 page insert booklet.
Part of Time - Life's History Of Rock 'N' Roll series. Mail Order Only.)
Disc contains the following Elvis selections:
Good Rockin' Tonight   Don't Be Cruel

[ ]   **ROCK 'N' ROLL LEGENDS** *(3 CD Set)*
Catalog# 211C RC7-211-1/2/3
(1996 Readers Digest Music Release. 3 CD Set. Contains 48 page insert booklet.
Mail Order Only.)
Discs contain the following Elvis selections:
That's All Right   Don't Be Cruel
All Shook Up   Jailhouse Rock
Hound Dog

[ ] **ROCK 'N' ROLL: THE EARLY DAYS**
Catalog# PCD1-5463   Value $ 15-20
(1985 First Pressing. RCA Release. Pressed in Japan for U.S. Release.)
Disc contains the following Elvis selection:
That's All Right

[ ] **ROCK 'N' ROLL: THE EARLY DAYS**
Catalog# PCD1-5463   Value $ 10-15
(1988 Second Pressing. RCA Release. Pressed in U.S.)

[ ] **ROCKIN' 60's**
Catalog# 44540   Value $ 6-8
(1997 BMG Special Products Release.)
Disc contains the following Elvis selection:
Suspicious Minds

[ ] **SHE DEVIL** *(Original Soundtrack)*
Catalog# 841583-2   Value $ 15-20
(1989 PolyGram Records Release.)
Disc contains the following Elvis selection:
(You're The) Devil In Disguise

[ ] **SOFTLY AS I LEAVE YOU**
Catalog# TR-1993 CD BG-121396-CD   Value $ 20-25
(1994 Collectors Edition CD from Tribute Records International, Hendersonville, TN. Sold by Home Shopping Network in Jan. 1997 for Elvis Birthdat Tribute. Songs by Shaun Nielsen, former Elvis backup singer. CD housed in 7" x 7" hard cover plastic case. Contains 4 page booklet.)
Disc contains the following Elvis selections:
Softly As I Leave You   Blue Spanish Eyes

[ ] **SOLID GOLD COUNTRY**   *(5 CD Radio Show)*
AUGUST GOLD
Catalog# 93-8   Value $ 30-35
(1993 Unistar Radio Network Inc. 5 CD Set with Cue sheets.)
Discs contain the following Elvis selection:
Wear My Ring Around Your Neck

[ ]   **SOLID GOLD COUNTRY**   *(5 CD Radio Show)*
CHRISTMAS WITH ELVIS PRESLEY
Catalog# 92-12   Value $ 30-35
(1992 Unistar Radio Network Inc. 5 CD Set with Cue sheets.)
Discs contain the following Elvis selections:

Here Comes Santa Claus	The First Noel
Santa Bring My Baby Back to Me	O Come, All Ye Faithful
Holly Leaves And Christmas Trees	I'll Be Home On Christmas Day
Winter Wonderland	I'll Be Home For Christmas
Santa Claus Is Back In Town	If I Get Home On Christmas Day
Merry Christmas Baby	Blue Christmas
O Little Town Of Bethlehem	Silent Night

[ ]   **SOLID GOLD COUNTRY**   *(5 CD Radio Show)*
The **COMPLETE 50's MASTERS**
Catalog# 92-11   Value $ 30-35
(1992 Unistar Radio Network Inc. 5 CD Set with Cue sheets.)
Discs contain the following Elvis selections:

Hard Headed Woman	A Fool Such As I
Heartbreak Hotel	That's All Right
One Night	Too Much
Jailhouse Rock	Baby Let's Play House
Love Me	Mystery Train
I Forgot To Remember To Forget	Hound Dog
Love Me Tender	I Was The One
Don't Be Cruel	Wear My Ring Around Your Neck

[ ]   **SOLID GOLD COUNTRY**   *(5 CD Radio Show)*
COUNTRY STARS WITH GOSPEL ROOTS
Catalog# 92-4   Value $ 30-35
(1992 Unistar Radio Network Inc. 5 CD Set with Cue sheets.)
Discs contain the following Elvis selection:
Suspicious Minds

[ ]   **SOLID GOLD COUNTRY**   *(5 CD Radio Show)*
ELVIS: WHAT HAPPENED?
Catalog# 92-7   Value $ 30-35
(1992 Unistar Radio Network Inc. 5 CD Set with Cue sheets.)
Discs contain the following Elvis selections:

Hound Dog	It's Now Or Never
Hurt	Moody Blue
Love Me Tender	Hard Headed Woman
Heartbreak Hotel	Memories
One Night	Are You Lonesome Tonight?
Too Much	Crying In The Chapel
Little Sister	My Way
I Forgot To Remember To Forget	

[ ]   **SOLID GOLD COUNTRY**   *(5 CD Radio Show)*
ELVIS PRESLEY AND TV
Catalog# 91-9   **Value $ 30-35**
(1991 Unistar Radio Network Inc. 5 CD Set with Cue sheets.)
Discs contain the following Elvis selections:

Don't Be Cruel	If I Can Dream
Love Me Tender	An American Trilogy
Too Much	Hound Dog
Heartbreak Hotel	I Want You, I Need You, I Love You
Blue Suede Shoes	My Way
I Was The One	Stuck On You
Shake, Rattle And Roll	Burning Love
Baby Let's Play House	

[ ]   **SOLID GOLD COUNTRY**   *(5 CD Radio Show)*
ELVIS PRESLEY BIRTHDAY TRIBUTE
Catalog# 92-1   **Value $ 30-35**
(1992 Unistar Radio Network Inc. 5 CD Set with Cue sheets.)
Discs contain the following Elvis selections:

Hound Dog	Suspicious Minds
Baby, Let's Play House	Burning Love
Crying In The Chapel	In The Ghetto
Jailhouse Rock	You Don't Have To Say You Love Me
Mystery Train	Memories
I Forgot To Remember To Forget	Always On My MInd
Heartbreak Hotel	Kentucky Rain
Don't Be Cruel	Promised Land
Love Me Tender	My Boy
Are You Lonesome Tonight?	Moody Blue
Hard Headed Woman	Way Down
Return To Sender	My Way
(Now And Then There's) A Fool Such As I	The Elvis Medley
It's Now Or Never	
Don't	
Little Sister	

[ ]   **SOLID GOLD COUNTRY**   *(5 CD Radio Show)*
ELVIS PRESLEY BIRTHDAY TRIBUTE
Catalog# 93-1   **Value $ 30-35**
(1993 Unistar Radio Network Inc. 5 CD Radio Show with Cue sheets.)
Discs contain the following Elvis selections:

Hard Headed Woman	In The Ghetto
Don't Be Cruel	Kentucky Rain
Don't	(Let Me Be Your) Teddy Bear
Baby Let's Play House	My Boy
All Shook Up	Burning Love
I Fortgot to Remember To Forget	Memories
Heartbreak Hotel	Suspicious Minds
Wear My Ring Around Your Neck	Don't Cry Daddy
(Now And Then There's) A Fool Such As I	If You Talk In Your Sleep
Love Me Tender	The Wonder Of You
Jailhouse Rock	Unchained Melody
Hound Dog	Way Down
Can't Help Falling In Love	Moody Blue
Are You Lonesome Tonight?	My Way
Return To Sender	
It's Now Or Never	

[ ] **SOLID GOLD COUNTRY** *(5 CD Radio Show)*
ELVIS PRESLEY'S GOLDEN RECORDS
Catalog# 91-11   Value $ 30-35
(1991 Unistar Radio Network Inc. 5 CD Radio Show with Cue sheets.)
Discs contain the following Elvis selections:

Don't Be Cruel	It's Now Or Never
Heartbreak Hotel	Ain't That Loving You Baby
Jailhouse Rock	(You're The) Devil In Disguise
Wear My Ring Around Your Neck	A Mess Of Blues
I Need Your Love Tonight	Moody Blue
(Now And Then There's) A Fool Such As I	Suspicious Minds
I Feel So Bad	Burning Love
Are You Lonesome Tonight?	

[ ] **SOLID GOLD COUNTRY** *(5 CD Radio Show)*
ELVIS PRESLEY'S GOLDEN RECORDS
Catalog# 93-2   Value $ 30-35
(1993 Unistar Radio Network Inc. 5 CD Radio Show with Cue sheets.)
Discs contain the following Elvis selections:

Hound Dog	Little Sister
Heartbreak Hotel	Good Luck Charm
Jailhouse Rock	It's Now Or Never
Don't Be Cruel	Ain't That Loving You Baby
Wear My Ring Around Your Neck	Devil In Disguise
I Beg Of You	Suspicious Minds
A Fool Such As I	Burning Love
I Need Your Love Tonight	Way Down

[ ] **SOLID GOLD COUNTRY** *(5 CD Radio Show)*
ELVIS PRESLEY: HIS FAVORITE WRITERS
Catalog# 91-7   Value $ 30-35
(1991 Unistar Radio Network Inc. 5 CD Set with Cue sheets.)
Discs contain the following Elvis selections:

Little Sister	Hound Dog
His Latest Flame	Treat Me Nice
A Mess Of Blues	Love Me
Viva Las Vegas	Return To Sender
Surrender	Paralyzed
Jailhouse Rock	Don't Be Cruel
	All Shook Up

[ ] **SOLID GOLD COUNTRY** *(5 CD Radio Show)*
ELVIS PRESLEY IN CONCERT
Catalog# 92-9   Value $ 30-35
(1992 Unistar Radio Network Inc. 5 CD Set with Cue sheets.)
Discs contain the following Elvis selections:

See See Rider	Fairytale
Little Sister	If You Love Me
Early Morning Rain	Jailhouse Rock
Hound Dog	Hurt
That's All Right	And I Love You So
Are You Lonesome Tonight?	Love Me
You Gave Me A Mountain	My Way
Teddy Bear/Don't Be Cruel	Can't Help Falling In Love

[ ] **SOLID GOLD COUNTRY** *(5 CD Radio Show)*
ELVIS PRESLEY IN NASHVILLE
Catalog# 92-4   Value $ 30-35
(1992 Unistar Radio Network Inc. 5 CD Set with Cue sheets.)
Discs contain the following Elvis selections:

Good Luck Charm	I Feel So Bad
Little Sister	Stuck On You
Crying In The Chapel	Guitar Man
I Want You, I Need You, I Love You	Devil In Disguise
You Don't Have to Say You Love Me	Lovin' Arms
A Fool Such As I	His Latest Flame
Surrender	Heartbreak Hotel
Are You Lonesome Tonight?	It's Now Or Never

[ ] **SOLID GOLD COUNTRY** *(5 CD Radio Show)*
ELVIS PRESLEY LIVE
Catalog# 92-6   Value $ 30-35
(1992 Unistar Radio Network Inc. 5 CD Set with Cue sheets.)
Discs contain the following Elvis selections:

Blue Suede Shoes	Steamroller Blues
Hound Dog	Suspicious Minds
Maybellene	An American Trilogy
All Shook Up	My Way
The Wonder Of You	Unchained Melody
Burning Love	Can't Help Falling In Love
Memories	

[ ] **SOLID GOLD COUNTRY** *(5 CD Radio Show)*
ELVIS PRESLEY'S LOVE SONGS
Catalog# 92-5   Value $ 30-35
(1992 Unistar Radio Network Inc. 5 CD Set with Cue sheets.)
Discs contain the following Elvis selections:

Love Me Tender	The Wonder Of You
A Big Hunk O' Love	All Shook Up
One Night	Always On My Mind
Teddy Bear	Unchained Melody
A Fool Such As I	Burning Love
Wear My Ring Around Your Neck	Too Much
Can't Help Falling In Love	It's Now Or Never

[ ]   **SOLID GOLD COUNTRY** *(5 CD Radio Show)*
ELVIS PRESLEY MEMORIAL TRIBUTE
Catalog# 91-8   Value $ 30-35
(1991 Unistar Radio Network Inc. 5 CD Set with Cue sheets.)
Discs contain the following Elvis selections:

Hound Dog	Teddy Bear
Don't Be Cruel	It's Now Or Never
Crying In The Chapel	Burning Love
Baby Let's Play House	Are You Lonesome Tonight?
Heartbreak Hotel	In The Ghetto
I Forgot To Remember To Forget	Guitar Man
Mystery Train	If I Can Dream
Love Me Tender	Always On My Mind
All Shook Up	Kentucky Rain
Good Luck Charm	Moody Blue
Hard Headed Woman	Way Down
Jailhouse Rock	Lovin' Arms
Wear My Ring Around Your Neck	Suspicious Minds
A Big Hunk O' Love	My Way
Little Sister	

[ ]   **SOLID GOLD COUNTRY** *(5 CD Radio Show)*
ELVIS PRESLEY MEMORIAL TRIBUTE
Catalog# 92-8   Value $ 30-35
(1992 Unistar Radio Network Inc. 5 CD Set with Cue sheets.)
Discs contain the following Elvis selections:

Hard Headed Woman	It's Now Or Never
Little Sister	(You're The) Devios In Disguise
All Shook Up	Kentucky Rain
(Let Me Be Your) Teddy Bear	Guitar Man
Hound Dog	In The Ghertto
I Forgot To Remember To Forget	Burning Love
Mystery Train	Memories
Heartbreak Hotel	Suspicious Minds
Wear My Ring Around Your Neck	Don't Cry Daddy
Are You Lonesome Tonight?	Promised Land
Crying In The Chapel	Way Down
Don't Be Cruel	Moody Blue
Baby, Lets Play House	(Now And Then There's) A Fool Such As I
Can't Help Falling In Love	The Wonder Of You
Return To Sender	My Way

[ ] **SOLID GOLD COUNTRY** *(5 CD Radio Show)*
ELVIS PRESLEY MEMORIAL TRIBUTE
Catalog# 93-8   **Value $ 30-35**
(1993 Unistar Radio Network Inc. 5 CD Set with Cue sheets.)
Discs contain the following Elvis selections:

Hard Headed Woman	Hound Dog
Mystery Train	Can't Help Falling In Love
Love Me Tender	Devil In Disguise
Jailhouse Rock	In The Ghetto
Don't Be Cruel	Are You Lonesome Tonight?
I Want You, I Need You, I Love You	Burning Love
Baby Let's Play House	Suspicious Minds
Heartbreak Hotel	Memories
All Shook Up	Guitar Man/What'd I Say
It's Now Or Never	Kentucky Rain
Treat Me Nice	Unchained Melody
Teddy Bear	Return To Sender
I Forgot To Remember To Forget	Moody Blue
Little Sister	Way Down
My Way	T-R-O-U-B-L-E

[ ] **SOLID GOLD COUNTRY** *(5 CD Radio Show)*
ELVIS PRESLEY SINGS LEIBER AND STOLLER
Catalog# 92-2   **Value $ 30-35**
(1992 Unistar Radio Network Inc. 5 CD Set with Cue sheets.)
Discs contain the following Elvis selections:

Girls, Girls, Girls	Trouble
Hound Dog	You're The Boss *(with Ann-Margret)*
Bossa Nova Baby	Saved
Just Tell Her Jim Said Hello	Loving You
Love Me	Little Egypt
Treat Me Nice	Don't
	Jailhouse Rock

[ ] **SOLID GOLD COUNTRY** *(5 CD Radio Show)*
MAC DAVIS BIRTHDAY SALUTE
Catalog# 92-1   **Value $ 30-35**
(1992 Unistar Radio Network Inc. 5 CD Radio Show with Cue sheets.)
Discs contain the following Elvis selections:

In The Ghetto	Memories
Don't Cry Daddy	

[ ]   **SOLID GOLD COUNTRY**   *(5 CD Radio Show)*
SALUTE TO RCA STUDIO B
Catalog# 92-11   Value $ 30-35
(1992 Unistar Radio Network Inc. 5 CD Set with Cue sheets.)
Discs contain the following Elvis selection:
It's Now Or Never

[ ]   **SOLID GOLD COUNTRY**   *(5 CD Radio Show)*
THIS WEEK IN 1977
Catalog# 91-9   Value $ 30-35
(1991 Unistar Radio Network Inc. 5 CD Set with Cue sheets.)
Discs contain the following Elvis selection:
Way Down

[ ]   **SOLID GOLD COUNTRY**   *(5 CD Radio Show)*
THIS WEEK IN 1977
Catalog# 92-9   Value $ 30-35
(1992 Unistar Radio Network Inc. 5 CD Set with Cue sheets.)
Discs contain the following Elvis selection:
Way Down

[ ]   **SOLID GOLD COUNTRY**   *(5 CD Radio Show)*
THIS WEEK IN 1978
Catalog# 92-1   Value $ 30-35
(1992 Unistar Radio Network Inc. 5 CD Set with Cue Sheets.)
Discs contain the following Elvis selection:
My Way

[ ]   **SOLID GOLD COUNTRY**   *(5 CD Radio Show)*
70 YEARS OF RCA COUNTRY
Catalog# 92-7   Value $ 30-35
(1992 Unistar Radio Network Inc. 5 CD Set with Cue sheets.)
Discs contain the following Elvis selections:

Suspicious Minds	I Forgot To Remember To Forget
Hound Dog	It's Now Or Never
Hurt	Moody Blue
Love Me Tender	Hard Headed Woman
Heartbreak Hotel	Memories
One Night	Are You Lonesome Tonight?
Too Much	Crying In The Chapel
Little Sister	My Way

[ ]   **SOLID GOLD HITS OF THE '50's**
Catalog# DPC1-0814   Value $ 20-25
(1988 RCA Special Products Release for AVON. Mail Order Only.
This title now deleted.)
Disc contains the following Elvis selection:
Hound Dog

[ ]   **SOLID GOLD HITS OF THE '60's**
Catalog# DPC1-0815   **Value $ 20-25**
(1988 RCA Special Products Release for AVON. Mail Order Only.
This title now deleted.)
Disc contains the following Elvis selection:
Stuck On You

[ ]   **SOLID GOLD HITS OF THE '70's**
Catalog# DPC1-0816   **Value $ 20-25**
(1989 RCA Special Products Release for AVON. Mail Order Only.
This title now deleted.)
Disc contains the following Elvis selection:
The Wonder Of You

[ ]   **SOLID GOLD SCRAPBOOK**   *(5 CD Radio Show)*
ELVIS GOLDEN DECADE 1956-1965
Catalog# 91-05   **Value $ 30-35**
(1991 Unistar Radio Network Inc. 5 CD Set with Cue sheets.)
Discs contain the following Elvis selections:

Heartbreak Hotel	Wear My Ring Around Your Neck
Don't Be Cruel	Hard Headed Woman
Hound Dog	One Night
Love Me Tender	A Fool Such As I
Too Much	A Big Hunk O' Love
All Shook Up	Surrender
Teddy Bear	I Feel So Bad
Jailhouse Rock	Little Sister
Don't	Crying In The Chapel

[ ]   **SOLID GOLD SCRAPBOOK**   *(5 CD Radio Show)*
ELVIS IN MEMPHIS
Catalog# 91-10   **Value $ 30-35**
(1991 Unistar Radio Network Inc. 5 CD Set with Cue sheets.)
Discs contain the following Elvis selections:

That's All Right	Rubberneckin'
Blue Moon Of Kentucky	Kentucky Rain
Good Rockin' Tonight	Any Day Now
Baby Let's Play House	If You Talk In Your Sleep
Mystery Train	Promised Land
In The Ghetto	My Boy
Suspicious Minds	Way Down
Don't Cry Daddy	

[ ] **SOLID GOLD SCRAPBOOK** *(5 CD Radio Show)*
ELVIS MOVIE MUSIC
Catalog# 91-09   Value $ 30-35
(1991 Unistar Radio Network Inc. 5 CD Set with Cue sheets.)
Discs contain the following Elvis selections:

Love Me Tender	Good Luck Charm
(Let Me Be) Your Teddy Bear	Return To Sender
Loving You	One Broken Heart for Sale
Jailhouse Rock	Bossa Nova Baby
Treat Me Nice	Kissin' Cousins
Hard Headed Woman	Kiss Me Quick
King Creole	Viva Las Vegas
Can't Help Falling In Love	Separate Ways
Rock-A-Hula Baby	

[ ] **SOLID GOLD SCRAPBOOK** *(5 CD Radio Show)*
SOLID GOLD ELVIS
Catalog# 91-11   Value $ 30-35
(1991 Unistar Radio Network Inc. 5 CD Set with Cue sheets.)
Discs contain the following Elvis selections:

Good Rockin' Tonight	Stuck On You
Don't	It's Now Or Never
Wear My Ring Around Your Neck	Are You Lonesome Tonight
One Night	Surrender
I Got Stung	I Feel So Bad
(Now And Then There's) A Fool Such As I	Little Sister
I Need Your Love Tonight	(Marie's The Name) His Latest Flame
A Big Hunk O' Love	Good Luck Charm
	She's Not You

[ ] **SONGS OF FAITH AND INSPIRATION** *(2 CD Set)*
Catalog# TCD-127A/B   Value $ 20-25
(1993 Time - Life Music Release. 2 CD Set. Mail Order Only.)
Discs contain the following Elvis selections:

His Hand In Mine	How Great Thou Art

[ ] **STEVE ALLEN ON THE AIR!**
THE CLASSIC COMEDY OF STEVE ALLEN
Catalog# VSD-5703   Value $ 15-20
(1996 Release from Varese Sarabande Records, Inc. Contains 8 page insert booklet. Features Elvis in "Ranch Roundup" skit from 7/1/56.)
Disc contains the following Elvis selection:
I Got A Horse - I Got A Gun

[ ] **STUDIO B HOME OF A THOUSAND HITS Vol. 1**
Catalog# CMF-098   Value $ 15-18
(1996 Country Music Foundation Records Release. Contains 4 page insert cover. Only available at RCA Studio B souvenir shop in Nashville.)
Disc contains the following Elvis Selection:
His Latest Flame

[ ] **STUDIO B HOME OF A THOUSAND HITS Vol. 2**
Catalog# CMF-099   Value $ 15-18
(1996 Country Music Foundation Records Release. Contains 4 page insert cover.
Only available at RCA Sudio B souvenir shop in Nashville.)
Disc contains the following Elvis selection:
It's Now Or Never

[ ] **SUMMER SONGS** *(2 CD Set)*
Catalog# DPC2-0981   Value $ 30-35
(1991 RCA Special Products Release for AVON. 2 CD Set. Mail Order Only.
This title now deleted.)
Discs contain the following Elvis selection:
(Let Me Be Your) Teddy Bear

[ ] The **SUN RECORDS COLLECTION**   *(3 CD Box Set)*
Catalog# R2 71780/DRC3-1211   Value $ 50-75
(1994 Rhino Records Release from RCA Special Products. Packaged in a special
longbox. Each CD has it's own jewel box with individual insert sleeve. Box
contains 32 page booklet. Black collectors sticker with white and gold printing
on shrink wrap.)
Discs contain the following Elvis selections:

That's All Right	Mystery Train
Good Rockin' Tonight	Down By The Riverside -
Baby Let's Play House	*(by The Million Dollar Quartet)*

[ ] The **SUN STORY**
Catalog# RNCD 75884   Value $ 10-15
(1987 First Pressing. A Rhino Records Release. Dark Yellow and Black Disc
with Black Print. Contains 12 page insert booklet. Booklet and back insert cover
printed in Canada.)
Disc contains the following Elvis selections:

Good Rockin' Tonight	That's All Right (Mama)

[ ] The **SUN STORY**
Catalog# RNCD 75884   Value $ 20-25
BMG Music Service Catalog# D 244534
(1988 Second Pressing. Mfg. for BMG Direct Marketing, Inc. Dark Yellow and
Black Disc with Black Print. BMG Music Service catalog number on disc and
back insert cover. Contains 12 page insert booklet. Booklet and back insert cover
printed in Canada. Only available from BMG Music CD Club. Mail Order Only.)

[ ] The **SUN STORY**
Catalog# RNCD 75884   Value $ 10-15
(1989 Third Pressing. A Rhino Records Release. Dark Yellow and Black Disc
with Black Print. Contains 12 page insert booklet. Booklet and back insert cover
printed in Canada.)

[ ]   **The SUN STORY**
        Catalog# RNCD 75884   **Value $20-25**
        BMG Music Service Catalog# D 244534
        (1995 Fourth Pressing. Mfg. for BMG Direct Marketing, Inc. Light Yellow and Black Disc with Black Print. BMG Music catalog number on disc and back insert cover. Contains 12 page insert booklet. Booklet and back insert cover printed in U.S. Only available from BMG Music CD Club. Mail Order Only.)

[ ]   **SUN'S GREATEST HITS**
        Catalog# 07863-66059-2   **Value $ 14-18**
        (1992 RCA Release. Contains 16 page insert booklet.)
        Disc contains the following Elvis selections:

That's All Right Mama	Mystery Train
Blue Moon Of Kentucky	Tomorrow Night

[ ]   **The SUPER '60's**   *(4 CD Set)*
        Catalog# RBD-037/CD1   **Value $ 55-60**
        (1990 Readers Digest Music Release. 4 CD Set. Contains 50 page booklet. Mail Order Only.)
        Discs contain the following Elvis selections:

It's Now Or Never	Love Letters
Such A Night	In The Ghetto
Crying In The Chapel	

[ ]   **SWEET DREAMS OF COUNTRY** *(4 CD Set)*
        Catalog# RCD-049/CD1   **Value $ 55-60**
        (1990 Reader's Digest Music Release. 4 CD Set. Mail Order Only.)
        Discs contain the following Elvis selections:

Are You Lonesome Tonight?	Take My Hand Precious Lord
Hawaiian Wedding Song	There Goes My Everything
I Want You, I Need You, I Love You	You Don't Have To Say You Love Me
Love Letters	

[ ]   **TAKE 2** *(Promo)*
        Catalog# FBO-1001   **Value $ 30-40**
        (1994 Precision Media Release. "For Broadcast Only". Contains 8 page insert booklet. Mail Order Only.)
        Disc contains the following Elvis selection:
        I Beg Of You *(Stereo Alternate Take)*

[ ]   **The TEENAGE YEARS 1957-1964**
        Catalog# TCD-161   **Value $ 15-20**
        (1993 Time - Life Music Release. Mail Order Only.)
        Disc contains the following Elvis selection:
        (Let Me Be Your) Teddy Bear

[ ] **THERE'S A RIOT GOIN' ON! -**
THE ROCK 'N' ROLL CLASSICS OF LEIBER & STOLLER
Catalog# R2-70593   Value $ 10-15
(1991 Rhino Records Release.)
Disc contains the following Elvis selections:
Love Me   Jailhouse Rock

[ ] **THESE WERE OUR SONGS:** *(3 CD Set)*
THE EARLY '60's
Catalog # RCD-100/CD1   Value $ 45-50
(1990 Reader's Digest Music Release. 3 CD Set. Contains 48 page insert
booklet. Mail Order Only.)
Discs contain the following Elvis selections:
Little Sister   Devil In Disguise
His Latest Flame   Return To Sender
She's Not You

[ ] **THOSE FABULOUS '50's** *(2 CD Set)*
Catalog# DVC2-0877-1,2   Value $ 20-25
(1989 RCA Special Products Release for Sessions Music. 2 CD Set.
Mail Order Only.)
Discs contain the following Elvis selection:
I Want You, I Need You, I Love You

[ ] **TIME-LIFE TREASURY OF CHRISTMAS Vol. 1** *(2 CD Set)*
Catalog# TCD-107-A/B   Value $ 25-30
(1987 Time-Life Music Release. 2 CD Set. Mail Order Only.)
Discs contain the following Elvis selections:
Here Comes Santa Claus   If Every Day Was Like Christmas

[ ] **TIME-LIFE TREASURY OF CHRISTMAS Vol. 2** *(2 CD Set)*
Catalog# TCD-108-A/B   Value $ 25-30
(1987 Time-Life Music Release. 2 CD Set. Mail Order Only.)
Discs contain the following Elvis selection:
Blue Christmas

[ ] **TO ELVIS, WITH LOVE** *(2 CD Set)*
Catalog# LG1000010/10   Value $ 25-35
(1992 Live Gold Productions Release. 2 CD Set. Contains 40 Novelty and
Tribute Songs. 4 page insert booklet. Pressed in Czechoslovakia for U.S.
Release.)
Contains Newscast About The Death Of Elvis

[ ] **TODAY'S HOT MOVIE HITS**
Catalog# SCD-5101   Value $ 5-8
(1993 Special Music Co. Release. The back cover lists the song "Can't Help
Falling In Love" by Elvis. It is actually an Elvis sound-alike. It is being sold as
an Elvis performance. Since this is not Elvis singing it is not listed in the
cross-reference.)

[ ]   **TREASURY OF COUNTRY** *(4 CD Set)*
      INSPIRATIONAL FAVORITES
      Catalog# RB7-063C-1,2,3,4   **Value $ 55-60**
      (1994 Reader's Digest Music Release. 4 CD Set with 48 page booklet.
      Mail Order Only.)
      Discs contain the following Elvis selections:
      It Is No Secret   Mansion Over The Hill Top
      Joshua Fit The Battle

[ ]   **UNFORGETTABLE FIFTIES** *(2 CD Set)*
      Catalog# DVC-0867-1 & 2   **Value $ 15-25**
      (1988 RCA Special Products Release for Heartland Music. 2 CD Set.
      Mail Order Only.)
      Discs contain the following Elvis selections:
      Love Me Tender   Don't Be Cruel

[ ]   **WCBS FM 101.1**
      THE ANNIVERSARY ALBUM THE 50's
      Catalog# COL-2514 DRC1-1879   **Value $ 15-20**
      (1997 BMG Special Products Release for Collectables Records Corp.
      Four-fold insert booklet.)
      Disc contains the following Elvis selections:
      Jailhouse Rock   Hound Dog
      Heartbreak Hotel

[ ]   **WE WISH YOU A MERRY CHRISTMAS**
      Catalog# 2294-2-R   **Value $ 12-15**
      (1990 RCA Release.)
      Disc contains the following Elvis selection:
      Santa Claus Is Back In Town

[ ]   **WE WISH YOU A MERRY CHRISTMAS**
      Catalog# DMC1-0992   **Value $ 20-25**
      *(1991 RCA Special Products Release for AVON. **This title has been deleted.***
      Mail Order Only.)
      Disc contains the following Elvis selection:
      Blue Christmas

[ ]   The **YEAR TO REMEMBER 1960**
      Catalog# RS7-601-1 CCD1-5671   **Value $ 50-75**
      (1995 Readers Digest Music Release. 6 page tri-fold insert booklet.
      Sent only to selected customers for test preview to determine possible general
      release. First in series "The Years To Remember 1960-1969".
      *This was a preview series to selected customers. **Series was deleted after third***
      ***release. Not available to general public.** Mail Order Only.)*
      Disc contains the following Elvis selections:
      Are You Lonesome Tonight?   It's Now Or Never

[ ]   The **YEAR TO REMEMBER 1969**
        Catalog# RS7-610-1 CCD1-5801   **Value $ 50-75**
        (1995 Reader's Digest Music Release. 6 page tri-fold insert booklet.
        Third in series "The Years To Remember 1960-1969". Second disc in series did
        *not have an Elvis selection. **After release of this disc, the series was suspended***
        ***due to non-response and further releases cancelled.** Mail Order Only.)*
        Disc contains the following Elvis selection:
        Suspicious Minds

[ ]   **YOUR EASY-LISTENING HIT PARADE:** *(4 CD Set)*
        OF THE '40s AND '50s
        Catalog# RB7-061-1,2,3,4   **Value $ 55-60**
        (1998 Readers Digest Music Release. Mfg. by BMG Direct Marketing, Inc.
        4 CD Set with 48 page booklet. Mail Order Only.)
        Discs contain the following Elvis selection:
        Loving You

[ ]   **YOUR GOODTIME OLDIES MAGAZINE:** *(3 CD Radio Show)*
        ON THE RADIO, Jan. 3, 1992
        Catalog# 92-01   **Value $ 20-25**
        (1992. A 3 CD Set from Westwood One Radio Networks, Inc. with Cue sheets.)
        Discs contain the following Elvis selection:
        All Shook Up

[ ]   **YOUR GOODTIMES OLDIES MAGAZINE:** *(3 CD Radio Show)*
        ON THE RADIO, Feb. 14, 1992
        Catalog# 92-07   **Value $ 20-25**
        (1992. A 3 CD Set from Westwood One Radio Networks, Inc. with Cue sheets.)
        Discs contain the following Elvis selection:
        Don't Be Cruel

[ ]   **YOUR GOODTIME OLDIES MAGAZINE:** *(3 CD Radio Show)*
        ON THE RADIO, March 20-22, 1992
        Catalog# 92-12   **Value $ 20-25**
        (1992. A 3 CD Set from Westwood One Radio Networks, Inc. with Cue sheets.)
        Discs contain the following Elvis selection:
        Hard Headed Woman

[ ]   **YOUR GOODTIME OLDIES MAGAZINE:** *(3 CD Radio Show)*
        ON THE RADIO, April 10, 1992
        Catalog# 92-15   **Value $ 20-25**
        (1992. A 3 CD Set from Westwood One Radio Networks, Inc. with Cue sheets.)
        Discs contain the following Elvis selection:
        Suspicious Minds

[ ]   **YOUR GOODTIME OLDIES MAGAZINE:** *(3 CD Radio Show)*
              ON THE RADIO, Aug. 16, 1992
              Catalog# 92-33   Value $ 20-25
              (1992. A 3 CD Set from Westwood One Radio Networks, Inc. with Cue sheets.)
              Discs contain the following Elvis selection:
              Burning Love

[ ]   **YOUR GOODTIME OLDIES MAGAZINE:** *(3 CD Radio Show)*
              ON THE RADIO, Sept. 18, 1992
              Catalog# 92-38   Value $20-25
              (1992. A 3 CD Set from Westwood One Radio Networks, Inc. with Cue sheets.)
              Discs contain the following Elvis selection:
              Return To Sender

[ ]   **YOUR GOODTIME OLDIES MAGAZINE:** *(3 CD Radio Show)*
              ON THE RADIO, Oct. 24, 1992
              Catalog# 92-43   Value $ 20-25
               (1992. A 3 CD Set from Westwood One Radio Networks, Inc. with Cue sheets.)
              Discs contain the following Elvis selection:
              Devil In Disguise

[ ]   **YOUR GOODTIME OLDIES MAGAZINE:** *(3 CD Radio Show)*
              ON THE RADIO, Nov. 6, 1992
              Catalog# 92-45   Value $20-25
               (1992. A 3 CD Set from Westwood One Radio Networks, Inc. with Cue sheets.)
              Discs contain the following Elvis selections:
              Wear My Ring Around Your Neck

[ ]   **YOUR GOODTIME OLDIES MAGAZINE:** *(3 CD Radio Show)*
              ON THE RADIO, Nov. 13, 1992
              Catalog# 92-46   Value $ 20-25
               (1992. A 3 CD Set from Westwood One Radio Networks, Inc. with Cue sheets.)
              Discs contain the following Elvis selections:
              Return To Sender

[ ]   **YOUR GOODTIME OLDIES MAGAZINE:** *(3 CD Radio Show)*
              ON THE RADIO, Feb. 19, 1993
              Catalog# 93-08   Value $ 20-25
               (1993. A 3 CD Set from Westwood One Radio Networks, Inc. with Cue sheets.)
              Discs contain the following Elvis selection:
              Teddy Bear

[ ]   **YOUR GOODTIME OLDIES MAGAZINE:** *(3 CD Radio Show)*
         ON THE RADIO, March 5, 1993
         Catalog# 93-10   **Value $ 20-25**
         (1993. A 3 CD Set from Westwood One Radio Networks, Inc. with Cue sheets.)
         Discs contain the following Elvis selection:
         Jailhouse Rock

[ ]   **YOUR GOODTIME OLDIES MAGAZINE:** *(3 CD Radio Show)*
         ON THE RADIO, March 20, 1993
         Catalog# 93-12   **Value $ 20-25**
         (1993. A 3 CD Set from Westwood One Radio Networks, Inc. with Cue sheets.)
         Discs contain the following Elvis selection:
         Good Luck Charm

[ ]   **YOUR GOODTIME OLDIES MAGAZINE:** *(3 CD Radio Show)*
         ON THE RADIO, April 3, 1993
         Catalog# 93-14   **Value $ 20-25**
         (1993. A 3 CD Set from Westwood One Radio Networks, Inc. with Cue sheets.)
         Discs contain the following Elvis selection:
         Return To Sender

[ ]   **YOUR GOODTIME OLDIES MAGAZINE:** *(3 CD Radio Show)*
         ON THE RADIO, May 7, 1993
         Catalog# 93-19   **Value $ 20-25**
         (1993. A 3 CD Set from Westwood One Radio Networks, Inc. with Cue sheets.)
         Discs contain the following Elvis selection:
         A Big Hunk O' Love

[ ]   **YOUR GOODTIME OLDIES MAGAZINE:** *(3 CD Radio Show)*
         ON THE RADIO, May 14, 1993
         Catalog# 93-20   **Value $ 20-25**
         (1993. A 3 CD Set from Westwood One Radio Networks, Inc. with Cue sheets.)
         Discs contain the following Elvis selection:
         Burning Love

[ ]   **YOUR GOODTIME OLDIES MAGAZINE:** *(3 CD Radio Show)*
         ON THE RADIO, Aug. 27, 1993
         Catalog# 93-35   **Value $ 20-25**
         (1993. A 3 CD Set from Westwood One Radio Networks, Inc. with Cue sheets.)
         Discs contain the following Elvis selection:
         Wear My Ring Around Your Neck

[ ]   **YOUR GOODTIME OLDIES MAGAZINE:** *(3 CD Radio Show)*
         ON THE RADIO, Feb. 5, 1994
         Catalog# 94-06   **Value $ 20-25**
         (1994. A 3 CD Set from Westwood One Radio Networks, Inc. with Cue sheets.)
         Discs contain the following Elvis selection:
         Burning Love

[ ]   **YOUR GOODTIME OLDIES MAGAZINE:** *(3 CD Radio Show)*
         ON THE RADIO, Feb. 12, 1994
         Catalog# 94-07   **Value $ 20-25**
         (1994. A 3 CD Set from Westwood One Radio Networks, Inc. with Cue sheets.)
         Discs contain the following Elvis selection:
         Don't Be Cruel

[ ]   **YOUR GOODTIME OLDIES MAGAZINE:** *(3 CD Radio Show)*
         ON THE RADIO, March 19, 1994
         Catalog# 94-12   **Value $ 20-25**
         (1994. A 3 CD Set from Westwood One Radio Networks, Inc. with Cue sheets.)
         Discs contain the following Elvis selection:
         Hard Headed Woman

[ ]   **YOUR GOODTIME OLDIES MAGAZINE:** *(3 CD Radio Show)*
         ON THE RADIO, April 30, 1994
         Catalog# 94-18   **Value $ 20-25**
         (1994. A 3 CD Set from Westwood One Radio Networks, Inc. with Cue sheets.)
         Discs contain the following Elvis selection:
         Return To Sender

[ ]   **YOUR GOODTIME OLDIES MAGAZINE:** *(3 CD Radio Show)*
         ON THE RADIO, May 7, 1994
         Catalog# 94-19   **Value $ 20-25**
         (1994. A 3 CD Set from Westwood One Radio Networks, Inc. with Cue sheets.)
         Discs contain the following Elvis selection:
         Burning Love

[ ]   **YOUR GOODTIME OLDIES MAGAZINE:** *(3 CD Radio Show)*
         ON THE RADIO, May 14, 1994
         Catalog# 94-20   **Value $ 20-25**
         (1994. A 3 CD Set from Westwood One Radio Networks, Inc. with Cue sheets.)
         Discs contain the following Elvis selection:
         Teddy Bear

[ ]   **YOUR GOODTIME OLDIES MAGAZINE:** *(3 CD Radio Show)*
ON THE RADIO, Aug. 13, 1994
Catalog# 94-33   Value $ 20-25
(1994. A 3 CD Set from Westwood One Radio Networks, Inc. with Cue sheets.)
Discs contain the following Elvis selection:
Are You Lonesome Tonight

[ ]   **YOUR GOODTIME OLDIES MAGAZINE:** *(3 CD Radio Show)*
ON THE RADIO, Aug. 27, 1994
Catalog# 94-34   Value # 20-25
(1994. A 3 CD Set from Westwood One Radio Networks, Inc. with Cue sheets.)
Discs contain the following Elvis selection:
Wear My Ring Around Your Neck

[ ]   **YOUR GOODTIME OLDIES MAGAZINE:** *(3 CD Radio Show)*
ON THE RADIO, Sept. 24, 1994
Catalog# 94-39   Value $ 20-25
(1994. A 3 CD Set from Westwood One Radio Networks, Inc. with Cue sheets.)
Discs contain the following Elvis selection:
All Shook Up

[ ]   **YOUR GOODTIME OLDIES MAGAZINE:** *(3 CD Radio Show)*
ON THE RADIO, April 22, 1995
Catalog# 95-17   Value $ 20-25
(1995. A 3 CD Set from Westwood One Radio Networks, Inc. with cue sheets.)
Discs contain the following Elvis selection:
Teddy Bear

[ ]   **YOUR GOODTIMES OLDIES MAGAZINE:** *(3 CD Radio Show)*
ON THE RADIO, June 24, 1995
Catalog# 95-26   Value $ 20-25
(1995. A 3 CD Set from Westwood One Radio Networks, Inc. with Cue sheets.)
Discs contain the following Elvis selection:
Hound Dog

[ ]   **YOUR GOODTIME OLDIES MAGAZINE:** *(3 CD Radio Show)*
ON THE RADIO, Aug. 12, 1995
Catalog# 95-33   Value $ 20-25
(1995. A 3 CD Set from Westwood One Radio Networks, Inc. with Cue sheets.)
Discs contain the following Elvis selection:
Are You Lonesome Tonight

[ ] **YOUR GOODTIME OLDIES MAGAZINE:** *(3 CD Radio Show)*
ON THE RADIO, Aug. 19, 1995
Catalog# 95-34   Value $ 20-25
(1995. A 3 CD Set from Westwood One Radio Networks, Inc. with Cue sheets.)
Discs contain the following Elvis selections:
Hound Dog

[ ] **YOUR GOODTIME OLDIES MAGAZINE:** *(3 CD Radio Show)*
ON THE RADIO, Aug. 26, 1995
Catalog# 95-35   Value $ 20-25
(1995. A 3 CD Set from Westwood One Radio Networks, Inc. with Cue sheets.)
Discs contain the following Elvis selection:
Wear My Ring Around Your Neck

[ ] **YOUR GOODTIME OLDIES MAGAZINE:** *(3 CD Radio Show)*
ON THE RADIO, Sept. 2, 1995
Catalog# 95-36   Value $ 20-25
(1995. A 3 CD Set from Westwood One Radio Networks, Inc. with Cue sheets.)
Discs contain the following Elvis selection:
Little Sister

[ ] **YOUR GOODTIME OLDIES MAGAZINE:** *(3 CD Radio Show)*
ON THE RADIO, Dec. 20, 1997
Catalog# 97-51   Value $ 20-25
(1997. A 3 CD Set from Global Media with Cue sheets.)
Discs contain the following Elvis selections.
Santa Claus Is Back In Town   Here Comes Santa Claus

[ ] **YOUR HIT PARADE: 1956**
Catalog# TCD-125   Value $ 15-20
(1990 Time - Life Music Release. Mail Order Only.)
Disc contains the following Elvis selection:
Love Me Tender

[ ] **YOUR HIT PARADE - THE '50's POP REVIVAL**
Catalog# TCD-137   Value $ 15-20
(1993 Time - Life Music Release. Mail Order Only.)
Disc contains the following Elvis selection:
Don't

[ ] **YULE FUEL -** *(Promo)*
1992 RHINO CHRISTMAS SAMPLER
Catalog# PRO2 90123   Value $ 25-35
(1992 Rhino Records Promo Only Release. "Not For Sale - For Promotional
Use Only" on back insert cover.)
Disc contains the following Elvis selection:
Blue Christmas

[ ] **YULE TRAIN-** *(Promo)*
A RHINO CHRISTMAS SAMPLER
Catalog# PRO2 90048   Value $ 25-35
(1990 Rhino Records Promo Only Release. "Not For Sale - Promotional Use
Only" on insert sleeve.)
Disc contains the following Elvis selection:
Blue Christmas

[ ] **14 #1 COUNTRY HITS**
Catalog# 7004-2-R   Value $ 12-15
(1989 RCA Release.)
Disc contains the following Elvis selection:
Guitar Man *(1980 Remix Version)*

[ ] **20 YEARS OF NO. 1 HITS, 1956-1975** *(4 CD Set)*
Catalog# RBD-243/CD1   Value $ 55-60
(1988 Reader's Digest Music Release. 4 CD Set with 64 page booklet.
Mail Order Only.)
Discs contain the following Elvis selections:

Hound Dog	Surrender
Don't Be Cruel	Good Luck Charm
Stuck On You	Suspicious Minds
Are You Lonesome Tonight?	

[ ] **50 BELOVED SONGS OF FAITH** *(2 CD Set)*
Catalog# BMD2-100   Value $ 25-30
(1990 Reader's Digest Music Release. 2 CD Set. Mail Order Only.)
Discs contain the following Elvis selection:
Crying In The Chapel

[ ]   **50 CHRISTMAS FAVORITES**   *(2 CD Set)*
                        Catalog# TCD-130-A/B   **Value $ 25-30**
                        (1990 Time - Life Music Release. 2 CD Set. Mail Order Only.)
                        Discs contain the following Elvis selections:
                        White Christmas   I'll Be Home For Christmas

[ ]   **60's**
                        Catalog# 5553   **Value $ 10-12**
                        (1998 Simitar Label Release.)
                        Disc contains the following Elvis selection:
                        Suspicious Minds

Section 111

Cross Reference

CROSS REFERENCE
ELVIS SONG TITLES TO DISC

"A"

A Big Hunk O' Love
A Touch Of Platinum - A Life In Music - Disc 1 *(alternate take 4)*
Aloha From Hawaii Via Satellite
Aloha From Hawaii Via Satellite - 25th Anniversary Edition
Alternate Aloha
Blue Suede Shoes (Original Soundtrack) - Disc 1
Elvis' Gold Records Vol. 2 - 50,000,000 Elvis Fans Can't Be Wrong
Elvis' Gold Records Vol. 2 - 50,000,000 Elvis Fans Can't Be Wrong (1997 Reissue)
Elvis' Greatest Jukebox Hits
Elvis! His Greatest Hits - Disc 2
Elvis - His Life & Music - Disc 2
Elvis In Nashville 1956-1971
(The) Elvis Presley Birthday Tribute 1992 - Disc 1
(The) Elvis Presley Collection - Rock 'N' Roll - Disc 2
Elvis Presley Radio Show (Promo)
Elvis Presley 1954 - 1961
Elvis Presley 50 Greatest Hits - Disc 2
Elvis The Legend - Disc 2
Elvis The Tribute - A Biography - Disc 1
Elvis 15th Anniversary Radio Show - Disc 3
Elvis 20th Anniversary Radio Show - Disc 3
Elvis 24 Karat Hits!
Elvis 50 Yrs 50 Hits - Disc 2
Elvis 50 Worldwide Gold Hits Vol 1 - Disc 1
Essential Elvis Vol 3/Hits Like Never Before *(alternate take 1)*
Good Rockin' Tonight - Disc 2
(The) King Of Rock 'N' Roll - 50's Masters - Disc 4
(The) Legend Lives On - Disc 1
Memories Of Elvis - 1991 - Disc 1
Memories Of Elvis - 1993 - Disc 2
(The) Number One Hits
Platinum - A Life In Music - Disc 1 *(alternate take 4)*
Platinum In-Store Sampler (Promo) *(alternate take 4)*
Platinum Sampler (Promo) *(alternate take 4)*
Shake Rattle & Roll (Promo)
(The) Top Ten Hits - Disc 1
Walk A Mile In My Shoes - 70's Masters - Disc 5
Various Artists
Billboard's Top Rock 'N' Roll Hits 1959
Billboard's Top Rock 'N' Roll Hits 1957-1961
Dick Clark's Rock Roll & Remember 1/3 - 1/5
(The) Elvis Presley Years - Disc 2
Solid Gold Country - Elvis Presley Love Songs
Solid Gold Country - Elvis Presley Memorial Tribute 91-8
Solid Gold Scrapbook - Elvis Golden Decade 1956-1965
Solid Gold Scrapbook - Solid Gold Elvis
Your Goodtime Oldies Magazine - 93-19

A Boy Like Me, A Girl Like You
Elvis Double Features - Kid Galahad & Girls, Girls, Girls

A Cane And A High Starch Collar
Elvis Double Features - Flaming Star, Wild In The Country & Follow That Dream

A Dog's Life
Elvis Aron Presley - Disc 2 *(alternate takes 4-6)*
Elvis Double Features - Frankie & Johnny & Paradise Hawaiian Style

(Now And Then There's) A Fool Such As I
Elvis Aron Presley -Disc 1
Elvis' Gold Records Vol. 2 - 50,000,000 Elvis Fans Can't Be Wrong
Elvis' Gold Records Vol. 2 - 50.000,000 Elvis Fans Can't Be Wrong (1997 Reissue)
Elvis! His Greatest Hits - Disc 2
Elvis His Life & Music - Elvis Gold Records Vol.2 - Disc 2
(The) Elvis Presley Birthday Tribute 1992 - Disc 3
(The) Elvis Presley Collection - Country - Disc 1
Elvis Presley 50 Greatest Hits - Disc 2
Elvis Presley 1954-1961
Elvis The Legend - Disc 2
Elvis The Tribute - A Biography - Disc 2
Elvis 20th Anniversary Radio Show - Disc 3
Elvis 50 Yrs 50 Hits - Disc 2
Elvis 50 Worldwide Gold Hits Vol. 1 - Disc 1
Essential Elvis Vol. 3 - Hits Like Never Before *(alternate take 3, unreleased version)*
Great Country Songs
(The) King Of Rock 'N' Roll 50's Masters - Disc 4
(The) Legend Of A King - Disc 1
Memories Of Elvis - 1991 - Disc 3
Memories Of Elvis - 1993 - Disc 2
(The) Top Ten Hits - Disc 1
Various Artists
Dick Clark's Rock Roll & Remember 08/12 - 08/14
Country Memories
Solid Gold Country - The Complete 50's Masters
Solid Gold Country - Elvis Presley Birthday Tribute 92-1
Solid Gold Country - Elvis Presley Birthday Tribute 93-1
Solid Gold Country - Elvis Presley's Golden Records 91-11
Solid Gold Country - Elvis Presley's Golden Records 93-2
Solid Gold Country - Elvis Presley In Nashville
Solid Gold Country - Elvis Presley Love Songs
Solid Gold Country - Elvis Presley Memorial Tribute 92-8
Solid Gold Scrapbook - Elvis Golden Decade 1956-1965
Solid Gold Scrapbook - Solid Gold Elvis

A House That Has Everything
An Elvis Double Feature: Speedway, Clambake
Elvis Double Features - Kissin' Cousins, Clambake & Stay Away Joe

A Hundred Years From Now
Essential Elvis Vol. 4 - A Hundred Years From Now *(alternate take 2)*
Walk A Mile In My Shoes - 70's Masters - Disc 3 (studio highlights)
Walk A Mile In My Shoes Out Of The Box Sampler (Promo)

A Little Bit Of Green
Back In Memphis
From Nashville To Memphis Disc 4

A Little Less Conversation
Almost In Love
Command Performances - 60's Masters - Disc 2
Elvis Double Features - Live A Little, Love A Little - Charro -The Trouble With Girls *(reg. version and album ver.)*
Memories - The '68 Comeback Special - Disc 1 *(previously unreleased)*

A Mess Of Blues
A Touch Of Platinum - A Life In Music - Disc 2 *(alternate take 1)*
Elvis' Gold Records Volume 4
Elvis' Gold Records Volume 4 (1997 Reissue)
Elvis! His Greatest Hits - Disc 2
Elvis His Life & Music - Disc 4
(The) Elvis Presley Collection - Rhythm & Blues - Disc 2

A MESS OF BLUES (cont'd)
Elvis The King 1954-1965
Elvis The Legend - Disc 2
Elvis 50 Worldwide Gold Hits Vol. 1 - Disc 2
From Nashville To Memphis - 60's Masters - Disc 1
Platinum - A Life In Music - Disc 2 *(alternate take 1)*
Return Of The Rocker
Various Artists
Solid Gold Country - Elvis Presley's Golden Records 91-11
Solid Gold Country - Elvis Presley: His Favorite Writers

A Thing Called Love
Amazing Grace: His Greatest Sacred Performances - Disc 2
He Touched Me

A Whistling Tune
Collectors Gold - Disc 1 *(alternate take 4)*
Elvis Double Features - Cannister Set - Disc 1
Elvis Double Features - Flaming Star - Wild In The Country - Follow That Dream
Elvis Double Features - Kid Galahad - Girls! Girls! Girls!

A World Of Our Own
Elvis Double Features - Cannister Set - Disc 2
Elvis Double Features - It Happened At The Worlds Fair & Fun In Acapulco

Adam And Evil
Elvis Double Features - Spinout and Double Trouble

After Loving You
A Touch Of Platinum - A Life In Music - Disc 2 -(Graceland & Palm Springs Segment) *(home recording)*
(The) Elvis Presley Collection - Rhythm & Blues - Disc 1
From Nashville To Memphis - 60's Masters - Disc 5
From Elvis In Memphis
(The) Memphis Record
Platinum - A Life In Music - Disc 2 (Graceland & Palm Springs Segment) *(home recording)*

Ain't That Loving You Baby
Don't Be Cruel *(fast version alternate take 11)*
Elvis' Gold Records Volume 4
Elvis' Gold Records Volume 4 (1997 Reissue)
Elvis! His Greatest Hits - Disc 3
Elvis His Life & Music - Disc 4
(The) Elvis Presley Collection - Rhythm & Blues - Disc 1 *(fast version alternate take 11)*
(The) Elvis Presley Collection - The Rocker - Disc 2
Elvis 50 Worldwide Gold Hits - Disc 1
Essential Elvis Vol.3 Hits Like Never Before *(alternate takes 5,11, unreleased fast versions)*
Essential Elvis Vol.3 Hits Like Never Before *(alternate take 1, unreleased mid tempo version)*
(The) King Of Rock 'N' Roll 50's Masters Disc 4
(The) King Of Rock 'N' Roll 50's Masters Disc 5 *(fast version, alternate take 11)*
Reconsider Baby *(alternate take)*
Various Artists
Solid Gold Country - Elvis Presley's Golden Records 91-11
Solid Gold Country - Elvis Presley's Golden Records 93-2

All I Needed Was The Rain
Elvis Double Features - Kissin' Cousins, Clambake & Stay Away Joe

All Shook Up
A Touch Of Platinum - A Life In Music - Disc 1
All Shook Up/ Are You Lonesome Tonight?

ALL SHOOK UP (cont'd)

An Afternoon In The Garden
Elvis Aron Presley - Disc 1
Elvis Aron Presley - Disc 4
Elvis As Recorded At Madison Square Garden
Elvis' Birthday Tribute Radio Program
Elvis' Golden Records
Elvis' Golden Records (1997 Reissue)
Elvis' Greatest Jukebox Hits
Elvis! His Greatest Hits -Disc 1
Elvis - His Life & Music - Disc 1
Elvis In Person At The International Hotel
Elvis/NBC TV Special
(The) Elvis Presley Birthday Tribute 1992 - Disc 1
(The) Elvis Presley Collection - Rock 'N' Roll - Disc 2
Elvis Presley Radio Special (Promo)
Elvis Presley 1954 - 1961
Elvis Presley - 50 Greatest Hits - Disc 1
Elvis The Legend - Disc 1
Elvis The Tribute - A Biography - Disc 1
Elvis 15th Anniversary Radio Show - Disc 4
Elvis 20th Anniversary Radio Show - Disc 2
Elvis 20th Anniversary Sampler
Elvis 20th Anniversary Singles Set -Disc 4
Elvis 24 Karat Hits!
Elvis 50 Worldwide Gold Hits - Vol. 1 - Disc 1
Elvis 50 Yrs 50 Hits - Disc 1
Essential Elvis Vol. 2 Stereo 57 *(alternate take 10)*
The Honeymoon Companion (Promo)
(The) King Of Rock 'N' Roll 50's Masters - Disc 2
(The) King Of Rock 'N' Roll 50's Masters - (Promo)
(The) Legend Lives On - Disc 1
(The) Legend Lives On - Disc 4
(The) Legend Of A King - Disc 1
Memories - The '68 Comeback Special - Disc 1
Memories Of Elvis - 1991 - Disc 4
Memories Of Elvis - 1993 - Disc 1
(The) Number One Hits
Out Of The Box (Promo)
Platinum - A Life In Music Disc 1
Pure Gold
Shake Rattle & Roll (Promo)
(The) Top Ten Hits - Disc 1
Virtual Graceland CD-ROM

Various Artists

Back To The 50's
Billboard's Top Rock 'N' Roll Hits 1957
Billboard's Top Rock 'N' Roll Hits 1957-1961
(The) Elvis Presley Years
Jukebox Favorites - Musical Memories of The 50's & 60's
Made In America
Rock 'N' Roll Legends
Solid Gold Country - Elvis Presley Birthday Tribute - 93-1
Solid Gold Country - Elvis Presley - His Favorite Writers
Solid Gold Country - Elvis Presley Live
Solid Gold Country - Elvis Presley's Love Songs
Solid Gold Country - Elvis Presley Memorial Tribute - 91-8
Solid Gold Country - Elvis Presley Memorial Tribute - 92-8
Solid Gold Country - Elvis Presley Memorial Tribute - 93-8
Solid Gold Scrapbook - Elvis' Golden Decade 1956-1965
The RCA Records Label - The First Note In Black Music
The RCA Records Label - The First Note In Black Music (Promo)
Your Goodtime Oldies Magazine - 92-01
Your Goodtime Oldies Magazine - 94-39

All That I Am
Command Performances 60's Masters - Disc 2
Elvis Double Features - Spinout & Double Trouble

Alla' En El "Rancho Grande"
Walk A Mile In My Shoes - 70's Masters - Disc 5 *(rehearsal)*

Almost
Elvis Double Features - Live A Little, Love A Little, The Trouble With Girls &Change Of Habit
Elvis Double Features - Live A Little, Love A Little, The Trouble With Girls & Change Of Habit *(undubbed)*

Almost Always True
Blue Hawaii
Blue Hawaii (1997 Reissue)
Blue Hawaii (1997 Reissue Collectors Edition)
(The) Blue Suede Box - Elvis: His Greatest Soundtracks - Disc 4

Almost In Love
Almost In Love
Command Performances - 60's Masters - Disc 2
Elvis Double Features - Live A Little, Love A Little, The Trouble With Girls & Change Of Habit

Aloha Oe
Blue Hawaii
Blue Hawaii (1997 Reissue)
Blue Hawaii (1997 Reissue Collectors Edition)
(The) Blue Suede Box - Elvis: His Greatest Soundtracks - Disc 4

Always On My Mind
A Touch Of Platinum Vol. 2 - A Life In Music - Disc 2 *(alternate take 2)*
Always On My Mind
Elvis At His Romantic Best
(The) Elvis Presley Collection - Love Songs - Disc 1
Elvis The Legend - Disc 3
Great Country Songs
(The) Great Performances
Heart & Soul
King Of The Whole Wide World - Collectors Set - The Elvis Medley
(The) Legend Lives On - Disc 3
Platinum - A Life In Music - Disc 4 *(alternate take 2)*
Platinum In-Store Sampler (Promo) *(alternate take 2)*
Separate Ways
Walk A Mile In My Shoes - 70's Masters - Disc 2
Various Artists
Country Soft 'N' Mellow
Do You Love Me? All Time Best Love Songs
Practical Magic (Original Soundtrack)
Solid Gold Country - Elvis Presley Birthday Tribute 92-1
Solid Gold Country - Elvis Presley's Love Songs
Solid Gold Country - Elvis Presley Memorial Tribute 91-8

Am I Ready
Burning Love & Hits From His Movies Vol .2
Collectors Gold - Disc 1 *(alternate take 1)*
Elvis Double Features - Spinout & Double Trouble
Elvis Presley - The King Of Rock & Roll At His Best - Disc 2

Amazing Grace
Amazing Grace - His Greatest Sacred Performances - Disc 2
(The) Elvis Presley Collection - Gospel - Disc 1
(The) Elvis Presley Gospel Treasury - Disc 1

AMAZING GRACE (cont'd)
(The) Elvis Presley Gospel Treasury (Special Edition)
He Touched Me
Selections From Amazing Grace - His Greatest Sacred Performances (Promo)
Walk A Mile In My Shoes - 70's Masters - Disc 3 *(alternate take 2)*
Various Artists
Driver's Favorite Songs

Amen
Elvis Aron Presley (medley I Got A Woman/Amen) Disc 4
Elvis In Concert (I Got A Woman/Amen)
(The) Legend Lives On (I Got A Woman/Amen) Disc 1

America The Beautiful
Elvis Aron Presley - Disc 3
Elvis 20th Anniversary Sampler
Various Artists
God Bless The U.S.A.

An American Trilogy
A Touch Of Platinum Vol. 2 - A Life In Music - Disc 2 (Alternate Aloha)
Aloha From Hawaii Via Satellite
Aloha From Hawaii Via Satellite - 25th Anniversary Edition
(The) Alternate Aloha
An Afternoon In The Garden
Elvis Aron Presley - Disc 3
Elvis Aron Presley - Disc 4
Elvis As Recorded At Madison Square Garden
(The) Elvis Presley Collection - From The Heart - Disc 2
Elvis Recorded Live On Stage In Memphis
Elvis The Legend - Disc 3
Elvis 20th Anniversary Radio Show - Disc 1
(The) Great Performances
(The) Legend Lives On - Disc 2
(The) Legend Of A King - Disc 2
Platinum - A Life In Music - Disc 4 (Alternate Aloha)
Walk A Mile In My Shoes - 70's Masters - Disc 1
Various Artists
Fifty Years of Hits
Reach Out & Touch
Solid Gold Country - Elvis Presley & TV
Solid Gold Country - Elvis Presley Live

An Evening Prayer
Amazing Grace - His Greatest Sacred Performances - Disc 2
An Afternoon In The Garden
He Touched Me
Various Artists
A Celebration Of Faith And Joy

And I Love You So
A Touch Of Platinum Vol. 2 - A Life In Music - Disc 2 *(alternate take 2)*
Elvis Aron Presley - Forever
Elvis At His Romantic Best
Elvis In Concert
(The) Elvis Presley Collection - The Romantic - Disc 2
Elvis Today
(The) Legend Lives On - Disc 3
Platinum - A Life In Music - Disc 4 *(alternate take 2)*
Various Artists
Solid Gold Country - Elvis Presley In Concert

And The Grass Won't Pay No Mind
Back In Memphis
From Nashville To Memphis - 60's Masters - Disc 4

Angel
Command Performances - 60's Masters - Disc 1
Elvis Double Features - Flaming Star, Wild In The Country & Follow That Dream
Elvis Sings For Children And Grownups Too!
(The) Elvis Presley Collection - The Romantic - Disc 1

Animal Instinct
Elvis Double Features - Cannister Set - Disc 4
Elvis Double Features - Harum Scarum And Girl Happy

Any Day Now
Elvis The Other Sides - Worldwide Gold Award Hits Volume 2 - Disc 2
(The) Elvis Presley Collection - From The Heart - Disc 2
From Elvis In Memphis
From Nashville To Memphis - 60's Masters - Disc 5
(The) Memphis Record
Various Artists
Solid Gold Scrapbook - Elvis In Memphis

Anyway You Want Me
Elvis At His Romantic Best
Elvis Golden Records
Elvis Golden Records (1997 Reissue)
Elvis! His Greatest Hits -Disc 1
Elvis His Life And Music - Disc 1
(The) Elvis Presley Collection - Love Songs - Disc 2
Elvis The King: 1954-1965
Elvis 15th Anniversary Radio Show - Disc 2
Elvis 50 Worldwide Gold Hits Vol. 1 - Disc 1
Elvis 56
Elvis 56 Advance Music (Promo)
Great Hits Of 1956-57
Heartbreak Hotel, Hound Dog & Top Ten Hits
(The) King Of Rock 'N' Roll - 50's Masters - Disc 2

Anyone (Could Fall In Love With You)
Elvis Double Features - Kissin' Cousins, Clambake & Stay Away Joe

Anyplace Is Paradise
Elvis
(The) Elvis Presley Collection - Rhythm & Blues - Disc 1
Elvis 56
Elvis 56 Advance Music (Promo)
(The) King Of Rock 'N' Roll - 50's Masters - Disc 2

Anything That's Part Of You
Elvis Golden Records Vol. 3
Elvis Golden Records Vol. 3 (1997 Reissue)
Elvis His Life & Music - Disc 3
Elvis In Nashville *(alternate take 1)*
(The) Elvis Presley Collection - Love Songs - Disc 1
Elvis 50 Worldwide Hits Vol. 1 - Disc 2 *(alternate take)*
From Nashville To Memphis - 60's Masters - Disc 2
Heart & Soul

Apron Strings
Platinum - Disc 1 (Bad Nauheim Medley)

Are You Lonesome Tonight
A Golden Celebration - Disc 4 - Elvis - Burbank, Calif. June 27, 1968
A Touch Of Platinum - A Life In Music - Disc 2
A Valentine Gift For You
All Shook Up/ Are You Lonesome Tonight?
Are You Lonesome Tonight/I Gotta Know (Jukebox Single)
Blue Suede Shoes (Original Soundtrack) - Disc 1
Collectors Gold - Disc 3
Commemorative Juke Box Series (5 CD Set)
Elvis Aron Presley - Disc 1
Elvis Aron Presley - Disc 3
Elvis' Golden Records Vol. 3
Elvis' Golden Records Vol. 3 (1997 Reissue)
Elvis! His Greatest Hits - Disc 2
Elvis - His Life And Music - Disc 3
Elvis In Person At The International Hotel
Elvis In Concert
(The) Elvis Presley Birthday Tribute 1992 - Disc 1
(The) Elvis Pressley Collection - Love Songs - Disc 1
Elvis Presley: 1954-1961
Elvis The Legend - Disc 2
Elvis The Tribute - A Biography - Disc 2
Elvis 15th Anniversary Radio Show - Disc 4
Elvis 20th Anniversary Singles Set - Disc 4
Elvis 24 Karat Hits!
Elvis 50 Worldwide Gold Hits Vol. 1 - Disc 2
From Nashville To Memphis - 60's Masters - Disc 1
(The) Honeymoon Companion (Promo)
Heart And Soul
(The) Legend Lives On - Disc 1
Love Songs
Memories - The '68 Comeback Special - Disc 2 *(previously unreleased)*
Memories Of Elvis - 1991 - Disc 4
Memories Of Elvis - 1993 - Disc 2
(The) Number One Hits
Platinum - A Life In Music Disc 2
Platinum In-Store Sampler (Promo)
Shake, Rattle & Roll
Sixties Legends - Elvis Presley Disc 1
Tiger Man
(The) Top Ten Hits - Disc 2
Virtual Graceland CD-ROM
Various Artists
Dick Clark's Rock Roll & Remember 1/3-1/5
Dick Clark's Rock Roll & Remember 08/12-08/14
Love Me Tender
Million Dollar Memories Of The 50's And 60's
Solid Gold Country - Elvis: What Happened?
Solid Gold Country - Elvis Presley Birthday Tribute - 92-1
Solid Gold Country - Elvis Presley Birthday Tribute - 93-1
Solid Gold Country - Elvis Presley's Golden Records - 91-11
Solid Gold Country - Elvis Presley In Concert
Solid Gold Country - Elvis Presley In Nashville
Solid Gold Country - Elvis Presley Memorial Tribute - 91-8
Solid Gold Country - Elvis Presley Memorial Tribute - 92-8
Solid Gold Country - Elvis Presley Memorial Tribute - 93-8
Solid Gold Country - 70 Years Of RCA Country
Solid Gold Scrapbook - Solid Gold Elvis
Sweet Dreams Of Country
The Year To Remember 1960
Your Goodtime Oldies Magazine 94-33
Your Goodtime Oldies Magazine 95-33
20 Years Of No. 1 Hits 1965-1975

Are You Sincere
A Touch Of Platinum Vol. 2 - A Life In Music - Disc 2 *(alternate take 2)*
(The) Elvis Presley Collection - Country - Disc 1
Platinum - A Life In Music Disc 4 *(alternate take 2)*
Raised On Rock
Walk A Mile In My Shoes -70's Masters - Disc 4
Various Artists
(The) Nashville Explosion Country Music's Greatest Hits (Promo)

As Long As I Have You
(The) Blue Suede Box - Elvis: His Greatest Soundtracks -Disc 3
(The) Blue Suede Box - Elvis: His Greatest Soundtracks -Disc 3 *(movie version take 4)*
(The) Blue Suede Box - Elvis: His Greatest Soundtracks -Disc 3 *(movie version take 8)*
(The) Elvis Presley Collection - Love Songs - Disc 2
Elvis The Other Sides - Worldwide Gold Award Hits - Volume 2 - Disc 1
Elvis 20th Anniversary Radio Show - Disc 3
Essential Elvis Vol. 3/Hits Like Never Before *(track N take 8 unreleased version)*
Essential Elvis Vol. 3/Hits Like Never Before *(track N take 4 unreleased version)*
Heart And Soul
King Creole
King Creole (1997 Reissue)
King Creole (1997 Reissue) *(movie version take 4)*
King Creole (1997 Reissue) *(movie version take 8)*
(The) King Of Rock 'N' Roll - 50's Masters - Disc 4
(The) King Of Rock 'N' Roll - 50's Masters - Disc 5 *(alternate take 8)*

As We Travel Along The Jerico Road
(The) Million Dollar Quartet

Ask Me
Collectors Gold - Disc 2 *(alternate take 2)*
Elvis' Gold Records Volume 4
Elvis' Gold Records Volume 4 (1997 Reissue)
Elvis! His Greatest Hits - Disc 3
Elvis His Life And Music - Disc 4
(The) Elvis Presley Collection - The Romantic - Disc 2
Elvis The Other Sides - Worldwide Gold Award Hits - Volume 2 - Disc 2
From Nashville To Memphis - 60's Masters - Disc 3
(The) Lost Album
Sixties Legends - Elvis Presley - Disc 2

"B"

(You're So Square) Baby I Don't Care
A Date With Elvis
(The) Blue Suede Box - Elvis: His Greatest Soundtracks - Disc 2
Elvis!Elvis!Elvis! - The King And His Movies
(The) Elvis Presley Collection - Movie Magic - Disc 1
Elvis Presley Sings Leiber & Stoller
Elvis The King 1954-1965
Elvis The Other Sides - Worldwide Gold Award Hits Volume 2 - Disc 1
Essential Elvis - The First Movies *(alternate takes 16 & 6)*
Jailhouse Rock and Love Me Tender
(The) King Of Rock 'N' Roll - 50's Masters - Disc 3
(The) King Of Rock 'N' Roll - 50's Masters - Promo
Rocker
Various Artists
Leiber & Stoller Music Publishing (6 CD Promo Set)

Baby, If You'll Give Me All Of Your Love
Elvis Double Features - Spinout & Double Trouble
Mahalo From Elvis

Baby Let's Play House
A Date With Elvis
A Golden Celebration - Disc 1 - Dorsey Bros. Show New York Feb. 4, 1956
A Golden Celebration - Disc 3 - Miss.-Alabama Dairy Show Tupelo Evening Sept. 26, 1956
A Touch Of Platinum Vol. 2 - A Life In Music - Disc 1 (Las Vegas Rehearsals)
Elvis Country *(1983 overdubbed version)*
Elvis' Golden Records (1997 Reissue)
Elvis' Greatest Jukebox Hits
Elvis! His Greatest Hits - Disc 4
(The) Elvis Presley Birthday Tribute 1992 - Disc 1
(The) Elvis Presley Collection - Rhythm & Blues - Disc 2
Elvis The Tribute - A Biography - Disc 3
Elvis 15th Anniversary Radio Show - Disc 1
Good Rockin' Tonight - Disc 1
(The) King Of Rock 'N' Roll - 50's Masters - Disc 1
(The) Louisiana Hayride - Anthologies Of Legends - Elvis Presley
(The) Louisiana Hayride Archives Volume 1 (8/20/55)
Memories Of Elvis - 1991 - Disc 3
Memories Of Elvis - 1993 - Disc 1
Platinum - A Life In Music - Disc 3 (Las Vegas Rehearsals)
(The) Private Presley CD
Raw Elvis
Remembering Elvis
(The) Sun Sessions CD
Vintage 55 Elvis
Various Artists
Solid Gold Country - Elvis Presley And TV
Solid Gold Country - Elvis Presley Birthday Tribute - 92-1
Solid Gold Country - Elvis Presley Birthday Tribute - 93-1
Solid Gold Country - Elvis Presley Memorial Tribute - 91-8
Solid Gold Country - Elvis Presley Memorial Tribute - 92-8
Solid Gold Country - Elvis Presley Memorial Tribute - 93-8
Solid Gold Country - The Complete 50's Masters
Solid Gold Scrapbook - Elvis In Memphis
The Sun Records Collection

#4 Baby What You Want Me To Do
A Golden Celebration - Disc 4 - Burbank, Calif. June 27, 1968 *(2 alternate takes)*
A Private Moment With The King *(home recording)*
A Touch Of Platinum Vol. 2 - A Life In Music- Disc 1 (Las Vegas 1969)
Collectors Gold - Disc 3 (Las Vegas 1969)
Elvis Aron Presley - Disc 2
Elvis A Legendary Performer Vol. 2
Elvis/NBC TV Special (Lawdy Miss Clawdy/Baby What You Want Me To Do)
Elvis/NBC TV Special (Baby What You Want Me To Do/That's All Right/Blue Christmas/One Night/Tiger Man)
(The) Elvis Presley Collection - Rhythm & Blues - Disc 2 (NBC TV Special)
(The) Elvis Presley Collection - Rock 'N' Roll - Disc 2 *(dressing room jam)*
Elvis Presley: Great Performances
Elvis Presley - The King Of Rock & Roll At His Best - Disc 4
(The) Legend Lives On - Disc 4
Memories - The '68 Comeback Special - Disc 1 *(previously unreleased)*
Memories - The '68 Comeback Special - Disc 2 *(previously unreleased rehearsal)*
Memories - The '68 Comeback Special - Disc 2 *(previously unreleased sit down show)*
Memories - The '68 Comeback Special - Disc 2
Platinum - A Life In Music - Disc 3 (Las Vegas 1969)
Platinum In-Store Sampler (Promo)
Tiger Man *(previously unreleased)*
Tiger Man (version 2) *(previously unreleased)*

Barefoot Ballad
Elvis Double Features - Kissin' Cousins, Clambake & Stay Away Joe

Beach Boy Blues
Blue Hawaii
Blue Hawaii (1997 Reissue)
Blue Hawaii (1997 Reissue) *(movie version alternate take 3)*
Blue Hawaii (1997 Reissue Collectors Edition)
Blue Hawaii (1997 Reissue Collectors Edition) *(movie version alternate take 3)*
(The) Blue Suede Box - Elvis: His Greatest Soundtracks - Disc 4
(The) Blue Suede Box - Elvis: His Greatest Soundtracks - Disc 4 *(movie version alternate take 3)*
Command Performances - 60's Masters - Disc 1

Beach Shack
Elvis Double Features - Spinout & Double Trouble

Because Of Love
Command Performances - 60's Masters - Disc 1
Elvis Double Features - Canister Set - Disc 1
Elvis Double Features - Kid Galahad & Girls! Girls! Girls!

Beginner's Luck
Elvis Double Features - Frankie & Johnnie & Paradise Hawaiian Style

Beyond The Bend
Collectors Gold - Disc 1 *(alternate takes 1 & 2)*
Elvis Double Features - Canister Set - Disc 2
Elvis Double Features - It Happened At the Worlds Fair & Fun In Acapulco

Beyond The Reef
Elvis Aron Presley - Disc 3
From Nashville To Memphis - 60's Masters - Disc 3 *(original undubbed master)*

Big Boots
(The) Blue Suede Box - Elvis: His Greatest Soundtracks - Disc 5
(The) Blue Suede Box - Elvis: His Greatest Soundtracks - Disc 5 *(fast version take 7)*
(The) Blue Suede Box - Elvis: His Greatest Soundtracks - Disc 5 *(acoustic version alternate take 2)*
Collectors Gold - Disc 1 *(alternate take 10)*
G.I. Blues
G.I. Blues (1997 Reissue)
G.I. Blues (1997 Reissue) *(fast version take 7)*
G.I. Blues (1997 Reissue) *(accoustic version alternate take 2)*
G.I. Blues (1997 Reissue Collectors Edition)
G.I. Blues (1997 Reissue Collectors Edition) *(fast version take 7)*
G.I. Blues (1997 Reissue Collectors Edition) *(accoustic version alternate take 2)*

Big Boss Man
An Elvis Double Feature: Speedway, Clambake
Blue Suede Shoes (Original Soundtrack) Disc 2
Double Dynamite
Elvis' Gold Records Volume 5 (1997 Reissue)
Elvis/NBC - TV Special Disc 3
(The) Elvis Presley Collection - Rhythm & Blues - Disc 1
Elvis Sings Hits From His Movies Volume 1
From Nashville To Memphis - 60's Masters - Disc 3
From Nashville To Memphis - 60's Masters - Disc 5 *(alternate take 2)*
Memories - The '68 Comeback Special - Disc 1
Various Artists
The Elvis Presley Years - Disc 3

Big Love Big Heartache
Elvis Double Features - Canister Set - Disc 3
Elvis Double Features - Viva Las Vegas & Roustabout

Bitter They Are Harder They Fall
Always On My Mind
From Elvis Presley Blvd. Memphis, Tennessee, Recorded Live

Black Star
Collectors Gold - Disc 1 *(take unknown)*
Elvis Double Features - Flaming Star, Wild In The Country & Follow That Dream

Blessed Jesus (Hold My Hand)
(The) Million Dollar Quartet

Blowin' In The Wind
A Touch Of Platinum - A Life In Music - Disc 2 - (Graceland & Palm Springs Segment) *(home recording)*
Platinum - A Life In Music - Disc 2 (Graceland & Palm Springs Segment) *(home recording)*

Blue Christmas
A Golden Celebration - Disc 4 - Elvis - Burbank, Calif. June 27, 1968
Blue Christmas
Country Christmas - Elvis Presley Country Christmas - Jim Reeves Holiday Hits
Christmas Classics
Christmas Wishes From Anne Murray, Glen Campbell & Elvis Presley
Christmas With Elvis
Don't Be Cruel
Elvis Aron Presley - Disc 2
Elvis Christmas Album
Elvis Christmas Album (Camden)
Elvis! His Greatest Hits - Disc 1
Elvis /NBC-TV Special
Elvis Presley & Jim Reeves Christmas Favorites
Elvis Presley Radio Special (Promo)
Elvis Sings The Wonderful World Of Christmas (bonus track)
If Every Day Was Like Christmas
If Every Day Was Like Christmas - Special Collectors Edition
(The) King Of Rock 'N' Roll - 50's Masters - Disc 3
(The) Legend Lives On - Disc 4
Merry Christmas
Memories - The '68 Comeback Special - Disc 2 *(previously unreleased)*
Memories Of Christmas
Tiger Man
Various Artists
American Gold With Dick Bartley 93-12 Show 51
American Gold With Dick Bartley 97-12 Show 51
Billboard Christmas 4 Pack
Billboard's Greatest Christmas Hits - 1955 - Present
Christmas Classics Volume 1
Country Christmas
Dick Clark's Rock 'N' Roll Christmas
Happy Holidays From ASCAP - The ASCAP Holiday Musical Special (Promo)
Holiday Music 1992 Collection
Honky Tonk Christmas With Alan Jackson
I Believe - Best Loved Stars Of Inspiration
K-Tel's Christmas Rock Greats
RCA Christmas 1996 (Promo)
RCA Christmas 1997 (Promo)
Solid Gold Christmas - Christmas With Elvis Presley
Time-Life Treasury Of Christmas Vol.2
We Wish You A Merry Christmas
Yule Fuel - 1992 Rhino Christmas Sampler (Promo)

BLUE CHRISTMAS (cont'd)
Yule Train - A Rhino Christmas Sampler (Promo)

Blue Eyes Crying In The Rain
(The) Elvis Presley Collection - Country - Disc 2
From Elvis Presley Blvd. Memphis, Tennessee, Recorded Live

Blue Hawaii
Aloha From Hawaii Via Satellite - 25th Anniversary Edition
(The) Alternate Aloha
Blue Hawaii
Blue Hawaii (1997 Reissue)
Blue Hawaii (1997 Reissue) *(alternate take 3)*
Blue Hawaii (1997 Reissue Collectors Edition)
Blue Hawaii (1997 Reissue Collectors Edition) *(alternate take 3)*
(The) Blue Suede Box - Elvis: His Greatest Soundtracks - Disc 4
(The) Blue Suede Box - Elvis: His Greatest Soundtracks - Disc 4 *(alternate take 3)*
Command Performances - 60's Masters - Disc 1
Elvis Aron Presley - Forever
Elvis A Legendary Performer Volume 2
Elvis! His Greatest Hits - Disc 3
(The) Elvis Presley Collection - Love Songs - Disc 2
Elvis Presley: Great Performances
Elvis Presley - (The) King Of Rock & Roll At His Best - Disc 4
Elvis Presley - 50 Greatest Hits - Disc 2
Elvis 50 Years - 50 Hits - Disc 2
(The) Honeymoon Companion (Promo)
Mahalo From Elvis

Blue Moon
A Touch Of Platinum - A Life In Music - Disc 1 *(alternate take 3)*
Elvis Presley
(The) Elvis Presley Collection - The Romantic - Disc 2
Elvis Presley - Collectors Edition
(The) King Of Rock 'N' Roll - 50's Masters - Disc 1
(The) King Of Rock 'N' Roll - 50's Masters - Disc 5 *(alternate take 1)*
(The) Legend Lives On - Disc 2
Platinum - A Life In Music - Disc 1 *(alternate take 3)*
(The) Sun Sessions CD (the master takes)
Various Artists
Mystery Train (Original Soundtrack)

Blue Moon Of Kentucky
A Date With Elvis
A Golden Celebration - Disc 1 *(alternate take 1)*
Elvis The Tribute - A Biography - Disc 1
(The) Elvis Presley Collection - Country - Disc 1
(The) Elvis Presley Collection - Treasures ' 53 To '58 - Disc 2 *(alternate take 1)*
Great Country Songs
(The) King Of Rock 'N' Roll - 50's Masters - Disc 1
(The) King Of Rock 'N' Roll - 50's Masters - Disc 5 *(alternate take)*
(The) Louisiana Hayride - Anthologies Of Legends - Elvis Presley
(The) Louisiana Hayride Archives Volume 1 (10/16/54)
(The) Private Presley CD
Raw Elvis
Remembering Elvis
(The) Sun Sessions CD (the master takes)
(The) Sun Sessions CD (the outtakes)
Vintage 55 Elvis
Various Artists
Country USA - 1954
Classic Country Music II - A Smithsonian Collection

BLUE MOON OF KENTUCKY (cont'd)
Solid Gold Scrapbook - Elvis In Memphis
Sun's Greatest Hits

Blue River
From Nashville To Memphis - 60's Masters - Disc 3
(The) Lost Album

Blue Suede Shoes
A Golden Celebration - Disc 1 - Dorsey Bros. Show New York Feb. 11, 1956
A Golden Celebration - Disc 1 - Dorsey Bros. Show New York March 17, 1956
A Golden Celebration - Disc 2 - Milton Berle Show San Diego April 3, 1956
A Golden Celebration - Disc 3 - Miss.-Alabama Dairy Show Tupelo Evening Sept. 26, 1956
A Golden Celebration - Disc 4 - Elvis - Burbank, Calif. June 27, 1968
Aloha From Hawaii Via Satellite
Aloha From Hawaii Via Satellite - 25th Anniversary Edition
(The) Alternate Aloha
An Afternoon In The Garden
(The) Blue Suede Box - Elvis: His Greatest Soundtracks - Disc 5
Blue Suede Shoes (Original Soundtrack) Disc 1
Blue Suede Shoes (Original Soundtrack) Disc 2 *(instrumental)*
Blue Suede Shoes/Tutti Frutti (Jukebox Single)
Collectors Gold - Disc 3 (Las Vegas 1969)
Commemorative Jukebox Series (5 CD Set) - Disc 4
Elvis A Legendary Performer Volume 2
Elvis Aron Presley Disc 1
Elvis Birthday Tribute & Radio Show
Elvis' Golden Records (1997 Reissue)
Elvis! His Greatest Hits - Disc 1
Elvis In Person At The International Hotel
Elvis / NBC - TV Special
(The) Elvis Presley Birthday Tribute 1992 - Disc 1
(The) Elvis Presley Collection - Rock 'N' Roll - Disc 2
Elvis Presley - Collectors Edition
Elvis Presley: Great Performances
Elvis Presley Radio Special
Elvis Presley The King Of Rock & Roll At His Best - Disc 4
Elvis The King: 1954-1965
Elvis The Legend - Disc 1
Elvis The Tribute - A Biography - Disc 1 *(live version)*
Elvis 15th Anniversary Radio Show - Disc 5
Elvis 20th Anniversary Radio Show - Disc 1
Elvis 56
Elvis 56 Advance Music (Promo)
Elvis Presley
G.I. Blues
G.I. Blues (1997 Reissue)
G.I. Blues (1997 Reissue Collectors Edition)
Good Rockin' Tonight - Disc 1
Great Hits Of 1956-57
(The) Great Performances
(The) King Of Rock 'N' Roll - 50's Masters - Disc 1
(The) King Of Rock 'N' Roll - 50's Masters - Disc 5 (Las Vegas 1956)
(The) Legend Lives On - Disc 4
Memories - The '68 Comeback Special - Disc 1 *(previously unreleased)*
Memories - The '68 Comeback Special - Disc 2
Memories Of Elvis - 1991 - Disc 3
Memories Of Elvis - 1993 - Disc 1
Rocker
Tiger Man
Various Artists
Heart Of Dixie (Original Soundtrack)
Heart Of Dixie (Original Soundtrack Promo)
Solid Gold Country - Elvis Presley & TV

BLUE SUEDE SHOES (cont'd)
Solid Gold Country - Elvis Presley Live

Blueberry Hill
A Touch Of Platinum - A Life In Music - Disc 1 *(1957 acetate)*
(The) Blue Suede Box - Elvis: His Greatest Soundtracks - Disc 1
Elvis Aron Presley - Forever
(The) Elvis Presley Collection - Treasures '53 To '58 - Disc 2
Elvis Recorded Live On Stage In Memphis
Essential Elvis Vol. 2 - Stereo 57 *(alternate takes 2,7)*
(The) King Of Rock 'N' Roll - 50's Masters - Disc 3
Loving You (1997 Reissue)
Platinum - A Life In Music - Disc 1 *(1957 acetate)*

Bosom Of Abraham
A Touch Of Platinum Vol. 2 - A Life In Music - Disc 2 *(alternate take 3)*
Amazing Grace - His Greatest Sacred Performances - Disc 2
Amazing Grace - His Greatest Sacres Performances - Disc 2 *(previously unreleased)*
(The) Elvis Presley Collection - Gospel - Disc 1
(The) Elvis Presley Gospel Treasury - Disc 1
He Touched Me
Platinum - A Life In Music - Disc 4 *(alternate take 3)*
Selections From Amazing Grace - His Greatest Sacred Performances (Promo)

Bossa Nova Baby
A Touch Of Platinum - A Life In Music - Disc 2 *(alternate take 2)*
Blue Suede Shoes (Original Soundtrack) - Disc 2
Command Performances - 60's Masters - Disc 1
Elvis Double Features - Canister Set - Disc 2
Elvis Double Features - It Happened At The Worlds Fair - Fun In Acapulco
Elvis' Gold Records Volume 4 (1997 Reissue)
Elvis! His Greatest Hits - Disc 3
(The) Elvis Presley Birthday Tribute 1992 - Disc 1
(The) Elvis Presley Collection - Movie Magic - Disc 2
Elvis Presley Sings Leiber & Stoller
Elvis The Legend - Disc 3
Elvis The Tribute - A Biography - Disc 3
Elvis 50 Worldwide Gold Hits Vol. 1 - Disc 2
Memories Of Elvis - 1991 - Disc 1
Memories Of Elvis - 1993 - Disc 3
Platinum - A Life In Music - Disc 2 *(alternate take 2)*
Platinum In-Store Sampler (Promo) *(alternate take 2)*
Sixties Legends - Elvis Presley - Disc 1
(The) Top Ten Hits - Disc 2
Various Artists
Leiber & Stoller The 60's, 70's, 80's (Promo)
Leiber & Stoller Publishing (6 CD Promo Set)
Solid Gold Country - Elvis Presley Sings Leiber And Stoller
Solid Gold Scrapbook - Elvis Movie Music

Bridge Over Troubled Water
A Touch Of Platinum Vol. 2 - A Life In Music - Disc 1 (Las Vegas 1970)
(The) Elvis Presley Collection - From The Heart - Disc 2
Essential Elvis Vol.4 - A Hundred Years From Now *(alternate take 5)*
Heart & Soul *(unreleased - undubbed version)*
(The) Legend Lives On - Disc 2
Platinum - A Life In Music - Disc 3 (Las Vegas 1970)
Platinum In-Store Sampler (Promo)
That's The Way It Is
That's The Way It Is - Original Master Recording
Walk A Mile In My Shoes - 70's Masters - Disc 3
Various Artists
Country Soft 'N' Mellow

Bringin' It Back
Elvis Aron Presley - Forever
Elvis Today
Walk A Mile In My Shoes - 70's Box Set - Disc 2

Britches
Elvis Double Features - Flaming Star, Wild In The Country & Follow That Dream

Brown Eyed Handsome Man
(The) Million Dollar Quartet (3 Performances)

Burning Love
A Touch Of Platinum Vol. 2 - A Life In Music - Disc 2 *(alternate take 1)*
Aloha From Hawaii Via Satellite
Aloha From Hawaii Via Satellite - 25th Anniversary Edition
(The) Alternate Aloha
Burning Love And Hits From His Movies Vol. 2
Double Dynamite
Elvis Aron Presley - Disc 4
Elvis' Gold Records Volume 5
Elvis' Gold Records Volume 5 (1997 Reissue)
Elvis' Greatest Jukebox Hits
Elvis! His Greatest Hits - Disc 4
(The) Elvis Presley Birthday Tribute 1992 - Disc 1
(The) Elvis Presley Collection - Rock 'N' Roll - Disc 1
(The) Elvis Presley Collection - The Rocker - Disc 2 *(alternate take)*
Elvis Presley - The King Of Rock & Roll At His Best - Disc 2
Elvis The Legend - Disc 3
Elvis The Tribute - A Biography - Disc 3
Elvis 15th Anniversary Radio Show - Disc 5
Elvis 20th Anniversary Sampler *(alternate take 1)*
(The) Honeymoon Companion (Promo)
King Of The Whole Wide World - Collectors Set - The Elvis Medley
(The) Legend Lives On - Disc 2
Memories Of Elvis - 1991 - Disc 3
Memories Of Elvis - 1993 - Disc 3
Platinum - A Life In Music - Disc 4 *(alternate take 1)*
Platinum In-Store Sampler (Promo) *(alternate take 1)*
(The) Top Ten Hits - Disc 2
Virtual Graceland CD-ROM
Walk A Mile In My Shoes - '70's Masters - Disc 1
Walk A Mile In My Shoes - Out Of The Box Sampler (Promo)
Various Artists
Dick Clark's Rock & Roll Remember 1/2-1/5
Dick Clark's Rock & Roll Remember 08/12-08/14
(The) Elvis Presley Years - Disc 4
Heartbreak Hotel (Original Soundtrack)
Keepin' The '70's Alive
Nipper's Greatest Hits - The '70's
(The) Oldies Countdown
Solid Gold Country - Elvis Presley And TV
Solid Gold Country - Elvis Presley Birthday Tribute - 92-1
Solid Gold Country - Elvis Presley Birthday Tribute - 93-1
Solid Gold Country - Elvis Presley's Golden Records - 91-11
Solid Gold Country - Elvis Presley's Golden Records - 93-2
Solid Gold Country - Elvis Presley Live
Solid Gold Country - Elvis Presley's Love Songs
Solid Gold Country - Elvis Presley Memorial Tribute - 91-8
Solid Gold Country - Elvis Presley Memorial Tribute - 92-8
Solid Gold Country - Elvis Presley Memorial Tribute - 93-8
Your Goodtime Oldies Magazine - 92-33
Your Goodtime Oldies Magazine - 93-20
Your Goodtime Oldies Magazine - 94-06

BURNING LOVE (cont'd)
Your Goodtime Oldies Magazine - 94-19

By And By
Amazing Grace - His Greatest Sacred Performances - Disc 1
(The) Elvis Presley Collection - Gospel - Disc 1
(The) Elvis Presley Gospel Treasury - Disc 2
How Great Thou Art

"C"

C'mon Everybody
Elvis Double Features - Canister Set - Disc 3
Elvis Double Features - Viva Las Vegas & Roustabout
(The) Elvis Presley Collection - Movie Magic - Disc 1

Can't Help Falling In Love
A Touch Of Platinum - A Life In Music - Disc 2
A Valentine Gift For You
Aloha From Hawaii Via Satellite
Aloha From Hawaii Via Satellite - 25th Anniversary Edition
(The) Alternate Hawaii
An Afternoon In The Garden
Blue Hawaii
Blue Hawaii (1997 Reissue)
Blue Hawaii (1997 Reissue) *(movie version take 23)*
Blue Hawaii (1997 Reissue Collectors Edition)
Blue Hawaii (1997 Reissue Collectors Edition) *(movie version take 23)*
(The) Blue Suede Box - Elvis: His Greatest Soundtracks - Disc 4
(The) Blue Suede Box - Elvis: His Greatest Soundtracks - Disc 4 *(movie version take 23)*
Can't Help Falling In Love/Rock A Hula Baby (Jukebox Single)
Command Performances - 60's Masters - Disc 1
Commemorative Juke Box Series (5 CD Set) - Disc 2
Don't Be Cruel/ Can't Help Falling In Love
Elvis Aron Presley - Disc 2 *(alternate take 24)*
Elvis Aron Presley - Disc 4
Elvis As Recorded Live At Madison Square Garden
Elvis A Legendary Performer Volume 1
Elvis!Elvis!Elvis! - The King And His Movies
Elvis' Golden Records Vol. 3 (1997 Reissue)
Elvis! His Greatest Hits - Disc 2
Elvis In Concert
Elvis In Person At The International Hotel
Elvis/ NBC - TV Special
(The) Elvis Presley Birthday Tribute 1992 - Disc 1
(The) Elvis Presley Collection - Love Songs - Disc 2
(The) Elvis Presley Collection - Movie Magic - Disc 2 *(movie version take 23)*
Elvis Presley: Great Performances
Elvis Presley - The King Of Rock & Roll At His Best - Disc 3
Elvis Presley: 1954-1961
Elvis Presley - 50 Greatest Hits - Disc 2
Elvis Recorded Live On Stage In Memphis
Elvis The Legend - Disc 2
Elvis The Tribute - A Biography - Disc 3
Elvis 15th Anniversary Radio Show
Elvis 20th Anniversary Radio Show - Disc 2
Elvis 20th Anniversary Sampler *(movie version take 23)*
Elvis 20th Anniversary Singles Set - Disc 3
Elvis 24 Karat Gold!
Elvis 50 Worldwide Gold Hits Vol. 1 - Disc 2
Elvis 50 Years 50 Hits - Disc 2
Heart & Soul
Honeymoon Companion (Promo)

Page 485

CAN'T HELP FALLING IN LOVE (cont'd)
(The) Legend Lives On - Disc 3
(The) Legend Of A King - Disc 1
Love Songs
Memories - The '68 Comeback Special - Disc 1
Memories Of Elvis - 1991 - Disc 4
Memories Of Elvis - 1993 - Disc 2
Platinum - A Life In Music - Disc 2
Sixties Legends - Elvis Presley - Disc 1
(The) Top Ten Hits - Disc 2
Various Artists
American Gold With Dick Bartley 95-2 Show 6
Dick Clark's Rock Roll & Remember 08/12-08/14
Easy Listening Hits Of The '60's & 70's
(The) Elvis Presley Years - Disc 2
Love Me Tender
Solid Gold Country - Elvis Presley Birthday Tribute 93-1
Solid Gold Country - Elvis Presley In Concert
Solid Gold Country - Elvis Presley Live
Solid Gold Country - Elvis Presley's Love Songs
Solid Gold Country - Elvis Presley Memorial Tribute - 92-8
Solid Gold Country - Elvis Presley Memorial Tribute - 93-8
Solid Gold Scrapbook - Elvis Movie Music
The Many Moods Of Romance - As Time Goes By

Carny Town
Elvis Double Features - Canister Set - Disc 3
Elvis Double Features - Viva Las Vegas & Roustabout

Catchin' On Fast
Elvis Double Features - Kissin' Cousins, Clambake & Stay Away Joe

Cattle Call
A Touch Of Platinum Vol. 2 - A Life In Music - Disc 1 (Las Vegas Rehearsals)
Platinum - A Life In Music - Disc 3 (Las Vegas Rehearsals)

Change Of Habit
Command Performances - 60's Masters - Disc 2
Elvis Double Features - Live A Little, Love A Little, Charro, The Trouble With Girls & Change Of Habit

Charro
Almost In Love
Command Performances - 60's Masters - Disc 2
Elvis Double Features - Live A Little, Love A Little, Charro, The Trouble With Girls & Change Of Habit

Chesay
Elvis Double Features - Frankie and Johnny & Paradise Hawaiian Style

Cindy, Cindy
Essential Elvis Vol. 4 - A Hundred Years From Now *(alternate take 1)*
Love Letters
Walk A Mile In My Shoes - 70's Masters - Disc 3

City By Night
Elvis Double Features - Spinout & Double Trouble

Clambake
An Elvis Double Feature: Speedway & Clambake
Command Performances - 60's Masters - Disc 2
Elvis Double Features - Kissin' Cousins, Clambake & Stay Away Joe
Elvis Double Features - Kissin' Cousins, Clambake & Stay Away Joe *(reprise)*

Clean Up Your Own Backyard

Almost In Love
Command Performances - 60's Masters - Disc 2
Elvis Double Features - Live A Little, Love A Little, Charro, The Trouble With Girls & Change Of Habit
Elvis Double Features - Live A Little Love, A Little, Charro, The Trouble With Girls & Change Of Habit (*Undub.*)
Elvis' Gold Records Volume 5
Elvis' Gold Records Volume 5 (1997 Reissue)

Come Along

Elvis Double Features - Frankie & Johnnie & Paradise Hawaiian Style

Come What May (You Are Mine)

Collectors Gold - Disc 2 (*alternate take 6*)
From Nashville To Memphis - 60's Masters - Disc 3 (*alternate take 7*)
Various Artists
Leiber & Stoller Music Publishing (Promo Set)

Confidence

Elvis Double Features - Kissin' Cousins, Clambake & Stay Away Joe
Elvis Sings Hits From His Movies Volume 1

Cotton Candy Land

Elvis Double Features - Canister Set - Disc 2
Elvis Double Features - It Happened At The Worlds Fair & Fun In Acapulco
Elvis Sings For Children & Growups Too!

Could I Fall In Love

Elvis Double Features - Spinout & Double Trouble

Crawfish

(The) Blue Suede Box - Elvis: His Greatest Soundtracks - Disc 3
Elvis!Elvis!Elvis! - The King And His Movies
(The) Elvis Presley Collection - Movie Magic - Disc1
Elvis The Other Sides - Worldwide Gold Award Hits Volume 2 - Disc 1
Essential Elvis Vol. 3 - Hits Like Never Before (*track F alternate take 7, full length version*)
King Creole
King Creole (1997 Reissue)
(The) King Of Rock 'N' Roll - 50's Masters - Disc 4

Crazy Arms

The Million Dollar Quartet (*2 Performances*)

Cross My Heart And Hope To Die

Elvis Double Features - Canister Set - Disc 4
Elvis Double Features - Harum Scarum & Girl Happy

Crying In The Chapel

Amazing Grace - His Greatest Sacred Performances - Disc 1
Elvis' Gold Records Volume 4 (1997 Reissue)
(The) Elvis Presley Birthday Tribute 1992 - Disc 1
(The) Elvis Presley Collection - Gospel - Disc 1
(The) Elvis Presley Gospel Treasury - Disc 1
(The) Elvis Presley Gospel Treasury (Special Edition)
Elvis Presley - 50 Greatest Hits - Disc 2
Elvis The King: 1954-1965
Elvis The Legend - Disc 3
Elvis The Tribute - A Biography - Disc 2
Elvis 15th Anniversary Radio Show - Disc 6
Elvis 24 Karat Hits!
Elvis 50 Yrs 50 Hits - Disc 2

CRYING IN THE CHAPEL (cont'd
Elvis 50 Worldwide Gold Hits - Disc 1
How Great Thou Art)
Memories Of Elvis - 1991 - Disc 2
Memories Of Elvis - 1993 - Disc 3
Sixties Legends - Elvis Presley - Disc 2
(The) Top Ten Hits - Disc 2
Various Artists
Classic Country 1965-1969
Country Memories
Dick Clarks Rock Roll & Remember 1/3-1/5
Dick Clarks Rock Roll & Remember 08/12-08/14
(The) Elvis Years - Disc 2
Solid Gold Country - Elvis: What Happened?
Solid Gold Country - Elvis Presley Birthday Tribute - 92-1
Solid Gold Country - Elvis Presley In Nashville
Solid Gold Country - Elvis Presley Memorial Tribute - 91-8
Solid Gold Country - Elvis Presley Memorial Tribute - 92-8
Solid Gold Country - 70 Years Of RCA Country
Solid Gold Scrapbook - Elvis Golden Decade 1956-1965
The Super 60's
50 Beloved Songs Of Faith

"D"

Dainty Little Moonbeams
Elvis Double Features - Canister Set
Elvis Double Features - Kid Galahad & Girls!Girls!Girls!

Danny
(The) Blue Suede Box - Elvis: His Greatest Soundtracks - Disc 3
(The) Elvis Presley Collection - Movie Magic - Disc 1
Essential Elvis Vol. 3 Hits Like Never Before
King Creole (1997 Reissue)
(The) King Of Rock 'N' Roll - 50's Masters - Disc 4

Danny Boy
A Golden Celebration - Disc 4 - Elvis At Home - Germany 1958-60
A Touch Of Platinum Vol. 2 - A Life In Music - Disc 2 *(alternate take 9)*
(The) Elvis Presley Collection - From The Heart - Disc 1
Elvis Presley - 50 Greatest Hits - Disc 1
Elvis 50 Yrs - 50 Hits - Disc 1
From Elvis Presley Boulevard - Memphis, Tennessee, Recorded Live
Platinum - A Life In Music - Disc 4 *(alternate take 9)*
Walk A Mile In My Shoes - 70's Masters - Disc 4

Dark Moon
A Golden Celebration - Disc 4 - Collectors Treasures - Graceland *(home recording)*

Datin'
Elvis Aron Presley - Disc 2 *(alternate takes 6-8, 11-12)*
Elvis Double Features - Frankie & Johnny & Paradise Hawaiian Style

(You're The) Devil In Disguise
Blue Suede Shoes (Original Soundtrack) Disc 1
Elvis' Gold Records Volume 4
Elvis' Gold Records Volume 4 (1997 Reissue)
Elvis' Greatest Jukebox Hits
Elvis! His Greatest Hits - Disc 3
Elvis His Life And Music - Disc 4
(The) Elvis Presley Birthday Tribute 1992 - Disc 4
(The) Elvis Presley Collection - Rock 'N' Roll - Disc 1
Elvis Presley - 50 Greatest Hits - Disc 1

(YOU'RE THE) DEVIL IN DISGUISE (cont'd)
Elvis The King: 1954-1965
Elvis The Legend - Disc 3
Elvis The Tribute A Biography - Disc 1
Elvis 15th Anniversary Radio Show - Disc 2
Elvis 20th Anniversary Radio Show - Disc 3
Elvis 24 Karat Hits!
Elvis 50 Worldwide Gold Hits - Disc 2
Elvis 50 Years 50 Hits - Disc 1
From Nashville To Memphis - 60's Masters - Disc 2
(The) Honeymoon Companion (Promo)
(The) Lost Album
Memories Of Elvis - 1991 - Disc 2
Memories Of Elvis - 1993 - Disc 3
Sixties Legends - Elvis Presley - Disc 1
(The) Top Ten Hits - Disc 2
Various Artists
Dick Clark's Rock Roll & Remember - 08/12-08/14
She Devil (Original Soundtrack)
Solid Gold Country - Elvis Presley's Golden Records - 91-11
Solid Gold Country - Elvis Presley's Golden Records - 93-2
Solid Gold Country - Elvis Presley In Nashville
Solid Gold Country - Elvis Presley Memorial Tribute - 92-8
Solid Gold Country - Elvis Presley Memorial Tribute - 93-8
These Were Our Songs: The Early 60's
Your Goodtime Oldies Magazine 92-43

Didja' Ever
(The) Blue Suede Box - Elvis: His Greatest Soundtracks - Disc 5
(The) Blue Suede Box - Elvis: His Greatest Soundtracks - Disc 5 *(alternate take 1)*
Elvis 15th Anniversary Radio Show - Disc 3
G I Blues
G.I. Blues (1997 Reissue)
G.I. Blues (1997 Reissue) *(alternate take 1)*
G.I. Blues (1997 Reissue Collectors Edition)
G.I. Blues (1997 Reissue Collectors Edition) *(alternate take 1)*

Dirty Dirty Feeling
Elvis Is Back
Elvis Is Back - 24 kt Gold Disc
(The) Elvis Presley Collection - The Rocker - Disc 1
Elvis Presley Sings Leiber & Stoller
From Nashville To Memphis - 60's Masters - Disc 1
Various Artists
Leiber & Stoller Music Publishing (6 CD Promo Set)

Dixieland Rock
(The) Blue Suede Box - Elvis: His Greatest Soundtracks - Disc 3
(The) Elvis Presley Collection - The Rocker - Disc 2
Elvis The Other Sides - Worldwide Gold Award Hits Volume 2 - Disc 1
King Creole
King Creole (1997 Reissue)
(The) King Of Rock 'N' Roll - 50's Masters - Disc 4

Do Not Disturb
Elvis Double Features - Canister Set - Disc 4
Elvis Double Features - Harum Scarum & Girl Happy

Do The Clam
Command Performances - 60's Masters - Disc 2
Elvis Double Features - Canister Set - Disc 4
Elvis Double Features - Harum Scarum & Girl Happy

Do The Vega
Elvis Double Features - Canister Set - Disc 3
Elvis Double Features - Viva Las Vegas & Roustabout

Do You Know Who I Am?
Back In Memphis
From Nashville To Memphis - 60's Masters - Disc 5

Doin' The Best I Can
(The) Blue Suede Box - Elvis: His Greatest Soundtracks - Disc 5
(The) Blue Suede Box - Elvis: His Greatest Soundtracks - Disc 5 *(alternate take 9)*
Command Performances - 60's Masters - Disc 1
(The) Elvis Presley Collection - The Romantic - Disc 2
G I Blues
G.I. Blues (1997 Reissue)
G.I. Blues (1997 Reissue) *(alternate take 9)*
G.I. Blues (1997 Reissue Collectors Edition)
G.I. Blues (1997 Reissue Collectors Edition) *(alternate take 9)*

Dominic

Elvis Double Features - Kissin' Cousins, Clambake & Stay Away Joe

Don't
A Touch Of Platinum Vol. 2 - A Life In Music - Disc 1 (Las Vegas Rehearsals)
Elvis' Gold Records Vol. 2 50,000,000 Elvis Fans Can't Be Wrong
Elvis' Gold Records Vol. 2 50,000,000 Elvis Fans Can't Be Wrong (1997 Reissue)
Elvis! His Greatest Hits - Disc 1
Elvis His Life And Music (Box Set) Disc 2
(The) Elvis Presley Birthday Tribute 1992 - Disc 1
(The) Elvis Presley Collection - Love Songs - Disc 1
Elvis Presley Sings Leiber & Stoller
Elvis Presley Radio Special
Elvis Presley - 50 Greatest Hits - Disc 1
Elvis Presley - 1954-1961
Elvis The Legend - Disc 1
Elvis 50 Years -50 Hits - Disc 1
Elvis 15th Anniversary Radio Show - Disc 2
Elvis 50 Worldwide Gold Hits Vol.1 - Disc 4
Heart And Soul
(The) King Of Rock 'N' Roll - 50's Masters - Disc 4
Memories Of Elvis - 1991 - Disc 1
Memories Of Elvis - 1993 - Disc 2
(The) Number One Hits
Platinum - A Life In Music - Disc 3 (Las Vegas Rehearsals)
Shake Rattle & Roll (Promo)
(The) Top Ten Hits - Disc 1
Various Artists
Country USA - 1958
Leiber & Stoller Music Publishing (6 CD Promo Set)
Leiber & Stoller - The Fifties - (Promo)
Solid Gold Country - Elvis Presley Sings Leiber And Stoller
The Many Moods Of Romance - My Heart Reminds Me
Solid Gold Country - Elvis Presley Birthday Tribute - 92-1
Solid Gold Country - Elvis Presley Birthday Tribute - 93-1
Solid Gold Scrapbook - Elvis Golden Decade 1956-1965
Solid Gold Scrapbook - Solid Gold Elvis
Your Hit Parade - The 50's Pop Revival

Don't Ask Me Why
(The) Blue Suede Box - Elvis: His Greatest Soundtracks - Disc 3
(The) Elvis Presley Collection - Treasures '53 To '58 - Disc 1
Elvis The Other Sides - Worldwide Gold Award Hits Volume 2 - Disc 1

DON'T ASK ME WHY (cont'd)
King Creole
King Creole (1997 Reissue)
(The) King Of Rock 'N' Roll - 50's Masters - Disc 4

Don't Be Cruel
A Golden Celebration - Disc 2 - Miss.-Alabama Dairy Show Tupelo Afternoon Sept. 26, 1956
A Golden Celebration - Disc 3 - Miss.-Alabama Dairy Show Tupelo Evening Sept. 26, 1956
A Golden Celebration - Disc 3 - Ed Sullivan Show New York Sept. 9, 1956
A Golden Celebration - Disc 3 - Ed Sullivan Show New York Oct. 28, 1956
A Golden Celebration - Disc 3 - Ed Sullivan Show New York Jan. 6, 1957
A Touch Of Platinum - A Life In Music - Disc 1
An Afternoon In The Garden
Blue Suede Shoes (Original Soundtrack) Disc 1
Collectors Gold - Disc 3 (Las Vegas 1969)
Commemorative Juke Box Series (5 CD Set) -Disc 1
Don't Be Cruel
Don't Be Cruel/ Can't Help Falling In Love
Elvis A Legendary Performer - Volume 1
Elvis Aron Presley - Disc 1
Elvis Aron Presley (medley Teddy Bear/Don't Be Cruel) Disc 4
Elvis As Recorded At Madison Square Garden
Elvis' Birthday Tribute Radio Program
Elvis' Golden Records
Elvis' Golden Records (1997 Reissue)
Elvis' Greatest Jukebox Hits
Elvis! His Greatest Hits - Disc 1
Elvis His Life & Music (Box Set) - Disc 1
Elvis In Concert
Elvis/NBC TV Special
(The) Elvis Presley Birthday Tribute 1992 - Disc 1
(The) Elvis Presley Collection - Rock 'N' Roll - Disc 2
Elvis Presley's Great Performances
Elvis Presley Radio Show
Elvis Presley The King Of Rock & Roll At His Best - Disc 3
Elvis Presley - 50 Greatest Hits
Elvis Presley: 1954-1961
Elvis The Legend - Disc 1
Elvis The Tribute - A Biography - Disc 1
Elvis 15th Anniversary Radio Show - Disc 1
Elvis 20th Anniversary Radio Show - Disc 3
Elvis 20th Anniversary Singles Set - Disc 3
Elvis 24 Karat Hits!
Elvis 50 Worldwide Gold Hits Vol. 1 - Disc 1
Elvis 50 Years 50 Hits -Disc 1
Elvis 56
Elvis 56 Advance Music (Promo)
Great Hits Of 1956-57
(The) Great Performances
Hound Dog/Don't Be Cruel (Jukebox Single)
Heartbreak Hotel, Hound Dog & Top Ten Hits
(The) King Of Rock 'N' Roll - 50's Masters - Disc 2
King Of The Whole Wide World - Collectors Set - The Elvis Medley
(The) Legend Lives On - Disc 1
(The) Legend Lives On - Disc 2
(The) Legend Of A King - Disc 1
(The) Million Dollar Quartet
(The) Million Dollar Quartet
(The) Million Dollar Quartet
Memories - The '68 Comeback Special - Disc 1 *(previously unreleased)*
Memories Of Elvis - 1991 - Disc 4
Memories Of Elvis - 1993 - Disc 1
(The) Number One Hits
Out Of The Box (Promo)

DON'T BE CRUEL (cont'd)
Platinum - A Life In Music - Disc 1
Pure Gold
Shake Rattle & Roll (Promo)
(The) Top Ten Hits - Disc 1
Virtual Graceland - CD-ROM
Various Artists
Billboard's Top Rock 'N' Roll Hits -1956
Country Memories
Dick Clark's Rock Roll & Remember 1/3-1/5
Dick Clark's Rock Roll & Remember 08/12-08/14
Diner (Movie Soundtrack)
Nippers Greatest Hits - The 50's Vol. 2
Rock 'N' Roll Classics 1954-1956
Rock 'N' Roll Legends
Solid Gold Country - The Complete 50's Masters
Solid Gold Country - Elvis Presley And TV
Solid Gold Country - Elvis Presley Birthday Tribute - 92-1
Solid Gold Country - Elvis Presley Birthday Tribute - 93-1
Solid Gold Country - Elvis Presley's Golden Records - 91-11
Solid Gold Country - Elvis Presley's Golden Records - 93-2
Solid Gold Country - Elvis Presley: His Favorite Writers
Solid Gold Country - Elvis Presley In Concert
Solid Gold Country - Elvis Presley Memorial Tribute - 91-8
Solid Gold Country - Elvis Presley Memorial Tribute - 92-8
Solid Gold Country - Elvis Presley Memorial Tribute - 93-8
Solid Gold Scrapbook - Elvis Golden Decade 1956-1965
The Legends Of Rock 'N' Roll
Unforgetable Fifties
Your Goodtime Oldies Magazine - 92-07
Your Goodtime Oldies Magazine - 94-07
20 Years Of No. 1 Hits - 1956-1975

Don't Cry Daddy
Always On My Mind
Elvis! His Greatest Hits - Disc 3
(The) Elvis Presley Birthday Tribute 1992 - Disc 1
(The) Elvis Presley Collection - From The Heart - Disc 2
Elvis Presley - 50 Greatest Hits - Disc 2
Elvis The Legend - Disc 3
Elvis The Tribute - A Biography - Disc 3
Elvis 15th Anniversary Radio Show - Disc 5
Elvis 20th Anniversary Radio Show - Disc 2
Elvis 50 Worldwide Gold Hits Vol. 1 - Disc 2
Elvis 50 Years - 50 Hits - Disc 2
From Nashville To Memphis - 60's Masters - Disc 4
(The) Legend Lives On - Disc 2
(The) Memphis Record
Memories Of Elvis - 1991 - Disc 3
Memories Of Elvis - 1993 - Disc 3
Sixties Legends - Elvis Presley - Disc 2
(The) Top Ten Hits - Disc 2
Various Artists
Country Memories
(The) Elvis Presley Years - Disc 3
Solid Gold Country - Elvis Presley Birthday Tribute - 93-1
Solid Gold Country - Elvis Presley Memorial Tribute - 92-8
Solid Gold Country - Mac Davis Birthday Salute
Solid Gold Scrapbook - Elvis In Memphis

Don't Forbid Me
(The) Million Dollar Quartet

Don't Leave Me Now
(The) Blue Suede Box - Elvis: His Greatest Soundtracks - Disc 1
(The) Blue Suede Box - Elvis: His Greatest Soundtracks - Disc 2
(The) Blue Suede Box - Elvis: His Greatest Soundtracks - Disc 2 *(alternate master)*
(The) Elvis Presley Collection - Treasures '53 To '58 - Disc 1
Essential Elvis - The First Movies *(take 22)*
Jailhouse Rock and Love Me Tender
Jailhouse Rock and Love Me Tender *(alternate master)*
(The) King Of Rock 'N' Roll - 50's Masters - Disc 3
(The) King Of Rock 'N' Roll - 50's Masters - Disc 3
(The) King Of Rock 'N' Roll - 50's Masters (Promo)
Loving You
Loving You (1997 Reissue)

Don't Think Twice, It's All Right
Elvis (aka) The Fool Album
Walk A Mile In My Shoes - 70's Masters - Disc 4 *(jam edit)*

Doncha' Think It's Time
Elvis' Gold Records Vol. 2 - 50,000,000 Fans Can't Be Wrong
Elvis' Gold Records Vol. 2 - 50,000,000 Fans Can't Be Wrong (1997 Reissue)
Elvis! His Greatest Hits - Disc 2
Elvis His Life And Music - Disc 2
(The) Elvis Presley Collection - The Rocker - Disc 1
Elvis The Other Sides - Worldwide Gold Award Hits Volume 2 - Disc 2
Essential Elvis Vol. 3 Hits Like Never Before *(alternate take 40)*
Essential Elvis Vol. 3 Hits Like Never Before *(spliced - original single version)*
(The) King Of Rock 'N' Roll - 50's Masters - Disc 4

Double Trouble
Command Performances - 60's Masters - Disc 2
Elvis Double Features - Spinout & Double Trouble
Elvis!Elvis!Elvis! - The King And His Movies
Elvis 15th Anniversary Radio Show - Disc 3

Down By The Riverside
Elvis Double Features - Frankie & Johnny & Paradise Hawaiian Style
Elvis Sings Hits From His Movies Volume 1
Elvis 15th Anniversary Radio Show - Disc 3
(The) Million Dollar Quartet
Various Artists
The Sun Records Collection (by Million Dollar Quartet)

Down In The Alley
(The) Elvis Presley Collection - Rhythm & Blues - Disc 2
From Nashville To Memphis - 60's Masters - Disc 3
From Nashville To Memphis - 60's Masters - Disc 5 *(alternate take 2)*
Good Rockin' Tonight - Disc 2
Reconsider Baby

Drums Of The Islands
Elvis Double Features - Frankie and Johnny & Paradise Hawaiian Style

Early Mornin' Rain
Aloha From Hawaii Via Satellite - 25th Anniversary Edition
Elvis Aron Presley - Forever
Elvis In Concert
Elvis In Nashville - 1956-1971
Elvis Now
(The) Elvis Presley Collection - Country - Disc 2
(The) Legend Lives On - Disc 4
Mahalo From Elvis
Various Artists
Solid Gold Country - Elvis Presley In Concert

Earth Angel
A Golden Celebration - Disc 4 - Elvis At Home - Germany - 1958-60

Earth Boy
Elvis Double Features - Canister Set - Disc 1
Elvis Double Features - Kid Galahad & Girls! Girls! Girls!

Easy Come, Easy Go
Command Performances - 60's Masters - Disc 2
Double Dynamite
Elvis Double Features - Easy Come, Easy Go & Speedway

(Such An) Easy Question
Elvis! His Greatest Hits - Disc 3
(The) Elvis Presley Collection - The Romantic - Disc 1
Elvis Presley 50 Greatest Hits - Disc 2
Elvis 50 Years - 50 Hits - Disc 2
From Nashville To Memphis - 60's Masters - Disc 2
Pot Luck With Elvis
Remembering Elvis

Echoes Of Love
From Nashville To Memphis - 60's Masters - Disc 2
(The) Lost Album

Edge Of Reality
Almost In Love
Command Performances - 60's Masters - Disc 2
Elvis Double Features - Live A Little, Love A Little, Charro, The Trouble With Girls & Change of Habit
Elvis' Gold Records Volume 5 (1997 Reissue)

The Elvis Medley
(The) Elvis Presley Birthday Tribute - 1992 - Disc 1
Elvis 20th Anniversary Radio Show - Disc 1
Elvis 20th Anniversary Radio Show - Disc 3
King Of The Whole Wide World - Collectors Set - The Elvis Medley
(The) Legend Lives On - Disc 4
Various Artists
Solid Gold Country - Elvis Presley Birthday Tribute - 92-1

El Toro
Elvis Double Features - Canister Set - Disc 2
Elvis Double Features - It Happened At The Worlds Fair & Fun In Acapulco

Everybody Come Aboard
Elvis Double Features - Frankie & Johnny & Paradise Hawaiian Style

Faded Love
Elvis Country - I'm 10,000 Years Old
Essential Elvis Vol. 4 - A Hundred Years From Now *(country version)*
Essential Elvis Vol. 4 - A Hundred Years From Now *(alternate take 3)*
Walk A Mile In My Shoes - 70's Masters - Disc 3 *(original unedited version)*
Walk A Mile In My Shoes - Out Of The Box (Promo) *(original unedited version)*

Fairytale
Elvis In Concert
Elvis Today
Great Country Songs *(alternate take 2)*
(The) Legend Lives On - Disc 2
Various Artists
Solid Gold Country - Elvis Presley In Concert

Fame And Fortune
A Touch Of Platinum - A Life In Music - Disc 2 - From "The Frank Sinatra Timex Special"
A Valentine Gift For You
Elvis' Golden Records Vol. 3
Elvis' Golden Records Vol. 3 (1997 Reissue)
Elvis! His Greatest Hits - Disc 2
Elvis His Life & Music - Disc 3
(The) Elvis Presley Collection - The Romantic - Disc 1
Elvis The Other Sides - Worldwide Gold Award Hits Volume 2 - Disc 2
From Nashville To Memphis 60's Masters - Disc 1
(The) Great Performances
Heart & Soul
Platinum - A Life In Music - Disc 2 - From "The Frank Sinatra Timex Special"
Various Artists
Dick Clark's Rock Roll & Remember 1/3-1/5
New Gold On CD: The Week Of July 13, 1992

Farther Along
Amazing Grace His Greatest Sacred Performances
(The) Elvis Presley Collection - Gospel - Disc 2
(The) Elvis Presley Gospel Treasury - Disc 1
(The) Elvis Presley Gospel Treasury (Special Edition)
How Great Thou Art
(The) Million Dollar Quartet

Fever
A Valentine Gift For You
Aloha From Hawaii Via Satallite
Aloha From Hawaii Via Satellite - 25th Anniversary Edition
(The) Alternate Aloha
Elvis At His Romantic Best
Elvis Is Back
Elvis Is Back - 24 kt Gold Disc
(The) Elvis Presley Collection - Rhythm & Blues - Disc 2
Elvis 15th Anniversary Radio Show - Disc 6
From Nashville To Memphis - 60's Masters - Disc 1
Good Rockin' Tonight - Disc 2
(The) Legend Lives On - Disc 1
Pure Gold
Various Artists
Leiber & Stoller Music Publishing Co. (6 CD Disc Promo Set)

Find Out What's Happening
Essential Elvis Vol. 5 - Rhythm And Country *(alternate take 6)*

FIND OUT WHAT'S HAPPENING (cont'd)
Raised On Rock

Finders Keepers, Losers Weepers
Elvis For Everyone
From Nashville To Memphis - 60's Masters - Disc 2
(The) Lost Album

First In Line
Elvis
(The) Elvis Presley Collection - Treasures '53 To '58 - Disc 2
(The) King Of Rock 'N' Roll - 50's Masters - Disc 2

Five Sleepy Heads
Elvis Double Features - Easy Come, Easy Go & Speedway
Elvis Sings For Children And Grownups Too!

Flaming Star
Double Dynamite
Elvis Double Features - Flaming Star, Wild In The Country & Follow That Dream
Elvis Double Features - Flaming Star, Wild In The Country & Follow that Dream *(end title version)*
Elvis! His Greatest Hits - Disc 2
(The) Elvis Presley Collection - Movie Magic - Disc 2
Sixties Legends - Elvis Presley - Disc 1

Flip Flop And Fly
Elvis Recorded Live On Stage In Memphis (part of Rock & Roll medley)
(The) Great Performances (medley Shake, Rattle & Roll/Flip Flop & Fly)
(The) Legend Lives On - Disc 2 (medley Shake, Rattle & Roll/Flip Fop & Fly)
Platinum - A Life In Music - Disc 1 (medley Shake, Rattle & Roll/Flip Flop & Fly)

Follow That Dream
Command Performances - 60's Masters - Disc 1 *(alternate take 2)*
Double Dynamite
Elvis Aron Presley - Disc 2 *(alternate take 2)*
Elvis Double Features - Wild In The Country & Follow That Dream
Elvis' Golden Records Vol. 3 (1997 Reissue)
Elvis! His Greatest Hits - Disc 3
(The) Elvis Presley Collection - Movie Magic - Disc 2
Elvis The Legend - Disc 2
Elvis 15th Anniversary Radio Show - Disc 5
Elvis 20th Anniversary Radio Show - Disc 3
Memories Of Elvis - 1991 - Disc 2
Return Of The Rocker
Sixties Legends - Elvis Presley - Disc 1

Fool
Elvis (aka "The Fool Album")
Elvis Aron Presley - Disc 3
(The) Elvis Presley Collection - From The Heart - Disc 1
(The) Legend Lives On - Disc 3
Walk A Mile In My Shoes - 70's Masters - Disc 2

Fool Fool Fool
(The) King Of Rock 'N' Roll - 50's Masters - Disc 5 *(1955 acetate)*

Fools Fall In Love
Double Dynamite
Elvis Presley Sings Leiber & Stoller
From Nashville To Memphis - 60's Masters - Disc 3

FOOLS FALL IN LOVE (cont'd)
Various Artists
Leiber & Stoller Music Publishing (6 CD Promo Set)

Fools Rush In (Where Angels Fear To Tread)
Elvis Now
(The) Elvis Presley Collection - From The Heart - Disc 2
Various Artists
Angels Among Us

(That's What You Get) For Lovin' Me
Elvis (aka "The Fool Album")
Walk A Mile In My Shoes - 70's Masters - Disc 3

For Ol' Times Sake
(The) Elvis Presley Collection - From The Heart - Disc 2
Essential Elvis Vol.5 - Rhythm And Country *(alternate take 3)*
Raised On Rock
Walk A Mile In My Shoes - 70's Masters - Disc 2

For The Good Times
An Afternoon In The Garden
Elvis As Recorded At Madison Square Garden
(The) Elvis Presley Collection - Love Songs - Disc 2
(The) Elvis Presley Collection - The Romantic - Disc 2 *(alternate take)*
(The) Legend Lives On - Disc 3
Platinum - A Life In Music - Disc 4 *(alternate take 3)*
Walk A Mile In My Shoes - 70's Masters - Disc 4 *(studio master)*
Welcome To My World

For The Heart
A Touch Of Platinum Vol. 2 - A Life In Music - Disc 2 *(alternate take 1)*
Elvis' Gold Records Volume 5
Elvis' Gold Records Volume 5 (1997 Reissue)
From Elvis Presley Boulevard Memphis, Tennessee, Recorded Live
Platinum - A life In Music - Disc 4 *(alternate take 1)*
Platinum In-Store Sampler (Promo) *(alternate take 1)*
Platinum Sampler (Promo) *(alternate take 1)*
Walk A Mile In My Shoes - 70's Masters - Disc 2

For The Millionth And The Last Time
Elvis For Everyone!
(The) Elvis Presley Collection - The Romantic - Disc 2
From Nashville To Memphis - 60's Masters - Disc 2

Forget Me Never
Elvis For Everyone!
Elvis Double Features - Flaming Star, Wild In The Country & Follow That Dream
Separate Ways

Fort Lauderdale Chamber Of Commerce
Elvis Double Features - Canister Set - Disc 4
Elvis Double Features - Harum Scarum & Girl Happy

Fountain Of Love
From Nashville To Memphis - 60's Masters - Disc 2
Pot Luck With Elvis
Remembering Elvis

Frankfort Special
(The) Blue Suede Box - Elvis: His Greatest Soundtracks - Disc 5
(The) Blue Suede Box - Elvis: His Greatest Soundtracks - Disc 5 *(fast version, alternate take 2)*
Blue Suede Shoes (Original Soundtrack) Disc 1
Elvis 15th Anniversary Radio Show - Disc 4
G.I. Blues
G.I. Blues (1997 Reissue)
G.I. Blues (1997 Reissue) *(fast version, alternate take 2)*
G.I. Blues (1997 Reissue Collectors Edition)
G.I. Blues (1997 Reissue Collectors Edition) *(fast version, alternate take 2)*

Frankie And Johnny
Command Performances - 60's Masters - Disc 2
Double Dynamite
Elvis Double Features - Frankie And Johnny & Paradise Hawaiian Style
Elvis Sings Hits From His Movies Volume 1

Froggy Went A Courtin'
Walk A Mile In My Shoes - 70's Masters - Disc 5 (rehearsal)

From A Jack To A King
Back In Memphis
(The) Elvis Presley Collection - Country - Disc 1
From Nashville To Memphis - 60's Masters - Disc 4
Great Country Songs

Fun In Acapulco
Command Performances - 60's Masters - Disc 1
Elvis Double Features - Canister Set - Disc 2
Elvis Double Features - It Happened At The Worlds Fair & Fun In Acapulco

Funny How Time Slips Away
A Touch Of Platinum Vol. 2 - A Life In Music - Disc 1
An Afternoon In The Garden
Collectors Gold - Disc 3 (Las Vegas 1969)
Elvis Aron Presley - Disc 4
Elvis As Recorded At Madison Square Garden
Elvis Country
Elvis Country "I'm 10,000 Years Old"
(The) Elvis Presley Collection - Country - Disc 2
Great Country Songs
(The) Legend Lives On - Disc 4
Platinum - A Life In Music - Disc 3
Walk A Mile In My Shoes - 70's Masters - Disc 3
Various Artists
American Country Countdown 94-10 Show 43

"G"

G. I. Blues
(The) Blue Suede Box - Elvis: His Greatest Soundtracks - Disc 5
Collectors Gold - Disc 1 *(alternate take 1)*
Elvis Command Performances - 60's Masters - Disc 1
Elvis 15th Anniversary Radio Show - Disc 3
G.I. Blues
G.I. Blues (1997 Reissue)
G.I. Blues (1997 Reissue Collectors Edition)
Memories Of Elvis - 1991 - Disc 1

Gentle On My Mind

(The) Elvis Presley Collection - Country - Disc 1
From Elvis In Memphis
From Nashville To Memphis - 60's Masters - Disc 4
Great Country Songs
(The) Memphis Record
Welcome To My World
Various Artists
A Celebration Of Country 'n' Pop Music

Gently

Collectors Gold - Disc 2 *(alternate take 3)*
From Nashville To Memphis - 60's Masters - Disc 1
Something For Everybody

Get Back

Elvis Aron Presley - Disc 3 (medley Little Sister/Get Back)

Girl Happy

Collectors Gold - Disc 1 *(alternate take 4)*
Command Performances - 60's Masters - Disc 2
Elvis Double Features - Canister Set - Disc 4
Elvis Double Features - Harum Scarum & Girl Happy

Girl Next Door Went A Walking

Elvis Is Back
Elvis Is Back - 24 kt Gold Disc
From Nashville To Memphis - 60's Masters - Disc 1

Girl Of Mine

Essential Elvis Vol. 5 - Rhythm And Country*(alternate take 9)*
Raised On Rock

Girls! Girls! Girls!

Command Performances - 60's Masters - Disc 1
Elvis Double Features - Canister Set - Disc 1
Elvis Double Features - Canister Set - Disc 1 *(end title version)*
Elvis Double Features - Kid Galahad & Girls! Girls! Girls!
Elvis Double Features - Kid Galahad & Girls! Girls! Girls! *(end title version)*
(The) Elvis Presley Collection - Movie Magic - Disc 1
Elvis Presley Sings Leiber & Stoller
Various Artists
Leiber & Stoller Music Publishing (6 CD Promo Set)
Solid Gold Country - Elvis Presley Sings Leiber And Stoller

Give Me the Right

A Valentine Gift For You
Collectors Gold - Disc 2 *(alternate take 1)*
(The) Elvis Presley Collection - The Romantic - Disc 2
From Nashville To Memphis - 60's Masters - Disc 1
Something for Everybody

Go East - Young Man

Elvis Double Features - Canister Set - Disc 4
Elvis Double Features - Harum Scarum & Girl Happy

Goin' Home

An Elvis Double Feature - Speedway, Clambake
Collectors Gold - Disc 2 *(alternate takes 24 & 21)*
Elvis Double Features - Kissin' Cousins, Clambake & Stay Away Joe

Page 499

Golden Coins
Elvis Double Features - Canister Set - Disc 4
Elvis Double Features - Harum Scarum & Girl Happy

Gonna Get Back Home Somehow
From Nashville To Memphis - 60's Masters - Disc 2
Pot Luck With Elvis
Remembering Elvis

Good Luck Charm
Elvis' Golden Records Vol. 3
Elvis' Golden Records Vol. 3 (1997 Reissue)
Elvis' Greatest Jukebox Hits
Elvis! His Greatest Hits - Disc 3
Elvis His Life And Music - Disc 3
(The) Elvis Presley Birthday Tribute 1992 - Disc 1
(The) Elvis Presley Collection - Rock 'N' Roll - Disc 2
Elvis Presley - 50 Greatest Hits - Disc 1
Elvis The King: 1954-1965
Elvis The Legend - Disc 2
Elvis The Tribute A Biography - Disc 3
Elvis 15th Anniversary Radio Show - Disc 5
Elvis 20th Anniversary Radio Show - Disc 3
Elvis 24 Karat Hits!
Elvis 50 Worldwide Gold Hits Vol. 1 - Disc 2
Elvis 50 Years 50 Hits - Disc 1
From Nashville To Memphis - 60's Masters - Disc 2
Love Songs
Memories Of Elvis - 1991 - Disc 2
Memories Of Elvis - 1993 - Disc 3
(The) Number One Hits
Shake Rattle & Roll (Promo)
Sixties Legends - Elvis Presley - Disc 1
(The) Top Ten Hits - Disc 2
Various Artists
Don Kirshner's 35th Anniversary Of Rock - Great Vocalists
(The) Elvis Presley Years - Disc 2
Goodtime Oldies Theme Party
Solid Gold Country - Elvis Presley's Golden Records 93-2
Solid Gold Country - Elvis Presley In Nashville
Solid Gold Country - Elvis Presley Memorial Tribute 91-8
Solid Gold Scrapbook - Elvis Movie Music
Solid Gold Scrapbook - Solid Gold Elvis
Your Goodtime Oldies Magazine - 93-12
20 Years Of No. 1 Hits, 1956-1975

Good Rockin' Tonight
A Date With Elvis
A Touch Of Platinum - A Life In Music - Disc 1
Elvis Greatest Jukebox Hits
(The) Elvis Presley Collection - Rock 'N' Roll - Disc 1
Elvis The King: 1954-1965
Elvis The Tribute A Biography - Disc 1
Elvis 15th Anniversary Radio Show - Disc 1
Good Rockin' Tonight - Disc 1
(The) King Of Rock 'N' Roll - 50's Masters - Disc 1
(The) Legend Of a King - Disc 1
(The) Legend Lives On - Disc 2
(The) Louisiana Hayride - Anthologies Of Legends - Elvis Presley
(The) Louisiana Hayride Archives Volume 1 (6/25/55)
Platinum - A Life In Music - Disc 1
(The) Private Presley CD
Raw Elvis

GOOD ROCKIN' TONIGHT (cont'd)
Remembering Elvis
(The) Sun Sessions
Vintage 55
Various Artists
(The) Elvis Presley Years - Disc 1
Leiber & Stoller Music Publishing (6 CD Promo Set)
Rock 'N' Roll Classics: 1954-1956
Solid Gold Scrapbook - Elvis In Memphis
Solid Gold Scrapbook - Solid Gold Elvis
The Sun Record Collection
The Sun Story

Good Time Charlie's Got The Blues

(The) Elvis Presley Collection - Country - Disc 1
Essential Elvis Vol. 5 - Rhythm And Country *(alternate take 8)*
Good Times
Walk A Mile In My Shoes - 70's Masters - Disc 4
Walk A Mile In My Shoes - Out Of The Box Sampler (Promo)

Got A Lot O' Livin' To Do!

(The) Blue Suede Box - Elvis: His Greatest Soundtracks - Disc 1
(The) Blue Suede Box - Elvis: His Greatest Soundtracks - Disc 1 *(finale)*
Blue Suede Shoes (Original Soundtrack) Disc 2
Elvis Aron Presley Forever
Elvis' Gold Records Vol. 2 - 50,000,000 Elvis Fans Can't Be Wrong (1997 Reissue)
(The) Elvis Presley Collection - Movie Magic - Disc 1
Elvis The Other Sides - Worldwide Gold Award Hits Volume 2 - Disc 1
Elvis 15th Anniversary Radio Show - Disc 4
Essential Elvis The First Movies
Essential Elvis The First Movies *(unreleased version take 13)*
Essential Elvis Vol. 2 - Stereo 57 *(alternate take 9)*
(The) Great Performances
(The) King Of Rock 'N' Roll - 50's Masters - Disc 2
Loving You
Loving You (1997 Reissue)
Loving You (1997 Reissue) *(finale)*
(The) Legend Lives On - Disc 2

Got My Mojo Working

(The) Elvis Presley Collection - Rhythm & Blues - Disc 1
Essential Elvis Vol. 4 - A Hundred Years From Now *(undubbed/unedited version)*
Love Letters From Elvis
Walk A Mile In My Shoes - 70's Masters - Disc 3

Green Green Grass Of Home

Elvis Aron Presley Forever
(The) Elvis Presley Collection - Country - Disc 2
Elvis Today
Great Country Songs *(alternate take 1)*
(The) Legend Lives On - Disc 3
Walk A Mile In My Shoes - 70's Masters - Disc 2

Guadalajara

Burning Love And Hits From His Movies Vol. 2
Elvis Double Features - Canister Set - Disc 2
Elvis Double Features - It Happened At The Worlds Fair & Fun In Acapulco
Elvis Presley - The King Of Rock & Roll At His Best - Disc 2

Guitar Man
A Touch Of Platinum - A Life In Music - Disc 2 *(alternate take 4)*
An Elvis Double Feature: Speedway, Clambake
Blue Suede Shoes (Original Soundtrack) - Disc 1 *(unedited version)*
Elvis' Gold Records Volume 5 (1997 Reissue)
Elvis In Nashville 1956-1971
Elvis/NBC - TV Special (3 Performances)
(The) Elvis Presley Birthday Tribute 1992 - Disc 2
(The) Elvis Presley Collection - Rock 'N' Roll - Disc 1
Elvis Sings Hits From His Movies Volume 1
Elvis The Legend - Disc 3
Elvis 15th Anniversary Radio Show - Disc 6
From Nashville To Memphis - 60's Masters - Disc 3
Great Country Songs *(1980 remixed version)*
Memories - The '68 Comeback Special - Disc 1
Memories - The '68 Comeback Special - Disc 1 *(previously unreleased)*
Memories - The '68 Comeback Special - Disc 1
Memories Of Elvis - 1991 - Disc 3
Platinum - A Life In Music - Disc 2 *(alternate take 4)*

Various Artists
Contemporary Country Volume 4 - The Early 80's - Hot Hits *(1980 remixed version)*
Nippers Greatest Hits - The 80's *(1980 remixed version)*
Solid Gold Country - Elvis Presley In Nashville
Solid Gold Country - Elvis Presley Memorial Tribute 91-8
Solid Gold Country - Elvis Presley Memorial Tribute 92-8
Solid Gold Country - Elvis Presley Memorial Tribute 93-8
14 #1 Country Hits *(1980 remixed version)*

"H"

Happy Ending
Elvis Double Features - Canister Set - Disc 2
Elvis Double Features - It Happened At The Worlds Fair & Fun In Acapulco
Mahalo From Elvis

Harbor Lights
A Golden Celebration - Disc 1
Elvis A Legendary Performer Volume 2
(The) Elvis Presley Collection - Treasures '53 To '58 - Disc 2
Elvis Presley The King Of Rock & Roll At His Best - Disc 4
Elvis 20th Anniversary Radio Show - Disc 1
(The) King Of Rock 'N' Roll - 50's Masters - Disc 1
(The) Sun Sessions CD - The Outtakes

Hard Headed Woman
(The) Blue Suede Box - Elvis: His Greatest Soundtracks - Disc 3
Blue Suede Shoes (Original Soundtrack) Disc 1
Elvis' Gold Records Vol. 2 - 50,000,000 Elvis Fans Can't Be Wrong (1997 Reissue)
Elvis' Greatest Jukebox Hits
Elvis! His Greatest Hits - Disc 2
(The) Elvis Presley Birthday Tribute 1992 - Disc 2
(The) Elvis Presley Collection - Rock 'N' Roll - Disc 1
Elvis Presley: 1954-1961
Elvis Presley - 50 Greatest Hits - Disc 2
Elvis 50 Worldwide Gold Hits Vol. 1 - Disc 1
Elvis 50 Years 50 Hits - Disc 2
Elvis 15th Anniversary Radio Show - Disc 1
Good Rockin' Tonight - Disc 1

HARD HEADED WOMAN (cont'd)
King Creole
King Creole (1997 Reissue)
(The) King Of Rock 'N' Roll - 50's Masters - Disc 4
King Of The Whole Wide World - Collectors Set - The Elvis Medley
Memories Of Elvis - 1991 - Disc 1
Memories Of Elvis - 1993 - Disc 2
(The) Number One Hits
Shake Rattle & Roll (Promo)
(The) Top Ten Hits - Disc 1
Various Artists
Billboard's Top Rock 'N' Roll Hits 1958
Billboard's Top Rock 'N' Roll Hits 1957-1961
Cruisin' America with Cousin Brucie 92-30
(The) Elvis Presley Years - Disc 1
Made In America
Nippers #1 Hits (1956-1986)
Solid Gold Country - Elvis: What Happened?
Solid Gold Country - Elvis Presley Birthday Tribute 92-1
Solid Gold Country - Elvis Presley Birthday Tribute 93-1
Solid Gold Country - Elvis Presley Memorial Tribute 91-8
Solid Gold Country - Elvis Presley Memorial Tribute 92-8
Solid Gold Country - Elvis Presley Memorial Tribute 93-8
Solid Gold Country - The Complete 50's Masters
Solid Gold Country - 70 Years Of RCA Country
Solid Gold Scrapbook - Elvis' Golden Decade 1956-1965
Solid Gold Scrapbook - Elvis Movie Magic
Your Goodtime Oldies Magazine 92-12

Hard Knocks
Elvis Double Features - Canister Set - Disc 3
Elvis Double Features - Viva Las Vegas & Roustabout

Hard Luck
Elvis Double Features - Frankie & Johnny & Paradise Hawaiian Style

Harem Holiday
Command Performances - 60's Masters - Disc 2
Elvis Double Features - Canister Set - Disc 4
Elvis Double Features - Harum Scarum & Girl Happy

Have A Happy
Elvis Double Features - Live A Little, Love A Little, Charro, The Trouble With Girls & Change Of Habit
Elvis Sings For Children And Grownups Too!

Have I Told You Lately That I Love You
(The) Blue Suede Box - Elvis: His Greatest Soundtracks - Disc 1
Elvis! His Greatest Hits - Disc 4
(The) Elvis Presley Collection - Country - Disc 2
Elvis 15th Anniversary Radio Show - Disc 4
Essential Elvis Vol. 2 Stereo 57 *(alternate take 2)*
Essential Elvis Vol. 2 Stereo 57 *(alternate take 6)*
Essential Elvis Vol. 2 Stereo 57 *(alternate takes 12,13)*
(The) King Of Rock 'N' Roll - 50's Masters - Disc 3
Loving You
Loving You (1997 Reissue)

Hawaiian Sunset
Blue Hawaii
Blue Hawaii (1997 Reissue)
Blue Hawaii (1997 Reissue Collectors Edition)
(The) Blue Suede Box - Elvis: His Greatest Soundtracks - Disc 4

Hawaiian Wedding Song
Aloha From Hawaii Via Satellite - 25th Anniversary Edition
(The) Alternate Aloha
Blue Hawaii
Blue Hawaii (1997 Reissue)
Blue Hawaii (1997 Reissue Collectors Edition)
(The) Blue Suede Box - Elvis: His Greatest Soundtracks - Disc 4
Command Performances - 60's Masters - Disc 1
Elvis Aron Presley Forever
Elvis In Concert
(The) Elvis Presley Collection - The Romantic - Disc 2
Mahalo From Elvis
Various Artists
Sweet Dreams Of Country

He Is My Everything
Amazing Grace His Greatest Sacred Performances - Disc 2
(The) Elvis Presley Collection - Gospel - Disc 1
He Touched Me
Various Artists
I Believe - Best Loved Stars Of Inspiration

He Knows Just What I Need
Amazing Grace His Greatest Sacred Performances - Disc 1
(The) Elvis Presley Collection - Gospel - Disc 2
(The) Elvis Presley Gospel Treasury - Disc 2
His Hand In Mine

He Touched Me
Amazing Grace His Greatest Sacred Performances - Disc 2
(The) Elvis Presley Collection - Gospel - Disc 1
(The) Elvis Presley Gospel Treasury - Disc 2
(The) Elvis Presley Gospel Treasury (Special Edition)
He Touched Me
Platinum - A Life In Music - Disc 4 *(alternate take 2)*
Various Artists
I Believe - Best Loved Stars Of Inspiration
Reach Out And Touch

He'll Have To Go
(The) Elvis Presley Collection - Country - Disc 1
Great Country Songs
Moody Blue
Walk A Mile In My Shoes - 70's Masters - Disc 4

He's Your Uncle Not Your Dad
Elvis Double Features - Easy Come, Easy Go & Speedway

Heart Of Rome
Love Letters From Elvis
Walk A Mile In My Shoes - 70's Masters - Disc 1

Hearts Of Stone
(The) Louisiana Hayride - Anthologies Of Legends - Elvis Presley
(The) Louisiana Hayride Archives Volume 1 (1/15/55)

Heartbreak Hotel
A Golden Celebration - Disc 1 - Dorsey Bros. Show New York Feb. 11, 1956
A Golden Celebration - Disc 1 - Dorsey Bros. Show New York March 17, 1956
A Golden Celebration - Disc 1 - Dorsey Bros. Show New York March 24, 1956

HEARTBREAK HOTEL (cont'd)
A Golden Celebration - Disc 2 - Milton Berle Show San Diego April 3, 1956
A Golden Celebration - Disc 2 - Miss.-Alabama Dairy Show Tupelo Afternoon. Sept. 26, 1956
A Golden Celebration - Disc 3 - Ed Sullivan Show New York Oct. 28, 1956
A Touch Of Platinum - A Life In Music - Disc 1 *(alternate take 6)*
An Afternoon In the Garden
Blue Suede Shoes (Original Soundtrack) Disc 2
Collectors Gold - Disc 3 (Las Vegas 1969)
Don't Be Cruel
Elvis A Legendary Performer Volume 1
Elvis Aron Presley - Live - Las Vegas 1956 - Disc 1
Elvis Aron Presley - Live - Hawaii 1961 - Disc 1
Elvis As Recorded At Madison Square Garden
Elvis Birthday Tribute Radio Special
Elvis' Golden Records
Elvis' Golden Records (1997 Reissue)
Elvis' Greatest Jukebox Hits
Elvis! His Greatest Hits - Disc 1
Elvis His Life And Music - Disc 1
Elvis/NBC-TV Special
(The) Elvis Presley Birthday Tribute 1992 - Disc 2
(The) Elvis Presley Collection - Rock 'N' Roll - Disc 2
Elvis Presley: Great Performances
Elvis Presley Radio Show (Promo)
Elvis Presley The King Of Rock & Roll At His Best - Disc 3
Elvis Presley: 1954-1961
Elvis Presley - 50 Greatest Hits - Disc 1
Elvis The Legend - Disc 1
Elvis The Tribute - A Biography - Disc 2
Elvis 15th Anniversary Radio Show - Disc 2
Elvis 20th Anniversary Radio Show - Disc 1
Elvis 20th Anniversary Singles Set - Disc 1
Elvis 24 Karat Hits!
Elvis 50 Worldwide Gold Hits Vol. 1
Elvis 50 Years 50 Hits - Disc 1
Elvis 56
Elvis 56 *(alternate take 5)*
Elvis 56 Advance Music (Promo)
Elvis 56 Advance Music (Promo) *(alternate take 5 - intro - previously unreleased)*
Good Rockin' Tonight - Disc 1
Great Hits Of 1956-57
(The) Great Performances
Heartbreak Hotel, Hound Dog And Top Ten Hits
Heartbreak Hotel - I Was The One
Heartbreak Hotel - I Was The One *(alternate take 5)*
Heartbreak Hotel/ It's Now Or Never
(The) Honeymoon Companion (Promo)
(The) King Of Rock 'N' Roll - 50's Masters - Disc 1
(The) King Of Rock 'N' Roll - 50's Masters - Disc 5 (Las Vegas 1956)
King Of The Whole Wide World - Collectors Set - The Elvis Medley
(The) Legend Lives On - Disc 2
(The) Legend Lives On - Disc 4
(The) Legend Of A King - Disc 1
Memories - The '68 Comeback Special - Disc 1
Memories - The '68 Comeback Special - Disc 2 *(previously unreleased)*
Memories Of Elvis - 1991 - Disc 4
Memories Of Elvis - 1993 - Disc 1
(The) Number One Hits
Platinum - A Life In Music - Disc 1 *(alternate take 6)*
Shake Rattle & Roll (Promo)
(The) Top Ten Hits - Disc 1
Tiger Man *(previously unreleased)*
Virtual Graceland - CD-ROM
Walk A Mile In My Shoes - 70's Masters - Disc 5 (The Elvis Presley Show)

HEARTBREAK HOTEL (cont'd)
Various Artists
Country USA -1956
Dick Clark's Rock Roll & Remember 1/3-1/5
Dick Clark's Rock Roll & Remember 8/12-8/14
(The) Elvis Presley Years
Heartbreak Hotel (Original Soundtrack)
Nippers Greatest Hits - The 50's Vol. 1
Solid Gold Country - (The) Complete 50's Masters
Solid Gold Country - Elvis: What Happened?
Solid Gold Country - Elvis Presley And TV
Solid Gold Country - Elvis Presley Birthday Tribute - 92-1
Solid Gold Country - Elvis Presley Birthday Tribute - 93-1
Solid Gold Country - Elvis Presley's Golden Records - 91-11
Solid Gold Country - Elvis Presley's Golden Records - 93-2
Solid Gold Country - Elvis Presley In Nashville
Solid Gold Country - Elvis Presley Memorial Tribute 91-8
Solid Gold Country - Elvis Presley Memorial Tribute 92-8
Solid Gold Country - Elvis Presley Memorial Tribute 93-8
Solid Gold Country - 70 Years Of RCA Country
Solid Gold Scrapbook - Elvis' Golden Decade 1956-1965
The Legends Of Rock 'N' Roll
WCBS FM 101.1 The Anniversary Album The 50's

Help Me
Amazing Grace His Greatest Sacred Performances - Disc 2
Elvis Recorded Live On Stage In Memphis
Promised Land

Help Me Make It Through The Night
Elvis At His Romantic Best
Elvis Now
(The) Elvis Presley Collection - Love Songs - Disc 2
Great Country Songs *(alternate take 3)*
(The) Legend Lives On - Disc 3
Welcome To My World

Here Comes Santa Claus
Christmas Wishes From Anne Murray, Glen Campbell & Elvis Presley
Christmas With Elvis
Elvis Presley's Country Christmas/Jim Reeves Holiday Hits
Elvis' Christmas Album
Elvis' Christmas Album - Camden
Elvis Presley & Jim Reeves Christmas Favorites
If Every Day Was Like Christmas
If Every Day Was Like Christmas - Collectors Edition
(The) King Of Rock 'N' Roll - 50's Masters - Disc 3
Various Artists
A Country Christmas
Happy Holidays Volume 28
Honkey Tonk Christmas With Alan Jackson
Nippers Greatest Christmas Hits
Solid Gold Country - Christmas With Elvis Presley
Time - Life Treasury Of Christmas Vol.1
Your Goodtime Oldies Magazine 97-51

Hey Hey Hey
An Elvis Double Feature - Speedway & Clambake
Elvis Double Features - Kissin' Cousins, Clambake & Stay Away Joe

Hey Jude
Elvis Now
From Nashville To Memphis - 60's Masters - Disc 4

Hey Little Girl
Elvis Double Features - Canister Set - Disc 4
Elvis Double Features - Harum Scarum & Girl Happy

Hi Heel Sneakers
Elvis Aron Presley - Disc 3 *(single version)*
(The) Elvis Presley Collection - Rock 'N' Roll - Disc 2
From Nashville To Memphis - 60's Masters - Disc 3 *(original undubbed master)*
Reconsider Baby

His Hand In Mine
A Touch Of Platinum - A Life In Music - Disc 2 *(alternate take 2)*
Amazing Grace His Greatest Sacred Performances - Disc 1
(The) Elvis Presley Collection - Gospel - Disc 1
(The) Elvis Presley Gospel Treasury - Disc 2
His Hand In Mine
Platinum - A Life In Music - Disc 2 *(alternate take 2)*
Various Artists
A Celebration Of Faith And Joy
Precious Memories
Songs Of Faith And Inspiration

(Marie's The Name) His Latest Flame
Elvis' Golden Records Vol. 3
Elvis' Golden Records Vol. 3 (1997 Reissue)
Elvis! His Greatest Hits - Disc 2
Elvis His Life And Music - Disc 3
(The) Elvis Presley Birthday Tribute 1992 - Disc 3
(The) Elvis Presley Collection - Rock 'N' Roll - Disc 1
Elvis The King: 1954-1965
Elvis The Legend - Disc 2
Elvis The Other Sides - Worldwide Gold Award Hits Volume 2 - Disc 2
Elvis 20th Anniversary Radio Show - Disc 3
Elvis 24 Karat Hits!
From Nashville To Memphis - 60's Masters - Disc 2
From Nashville To Memphis - 60's Masters - Disc 5 *(alternate take 4)*
Good Rockin' Tonight - Disc 2
Memories Of Elvis - 1991 - Disc 1
Memories Of Elvis - 1993 - Disc 2
Out Of The Box - 6 From The 60's - (Promo) *(alternate take 4)*
Return Of The Rocker
Sixties Legends - Elvis Presley - Disc 1
(The) Top Ten Hits - Disc 2
Various Artists
Dick Clark's Rock Roll & Remember - 08/12-08/14
Solid Gold Country - Elvis Presley: His Favorite Writers
Solid Gold Country - Elvis Presley In Nashville
Solid Gold Scrapbook - Solid Gold Elvis
Studio B Home Of A Thousand Hits Vol. 1
These Were Our Songs: The Early 60's

Holly Leaves And Christmas Trees
Christmas With Elvis
Elvis Sings The Wonderful World Of Christmas
If Every Day Was Like Christmas
If Every Day Was Like Christmas *(unreleased alternate take 8)*
If Every Day Was Like Christmas - Special Collectors Edition
If Every Day Was Like Christmas - Special Collectors Edition *(unreleased alternate take 8)*

HOLLY LEAVES AND CHRISTMAS TREES (cont'd)
Various Artists
Solid Gold Country - Christmas With Elvis

Home Is Where The Heart Is
Elvis Double Features - Canister Set - Disc 1
Elvis Double Features - Kid Galahad & Girls! Girls! Girls!
(The) Elvis Presley Collection - Movie Magic - Disc 1

Hot Dog
(The) Blue Suede Box - Elvis: His Greatest Soundtracks - Disc 1
Blue Suede Shoes (Original Soundtrack) Disc 1
(The) Elvis Presley Collectiuon - The Rocker - Disc 2
Elvis Presley Sings Leiber & Stoller
Elvis The Other Sides - Worldwide Gold Award Hits Volume 2 - Disc 1
Essential Elvis - The First Movies
(The) King Of Rock 'N' Roll - 50's Masters - Disc 3
Loving You
Loving You (1997 Reissue)
Various Artists
Leiber & Stoller Music Publishing (6 CD Promo Set)

Hound Dog
A Golden Celebration - Disc 2 - Milton Berle Show Hollywood June 5, 1956
A Golden Celebration - Disc 2 - Steve Allen Show New York July 1, 1956
A Golden Celebration - Disc 2 - Miss. - Alabama Dairy Show Tupelo Afternoon Sept. 26, 1956
A Golden Celebration - Disc 3 - Miss. - Alabama Dairy Show Tupelo Evening Sept. 26, 1956
A Golden Celebration - Disc 3 - Ed Sullivan Show New York Sept. 9, 1956
A Golden Celebration - Disc 3 - Ed Sullivan Show New York Oct. 28, 1956
A Golden Celebration - Disc 3 - Ed Sullivan Show New York Jan. 6, 1957
A Touch Of Platinum - A Life In Music - Disc 1 - Milton Berle Show Hollywood June 5, 1956
Aloha From Hawaii Via Satellite
Aloha From Hawaii Via Satellite - 25th Anniversary Edition
(The) Alternate Aloha
An Afternoon In The Garden
Blue Suede Shoes (Original Soundtrack) Disc 2 *(instrumental)*
Commemorative Jukebox Series (5 CD Set)
Elvis Aron Presley - Disc 1
Elvis Aron Presley - Disc 4
Elvis As Recorded At Madison Square Garden
Elvis Birthday Tribute Radio Special
Elvis' Golden Records
Elvis' Golden Records (1997 Reissue)
Elvis' Greatest Jukebox Hits
Elvis! His Greatest Hits - Disc 1
Elvis His Life And Music - Disc 1
Elvis In Concert
Elvis In Person At The International Hotel
Elvis/NBC-TV Special
(The) Elvis Presley Birthday Tribute 1992 - Disc 2
(The) Elvis Presley Collection - Rock 'N' Roll - Disc 1
Elvis Presley Radio Special (Promo)
Elvis Presley Sings Leiber & Stoller
Elvis Presley: 1954-1961
Elvis Presley - 50 Greatest Hits - Disc 1
Elvis Recorded Live On Stage In Memphis
Elvis The Legend - Disc 1
Elvis The Tribute - A Biography - Disc 3
Elvis 20th Anniversary Radio Show - Disc 2
Elvis 20th Anniversary Singles Set - Disc 2
Elvis 24 Karat Hits!
Elvis - 50 Years - 50 Hits -Disc 1
Elvis 56

HOUND DOG (cont'd)
Elvis 56 Advance Music (Promo)
Elvis 50 Worldwide Gold Hits Vol. 1 - Disc 1
Great Hits Of 1956-57
Good Rockin' Tonight - Disc 1
(The) Honeymoon Companion
Hound Dog / Don't Be Cruel (Jukebox Single)
Hound Dog/ It's Now Or Never
Heartbreak Hotel, Hound Dog & The Top Ten Hits
(The) King Of Rock 'N' Roll - 50's Masters - Disc 2
King Of The Whole Wide World - Collectors Set - The Elvis Medley
(The) Legend Lives On - Disc 2
(The) Legend Lives On - Disc 4
(The) Louisisna Hayride - Anthologies of Legends - Elvis Presley
(The) Louisiana Hayride Archives Volume 1 (12/15/56)
Memories - The '68 Comeback Special - Disc 1
Memories Of Elvis - 1991 - Disc 4
Memories Of Elvis - 1993 - Disc 1
(The) Number One Hits
Out Of The Box (Promo)
Platinum - A Life In Music - Disc 1 - Milton Berle Show Hollywood June 5, 1956
Rocker
Shake Rattle & Roll (Promo)
(The) Top Ten Hits - Disc 1
Virtual Graceland CD-ROM
Various Artists
Billboard's Top Rock 'N' Roll Hits - 1956
Dick Clark's Rock Roll & Remember 1/3-1/5
Dick Clark's Rock Roll & Remember 8/12-8/14
Forrest Gump (Original Soundtrack)
Greatest Hits Of The '50's
Leiber & Stoller - The Fifties (Promo)
RCA Nashville - 60 Years 1928 - 1988
Rock 'N' Roll Legends
Solid Gold Country - (The) Complete 50's Masters
Solid Gold Country - Elvis: What Happened?
Solid Gold Country - Elvis Presley And TV
Solid Gold Country - Elvis Presley Birthday Tribute 92-1
Solid Gold Country - Elvis Presley Birthday Tribute 93-1
Solid Gold Country - Elvis Presley's Golden Records 93-2
Solid Gold Country - Elvis Presley: His Favoirte Writers
Solid Gold Country - Elvis Presley In Concert
Solid Gold Country - Elvis Presley Live
Solid Gold Country - Elvis Presley Memorial Tribute 91-8
Solid Gold Country - Elvis Presley Memorial Tribute 92-8
Solid Gold Country - Elvis Presley Memorial Tribute 93-8
Solid Gold Country - Elvis Presley Sings Leiber And Stoller
Solid Gold Country - 70 Years Of RCA Country
Solid Gold Hits Of The '50's
Solid Gold Scrapbook - Elvis Golden Decade 1956-1965
The Golden Days Of Rock 'N' Roll
WCBS FM 101.1 The Anniversary Album The 50's
Your Goodtime Oldies Magazine 95-26
Your Goodtime Oldies Magazine 95-34
20 Years Of No. 1 Hits, 1956-1975

House Of Sand
Elvis Double Features - Frankie And Johhny & Paradise Hawaiian Style

How Can You Lose What You Never Had
An Elvis Double Feature - Speedway & Clambake
Collectors Gold - Disc 1 *(alternate takes 1 & 3)*
Elvis Double Features - Kissin' Cousins, Clambake & Stay Away Joe

How Do You Think I Feel
Elvis
(The) Elvis Presley Collection - Treasures '53 To '58 - Disc 1
(The) King Of Rock 'N' Roll - 50's Masters - Disc 2

How Great Thou Art
A Touch Of Platinum - A Life In Music - Disc 2 *(alternate take 4)*
Amazing Grace His Greatest Sacres Performances - Disc 1
Amazing Grace His Greatest Sacred Performances - Disc 2 *(live version)*
Elvis A Legendary Performer Vol. 2
Elvis Aron Presley - Disc 4
(The) Elvis Presley Collection - Gospel - Disc 1
(The) Elvis Presley Gospel Treasury - Disc 1
(The) Elvis Presley Gospel Treasury (Special Edition)
Elvis Presley The King Of Rock & Roll At His Best - Disc 4
Elvis Recorded Live On Stage In Memphis
Elvis In Concert
Elvis 15th Anniversary Radio Show - Disc 6
How Great Thou Art
(The) Legend Of A King - Disc 2
Platinum - A Life In Music - Disc 2 *(alternate take 4)*
Various Artists
Reach Out And Touch
Precious Memories
Songs Of Faith And Inspiration

How The Web Was Woven
That's The Way It Is
That's The Way It Is - Original Master Recording
Walk A Mile In My Shoes - 70's Masters - Disc 1

How Would You Like To Be
Elvis Double Features - Canister Set - Disc 2
Elvis Double Features - It Happened At The Worlds Fair & Fun In Acapulco
Elvis Sings For Children And Grownups Too!
Elvis Sings Hits From His Movies Volume 1
Various Artists
The Hollywood Men
Hooray For Hollywood

How's The World Treating You
Elvis
(The) Elvis Presley Collection - Treasures '53 To '58 - Disc 1
(The) King Of Rock 'N' Roll - 50's Masters - Disc 2

Hurt
A Touch Of Platinum Vol. 2 - A Life In Music - Disc 2 *(alternate take 2)*
Always On My Mind
Elvis In Concert
(The) Elvis Presley Collection - From The Heart - Disc 1
Elvis 15th Anniversary Radio Show - Disc 3
From Elvis Presley Boulevard, Memphis, Tennessee, Recorded Live
(The) Legend Lives On - Disc 3
Platinum - A Life In Music - Disc 4 *(alternate take 2)*
Walk A Mile In My Shoes - 70's Masters - Disc 2
Various Artists
Solid Gold Country - Elvis: What Happened?
Solid Gold Country - Elvis Presley In Concert
Solid GoldCountry - 70 Years Of RCA Country

I Asked The Lord (He's Only A Prayer Away)
A Golden Celebration - Disc 4 - Elvis At Home - Germany 1958-60

I Beg Of You
(The) Blue Suede Box - Elvis: His Greatest Soundtracks - Disc 1 *(alternate master, take 12)*
Elvis' Gold Records Volume 2 - 50,000,000 Elvis Fans Can't Be Wrong
Elvis Gold Records Volume 2 - 50,000,000 Elvis Fans Can't Be Wrong (1997 Reissue)
Elvis! His Greatest Hits - Disc 1
Elvis His Life And Music - Disc 2
(The) Elvis Presley Birthday Tribute 1992 - Disc 2
(The) Elvis Presley Collection - The Rocker - Disc 1
Elvis Presley - 50 Greatest Hits - Disc 2
Elvis 50 Worldwide Gold Hits Vol. 1
Elvis 50 Years 50 Hits - Disc 2
Essential Elvis Vol. 2 Stereo 57 *(alternate take 1)*
Essential Elvis Vol. 2 Stereo 57 *(alternate takes 6 & 8)*
Essential Elvis Vol. 2 Stereo 57 *(alternate take 22)*
(The) King Of Rock' N' Roll - 50's Masters - Disc 3
(The) King Of Rock 'N' Roll - 50's Masters - Disc 5 *(alternate master, take 12)*
Loving You (1997 Reissue) *(alternate master, take 12)*
Memories Of Elvis - 1991 - Disc 1
Memories Of Elvis - 1993 - Disc 2
(The) Top Ten Hits - Disc 1
Various Artists
Solid Gold Country - Elvis Presley Golden Records - 93-2
Take 2 (Promo) *(stereo alternate take)*

I Believe
Amazing Grace His Greatest Sacred Performances - Disc 1
Elvis Christmas Album
(The) Elvis Presley Collection - Gospel - Disc 1
(The) Elvis Presley Gospel Treasury - Disc 1
Elvis Presley - The King Of Rock & Roll At His Best - Disc 1
Elvis 15th Anniversary Radio Show - Disc 3
Essential Elvis Vol. 2 Stereo 57 *(alternate take 4)*
(The) King Of Rock 'N' Roll - 50's Masters - Disc 2
You'll Never Walk Alone

I Believe In The Man In The Sky
Amazing Grace His Greatest Sacres Performances - Disc 1
Elvis Gospel 1957-1971: Known Only To Him
(The) Elvis Presley Collection - Gospel - Disc 1
Elvis The Other Sides - Worldwide Gold Award Hits Volume 2 - Disc 2
His Hand In Mine

I Can Help
Elvis Aron Presley Forever
Elvis Today
Walk A Mile In My Shoes - 70's Masters - Disc 4

I Can't Help It
Platinum -A Life In Music - Disc 2 (Graceland & Palm Springs Segment) *(home recording)*

I Can't Stop Loving You
Aloha From Hawaii Via Satellite
Aloha From Hawaii Via Satellite - 25th Anniversary Edition
An Afternoon In The Garden
Elvis As Recorded At Madison Square Garden
Elvis! His Greatest Hits - Disc 4
Elvis In Person At The International Hotel
Elvis Recorded Live On Stage In Memphis
Elvis 20th Anniversary Radio Show - Disc 1
From Nashville To Memphis -60's Masters- Disc 5 (medley This Time/I Can't StopLovingYou)*(inf. recording)*
(The) Legend Lives On - Disc 3
Welcome To My World

I Didn't Make It On Playing Guitar
Essential Elvis Vol. 4 - A Hundred Years From Now *(informal jam)*

I Don't Care If The Sun Don't Shine
A Golden Celebration - Disc 1 *(alternate take)*
(The) Elvis Presley Collection - Treasures '53 To '58 - Disc 1
(The) King Of Rock 'N' Roll - 50's Masters - Disc 1
(The) Louisiana Hayride - Anthologies Of Legends - Elvis Presley
(The) Louisiana Hayride Archives Volume 1 (1/22/55)
(The) Sun Sessions - The Master Takes
(The) Sun Sessions - The Outtakes

I Don't Wanna Be Tied
Elvis Double Features - Canister Set - Disc 1
Elvis Double Features - Kid Galahad & Girls! Girls! Girls!

I Don't Want To
Elvis Double Features - Canister Set - Disc 1
Elvis Double Features - Kid Galahad & Girls! Girls! Girls!

I Feel I've Known You Forever
From Nashville To Memphis - 60's Masters - Disc 2
Pot Luck With Elvis
Remembering Elvis

I Feel So Bad
A Touch Of Platinum - A Life In Music - Disc 2 *(alternate take 1)*
Elvis' Golden Records Volume 3
Elvis' Golden Records Volume 3 (1997 Reissue)
Elvis! His Greatest Hits - Disc 2
Elvis His Life And Music - Disc 3
(The) Elvis Presley Birthday Tribute 1992 - Disc 2
(The) Elvis Presley Collection - Rhythm & Blues - Disc 1
Elvis The King: 1954-1965
Elvis 50 Worldwide Gold Hits Vol. 1 - Disc 2
From Nashville To Memphis - 60's Masters - Disc 1
Good Rockin' Tonight - Disc 1
Memories Of Elvis - 1991 - Disc 2
Platinum - A Life In Music - Disc 2 *(alternate take 1)*
Reconsider Baby
Sixties Legends - Elvis Presley - Disc 1
(The) Top Ten Hits - Disc 2
Various Artists
Solid Gold Country - Elvis Presley's Golden Records - 91-11
Solid Gold Country - Elvis Presley In Nashville
Solid Gold Scrapbook - Elvis Golden Decade - 1956-1965
Solid Gold Scrapbook - Solid Gold Elvis

I Forgot To Remember To Forget
A Date With Elvis
Elvis! His Greatest Hits - Disc 4
(The) Elvis Presley Collection - Country - Disc 2
Great Country Songs
(The) King Of Rock 'N' Roll - 50's Masters - Disc 1
Remembering Elvis
The Sun Sessions CD - The Masters Outtakes
Various Artists
Country USA - 1955
Solid Gold Country - Elvis: What Happened?
Solid Gold Country - Elvis Presley Birthday Tribute 92-1
Solid Gold Country - Elvis Presley Birthday Tribute 93-1
Solid Gold Country - Elvis Presley Memorial Tribute 91-8
Solid Gold Country - Elvis Presley Memorial Tribute 92-8
Solid Gold Country - Elvis Presley Memorial Tribute 93-8
Solid Gold Country - The Complete 50's Masters
Solid Gold Country - 70 Years Of RCACountry

I Got A Feelin' In My Body
Essential Elvis Vol. 5 - Rhythm And Country *(alternate take 1)*
Good Times
Walk A Mile In My Shoes - 70's Masters - Disc 4

I Got A Woman
A Golden Celebration - Disc 1 - Dorsey Bros. Show New York Jan. 28, 1956
A Golden Celebration - Disc 2 - Miss.-Alabama Dairy Show Tupelo Afternoon Sept. 26, 1956
A Golden Celebration - Disc 3 - Miss.-Alabama Dairy Show Tupelo Evening Sept. 26, 1956
A Touch Of Platinum - A Life In Music - Disc 1 *(alternate take)*
Collectors Gold - Disc 3 (Las Vegas 1969)
Elvis Aron Presley - Disc 1
Elvis Aron Presley - Disc 4 (medley I Got A Woman/Amen)
Elvis In Concert
Elvis In Nashville
Elvis Presley
Elvis Presley - Collectors Edition
Elvis Recorded Live On Stage In Memphis
Elvis 15th Anniversary Radio Show - Disc 3
Elvis 20th Anniversary Radio Show - Disc 3
Elvis 56
Elvis 56 Advance Music (Promo)
Good Rockin' Tonight - Disc 1
(The) King Of Rock 'N' Roll - 50's Masters - Disc 1
(The) Legend Lives On - Disc 1
(The) Louisiana Hayride - Anthologies Of Legends - Elvis Presley
(The) Louisiana Hayride Archives Volume 1 (4/9/55)
Platinum - A Life In Music - Disc 1 *(alternate take)*
Platinum - A Life In Music - Disc 3 ('68 Comeback Special rehearsal)
(The) Private Presley CD
Pure Gold
Raw Elvis
Rocker
Vintage 55

I Got Lucky
Elvis Command Performances - 60's Masters - Disc 1
Elvis Double Features - Canister Set - Disc 1
Elvis Double Features - Kid Galahad & Girls! Girls! Girls!

I Got Stung
Elvis' Gold Records Vol. 2 - 50,000,000 Elvis Fans Can't Be Wrong
Elvis' Gold Records Vol. 2 - 50,000,000 Elvis Fans Can't Be Wrong (1997 Reissue)

I GOT STUNG (cont'd)
Elvis' Greatest Jukebox Hits
Elvis! His Greatest Hits - Disc 2
Elvis His Life And Music - Disc 2
(The) Elvis Presley Birthday Tribute 1992 - Disc 2
(The) Elvis Presley Collection - The Rocker - Disc 1
Elvis Presley - 50 Greatest Hits - Disc 2
Elvis The King: 1954 - 1965
Elvis The Legend - Disc 2
Elvis The Tribute - A Biography - Disc 1
Elvis 50 Worldwide Gold Hits Vol. 1 - Disc 1
Elvis 50 Years - 50 Hits - Disc 2
Essential Elvis Vol. 3 / Hits Like Never Before *(alternate take 1, unreleased version)*
Essential Elvis Vol. 3 / Hits Like Never Before *(alternate takes 13,14, unreleased version, false start)*
Essential Elvis Vol. 3 / Hits Like Never Before *(alternate take 12, unreleased version)*
Good Rockin' Tonight - Disc 1
(The) King Of Rock 'N' Roll - 50's Masters - Disc 4
Memories Of Elvis - 1991 - Disc 1
Memories Of Elvis - 1993 - Disc 2
(The) Top Ten Hits - Disc 1
Various Artists
Monster Rock 'N' Roll Show
Solid Gold Scrapbook - Solid Gold Elvis

I Gotta Horse - I Gotta Gun (Comedy Skit)
Various Artists
Steve Allen On The Air!

I Gotta Know
Are You Lonesome Tonight/I Gotta Know (Jukebox Single)
Commemorative Jukebox Series (5 CD Set)
Elvis' Golden Records Vol. 3
Elvis' Golden Records Vol. 3 (1997 Reissue)
Elvis! His Greatest Hits - Disc 2
Elvis His Life And Music - Disc 3
(The) Elvis Presley Birthday Tribute 1992 - Disc 2
(The) Elvis Presley Collection - The Rocker - Disc 2
Elvis 50 Worldwide Gold Hits Vol. 1 - Disc 2
From Nashville To Memphis - 60's Masters - Disc 1

I Hear A Sweet Voice Calling
(The) Million Dollar Quartet

I, John
Amazing Grace His Greatest Sacred Performances - Disc 2
Amazing Grace His Greatest Sacred Performances - Disc 2 *(previously unreleased)*
Elvis In Nashville - 1956-1971
He Touched Me
Selections From Amazing Grace (Promo)

I Just Can't Help Believin'
Elvis The Legend - Disc 3
(The) Elvis Presley Collection - Love Songs - Disc 2
Heart And Soul
(The) Legend Lives On - Disc 1
That's The Way It Is
That's The Way It Is - Original Master Recording
Walk A Mile In My Shoes - 70's Masters - Disc 1
Walk A Mile In My Shoes - Out Of The Box Sampler (Promo)

I Just Can't Make It By Myself
(The) Million Dollar Quartet

I Love Only One Girl
Burning Love And Hits From His Movies
Elvis Double Features - Spinout & Double Trouble
Elvis Presley The King Of Rock & Roll At His Best - Disc 2

I Love You Because
Elvis Presley
Elvis Presley - Collectors Edition
(The) Elvis Presley Collection - Treasures '53 To '58 - Disc 1
(The) King Of Rock 'N' Roll - 50's Masters - Disc 1
(The) Sun Sessions - The Master Takes
(The) Sun Sessions - The Outtakes *(alternate take 2)*
(The) Sun Sessions - The Alternate Takes *(alternate take 3)*
(The) Sun Sessions - The Alternate Takes *(alternate take 5)*

I Met Her Today
Collectors Gold - Disc 2 *(alternate take 1)*
Elvis For Everyone
From Nashville To Memphis - 60's Masters - Disc 2
Separate Ways

I Miss You
Always On My Mind
Raised On Rock

I Need Somebody To Lean On
A Valentine Gift For You
Elvis Double Features - Canister Set - Disc 3
Elvis Double Features - Viva Las Vegas & Roustabout
(The) Elvis Presley Collection - The Romantic - Disc 2

I Need You So
(The) Blue Suede Box - Elvis: His Greatest Soundtracks - Disc 1
(The) Elvis Presley Collection - Rhythm & Blues - Disc 2
(The) King Of Rock 'N' Roll - 50's Masters - Disc 3
Loving You
Loving You (1997 Reissue)

I Need Your Love Tonight
A Touch Of Platinum - A Life In Music - Disc 1 *(alternate take 7)*
Elvis Aron Presley - Disc 1
Elvis' Gold Records Volume 2 - 50,000,000 Elvis Fans Can't Be Wrong
Elvis' Gold Records Volume 2 - 50,000,000 Elvis Fans Can't Be Wrong (1997 Reissue)
Elvis! His Greatest Hits - Disc 2
Elvis His Life And Music - Disc 2
(The) Elvis Presley Birthday Tribute 1992 - Disc 2
(The) Elvis Presley Collection - Rock 'N' Roll - Disc 1
Elvis Presley - 50 Greatest Hits - Disc 1
Elvis The Other Sides - Worldwide Gold Award Hits Volume 2 - Disc 2
Elvis The King: 1954-1965
Elvis The Tribute - A Biography - Disc 1
Elvis 50 Years 50 Hits - Disc 1
Elvis 15th Anniversary Radio Show - Disc 3
Essential Elvis Volume 3/ Hits Like Never Before *(alternate takes 2 & 10, unreleased false start & complete take)*
Essential Elvis Volume 3/ Hits Like Never Before *(alternate take 5, unreleased version)*
(The) King Of Rock 'N' Roll - 50's Masters - Disc 4
Memories Of Elvis - 1991 - Disc 1
Memories Of Elvis - 1993 - Disc 2
Platinum - A Life In Music - Disc 1 *(alternate take 7)*

I NEED YOUR LOVE TONIGHT (cont'd)
(The) Top Ten Hits - Disc 1
Various Artists
(The) Elvis Presley Years - Disc 2
Solid Gold Country - Elvis Presley's Golden Records 91-11
Solid Gold Country - Elvis Presley's Golden Records 93-2
Solid Gold Scrapbook - Solid Gold Elvis

I Really Don't Want to Know
Elvis At His Romantic Best
Elvis Country - I'm 10,000 Years Old
Elvis! His Greatest Hits - Disc 4
Elvis In Concert
(The) Elvis Presley Collection - Country - Disc 2
Elvis The Other Sides - Worldwide Gold Award Hits Volume 2 - Disc 2
Great Country Songs
Walk A Mile In My Shoes - 70's Masters - Disc 1
Welcome To My World
Various Artists
Dick Clark's Rock Roll & Remember 08/12-08/14
Country Songs That Will Last Forever

I Shall Be Released
Walk A Mile In My Shoes - 70's Masters - Disc 4 *(informal recording)*

I Shall Not Be Moved
(The) Million Dollar Quartet

I Slipped, I Stumbled, I Fell
Collectors Gold - Disc 1 *(alternate take 18)*
Elvis Double Features - Flaming Star, Wild In The Country & Follow That Dream
Elvis Double Features - Flaming Star, Wild In The Country & Follow That Dream *(alternate master)*
Something For Everybody
Separate Ways

I Think I'm Gonna Like It Here
Elvis Double Features - Canister Set - Disc 2
Elvis Double Features - It Happened At The Worlds Fair & Fun In Acapulco

I Want To Be Free
A Date With Elvis
(The) Blue Suede Box - Elvis: His Greatest Soundtracks - Disc 2
(The) Blue Suede Box - Elvis: His Greatest Soundtracks - Disc 2 *(movie version)*
Elvis The Other Sides - Worldwide Gold Award Hits Volume 2 - Disc 1
(The) Elvis Presley Collection - Movie Magic - Disc 2
Elvis Presley Sings Leiber & Stoller
Essential Elvis - The First Movies *(original version alternate take 11)*
Jailhouse Rock and Love Me Tender
Jailhouse Rock and Love Me Tender *(movie version)*
(The) King Of Rock 'N' Roll - 50's Masters - Disc 3
(The) King Of Rock 'N' Roll - 50's Masters - Disc 5 *(alternate take 10)*
Remembering Elvis
Various Artists
Leiber & Stoller Music Publishing (6 CD Promo Set)

I Want You, I Need You, I Love You
A Golden Celebration - Disc 2 - Milton Berle Show Hollywood June 5, 1956
A Golden Celebration - Disc 2 - Steve Allen Show New York July 1, 1956
A Golden Celebration - Disc 2 - Miss.-Alabama Dairy Show Tupelo Afternoon Sept. 26, 1956
A Touch Of Platinum - A Life In Music - Disc 1 *(alternate take 4)*
Blue Suede Shoes (Original Soundtrack) - Disc 1 *(alternate take)*

I WANT YOU, I NEED YOU, I LOVE YOU (cont'd)
Elvis A Legendary Performer Vol. 2
Elvis' Golden Records
Elvis' Golden Records (1997 Reissue)
Elvis! His Greatest Hits - Disc 1
Elvis His Life & Music - Disc 1
(The) Elvis Presley Birthday Tribute 1992 - Disc 2
(The) Elvis Presley Collection - Love Songs - Disc 2
Elvis Presley The King Of Rock & Roll At His Best - Disc 4
Elvis Presley Great Performances
Elvis Presley - 50 Greatest Hits -Disc 1
Elvis Presley: 1954-1961
Elvis The Legend - Disc 1
Elvis 20th Anniversary Radio Show - Disc 1
Elvis 50 Years 50 Hits - Disc 1
Elvis 56
Elvis 56 Advance Music (Promo)
Elvis 50 Worldwide Gold Hits Vol. 1 - Disc 1
Great Hits Of 1956-57
Heart And Soul
(The) King Of Rock 'N' Roll - 50's Masters - Disc 2
(The) King Of Rock 'N' Roll - 50's Masters - Disc 5 *(alternate take 16)*
Memories Of Elvis - 1991 - Disc 4
Memories Of Elvis - 1993 - Disc 1
(The) Number One Hits
Platinum - A Life In Music - Disc 1 *(alternate take 4)*
Shake Rattle & Roll (Promo)
(The) Top Ten Hits - Disc 1
Various Artists
Country U.S.A. 1956
Dick Clark's Rock Roll & Remember 9/2-9/4
Heart Of Dixie (Original Soundtrack)
Heart Of Dixie (Original Soundtrack) (Promo)
Solid Gold Country - Elvis Presley & TV
Solid Gold Country - Elvis Presley In Nashville
Solid Gold Country - Elvis Presley Memorial Tribute 93-8
Sweet Dreams Of Country
The Heart 'N' Soul Of Rock 'N' Roll
Those Fabulous 50's

I Want You With Me
Collectors Gold - Disc 2 *(alternate take 1)*
From Nashville to Memphis - 60's Masters - Disc 1
Good Rockin' Tonight - Disc 2
Return Of The Rocker
Something For Everybody

I Was Born About Ten Thousand Years Ago
Elvis Now
Walk A Mile In My Shoes - 70's Masters - Disc 3

I Was The One
A Golden Celebration - Disc 1 - Dorsey Bros. Show New York Feb. 18, 1956
A Golden Celebration - Disc 2 - Miss.-Alabama Dairy Show Tupelo Afternoon Sept. 26, 1956
A Golden Celebration - Disc 3 - Miss.-Alabama Dairy Show Tupelo Evening Sept. 26, 1956
A Touch O Platinum Vol. 2 - A Life In Music - Disc 1 (Las Vegas Rehearsals)
A Valentine Gift For You
Elvis' Golden Records (1997 Reissue)
Elvis! His Greatest Hits - Disc 1
(The) Elvis Presley Collection - Love Songs - Disc 2
(The) Elvis Presley Collection - Treasures '53 To '58 - Disc 2 *(alternate take 3)*
Elvis The Legend - Disc 1
Elvis 56

I WAS THE ONE (cont'd)
Elvis 56 Advance Music (Promo)
Elvis 50 Worldwide Gold Hits Vol. 1 - Disc 1
For LP Fans Only
Good Rockin' Tonight - Disc 2
Great Hits: 1956-57
Heartbreak Hotel - I Was The One
Heartbreak Hotel - I Was The One *(alternate take 2)*
(The) King Of Rock 'N' Roll - 50's Masters - Disc 1
(The) Louisiana Hayride - Anthologies Of Legends - Elvis Presley
(The) Louisiana Hayride Volume 1 (12/15/56)
Memories Of Elvis - 1991 - Disc 2
Platinum - A Life In Music - Disc 3 (Las Vegas Rehearsals)
Walk A Mile In My Shoes - 70's Masters - Disc 5 (The Elvis Presley Show)
Various Artists
Solid Gold Country - Elvis Presley & TV

I Washed My Hands In Muddy Waters
A Touch Of Platinum Vol. 2 - A Life In Music - Disc 1 (Las Vegas Rehearsals)
Elvis Country - I'm 10,000 Years Old
(The) Elvis Presley Collection - The Rocker - Disc 1
Essential Elvis Vol. 4 - A Hundred Years From Now *(undubbed/unedited)*
Platinum - A Life In Music - Disc 3 (Las Vegas Rehearsals)
Walk A Mile In My Shoes - 70's Masters - Disc 3 *(long version)*

I Will Be Home Again
Elvis Is Back
Elvis Is Back - 24 kt Gold Disc
(The) Elvis Presley Collection - The Romantic - Disc 1
From Nashville To Memphis - 60's Masters - Disc 1

I Will Be True
Elvis (aka 'The Fool Album")
Elvis Aron Presley - Disc 3
Platinum - A Life In Music - Disc 1 (Bad Nauheim Medley) *(home recording)*
Walk A Mile In My Shoes - 70's Masters - Disc 4

I'll Be Back
Command Performances - 60's Masters - Disc 2
Double Dynamite
Elvis Double Features - Spinout & Double Trouble
(The) Elvis Presley Collection - Movie Magic - Disc 2

I'll Be Home For Christmas
Blue Christmas
Christmas With Elvis
Country Christmas-Elvis Presley Country Christmas/Jim Reeves Holiday Hits
Christmas Classics
Christmas Wishes From Anne Murray, Glen Campbell & Elvis Presley
Elvis Christmas Album
Elvis Christmas Album - Camden
Elvis Presley & Jim Reeves Christmas Favorites
If Every Day Was Like Christmas
If Every Day Was Like Christmas - Special Collectors Edition
(The) King Of Rock 'N' Roll - 50's Masters - Disc 3
Merry Christmas
Various Artists
Country Christmas
Solid Gold Country - Christmas With Elvis Presley
The Family Christmas Collection
50 Christmas Favorites

I'll Be Home On Christmas Day
A Touch Of Platinum Vol. 2 - A Life In Music - Disc 2 *(alternate take 4)*
Christmas With Elvis
Elvis Sings The Wonderful World Of Christmas
If Every Day Was Like Christmas
If Every Day Was Like Christmas *(alternate version)*
If Every Day Was Like Christmas - Special Collectors Edition
If Every Day Was Like Christmas - Special Collectors edition *(alternate version)*
Memories Of Christmas
Platinum - A Life In Music - Disc 4 *(alternate take 4)*
Various Artists
Solid Gold Country - Christmas With Elvis Presley

I'll Be There
From Nashville to Memphis - 60's Masters - Disc 4

I'll Hold You In My Heart
(The) Elvis Presley Collection - The Romantic - Disc 1
From Elvis In Memphis
From Nashville To Memphis - 60's Masters - Disc 4
Great Country Songs
(The) Memphis Record

I'll Never Fall In Love Again
(The) Elvis Presley Collection - From The Heart - Disc 2
From Elvis Presley Boulevard, Memphis, Tennessee, Recorded Live

I'll Never Know
Love Letters From Elvis

I'll Never Let You Go (Little Darlin')
A Golden Celebration - Disc 1 *(alternate take)*
Elvis Presley
Elvis Presley - Collectors Edition
(The) Elvis Presley Collection - Treasures '53 To '58 - Disc 2
(The) King Of Rock 'N' Roll - 50's Masters - Disc 1
(The) Sun Sessions - The Master Takes
(The) Sun Sessions - The Outtakes

I'll Never Stand In Your Way
A Touch Of Platinum - A Life In Music - Disc 1 *(1954 acetate)*
Platinum - A Life In Music - Disc 1 *(1954 acetate)*
Platinum In-Store Sampler (Promo) *(1954 acetate)*
Platinum Sampler (Promo) *(1954 acetate)*

I'll Remember You
Aloha From Hawaii Via Satellite
Aloha From Hawaii Via Satellite - 25th Anniversary Edition
Aloha Via Satellite
(The) Alternate Aloha
An Afternoon In The Garden
Elvis Aron Presley - Disc 2
Elvis Birthday Tribute Radio Program
Elvis 20th Anniversary Radio Show - Disc 2
From Nashville To Memphis - 60's Masters - Disc 3 *(original unedited master)*
Walk A Mile In My Shoes - 70's Masters - Disc 5 (The Elvis Presley Show)

I'll Take Love
Elvis Double Features - Easy Come, Easy Go & Speedway

I'll Take You Home Again Kathleen
Elvis (aka "The Fool Album")
Elvis Aron Presley - Disc 3
Platinum - A Life In Music - Disc 1 (Bad Nauheim Medley) *(home recording)*
Walk A Mile In My Shoes - 70's Masters - Disc 4 *(original undubbed version)*

I'm Beginning To Forget You
A Touch Of Platinum - A Life In Music - Disc 2 (Graceland & Palm Springs Segment) *(home recording)*
Platinum - A Life In Music - Disc 2 (Graceland & Palm Springs Segment) *(home recording)*

I'm Comin' Home
A Touch Of Platinum - A Life In Music - Disc 2 *(alternate take 3)*
(The) Elvis Presley Collection - The Rocker - Disc 2
From Nashville To Memphis - 60's Masters - Disc 1
Platinum - A Life In Music - Disc 2 *(alternate take 3)*
Return Of The Rocker
Something For Everybody

I'm Counting On You
A Touch Of Platinum - A Life In Music - Disc 1 *(alternate take 13)*
Elvis Presley
Elvis Presley - Collectors Edition
(The) Elvis Presley Collection - Treasures '53 To '58 - Disc 2
(The) King Of Rock 'N' Roll - 50's Masters - Disc 1
Platinum - A Life In Music - Disc 1 *(alternate take 13)*

I'm Falling In Love Tonight
Command Performances - 60's Masters - Disc 1
Elvis Aron Presley- Disc 2 *(alternate takes 1-4)*
Elvis Double Features - Canister Set - Disc 2
Elvis Double Features - It Happened At The Worlds Fair & Fun In Acapulco

I'm Gonna Bid My Blues Goodby
(The) Million Dollar Quartet

I'm Gonna Sit Right Down And Cry
Elvis Presley
Elvis Presley - Collectors Edition
(The) Elvis Presley Collection - Treasures '53 To '58 - Disc 1
(The) King Of Rock 'N' Roll - 50's Masters - Disc 1
Various Artists
RCA 24 kt Gold Sampler (Promo)

I'm Gonna Walk Dem Golden Stairs
Amazing Grace His Greatest Sacred Performances - Disc 1
Elvis Gospel 1957-1971: Known Only to Him
(The) Elvis Presley Collection - Gospel - Disc 2
(The) Elvis Presley Gospel Treasury - Disc 1
His Hand In Mine

I'm Leavin'
Elvis Aron Presley - Disc 3
(The) Elvis Presley Collection - From The Heart - Disc 1
(The) Legend Lives On - Disc 4
Love Songs
Walk A Mile In My Shoes - 70's Masters - Disc 1

I'm Left, You're Right, She's Gone
A Golden Celebration - Disc 1 *(slow version)*
Elvis! His Greatest Hits - Disc 4

I'M LEFT, YOUR RIGHT, SHE'S GONE (cont'd)
(The) Elvis Presley Collection - Treasures '53 To '58 - Disc 1
For LP Fans Only
(The) King Of Rock 'N' Roll - 50's Masters - Disc 1
(The) King Of Rock 'N' Roll - 50's Masters - Disc 5 *(alternate take 11)*
(The) Sun Sessions - The Master Takes
(The) Sun Sessions - The Outtakes *(alternate take 9)*
(The) Sun Sessions - The Alternate Takes *(alternate take 7)*
(The) Sun Sessions - The Alternate Takes *(alternate take 22)*

I'm Movin' On
(The) Elvis Presley Collection - Country - Disc 2
From Elvis In Memphis
From Nashville To Memphis - 60's Masters - Disc 4
(The) Memphis Record

I'm Not The Marrying Kind
Elvis Double Features - Flaming Star, Wild In The Country & Follow That Dream

I'm So Lonesome I Could Cry
A Private Moment With The King *(home recording)*
Aloha From Hawaii Via Satellite
Aloha From Hawaii Via Satellite - 25th Anniversary Edition
(The) Alternate Aloha
(The) Elvis Presley Collection - Country - Disc 1
(The) Legend Lives On - Disc 3
Walk A Mile In My Shoes - 70's Masters - Disc 5 (The Elvis Presley Show)
Welcome To My World

I'm With A Crowd But So Alone
(The) Million Dollar Quartet

I'm Yours
(The) Elvis Presley Birthday Tribute 1992 - Disc 2
(The) Elvis Presley Collection - Love Songs - Disc 1
From Nashville To Memphis - 60's Masters - Disc 2
From Nashville To Memphis - 60's Masters - Disc 5 *(alternate take 1 undubbed)*
Pot Luck With Elvis

I've Got A Thing About You Baby
A Touch Of Platinum Vol. 2 - A Life In Music - Disc 2
(The) Elvis Presley Collection - Country - Disc 1
Essential Elvis Vol. 5 - Rhythm And Country *(alternate take 14)*
Platinum - A Life In Music - Disc 4
Walk A Mile In My Shoes - 70's Masters - Disc 2

I've Got Confidence
Amazing Grace His Greatest Sacred Performances - Disc 2
He Touched Me

I've Got To Find My Baby
Elvis Double Features - Canister Set - Disc 4
Elvis Double Features - Harum Scarum & Girl Happy
Good Times

I've Lost You
Always On My Mind
Elvis The Other Sides - Worldwide Gold Award Hits Volume 2 - Disc 2
(The) Elvis Presley Collection - From The Heart - Disc 1
Essential Elvis Vol. 4 - A Hundred Years From Now *(alternate take 6)*
Heart And Soul *(unreleased stereo)*

I'VE LOST YOU (cont'd)
(The) Legend Lives On - Disc 3
That's The Way It Is
That's The Way It Is - Original Master Recording
Walk A Mile In My Shoes - 70's Masters - Disc 1

If Every Day Was Like Christmas
Christmas Wishes From Anne Murray, Glen Campbell & Elvis Presley
Christmas With Elvis
Elvis Christmas Album (Camden)
From Nashville To Memphis - 60's Masters - Disc 3
If Every Day Was Like Christmas
If Every Day Was Like Christmas - Special Collectors Edition
Memories Of Christmas *(unreleased undubbed version)*
Various Artists
A Fireside Christmas
Country Christmas
Dick Clark's Rock 'N' Roll Christmas
Happy Holidays Volume 25
Holiday Music 1992 Collection
Time-Life Treasury Of Christmas - Vol. 1
The Family Christmas Collection

If I Can Dream
A Touch Of Platinum Vol. 2 - A Life In Music - Disc 1 *(alternate take 1)*
Elvis A Legendary Performer Volume 2
Elvis' Gold Records Volume 5
Elvis' Gold Records Volume 5 (1997 Reissue)
Elvis! His Greatest Hits - Disc 3
Elvis / NBC-TV Special
(The) Elvis Presley Birthday Tribute 1992 - Disc 2
(The) Elvis Presley Collection - From The Heart - Disc 2
Elvis Presley: Great Performances
Elvis Presley The King Of Rock & Roll At His Best - Disc 4
Elvis Presley - 50 Greatest Hits - Disc 1
Elvis The Legend - Disc 3
Elvis The Tribute A Biography Disc 3
Elvis 20th Anniversary Radio Show - Disc 2
Elvis 50 Worldwide Gold Hits Vol. 1 - Disc 2
Elvis 50 Years 50 Hits - Disc !
Elvis 15th Anniversary Radio Show - Disc 5
(The) Great Performances
(The) Legend Of A King - Disc 2
Memories - The '68 Comeback Special - Disc 1
Memories - The '68 Comeback Special - Disc 2 *(previously unreleased)*
Memories Of Elvis - 1991 - Disc 3
Memories Of Elvis - 1993 - Disc 3
Platinum - A Life In Music - Disc 3 *(alternate take 1)*
Sixties Legends - Elvis Presley - Disc 2
Various Artists
American Country Countdown 91-1 Show 1
Dick Clark's Rock Roll & Remember 1/3-1/5
(The) Elvis Presley Years - Disc 3
Heartbreak Hotel (Original Soundtrack)
I Believe - Best Loved Stars Of Inspiration *(alternate take)*
Solid Gold Country - Elvis Presley & TV
Solid Gold Country - Elvis Presley Memorial Tribute 91-8

If I Get Home On Christmas Day
Christmas With Elvis
Elvis Sings The Wonderful World Of Christmas
If Every Day Was Like Christmas
If Every Day Was Like Christmas - Special Collectors Edition

IF I GET HOME ON CHRISTMAS DAY (cont'd)
Various Artists
Solid Gold Country - Christmas With Elvis Presley

If I Loved You
(The) Elvis Presley Collection - Love Songs - Disc 2 *(home recording)*

If I Were You
Essential Elvis Vol. 4 - A Hundred Years From Now *(alternate take 5)*
Love Letters From Elvis

If I'm A Fool (For Lovin' You)
(The) Elvis Presley Collection - The Romantic - Disc 1
From Nashville To Memphis - 60's Masters - Disc 5

If That Isn't Love
Amazing Grace His Greatest Sacred Performances - Disc 2
Essential Elvis Vol. 5 - Rhythm And Country *(alternate take 1)*
Good Times

If The Lord Wasn't Walking By My Side
Amazing Grace His Greatest Sacred Performances - Disc 1
How Great Thou Art

If We Never Meet Again
Amazing Grace His Greatest Sacred Performances - Disc 1
(The) Elvis Presley Collection - Gospel - Disc 2
(The) Elvis Presley Gospel Treasury - Disc 2
His Hand In Mine

If You Don't Come Back
Essential ElvisVol. 5 - Rhythm And Country *(alternate take 3)*
Raised On Rock

If You Love Me (Let Me Know)
Elvis Aron Presley - Disc 4
Elvis In Concert
Moody Blue
Various Artists
Solid Gold Country - Elvis Presley In Concert

If You Talk In Your Sleep
Elvis' Gold Records Volume 5
Elvis' Gold Records Volume 5 (1997 Reissue)
Promised Land
Walk A Mile In My Shoes - 70's Masters - Disc 2
Various Artists
Solid Gold Country - Elvis Presley Birthday Tribute 93-1
Solid Gold Scrapbook - Elvis In Memphis

If You Think I Don't Need You
Elvis Double Features - Canister Set - Disc 3
Elvis Double Features - Viva Las Vegas & Roustabout

In My Fathers House
Amazing Grace His Greatest Sacred Performances - Disc 1
His Hand In Mine

In My Way
Elvis Double Features - Flaming Star, Wild In The Country & Follow That Dream
Elvis For Everyone *(alternate take)*
Separate Ways

In The Garden
Amazing Grace His Greatest Sacred Performances - Disc 1
(The) Elvis Presley Collection - Gospel - Disc 2
(The) Elvis Presley Gospel Treasury - Disc 1
(The) Elvis Presley Gospel Treasury (Special Edition)
How Great Thou Art

In The Ghetto
A Touch Of Platinum Vol. 2 - A Life In Music - Disc 1 *(alternate take 3)*
Blue Suede Shoes (Original Soundtrack) Disc 2
Elvis Aron Presley - Disc 3
Elvis' Gold Records Volume 5
Elvis' Gold Records Volume 5 (1997 Reissue)
Elvis! His Greatest Hits - Disc 4
Elvis In Person At The International Hotel
(The) Elvis Presley Birthday Tribute 1992 - Disc 2
(The) Elvis Presley Collection - From The Heart - Disc 1
Elvis Presley 50 Greatest Hits - Disc 2
Elvis The Legend - Disc 3
Elvis The Tribute A Biography - Disc 3
Elvis 20th Anniversary Radio Show - Disc 2
Elvis 20th Anniversary Singles Set - Disc 5
Elvis 24 Karat Hits!
Elvis 50 Worldwide Gold Hits Vol. 1 - Disc 2
Elvis 50 Years 50 Hits - Disc 2
From Elvis In Memphis
From Nashville To Memphis - 60's Masters - Disc 4
From Nashville To Memphis - 60's Masters - Disc 5 *(alternate take 4)*
In The Ghetto/ Stuck On You
(The) Legend Lives On - Disc 1
Memories Of Elvis - 1991 - Disc 3
Memories Of Elvis - 1993 - Disc 3
(The) Memphis Record
Platinum - A Life In Music - Disc 3 *(alternate take 3)*
Platinum In-Store Sampler (Promo) *(alternate take 3)*
Pure Gold
Sixties Legends - Elvis Presley - Disc 2
(The) Top Ten Hits - Disc 2
Various Artists
Gold Disc 1001
Solid Gold Country - Elvis Presley Birthday Tribute 92-1
Solid Gold Country - Elvis Presley Birthday Tribute 93-1
Solid Gold Country - Elvis Presley Memorial Tribute 91-8
Solid Gold Country - Elvis Presley Memorial Tribute 92-8
Solid Gold Country - Elvis Presley Memorial Tribute 93-8
Solid Gold Country - Mac Davis Birthday Salute
Solid Gold Scrapbook - Elvis In Memphis
The Super 60's

In Your Arms
From Nashville To Memphis - 60's Masters - Disc 1
Something For Everybody

Indescribably Blue
Elvis' Gold Records Volume 4
Elvis' Gold Records Volume 4 (1997 Reissue)
Elvis His Life And Music - Disc 4
(The) Elvis Presley Collection - The Romantic - Disc 2

INDESCRIBABLY BLUE (cont'd)
From Nashville To Memphis - 60's Masters - Disc 3
(The) Legend Lives On - Disc 3

Inherit The Wind
Back In Memphis
Collectors Gold - Disc 3 (Las Vegas 1969)
From Nashville To Memphis - 60's Masters - Disc 4
(The) Memphis Record

Is It So Strange
A Date With Elvis
(The) Blue Suede Box - Elvis: His Greatest Soundtracks - Disc 1
(The) Elvis Presley Collection - Treasures '53 To '58 - Disc 1
Essential Elvis Vol. 2 - Stereo 57 *(alternate take 1)*
Essential Elvis Vol. 2 - Stereo 57 *(alternate takes 7,12)*
(The) King Of Rock 'N' Roll - 50's Masters Disc 3
Loving You (1997 Reissue)
(The) Million Dollar Quartet
Separate Ways

Island Of Love
Blue Hawaii
Blue Hawaii (1997 Reissue)
Blue Hawaii (1997 Reissue Collectors Edition)
(The) Blue Suede Box - Elvis: His Greatest Soundtracks - Disc 4

It Ain't No Big Thing (But It's Growing)
Essential Elvis Vol. 4 - A Hundred Years From Now *(alternate take 2)*
Love Letters From Elvis
Walk A Mile In My Shoes - 70's Masters - Disc 3

It Feels So Right
A Valentine Gift For You
Elvis Is Back
Elvis Is Back - 24 kt GoldDisc
(The) Elvis Presley Collection - Rhythm & Blues - Disc 1
From Nashville To Memphis - 60's Masters - Disc 1
Good Rockin' Tonight - Disc 2
Platinum - A Life In Music - Disc 2 *(alternate take 3)*

It Hurts Me
Elvis' Gold Records Volume 4
Elvis' Gold Records Volume 4 (1997 Reissue)
Elvis / NBC-TV Special
Elvis His Life And Music - Disc 4
(The) Elvis Presley Collection - The Romantic - Disc 1
Elvis The Other Sides - Worldwide Gold Award Hits Volume 2 - Disc 2
From Nashville To Memphis - 60's Masters - Disc 3
Heart And Soul
(The) Lost Album
Memories - The '68 Comeback Special - Disc 1

It Is No Secret (What God Can Do)
Amazing Grace His Greatest Sacred Performances - Disc 1
Country Christmas - Elvis Presley's Country Christmas/Jim Reeves Holiday Hits
Elvis Christmas Album
(The) Elvis Presley Collection - Gospel - Disc 2
(The) Elvis Presley Gospel Treasury - Disc 1
Elvis Presley The King Of Rock & Roll At His Best - Disc 1
Essential Elvis Vol. 2 Stereo 57 *(alternate takes 1,2,3)*
His Hand In Mine (bonus track)

IT IS NO SECRET (cont'd)
(The) King Of Rock 'N' Roll - 50's Masters - Disc 3
You'll Never Walk Alone
Various Artists
Treasury Of Country - Inspirational Favorites

It Keeps Right On A-Hurtin'
(The) Elvis Presley Collection - Country - Disc 1
From Elvis In Memphis
From Nashville To Memphis - 60's Masters - Disc 5
Great Country Songs
(The) Memphis Record
Various Artists
Country Sweet 'N' Sentimental

It Won't Be Long
Elvis Double Features - Spinout & Double Trouble

It Won't Seem Like Christmas (Without You)
Christmas With Elvis
Elvis Sings The Wonderful World Of Christmas
If Every Day Was Like Christmas
If Every Day Was Like Christmas *(unreleased alternate take 6)*
If Every Day Was Like Christmas - Special Collectors Edition
If Every Day Was Like Christmas - Special Collectors Edition *(unreleased alternate take 6)*

It's A Matter Of Time
Burning Love And Hits From His Movies Vol. 2
Double Dynamite
Elvis Presley - The King Of Rock & Roll At His Best - Disc 2
Walk A Mile In My Shoes - 70's Masters - Disc 1

It's A Sin
From Nashville to Memphis - 60's Masters - Disc 1
Something For Everybody

It's A Wonderful World
Elvis Double Features - Canister Set - Disc 3
Elvis Double Features - Viva Las Vegas & Roustabout

It's Been So Long Darling
Platinum - A Life In Music - Disc 1 (Bad Nauheim Medley) *(home recording)*

It's Carnival Time
Elvis Double Features - Canister Set - Disc 3
Elvis Double Features - Viva Las Vegas & Roustabout

It's Different Now
Walk A Mile In My Shoes - 70's Masters - Disc 4 *(rehearsal)*

It's Easy For You
Moody Blue

It's Impossible
Elvis (aka "The Fool Album")
(The) Elvis Presley Collection - From The Heart - Disc 2
(The) Legend Lives On - Disc 2
Pure Gold
Walk A Mile In My Shoes - 70's Masters - Disc 5 (The Elvis Presley Show)

It's Midnight
Always On My Mind
(The) Elvis Presley Collection - The Romantic - Disc 2
Platinum - A Life In Music - Disc 4 *(alternate take 10)*
Promised Land
Walk A Mile In My Shoes - 70's Masters - Disc 2

It's Now Or Never
A Touch Of Platinum - A Life In Music - Disc 2
Elvis A Legendary Performer Volume 2
Elvis Aron Presley - Disc 1
Elvis' Golden Records Volume 3
Elvis' Golden Records Volume 3 (1997 Reissue)
Elvis' Greatest Jukebox Hits
Elvis! His Greatest Hits - Disc 2
Elvis His Life And Music - Disc 3
Elvis In Concert
(The) Elvis Presley Birthday Tribute 1992 - Disc 2
(The) Elvis Presley Collection - Love Songs - Disc 1
Elvis Presley: Great Performances
Elvis Presley The King Of Rock & Roll At His Best - Disc 4
Elvis Presley: 1954-1961
Elvis Presley - 50 Greatest Hits - Disc 2
Elvis The Legend - Disc 2
Elvis The Tribute - A Biography - Disc 2
Elvis 15th Anniversary Radio Show - Disc 4
Elvis 20th Anniversary Radio Show - Disc 1
Elvis 20th Anniversary Singles Set - Disc 2
Elvis 24 Karat Hits!
Elvis 50 Worldwide Gold Hits Vol. 1 - Disc 2
Elvis 50 Years 50 Hits - Disc 2
From Nashville To Memphis - 60's Masters - Disc 1
From Nashville To Memphis - 60's Masters - Disc 5 *(original undubbed master)*
Heart And Soul
Hound Dog/ It's Now Or Never
(The) Legend Lives On - Disc 1
(The) Legend Of A King - Disc 1
Love Songs
Memories Of Elvis - 1991 - Disc 3
Memories Of Elvis - 1993 - Disc 2
(The) Number One Hits
Out Of The Box - 6 From The 60's (Promo) *(original undubbed master)*
Platinum - A Life In Music - Disc 2
Shake, Rattle & Roll (Promo)
Sixties Legends - Elvis Presley - Disc 1
(The) Top Ten Hits - Disc 2
Various Artists
Billboard's Top Rock 'N Roll Hits 1960
Billboard's Top Rock 'N' Roll Hits 1957-1961
Dick Clark's Rock Roll & Remember 1/3-1/5
Dick Clark's Rock Roll & Remember 8/12-8/14
(The) Elvis Presley Years - Disc 2
Nippers Greatest Hits - The 60's - Vol. 1
Solid Gold Country - Elvis: What Happened?
Solid Gold Country - Elvis Presley Birthday Tribute 92-1
Solid Gold Country - Elvis Presley Birthday Tribute 93-1
Solid Gold Country - Elvis Presley's Golden Years 93-11
Solid Gold Country - Elvis Presley's Golden Years 93-2
Solid Gold Country - Elvis Presley In Nashville
Solid Gold Country - Elvis Presley's Love Songs
Solid Gold Country - Elvis Presley Memorial Tribute 91-8
Solid Gold Country - Elvis Presley Memorial Tribute 92-8
Solid Gold Country - Elvis Presley Memorial Tribute 93-8
Solid Gold Country - Salute To RCA Studio B

IT'S NOW OR NEVER (cont'd)
Solid Gold Country - 70 Years Of RCA Country
Solid Gold Scrapbook - Solid Gold Elvis
Studio B Home Of A Thousand Hits Vol. 2
The Super 60's
The Year To Remember 1960

It's Only Love
Elvis Aron Presley - Disc 3
(The) Elvis Presley Collection - From The Heart - Disc 1
Elvis The Legend - Disc 3
Essential Elvis Vol. 4 - A Hundred Years From Now *(alternate take 9)*
Walk A Mile In My Shoes - 70's Masters - Disc 1

It's Over
Aloha From Hawaii Via Satellite
Aloha From Hawaii Via Satellite - 25th Anniversary Edition
Aloha Via Satellite
(The) Alternate Aloha
Walk A Mile In My Shoes - 70's Masters - Disc 5 (The Elvis Presley Show)

It's Still Here
Elvis (aka "The Fool Album")
Elvis Aron Presley - Disc 3
Elvis In Nashville 1956-1971
Walk A Mile In My Shoes - 70's Masters - Disc 4 *(original unedited version)*

It's Your Baby You Rock It
Elvis Country - I'm 10,000 Years Old
Elvis In Nashville 1956-1971
Walk A Mile In My Shoes - 70's Masters - Disc 3

Ito Eats
Blue Hawaii
Blue Hawaii (1997 Reissue)
Blue Hawaii (1997 Reissue Collectors Edition)
(The) Blue Suede Box - Elvis: His Greatest Soundtracks - Disc 4

"J"

Jailhouse Rock
A Touch Of Platinum - A Life In Music - Disc 1
(The) Blue Suede Box - Elvis: His Greatest Soundtracks - Disc 2
(The) Blue Suede Box - Elvis: His Greatest Soundtracks - Disc 2 *(movie version)*
Blue Suede Shoes (Original Soundtrack) Disc 2 *(sax overdub)*
Collectors Gold - Disc 3 (Las Vegas 1969)
Commemorative Jukebox Series (5 CD Set) - Disc 3
Elvis Aron Presley - Disc 2
Elvis A Legendary Performer Volume 2
Elvis Birthday Tribute Radio Program
Elvis!Elvis!Elvis! - The King And His Movies
Elvis' Golden Records
Elvis' Golden Records (1997 Reissue)
Elvis' Greatest Jukebox Hits
Elvis! His Greatest Hits - Disc 1
Elvis His Life And Music - Disc 1
Elvis In Concert
Elvis/NBC-TV Special
(The) Elvis Presley Birthday Tribute 1992 - Disc 2
(The) Elvis Presley Collection - Movie Magic - Disc 2 *(movie version)*
(The) Elvis Presley Collection - Rock 'N' Roll - Disc 1
Elvis Presley Radio Show (Promo)

JAILHOUSE ROCK (cont'd)
Elvis Presley Sings Leiber & Stoller
Elvis Presley The King Of Rock & Roll At His Best - Disc 4
Elvis Presley Great Performances
Elvis Presley: 1954-1961
Elvis Recorded Live On Stage In Memphis
Elvis The Legend - Disc 1
Elvis The Tribute - A Biography - Disc 1
Elvis 20th Anniversary Sampler
Elvis 24 Karat Hits!
Elvis 50 Worldwide Gold Hits Vol. 1 - Disc 1
Essential Elvis The First Movies *(vocal overdub take 6)*
Essential Elvis The First Movies *(unreleased version take 5)*
(The) Great Performances
Good Rockin' Tonight - Disc 1
Heartbreak Hotel, Hound Dog & Top Ten Hits
(The) Honeymoon Companion (Promo)
Jailhouse Rock and Love Me Tender
Jailhouse Rock and Love Me Tender *(movie version)*
Jailhouse Rock/Treat Me Nice (Jukebox Single)
(The) King Of Rock 'N' Roll - 50's Masters - Disc 3
King Of The Whole Wide World - Collectors Set - The Elvis Medley
(The) Legend Lives On - Disc 1
(The) Legend Of A King - Disc 1
Memories - The '68 Comeback Special - Disc 1 *(previously unreleased)*
Memories Of Elvis - 1991 - Disc 4
Memories Of Elvis - 1993 - Disc 1
(The) Number One Hits
Out Of The Box (Promo)
Platinum - A Life In Music - Disc 1
Pure Gold
Rocker
Shake, Rattle & Roll (Promo)
(The) Top Ten Hits - Disc 1
Virtual Graceland CD-ROM

Various Artists
American Bandstand - 40th Anniversary Special
American Gold - With Dick Bartley 96-3 Show 10
Billboard's Top Rock 'N' Roll Hits 1957
Billboard's Top Rock 'N' Roll Hits 1957-1961
Dick Clark's Rock Roll & Remember 1/3-1/5
Dick Clark's Rock Roll & Remember 8/12-8/14
Goodtime Oldies Theme Party
Leiber & Stoller The Fifties (Promo)
Leiber & Stoller Music Publishing (6 CD Promo Set)
Made In America
Rock 'N' Roll Legends
Solid Gold Country - Elvis Presley Birthday Tribute 92-1
Solid Gold Country - Elvis Presley Birthday Tribute 93-1
Solid Gold Country - Elvis Presley's Golden Records 91-11
Solid Gold Country - Elvis Presley's Golden Records 93-2
Solid Gold Country - Elvis Presley Memorial Tribute 91-8
Solid Gold Country - Elvis Presley Memorial Tribute 93-8
Solid Gold Country - The Complete 50's Masters
Solid Gold Country - Elvis Presley's Golden Records
Solid Gold Country - Elvis Presley: His Favorite Writers
Solid Gold Country - Elvis Presley In Concert
Solid Gold Country - Elvis Presley Sings Leiber And Stoller
Solid Gold Scrapbook - Elvis Golden Decade 1956-1965
Solid Gold Scrapbook - Elvis Movie Magic
There's A Riot Goin' On The Rock & Roll Classics Of Leiber & Stoller
WCBS FM 101.1 The Anniversary Album The 50's
Your Goodtime Oldies 93-03

Jesus Walked That Lonesome Valley
(The) Million Dollar Quartet

Johnny B. Goode
A Touch Of Platinum Vol. 2 - A Life In Music - Disc 1 (Las Vegas 1969)
Aloha From Hawaii Via Satellite
Aloha From Hawaii Via Satellite - 25th Anniversary Edition
Elvis Aron Presley - Disc 4
Elvis In Concert
Elvis In Person At The International Hotel
Elvis 15th Anniversary Radio Show
(The) Legend Lives On - Disc 1
(The) Legend Of A King - Disc 2
Platinum - A Life In Music - Disc 3 (Las Vegas 1969)

Joshua Fit The Battle
Amazing Grace His Greatest Sacred Performances - Disc 1
(The) Elvis Presley Collection - Gospel - Disc 1
Elvis Gospel 1957-1971: Known Only To Him
(The) Elvis Presley Gospel Treasury - Disc 1
(The) Elvis Presley Gospel Treasury (Special Edition)
His Hand In Mine
Various Artists
A Celebration Of Faith & Joy
Treasury Of Christmas - Inspirational Favorites

Judy
Elvis In Nashville - 1956-1971
From Nashville To Memphis - 60's Masters - Disc 2
Something For Everybody

Just A Little Bit
(The) Elvis Presley Collection - Rhythm & Blues - Disc 2
Raised On Rock
Walk A Mile In My Shoes - 70's Masters - Disc 4

Just A Little Talk With Jesus
(The) Million Dollar Quartet

Just Because
Elvis The King Of Rock 'N' Roll - 50's Masters - Disc 1
Elvis Presley
Elvis Presley - Collectors Edition
(The) Elvis Presley Collection - Treasures '53 To '58 - Disc 2
(The) Sun Sessions - The Master Takes

Just Call Me Lonesome
An Elvis Double Feature - Speedway & Clambake
Elvis In Nashville: 1956-1971
(The) Elvis Presley Collection - Country - Disc 2
From Nashville To Memphis - 60's Masters - Disc 3
Great Country Songs *(alternate take 6)*

Just For Old Times Sake
From Nashville To Memphis - 60's Masters - Disc 2
Pot Luck with Elvis
Remembering Elvis

Just Pretend
(The) Elvis Presley Collection - The Romantic - Disc 1
Essential Elvis Vol. 4 - A Hundred Years From Now *(alternate take 2)*
That's The Way It Is
That's The Way It Is - Original Master Recording
Walk A Mile In My Shoes - 70's Masters - Disc 3

Just Tell Her Jim Said Hello
Collectors Gold - Disc 2 *(alternate take 1)*
Elvis' Gold Records Volume 4
Elvis' Gold Records Volume 4 (1997 Reissue)
Elvis His Life And Music - Disc 4
Elvis Presley Sings Leiber & Stoller
Elvis The Other Sides - Worldwide Gold Award Hits Volume 2 - Disc 2
From Nashville To Memphis - 60's Masters - Disc 2
Various Artists
Leiber & Stoller Music Publishing (6 CD Promo Set)
Solid Gold Country - Elvis Presley Sings Leiber And Stoller

"K"

Kentucky Rain
Elvis Aron Presley - Disc 3
Elvis' Gold Records Volume 5
Elvis' Gold Records Volume 5 - (1997 Reissue)
Elvis! His Greatest Hits - Disc 4
(The) Elvis Presley Birthday Tribute 1992 - Disc 3
(The) Elvis Presley Collection - Country - Disc 1
Elvis Presley 50 Greatest Hits - Disc 2
Elvis The Tribute - A Biography - Disc 2
Elvis 20th Anniversary Radio Show - Disc 2
Elvis 50 Worldwide Gold Hits Vol. 1 - Disc 2
Elvis 50 Years 50 Hits - Disc 2
From Nashville ToMemphis - 60's Masters - Disc 5
From Nashville To Memphis - 60's Masters - Disc 5 *(alternate take 5)*
Great Country Songs
(The) Legend Lives On - Disc 2
Love Songs
Memories Of Elvis - 1991 - Disc 4
(The) Memphis Record
Pure Gold
Various Artists
Country Memories
Dick Clark's Rock Roll & Remember 1/3-1/5
(The) Elvis Presley Years - Disc 3
Golden Country Oldies (Promo) *(unreleased 1980 remixed version)*
Solid Gold Country - Elvis Presley Birthday Tribute 92-1
Solid Gold Country - Elvis Presley Birthday Tribute 93-1
Solid Gold Country - Elvis Presley Memorial Tribute 91-8
Solid Gold Country - Elvis Presley Memorial Tribute 92-8
Solid Gold Country - Elvis Presley Memorial Tribute 93-8
Solid Gold Scrapbook - Elvis In Memphis

King Creole
(The) Blue Suede Box - Elvis: His Greatest Soundtracks - Disc 3
(The) Blue Suede Box - Elvis: His Greatest Soundtracks - Disc 3 *(alternate take 18)*
(The) Blue Suede Box - Elvis: His Greatest Soundtracks - Disc 3 *(alternate take 3)*
Elvis!Elvis!Elvis! - The King And His Movies
Elvis' Gold Records Vol. 2 - 50,000,000 Elvis Fans Can't Be Wrong (1997 Reissue)
Elvis! His Greatest Hits - Disc 2
(The) Elvis Presley Collection - Movie Magic - Disc 2

KING CREOLE (cont'd)
Elvis Presley Sings Leiber & Stoller
Elvis The Legend - Disc 1
Elvis The Other Sides - Worldwide Gold Award Hits Volume 2 - Disc 1
Elvis The Tribute - A Biography - Disc 3 *(alternate take)*
Essential Elvis Vol. 3/ Hits Like Never Before *(track E take 18, unreleased master recording)*
Essential Elvis Vol. 3/ Hits Like Never Before *(track E take 3, unreleased version)*
Essential Elvis Vol. 3/ Hits Like Never Before *(track R take 8, main title instrumental version)*
(The) Great Performances
King Creole
King Creole (1997 Reissue)
King Creole (1997 Reissue) *(alternate take 18)*
King Creole (1997 Reissue) *(alternate take 3)*
(The) King Of Rock 'N' Roll - 50's Masters - Disc 4
(The) King Of Rock 'N' Roll - 50's Masters - Disc 5 *(alternate take 3)*
Various Artists
Leiber & Stoller Music Publishing (6 CD Promo Set)
Solid Gold Scrapbook - Elvis' Movie Music

King Of The Whole Wide World
Command Performances - 60's Masters - Disc 1
Elvis Double Features - Canister Set - Disc 1
Elvis Double Features - Kid Galahad & Girls! Girls! Girls!
Elvis!Elvis!Elvis! - The King And His Movies
Elvis' Golden Records Vol. 3 (1997 Reissue)
Elvis! His Greatest Hits - Disc 3
(The) Elvis Presley Collection - Movie Magic - Disc 1
Return Of The Rocker

Kismet
Elvis Double Features - Canister Set - Disc 4
Elvis Double Features - Harum Scarum & Girl Happy

Kiss Me Quick
Elvis! His Greatest Hits - Disc 3
(The) Elvis Presley Collection - The Romantic - Disc 2
From Nashville To Memphis - 60's Masters - Disc 2
Pot Luck With Elvis
Remembering Elvis
Various Artists
Solid Gold Scrapbook - Elvis Movie Music

Kissin' Cousins
Command Performances - 60's Masters - Disc 1
Elvis Double Features - Kissin' Cousins, Clambake & Stay Away Joe *(number 2)*
Elvis Double Features - Kissin' Cousins, Clambake & Stay Away Joe
Elvis' Gold Records Volume 4 (1997 Reissue)
Elvis! His Greatest Hits - Disc 3
(The) Elvis Presley Collection - The Rocker - Disc 1
Elvis Presley - 50 Greatest Hits - Disc 1
Elvis The Tribute - A Biography - Disc 3
Elvis 50 Worldwide Gold Hits Vol. 1 - Disc 2
Elvis 50 Years 50 Hits - Disc 1
Various Artists
Solid Gold Scrapbook - Elvis Movie Music

Known Only To Him
Amazing Grace His Greatest Sacred Performances - Disc 1
Elvis Gospel 1957-1971: Known Only To Him
(The) Elvis Presley Collection - Gospel - Disc 2
His Hand In Mine

Ku-U-I-Po

Aloha From Hawaii Via Satellite - 25th Anniversary Edition
(The) Alternate Aloha
Blue Hawaii
Blue Hawaii (1997 Reissue)
Blue Hawaii (1997 Reissue Collectors Edition)
(The) Blue Suede Box - Elvis: His Greatest Soundtracks - Disc 4
Mahalo From Elvis

"L"

Lady Madonna

Walk A Mile In My Shoes - 70's Masters - Disc 3 *(informal recording)*

Lawdy, Miss Clawdy

A Golden Celebration - Disc 4 - Elvis - Burbank, Calif. June 27, 1968
A Touch Of Platinum - A Life In Music - Disc 1 *(alternate take 1)*
Elvis Aron Presley - Disc 2
Elvis Recorded Live On Stage In Memphis
Elvis, The King: 1954-1965
Elvis/NBC-TV Special
(The) Elvis Presley Collection - Rhythm & Blues - Disc 2 (NBC TV Special)
(The) Elvis Presley Collection - Rock 'N' Roll - Disc 2
Elvis 15th Anniversary Radio Show - Disc 5
Elvis 20th Anniversary Radio Show - Disc 2
Elvis 56
Elvis 56 Advance Music (Promo)
For LP Fans Only
Good Rockin' Tonight - Disc 1
(The) King Of Rock 'N' Roll - 50's Masters - Disc 2
(The) King Of Rock 'N' Roll -50's Masters - Disc 5 *(alternate take 3)*
(The) Legend Lives On - Disc 4
Memories - The '68 Comeback Special - Disc 2 *(previously unreleased rehearsal)*
Memories - The '68 Comeback Special - Disc 2 *(previously unreleased sit down show)*
Platinum - A Life In Music - Disc 1 *(alternate take 1)*
Rocker
Tiger Man

Lead Me, Guide Me

Amazing Grace His Greatest Sacred Performances - Disc 2
Amazing Grace His Greatest Sacred Performances - Disc 2 *(previously unreleased)*
Elvis Gospel 1957-1971 : Known Only To Him
Selections From Amazing Grace His Greatest Sacred Performances (Promo)
Virtual Graceland CD-ROM

Let It Be Me (Je T' Appartiens)

Elvis At His Romantic Best
(The) Elvis Presley Collection - From The Heart - Disc 1
He Touched Me
(The) Legend Lives On - Disc 1
On Stage February 1970 (Je T' Appartiens)
Walk A Mile In My Shoes - 70's Masters - Disc 5 (The Elvis Presley Show)

Let Me

(The) Blue Suede Box - Elvis: His Greatest Soundtracks - Disc 2
(The) Blue Suede Box - Elvis: His Greatest Soundtracks - Disc 2 *(solo)*
(The) Elvis Presley Collection - Treasures '53 To '58 - Disc 2
Elvis The Other Sides - Worldwide Gold Award Hits Volume 2 - Disc 1
Essential Elvis - The First Movies
Jailhouse Rock and Love Me Tender

LET ME (cont'd)
Jailhouse Rock and Love Me Tender *(solo)*
(The) King Of Rock 'N' Roll - 50's Masters - Disc 2

Let Me Be There
Elvis Aron Presley - Disc 4
Elvis Recorded Live On Stage In Memphis
(The) Legend Lives On - Disc 2
Moody Blue

Let Us Pray
Elvis Double Features - Live A Little, Love A Little, Charro, The Trouble With Girls, Change Of Habit
Elvis Presley The King Of Rock & Roll At His Best - Disc 1
You'll Never Walk Alone

Let Yourself Go
An Elvis Double Feature - Speedway & Clambake
Command Performances - 60's Masters - Disc 2
Elvis Double Features - Easy Come, Easy Go & Speedway
Elvis/NBC-TV Special
(The) Elvis Presley Collection - Movie Magic - Disc 1
Memories - The '68 Comeback Special - Disc 1

Let's Be Friends
Elvis Double Features - Live A Little, Love A Little, Charro, The Trouble With Girls & Change Of Habit

Let's Forget About The Stars
Elvis Double Features - Live A Little, Love A Little, Charro, The Trouble With Girls & Change Of Habit

Life
(The) Legend Lives On -Disc 4
Love Letters From Elvis
Walk A Mile In My Shoes - 70's Masters - Disc 1

Like A Baby
Collectors Gold - Disc 2 *(alternate takes 1 & 2)*
Elvis Is Back
Elvis Is Back - 24 kt Gold Disc
(The) Elvis Presley Collection - Rhythm & Blues - Disc 1
From Nashville To Memphis - 60's Masters - Disc 1
Good Rockin' Tonight - Disc 2
Return Of The Rocker

Little Cabin On The Hill
Elvis Country - I'm 10,000 Years Old
Elvis In Nashville 1956-1971
Essential Elvis Vol. 4 - A Hundred Years From Now *(alternate take 1)*
(The) Million Dollar Quartet
Walk A Mile In My Shoes - 70's Masters - Disc 3

Little Darlin'
Elvis Aron Presley - Disc 4
(The) Legend Lives On - Disc 1
Moody Blue

Little Egypt
Command Performances - 60's Masters - Disc 2
Elvis Double Features - Canister Set - Disc 3
Elvis Double Features - Viva Las Vegas & Roustabout
Elvis/NBC-TV Special

LITTLE EGYPT (cont'd)
(The) Elvis Presley Collection - Movie Magic - Disc 2 *(alternate take 21)*
Elvis Presley Sings Leiber & Stoller
Memories - The '68 Comeback Special - Disc 1
Various Artists
Leiber & Stoller Music Publishing (6 CD Promo Set)
Solid Gold Country - Elvis Presley Sings Leiber And Stoller

Little Sister
Elvis Aron Presley Disc 3 (medley Little Sister/Get Back)
Elvis' Golden Records Vol. 3
Elvis' Golden Records Vol. 3 (1997 Reissue)
Elvis' Greatest Jukebox Hits
Elvis! His Greatest Hits - Disc 2
Elvis His Life And Music - Disc 3
Elvis In Concert
(The) Elvis Presley Birthday Tribute 1992 - Disc 3
(The) Elvis Presley Collection - Rock 'N' Roll - Disc 2
Elvis Presley: 1954-1961
Elvis The Tribute - A Biography - Disc 1
Elvis 24 Karat Hits!
Elvis 50 Worldwide Gold Hits Vol. 1 - Disc 2
From Nashville To Memphis - 60's Masters - Disc 2
Good Rockin' Tonight - Disc 1
(The) Legend Lives On - Disc 1
Memories Of Elvis - 1991 - Disc 3
Memories Of Elvis - 1993 - Disc 2
Return Of The Rocker
Sixties Legends - Elvis Presley - Disc 1
(The) Top Ten Hits - Disc 2
Various Artists
Solid Gold Country - Elvis: What Happened?
Solid Gold Country - Elvis Presley Birthday Tribute 92-1
Solid Gold Country - Elvis Presley Golden Records 93-2
Solid Gold Country - Elvis Presely: His Favorite Writers
Solid Gold Country - Elvis Presley In Concert
Solid Gold Country - Elvis Presley In Nashville
Solid Gold Country - Elvis Presley Memorial Tribute 91-8
Solid Gold Country - Elvis Presley Memorial Tribute 92-8
Solid Gold Country - Elvis Presley Memorial Tribute 93-8
Solid Gold Country - 70 Years Of RCA Country
Solid Gold Scrapbook - Elvis Golden Decade 1956-1965
Solid Gold Scrapbook - Solid Gold Elvis
These Were Our Songs - The Early 60's
Your Goodtime Oldies Magazine 95-36

Lonely Man
Collectors Gold - Disc 1 *(alternate take 4)*
Command Performances - 60's Masters - Disc 1
Elvis Double Features - Flaming Star, Wild In The Country & Follow That Dream
Elvis Double Features - Flaming Star, Wild In The Country & Follow That Dream *(solo)*
Elvis' Gold Records Volume 4
Elvis' Gold Records Volume 4 (1997 Reissue)
Elvis His Life And Music - Disc 4
Elvis The Other Sides - Worldwide Gold Award Hits Volume 2 - Disc 2

Lonesome Cowboy
(The) Blue Suede Box - Elvis: His Greatest Soundtracks - Disc 1
Elvis!Elvis!Elvis! - The King And His Movies
Elvis The Other Sides - Worldwide Gold Award Hits Volume 2 - Disc 1
(The) Elvis Presley Collection - Movie Magic - Disc 1
Essential Elvis - The First Movies
(The) King Of Rock 'N' Roll - 50's Masters - Disc 3

LONESOME COWBOY (cont'd)
Loving You
Loving You (1997 Reissue)

Long Black Limousine
From Elvis In Memphis
From Nashville To Memphis - 60's Masters - Disc 4
(The) Memphis Record

Long Legged Girl (With A Short Dress On)
Almost In Love
Command Performances - 60's Masters - Disc 2
Elvis Double Features - Spinout & Double Trouble
Elvis Sings Hits From His Movies Vol. 1

(It's A) Long Lonely Highway
Blue Suede Shoes (Original Soundtrack) Disc 2
From Nashville To Memphis - 60's Masters - Disc 3
(The) Lost Album

Long Tall Sally
A Golden Celebration - Disc 2 - Miss.-Alabama Dairy Show Tupelo Afternoon Sept 26, 1956
Aloha From Hawaii Via Satellite
Aloha From Hawaii Via Satellite - 25th Anniversary Edition
Blue Suede Shoes (Original Soundtrack) Disc 2
Elvis
Elvis Aron Presley - Disc 1
(The) Elvis Presley Collection - The Rocker - Disc 1
Elvis Recorded Live On Stage In Memphis
Elvis 15th Anniversary Radio Show - Disc 1
Elvis 15th Anniversary Radio Show - Disc 4
(The) King Of Rock 'N' Roll - 50's Masters - Disc 2
(The) King Of Rock 'N' Roll - 50's Masters - Disc 5 (Las Vegas 1956)
(The) Legend Lives On - Disc 1
Rocker

Look Out Broadway
Elvis Double Features - Frankie And Johnny & Paradise Hawaiian Style

Love Coming Down
From Elvis Presley Boulevard Memphis, Tennessee, Recorded Live
Walk A Mile In My Shoes - 70's Masters - Disc 4

Love Letters
A Valentine Gift For You
Collectors Gold - Disc 2 *(alternate takes 4 & 7)*
Elvis At His Romantic Best
Elvis' Gold Records Volume 4
Elvis' Gold Records Volume 4 (1997 Reissue)
Elvis His Life And Music - Disc 4
(The) Elvis Presley Collection - Love Songs - Disc 2
Elvis The Legend - Disc 3
From Nashville To Memphis - 60's Masters - Disc 3
Heart And Soul
Love Letters From Elvis
(The) Legend Lives On - Disc 3
Various Artists
(The) Elvis Presley Years - Disc 3
Sweet Dreams Of Country
The Super 60's

Love Me
A Golden Celebration - Disc 3 - Ed Sullivan Show New York Oct 28, 1956
A Golden Celebration - Disc 4 - Elvis - Burbank, Calif. June 27, 1968
Aloha From Hawaii Via Satellite
Aloha From Hawaii Via Satellite - 25th Anniversary Edition
(The) Alternate Aloha
An Afternoon In The Garden
Elvis
Elvis Aron Presley - Disc 1
Elvis Aron Presley - Disc 4
Elvis As Recorded At Madison Square Garden
Elvis At His Romantic Best
Elvis' Golden Records
Elvis' Golden Records (1997 Reissue)
Elvis! His Greatest Hits - Disc 1
Elvis His Life And Music - Disc 1
Elvis In Concert
(The) Elvis Presley Birthday Tribute 1992 - Disc 3
(The) Elvis Presley Collection - Love Songs - Disc 1
Elvis Presley Radio Show
Elvis Presley Sings Leiber & Stoller
Elvis Presley: 1954-1961
Elvis Presley - 50 Greatest Hits - Disc 2
Elvis Recorded Live On Stage In Memphis
Elvis The Legend - Disc 1
Elvis The Other Sides - Worldwide Gold Award Hits Volume 2 - Disc 1
Elvis 15th Anniversary Radio Show
Elvis 20th Anniversary Radio Show - Disc 3
Elvis 24 Karat Hits!
Elvis 50 Years 50 Hits - Disc 2
Elvis 56
Elvis 56 Advance Music (Promo)
Great Hits: 1956-57
Heart And Soul
(The) King Of Rock 'N' Roll - 50's Masters - Disc 2
(The) Legend Lives On - Disc 1
Memories - The '68 Comeback Special - Disc 2 *(previously unreleased)*
Memories Of Elvis - 1991 - Disc 1
Memories Of Elvis - 1993 - Disc 1
(The) Top Ten Hits - Disc 1
Tiger Man
Various Artists
Leiber & Stoller The 50's (Promo)
Leiber & Stoller Music Publishing (6 CD Promo Set)
Solid Gold Country - The Complete 50's Masters
Solid Gold Country - Elvis Presley His Favorite Writers
Solid Gold Country - Elvis Presley In Concert
Solid Gold Country - Elvis Presley Sings Leiber And Stoller
There's A Riot Goin' On - The Rock & Roll Classics Of Leiber & Stoller

Love Me, Love The Life I Lead
Elvis (aka "The Fool Album")
(The) Legend Of A King - Disc 2

Love Me Tender
A Golden Celebration - Disc 2 - Miss.-Alabama Dairy Show Tupelo Afternoon Sept. 26, 1956
A Golden Celebration - Disc 3 - Miss.-Alabama Dairy Show Tupelo Evening Sept. 26, 1956
A Golden Celebration - Disc 3 - Ed Sullivan Show New York Sept. 9, 1956
A Golden Celebration - Disc 3 - Ed Sullivan Show New York Oct. 28, 1956
A Golden Celebration - Disc 3 - Ed Sullivan Show New York Jan 6, 1957
A Touch Of Platinum - A Life In Music - Disc 1 - Ed Sullivan Show New York Sept. 9, 1956
An Afternoon In The Garden
(The) Blue Suede Box - Elvis: His Greatest Soundtracks - Disc 2

LOVE ME TENDER (cont'd)

(The) Blue Suede Box - Elvis: His Greatest Soundtracks - Disc 2 (*end title version*)
(The) Blue Suede Box - Elvis: His Greatest Soundtracks - Disc 2 (*stereo*)
Blue Suede Shoes (Original Soundtrack) Disc 1
Collectors Gold - Disc 3 (Las Vegas 1969)
Don't Be Cruel
Elvis A Legendary Performer Volume 1
Elvis Aron Presley - Disc 4
Elvis As Recorded At Madison Square Garden
Elvis Birthday Tribute Radio Program
Elvis!Elvis!Elvis! - The King And His Movies
Elvis' Golden Records
Elvis' Golden Records (1997 Reissue)
Elvis! His Greatest Hits - Disc 1
Elvis His Life And Music - Disc 1
Elvis/NBC-TV Special
(The) Elvis Presley Birthday Tribute 1992 - Disc 3
(The) Elvis Presley Collection - Love Songs - Disc 2
Elvis Presley Radio Show (Promo)
Elvis Presley The King Of Rock & Roll At His Best - Disc 3
Elvis Presley: Great Performances
Elvis Presley: 1954-1961
Elvis Presley - 50 Greatest Hits - Disc 1
Elvis The Legend - Disc 1
Elvis The Tribute - A Biography - Disc 2
Elvis 15th Anniversary Radio Show - Disc 2
Elvis 20th Anniversary Radio Show - Disc 1
Elvis 20th Anniversary Singles Set - Disc 1
Elvis 24 Karat Hits! (*stereo*)
Elvis 50 Worldwide Gold Hits Vol. 1 - Disc 1
Elvis 50 Years 50 Hits - Disc 1
Essential Elvis - The First Movies
Essential Elvis - The First Movies (*unreleased version*)
From Nashville To Memphis - 60's Masters - Disc 5 - from "the Frank Sinatra Timex Special"
Great Hits of 1956-57
Heartbreak Hotel, Hound Dog & Top Ten Hits
Heartbreak Hotel/ Love Me Tender
(The) Honeymoon Companion (Promo)
Heart And Soul (*unreleased stereo version*)
Jailhouse Rock and Love Me Tender
Jailhouse Rock and Love Me Tender (*end title version*)
Jailhouse Rock and Love Me Tender (*stereo*)
(The) King Of Rock 'N' Roll - 50's Masters - Disc 2
(The) Legend Lives On - Disc 4
(The) Legend Of A King - Disc 1
(The) Lost Album
(The) Louisiana Hayride - Anthologies Of Legends - Elvis Presley
(The) Louisiana Hayride Archives Volume 1 (12/15/56)
Love Me Tender - Shaped Disc (*stereo*)
Love Songs (*stereo*)
Memories - The '68 Comeback Special - Disc 1 (*previously unreleased*)
Memories Of Elvis - 1991 - Disc 4
Memories Of Elvis - 1993 - Disc 1
(The) Number One Hits
Platinum - A Life In Music - Disc 1 - Ed Sullivan Show New York Sept. 9, 1956
Pure Gold
Shake, Rattle & Roll (Promo)
(The) Top Ten Hits - Disc 1
Virtual Graceland CD-ROM

Various Artists

Country Memories
Dick Clark's Rock Roll & Remember 1/3-1/5
(The) Elvis Presley Years - Disc 1
Love Me Tender

LOVE ME TENDER (cont'd)
Solid Gold Country - (The) Complete 50's Masters
Solid Gold Country - Elvis: What Happened?
Solid Gold Country - Elvis Presley And TV
Solid Gold Country - Elvis Presley Birthday Tribute 92-1
Solid Gold Country - Elvis Presley Birthday Tribute 93-1
Solid Gold Country - Elvis Presley Love Songs
Solid Gold Country - Elvis Presley Memorial Tribute 91-8
Solid Gold Country - Elvis Presley Memorial Tribute 93-8
Solid Gold Country - 70 Years Of RCA Country
Solid Gold Scrapbook - Elvis Golden Decade 1956-1965
Solid Gold Scrapbook - Elvis Movie Music
Unforgettable Fifties
Your Hit Parade: 1956

Love Me Tonight
Collectors Gold - Disc 2 *(alternate take 1)*
From Nashville To Memphis - 60's Masters - Disc 2

Love Song Of The Year
Promised Land

Lover Doll
(The) Blue Suede Box - Elvis: His Greatest Soundtracks - Disc 3
(The) Blue Suede Box - Elvis: His Greatest Soundtracks - Disc 3 *(undubbed)*
(The) Elvis Presley Collection - Treasures '53 To '58 - Disc 1
Elvis The Other Sides - Worldwide Gold Award Hits Volume 2 - Disc 1
Essential Elvis Vol. 3/ Hits Like Never Before *(track H-take 7, original undubbed version)*
King Creole
King Creole (1997 Reissue)
King Creole (1997 Reissue) *(undubbed)*
(The) King Of Rock 'N' Roll - 50's Masters - Disc 4

Loving Arms
Elvis Country *(1980 remixed version)*
(The) Elvis Presley Collection - Love Songs - Disc 2
Essential Elvis Vol. 5 - Rhythm And Country *(alternate take 2)*
Good Times
(The) Legend Lives On - Disc 4
Walk A Mile In My Shoes - 70's Masters - Disc 2
Various Artists
Solid Gold Country - Elvis Presley In Nashville
Solid Gold Country - Elvis Presley Memorial Tribute 91-8

Loving You
(The) Blue Suede Box - Elvis: His Greatest Soundtracks - Disc 1
(The) Blue Suede Box - Elvis: His Greatest Soundtracks - Disc 1 *(uptempo version, alternate take 13)*
Collectors Gold - Disc 3 (Las Vegas 1969)
Elvis Aron Presley Forever
Elvis' Golden Records
Elvis' Golden Records (1997 Reissue)
Elvis! His Greatest Hits - Disc 1
Elvis His Life And Music - Disc 1
(The) Elvis Presley Birthday Tribute 1992 - Disc 3
(The) Elvis Presley Collection - Love Songs - Disc 1
(The) Elvis Presley Collection - Movie Magic - Disc 2 *(fast version)*
(The) Elvis Presley Collection - Treasures '53 To '58 - Disc 2 *(uptempo version, alternate take 13)* _
Elvis Presley Sings Leiber & Stoller
Elvis Presley - 50 Greatest Hits - Disc 1
Elvis The King: 1954-1965
Elvis The Legend - Disc 1
Elvis The Tribute - A Biography - Disc 2

LOVING YOU (cont'd)
Elvis 15th Anniversary Radio Show - Disc 3
Elvis 15th Anniversary Radio Show - Disc 4
Elvis 50 Worldwide Gold Hits Vol. 1 - Disc 1
Elvis 50 Years 50 Hits - Disc 1
Essential Elvis - The First Movies - *(slow version, alternate take 10)*
Essential Elvis - The First Movies - *(fast version, alternate takes 20,21)*
Essential Elvis - The First Movies - *(slow version, alternate take 1)*
Essential Elvis - The First Movies - *(fast version, alternate take 8)*
Essential Elvis - The First Movies - *(fast version, alternate take 1)*
Heart And Soul
(The) King Of Rock 'N' Roll - 50's Masters - Disc 3
(The) King Of Rock 'N' Roll - 50's Masters - Disc 5 *(slow version, alternate take 12)*
(The) King Of Rock 'N' Roll - 50's Masters - Disc 5 *(uptempo version, alternate take 13)*
Loving You
Loving You (1997 Reissue)
Loving You (1997 Reissue) *(uptempo version, alternate take 13)*
Memories Of Elvis - 1991 - Disc 1
Memories Of Elvis - 1993 - Disc 1
Pure Gold

Various Artists
Leiber & Stoller - The Fifties (Promo)
Leiber & Stoller Music Publishing (6 CD Promo Set)
Solid Gold Scrapbook - Elvis Movie Music
Solid Gold Scrapbook - Elvis Presley Sings Leiber And Stoller
Your Easy-Listening Hit Parade Of the 40's And 50's - Disc 4

"M"

Make Me Know It
Elvis Is Back
Elvis Is Back - 24 kt Gold Disc
(The) Elvis Presley Collection - The Rocker - Disc 1
From Nashville To Memphis - 60's Masters - Disc 1
Return Of The Rocker

Make The World Go Away
Elvis Country - I'm 10,000 Years Old
(The) Elvis Presley Collection - Country - Disc 1
Great Country Songs
Walk A Mile In My Shoes - 70's Masters - Disc 3
Welcome To My World

Mama
Double Dynamite
Elvis Double Features - Canister Set - Disc 1
Elvis Double Features - Kid Galahad & Girls!Girls!Girls!

Mama Don't Dance
Elvis Recorded Live On Stage In Memphis

Mama Liked The Roses
Blue Suede Shoes (Original Soundtrack) Disc 2 *(chimes intro)*
Christmas Wishes From Anne Murray, Glen Campbell & Elvis Presley
Elvis Christmas Album
(The) Elvis Presley Collection - From The Heart - Disc 1
From Nashville To Memphis - 60's Masters - Disc 4
(The) Memphis Record

Mansion Over The Hill
Amazing Grace His Greatest Sacred Performances - Disc 1
(The) Elvis Presley Collection - Gospel - Disc 1
(The) Elvis Presley Gospel Treasury - Disc 2
His Hand In Mine
Various Artists
Treasury Of Country - Inspirational Favorites

Marguereta
Command Performances - 60's Masters - Disc 1
Elvis Double Features - Canister Set - Disc 2
Elvis Double Features - It Happened At The Worlds Fair & Fun In Acapulco

Mary In The Morning
(The) Elvis Presley Collection - From The Heart - Disc 1
(The) Legend Lives On - Disc 3
That's The Way It Is
That's The Way It Is - Original Master Recording
Walk A Mile In My Shoes - 70's Masters - Disc 3

Maybellene
(The) King Of Rock 'N' Roll - 50's Masters - Disc 5 (Louisiana Hayride 1955)
(The) Louisiana Hayride - Anthologies Of Legends - Elvis Presley
(The) Louisiana Hayride Archives Volume 1 (8/20/55)
(The) Private Presley CD
Various Artists
Solid Gold Country - Elvis Presley Live

Mean Woman Blues
(The) Blue Suede Box - Elvis: His Greatest Soundtracks - Disc 1
Elvis Aron Presley Forever
Elvis!Elvis!Elvis! - The King And His Movies
Elvis' Gold Records Volume 2 - 50,000,000 Elvis Fans Can't Be Wrong (1997 Reissue)
(The) Elvis Presley Collection - Movie Magic - Disc 2
Elvis The Other Sides - Worldwide Gold Award Hits Volume 2 - Disc 1
Essential Elvis - The First Movies
Essential Elvis - The First Movies *(alternate film version)*
Essential Elvis Vol. 2 Stereo 57 *(alternate take 14)*
Good Rockin' Tonight - Disc 1
(The) King Of Rock 'N' Roll - 50's Masters - Disc 2
Loving You
Loving You (1997 Reissue)

Memories
Collectors Gold - Disc 3 (Las Vegas 1969)
Elvis' Gold Records Volume 5 (1997 Reissue)
Elvis/NBC-TV Special
(The) Elvis Presley Collection - From The Heart - Disc 1
Elvis Presley - 50 Greatest Hits - Disc 2
Elvis The Tribute - A Biography - Disc 3
Elvis 15th Anniversary Radio Show - Disc 6
Elvis 20th Anniversary Radio Show - Disc 3
Elvis 50 Years 50 Hits - Disc 2
(The) Greatest Performances
(The) Legend Lives On - Disc 4
(The) Legend Of A King - Disc 2
Memories - The '68 Comeback Special - Disc 1
Memories - The '68 Comeback Special - Disc 2 *(previously unreleased)*
Tiger Man *(previously unreleased)*
Various Artists
Country Soft 'N' Mellow
Easy Listening Hits Of the 60's & 70's

MEMORIES(cont'd)
Solid Gold Country - Elvis: What Happened?
Solid Gold Country - Elvis Presley Birthday Tribute 92-1
Solid Gold Country - Elvis Presley Birthday Tribute 93-1
Solid Gold Country - Elvis Presley Live
Solid Gold Country - Elvis Presley Memorial Tribute 92-8
Solid Gold Country - Elvis Presley Memorial Tribute 93-8
Solid Gold Country - Mac Davis Birthday Salute
Solid Gold Country - 70 Years Of RCA Country

Memphis, Tennessee
Collectors Gold - Disc 2 *(alternate take 2)*
Elvis For Everyone
(The) Elvis Presley Collection - Rhythm & Blues - Disc 1
From Nashville To Memphis - 60's Masters - Disc 3
From Nashville To Memphis - 60's Masters - Disc 5 *(alternate take 1 from 1963 session)*
(The) Lost Album
Out Of The Box - 6 From The 60's (Promo) *(alternate take 1)*

Men With Broken Hearts
Walk A Mile In My Shoes - 70's Masters - Disc 5 (The Elvis Presley Show) *(short poem)*

Merry Christmas Baby
Christmas With Elvis
Elvis Sings The Wonderful World Of Christmas *(extended version)*
Elvis Walk A Mile In My Shoes - 70's Masters - Disc 4
If Every Day Was Like Christmas
If Every Day Was Like Christmas - Special Collectors Edition
Merry Christmas
Memories Of Christmas *(unreleased complete studio performance)*
Reconsider Baby *(alternate edit)*
Various Artists
December Songs (Promo)
Happy Holidays (Promo)
Holiday Music Collection
Solid Gold Country - Christmas With Elvis Presley

Mexico
Command Performances - 60's Masters - Disc 1
Elvis Double Features - Canister Set - Disc 2
Elvis Double Features - It Happened At The Worlds Fair & Fun In Acapulco

Milkcow Blues Boogie
A Date With Elvis
(The) Elvis Presley Collection - Rhythm & Blues - Disc 1
(The) King Of Rock 'N' Roll - 50's Masters - Disc 1
Remembering Elvis
(The) Sun Sessions

Milky White Way
A Touch Of Platinum - A Life In Music - Disc 2 *(alternate take 3)*
Amazing Grace His Greatest Sacred Performances - Disc 1
(The) Elvis Presley Collection - Gospel - Disc 2
(The) Elvis Presley Gospel Treasury - Disc 1
(The) Elvis Presley Gospel Treasury (Special Edition)
His Hand In Mine
Platinum - A Life In Music - Disc 2 *(alternate take 3)*
Selections From Amazing Grace His Greatest Sacred Performances

Mine
From Nashville To Memphis - 60's Masters - Disc 3

Miracle Of The Rosary
A Touch Of Platinum Vol. 2 - A Life In Music - Disc 2 (*alternate take 1*)
Amazing Grace His Greatest Sacred Performances - Disc 2
Elvis Now
Platinum - A Life In Music - Disc 4 (*alternate take 1*)

Mirage
Elvis Double Features - Canister Set - Disc 4
Elvis Double Features - Harum Scarum & Girl Happy

Money Honey
A Golden Celebration - Disc 1 - Dorsey Bros. Show, New York, March 24, 1956
A Touch Of Platinum Vol. 2 - A Life In Music - Disc 1 (Las Vegas Rehearsals)
Elvis Aron Presley - Disc 1
Elvis Presley
Elvis Presley - Collectors Edition
(The) Elvis Presley Collection - The Rocker - Disc 2
(The) Elvis Presley Collection - Treasures '53 To '58 - Disc 1 - Dorsey Bros. Show, New York, March 24, 1956
Elvis The King: 1954-1965
Elvis The Tribute - A Biography - Disc 3
Elvis 15th Anniversary Radio Show - Disc 2
Elvis 56
Elvis 56 Advance Music (Promo)
Good Rockin' Tonight - Disc 2
(The) King Of Rock 'N' Roll - 50's Masters - Disc 1
(The) King Of Rock 'N' Roll -50's Masters - Disc 5 (Las Vegas 1956)
(The) Legend Lives On - Disc 2
(The) Louisiana Hayride - Anthologies Of Legends - Elvis Presley
(The) Louisiana Hayride Archives Volume 1 (1/22/55)
Platinum - A Life In Music - Disc 3 (Las Vegas Rehearsals)
Rocker

Moody Blue
A Touch Of Platinum Vol. 2 - A Life In Music - Disc 2
Elvis' Gold Records Volume 5
Elvis' Gold Records Volume 5 (1997 Reissue)
Elvis 50 Years 50 Hits - Disc 2
Elvis 15th Anniversary Radio Show - Disc 2
(The) Elvis Presley Birthday Tribute 1992 - Disc 3
(The) Elvis Presley Collection - Country - Disc 2
Elvis Presley - 50 Greatest Hits - Disc 2
(The) Legend Lives On - Disc 4
(The) Legend Of a King - Disc 2
Moody Blue
Platinum - A Life In Music - Disc 4
Walk A Mile In My Shoes - 70's Masters - Disc 2
Various Artists
American Country Countdown 94-6 Show 25
Contempory Country Volume 1
Solid Gold Country - Elvis: What Happened?
Solid Gold Country - Elvis Presley Birthday Tribute 92-1
Solid Gold Country - Elvis Presley Birthday Tribute 93-1
Solid Gold Country - Elvis Presley's Golden Records 91-11
Solid Gold Country - Elvis Presley Memorial Tribute 91-8
Solid Gold Country - Elvis Presley Memorial Tribute 92-8
Solid Gold Country - Elvis Presley Memorial Tribute 93-8
Solid Gold Country - 70 Years Of RCA Country

Moonlight Swim
Blue Hawaii
Blue Hawaii (1997 Reissue)
Blue Hawaii (1997 Reissue Collectors Edition)

MOONLIGHT SWIM (cont'd)
(The) Blue Suede Box - Elvis: His Greatest Soundtracks - Disc 4

Mr. Songman
Promised Land
Walk A Mile In My Shoes - 70's Masters - Disc 2

My Babe
Elvis Aron Presley - Disc 3
Elvis In Person At The International Hotel
(The) Elvis Presley Collection - Rhythm & Blues - Disc 2
Elvis 15th Anniversary Radio Show - Disc 2

My Baby Left Me
Elvis' Golden Records (1997 Reissue)
(The) Elvis Presley Collection - Rhythm & Blues - Disc 1
Elvis Recorded Live On Stage In Memphis
Elvis The King: 1954-1965
Elvis The Legend - Disc 1
Elvis The Other Sides - Worldwide Gold Award Hits Volume 2 - Disc 1
Elvis 15th Anniversary Radio Show - Disc 5
Elvis 56
Elvis 56 Advance Music (Promo)
For LP Fans Only
(The) King Of Rock 'N' Roll - 50's Masters - Disc 1
Reconsider Baby

My Boy
Always On My Mind
(The) Elvis Presley Collection - From The Heart - Disc 2
Good Times
Memories Of Elvis - 1991 - Disc 2
Walk a Mile In My Shoes - 70's Masters - Disc 2
Various Artists
(The) Elvis Presley Years - Disc 4
Solid Gold Country - Elvis Presley Birthday Tribute 92-1
Solid Gold Country - Elvis Presley Birthday Tribute 93-1
Solid Gold Scrapbook - Elvis In Memphis

My Desert Serenade
Elvis Double Features - Canister Set - Disc 4
Elvis Double Features - Harum Scarum & Girl Happy

My Happiness
Elvis The King Of Rock 'N' Roll -50's Masters - Disc 1 *(1953 acetate)*
Elvis 15th Anniversary Radio Show - Disc 1 *(1953 acetate)*
(The) Great Performances *(1953 acetate)*
My Happiness (Promo) *(1953 acetate)*
Various Artists
The Music That Made Memphis *(1953 acetate)*

My Heart Cries For You
A Golden Celebration - Disc 4 - Collectors Treasures - Graceland *(home recording)*

My Little Friend
Almost In Love
From Nashville To Memphis - 60's Masters - Disc 4

My Way
A Touch Of Platinum Vol. 2 - A Life In Music - Disc 2 *(unreleased live performance)*
Aloha From Hawaii Via Satellite

MY WAY (cont'd)
Aloha From Hawaii Via Satellite - 25th Anniversary Edition
(The) Alternate Aloha
Elvis Aron Presley - Disc 2
Elvis Birthday Tribute Radio Show
Elvis! His Greatest Hits - Disc 4
Elvis In Concert
(The) Elvis Presley Birthday Tribute 1992 - Disc 3
(The) Elvis Presley Collection - From The Heart - Disc 1 *(studio master)*
(The) Legend Lives On - Disc 2
Memories Of Elvis - 1991 - Disc 4
Memories Of Elvis - 1993 - Disc 3
Platinum - A Life In Music - Disc 4 (unreleased live performance)
Walk A Mile In My Shoes - 70's Masters - Disc 4 *(studio master)*
Walk A Mile In My Shoes - Out Of The Box Sampler (Promo) *(studio master)*
Various Artists
Easy Listening Hits Of The 60's & 70's
(The) Elvis Presley Years - Disc 4
God Bless The USA
Solid Gold Country - Elvis: What Happened?
Solid Gold Country - Elvis Presley And TV
Solid Gold Country - Elvis Presley Birthday Tribute 92-1
Solid Gold Country - Elvis Presley Birthday Tribute 93-1
Solid Gold Country - Elvis Presley In Concert
Solid Gold Country - Elvis Presley Memorial Tribute 91-8
Solid Gold Country - Elvis Presley Memorial Tribute 92-8
Solid Gold Country - Elvis Presley Memorial Tribute 93-8
Solid Gold Country - Elvis Presley Live
Solid Gold Country - This Week In 1978
Solid Gold Country - 70 Years Of RCA Country

My Wish Came True
Elvis' Gold Records Volume 2 - 50,000,000 Elvis Fans Can't Be Wrong
Elvis' Gold Records Volume 2 - 50,000,000 Elvis Fans Can't Be Wrong (1997 Reissue)
Elvis! His Greatest Hits - Disc 2
Elvis His Life And Music - Disc 2
(The) Elvis Presley Collection - The Romantic - Disc 1
Elvis Presley 50 Greatest Hits - Disc 2
Elvis The Legend - Disc 2
Elvis The Other Sides - Worldwide Gold Award Hits Volume 2 - Disc 1
Elvis 50 Years 50 Hits - Disc 2
(The) King Of Rock 'N' Roll - 50's Masters - Disc 4
(The) Legend Of A King - Disc 1
Memories Of Elvis - 1991 - Disc 1

Mystery Train
A Touch Of Platinum - A Life In Music - Disc 1
Collectors Gold - Disc 3 (Las Vegas 1969)
Elvis Aron Presley - Disc 4 (medley Mystery Train/Tiger Man)
Elvis' Golden Records (1997 Reissue)
Elvis! His Greatest Hits - Disc 4
Elvis In Person At The International Hotel
(The) Elvis Presley Birthday Tribute 1992 - Disc 3
(The) Elvis Presley Collection - The Rocker - Disc 1
Elvis Presley Radio Show (Promo)
Elvis The King: 1954-1965
Elvis The Tribute - A Biography - Disc 1
Elvis 15th Anniversary Radio Special - Disc 6 (music fades)
For LP Fans Only
Good Rockin' Tonight - Disc 2
(The) King Of Rock 'N' Roll - 50's Masters - Disc 1
(The) King Of Rock 'N' Roll - 50's Masters - (Promo)
(The) Legend Lives On - Disc 1
(The) Legend Of A King - Disc 1

MYSTERY TRAIN (cont'd)
Memories Of Elvis - 1991 - Disc 2
Memories Of Elvis - 1993 - Disc 1
Platinum - A Life In Music - Disc 1
(The) Sun Sessions CD - The Master Takes
Various Artists
Country USA - 1955
Mystery Train (Original Soundtrack)
Solid Gold Country - Elvis Presley Birthday Tribute 92-1
Solid Gold Country - Elvis Presley Memorial Tribute 91-8
Solid Gold Country - Elvis Presley Memorial Tribute 92-8
Solid Gold Country - Elvis Presley Memorial Tribute 93-8
Solid Gold Country - The Complete 50's Masters
Sun's Greatest Hits
The Sun Records Collection
Solid Gold Scrapbook - Elvis In Memphis

"N"

Nearer My God To Thee
Amazing Grace His Greatest Sacred Performances - Disc 2 *(previously unreleased)*
Selections From Amazing Grace His Greatest Sacred Performances (Promo)

Never Again
From Elvis Presley Boulevard Memphis, Tennessee, Recorded Live

Never Been To Spain
An Afternoon In The Garden
Elvis As Recorded At Madison Square Garden
Walk A Mile In My Shoes - 70's Masters - Disc 5 (The Elvis Presley Show)

Never Ending
From Nashville To Memphis - 60's Masters - Disc 2
(The) Lost Album

Never Say Yes
Elvis Double Features - Spinout & Double Trouble

New Orleans
(The) Blue Suede Box - Elvis: His Greatest Soundtracks - Disc 3
(The) Elvis Presley Collection - Treasures '53 To '58 - Disc 1
Elvis The Other Sides - Worldwide Gold Award Hits Volume 2 - Disc 1
King Creole
King Creole (1997 Reissue)
(The) King Of Rock 'N' Roll - 50's Masters - Disc 4
Platinum - A Life In Music - Disc 1

Night Life
Elvis Double Features - Canister Set - Disc 3
Elvis Double Features - Viva Las Vegas & Roustabout

Night Rider
Collectors Gold - Disc 2 *(alternate takes 1 & 2)*
Elvis In Nashville 1956-1971
From Nashville To Memphis - 60's Masters - Disc 2
Pot Luck With Elvis
Remembering Elvis

No More
Aloha From Hawaii Via Satellite - 25th Anniversary Edition
Blue Hawaii
Blue Hawaii (1997 Reissue)
Blue Hawaii (1997 Reissue) *(alternate take 7)*
Blue Hawaii (1997 Reissue Collectors Edition)
Blue Hawaii (1997 Reissue Collectors Edition) *(alternate take 7)*
(The) Blue Suede Box - Elvis: His Greatest Soundtracks - Disc 4
(The) Blue Suede Box - Elvis: His Greatest Soundtracks - Disc 4 *(alternate take 7)*
Burning Love And Hits From His Movies Vol. 2
Elvis Aron Presley Forever
Elvis Presley - The King Of Rock & Roll At His Best - Disc 2
Mahalo From Elvis

(There's) No Room to Rhumba In A Sports Car
Elvis Double Features - Canister Set - Disc 2
Elvis Double Features - It Happened At The Worlds Fair & Fun In Acapulco

Nothingville
Elvis/NBC-TV Special
Memories - The '68 Comeback Special - Disc 1

"O"

O Come All Ye Faithful
Blue Christmas
Christmas Classics
Christmas Memories From Elvis & Alabama
Christmas With Elvis
Country Christmas - Elvis Presley's Country Style Christmas
Elvis Sings The Wonderful World Of Christmas
If Every Day Was Like Christmas
If Every Day Was Like Christmas - Special Collectors Edition
Memories Of Christmas *(unreleased version)*
Merry Christmas
Various Artists
Mistletoe And Memories
Solid Gold Country - Christmas With Elvis Presley

O Little Town Of Bethlehem
Christmas Classics
Christmas Wishes From Anne Murray, Glen Campbell & Elvis Presley
Christmas With Elvis
Elvis Christmas Album
Elvis Christmas Album - Camden Classics
If Every Day Was Like Christmas
If Every Day Was Like Christmas - Special Collectors Edition
(The) King Of Rock 'N' Roll 50's Masters - Disc 3
Merry Christmas
Various Artists
I Believe - Best Loved Stars Of Inspiration
Solid Gold Country - Christmas With Elvis Presley

O Sole Mio
Elvis In Concert
(The) Legend Lives On - Disc 1

Oh How I Love Jesus
A Touch Of Platinum - A Life In Music - Disc 2 (Graceland & Palm Springs Segment) *(home recording)*
Platinum - A Life In Music - Disc 2 (Graceland & Palm Springs Segment) *(home recording)*
Platinum In-Store Sampler (Promo) *(home recording)*
Platinum Sampler (Promo) *(home recording)*

Old MacDonald
Elvis Double Features - Spinout & Double Trouble
Elvis Sings For Children And Grownups Too!
Elvis Sings Hits From His Movies Volume 1

Old Shep
Double Dynamite
Elvis
(The) Elvis Presley Collection - Country - Disc 2
Elvis Presley - 50 Greatest Hits - Disc 1
Elvis Sings For Children And Grownups Too
Elvis 15th Anniversary Radio Show - Disc 1
Elvis 50 Years 50 Hits - Disc 1
Great Country Songs
(The) King Of Rock 'N'Roll - 50's Masters - Disc 2
(The) King Of Rock 'N' Roll - 50's Masters - Disc 5 *(alternate take 5)*
(The) Legend Of A King - Disc 1
Separate Ways
Various Artists
Feel 21 Again/ Rarities Volume 4 (Promo) *(alternate take)*

On A Snowy Christmas Night
Christmas With Elvis
Elvis Sings The Wonderful World Of Christmas
If Every Day Was Like Christmas
If Every Day Was Like Christmas - Special Collectors Edition
Various Artists
EMI Publishing Christmas Songs (Promo)

Once Is Enough
Command Performances - 60's Masters - Disc 1
Elvis Double Features - Kissin' Cousins, Clambake & Stay Away Joe

One Boy, Two Little Girls
Command Performances - 60's Masters - Disc 1
Elvis Double Features - Kissin' Cousins, Clambake & Stay Away Joe

One Broken Heart For Sale
Collectors Gold - Disc 1 *(alternate take 1)*
Command Performances - 60's Masters - Disc 1
Elvis Double Features - Canister Set - Disc 2 *(film version)*
Elvis Double Features - Canister Set - Disc 2 *(single version)*
Elvis Double Features - It Happened At The Worlds Fair & Fun in Acapulco *(film version)*
Elvis Double Features - It Happened At The Worlds Fair & Fun In Acapulco *(single version)*
Elvis! His Greatest Hits - Disc 3
(The) Elvis Presley Birthday Tribute 1992 - Disc 3
(The) Elvis Presley Collection - Movie Magic - Disc 2
Elvis Presley - 50 Greatest Hits - Disc 1
Elvis 50 Worldwide Gold Hits Vol. 1 - Disc 2
Elvis 50 Years - 50 Hits - Disc 1
Mahalo From Elvis
Memories Of Elvis - 1991 - Disc 1
Various Artists
Solid Gold Scrapbook - Elvis Movie Music

One Night
A Golden Celebration - Disc 4 - Elvis - Burbank, Calif. June 27, 1968
Elvis Aron Presley - Disc 1
Elvis At His Romantic Best
Elvis' Gold Records Vol. 2 - 50,000,000 Elvis Fans Can't Be Wrong
Elvis' Gold Records Vol. 2 - 50,000,000 Elvis Fans Can't Be Wrong (1997 Reissue)
Elvis! His Greatest Hits - Disc 2
Elvis His Life And Music - Disc 2
Elvis/NBC-TV Special
(The) Elvis Presley Birthday Tribute 1992 - Disc 3
(The) Elvis Presley Collection - Rock 'N' Roll - Disc 1
Elvis Presley - 50 Greatest Hits - Disc 2
Elvis Presley: 1954-1961
Elvis The Legend - Disc 1
Elvis The Other Sides - Worldwide Gold Award Hits Volume 2 - Disc 1
Elvis The Tribute - A Biography - Disc 2
Elvis 50 Years 50 Hits - Disc 2
Good Rockin' Tonight - Disc 2
(The) King Of Rock 'N' Roll - 50's Masters - Disc 3
(The) Legend Lives On - Disc 4
Memories - The '68 Comeback Special - Disc 2 *(previously unreleased)*
Memories - The '68 Comeback Special - Disc 2
Memories Of Elvis - 1991 - Disc 2
Memories Of Elvis - 1993 - Disc 2
Reconsider Baby *(alternate take)*
(The) Top Ten Hits - Disc 1
Tiger Man *(previously unreleased)*
Walk A Mile In My Shoes - 70's Masters - Disc 5 (The Elvis Presley Show)
Various Artists
Dick Clark's Rock Roll & Remember 1/3-1/5
Heartbreak Hotel - (Original Soundtrack)
Monster Rock And Roll Show
Solid Gold Country - (The) Complete 50's Masters
Solid Gold Country - Elvis: What Happened?
Solid Gold Country - Elvis Presley's Love Songs
Solid Gold Country - 70 Years Of RCA Country
Solid Gold Scrapbook - Elvis Golden Decade 1956-1965
Solid Gold Scrapbook - Solid Gold Elvis
The Great American Vocalists

One Night Of Sin
(The) Blue Suede Box - Elvis: His Greatest Soundtracks - Disc 1
Blue Suede Shoes (Original Soundtrack) Disc 2 *(sax overdub)*
(The) Elvis Presley Collection - Rhythm & Blues - Disc 1
Elvis Presley Radio Show (Promo)
Elvis 15th Anniversary Radio Show - Disc 3
(The) King Of Rock 'N' Roll - 50's Masters - Disc 3
Loving You (1997 Reissue)

One Track Heart
Elvis Double Features - Canister Set - Disc 3
Elvis Double Features - Viva Las Vegas & Roustabout

One-Sided Love Affair
Elvis Presley
Elvis Presley - Collectors Edition
(The) Elvis Presley Collection - The Rocker - Disc 2
Elvis 15th Anniversary Radio Show - Disc 5
Elvis 56
Elvis 56 Advance Music (Promo)
(The) King Of Rock 'N' Roll - 50's Masters - Disc 1
(The) Legend Lives On - Disc 2

Only Believe
Amazing Grace His Greatest Sacred Performances - Disc 2
Love Letters From Elvis

Only The Strong Survive
(The) Elvis Presley Collection - From The Heart - Disc 2
From Elvis In Memphis
From Nashville To Memphis - 60's Masters - Disc 5
(The) Memphis Record

Out Of Sight Out Of Mind
(The) Million Dollar Quartet

"P"

Padre
Elvis (aka "The Fool Album")

Paradise Hawaiian Style
Command Performances - 60's Masters - Disc 2
Elvis Double Features - Frankie And Johnny & Paradise Hawaiian Style

Paralyzed
Elvis
Elvis Country *(1983 overdubbed version)*
Elvis' Gold Records Volume 2 - 50,000,000 Elvis Fans Can't Be Wrong (1997 Reissue)
(The) Elvis Presley Collection - The Rocker - Disc 1
Elvis The Other Sides - Worldwide Gold Award Hits Volume 2 - Disc 1
Elvis 56
Elvis 56 Advance Music (Promo)
(The) King Of Rock 'N' Roll - 50's Masters - Disc 2
(The) Million Dollar Quartet
Various Artists
Solid Gold Country - Elvis Presley: His Favorite Writers

Party
(The) Blue Suede Box - Elvis: His Greatest Soundtracks - Disc 1
(The) Blue Suede Box - Elvis: His Greatest Soundtracks - Disc 1 *(alternate master, take 7)*
Elvis' Gold Records Volume 2 - 50,000,000 Elvis Fans Can't Be Wrong (1997 Reissue)
(The) Elvis Presley Collection - Movie Magic - Disc 1
Elvis The King: 1954-1965
Elvis The Legend - Disc 1
Essential Elvis - The First Movies
Essential Elvis - The First Movies *(alternate master, take 7)*
(The) King Of Rock 'N' Roll - 50's Masters - Disc 3
Loving You
Loving You (1997 Reissue)
Loving You (1997 Reissue) *(alternate master, take 7)*

Patch It Up
Elvis The Other Sides - Worldwide Gold Award Hits Volume 2 - Disc 2
(The) Elvis Presley Collection - The Rocker - Disc 2
Essential Elvis Vol. 4 - A Hundred Years From Now *(alternate take 9)*
Thats The Way It Is
Thats The Way It Is - Original Master Recording
Walk A Mile In My Shoes - 70's Masters - Disc 1

(There'll Be) Peace In The Valley (For Me)

A Golden Celebration - Disc 3 - Ed Sullivan Show New York Jan 6. 1957
A Touch Of Platinum - A Life In Music - Disc 1 *(alternate take 3)*
Amazing Grace His Greatest Sacred Performances - Disc 1
Country Christmas - Elvis Presley Country Christmas
Double Dynamite
Elvis A Legendary Performer Volume 1
Elvis Christmas Album
Elvis' Gold Records Volume 2 - 50,000,000 Elvis Fans Can't Be Wrong (1997 Reissue)
Elvis Gospel: 1957-1971 - Known Only To Him
(The) Elvis Presley Collection - Gospel - Disc 1
(The) Elvis Presley Gospel Treasury - Disc 1
(The) Elvis Presley Gospel Treasury (Special Edition)
Elvis Presley: Great Performances
Elvis Presley/Jim Reeves Country Favorites
Elvis Presley - The King Of Rock & Roll At His Best - Disc 1
Elvis Presley - The King Of Rock & Roll At His Best - Disc 3
Elvis The Legend - Disc 1
Elvis 15th Anniversary Radio Show - Disc 3
Essential Elvis Vol. 2 Stereo 57 *(alternate take 7)*
Essential Elvis Vol. 2 Stereo 57 *(alternate takes 2,3)*
How Great Thou Art (bonus track)
(The) King Of Rock 'N' Roll - 50's Masters - Disc 2
Merry Christmas
(The) Million Dollar Quartet
Platinum - A Life In Music - Disc 1 *(alternate take 3)*
You'll Never Walk Alone

Petunia, The Gardeners Daughter

Elvis Double Features - Frankie And Johnny & Paradise Hawaiian Style

Pieces Of My Life

Always On My Mind
Elvis Aron Presley - Forever
Elvis Today
(The) Elvis Presley Collection - From The Heart - Disc 2
Walk A Mile In My Shoes- 70's Masters - Disc 2

Plantation Rock

Elvis Double Features - Canister Set - Disc 1
Elvis Double Features - Kid Galahad & Girls!Girls!Girls!

Playing For Keeps

A Valentine Gift For You
Elvis' Gold Records Volume 2 - 50,000,000 Elvis Fans Can't Be Wrong (1997 Reissue)
Elvis! His Greatest Hits - Disc 1
(The) Elvis Presley Collection - The Romantic - Disc 2
Elvis 50 Worldwide Gold Hits Vol. 1 - Disc 1
For LP Fans Only
Great Hits Of 1956-57
(The) King Of Rock 'N' Roll - 50's Masters - Disc 2

Please Don't Drag That String Around

Elvis' Gold Records Volume 4
Elvis' Gold Records Volume 4 - 1997 Reissue
Elvis His Life And Music - Disc 4
Elvis The Other Sides - Worldwide Gold Award Hits Volume 2 - Disc 2
From Nashville To Memphis - 60's Masters - Disc 2
(The) Lost Album

Please Don't Stop Loving Me
Command Performances - 60's Masters - Disc 2
Elvis Double Features - Frankie And Johnny & Paradise Hawaiian Style
(The) Elvis Presley Collection - The Romantic - Disc 1

Pledging My Love
A Touch Of Platinum Vol. 2 - A Life In Music - Disc 2 *(alternate take 3)*
(The) Elvis Presley Collection - From The Heart - Disc 2
Moody Blue
Platinum - A Life In Music - Disc 4 *(alternate take 3)*
Walk a Mile In My Shoes - 70's Masters - Disc 2

Pocket Full Of Rainbows
(The) Blue Suede Box - Elvis: His Greatest Soundtracks - Disc 5
(The) Blue Suede Box - Elvis: His Greatest Soundtracks - Disc 5 *(alternate take 2)*
Collectors Gold - Disc 1 *(alternate takes 22 & 17)*
(The) Elvis Presley Collection - Movie Magic - Disc 2
G I Blues
G.I. Blues (1997 Reissue)
G.I. Blues (1997 Reissue) *(alternate take 2)*
G.I. Blues (1997 Reissue Collectors Edition)
G.I. Blues (1997 Reissue Collectors Edition) *(alternate take 2)*
Various Artists
Jerry Maguire (Original Soundtrack) *(alternate take)*

Poison Ivy League
Command Performances - 60's Masters - Disc 2
Elvis Double Features - Canister Set - Disc 3
Elvis Double Features - Viva Las Vegas & Roustabout

Polk Salad Annie
An Afternoon In The Garden
Elvis Aron Presley - Disc 3
Elvis As Recorded At Madison Square Garden
(The) Elvis Presley Collection - The Rocker - Disc 2
Elvis 15th Anniversary Radio Show - Disc 3
On Stage February 1970
Walk A Mile In My Shoes - 70's Masters - Disc 5 (The Elvis Presley Show)

Poor Boy
(The) Blue Suede Box - Elvis: His Greatest Soundtracks - Disc 2
(The) Blue Suede Box - Elvis: His Greatest Soundtracks - Disc 2 *(stereo)*
(The) Elvis Presley Collection - Treasures '53 To '58 - Disc 2
Elvis The Other Sides - Worldwide Gold Award Hits Volume 2 - Disc 1
Essential Elvis - The First Movies
For LP Fans Only
Jailhouse Rock and Love Me Tender
Jailhouse Rock and Love Me Tender *(stereo)*
(The) King Of Rock 'N' Roll - 50's Masters - Disc 2

Power Of My Love
From Nashville To Memphis - 60's Masters - Disc 4
From Elvis In Memphis
(The) Memphis Record
Platinum - A Life In Music - Disc 3 *(alternate take 3)*

Promised Land
A Touch Of Platinum Vol. 2 - A Life In Music - Disc 2 *(alternate take 5)*
(The) Elvis Presley Birthday Tribute 1992 - Disc 3
(The) Elvis Presley Collection - Rock 'N' Roll - Disc 2
Essential Elvis Vol. 5 - Rhythm And Country *(alternate take 4)*

PROMISED LAND (cont'd)
(The) Legend Lives On - Disc 4
Memories Of Elvis - 1991 - Disc 2
Platinum - A Life In Music - Disc 4 *(alternate take 5)*
Promised Land
Walk A Mile In My Shoes - 70's Masters - Disc 2
Walk A Mile In My Shoes - Out Of The Box Sampler (Promo)
Various Artists
(The) Elvis Presley Years - Disc 4
Solid Gold Country - Elvis Presley Birthday Tribute 92-1
Solid Gold Country - Elvis Presley Memorial Tribute 92-8
Solid Gold Scrapbook - Elvis In Memphis

Proud Mary
An Afternoon In The Garden
Elvis As Recorded At Madison Square Garden
On Stage February 1970
Walk A Mile In My Shoes - 70's Masters - Disc 5 (The Elvis Presley Show)

Puppet On A String
Command Performances - 60's Masters - Disc 2
Elvis Double Features - Canister Set - Disc 4
Elvis Double Features - Harum Scarum & Girl Happy
Elvis! His Greatest Hits - Disc 3
(The) Elvis Presley Collection - Love Songs - Disc 2
Elvis Presley - 50 Greatest Hits - Disc 2
Elvis Sings For Children And Grownups Too!
Elvis The Other Sides - Worldwide Gold Award Hits Volume 2 - Disc 2
Elvis 50 Years 50 Hits - Disc 2
Love Songs

Put The Blame On Me
(The) Elvis Presley Collection - The Rocker - Disc 2
From Nashville To Memphis - 60's Masters - Disc 2
Something For Everybody

Put Your Hand In The Hand
Amazing Grace His Greatest Sacred Performances - Disc 2
Elvis Now
Various Artists
Country Sweet 'N' Sentimental

"Q"

Queenie Wahine's Papaya
Elvis Double Features - Frankie And Johnny & Paradise Hawaiian Style

"R"

Rags To Riches
Elvis Aron Presley - Disc 3
(The) Elvis Presley Collection - From The Heart - Disc 2
Elvis The Legend - Disc 3
Elvis 15th Anniversary Radio Show - Disc 3
Essential Elvis Vol. 4 - A Hundred Years From Now *(alternate take 3)*
Walk A Mile In My Shoes - 70's Masters - Disc 1

Raised On Rock

Raised On Rock
Walk A Mile In My Shoes - 70's Masters - Disc 2

Reach Out To Jesus

Amazing Grace His Greatest Sacred Performances - Disc 2
(The) Elvis Presley Collection - Gospel - Disc 2
(The) Elvis Presley Gospel Treasury - Disc 2
He Touched Me

Ready Teddy

A Golden Celebration - Disc 2 - Miss.-Alabama Dairy Show Tupelo Afternoon Sept. 26, 1956
A Golden Celebration - Disc 3 - Ed Sullivan Show New York Sept. 9, 1956
Elvis
(The) Elvis Presley Collection - Rock 'N' Roll - Disc 2
Elvis 56
Elvis 56 Advance Music (Promo)
Good Rockin' Tonight - Disc 2
(The) Great Performances
(The) King Of Rock 'N' Roll - 50's Masters - Disc 2
(The) Legend Lives On - Disc 2
Rocker

Various Artists

Dick Clark's Rock Roll & Remember 1/3-1/5
Heartbreak Hotel - (Original Soundtrack)

Reconsider Baby

A Touch Of Platinum - A Life In Music - Disc 2
An Afternoon In The Garden
Collectors Gold - Disc 3 (Las Vegas 1969)
Elvis Aron Presley - Disc 1
Elvis Is Back
Elvis Is Back - 24 kt Gold Disc
(The) Elvis Presley Collection - Rhythm & Blues - Disc 2
From Nashville To Memphis - 60's Masters - Disc 1
(The) King Of Rock 'N' Roll - 50's Masters - Disc 5 (Million Dollar Quartet)
Platinum - A Life In Music - Disc 2
Reconsider Baby
Walk A Mile In My Shoes - 70's Masters - Disc 5 (The Elvis Presley Show)

Relax

Elvis Double Features - Canister Set - Disc 2
Elvis Double Features - It Happened At The Worlds Fair & Fun In Acapulco
Elvis!Elvis!Elvis! - The King And His Movies
Mahalo From Elvis

Release Me (And Let Me Love Again)

A Touch Of Platinum Vol. 2 - A Life In Music - Disc 1 (Las Vegas 1970)
(The) Legend Lives On - Disc 3
On Stage February 1970
Platinum - A Life In Music - Disc 3 (Las Vegas 1970)
Welcome To My World

Return To Sender

A Touch Of Platinum - A Life In Music - Disc 2
Command Performances - 60's Masters - Disc 1
Elvis Double Features - Canister Set - Disc 1
Elvis Double Features - Kid Galahad & Girls!Girls!Girls!
Elvis' Gold Records Volume 4 (1997 Reissue)
Elvis' Greatest Jukebox Hits
Elvis! His Greatest Hits - Disc 3

RETURN TO SENDER (cont'd)
(The) Elvis Presley Birthday Tribute 1992 - Disc 4
(The) Elvis Presley Collection - Rock 'N' Roll - Disc 1
Elvis Presley - 50 Greatest Hits - Disc 1
Elvis The King: 1954-1965
Elvis The Legend - Disc 2
Elvis The Tribute - A Biography - Disc 2
Elvis 15th Anniversary Radio Show - Disc 2
Elvis 20th Anniversary Radio Show - Disc 2
Elvis 24 Karat Hits!
Elvis 50 Worldwide Gold Hits - Disc 2
Elvis 50 Years 50 Hits - Disc 1
(The) Great Performances
(The) Legend Of A King - Disc 1
Memories Of Elvis - 1991 - Disc 3
Memories Of Elvis - 1993 - Disc 3
Platinum - A Life In Music - Disc 2
Return Of The Rocker
Sixties Legends - Elvis Presley - Disc 1
(The) Top Ten Hits - Disc 2

Various Artists
(The) Elvis Presley Years - Disc 2
Good Time Oldies Theme Party
Jukebox Favorites - Musical Memories From The 50's & 60's
Solid Gold Country - Elvis Presley Birthday Tribute 92-1
Solid Gold Country - Elvis Presley Birthday Tribute 93-1
Solid Gold Country - Elvis Presley Memorial Tribute 92-8
Solid Gold Country - Elvis Presley Memorial Tribute 93-8
Solid Gold Country - His Favorite Writers
Solid Gold Scrapbook - Elvis Movie Music
The Legends Of Rock 'N' Roll
These Were Our Songs - The Early 60's
Your Goodtime Oldies Magazine - 92-46
Your Goodtime Oldies Magazine - 93-14
Your Goodtime Oldies Magazine - 94-18

Riding The Rainbow
Elvis Double Features - Canister Set - Disc 1
Elvis Double Features - Kid Galahad & Girls!Girls!Girls!

Rip It Up
A Touch Of Platinum - A Life In Music - Disc 1 *(alternate take 15)*
Blue Suede Shoes (Original Soundtrack) Disc 2
Elvis
Elvis Country *(1983 overdubbed version)*
(The) Elvis Presley Collection - The Rocker - Disc 2
Elvis The Other Sides - Worldwide Gold Award Hits Volume 2 - Disc 1
Elvis 56
Elvis 56 Advance Music (Promo)
Good Rockin' Tonight - Disc 2
(The) King Of Rock 'N' Roll - 50's Masters - Disc 2
(The) Legend Lives On - Disc 2
(The) Million Dollar Quartet
Platinum - A Life In Music - Disc 1 *(alternate take 15)*
Rocker

Rock A Hula Baby
Blue Hawaii
Blue Hawaii (1997 Reissue)
Blue Hawaii (1997 Reissue) *(alternate take 1)*
Blue Hawaii (1997 Reissue Collectors Edition)
Blue Hawaii (1997 Reissue Collectors Edition) *(alternate take 1)*
(The) Blue Suede Box - Elvis: His Greatest Soundtracks - Disc 4

ROCK A HULA BABY (cont'd)
(The) Blue Suede Box - Elvis: His Greatest Soundtracks - Disc 4 *(alternate take 1)*
Can't Help Falling In Love/Rock-A Hula Baby - (Jukebox Single)
Command Performances - 60's Masters - Disc 1
Commerative Jukebox Series - 5 CD Set - Disc 2
Elvis' Gold Records Volume 4 (1997 Reissue)
Elvis! His Greatest Hits - Disc 3
(The) Elvis Presley Collection - The Rocker - Disc 1
Elvis The Legend - Disc 2
Elvis 15th Anniversary Radio Show - Disc 4
Elvis 50 Worldwide Gold Hits Vol. 1 - Disc 2
Various Artists
Solid Gold Scrapbook - Elvis Movie Music

Roustabout
Collectors Gold - Disc 1 *(alternate take 6)*
Command Performances - 60's Masters - Disc 2
Elvis Double Features - Canister Set - Disc 3
Elvis Double Features - Viva Las Vegas & Roustabout

Rubberneckin'
Almost In Love
Collectors Gold - Disc 3 (Las Vegas 1969)
Double Dynamite
Elvis Double Features - Live A Little, Love A Little - Charro - The Trouble With Girls - Change of Habit
From Nashville To Memphis - 60's Masters - Disc 4
(The) Memphis Record
Various Artists
Solid Gold Scrapbook - Elvis In Memphis

Run On
Amazing Grace His Greatest Sacred Performances - Disc 1
Elvis Gospel 1957-1971: Known Only To Him
(The) Elvis Presley Collection - Gospel - Disc 2
How Great Thou Art
Selections From Amazing Grace His Greatest Sacred Performances (Promo)

Runaway
Collectors Gold - Disc 3 (Las Vegas 1969)
On Stage February 1970

"S "

Sand Castles
Elvis Double Features - Frankie And Johnny & Paradise Hawaiian Style

Santa Bring My Baby Back (To Me)
Christmas Wishes From Anne Murray, Glen Campbell And Elvis Presley
Christmas With Elvis
Elvis Christmas Album
Elvis Christmas Album (Camden)
Elvis' Gold Records Volume 2 - 50,000,000 Elvis Fans Can't Be Wrong (1997 Reissue)
If Every Day Was Like Christmas
If Every Day Was Like Christmas - Special Collectors Edition
(The) King Of Rock 'N' Roll - 50's Masters - Disc 3
Various Artists
December Songs (Promo)
Happy Holidays Volume 28
Solid Gold Country - Christmas With Elvis Presley
The Album Network Christmas CD Tune Up (Promo)

Santa Claus Is Back In Town
Christmas Wishes From Anne Murray, Glen Campbell And Elvis Presley
Christmas With Elvis
Country Christmas - Elvis Presley Country Style Christmas
Elvis Christmas Album
Elvis Christmas Album (Camden)
Elvis' Gold Records Volume 2 - 50,000,000 Elvis Fans Can't Be Wrong (1997 Reissue)
Elvis Presley Sings Leiber & Stoller
If Every Day Was Like Christmas
If Every Day Was Like Christmas - Special Collectors Edition
(The) King Of Rock 'N' Roll - 50's Masters - Disc 3
Merry Christmas
Memories Of Christmas
Santa Claus Is Back In Town - 1997 Seasons Greetings From Graceland
Tiger Man (*previously unreleased*)
Various Artists
A Holiday Happening - Christmas Rarities On CD Vol. 8 (Promo)
American Gold With Dick Bartley 93-13 Show 51
American Gold With Dick Bartley 97-12 Show 51
Christmas Classics Volume 2
Dick Clark's Rock 'N' Roll Christmas
Leiber & Stoller - The Fifties (Promo)
Leiber & Stoller Music Publishing (6 CD Promo Set)
Miracle On 34th Street (Original Soundtrack)
Solid Gold Country - Christmas With Elvis Presley
We Wish You A Merry Christmas
Your Goodtime Oldies Magazine 97-51

Santa Lucia
Burning Love And Hits From His Movies
Elvis Double Features - Canister Set - Disc 3 (traditional)
Elvis Double Features - Viva Las Vegas & Roustabout (traditional)
Elvis For Everyone
Elvis Presley The King Of Rock 'N' Roll At His Best - Disc 2

Saved
Elvis/ NBC-TV Special
Elvis Presley Sings Leiber & Stoller
Memories - The '68 Comeback Special - Disc 1
Various Artists
Leiber & Stoller Music Publishing (6 CD Promo Set)
Solid Gold Country - Elvis Presley Sings Leiber And Stoller

Scratch My Back
Elvis Double Features - Frankie And Johnny & Paradise Hawaiian Style

See See Rider (C.C.Rider)
A Private Moment With The King (*home recording*)
A Touch Of Platinum Vol. 2 - A Life In Music - Disc 1 (Las Vegas 1970)
Aloha From Hawaii Via Satellite
Aloha From Hawaii Via Satellite - 25th Anniversary Edition
(The) Alternate Aloha
Elvis Aron Presley - Disc 4
Elvis In Concert
(The) Elvis Presley Collection - The Rocker - Disc 1
Elvis Recorded Live On Stage In Memphis
Elvis 15th Anniversary Radio Show - Disc 6
(The) Legend Lives On - Disc 1
On Stage February, 1970
Platinum - A Life In Music - Disc 3 (Las Vegas 1970)
Walk A Mile In My Shoes - 70's Masters - Disc 5 (The Elvis Presley Show)

SEE SEE RIDER (cont'd)
Various Artists
Solid Gold Country - Elvis Presley In Concert

Seeing Is Believing
Amazing Grace His Greatest Sacred Performances - Disc 2
He Touched Me

Sentimental Me
From Nashville To Memphis - 60's Masters - Disc 2
Separate Ways
Something For Everybody

Separate Ways
A Touch Of Platinum Vol. 2 - A Life In Music - Disc 2 *(alternate take 25)*
Always On My Mind
Double Dynamite
(The) Elvis Presley Birthday Tribute 1992 - Disc 4
(The) Elvis Presley Collection - From The Heart - Disc 2 *(alternate take)*
(The) Legend Lives On - Disc 3
(The) Legend Of A King - Disc 2
Love Songs
Memories Of Elvis - 1991 - Disc 3
Memories Of Elvis - 1993 - Disc 3
Platinum - A Life In Music - Disc 4 *(alternate take 25)*
Separate Ways
Walk A Mile In My Shoes - 70's Masters - Disc 1
Various Artists
Solid Gold Scrapbook - Elvis Movie Music

Shake A Hand
Elvis Aron Presley - Forever
(The) Elvis Presley Collection - Rhythm & Blues - Disc 1
Elvis Today
Walk A Mile In My Shoes - 70's Masters - Disc 4

Shake Rattle And Roll
A Golden Celebration - Disc 1 - Dorsey Bros. Show New York Jan. 28, 1956
Blue Suede Shoes (Original Soundtrack) Disc 2 *(instrumental)*
(The) Elvis Presley Collection - The Rocker - Disc 2
Elvis The Tribute - A Biography - Disc 3
Elvis 15th Anniversary Radio Show - Disc 1
Elvis 56 *(alternate take 8)*
Elvis 56 Advance Music (Promo) *(alternate take 8)*
For LP Fans Only
(The) Great Performances
(The) King Of Rock 'N' Roll - 50's Masters - Disc 2
(The) King Of Rock 'N' Roll - 50's Masters - Disc 5 *(1955 acetate)*
(The) King Of Rock 'N' Roll - 50's Masters - Disc 5 *(alternate take 5)*
(The) King Of Rock 'N' Roll - 50's Masters (Promo)
(The) Legend Lives On - Disc 2
Platinum - A Life In Music - Disc 1 - From Dorsey Bros. TV Stage Show
Rocker
Various Artists
Solid Gold Country - Elvis Presley And TV

Shake That Tambourine
Elvis Double Features - Canister Set - Disc 4
Elvis Double Features - Harum Scarum & Girl Happy

She Thinks I Still Care
Elvis Country *(1980 remixed version)*
(The) Elvis Presley Collection - Country - Disc 1
Moody Blue
Walk A Mile In My Shoes - 70's Masters - Disc 2
Walk A Mile In My Shoes - 70's Masters - Disc 4 *(alternate take 28)*
Various Artists
Country Songs That Will Last Forever

She Wears My Ring
Essential Elvis Vol. 5 - Rhythm And Country *(alternate take 8)*
Good Times

She's A Machine
Elvis Double Features - Easy Come, Easy Go & Speedway
Elvis Double Features - Easy Come, Easy Go & Speedway *(alternate take 13)*

She's All Mine (What's She Really Like)
G.I. Blues

She's Not You
Elvis' Golden Records Vol. 3
Elvis' Golden Records Vol. 3 (1997 Reissue)
Elvis' Greatest Jukebox Hits
Elvis! His Greatest Hits - Disc 3
Elvis His Life And Music - Disc 3
(The) Elvis Presley Birthday Tribute 1992 - Disc 4
(The) Elvis Presley Collection - Love Songs - Disc
Elvis Presley - 50 Greatest Hits - Disc 2
Elvis The Legend - Disc 2
Elvis 15th Anniversary Radio Show - Disc 5
Elvis 24 Karat Hits!
Elvis 50 Worldwide Gold Hits Vol. 1 - Disc 2
From Nashville To Memphis - 60's Masters - Disc 2
Heart And Soul
Love Songs
Memories Of Elvis - 1991 - Disc 2
Sixties Legends - Elvis Presley - Disc 1
(The) Top Ten Hits - Disc 2
Various Artists
Dick Clark's Rock Roll & Remember 8/12-8/14
Leiber & Stoller The 60's, 70's & 80's (Promo)
Leiber & Stoller Music Publishing (6 CD Promo Set)
Solid Gold Scrapbook - Solid Gold Elvis
Those Were Our Songs - The Early 60's

Shoppin' Around
(The) Blue Suede Box - Elvis: His Greatest Soundtracks - Disc 5
(The) Blue Suede Box - Elvis: His Greatest Soundtracks - Disc 5 *(alternate take 11)*
Command Performances - 60's Masters - Disc 1
Elvis Aron Presley - Disc 2 *(alternate takes 3,5)*
(The) Elvis Presley Collection - Movie Magic - Disc 2
G.I. Blues
G.I. Blues (1997 Reissue)
G.I. Blues (1997 Reissue) *(alternate take 11)*
G.I. Blues (1997 Reissue Collectors Edition)
G.I. Blues (1997 Reissue Collectors Edition) *(alternate take 11)*

Shout It Out
Elvis Double Features - Frankie And Johnny & Paradise Hawaiian Style

Signs Of The Zodiac
Elvis Double Features - Live A Little, Love A Little, Charro, The Trouble With Girls & Change Of Habit

Silent Night
Blue Christmas
Christmas Classics
Christmas Memories From Elvis & Alabama
Christmas Wishes From Anne Murray, Glen Campbell & Elvis Presley
Christmas With Elvis
Country Christmas - Elvis Presley's Country Style Christmas/ Alabama
Elvis' Christmas Album
Elvis Christmas Album (Camden)
If Every Day Was Like Christmas
If Every Day Was Like Christmas - Special Collectors Edition
(The) King Of Rock 'N' Roll - 50's Masters - Disc 3
Merry Christmas
Memories Of Christmas
Various Artists
Christmas In America
Solid Gold Country - Christmas With Elvis Presley

Silver Bells
Blue Christmas
Christmas Classics
Christmas Memories From Elvis & Alabama
Christmas With Elvis
Country Christmas - Elvis Presley's Country Style Christmas/ Alabama
Elvis Sings The Wonderful World Of Christmas
If Every Day Was Like Christmas
If Every Day Was Like Christmas *(alternate take 1)*
If Every Day Was Like Christmas - Special Collectors Edition
If Every Day Was Like Christmas - Special Collectors Edition *(alternate take 1)*
Memories Of Christmas
Various Artists
A Country Christmas Volume 2
Nippers Holiday Favorites (Promo) *(alternate take)*
Nippers Holiday Favorites II (Promo) *(alternate take)*
The Best Of Christmas

Sing You Children
Elvis Double Features - Easy Come, Easy Go & Speedway
Elvis Double Features - Easy Come, Easy Go & Speedway *(alternate take 1)*
Elvis Presley The King Of Rock & Roll At His Best - Disc 1
You'll Never Walk Alone

Singing Tree
From Nashville To Memphis - 60's Masters - Disc 3

Slicin' Sand
Blue Hawaii
Blue Hawaii (1997 Reissue)
Blue Hawaii (1997 Reissue) *(alternate take 4)*
Blue Hawaii (1997 Reissue Collectors Edition) *(alternate take 4)*
(The) Blue Suede Box - Elvis: His Greatest Soundtracks - Disc 4
(The) Blue Suede Box - Elvis: His Greatest Soundtracks - Disc 4 *(alternate take 4)*

Slowly But Surely
From Nashville To Memphis - 60's Masters - Disc 3
(The) Lost Album

Smokey Mountain Boy
Elvis Double Features - Kissin' Cousins, Clambake & Stay Away Joe

Smorgasbord
Elvis Double Features - Spinout & Double Trouble

Snowbird
Elvis Country - I'm 10,000 Years Old
(The) Elvis Presley Collection - Country - Disc 2 *(undubbed master)*
Walk A Mile In My Shoes - 70's Masters - Disc 3

So Close Yet So Far (From Paradise)
Collectors Gold - Disc 1 *(alternate take 4)*
Command Performances - 60's Masters - Disc 2
Elvis Double Features - Canister Set - Disc 4
Elvis Double Features - Harum Scarum & Girl Happy
Mahalo From Elvis

So Glad You're Mine
Elvis
(The) Elvis Presley Collection - Rhythm & Blues - Disc 2
Elvis 56
Elvis 56 Advance Music (Promo)
Good Rockin' Tonight - Disc 2
(The) King Of Rock 'N' Roll - 50's Masters - Disc 1
Reconsider Baby

So High
Amazing Grace His Greatest Sacred Performances - Disc 1
Elvis Gospel 1957-1971 Known Only to Him
How Great Thou Art

Softly And Tenderly
(The) Million Dollar Quartet

Softly As I Leave You
Elvis Aron Presley - Disc 3
Walk A Mile In My Shoes - 70's Masters - Disc 5
Various Artists
Softly As I Leave You

Soldier Boy
A Golden Celebration - Disc 4 - Elvis At Home - Germany - 1958-60
Blue Suede Shoes (Original Soundtrack) Disc 1
Elvis Is Back
Elvis Is Back - 24 kt Gold Disc
(The) Elvis Presley Collection - The Romantic - Disc 2
From Nashville To Memphis - 60's Masters - Disc 1
Good Rockin' Tonight - Disc 2

Solitaire
Always On My Mind
From Elvis Presley Boulevard, Memphis, Tennessee, Recorded Live

Somebody Bigger Than You And I
Amazing Grace His Greatest Sacred Performances - Disc 1
How Great Thou Art
Various Artists
A Celebration Of Faith And Joy

Something

Aloha From Hawaii Via Satellite
Aloha From Hawaii Via Satellite - 25th Anniversary Edition
(The) Alternate Aloha
Elvis 15th Anniversary Radio Show - Disc 5
Walk a Mile In My Shoes - 70's Masters - Disc 5 (The Elvis Presley Show)

Something Blue

A Touch Of Platinum - A Life In Music - Disc 2 *(alternate take 1)*
(The) Elvis Presley Collection - The Romantic - Disc 1
From Nashville To Memphis - 60's Masters - Disc 2
Platinum - A Life In Music - Disc 2 *(alternate take 1)*
Pot Luck With Elvis

Song Of The Shrimp

Elvis Double Features - Canister Set - Disc 1
Elvis Double Features - Kid Galahad & Girls!Girls!Girls!

Sound Advice

Elvis Double Features - Flaming Star, Wild In The Country & Follow That Dream
Elvis For Everyone

Spanish Eyes

A Private Moment With The King *(home recording)*
(The) Elvis Presley Collection - From The Heart - Disc 1
Essential Elvis Vol. 5 - Rhythm And Country *(alternate take 2)*
Good Times
Love Songs

Various Artists

(The) Boy From Tupelo *(home recording)*
(Blue Spanish Eyes) Softly As I Leave You *(home recording)*

Speedway

An Elvis Double Feature - Speedway & Clambake
Command Performances - 60's Masters - Disc 2
Elvis Double Features - Easy Come, Easy Go & Speedway

Spinout

Command Performances - 60's Masters - Disc 2
Elvis Double Features - Spinout & Double Trouble
Elvis!Elvis!Elvis! - The King And His Movies

Spring Fever

Elvis Double Features - Canister Set - Disc 4
Elvis Double Features - Harum Scarum & Girl Happy

Stand By Me

Amazing Grace His Greatest Sacred Performances - Disc 1
Elvis Gospel 1957-1971: Known Only To Him
(The) Elvis Presley Collection - Gospel - Disc 1
(The) Elvis Presley Gospel Treasury - Disc 2
How Great Thou Art

Startin' Tonight

Elvis Double Features - Canister Set - Disc 4
Elvis Double Features - Harum Scarum & Girl Happy

Starting Today

Blue Suede Shoes (Original Soundtrack) Disc 2
(The) Elvis Presley Collection - Love Songs - Disc 1

STARTING TODAY (cont'd)
(The) Elvis Presley Collection - The Romantic - Disc 1
From Nashville To Memphis - 60's Masters - Disc 2
Something For Everybody

Stay Away
Almost In Love
Elvis Double Features - Kissin' Cousins & Stay Away Joe

Stay Away, Joe
Command Performances - 60's Masters - Disc 2
Elvis Double Features - Kissin' Cousins & Stay Away Joe

Steadfast Loyal And True
(The) Blue Suede Box - Elvis: His Greatest Soundtracks - Disc 3
(The) Blue Suede Box - Elvis: His Greatest Soundtracks - Disc 3 *(alternate master)*
Blue Suede Shoes (Original Soundtrack) Disc 1
(The) Elvis Presley Collection - Treasures '53 To '58 - Disc 2
Elvis Presley Sings Leiber & Stoller
Essential Elvis Vol. 3/ Hits Like Never Before *(track M take 6 unreleased version)*
King Creole
King Creole (1997 Reissue)
King Creole (1997 Reissue) *(alternate master)*
(The) King Of Rock 'N' Roll - 50's Masters - Disc 4
Various Artists
Leiber & Stoller Music Publishing (6 CD Promo Set)

Steamroller Blues
A Touch Of Platinum Vol. 2 - A Life In Music - Disc 2 *(unreleased live performance)*
Aloha From Hawaii Via Satellite
Aloha From Hawaii Via Satellite - 25th Anniversary Edition
Aloha Via Satellite
(The) Alternate Aloha
Elvis! His Greatest Hits - Disc 4
(The) Elvis Presley Birthday Tribute 1992 - Disc 4
(The) Elvis Presley Collection - Rhythm & Blues - Disc 1
Elvis 20th Anniversary Radio Show - Disc 2
(The) Legend Lives On - Disc 2
Memories Of Elvis - 1991 - Disc 1
Platinum - A Life In Music - Disc 4 *(unreleased live performance)*
Walk A Mile In My Shoes - 70's Masters - Disc 2
Various Artists
(The) Elvis Presley Years - Disc 4
Solid Gold Country - Elvis Presley Live

Steppin' Out Of Line
Blue Hawaii (1997 Reissue)
Blue Hawaii (1997 Reissue) *(movie version, alternate take 19)*
Blue Hawaii (1997 Reissue Collectors Edition)
Blue Hawaii (1997 Reissue Collectors Edition) *(movie version, alternate take 19)*
(The) Blue Suede Box - Elvis: His Greatest Soundtracks - Disc 4
(The) Blue Suede Box - Elvis: His Greatest Soundtracks - Disc 4 *(movie version, alternate take 19)*
Pot Luck With Elvis

Stop Look And Listen
Collectors Gold - Disc 1 *(alternate take 3)*
Elvis Double Features - Spinout & Double Trouble

Stop Where You Are
Elvis Double Features - Frankie And Johnny & Paradise Hawaiian Style

Stranger In My Own Home Town

Back In Memphis
Blue Suede Shoes (Original Soundtrack) Disc 2
From Nashville To Memphis - 60's Masters - Disc 4
(The) Memphis Record
Reconsider Baby *(alternate mix)*
Walk A Mile In My Shoes - 70's Masters - Disc 5 *(informal rehearsal)*

Stranger In A Crowd

That's The Way It Is
That's The Way It Is - Original Master Recording
Walk A Mile In My Shoes - 70's Masters - Disc 3

Stuck On You

A Touch Of Platinum - A Life In Music - Disc 2 - From "the Frank Sinatra Timex Special"
Blue Suede Shoes (Original Soundtrack) Disc 1
Elvis' Golden Records Vol. 3
Elvis' Golden Records Vol. 3 (1997 Reissue)
Elvis' Greatest Jukebox Hits
Elvis! His Greatest Hits - Disc 2
Elvis His Life And Music - Disc 3
(The) Elvis Presley Birthday Tribute 1992 - Disc 4
(The) Elvis Presley Collection - Rock 'N' Roll - Disc 2
Elvis Presley - 50 Greatest Hits - Disc 2
Elvis Presley : 1954-1961
Elvis The Legend - Disc 2
Elvis The Tribute - A Biography - Disc 3
Elvis 20th Anniversary Singles Set - Disc 5
Elvis 24 Karat Hits!
Elvis 50 Worldwide Gold Hits Vol. 1 - Disc 2
Elvis 50 Years - 50 Hits - Disc 2
Elvis 15th Anniversary Radio Show - Disc 4
From Nashville To Memphis - 60's Masters - Disc 1
In The Ghetto/Stuck On You
Memories Of Elvis - 1991 - Disc 2
Memories Of Elvis - 1993 - Disc 2
(The) Number One Hits
Platinum - A Life In Music - Disc 2 - From "the Frank Sinatra Timex Special"
Return Of The Rocker
Shake Rattle And Roll (Promo)
Sixties Legends - Elvis Presley - Disc 1
(The) Top Ten Hits - Disc 2

Various Artists

Billboard's Top Rock 'N' Roll Hits 1960
Billboard's Top Rock 'N' Roll Hits 1957-1961
Made In America 93-27
Solid Gold Country - Elvis Presley And TV
Solid Gold Country - Elvis Presley In Nashville
Solid Gold Hits Of The 60's
Solid Gold Scrapbook - Solid Gold Elvis
20 Years Of No. 1 Hits 1956-1975

Such A Night

Elvis A Legendary Performer Volume 2
Elvis Aron Presley - Disc 1
Elvis! His Greatest Hits - Disc 3
Elvis Is Back
Elvis Is Back - 24 kt Gold Disc
(The) Elvis Presley Collection - Rhythm & Blues - Disc 1
Elvis Presley - Great Performances
Elvis Presley - The King Of Rock & Roll At His Best - Disc 4
Elvis Presley - 50 Greatest Hits - Disc 2
Elvis The King: 1954-1965

SUCH A NIGHT (cont'd)
Elvis The Legend - Disc 3
Elvis The Tribute - A Biography - Disc 1
Elvis 50 Years - 50 Hits - Disc 2
From Nashville To Memphis - 60's Masters - Disc 1
Love Songs
Memories Of Elvis - 1991 - Disc 2
Sixties Legends - Elvis Presley - Disc 1
Various Artists
(The) Elvis Presley Years - Disc 2
The Super 60's

Summer Kisses Winter Tears
Collectors Gold - Disc 1 *(alternate takes 1 & 14)*
Elvis Double Features - Flaming Star, Wild In The Country & Follow That Dream
Elvis Double Features - Flaming Star, Wild In The Country & Follow That Drream *(movie version)*
Elvis For Everyone

Summertime Is Past And Gone
(The) Million Dollar Quartet

Suppose
A Golden Celebration - Disc 4 - Collectors Treasures - Graceland - *(home recording)*
An Elvis Double Feature: Speedway & Clambake
Elvis Double Features - Easy Come, Easy Go & Speedway *(alternate master)*
Elvis Double Features - Easy Come, Easy Go & Speedway
From Nashville To Memphis - 60's Masters - Disc 3 *(master)*

Surrender
Collectors Gold - Disc 3 (Las Vegas 1969)
Elvis' Golden Records Vol.3
Elvis' Golden Records Vol. 3 (1997 Reissue)
Elvis! His Greatest Hits - Disc 2
Elvis His Life And Music - Disc 3
(The) Elvis Presley Birthday Tribute 1992 - Disc 4
(The) Elvis Presley Collection - Love Songs - Disc 1
Elvis Presley - 50 Greatest Hits - Disc 2
Elvis The Legend - Disc 2
Elvis 24 Karat Hits!
Elvis 50 Years 50 Hits - Disc 2
Elvis 50 Worldwide Gold Hits Vol. 1 - Disc 2
From Nashville To Memphis - 60's Masters - Disc 1
From Nashville To Memphis - 60's Masters - Disc 5 *(alternate take)*
Love Songs
Memories Of Elvis - 1991 - Disc 2
Memories Of Elvis - 1993 - Disc 2
(The) Number One Hits
Shake, Rattle & Roll (Promo)
Sixties Legends - Elvis Presley - Disc 1
(The) Top Ten Hits - Disc 2
Various Artists
Dick Clark's Rock Roll & Remember 1/3-1/5
Dick Clark's Rock Roll & Remember 8/12-8/15
Solid Gold Country - Elvis Presley In Nashville
Solid Gold Country - Elvis Presley: His Favorite Writers
Solid Gold Scrapbook - Elvis' Golden Decade 1956-1965
Solid Gold Scrapbook - Solid Gold Elvis
20 Years Of No. 1 Hits, 1956-1975

Susan When She Tried
Elvis Today
Great Country Songs

Walk A Mile In My Shoes - 70's Masters - Disc 4

Suspicion
Elvis 50 Years 50 Hits - Disc 1
(The) Elvis Presley Collection - Love Songs - Disc 2
Elvis Presley 50 Greatest Hits - Disc 1
From Nashville To Memphis - 60's Masters - Disc 2
Out Of The Box - 6 From The 60's - (Promo)
Pot Luck With Elvis
Remembering Elvis

Suspicious Minds
A Touch Of Platinum Vol. 2 - A Life In Music - Disc 1 *(alternate take 7)*
Aloha From Hawaii Via Satellite
Aloha From Hawaii Via Satellite - 25th Anniversary Edition
(The) Alternate Aloha
An Afternoon In The Garden
Elvis Aron Presley - Disc 2
Elvis As Recorded At Madison Square Garden
Elvis Birthday Tribute Radio Program
Elvis' Gold Records Volume 5
Elvis' Gold Records Volume 5 (1997 Reissue)
Elvis' Greatest Jukebox Hits
Elvis! His Greatest Hits - Disc 4
Elvis In Person At The International Hotel
(The) Elvis Presley Birthday Tribute 1992 - Disc 4
(The) Elvis Presley Collection - Love Songs - Disc 1
Elvis Presley 50 Greatest Hits - Disc 1
Elvis The Legend - Disc 3
Elvis The Tribute - A Biography - Disc 3
Elvis 20th Anniversary Radio Show - Disc 3
Elvis 24 Karat Hits!
Elvis 50 Worldwide Gold Hits Vol. 1 - Disc 2
Elvis 50 Years 50 Hits - Disc 1
Elvis 15th Anniversary Radio Show - Disc 6
From Nashville To Memphis - 60's Masters - Disc 4
From Nashville To Memphis - 60's Masters - Disc 5 *(alternate take 6)*
Heart And Soul
(The) Honeymoon Companion (Promo)
King Of The Whole Wide World - Collectors Set - The Elvis Medley
(The) Legend Lives On - Disc 1
(The) Legend Of A King - Disc 2
Love Songs
Memories Of Elvis - 1991 - Disc 4
Memories Of Elvis - 1993 - Disc 3
(The) Memphis Record
(The) Number One Hits
Out Of The Box - 6 From The 60's (Promo) *(alternate take 6)*
Platinum - A Life In Music - Disc 3 *(alternate take 7)*
Shake, Rattle & Roll (Promo)
Sixties Legends - Elvis Presley - Disc 2
(The) Top Ten Hits - Disc 2
Virtual Graceland CD-ROM
Walk A Mile In My Shoes - 70's Masters - Disc 5 (The Elvis Presley Show)
Various Artists
A Gift Of Music (Promo) *(alternate take)*
American Gold - With Dick Bartley 96-3 Show 10
Classic Country 1965-1969
Country USA - 1969
Dick Clark's Rock Roll & Remember 8/12-8/15
Gold & Platinum -The Ultimate Rock Collection
Golden Country Oldies (Promo)

SUSPICIOUS MINDS (cont'd)
Made In America 93-27
Made In America 94-27
Nippers Greatest Hits - The 60's Volume 2
Nippers #1 Hits (1956-1986)
Rockin' 60's
Solid Gold Country - Elvis Presley Birthday Tribute 92-1
Solid Gold Country - Elvis Presley Birthday Tribute 93-1
Solid Gold Country - Elvis Presley's Golden Records 91-11
Solid Gold Country - Elvis Presley's Golden Records 93-2
Solid Gold Country - Elvis Presley Live
Solid Gold Country - Elvis Presley Memorial Tribute 91-8
Solid Gold Country - Elvis Presley Memorial Tribute 92-8
Solid Gold Country - Elvis Presley Memorial Tribute 93-8
Solid Gold Country - Country Stars With Gospel Roots
Solid Gold Country - 70 Years Of RCA Country
Solid Gold Scrapbook - Elvis In Memphis
The Year To Remember - 1969
Your Goodtime Oldies Magazine April 10. 1992 - 92-15
20 Years Of No. 1 Hits 1956-1975
60's

Sweet Angeline
Raised on Rock

Sweet Caroline
Elvis Aron Presley - Disc 3
On Stage February 1970

Sweetheart You Done Me Wrong
(The) Million Dollar Quartet

Swing Down Sweet Chariot
Amazing Grace His Greatest Sacred Performances - Disc 1
Elvis Aron Presley - Disc 1
Elvis Double Features - Live A Little, Charro, The Trouble With Girls & Change Of Habit
Elvis Gospel 1957-1971: Known Only To Him
(The) Elvis Presley Collection - Gospel - Disc 2
(The) Elvis Presley Gospel Treasury - Disc 2
His Hand In Mine
Various Artists
I Believe - Best Loved Stars Of Inspiration

Sylvia
Elvis Now

"T"

T-R-O-U-B-L-E
A Touch Of Platinum Vol. 2 - A Life In Music - Disc 2
Elvis Aron Presley - Disc 4
Elvis Aron Presley Forever
(The) Elvis Presley Collection - Rock 'N' Roll - Disc 2
Elvis Today
Platinum - A Life In Music - Disc 4
Walk A Mile In My Shoes - 70's Masters - Disc 2
Walk A Mile In My Shoes - Out Of The Box Sampler (Promo)
Various Artists
Solid Gold Country - Elvis Presley Memorial Tribute 93-8

Take Good Care Of Her
A Touch Of Platinum Vol. 2 - A Life In Music - Disc 2 *(alternate take 4)*
(The) Elvis Presley Collection - Country - Disc 2
Good Times
Platinum - A Life In Music - Disc 4 *(alternate take 4)*
Walk A Mile In My Shoes - 70's Masters - Disc 2

Take Me To The Fair
Elvis Double Features - Canister Set - Disc 2
Elvis Double Features - It Happened At The Worlds Fair & Fun In Acapulco

Take My Hand Precious Lord
Amazing Grace His Greatest Sacred Performances - Disc 1
Country Christmas - Elvis Presley Country Christmas/Jim Reeves
Elvis Christmas Album
Elvis Gospel 1957-1971: Known Only To Him
Elvis Presley & Jim Reeves Christmas Favorites
(The) Elvis Presley Collection - Gospel - Disc 2
(The) Elvis Presley Gospel Treasury - Disc 2
(The) Elvis Presley Gospel Treasury (Special Edition)
Elvis Presley - The King Of Rock & Roll At His Best - Disc1
Essential Elvis Vol. 2 Stereo 57 *(alternate take 14)*
(The) King Of Rock 'N' Roll - 50's Masters - Disc 3
You'll Never Walk Alone
Various Artists
Sweet Dreams Of Country

Talk About The Good Times
Essential Elvis Vol. 5 - Rhythm And Country *(alternate take 3)*
Good Times
Walk A Mile In My Shoes - 70's Masters - Disc 4

Tear Drops
A Private Moment With The King *(home recording - with Linda Thompson)*

(Let Me Be Your) Teddy Bear
A Touch Of Platinum - A Life In Music - Disc 1
An Afternoon In The Garden
(The) Blue Suede Box - Elvis: His Greatest Soundtracks - Disc 1
Blue Suede Shoes (Original Soundtrack) Disc 1
Elvis Aron Presley - Disc 4 (medley Teddy Bear/Don't Be Cruel)
Elvis As Recorded At Madison Square Garden
Elvis Birthday Tribute Radio Program
Elvis' Golden Records
Elvis' Golden Records (1997 Reissue)
Elvis' Greatest Jukebox Hits
Elvis! His Greatest Hits - Disc 1
Elvis His Life & Music - Disc 1
Elvis In Concert
(The) Elvis Presley Birthday Tribute 1992 - Disc 3
(The) Elvis Presley Collection - Rock 'N' Roll - Disc 1
Elvis Presley Radio Special (Promo)
Elvis Presley: 1954-1961
Elvis Presley -50 Greatest Hits - Disc 1
Elvis Sings For Children And Grownups Too!
Elvis The Legend - Disc 1
Elvis The Tribute - A Biography - Disc 1
Elvis 15th Anniversary Radio Show -Disc 4
Elvis 24 Karat Hits!
Elvis 50 Worldwide Gold Hits Vol. 1 - Disc 1
Elvis 50 Years 50 Hits - Disc 1

TEDDY BEAR (cont'd)
Essential Elvis - The First Movies
Great Hits Of 1956-57
(The) Great Performances
Heartbreak Hotel, Hound Dog & The Top Ten Hits
(The) King Of Rock 'N' Roll - 50's Masters - Disc 3
King Of The Whole Wide World - Collectors Set - The Elvis Medley
Loving You
Loving You (1997 Reissue)
(The) Legend Lives On - Disc 1
Memories Of Elvis - 1991 - Disc 3
Memories Of Elvis - 1993 - Disc 1
(The) Number One Hits
Platinum - A Life In Music - Disc 1
Shake Rattle & Roll (Promo)
(The) Top Ten Hits - Disc 1
Virtual Graceland CD-ROM

Various Artists
Back To The 50's
Dick Clark's Rock Roll & Remember 1/3-1/5
Dick Clark's Rock Roll & Remember 8/12-8/14
(The) Elvis Presley Years
Solid Gold Country - Elvis Presley Birthday Tribute 93-1
Solid Gold Country - Elvis Presley In Concert
Solid Gold Country - Elvis Presley's Love Songs
Solid Gold Country - Elvis Presley Memorial Tribute 91-8
Solid Gold Country - Elvis Presley Memorial Tribute 92-8
Solid Gold Country - Elvis Presley Memorial Tribute 93-8
Solid Gold Scrapbook - Elvis Golden Decade 1956-1965
Solid Gold Scrapbook - Elvis' Movie Music
Summer Songs
The Golden Days Of Rock 'N' Roll
The Teen Age Years 1957-1964
Your Goodtime Oldies Magazine 93-03
Your Goodtime Oldies Magazine 94-20
Your Goodtime Oldies Magazine 95-17

Tell Me Why
A Valentine Gift For You
(The) Blue Suede Box - Elvis: His Greatest Soundtracks - Disc 1
(The) Elvis Presley Collection - Rhythm & Blues - Disc 2
Elvis The Other Sides - Worldwide Gold Award Hits Volume 2 - Disc 1
Essential Elvis Vol. 2 - Stereo 57 *(alternate take 5)*
(The) King Of Rock 'N' Roll - 50's Masters - Disc 2
Loving You (1997 Reissue)

Tender Feelings
Burning Love And Hits From His Movies Vol. 2
Elvis Double Features - Kissin' Cousins, Clambake & Stay Away Joe
Elvis Presley - The King Of Rock & Roll At His Best - Disc 2

Tennessee Waltz
A Touch Of Platinum - A Life In Music - Disc 2 (Graceland & Palm Springs Segment) *(home recording)*
Platinum - A Life In Music - Disc 2 (Graceland & Palm Springs Segment) *(home recording)*

Thanks To The Rolling Sea
Elvis Aron Presley - Disc 2 *(alternate take10)*
Elvis Double Features - Canister Set - Disc 1
Elvis Double Features - Kid Galahad & Girls!Girls!Girls!

That's All Right (Mama)
A Golden Celebration - Disc 1 *(alternate takes 1,2,3)*
A Golden Celebration - Disc 4 - Elvis - Burbank, Calif. June 27, 1968
A Private Moment With The King *(home recording)*
A Touch Of Platinum - A Life In Music - Disc 1 *(alternate takes 1,2,3)*
An Afternoon In The Garden
Elvis Aron Presley - Disc 1
Elvis A Legendary Performer Volume 1
Elvis As Recorded At Madison Square Garden
Elvis Birthday Tribute Radio Program
...vis' Golden Records (1997 Reissue)
Elvis! His Greatest Hits - Disc 4
Elvis In Concert
Elvis/NBC-TV-Special
(The) Elvis Presley Birthday Tribute 1992 - Disc 4
(The) Elvis Presley Collection - Rock 'N' Roll - Disc 2
Elvis Presley: Great Performances
Elvis Presley Radio Special (Promo)
Elvis Presley The King Of Rock & Roll At His Best - Disc 3
Elvis Presley: 1954-1961
Elvis The Legend - Disc 1
Elvis The Tribute - A Biography - Disc 2
Elvis 15th Anniversary Radio Show
Elvis 20th Anniversary Radio Show - Disc 1
For LP Fans Only
Good Rockin' Tonight - Disc 1
(The) Great Performances
(The) Honeymoon Companion (Promo)
(The) King Of Rock 'N' Roll - 50's Masters - Disc 1
(The) Legend Lives On - Disc 1
(The) Legend Of A King - Disc 1
(The) Louisiana Hayride - Anthologies Of Legends - Elvis Presley
(The) Louisiana Hayride - Anthologies Of Legends - Elvis Presley *(version 2)*
(The) Louisiana Hayride Archives Volume 1 (10/16/54)
(The) Louisiana Hayride Archives Volume 1 (1*1/19/55)*
Memories - The '68 Comeback Special - Disc 2 *(previously unreleased)*
Memories Of Elvis - 1991 - Disc 3
Memories Of Elvis - 1993 - Disc 1
Platinum - A Life In Music - Disc 1 *(alternate takes 1,2,3)*
(The) Private Presley CD
Raw Elvis
(The) Sun Sessions CD - The Master Takes
(The) Sun Sessions CD - The Outtakes
Tiger Man
Vintage 55
Virtual Graceland CD-ROM
Various Artists
Blues Notes And Black: Blues Sur
Dick Clark's Rock Roll & Remember 1/3-1/5
(The) Elvis Presley Years - Disc 1
Reelin' In The Years
Rock 'N' Roll: The Early Years
Rock 'N' Roll Legends
Solid Gold Country - The Complete 50's Masters
Solid Gold Country - Elvis Presley In Concert
Solid Gold Scrapbook - Elvis In Memphis
Sun's Greatest Hits
The Sun Records Collection
The Sun Story

That's Someone You Never Forget
(The) Elvis Presley Collection - Love Songs - Disc 1
From Nashville To Memphis - 60's Masters - Disc 2
From Nashville To Memphis - 60's Masters - Disc 5 *(alternate take 1)*

THAT'S SOMEONE YOU NEVER FORGET (cont'd)
Love Songs
Pot Luck With Elvis

That's When Your Heartaches Begin
Elvis' Golden Records
Elvis' Golden Records (1997 Reissue)
Elvis! His Greatest Hits - Disc 1
Elvis His Life And Music - Disc 1
(The) Elvis Presley Collection - The Romantic - Disc 1
(The) Elvis Presley Collection - Treasures '53 To '58 - Disc 1 *(1953 acetate)*
Elvis Presley Radio Special (Promo)
Elvis The King: 1954-1965
Elvis The Legend - Disc 1
Elvis 15th Anniversary Radio Show - Disc 1
Elvis 50 Worldwide Gold Hits Vol. 1
Essential Elvis Vol. 2 Stereo 57 *(alternate takes 4,5,6)*
Heartbreak Hotel, Hound Dog & Top Ten Hits
(The) King Of Rock 'N' Roll - 50's Masters - Disc 3
(The) King Of Rock 'N' Roll - 50's Masters - Disc 5 *(1953 acetate)*
(The) Million Dollar Quartet
Various Artists
The Music That Made Memphis *(1953 acetate)*

The Bullfighter Was A Lady
Elvis Double Features - Canister Set - Disc 2
Elvis Double Features - It Happened At The Worlds Fair & Fun In Acapulco

The Fair Is Moving On
Back In Memphis
From Nashville To Memphis - 60's Masters - Disc 5
(The) Memphis Record

The First Noel
Blue Christmas
Christmas Classics
Christmas With Elvis
Elvis Sings The Wonderful World Of Christmas
If Every Day Was Like Christmas
If Every Day Was Like Christmas - Special Collectors Edition
Merry Christmas
Various Artists
Solid Gold Country - Christmas With Elvis Presley

The First Time Ever I Saw Your Face
Elvis Aron Presley - Disc 3
Walk A Mile In My Shoes - 70's Masters - Disc 1

The Fool
A Golden Celebration - Disc 4 - Elvis At Home - Germany - 1958-60 *(home recording)*
Elvis Country - I'm 10,000 Years Old
(The) Elvis Presley Collection - The Rocker - Disc 1
Elvis 20th Anniversary Sampler *(home recording)*
Essential Elvis Vol. 4 - A Hundred Years From Now *(alternate take 1)*
Walk a Mile In My Shoes - 70's Masters - Disc 3

The Girl I Never Loved
An Elvis Double Feature - Speedway & Clambake
Elvis Double Features - Kissin' Cousins, Clambake & Stay Away Joe

The Girl Of My Best Friend
Elvis' Golden Records Vol. 3 (1997 Reissue)
Elvis Is Back
Elvis Is Back - 24 kt Gold Disc
(The) Elvis Presley Collection - The Rocker - Disc 1
Elvis The Legend - Disc 2
From Nashville To Memphis - 60's Masters - Disc 1
Heart And Soul
Out Of The Box - 6 From The 60's (Promo)

The Impossible Dream
Elvis As Recorded At Madison Square Garden
Elvis 20th Anniversary Radio Show - Disc 3
(The) Legend Lives On - Disc 2
Walk A Mile In My Shoes - 70's Masters - Disc 5 (The Elvis Presley Show)

The Lady Loves Me
Elvis Double Features - Canister Set - Disc 3 (with Ann-Margret)
Elvis Double Features - Viva Las Vegas & Roustabout (with Ann-Margret)
(The) Elvis Presley Collection - Movie Magic - Disc 2 (with Ann-Margret)
Various Artists
The Great Victor Duets (with Ann-Margret)

The Last Farewell
(The) Elvis Presley Collection - From The Heart - Disc 2
Elvis 15th Anniversary Radio Show - Disc 4
From Elvis Presley Boulevard Memphis, Tennessee, Recorded Live

The Lord's Prayer
Essential Elvis Vol. 4 - A Hundred Years From Now *(informal performance)*

The Love Machine
Elvis Double Features - Easy Come, Easy Go & Speedway
Elvis Double Features - Easy Come, Easy Go & Speedway *(alternate take 11)*

The Meanest Girl In Town
Elvis Double Features - Canister Set - Disc 4
Elvis Double Features - Harum Scarum & Girl Happy

The Next Step Is Love
Elvis The Other Sides - Worldwide Gold Award Hits Volume 2 - Disc 2
That's The Way It Is
That's The Way It Is - Original Master Recording
Walk A Mile In My Shoes - 70's Masters - Disc 1

The Sound Of Your Cry
Platinum - A Life In Music - Disc 3 *(alternate take 3)*
Walk A Mile In My Shoes - 70's Masters - Disc 1

The Twelfth Of Never
Elvis 20th Anniversary Radio Show - Disc 1
Walk A Mile In My Shoes - 70's Masters - Disc 5 *(rehearsal)*
Walk A Mile In My Shoes - Out Of The Box Sampler (Promo) *(rehearsal)*

The Walls Have Ears
Elvis Double Features - Canister Set - Disc 1
Elvis Double Features - Kid Galahad & Girls!Girls!Girls!

The Whiffenpoof Song
Elvis Double Features - Live A Little, Love A Little, Charro, The Trouble With Girls & Change Of Habit

The Wonder Of You
A Touch Of Platinum Vol. 2 - A Life In Music - Disc 1 (Las Vegas 1970)
Elvis Aron Presley - Disc 4
Elvis At His Romantic Best
Elvis! His Greatest Hits - Disc 4
(The) Elvis Presley Birthday Tribute 1992 - Disc 4
(The) Elvis Presley Collection - Love Songs - Disc 1
Elvis Presley - 50 Greatest Hits - Disc 1
Elvis The Legend - Disc 3
Elvis The Other Sides - Worldwide Gold Award Hits Volume 2 - Disc 2
Elvis The Tribute - A Biography - Disc 2
Elvis 50 Years 50 Hits - Disc 1
Elvis 15th Anniversary Radio Show - Disc 2
Elvis 20th Anniversary Radio Show - Disc 2
Love Songs
Memories Of Elvis - 1991 - Disc 4
Memories Of Elvis - 1993 - Disc 3
On Stage February 1970
Platinum - A Life In Music - Disc 3 (Las Vegas 1970)
Sixties Legends - Elvis Presley - Disc 2
(The) Top Ten Hits - Disc 2
Walk A Mile In My Shoes -70's Masters - Disc 1
Various Artists
(The) Elvis Presley Years - Disc 3
Solid Gold Country - Elvis Presley Birthday Tribute 93-1
Solid Gold Country - Elvis Presley Live
Solid Gold Country - Elvis Presley's Love Songs
Solid Gold Country - Elvis Presley Memorial Tribute 92-8
Solid Gold Hits Of The '70's

The Wonderful World Of Christmas
Christmas With Elvis
Elvis Sings The Wonderful World Of Christmas
If Every Day Was Like Christmas
If Every Day Was Like Christmas - Special Collectiors Edition
The Yellow Rose Of Texas/The Eyes Of Texas
Elvis Double Features - Canister Set - Disc 3
Elvis Double Features - Viva Las Vegas & Roustabout
Double Dynamite

There Ain't Nothing Like A Song
An Elvis Double Feature - Speedway & Clambake (with Nancy Sinatra)
Elvis Double Features - Easy Come, Easy Go & Speedway (with Nancy Sinatra)
Elvis!Elvis!Elvis! - The King And His Movies (with Nancy Sinatra)

There Goes My Everything
Elvis Country -I'm 10,000 Years Old
Elvis! His Greatest Hits - Disc 4
(The) Elvis Presley Collection - Country - Disc 2
Elvis The Legend - Disc 3
Elvis The Other Sides - Worldwide Gold Award Hits Volume 2 - Disc 2
Elvis 20th Anniversary Radio Show - Disc 3
Great Country Songs *(alternate take 1)*
Walk A Mile In My Shoes - 70's Masters - Disc 1
Various Artists
Sweet Dreams Of Country

There Is No God But God
Amazing Grace His Greatest Sacred Performances - Disc 2
He Touched Me

There Is So Much World To See
Elvis Double Features - Spinout & Double Trouble

There's A Brand New Day On The Horizon
Command Performances - 60's Masters - Disc 2
Elvis Double Features - Canister Set - Disc 3
Elvis Double Features - Viva Las Vegas & Roustabout

There's A Honky Tonk Angel
Essential Elvis Vol. 5 - Rhythm And Country *(alternate take 1)*
Promised Land

There's Always Me
Collectors Gold - Disc 2 *(alternate take 4)*
(The) Elvis Presley Collection - The Romantic - Disc 2
From Nashville To Memphis - 60's Masters - Disc 1
Something For Everybody

There's Gold In The Mountains
Elvis Double Features - Kissin' Cousins, Clambake & Stay Away Joe

There's No Place Like Home
(The) Million Dollar Quartet

There's No Tomorrow
Platinum - A Life In Music - Disc 1 (Bad Nauheim medley) *(home recording)*

They Remind Me Too Much Of You
Command Performances - 60's Masters - Disc 1
Elvis Aron Presley- Disc 2 *(alternate take 1)*
Elvis Double Features - Canister Set - Disc 2
Elvis Double Features - It Happened At The Worlds Fair & Fun In Acapulco
(The) Elvis Presley Collection - Movie Magic - Disc 1
Elvis Sings Hits From His Movies Volume 1
Elvis The Other Sides - Worldwide Gold Award Hits Volume 2 - Disc 2

Thinking About You
Essential Elvis Vol. 5 - Rhythm And Country *(alternate take 4)*
Promised Land
Walk A Mile In My Shoes - 70's Masters - Disc 2

This Is Living
Elvis Double Features - Canister Set - Disc 1
Elvis Double Features - Kid Galahad & Girls!Girls!Girls!

This Is My Heaven
Command Performances - 60's Masters - Disc 2
Elvis Double Features - Frankie And Johnny & Paradise Hawaiian Style

This Is Our Dance
Love Letters From Elvis

This Is The Story
Back In Memphis
Collectors Gold - Disc 3 (Las Vegas 1969)
From Nashville To Memphis - 60's Masters - Disc 4

This Time
From Nashville To Memphis-60's Masters-Disc 5(medley This Time/I Can't Stop Loving You) *(inf. recording)*

Three Corn Patches
Essential Elvis Vol. 5 - Rhythm And Country (*alternate take 14*)
Raised On Rock

Thrill Of Your Love
Elvis Is Back
Elvis Is Back - 24 kt Gold Disc
From Nashville To Memphis - 60's Masters - Disc 1

Tiger Man
A Golden Celebration - Disc 4 - Elvis - Burbank. Calif. June 27, 1968
A Touch Of Platinum Vol. 2 - A Life In Music - Disc 1 ('68 Comeback Special rehearsal)
Collectors Gold - Disc 3 (Las Vegas 1969)
Elvis Aron Presley (medley Mystery Train/Tiger Man) Disc 4
Elvis/NBC - TV Special
Elvis In Person At The International Hotel
(The) Elvis Presley Collection - Rhythm & Blues - Disc 2 (NBC TV Special)
(The) Legend Lives On - Disc 1
Platinum - A Life In Music - Disc 3 ('68 Comeback Special rehearsal)
Tiger Man
Walk A Mile In My Shoes - 70's Masters - Disc 4 (*studio jam*)

Today Tomorrow And Forever
Elvis Double Features - Canister Set - Disc 3
Elvis Double Features - Viva Las Vegas & Roustabout

Tomorrow Is A Long Time
A Valentine Gift For You
From Nashville To Memphis - 60's Masters - Disc 3

Tomorrow Never Comes
Elvis Country - I'm 10,000 Years Old
Walk A Mile In My Shoes - 70's Masters - Disc 3 (*includes false start*)

Tomorrow Night
Elvis For Everyone
(The) Elvis Presley Collection - Treasures '53 To '58 - Disc 1
(The) King Of Rock 'N' Roll - 50's Masters - Disc 1
Reconsider Baby (*unreleased Sun Master*)
(The) Sun Sessions CD - The Master Takes
Various Artists
Sun's Greatest Hits

Tonight Is So Right For Love
(The) Blue Suede Box - Elvis: His Greatest Soundtracks - Disc 5
Burning Love And Hits From His Movies
(The) Elvis Presley Collection - The Romantic - Disc 1
Elvis Presley: The King Of Rock & Roll At His Best - Disc 2
G.I. Blues
G.I. Blues (*alternate version*)
G.I. Blues (1997 Reissue)
G.I. Blues (1997 Reissue Collectors Edition)
Platinum - A Life In Music - Disc 2 (*alternate take 3*)

Tonight's All Right For Love
(The) Blue Suede Box - Elvis: His Greatest Soundtracks - Disc 5
G.I. Blues (1997 Reissue)
G.I. Blues (1997 Reissue Collectors Edition)
Elvis Aron Presley - Disc 2 (*alternate takes 3,4,7,8*)
Elvis A Legendary Performer Volume 1

TONIGHT'S ALL RIGHT FOR LOVE (cont'd)
Elvis Presley - The King Of Rock & Roll At His Best - Disc 3
Elvis Presley: Great Performances

Too Much
A Golden Celebration - Disc 3 - Ed Sullivan Show New York Jan. 6, 1957
Elvis' Golden Records
Elvis' Golden Records (1997 Reissue)
Elvis' Greatest Jukebox Hits
Elvis! His Greatest Hits - Disc 1
Elvis His Life And Music - Disc 1
(The) Elvis Presley Birthday Tribute 1992 - Disc 4
(The) Elvis Presley Collection - Rock 'N' Roll - Disc 1
(The) Elvis Presley Collection - Treasures '53 To '58 - Disc 2 - Ed Sullivan Show New York Jan. 6,1957
Elvis Presley 1954-1961
Elvis Presley - 50 Greatest Hits - Disc 1
Elvis The Tribute - A Biography - Disc 1
Elvis 15th Anniversary Radio Show - Disc 2
Elvis 20th Anniversary Radio Show - Disc 2
Elvis 50 Worldwide Gold Hits - Vol. 1 - Disc 1
Elvis 50 Years 50 Hits - Disc 1
Elvis 56
Elvis 56 Advance Music (Promo)
Good Rockin' Tonight - Disc 2
Great Hits Of 1956-57
(The) King Of Rock 'N' Roll - 50's Masters - Disc 2
Memories Of Elvis - 1991 - Disc 2
Memories Of Elvis - 1993 - Disc 1
(The) Number One Hits
Shake, Rattle & Roll (Promo)
(The) Top Ten Hits - Disc 1
Various Artists
Solid Gold Country - Elvis: What Happened?
Solid Gold Country - Elvis Presley & TV
Solid Gold Country - Elvis Presley's Love Songs
Solid Gold Country - The Complete 50's Masters
Solid Gold Country - 70 Years Of RCA Country
Solid Gold Scrapbook - Elvis Golden Decade 1956-1965

Too Much Monkey Business
(The) Elvis Presley Collection - The Rocker - Disc 2
From Nashville To Memphis - 60's Masters - Disc 3
(The) Million Dollar Quartet

Treat Me Nice
(The) Blue Suede Box - Elvis: His Greatest Soundtracks - Disc 2
(The) Blue Suede Box - Elvis: His Greatest Soundtracks - Disc 2 *(movie version)*
Commerative Jukebox Series - 5 CD Set - Disc 3
Elvis' Golden Records
Elvis' Golden Records (1997 Reissue)
Elvis! His Greatest Hits - Disc 1
Elvis His Life And Music - Disc 1
(The) Elvis Presley Birthday Tribute 1992 - Disc 4
(The) Elvis Presley Collection - Movie Magic - Disc 1
Elvis Presley Radio Special (Promo)
Elvis Presley Sings Leiber & Stoller
Elvis Presley - 50 Greatest Hits - Disc 1
Elvis The Tribute - A Biography - Disc 2
Elvis The King: 1954-1965
Elvis 15th Anniversary Radio Show - Disc 2
Elvis 20th Anniversary Radio Show - Disc 2
Elvis 50 Worldwide Gold Hits Vol.1 - Disc 1
Elvis 50 Years 50 Hits - Disc 1

TREAT ME NICE (cont'd)
Essential Elvis - The First Movies *(unreleased version take 10)*
Essential Elvis - The First Movies
(The) Great Performances *(stereo)*
Jailhouse Rock and Love Me Tender
Jailhouse Rock and Love Me Tender *(movie version)*
Jailhouse Rock/ Treat Me Nice (Jukebox Single)
(The) King Of Rock 'N' Roll - 50's Masters - Disc 4
Memories Of Elvis - 1991 - Disc 1
Memories Of Elvis - 1993 - Disc 2
Various Artists
Leiber & Stoller - The Fifties (Promo)
Leiber & Stoller Music Publishing (6 CD Promo Set)
Solid Gold Country - Elvis Presley: His Favorite Writers
Solid Gold Country - Elvis Presley Memorial Tribute 93-8
Solid Gold Country - Elvis Presley Sings Leiber And Stoller
Solid Gold Scrapbook - Elvis' Movie Music
My Fellow Americans (Original Soundtrack)

Trouble
(The) Blue Suede Box - Elvis: His Greatest Soundtracks - Disc 2
Blue Suede Shoes (Original Soundtrack) Disc 2 *(drum intro)*
Elvis!Elvis!Elvis! - The King And His Movies
Elvis/NBC - TV Special
Elvis/NBC - TV Special
(The) Elvis Presley Collection - Movie Magic - Disc 2
Elvis Presley Sings Leiber & Stoller
Elvis The Other Sides - Worldwide Gold Award Hits Volume 2 - Disc 2
Elvis 15th Anniversary Radio Show - Disc 1
(The) Great Performances
King Creole
King Creole (1997 Reissue)
(The) King Of Rock 'N' Roll - 50's Masters - Disc 4
(The) King Of Rock 'N' Roll - 50's Masters (Promo)
(The) Legend Of A King - Disc 1
Memories - The '68 Comeback Special - Disc 1
Memories - The '68 Comeback Special - Disc 1 *(previously unreleased)*
Memories - The '68 Comeback Special - Disc 1
Various Artists
Leiber & Stoller Music Publishing (6 CD Promo Set)
Leiber & Stoller - The Fifties (Promo)
Solid Gold Country - Elvis Presley Sings Leiber And Stoller

True Love
(The) Blue Suede Box - Elvis: His Greatest Soundtracks - Disc 1
(The) Elvis Presley Collection - The Romantic - Disc 1
(The) King Of Rock 'N' Roll - 50's Masters - Disc 3
Loving You
Loving You (1997 Reissue)

True Love Travels On A Gravel Road
From Elvis In Memphis
From Nashville To Memphis - 60's Masters - Disc 4
(The) Memphis Record

Trying To Get To You
A Golden Celebration - Disc 4 - Elvis - Burbank, Calif. June 27, 1968
A Touch Of Platinum Vol. 2 - A Life In Music - Disc 1 ("68 Comeback Special) *(alternate take)*
Elvis Aron Presley - Disc 2
Elvis A Legendary Performer Volume 1
Elvis In Concert
Elvis/NBC - TV Special

TRYING TO GET TO YOU (cont'd)
Elvis Presley
(The) Elvis Presley Collection - Rhythm & Blues - Disc 1 (NBC TV Special)
(The) Elvis Presley Collection - Rock 'N Roll - Disc 1
Elvis Presley - Collectors Edition
Elvis Presley: Great Performances
Elvis Presley - The King Of Rock & Roll At His Best - Disc 3
Elvis Recorded Live On Stage In Memphis
Good Rockin' Tonight - Disc 1
(The) King Of Rock 'N' Roll - 50's Masters - Disc 1
(The) Legend Lives On - Disc 2
Memories - The '68 Comeback Special - Disc 2 *(previously unreleased)*
Platinum - A Life In Music - Disc 3 ('68 Comeback Special) *(alternate take)*
(The) Sun Sessions - The Master Takes
Tiger Man

Turn Your Eyes Upon Jesus
Amazing Grace - His Greatest Sacred Performances - Disc 2 *(previously unreleased)*
Selections From Amazing Grace - His Greatest Sacred Performances (Promo)

Tutti Frutti
A Golden Celebration - Disc 1 - Dorsey Bros Show New York Feb. 4, 1956
A Golden Celebration - Disc 1 - Dorsey Bros. Show New York Feb. 18, 1956
Blue Suede Shoes (Original Soundtrack) - Disc 1
Blue Suede Shoes/Tutti Frutti (Jukebox Single)
Commemorative Jukebox Series (5 CD Set) Disc 4
Elvis Presley
Elvis Presley - Collectors Edition
(The) Elvis Presley Collection - The Rocker - Disc 1
Elvis The Tribute - A Biography - Disc 1
Elvis 15th Anniversary Radio Show - Disc 3
Elvis 56
Elvis 56 Advance Music (Promo)
Good Rockin' Tonight - Disc 1
(The) King Of Rock 'N' Roll - 50's Masters - Disc 1
Rocker
Various Artists
RCA 24 Karat Gold Sampler (Promo)

Tweedle Dee
(The) King Of Rock 'N' Roll - 50's Masters - Disc 5 (Texas 1954)
(The) Louisiana Hayride - Anthologies Of Legends - Elvis Presley
(The) Louisiana Hayride - Anthologies Of Legends - Elvis Presley *(version 2)*
(The) Louisiana Hayride Archives Volume 1 (4/30/55)
(The) Louisiana Hayride Archives Volume 1 (12/17/55)
(The) Private Presley CD

Twenty Days And Twenty Nights
That's The Way It Is
That's The Way It Is - Original Recording
Walk A Mile In My Shoes - 70's Masters - Disc 3

"U"

U.S. Male
Almost In Love
Double Dynamite
Elvis' Gold Records Volume 5 (1997 Reissue)
(The) Elvis Presley Collection - Rock 'N' Roll - Disc 1
Elvis The Legend - Disc 3
From Nashville To Memphis - 60's Masters - Disc 3
(The) Legend Lives On - Disc 4

Unchained Melody
Always On My Mind
Elvis Aron Presley - Disc 3
Elvis At His Romantic Best
Elvis 15th Anniversary Radio Show - Disc 6
(The) Great Performances
(The) Legend Lives On - Disc 1
Love Songs
Moody Blue
Virtual Graceland CD-ROM
Walk A Mile In My Shoes - 70's Masters - Disc 5 (The Elvis Presley Show)
Various Artists
God Bless The U.S.A.
Solid Gold Country - Elvis Presley Birthday Tribute 93-1
Solid Gold Country - Elvis Presley Live
Solid Gold Country - Elvis Presley's Love Songs
Solid Gold Country - Elvis Presley Memorial Tribute 93-8

Until It's Time For You To Go
An Afternoon In The Garden
Elvis At His Romantic Best
Elvis Now
(The) Elvis Presley Collection - Love Songs - Disc 1
Essential Elvis Vol. 4 - A Hundred Years From Now *(alternate master take 10)*
(The) Legend Lives On - Disc 3
Walk A Mile In My Shoes - 70's Masters - Disc 1
Various Artists
Easy Listening Hits Of The 60's & 70's

Up Above My Head
Elvis/NBC - TV Special
Memories - The '68 Comeback Special - Disc 1

"V"

Vino Dinero Y Amor
Elvis Double Features - Canister Set - Disc 2
Elvis Double Features - It Happened At The Worlds Fair & Fun In Acapulco

Violet
Elvis Double Features - Live A Little, Love A Little, Charro, The Trouble With Girls & Change Of Habit

Viva Las Vegas
Command Performances - 60's Masters - Disc 1
Elvis' Double Features - Canister Set - Disc 3
Elvis' Double Features - Viva Las Vegas & Roustabout
Elvis!Elvis!Elvis! - The King And His Movies
Elvis" Gold Records Volume 4 (1997 Reissue)
Elvis' Greatest Jukebox Hits
Elvis! His Greatest Hits - Disc 3
(The) Elvis Presley Birthday Tribute 1992 - Disc 4
(The) Elvis Presley Collection - Movie Magic - Disc 1
Elvis Presley - 50 Greatest Hits - Disc 1
Elvis The Tribute - A Biography - Disc 2
Elvis 15th Anniversary Radio Show - Disc 2
Elvis 50 Worldwide Hits Vol. 1 - Disc 1
Elvis 50 Years 50 Hits - Disc 1
Memories Of Elvis - 1991 - Disc 2
Various Artists
Solid Gold Country - Elvis Presley: His Favorite Writers
Solid Gold Scrapbook - Elvis Movie Music

Walk A Mile In My Shoes
On Stage February, 1970
Walk A Mile In My Shoes - 70's Masters - Disc 5 (The Elvis Presley Show)
Walk A Mile In My Shoes - Out Of The Box Sampler (Promo)
Various Artists
Lowery Country Gold Vol. 3 (Promo)

Way Down
A Touch Of Platinum Vol. 2 - A Life In Music - Disc 2 *(alternate take 2)*
Elvis' Gold Records Volume 5
Elvis' Gold Records Volume 5 (1997 Reissue)
Elvis' Greatest Jukebox Hits
(The) Elvis Presley Birthday Tribute 1992 - Disc 4
(The) Elvis Presley Collection - The Rocker - Disc 1
Elvis 15th Anniversary Radio Show - Disc 6
(The) Legend Lives On - Disc 4
(The) Legend Of A King - Disc 2
Moody Blue
Memories Of Elvis - 1991 - Disc 3
Memories Of Elvis - 1993 - Disc 3
Platinum - A Life In Music - Disc 4 *(alternate take 2)*
Walk A Mile In My Shoes - 70's Masters - Disc 2
Various Artists
Contempory Country Volume 3 - The Late 70's Hot Hits
(The) Elvis Presley Years - Disc 4
Solid Gold Country - Elvis Presley Birthday Tribute 92-1
Solid Gold Country - Elvis Presley Birthday Tribute 93-1
Solid Gold Country - Elvis Presley's Golden Records 93-2
Solid Gold Country - Elvis Presley Memorial Tribute 91-8
Solid Gold Country - Elvis Presley Memorial Tribute 92-8
Solid Gold Country - Elvis Presley Memorial Tribute 93-8
Solid Gold Country - This Week In 1977 - 91-9
Solid Gold Country - This Week In 1977 - 92-9
Solid Gold Scrapbook - Elvis In Memphis

We Call On Him
Amazing Grace His Greatest Sacred Performances - Disc 2
Elvis Gospel 1957-1971: Known Only to Him
(The) Elvis Presley Collection - Gospel - Disc 2 *(alternate take)*
Elvis Presley The King Of Rock & Roll At His Best - Disc 1
You'll Never Walk Alone

We Can Make The Morning
Elvis Now
Walk A Mile In My Shoes - 70's Masters - Disc 1

We'll Be Together
Burning Love And Hits From His Movies Vol. 2
Elvis Double Features - Canister Set - Disc 1
Eovis Double Features - Kid Galahad & Girls!Girls!Girls!
Elvis Presley - The King Of Rock & Roll At His Best - Disc 2

We're Coming In Loaded
Elvis Double Features - Canister Set - Disc 1
Elvis Double Features - Kid Galahad & Girls!Girls!Girls!

We're Gonna Move

A Date With Elvis
(The) Blue Suede Box - Elvis: His Greatest Soundtracks - Disc 2
(The) Blue Suede Box - Elvis: His Greatest Soundtracks - Disc 2 *(stereo alternate take 9)*
(The) Elvis Presley Collection - Treasures '53 To '58 - Disc 1
Elvis The Other Sides - Worldwide Gold Award Hits Volume 2 - Disc 1
Essential Elvis - The First Movies
Jailhouse Rock and Love Me Tender
Jailhouse Rock and Love Me Tender *(stereo alternate take 9)*
(The) King Of Rock 'N' Roll - 50's Masters - Disc 2
(The) King Of Rock 'N' Roll - 50's Masters - Disc 5 *(alternate take 4)*
Remembering Elvis

Wear My Ring Around Your Neck

Blue Suede Shoes (Original Soundtrack) Disc 1
Elvis' Gold Records Volume 2 - 50,000,000 Elvis Fans Can't Be Wrong
Elvis' Gold Records Volume 2 - 50,000,000 Elvis Fans Can't Be Wrong (1997 Reissue)
Elvis! His Greatest Hits - Disc 1
Elvis His Life And Music - Disc 2
(The) Elvis Presley Birthday Tribute 1992 - Disc 4
(The) Elvis Presley Collection - Rock 'N' Roll - Disc 1
Elvis Presley 1954-1961
Elvis Presley 50 Greatest Hits - Disc 2
Elvis The Legend - Disc 2
Elvis The Tribute - A Biography - Disc 3
Elvis 15th Anniversary Radio Show - Disc 5
Elvis 20th Anniversary Radio Show - Disc 1
Elvis 24 Karat Hits!
Elvis 50 Worldwide Gold Hits Vol. 1 - Disc 1
Elvis 50 Years 50 Hits - Disc 2
Essential Elvis Vol. 3/Hits Like Never Before *(take 22 original undubbed version)*
Essential Elvis Vol. 3/Hits Like Never Before *(take 22 original single version)*
(The) Honeymoon Companion (Promo)
(The) King Of Rock 'N' Roll - 50's Masters - Disc 4
Memories Of Elvis - 1991 - Disc 3
Memories Of Elvis - 1993 - Disc 2
(The) Top Ten Hits - Disc 1
Various Artists
(The) Elvis Presley Years - Disc 1
Solid Gold Country - August Gold
Solid Gold Country - Elvis Presley Birthday Tribute 93-1
Solid Gold Country - Elvis Presley's Golden Records 91-11
Solid Gold Country - Elvis Presley's Golden Records 93-2
Solid Gold Country - Elvis Presley's Love Songs
Solid Gold Country - Elvis Presley Memorial Tribute 92-8
Solid Gold Country - The Complete 50's Masters
Solid Gold Scrapbook - Elvis' Golden Decade 1956-1965
Solid Gold Scrapbook - Solid Gold Elvis
Your Goodtime Oldies Magazine 92-45
Your Goodtime Oldies Magazine 93-35
Your Goodtime Oldies Magazine 94-34
Your Goodtime Oldies Magazine 95-35

Wearin' That Loved On Look

(The) Elvis Presley Collection - Rhythm & Blues - Disc 2 *(alternate take)*
From Elvis In Memphis
From Nashville To Memphis - 60's Masters - Disc 4
(The) Memphis Record

Welcome To My World

Aloha From Hawaii Via Satellite
Aloha From Hawaii Via Satellite - 25th Anniversary Edition
Aloha Via Satellite

WELCOME TO MY WORLD (cont'd)
(The) Alternate Aloha
Elvis Aron Presley - Disc 2
(The) Elvis Presley Collection - Country - Disc 2
Elvis 15th Anniversary Radio Show - Disc 5
(The) Legend Lives On - Disc 3
Welcome To My World

Western Union
An Elvis Double Feature - Speedway & Clambake
From Nashville To Memphis - 60's Masters - Disc 3
(The) Lost Album

What A Wonderful Life
Collectors Gold - Disc 1 *(alternate takes 2 & 1)*
Elvis Double Features - Flaming Star, Wild In The Country & Follow That Dream

What Every Woman Lives For
Elvis Double Features - Frankie And Johnny & Paradise Hawaiian Style

What Now, What Next, Where To
From Nashville To Memphis - 60's Masters - Disc 2
(The) Lost Album
Separate Ways

What Now My Love
Aloha From Hawaii Via Satellite
Aloha From Hawaii Via Satellite - 25th Anniversary Edition
Aloha Via Satellite
(The) Alternate Aloha
Elvis 15th Anniversary Radio Show - Disc 6
(The) Legend Lives On - Disc 1

What'd I Say
A Touch Of Platinum Vol. 2 - A Life In Music - Disc 1 (Las Vegas Rehearsals)
Collectors Gold - Disc 3 (Las Vegas 1969)
Command Performances - 60's Masters - Disc 1
Elvis Double Features - Canister Set - Disc 3
Elvis Double Features - Viva Las Vegas & Roustabout
Elvis' Gold Records Volume 4
Elvis' Gold Records Volume 4 (1997 Reissue)
Elvis! His Greatest Hits - Disc 3
Elvis His Life And Music - Disc 4
Elvis In Concert
(The) Elvis Presley Collection - Rhythm & Blues - Disc 2
Elvis Presley - 50 Greatest Hits - Disc 1
Elvis 20th Anniversary Radio Show - Disc 1
Elvis 50 Years 50 Hits - Disc 4
From Nashville To Memphis - 60's Masters - Disc 3 (medley Guitar Man/What'd I Say) *(original unedited master)*
Platinum - A Life In Music - Disc 3 (Las Vegas Rehearsals)
Various Artists
Solid Gold Country - Elvis Presley Memorial Tribute 93-8

What's She Really Like
(The) Blue Suede Box - Elvis: His Greatest Soundtracks - Disc 5
(The) Blue Suede Box - Elvis: His Greatest Soundtracks - Disc 5 *(alternate take 7)*
G. I. Blues (See "She's All Mine")
G.I. Blues (1997 Reissue)
G.I. Blues (1997 Reissue) *(alternate take 7)*
G.I. Blues (1997 Reissue Collectors Edition)
G.I. Blues (1997 Reissue Collectors Edition) *(alternate take 7)*

Wheels On My Heels
Elvis Double Features - Canister Set - Disc 3
Elvis Double Features - Viva Las Vegas & Roustabout

When God Dips His Love In My Heart
(The) Million Dollar Quartet

When I'm Over You
Love Letters From Elvis

When It Rains It Really Pours
A Golden Celebration - Disc 1 *(alternate take)*
(The) Blue Suede Box - Elvis: His Greatest Soundtracks - Disc 1
Elvis For Everyone
(The) Elvis Presley Collection - Rhythm & Blues - Disc 2
(The) King Of Rock 'N' Roll - 50's Masters - Disc 1
(The) King Of Rock 'N' Roll - 50's Masters - Disc 3
Loving You (1997 Reissue)
Memories - The '68 Comeback Special - Disc 2 *(previously unreleased)*
Reconsider Baby
(The) Sun Sessions - The Outtakes

When My Blue Moon Turns To Gold Again
A Golden Celebration - Disc 3 - Ed Sullivan Show New York Jan 6, 1957
A Touch Of Platinum Vol. 2 - A Life In Music - Disc 1 ('68 Comeback Special) *(alternate take)*
Elvis
Elvis! His Greatest Hits - Disc 4
(The) Elvis Presley Collection - Country - Disc 1
Elvis The Other Sides - Worldwide Gold Award Hits Volume 2 - Disc 1
Elvis 15th Anniversary Radio Show - Disc 4
Great Country Songs
(The) King Of Rock 'N' Roll - 50's Masters - Disc 2
Memories - The '68 Comeback Special - Disc 2 *(previously unreleased)*
Memories Of Elvis - 1991 - Disc 1
Platinum - A Life In Music - Disc 3 ('68 comeback Special) *(alternate take)*
Tiger Man *(previously unreleased)*
Various Artists
Cruisin' America with Cousin Brucie 92-32

When The Saints Go Marchin' In
A Touch Of Platinum - A Life In Music - Disc 1 *(home recording)*
Elvis Double Features - Frankie And Johnny & Paradise Hawaiian Style
Elvis Sings Hits From His Movies Volume 1
(The) Million Dollar Quartet
Platinum - A Life In Music - Disc 1 *(home recording)*
Platinum In-Store Sampler (Promo) *(home recording)*

Where Could I Go But To The Lord
Amazing Grace His Greatest Sacred Performances - Disc 1
Elvis Gospel 1957-1971: Known Only To Him
Elvis/NBC - TV Special
(The) Elvis Presley Collection - Gospel - Disc 2
(The) Elvis Presley Gospel Treasury - Disc 2
(The) Elvis Presley Gospel Treasury (Special Edition)
How Great Thou Art
Memories - The '68 Comeback Special - Disc 1

Where Did They Go Lord
Essential Elvis Vol. 4 - A Hundred Years From Now *(alternate take 1)*
Walk A Mile In My Shoes - 70's Masters - Disc 1

Where Do I Go From Here
Elvis (aka "The Fool Album")

Where Do You Come From
Elvis Double Features - Canister Set - Disc 1
Elvis Double Features - Kid Galahad & Girls!Girls!Girls!
Elvis 50 Worldwide Gold Hits Vol. 1 - Disc 2

Where No One Stands Alone
Amazing Grace His Greatest Sacred Performances - Disc 1
Elvis In Nashville 1956-1971
(The) Elvis Presley Collection - Gospel - Disc 2
(The) Elvis Presley Gospel Treasury - Disc 1
How Great Thou Art

White Christmas
Blue Christmas
Christmas Classics
Christmas Memories From Elvis And Alabama
Christmas Wishes From Anne Murray, Glen Campbell And Elvis Presley
Christmas With Elvis
Country Christmas - Elvis Presley's Country Style Christmas/Alabama
Elvis Christmas Album
Elvis Christmas Album (Camden)
Elvis The King Of Rock 'N' Roll - 50's Masters - Disc 3
If Every Day Was Like Christmas
If Every Day Was Like Christmas - Special Collectors Edition
Merry Christmas
Various Artists
A Country Christmas
The Family Christmas Collection
50 Christmas Favorites

Who Am I
Elvis Gospel 1957-1971: Known Only To Him
Elvis Presley The King Of Rock & Roll At His Best - Disc 1
From Nashville To Memphis - 60's Masters - Disc 5
His Hand In Mine (bonus track)
You'll Never Walk Alone

Who Are You (Who Am I)
An Elvis Double Feature: Speedway & Clambake
Elvis Double Features - Easy Come, Easy Go & Speedway

Who Needs Money
Elvis Double Features - Kissin' Cousins, Clambake & Stay Away Joe

Whole Lot-ta Shakin' Goin' On
Aloha From Hawaii Via Satellite
Aloha From Hawaii Via Satellite - 25th Anniversary Edition
Elvis Country
Elvis Country - I'm 10,000 Years Old
Elvis Recorded Live On Stage In Memphis
Essential Elvis Vol. 4 - A Hundred Years From Now *(undubbed/unedited master)*
(The) Legend Lives On - Disc 1
Walk A Mile In My Shoes - 70's Masters - Disc 3

Why Me Lord
Amazing Grace His Greatest Sacred Performances - Disc 2
Elvis Aron Presley - Disc 4
Elvis Recorded Live On Stage In Memphis

Wild In The Country
Command Performances - 60's Masters - Disc 1
Elvis Aron Presley - Disc 2 *(alternate take 16)*
Elvis Double Features - Flaming Star, Wild In The Country & Follow That Dream
Elvis' Golden Records Vol. 3 (1997 Reissue)
(The) Elvis Presley Collection - The Romantic - Disc 2
Elvis The Legend - Disc 2
Elvis The Other Sides - Worldwide Gold Award Hits Volume 2 - Disc 2

Winter Wonderland
Blue Christmas
Country Christmas - Elvis Presley's Country Style Christmas/Alabama
Christmas Classics
Christmas Memories With Elvis And Alabama
Christmas With Elvis
Elvis Sings The Wonderful World Of Christmas
If Every Day Was Like Christmas
If Every Day Was Like Christmas - Special Collectors Edition
Various Artists
Solid Gold Country - Christmas With Elvis

Wisdom Of The Ages
Elvis Double Features - Canister Set - Disc 4
Elvis Double Features - Harum Scarum & Girl Happy

Witchcraft (Bartholemew/King)
Collectors Gold - Disc 2 *(alternate take 1)*
Elvis' Gold Records Volume 4
Elvis' Gold Records Volume 4 (1997 Reissue)
Elvis His Life And Music - Disc 4
(The) Elvis Presley Collection - The Rocker - Disc 2
Elvis The Other Sides - Worldwide Gold Award Hits Volume 2 - Disc 2
From Nashville To Memphis - 60's Masters - Disc 2
(The) Lost Album
Return Of The Rocker

Witchcraft (C. Coleman/C. Leigh)
From Nashville To Memphis - 60's Masters - Disc 5 - from "the Frank Sinatra Timex Special"

Without Him
Amazing Grace His Greatest Sacred Performances - Disc 1
How Great Thou Art

Without Love (There Is Nothing)
Back In Memphis
(The) Elvis Presley Collection - From The Heart - Disc 1
From Nashville To Memphis - 60's Masters - Disc 4
(The) Memphis Record

Wolf Call
Elvis Double Features - Canister Set - Disc 4
Elvis Double Features - Harum Scarum & Girl Happy

Woman Without Love
Elvis Aron Presley - Forever
Elvis Today

Wonderful World
Elvis Double Features - Live A Little, Love A Little, Charro, The Trouble With Girls & Change Of Habit

Wooden Heart
(The) Blue Suede Box - Elvis: His Greatest Soundtracks - Disc 5
Blue Suede Shoes -Original Soundtrack - Disc 1 *(music box intro)*
Command Performances - 60's Masters - Disc 1
Elvis' Golden Records Vol. 3 (1997 Reissue)
Elvis! His Greatest Hits - Disc 3
(The) Elvis Presley Collection - Movie Magic - Disc 1
Elvis Sings For Children And Grownups Too!
Elvis The Legend - Disc 2
Elvis 15th Anniversary Radio Show - Disc 4
Elvis 50 Worldwide Gold Hits Vol. 1 - Disc 2
G.I. Blues
G.I. Blues (1997 Reissue)
G.I. Blues (1997 Reissue Collectors Edition)

Words
A Touch Of Platinum Vol. 2 - A Life In Music- Disc 1 (Las Vegas 1969)
Elvis In Person At The International Hotel
Platinum - A Life In Music - Disc 3 (Las Vegas 1969)

Working On The Building
Amazing Grace His Greatest Sacred Performances - Disc 1
Elvis In Nashville 1956-1971
(The) Elvis Presley Collection - Gospel - Disc 1
(The) Elvis Presley Gospel Treasury - Disc 2
(The) Elvis Presley Gospel Treasury (Special Edition)
His Hand In Mine

Write To Me From Naples
A Golden Celebration - Collectors Treasures - Graceland - Disc 4 *(home recording)*

"Y"

Yesterday
Elvis Aron Presley - Disc 3
(The) Legend Lives On - Disc 4
On Stage

Yoga Is As Yoga Does
Elvis Double Features - Easy Come, Easy Go & Speedway

You Asked Me To
Elvis Country *(1980 remixed version)*
Essential Elvis Vol. 5 - Rhythm And Country *(alternate take 2)*
Great Country Songs
Promised Land
Walk A Mile In My Shoes - 70's Masters - Disc 4

You Better Run
Amazing Grace His Greatest Sacred Performances - Disc 2 *(previously unreleased)*
Selections From Amazing Grace His Greatest Sacred Performances (Promo)

You Can't Say No In Acapulco
Elvis Double Features - Canister Set - Disc 2
Elvis Double Features - It Happened At The Worlds Fair & Fun In Acapulco

You Don't Have To Say You Love Me
A Touch Of Platinum Vol. 2 - A Life In Music - Disc 1
An Afternoon In The Garden

YOU DON'T HAVE TO SAY YOU LOVE ME (cont'd)
Elvis As Recorded At Madison Square Garden
Elvis' Gold Records Volume 5 (1997 Reissue)
Elvis! His Greatest Hits - Disc 4
(The) Elvis Presley Collection - From The Heart - Disc 1
Elvis Presley 50 Greatest Hits - Disc 2
Elvis The Legend - Disc 3
Elvis The Other Sides - Worldwide Gold Award Hits Volume 2 - Disc 2
Elvis 50 Years 50 Hits - Disc 2
Essential Elvis Vol. 4 - A Hundred Years From Now *(alternate take 2)*
Heart And Soul
(The) Legend Lives On - Disc 1
Memories Of Elvis - 1991 - Disc 1
Platinum - A Life In Music - Disc 3
That's The Way It Is
That's The Way It Is - Original Master Recording
Walk A Mile In My Shoes - 70's Masters - Disc 1
Various Artists
Solid Gold Country - Elvis Presley BirthdayTribute 92-1
Solid Gold Country - Elvis Presley In Nashville
Sweet Dreams Of Country

You Don't Know Me
Command Performances - 60's Masters - Disc 2
Elvis At His Romantic Best
Elvis Double Features - Kissin' Cousins, Clambake & Stay Away Joe *(original film version)*
(The) Elvis Presley Collection - Country - Disc 1
Elvis Sings Hits From His Movies Volume 1
From Nashville To Memphis - 60's Masters - Disc 3
Various Artists
A Celebration Of Country 'n' Pop Music

You Gave Me A Mountain
Aloha From Hawaii Via Satellite
Aloha From Hawaii Via Satellite - 25th Anniversary Edition
(The) Alternate Aloha
Always On My Mind
Elvis Aron Presley - Disc 2
Elvis In Concert
Elvis 20th Anniversary Radio Show - Disc 3
(The) Legend Lives On - Disc 2
Love Songs
Walk A Mile In My Shoes - 70's Masters - Disc 5 (The Elvis Presley Show)
Walk A Mile In My Shoes - Out Of The Box Sampler - (Promo)
Various Artists
Solid Gold Country - Elvis Presley In Concert

You Gave Me A Moehill
Elvis 15th Anniversary Radio Show - Disc 6

You Gotta Stop
Elvis Double Features - Easy Come, Easy Go & Speedway

You'll Be Gone
From Nashville To Memphis - 60's Masters - Disc 2

You'll Never Walk Alone
A Touch Of Platinum - A Life In Music - Disc 2 *(alternate take 2)*
Amazing Grace His Greatest Sacred Performances - Disc 2
(The) Elvis Presley Collection - Gospel - Disc 1
(The) Elvis Presley Gospel Treasury - Disc 2

YOU'LL NEVER WALK ALONE (cont'd)
Elvis Presley The King Of Rock & Roll At His Best - Disc 1
His Hand In Mine (bonus track)
Platinum - A Life In Music - Disc 2 *(alternate take 2)*
You'll Never Walk Alone
Various Artists
Reach Out And Touch

You'll Think Of Me
Back In Memphis
Elvis The Other Sides - Worldwide Gold Award Hits Volume 2 - Disc 2
From Nashville To Memphis - 60's Masters - Disc 4
(The) Memphis Record

You're A Heartbreaker
Elvis! His Greatest Hits - Disc 4
(The) Elvis Presley Collection - Treasures '53 To '58 - Disc 2
Elvis 15th Anniversary Radio Show - Disc 3
For LP Fans Only
(The) King Of Rock 'N' Roll - 50's Masters - Disc 1
(The) Sun Sessions CD - The Master Takes

You're The Boss
Collectors Gold - Disc 1 (with Ann-Margret) *(take unknown)*
Elvis Double Features - Canister Set - Disc 3 (with Ann-Margret)
Elvis Double Features - Viva Las Vegas & Roustabout (with Ann-Margret)
Elvis Sings Leiber & Stoller (with Ann-Margret)
Various Artists
Leiber & Stoller Music Publishing (6 CD Promo Set) (with Ann-Margret)
Solid Gold Country - Elvis Presley Sings Leiber And Stoller (with Ann-Margret)

You're The Only Star In My Blue Heaven
(The) Million Dollar Quartet

You've Lost That Lovin' Feelin'
An Afternoon In The Garden
Elvis Aron Presley - Disc 3
Elvis As Recorded At Madison Square Garden
(The) Legend Lives On - Disc 1
That's The Way It Is
That's The Way It Is - Original Master Recording
Walk A Mile In My Shoes - 70's Masters - Disc 5 (The Elvis Presley Show)

Young And Beautiful
A Date With Elvis
A Valentine Gift For You
(The) Blue Suede Box - Elvis: His Greatest Soundtracks - Disc 2
(The) Blue Suede Box - Elvis: His Greatest Soundtracks - Disc 2 *(movie version)*
Blue Suede Shoes - Original Soundtrack - Disc 1 *(music box intro)*
(The) Elvis Presley Collection - Love Songs - Disc 1
Elvis The Other Sides - Worldwide Gold Award Hits Volume 2 - Disc 1
Elvis 15th Anniversary Radio Show - Disc 4
Essential Elvis - The First Movies *(unreleased version take 12)*
Heart And Soul
Jailhouse Rock and Love Me Tender
Jailhouse Rock and Love Me Tender *(movie version)*
(The) King Of Rock 'N' Roll - 50's Masters - Disc 3
(The) King Of Rock 'N' Roll - 50's Masters - Disc 5 *(alternate take 3)*
Remembering Elvis

Young Dreams
(The) Blue Suede Box - Elvis: His Greatest Soundtracks - Disc3
(The) Elvis Presley Collection - Treasures '53 To '58 - Disc 2
Elvis The Other Sides - Worldwide Gold Award Hits Volume 2 - Disc 2
King Creole
King Creole (1997 Reissue)
(The) King Of Rock 'N' Roll - 50's Masters - Disc 4

Your Cheatin' Heart
Elvis For Everyone
Elvis! His Greatest Hits - Disc 4
(The) Elvis Presley Collection - Country - Disc 2
Essential Elvis Volume 3/ Hits Like Never Before *(alternate take 9)*
Essential Elvis Volume 3/ Hits Like Never Before *(alternate take 10, original master)*
Great Country Songs *(alternate take 9)*
(The) King Of Rock 'N' Roll - 50's Masters - Disc 4
Welcome To My World *(alternate take)*

Your Life Has Just Begun
A Private Moment With The King *(home recording - with Linda Thompson)*

Your Love's Been A Long Time Coming
Essential Elvis Vol. 5 - Rhythm And Country *(alternate take 4)*
Promised Land

Your Time Hasn't Come Yet Baby
Command Performances - 60's Masters - Disc 2
Elvis Double Features - Easy Come, Easy Go & Speedway

WE HAVE /LS/ES/CP/SX/RA,SHP
with OBI, and a lot more rare Japanese stuff!

私達はエルウィスが好き

WE SELL!!
JAPANESE ELVIS CDS & RECORDS

PLEASE SEND US YOUR ADDRESS
AND PHONE NUMBER FOR FREE CATALOG!
THE JAPAN'S ELVIS PRESLEY COLLECTOR'S SHOP

LOVE ME TENDER

1-8-21 JINGUMAE SHIBUYA-KU
TOKYO 150-0001 JAPAN
TEL:813-3408-9225 FAX:813-3408-6745
E-mail:jtr@rrm.co.jp
HP:http://www.rrm.co.jp/world/

ELVIS PRESLEY

(RECORDS BY MAIL)

LPs, COMPACT DISCS, SINGLES, CASSETTES, BOX-SETS ETC. FROM ALL OVER THE WORLD VIDEOS, MAGAZINES ETC.

ALL BMG RELEASES STOCKED

CD PROMOS FROM £10.00 - CDs FROM £1.99 - VIDEOS FROM £3.99

MASTER LIST 4 TIMES A YEAR - UPDATES EVERY MONTH

VISA - MASTERCARD - EUROCARD ACCEPTED

MASSIVE CD LIST - JAPAN, USA ETC.

LPs FROM USA, RUSSIA ETC.

SAE OR 2 IRCs FOR LISTS AND DETAILS

JOIN OUR RECORD CLUB (ask for details)

PAY ONCE FOR LIFETIME MEMBERSHIP - 10% DISCOUNT OFF MOST ITEMS FOR MEMBERS

Write to: ELVIS PRESLEY (RECORDS BY MAIL),
103 BLITHEMEADOW DRIVE,
SPROWSTON, NORWICH, NORFOLK NR7 8PZ, U.K.
Telephone: (01603 488744)   Fax: (01603 787239)

Elvis lebt

in seiner Musik und seinen Filmen, welche er uns hinterlassen hat!

Deutschlands größter Elvis-Versand mit Riesenangebot an Schallplatten, CDs, Büchern, Videos, Magazinen, Kalendern, Postern, Souvenirs, Sammlerraritäten.

Bitte kostenlosen Gesamtkatalog anfordern!

Collectors Service – Ihr korrekter Elvis-Versand seit 1979!

Riesenauswahl, günstige Preise, prompte Lieferung und professioneller Service sind unsere Stärken – und Ihr Vorteil!

Wir sind die Nummer eins, wenn's um Elvis geht!!!

COLLECTORS SERVICE

ELVIS-VERSAND · Verlags- und Vertriebs-GmbH
Postfach 1228 · D-96003 Bamberg Germany

Since 1979!
We have all, please contact us
by mail or fax 0049951/203103
we send our great offers +
catalogs!

WORLDWIDE ELVIS

BOX 17998 • SARASOTA, FL 34276-0998
(941) 346-1930 • FAX (941) 346-8139
E mail: wwelvis@gte.net
www.worldwideelvis.com

NOW FEATURING:

• *A TOUCH OF MARBLE BOX SET* •
• *KING OF THE WHOLE WIDE WORLD BOX SET* •
• *King Of The Whole Wide World /
King Creole* (U.S.) single •
• *INSIDE JAILHOUSE ROCK* book
(1999 edition)
• Original records / CD's
from over 60 countries •

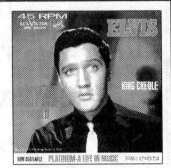

CATALOG: $10 u.s. / $15 FOREIGN

VISA /MASTERCARD ACCEPTED